Sparkling Recipes
For Every Occasion

from

Mumm Cuvée Napa

&

A Selection of Favorite Recipes
from
Napa Valley Chefs

We wish to acknowledge the contributions of Desktop Miracles for their creative and technical coordination of this book. Our thanks to Riedel Crystal of America for the pictures of their glasses, and the Pork Institute of America for the ham illustration.

The Hoffman Press, P.O. Box 2868, Santa Rosa CA 95404-2868
Phone: 707-538-5527, Fax: 707-538-7371, Email: rph@foodandwinebooks.com

Printed in Korea

Mother Nature determines each year what basic ingredients I will be working with for winemaking, just as she determines the fresh produce in my local market. I approach winemaking in much the same way the great chefs of the world begin cooking in the kitchen, with only the freshest of ingredients. I require that all Mumm Cuvée Napa grapes ripen naturally on the vine and are picked only when they yield the depth of flavor and perfection of ripeness that is worthy of a grape grown in the Napa Valley.

After the harvest, the art of making the pressed juice into a sparkling wine worthy of the Mumm Cuvée Napa label begins. As with any great dish, our winemaking team creates a sparkling wine that has complex aromas, flavors and textures. Each year we blend over 100 separate wines from particular and specific vineyard locations to create a cuvée that is elegant and expresses the elegance of the Napa Valley.

In the end, the satisfaction of opening a bottle of Mumm Cuvée Napa sparkling wine to enjoy with a meal is worth the effort. Sparkling wines in general are versatile with foods and our sparkling wines in particular, with their rich fruit focus and crisp acidity offer a perfect match. We trust that as you explore the recipes found within this book, that your experience of sparkling wine and food pairing has just begun.

Rob McNeill

Rob McNeill
Senior Winemaker
Mumm Cuvée Napa

Mumm Cuvée Napa Sparkling Wines

With the first release of sparkling wines into wine shops and fine dining establishments in 1986, Mumm Cuvée Napa developed a following for its award-winning and approachable wines. Today, Mumm Cuvée Napa sparkling wines are known for their expressions of California style—wines that have character and speak to the land from which they are grown.

Each vintage of wines has been made from grapes within the Napa Valley, which boasts 14 different growing regions that each has a distinct microclimate and a unique combination of weather and soil. Within these microclimates, the classic Champagne grapes Chardonnay and Pinot Noir flourish in the Napa Valley's long hot days and cool nights. Grapes from each vineyard within these distinct growing areas provide the foundation for Mumm Cuvée Napa's final blend. This small parcel of land in Northern California wine country is truly a winemaker's paradise.

Led by the winemaker, Rob McNeill, the Mumm Cuvée Napa winemaking team are masters at combining these distinct flavors into a cuvée, or blend, that celebrates the best of California's prestigious vineyards. Each Mumm Cuvée Napa wine showcases bright, ripe fruit and maintains fine balance and structure. The essential balance and harmony of Mumm Cuvée Napa will make your moments and meals with family and friends sparkle!

This Cookbook . . .

. . . is a little different from other cookbooks, for several reasons, and we thought we should point them out here before you get into reading the menus and recipes.

First, we have simplified the recipes so that you, with the demands that you have on your time and energies, can prepare a memorable meal without doing a great deal of work. For example: While it is admirable to make pie crusts from scratch you can find perfectly acceptable ones, ready for the filling and oven, in your supermarket refrigerated foods department.

Second, we don't think that everyone has little ethnic grocery stores, that carry exotic ingredients, available to them. And even if they do, many people do not have the time to shop two or three stores for the ingredients for a meal . . . even if it is a very special meal. So, we have, wherever possible, provided alternatives for these hard-to-find items that are available in most supermarkets.

Third, our beverage recommendations are simple. All of them call for one of four Mumm Cuvée Napa Sparkling Wines: Brut Prestige, Blanc de Blancs, Blanc de Noirs, and DVX. We want you to experience the pleasure of enjoying sparkling wine on many different occasions and with many different foods. Unlike most other wines, Sparkling Wine pairs so well with most foods, whether it be soup, salad, meat, poultry, fish, or desserts.

And, for those of you with a bit more time who truly enjoy the challenges of recipes that are more complex, we have included the favorite recipes of chefs in some of the finest restaurants here in the Napa Valley.

The Editors

Contents

Brunch for the Bunch

Page 11

The "Bunch" may be friends from the office, the PTA, a reunion party, or any occasion. The menu is simple and easy to prepare. Most of it can be done a day or two before. Serve it individually or as a mini-buffet.

Friday Festivities

Page 23

This menu is for those times when you want to celebrate the end of the week, whether it be with friends or family . . . or both . . . without making a project out of it. The special feature of this menu is that it may be made a few days ahead, refrigerated and reheated to serve. This is a great menu for a very informal get-together.

A Tailgate Party

Page 33

Football, baseball, polo or soccer, this menu fits any tailgate party perfectly. If you choose not to barbeque, it will be just as good cooked at home and brought to the parking lot in an insulated container. And, if you want to hold it in your backyard, that's OK too.

A Bridal Shower

Page 43

We designed this menu for a bridal shower, hosted by a friend or family member who may, or may not, have great culinary skills, but wants to do something special for the bride-to-be. If there is no bride-to-be, it's a very nice menu for any group to enjoy.

A Summer Picnic

Page 51

Summer without at least one picnic simply isn't summer! The ingredients of this picnic are all easily assembled and prepared a few days in advance for truly carefree entertaining. Do remember to bring enough ice so that the sparkling wine is properly chilled!

A Traditional Thanksgiving
Page 61

We've made it easy for you by gathering all the classic components of a traditional Thanksgiving dinner into this menu, but providing shortcuts so you can enjoy the event, too.

New Year's Eve at Home for Two
Page 71

This menu is for the truly romantic couple who want to share the passing of the old year and the birth of the new, together, at home. The menu is elegant. But, the preparation is not. The results are well worth the effort.

Sunday Supper
Page 81

This is pure and simple comfort food! This is the kind of food that your mother and grandmother may have cooked . . . but they took all day to do it. We've made it a lot easier to achieve, without losing the "hominess" of the flavors.

A Christmas Dinner
Page 91

We've included a traditional Southern Christmas Dinner for you because it is a bit different than the roasted turkey that takes four to five hours to roast. The ham is pre-cooked and pre-sliced . . . all you do is glaze it and warm it in the oven for about an hour.

Serving Sparkling Wine
Page 99

Some suggestions on glassware and serving sparkling wine.

The Chefs of the Valley
A Selection of Favorite Recipes from Napa Valley Chefs
Page 101

The Napa Valley, where we produce Mumm Cuvée Napa sparkling wines, is blessed with some of the finest restaurants in America. Here is a sampling of some of their favorite recipes, chosen to accompany their selections of our sparkling wines.

Menu

Brunch for the Bunch
for Eight

Ham Patties with Pineapple Relish

Mushroom Quiche

Cabbage and Orange Slaw

Sweet Potato Biscuits

Strawberry Rhubarb Crisp

Mumm Cuvée Napa Blanc de Noirs

Ham Patties with Pineapple Relish

1 pound lean ground smoked ham
1 pound lean ground loin of pork
2 cups bread crumbs, plain
½ teaspoon salt
½ teaspoon black pepper
½ teaspoon dried sage

½ cup onion, finely minced
1 teaspoon dried thyme
2 tablespoons Dijon mustard
2 eggs, beaten
Vegetable oil for brushing on grill rack
    or pan

Mix ham, pork, bread crumbs, salt, pepper, sage, onions, thyme, mustard and eggs. Divide the meat mixture into 8 equal portions and shape into round patties, approximately ½" thick. Place on waxed paper, separated, and refrigerate until grill is ready.

In a grill with a cover, prepare a medium-hot fire for direct-heat cooking. Brush the grill rack with vegetable oil. Place the patties on the grill and cook, turning once, until done to your preference, 5 to 8 minutes on each side.

Patties may be broiled in your oven, if you prefer.

Pineapple Relish

1 20-ounce can crushed pineapple
    (2½ cups) drained — reserve juice.
½ cup brown sugar
½ teaspoon salt
1 teaspoon fresh grated ginger

1 teaspoon fresh grated orange peel
1 cup reserved pineapple juice
½ cup raspberry vinegar
½ cup orange marmalade (preferably
    Seville or English bitter orange)

In medium saucepan over medium heat, combine pineapple, sugar, salt, ginger and orange peel. Add pineapple juice and vinegar. Simmer for 15 minutes until bubbling. Add orange marmalade and cook an additional 10 minutes. (Thin with additional pineapple juice if necessary.) Refrigerate until ready to serve. Serve warm over ham patties.

Mushroom Quiche

1 prepared 9" pie crust
½ cup shredded mozzarella cheese
2 tablespoons butter or margarine
½ cup sliced green onions
1 cup sliced mushrooms
2 tablespoons sliced pimentos, drained

5 eggs
1 cup half and half cream
¼ teaspoon salt
¼ teaspoon black pepper
Sprinkle of nutmeg

Preheat oven to 400 degrees. Line quiche pan with pastry crust. Flute the edges and prick bottom with a fork. Bake in preheated oven for 6 to 8 minutes. (Note: Pastry will still be pale.) Remove and cool.

Reduce oven temperature to 350 degrees. Heat butter in skillet over medium heat and cook mushrooms and onions for 5 minutes.

Sprinkle half the cheese on the bottom of the pastry shell. Spread onion and mushroom mixture over the cheese, and sprinkle remaining cheese on top.

Lightly beat eggs, cream and spice together. Stir in the pimento and pour over the cheese and mushroom mixture. Bake 35 to 40 minutes, until set and golden.

Note: This may be made a day ahead of your event, and reheated just before serving.

Cabbage and Orange Slaw

2 (11-ounce) cans mandarin orange
   segments, drained; reserve liquid
½ cup mayonnaise
2 tablespoons reserved orange syrup
1 tablespoon raspberry vinegar
1 teaspoon grated fresh orange peel

1 medium head new green cabbage,
   thinly sliced
½ cup sliced green onions including
   small portion of green tops
Salt and pepper

In a large bowl, mix mayonnaise, 2 tablespoons orange reserved liquid, vinegar and orange peel. Add cabbage, onions; toss to coat. Season with salt and pepper. Add orange segments, toss lightly, cover and chill. (Slaw may be made ahead, adding oranges before serving.)

Sweet Potato Biscuits

1 can (1 pound) sweet potatoes, mashed
2¼ cups buttermilk biscuit mix
½ cup firmly packed brown sugar
1 teaspoon ground cinnamon

½ teaspoon ground ginger
½ teaspoon ground nutmeg
3 tablespoons water

Preheat oven to 350 degrees.

Grease a large baking sheet. Put mashed sweet potatoes in a bowl. Stir in buttermilk biscuit mix, sugar and spices. Add enough water, by tablespoons, to form soft dough.

Turn out the dough onto a lightly floured surface. Pat the dough into ½" thick round. Cut out the biscuits using a small round biscuit or cookie cutter.

Transfer biscuits to the prepared baking sheet, spacing evenly. Bake until golden brown, about 18 minutes (biscuits will rise only slightly). Transfer biscuits to racks. Serve warm or at room temperature. May be made several days in advance. Place in plastic bag. Warm before serving.

Strawberry-Rhubarb Crisp

4 cups strawberries, cleaned and cut into
   halves or quarters

3 cups sliced rhubarb, ¼" wide

¾ cup sugar

½ cup plus 1 tablespoon flour

1 tablespoon cornstarch

¾ teaspoon cinnamon

½ teaspoon nutmeg

½ cup rolled oats

½ cup butter (softened)

Heat oven to 400 degrees. Grease an 8" by 8" baking dish. Mix strawberries and rhubarb with the sugar, 1 tablespoon of the flour, cornstarch, cinnamon and nutmeg. Arrange in the baking dish.

Mix remaining ½ cup flour, rolled oats and butter with your hands until mixture is blended and crumbly to make topping. Cover evenly over fruit. Bake about 40 minutes, until fruit is bubbly and topping is lightly browned. Cool slightly and serve with ice cream or whipped cream.

Make this the day before, if you like, and warm it just before serving.

Blanc de Blancs

Mumm Cuvée Napa's Blanc de Blancs is a unique wine. It is the only sparkling wine produced in the United States with a varietal make-up of 70% Chardonnay and 30% Pinot Gris. The crisp acidity of Chardonnay is broadened out on the palate with the spiciness of Pinot Gris to make this a wine that will age very well. The result is an unusual, attractive combination of distinctive fresh crispness with a depth one would not expect from a wine with such a pale gold green tint.

As is true with each Mumm Cuvée Napa wine, the philosophy of "Californian fruit to the forefront" shines through. The lots from individual vineyards are kept separate during initial fermentation in order to highlight vineyard differences and to maximize their individual characteristics.

The refreshing Blanc de Blancs shows nuances of apple and pear with a toastiness mid-palate. The firm acidity is complemented by a gentle mousse that highlights the pale straw color. This is a wine that ages well with proper cellaring.

For perfect food pairing, serve it with shellfish, sole, trout, sashimi, calamari, veal scaloppini, and angel hair pasta with a cream sauce.

Menu

Friday Festivities
for Eight

Young Salad Greens
with
Orange and Sweet Onions

Seafood Stew

Crusty French Bread — Crusty Garlic Bread

Caramel Apple Pie
with
French Vanilla Ice Cream

Mumm Cuvée Napa Blanc de Blancs

Seafood Stew

2 tablespoons butter
2 tablespoons olive oil
1 garlic clove, minced
1 large onion, minced
4 green onions, cut into 2" lengths,
   including some of green tops
3 medium carrots, peeled, cut into
   ¼" slices
4 cups clam juice
1 cup white wine
¼ cup parsley, chopped

1 tablespoon dried oregano
2 cans peeled, cut tomatoes, including juice
1 cup light cream
1½ cups frozen corn niblets
1 pound sea bass or red snapper fillet,
   skinned and boned
1 pound salmon fillet, skinned and boned
½ pound sea scallops
½ pound medium shrimp, cooked, frozen
1 cup cooked broccoli florets
1 cup blanched pea pods

Melt olive oil and butter in skillet over moderate heat. Saute onion, garlic and carrots for about 5 minutes, being careful not to brown them. Transfer to a large stew pot. Add clam juice, wine, parsley, oregano, and tomatoes. Bring to simmer. Add cream and corn. Continue to simmer.

Cut the fish into cubes approximately the same size as the scallops. (Cut scallops in half if very large.) Add to stew. Bring to a simmer over low heat, then cover and continue cooking for 10 minutes. Check to see if fish is cooked. Do not overcook. Add broccoli and pea pods. Season to taste with salt and pepper, if needed.

Note: This recipe can be made one day ahead, and stored in the refrigerator.

Crusty French Bread

3 baguettes or 2 loaves of French bread, unsliced   ½ cup extra virgin olive oil

Slice the bread horizontally, then cut into pieces about 4" long.

Brush olive oil thinly over the cut sides of bread, and toast briefly. If desired, this can be done a few days prior to the event, if placed in an airtight plastic bag or container. Reheat prior to serving.

Crusty Garlic Bread

3 baguettes or 2 loaves of French bread, unsliced   ½ cup extra virgin olive oil or butter
                                                           2 cloves garlic, finely minced

Slice the bread horizontally, then cut into pieces about 4" long.

Sauté garlic cloves for a few minutes in a small amount of olive oil or butter. After garlic has been sautéed, add all to the remainder of the olive oil or butter, and mix.

Brush mixture over the cut sides of bread. If desired, this can be done a few days prior to the event, if placed in an airtight plastic bag or container. Reheat prior to serving.

Young Salad Greens with Orange and Sweet Onions

8 cups mixed young greens
1 tablespoon fresh basil, chopped
1 tablespoon fresh tarragon, chopped
½ cup sweet onion (such as Vidalia),
   thinly sliced

4 oranges, peeled with pith removed
¼ cup sliced almonds, toasted
Orange Vinaigrette dressing (recipe below)

Orange Vinaigrette Dressing:

½ teaspoon orange zest, minced
4 tablespoons fresh orange juice
1 tablespoon balsamic vinegar

¼ teaspoon salt
¼ teaspoon black pepper
6 tablespoons light olive oil

Combine all vinaigrette ingredients in small bowl and whisk. Set aside.

Arrange greens on plates. Sprinkle with basil and tarragon. Cut orange segments in bite-size pieces and place around greens. Top greens with onion slices and drizzle with dressing. Top with sliced almonds.

Caramel Apple Pie with French Vanilla Ice Cream

1 15-ounce package refrigerated pie crusts
6 cups thinly sliced, peeled apples
¾ cup sugar
2 tablespoons flour
¾ teaspoon cinnamon

¼ teaspoon salt
⅛ teaspoon nutmeg
1 tablespoon lemon juice
1 cup prepared caramel dip
   (used for candied apples)

Prepare pie crust according to package directions for 2-crust pie using 9" pie pan. Dust bottom crust with flour.

Heat oven to 425 degrees. In large bowl, combine apples, ¾ cup sugar, flour, cinnamon, salt, nutmeg, and lemon juice. Mix lightly. Spoon into crust-lined pan. Spread caramel sauce over apples.

Top with remaining crust; fold edge of top crust under bottom crust. Press together to seal; flute edge. Cut slits in top crust. Brush crust lightly with water and sprinkle with 1 tablespoon sugar and a sprinkle of cinnamon.

Bake at 425 degrees for 40 to 50 minutes or until apples are tender and crust is golden brown. Cover edge of crust with strips of foil after 15 to 20 minutes of baking to prevent excessive browning. Let cool. Top with French Vanilla ice cream.

Pie may be made ahead and reheated.

Blanc de Noirs

Blanc de Noirs, literally "a white wine from red grapes" is a sparkling wine made primarily from dark-skinned grapes. In California sparkling winemaking, *blanc de noirs* is used to describe slightly colored wines that range from light golden colors to rosé.

It is a delicate balancing act to create a superior Blanc de Noirs — the grape skins must be quickly removed from the juice after the grapes have been crushed to prevent the grape's dark skin from transferring too much color to the wine. This wine is a triumph of the skill of Rob McNeill and his winemaking team.

A charming, pale salmon color introduces this wine, and follows with a bouquet of ripe Pinot Noir fruit. Part of the wine is initially fermented in the press, producing a soft, fruity character that gives Blanc de Noirs its directness, while a small percentage of Chardonnay gives the wine power and structure.

This more robust quality makes Blanc de Noirs a wonderful wine with many kinds of cuisine, ranging from Thai to Italian. Pair it with caviar, smoked fish, avocado and crab salad, or sauced shellfish, and vegetable and cheese soufflés.

Menu

Tailgate Party
for Eight

Spicy Barbecued Chicken

Chili Beans

Carrot and Cabbage Slaw

Toasted, Buttered Dinner Rolls

Chocolate Fruit-Nut Brownies

Mumm Cuvée Napa Blanc de Noirs

Spicy Barbecued Chicken

6 chicken breast halves
6 chicken drumsticks
6 chicken thighs

Barbeque Sauce:

1 cup catsup
1 cup chili sauce
3 tablespoons olive oil
3 tablespoons brown sugar
3 tablespoons minced onion

1 tablespoon Worcestershire sauce
1 tablespoon prepared mustard
½ teaspoon black pepper
2 tablespoons wine vinegar

Combine in a bowl. Set aside ½ cup sauce.

Prepare a lightly greased grill for chicken. Place chicken on grill.

Grill chicken, uncovered, 5 to 6" over medium-hot coals for about 30 minutes or until cooked through, turning and basting with sauce 3 to 4 times during grilling. Serve reserved ½ cup sauce as a condiment with grilled chicken.

Chili Beans

2 tablespoons olive oil
½ pound Canadian bacon,
  cut into ½" pieces
2 cups chopped onions
½ cup chili sauce
2 cups red wine
3 tablespoons chili powder
1 tablespoon ground cumin
1 tablespoon dried oregano leaves
½ cup brown sugar

4 tablespoons light molasses
2 (15-ounce) cans ready-cut peeled
  tomatoes, including juice
2 (15-ounce) cans red kidney beans,
  drained
1 (15-ounce) can black kidney beans,
  drained
1 (15-ounce) can prepared chili with beans
Salt and pepper

Heat oil in large dutch oven or heavy pot over medium heat. Add bacon and onions. Sauté until brown, about 8 to 10 minutes. Add chili sauce and wine. Mix in chili powder, cumin and oregano. Add brown sugar and molasses. Simmer, stirring until well blended. Add tomatoes. Bring to simmer. Add beans. Simmer on low until thickened, about 30 minutes, stirring to prevent sticking. Add salt and pepper, if needed.

Can be prepared 2 to 3 days ahead and stored covered in refrigerator. Heat before serving.

Carrot and Cabbage Slaw

1 large head cabbage, shredded
2 medium carrots, peeled and shredded
2 teaspoons celery seed
¾ cup mayonnaise
2 teaspoons sugar
2 tablespoons raspberry vinegar

2 tablespoons fresh lemon juice
½ teaspoon salt
½ teaspoon black pepper
2 teaspoons prepared mustard
1 medium onion, quartered

In a large bowl, toss cabbage, carrots and celery seed. Place the remaining ingredients in a blender or food processor; cover and process until combined. Pour over cabbage mixture and toss to coat. Cover and refrigerate for at least 2 hours or until time for game.

Chocolate Fruit-Nut Brownies

½ cup butter

4 ounces unsweetened chocolate

2 cups sugar

4 eggs

1 teaspoon rum extract

2 teaspoons ground cinnamon

½ teaspoon salt

1 ¼ cups flour

1 cup chopped walnuts

1 (7.5-ounce) jar glacé cherries

Melt butter and chocolate in saucepan. Let cool. In separate bowl, mix next 5 ingredients. Gradually add flour. Beat until smooth. Mix in chocolate. Then add nuts and cherries. Spread mixture in 9" by 13" greased pan. Bake 35 minutes at 350 degrees. Cool before cutting 2" squares from pan. Makes approximately 24.

Brut Prestige

If winemaker Rob McNeill were to pick one sparkling wine above all others to represent the Napa Valley, it would be Brut Prestige. The region's unique microclimates and diverse soil types provide the ideal conditions to grow Pinot Noir, Pinot Meunier, and Chardonnay.

The grapes from over 50 different vineyards are pressed and individual lots of wines are kept separate during the initial fermentation. This gives the winemaker tremendous flexibility in crafting a beautifully balanced and complex cuvée. The result is the signature cuvée, Brut Prestige, a very popular award-winning wine.

With an excellent mousse, a golden peach color, and tantalizing hints of melon, spice and toasty vanilla on the nose, the Brut Prestige reveals crisp, yet creamy qualities on the palate with a rich lingering finish. It pairs beautifully with grilled poultry, fish, shellfish, and creamy pastas.

Menu

Bridal Shower
for Eight

Mushroom Bisque with Sherry

Asian Chicken Salad

Croissants

*Chocolate Pecan Pie
with Cinnamon Whipped Cream*

*Mumm Cuvée Napa Blanc de Blancs
and
Mumm Cuvée Napa Blanc de Noirs*
with dessert

Mushroom Bisque with Sherry

1 pound fresh mushrooms	Salt and pepper
4 tablespoons butter	2 tablespoons flour
½ cup onion, minced	6 cups chicken stock or broth
¼ cup celery, minced	½ cup dry Sherry
¼ cup white wine	1 cup cream
1 teaspoon grated fresh lemon peel	Ground nutmeg

Clean and finely chop mushrooms. Put aside. Melt butter in skillet and sauté onion and celery until soft. Add mushrooms and cook until slightly browned, stirring. Add salt, pepper, lemon peel, and wine. Sprinkle with flour and blend into mushroom mixture for 4 to 5 minutes.

Gradually add stock and whisk until smooth and slightly thickened. Cover and simmer on low for 30 minutes. Add Sherry and cool slightly before slowly blending in cream.

Reheat, but do not boil. Serve with a sprinkling of nutmeg.

Asian Chicken Salad

3 cups celery cut diagonally into ½" strips

2 red bell peppers cut into ½" strips

4 cooked chicken breasts, cut into ½"
wide and 2" long strips

6 cups shredded lettuce

½ cup chopped roasted peanuts

Dressing:

¼ cup white wine vinegar

¼ cup light olive oil

1 teaspoon fresh grated ginger

2 tablespoons soy sauce

1 small garlic clove, finely minced

5 tablespoons peanut butter

Combine all dressing ingredients in a blender and blend for one minute. Pour into a small pan and set aside. (May be made a day or two in advance)

Put celery, peppers and chicken in a bowl. Put aside.

Heat salad dressing over low heat, mixing while it is heating. When dressing is hot, but not boiling, pour over celery, peppers, and chicken. Fold into mixture.

To serve: Arrange ¾ cup of lettuce on plates, top with chicken mixture. Sprinkle chopped peanuts on top.

Chocolate Pecan Pie with Cinnamon Whipped Cream

Filling:

1 cup light corn syrup

½ cup sugar

¼ cup margarine or butter, melted

1 teaspoon vanilla extract

1 teaspoon ground cinnamon

3 eggs

1 (6-ounce) package (1 cup) semi-sweet
  chocolate chips

1½ cups pecan halves

Pastry for a single pie crust

Topping:

Whipped cream

½ teaspoon ground cinnamon

1 teaspoon confectioners' sugar

Heat oven to 325 degrees.

In a large bowl, combine corn syrup, sugar, margarine, vanilla, cinnamon, and eggs and beat well. Stir in the chocolate chips and pecans.

Spread the mixture evenly in a pie crust-lined pan. Bake for 55 to 65 minutes or until the filling is set. Cover edge of pie crust with strip of foil after 15 or 20 minutes of baking to prevent excessive browning. Cool completely.

Garnish pie with whipped cream to which you have added the cinnamon and powdered sugar. Keep pie refrigerated until serving time.

Menu

A Summer Picnic
for Eight

Cold Dilled Cucumber Soup

Roast Beef Roll-ups

Ham and Cheese Roll-ups

Turkey Ranch Roll-ups

South of the Border Beans and Cheese Roll-ups

A Summer Potato Salad

Champagne Fruit Bowl

Mumm Cuvée Napa Blanc de Noirs

Cold Dilled Cucumber Soup

2 cups chicken stock
4 cucumbers, peeled, seeded and sliced
  (about 6 cups)
2 tablespoons chopped onion
1 tablespoon minced fresh dill
  (or 2 teaspoons dried)

Salt and freshly ground pepper
2 cups plain yogurt
½ cup finely chopped toasted walnuts
Thin slices of unpeeled cucumber
Crackers

In a 4-quart saucepan, combine stock, cucumbers and onion. Bring to a boil; reduce heat and simmer until cucumbers are just tender, about 5 to 7 minutes. Cool.

In a food processor, purée stock mixture, dill, salt and pepper until smooth (in batches if necessary). Add yogurt. Chill and adjust seasonings.

Before serving, stir in toasted walnuts. Serve cold, garnished with paper-thin slices of cucumber and crackers on the side.

Serves 8.

Roast Beef Roll-ups

¼ cup sour cream
½ cup mayonnaise
¼ cup minced curly leaf parsley
2 tablespoons chopped pimento

¼ cup toasted chopped almonds
Salt and black pepper to taste
4-8" flour tortillas
1 pound thinly sliced roast beef

Combine sour cream, mayonnaise, parsley, pimento and almonds, with salt and pepper to taste. Spread generously over tortillas. Top with slices of roast beef. Roll up tightly and secure with toothpicks. Cut in half. Wrap each half in foil or plastic wrap and refrigerate. Keep cold until served.

Ham and Cheese Roll-ups

1 package (3 ounces) cream cheese, softened
2 teaspoons prepared mustard
1 cup tart apple, peeled and shredded

4-8" flour tortillas
¼ cup chopped sweet red pepper
2 green onions, thinly sliced

Combine cream cheese and mustard. Stir in apple. Spread about 2 tablespoons on each tortilla. Layer with the red pepper, onions and ham. Roll up tightly. Secure with toothpicks. Cut in half. Wrap each half in foil or plastic wrap and refrigerate. Keep cold until served.

Turkey Ranch Roll-ups

8 thin slices of cooked turkey

4-8" flour tortillas

1 large tomato, thinly sliced

1 medium green pepper, cut into thin strips

1 cup shredded lettuce

1 cup (4 ounces) shredded cheddar cheese

⅓ cup ranch salad dressing

Place 2 slices of turkey on each tortilla. Layer with tomato, green pepper, lettuce and cheese. Drizzle with salad dressing. Roll up tightly and secure with toothpicks. Cut in half. Wrap each half in foil or plastic wrap and refrigerate. Keep cold until served.

South of the Border Beans and Cheese Roll-ups

1 cup canned red kidney beans, rinsed and drained

¼ cup chunky tomato salsa

2 tablespoons green onions, finely chopped

2 tablespoons cilantro, finely chopped

4-8" flour tortillas

2 medium tomatoes, chopped

1 cup lettuce, shredded

1½ cups shredded Monterey Jack Cheese

In a bowl, mash beans slightly. Add salsa, green onion and cilantro. Spread over tortillas. Sprinkle with tomatoes, lettuce and cheese. Roll up tightly. Secure with toothpicks. Cut in half. Wrap each half in foil or plastic wrap and refrigerate. Keep cold until served.

A Summer Potato Salad

2 pounds small red potatoes, quartered
3 tablespoons crumbled blue cheese
4 tablespoons plain yogurt
4 tablespoons mayonnaise
2 tablespoons fresh lemon juice
2 tablespoons fresh basil, chopped

Salt and black pepper to taste
½ stalk celery, finely chopped
4 tablespoons green onions, thinly sliced
2 tablespoons fresh parsley, chopped
4 hardboiled eggs, peeled and chopped

Bring water to a boil in a large pot. Add potatoes and boil for 15 to 20 minutes.

While potatoes are cooking, prepare the dressing by blending the blue cheese into the yogurt and mayonnaise. Add the lemon juice and basil. Season to taste with salt and pepper. If dressing is too thick, add wine vinegar to thin.

Drain potatoes and cool. Place in bowl. Pour dressing over potatoes and toss. Add celery, green onions, eggs and parsley, tossing well. Refrigerate, covered, until ready to serve.

Chive Cucumber Salad

4 large cucumbers, peeled and thinly sliced
½ cup sour cream
3 tablespoons freshly snipped chives
2 tablespoons raspberry vinegar

4 tablespoons mayonnaise
2 tablespoons chopped green onions
⅛ teaspoon cracked black pepper
Salt to taste

In a bowl, combine cucumbers and sour cream. Cover and refrigerate for at least an hour. Stir in the remaining ingredients just before serving.

Champagne Fruit Bowl

1 10-pound ripe watermelon

3 apples, cored and sliced into wedges

2 peaches, pit removed and sliced into wedges

2 kiwi fruit peeled, halved and thinly sliced

2 cups green grapes, stemmed

¼ cup freshly squeezed lemon juice

¼ cup freshly squeezed lime juice

1 cup (½ pint) blueberries

3 cups strawberries, hulled and halved

1 cup raspberries or blackberries

⅓ cup white sugar

⅓ cup brown sugar

⅓ cup water

Mix sugars and water in a small saucepan and bring to a boil; lower to simmer and cook for 5 minutes. Remove from heat to cool, and set aside.

To prepare watermelon bowl, measure one third down on sides and cut top third off, using a large knife. Retain. Scoop out the flesh of the melon with a melon baller, and set aside in a large glass bowl. Serrate the cut edge of the melon, cover with plastic wrap and place in refrigerator.

In a large bowl combine the apples, peaches and kiwi with the lemon and lime juices, mixing gently to avoid bruising. Add the watermelon balls, the rest of the fruit and the sugar syrup. Toss gently and refrigerate, covered.

When ready to serve, place all fruit in the watermelon bowl and pour half a bottle of sparkling wine over the fruit. Note: To prevent the bowl from tipping, and to maintain the cool temperature, place in a larger receptacle with ice.

DVX

DVX is carefully crafted from the very best Chardonnay and Pinot Noir grapes in the Napa Valley. Of the hundreds of individual vineyards, grapes from fewer than ten meet the stringent requirements of DVX. These base wines then undergo meticulous blending before resting in the Mumm Cuvée cellars for more than three years.

The result is a masterpiece, a winemaker's work of art that pays homage to the art of making Sparkling Wine. DVX is named for the late Guy Devaux, the founding winemaker of Mumm Cuvée Napa.

As is true of all Mumm Cuvée Napa wines, the natural ripeness of the fruit is accentuated. In appearance the wine is pale yellow with hints of gold. Very fine bubbles rise to a persistent mousse. The aromas are elegant and complex with fresh fruit aromas of red apple, lemon, orange peel, and berry. A layer of freshly baked bread melds pleasantly with the fruit.

The creamy texture on the palate has hints of cherries and plums, complemented by cocoa and citrus. The finish is long with nuances of plum, dried apricots, and butter.

Overall, DVX balances perfectly between the richness and complexity in the creation of an elegant wine. It has a solid backbone of tightly knit fruit supported by a refreshing acidity which will continue to develop in years to come.

The elegant DVX bottle is imported from France and reflects traditional 18th century champagne bottles with its long, slender neck and sturdy base. Each bottle is labeled by hand and features a distinctive Nicole Miller ribbon and special flute charm.

Menu

Traditional Thanksgiving Dinner
for Eight

Oysters on the Half Shell

Creamed Corn Bisque

Roast Turkey with a Molasses Glaze

Cornbread Sage Dressing

Mashed Potatoes — Giblet Gravy

Onions in Cream — Peppery Succotash

Fresh Cranberry Relish

Pumpkin Pie

Mumm Cuvée Napa Brut Prestige
and
Mumm Cuvée Napa Sparkling Pinot Noir

Oysters on the Half Shell

4 to six small oysters per person
8 lemon wedges

1 pound of rock salt

Hot Sauce Ingredients:
½ cup catsup
2 tablespoons chili sauce
2 tablespoons Worcestershire sauce

2 tablespoons prepared horseradish
¼ teaspoon salt

Have the store open the oyster shells and pack the oysters in ice for the trip home. Keep very cold until ready to serve. Serve, open, on a bed of rock salt (the salt keeps the shells from tipping). If fresh oysters are not available, serve bottled oysters in small glass bowls. Embed in ice instead of rock salt, with lemon wedges and hot sauce on the side.

Creamed Corn Bisque

3 tablespoons butter
1 medium onion, thinly sliced
½ cup green pepper, finely diced
2 potatoes, thinly sliced
2 cups boiling water
1 cup milk

1 cup half and half cream
1 tablespoon flour
½ bay leaf
1 teaspoon salt
¼ teaspoon pepper
1 can (19 oz.) of cream style corn

Heat butter in saucepan, add onion and green pepper, and cook gently over medium-low heat for 3 minutes, stirring frequently. Add potatoes and water. Boil for 15 minutes or until potatoes are tender. Mix ⅓ cup of the milk with the flour, stirring until smooth. Add to boiling mixture. Add the rest of the milk, half and half, bay leaf, salt, pepper and corn.

Simmer for 15 minutes, stirring frequently. Remove bay leaf. Place soup in blender and whip for a minute or until creamy. Remove. Heat again or serve cold. May be made several days ahead, if desired.

Roast Turkey with a Molasses Glaze

1 whole turkey, approximately 15 pounds
Salt and Pepper
Poultry seasoning
1 onion, peeled
3 tablespoons butter, melted

2 cups plus 2 tablespoons of chicken stock
1 tablespoon dark molasses
1 teaspoon red wine vinegar
½ pound red grapes
Celery leaves

Preheat oven to 350 degrees. Rinse turkey inside and out. Set aside neck and giblets. Dry thoroughly. Discard any fat in neck or main cavity. Season neck cavity with salt and pepper. Fold neck skin over and secure to body with skewers. Season main body cavity with salt, pepper, and poultry seasoning. Place onion in cavity. Skewer main cavity closed. Tuck wings under body. Tie legs together.

Place turkey, breast side up, on rack in large roasting pan. Brush 2 tablespoons of the melted butter over turkey. Pour ½ cup of stock into pan.

Roast turkey 2½ hours, basting with the pan juices, and adding ½ cup of chicken stock to pan every 45 minutes. Combine remaining butter with molasses and vinegar and brush over the turkey.

Roast turkey for another 30 minutes, until meat thermometer, inserted in thigh, registers 175 degrees. Move turkey to platter and tent with foil. Let stand for 20 to 30 minutes before carving. Garnish with grapes and celery leaves.

Cornbread & Sage Dressing

5 cups cornbread crumbs
7 tablespoons butter
3 large celery stalks, chopped coarsely
2 medium onions, chopped coarsely
3 tablespoons fresh sage, chopped, or
   1 tablespoon dried, crumbled sage

¾ teaspoon salt
½ teaspoon pepper
4 cups ½" cubes white bread
¾ cup chicken stock or canned
   low-salt broth
1 egg, beaten

Preheat oven to 350 degrees. Butter one large or two medium casserole dishes. (To make cornbread crumbs, crumble cornbread coarsely onto a large cookie sheet. Let stand uncovered at room temperature overnight to dry.)

Melt butter in large heavy skillet over medium heat. Add celery and onions to cook until tender, stirring frequently, about 12 minutes. Transfer mixture to large bowl, and mix in sage, salt, and pepper. Add cornbread crumbs and the bread cubes to vegetables. Combine the stock or broth with the egg in a small bowl. Stir into the dressing. Place dressing in buttered casserole and bake in oven for 30 to 45 minutes at 350 degrees.

Fresh Cranberry Relish

1 (12 ounce) package fresh cranberries
¼ cup water
1½ cups sugar
½ cup raspberry vinegar
½ cup golden raisins

2 teaspoons fresh grated ginger
2 cups diced apples
1 teaspoon cinnamon
½ teaspoon nutmeg
¼ teaspoon cloves

Simmer fresh cranberries, water, sugar and vinegar until soft, about 10 minutes. Add raisins, ginger, diced apples, cinnamon, nutmeg and cloves. Continue to cook an additional 15 minutes to blend all flavors. Cool and chill in refrigerator. (*Note: May be made several days in advance.*)

Mashed Potatoes

6 medium potatoes, 2 pounds
2 tablespoons butter
¼ cup warm milk

¼ teaspoon pepper
¼ teaspoon salt

Peel and quarter potatoes, removing any eyes, dark areas, or other blemishes. Boil for 20 to 25 minutes until tender, drain. Mash with mixer at low speed or with a potato masher until lumps are completely gone. Add butter and warm milk as you mash and finish with salt and pepper. *(Note: Use a mashed potatoes mix, if you prefer, but use milk instead of water to cook potatoes.)*

Giblet Gravy

Neck and giblets of turkey
4 cups boiling water
2 cups white wine
1 teaspoon salt
4 whole peppercorns
1 sprig parsley

1 medium onion
2 whole cloves
1 carrot
5 tablespoons flour
Salt and pepper

Cover neck and giblets in a saucepan with the 4 cups boiling water and all ingredients except the flour. Boil for 1 minute. Skim residue, cover, and lower heat to simmer contents for 1 hour. Strain the broth to remove the spices, onion and carrot.

Remove meat from neck and mince giblets and neck meat. Reserve.

Pour off all but 6 tablespoons of the fat from the drippings in the turkey pan. Place roasting pan over low heat and stir in the flour. Cook until thickened and bubbling. Add the broth, stirring. Add chopped neck meat and giblets just before serving. Add salt and pepper to taste.

Onions in Cream

3 pounds small yellow onions
2 cups chicken broth
2 tablespoons butter
6 tablespoons flour

⅓ cup dry Sherry
1 cup half and half cream
¼ teaspoon ground nutmeg
¼ teaspoon fresh parsley, chopped

Preheat oven to 375 degrees. Trim and peel onions, placing them in a saucepan. Add the chicken broth and bring to a boil. Cover and simmer for 10 minutes or until just tender. Strain, remove onions, and put them aside. Continue simmering stock.

Melt the butter in a small frying pan and add flour. Cook together for a few minutes, but do not allow to brown. Add this to the stock and stir until thickened and smooth. Stir in the Sherry and half and half cream. Simmer for 2 minutes more. Add nutmeg and parsley. *(This stage can be done 2 to 3 days prior to serving.)*

Combine the onions with the sauce in a casserole and bake for 40 to 45 minutes at 375 degrees, until it is bubbling. Brown, if you wish, under the broiler.

Peppery Succotash

2 to 3 tablespoons butter
1 green bell pepper, seeded and diced
1 red bell pepper, seeded and diced
¾ cup green onion, thinly sliced

2 packages (10 ounces each) frozen
  succotash
1 cup water
Salt and pepper to taste

Melt the butter in a saucepan. Add the diced pepper and ½ cup of the green onions; sauté 2 minutes. Add succotash and water; bring to a boil. Cover, reduce heat to medium-low and simmer 5 to 7 minutes until succotash is tender.

Sprinkle remaining green onion over succotash; season with salt and pepper to taste.

Pumpkin Pie

Pastry for a single crust pie*
2 eggs, slightly beaten
¾ cup sugar
1½ teaspoons ground cinnamon
½ teaspoon ground nutmeg
1 teaspoon ground ginger
¼ teaspoon ground allspice
¼ teaspoon ground cloves

½ teaspoon salt
1 can (16 oz.) pumpkin
3 tablespoons molasses
2 cans (6 oz. each) evaporated milk
1 egg white, unbeaten
¼ cup pecans, finely chopped
8 whole pecan halves
Whipped cream (optional)

Preheat oven to 400 degrees.

To make the filling, combine eggs, sugar, spices, salt, pumpkin, molasses, and evaporated milk in a large bowl. Combine with a wooden spoon or mixer on low speed, until mixture is smooth.

Lightly brush pie shell with egg white. Sprinkle chopped pecans evenly in the bottom of pie shell. Fill with pumpkin mixture. Gently arrange pecan halves evenly on the filling, around edge of pie.

Bake 55 to 60 minutes, or until tip of sharp knife inserted in center comes out clean. Let cool on wire rack. Serve at room temperature, garnished with whipped cream, if desired.

*Purchase a refrigerated pie shell, or use your favorite pie pastry recipe.

Menu

New Year's Eve at Home
for Two

Smoked Salmon on Toast Points

Lobster Bisque

Bibb Lettuce Salad
with Mushrooms and Pine Nuts

Brandied Orange Cornish Game Hens

Fruit-Nut Pilaf

Glazed Snow Peas — Fruit Relish

Caramel Nut Brownie Squares
with French Vanilla Ice Cream

Mumm Cuvée Napa DVX

Smoked Salmon on Toast Points

3 tablespoons cream cheese, softened
Freshly squeezed lemon juice
2 teaspoons minced fresh dill
1 teaspoon minced fresh chives
Black pepper

2 slices of toasted white bread
8 thin cucumber slices
¼ pound thinly sliced smoked salmon
Fresh dill sprigs for garnish

Place cream cheese in small bowl. Add tablespoon lemon juice and mix until cheese is soft and spreadable. (Add more lemon juice, if necessary.) Add minced dill and chives, mixing well. Season to taste with pepper.

Cut crust off toast and slice diagonally to make 2 triangles of each piece. Spread triangles with cheese and place 2 cucumber slices on each. Top with smoked salmon. Garnish with dill sprigs. (Makes 4 pieces.)

Lobster Bisque

2 teaspoons minced onion
1 ½ tablespoons butter
1 ½ tablespoons flour
1 tablespoon tomato paste
1 ½ cups hot chicken broth

½ cup milk
1 cup minced, cooked lobster meat
2 cups cream
Salt and cayenne pepper

Sauté the onion in the butter until tender. Add the flour and tomato paste. Stir until completely blended. Add broth. Cool until slightly thickened, stirring all the time. Add milk and lobster meat. Stir until well mixed.

Cook over low heat for 10 minutes. Stir in cream. Continue heating mixture. Do not let boil. Season with salt and cayenne pepper before serving.

Bibb Lettuce Salad
with Mushrooms and Pine Nuts

Dressing:
1 tablespoon olive oil
2 tablespoons raspberry vinegar
¼ teaspoon salt
¼ teaspoon sugar
Black pepper to taste

Salad:
1 head Bibb lettuce (butter lettuce)
4 mushrooms, thinly sliced
1 tablespoon pine nuts, toasted

In a small bowl, combine olive oil, vinegar, salt and sugar together. Whisk until well blended. Add pepper to taste. Place cleaned and sliced mushrooms in bowl with vinaigrette dressing.

Discard any discolored or bruised leaves from lettuce, retaining only center leaves. Handling gently, wash and dry to prevent bruising. Place a small handful on each plate. Remove mushrooms from vinaigrette and place on top of leaves. Drizzle salad greens with remaining dressing. Sprinkle toasted pine nuts on salads.

Brandied Orange Cornish Game Hens

2 Cornish game hens
Salt and pepper
2 tablespoons butter, softened

¼ cup orange marmalade
2 tablespoons brandy

Rinse game hens and pat dry. Salt and pepper cavity. Secure legs with kitchen string and place hens in a roasting pan. Brush hens with softened butter and roast for 30 minutes in preheated 350 degree oven.

Mix and heat orange marmalade with the brandy. Raise oven temperature to 400 degrees. Baste hens with marmalade mixture and continue roasting an additional 20 or 30 minutes, or until juices run clear and hens are browned. Baste occasionally with the marmalade mixture. If the hens start to darken too much, cover with aluminum foil.

Fruit-Nut Pilaf

2 cups chicken stock
½ teaspoon salt
1 tablespoon butter
¼ teaspoon ground cardamom
¼ teaspoon ground cinnamon

1 teaspoon orange rind, freshly grated
1 cup long grain white rice
½ cup chopped pitted dates
½ cup chopped pecans

Bring chicken stock, salt, butter, cinnamon, cardamom and orange rind to a boil. Add rice, cover and reduce heat. Simmer 20 minutes and let stand 5 minutes. Fluff with fork and stir in dates and pecans.

Glazed Snow Peas

½ pound fresh snow peas
  (Chinese pea pods)
Water to cover
2 tablespoons butter

1 tablespoon fresh toasted
  chopped almonds
Salt and pepper to taste

Trim both ends off pea pods. Place in small saucepan with enough hot water to cover. Bring water to fast boil for 1 minute. Remove and place beans in cold water to stop cooking process. Cool beans and drain well.

In a small skillet heat butter over moderately high heat. Add the peas, stirring. Toss with nuts and salt and pepper for 1 minute until peas are hot and ready to serve.

Fruit Relish

2 red delicious apples, cored and diced
1 firm red pear, peeled, cored and diced
1 cup freshly squeezed orange juice
2 teaspoons fresh grated orange rind
¼ cup brown sugar (4 tablespoons)

¼ cup orange marmalade (4 tablespoons)
½ teaspoon ground cinnamon
¼ teaspoon ground nutmeg
¼ teaspoon salt
¼ cup raspberry vinegar (4 tablespoons)

In a saucepan combine pear and apples with remaining ingredients and bring to a simmer, stirring gently. Simmer, covered, stirring occasionally, until fruit is tender, 10 to 15 minutes; cool. May be made ahead and refrigerated. Serve chilled.

Caramel Nut Chocolate Brownie Squares
with French Vanilla Ice Cream

1 package (20 ½ ounce) brownie mix   ½ cup chopped pecans
1 package (14 ounce) caramels   ¼ cup semi-sweet chocolate chips
⅓ cup heavy cream   ¼ cup pecan halves

Heat oven to 350 degrees.

Prepare brownie mix as directed on package. Spread ½ of batter in greased and foil-lined 13" by 9" baking pan. Bake in 350 degree oven for 20 to 25 minutes, until batter is firm to touch.

Meanwhile, microwave caramels and cream in microwaveable bowl on high for 3 minutes or until caramels begin to melt. Whisk until smooth. Gently spread caramel mixture over partly baked batter in pan. Sprinkle chopped pecans and chocolate chips over caramel.

Pour remaining batter mix over nuts and caramel layer. Some caramel and nuts may peek through. Place remaining pecan halves on top of brownie mixture. Bake for 30 to 35 minutes more.

Cool in pan. Run knife around edge of pan to loosen from side of pan. Using foil lining lift from pan. Cut into squares. This recipe makes 12 brownies approximately 3" x 4".

Serve with French Vanilla ice cream.

Menu

Sunday Supper
for Six

Old-Fashioned Meat Loaf

Lemon-Parsleyed Potatoes

Buttered Peas — Gingered Baby Carrots

*Red-Leaf Lettuce and Cucumber Salad
with Mustard Dressing*

Dinner Rolls

Black Forest Chocolate Cream Pie

Mumm Cuvée Napa Blanc de Noirs

Old-Fashioned Meat Loaf

2 cups finely chopped onion
¼ cup celery, chopped fine
2 carrots, finely chopped
4 tablespoons chopped pimento
2 tablespoons unsalted butter
2 teaspoons salt
1½ teaspoons freshly ground black pepper

2 teaspoons Worcestershire sauce
1 cup ketchup
1½ pounds ground chuck
¾ pound ground pork
1 cup fresh bread crumbs
2 large eggs, beaten lightly
⅓ cup minced fresh parsley leaves

Preheat oven to 350 degrees.

In a large, heavy skillet cook onion, celery, and carrot in butter over moderate heat, stirring, 5 minutes. Cover vegetables and cook, stirring occasionally, until carrot is tender, about 5 minutes more. Stir in salt, pepper, Worcestershire sauce, ½ cup of ketchup and pimento. Cook, stirring, 1 minute.

In a large bowl combine vegetables, meat, bread crumbs, eggs, and parsley. Place meat mixture into an oiled (10" by 5") loaf baking pan, packing meat mixture tightly into pan. Spread remaining ½ cup of ketchup over loaf.

Bake meatloaf in oven 1 hour, or until a meat thermometer inserted in center registers 155 degrees.

Buttered Peas

2 tablespoons butter
½ cup onion, minced
1 ½ teaspoons lemon zest, grated

2 (10-ounce) boxes frozen tiny peas,
  thawed
Salt and pepper to taste

In a medium saucepan, melt butter over low heat. Add the onion and lemon zest; cook gently, stirring occasionally, until onion is soft but not browned, about 4 minutes.

Add the peas to the pot, stir to combine thoroughly. Season with salt and pepper and cook, stirring, for about 5 minutes, or until the peas are heated through.

Gingered Baby Carrots

1 ½ pounds baby carrots, scraped and
  trimmed
3 tablespoons brown sugar
3 tablespoons butter

1 tablespoon fresh ginger, peeled
  and finely chopped
Salt and pepper

Cover carrots with salted water by 2" and boil, uncovered, until tender, about 10 minutes. While carrots are cooking, in a small saucepan cook brown sugar, butter, and ginger over moderate heat, stirring, until butter is melted. Drain carrots well and toss them with the brown sugar glaze and salt and pepper.

Lemon-Parsleyed Potatoes

2 pounds new red potatoes, scrubbed and
   quartered
¼ cup butter

¼ cup minced parsley
1 tablespoon lemon juice
Salt and pepper

Cook potatoes, covered in boiling salted water until tender, 20 to 25 minutes. Drain. Meanwhile, melt butter, stir in parsley and lemon juice. Pour over potatoes. Toss lightly to coat. Season with the salt and pepper to taste.

Red Leaf Lettuce and Cucumber Salad with Mustard Dressing

½ cup sour cream
¼ cup mayonnaise
1 garlic clove, minced and mashed to a paste
1 teaspoon prepared mustard
¼ teaspoon salt
Black pepper to taste

1 large head Red Leaf curly lettuce
   (washed and dried), torn into pieces
½ medium red onion, thinly sliced
1 English cucumber, thinly sliced
Cherry tomatoes

In a small bowl, whisk together sour cream, mayonnaise, garlic, mustard, and salt and pepper to taste.

In a large bowl, toss lettuce, onion and cucumber with dressing. Garnish with cherry tomatoes.

Black Forest Chocolate Cream Pie

1-9" pie crust
1 can (14 ounces) sweetened condensed
  milk
1½ cups semi-sweet chocolate chips

¼ teaspoon salt
1 can (21 ounces) red cherry pie filling
½ pint whipping cream (2 cups whipped)

Bake pie crust until golden brown, according to package directions. Cool.

In a saucepan, combine milk, chocolate chips, and salt. Cook over low heat stirring until chocolate melts. Add cherry pie filling and stir until combined. Pour into crust. Chill for 2 to 3 hours. Serve topped with whipped cream.

Serves 6 to 8.

Menu

A Christmas Dinner
for Eight

Watercress Soup

Baked Ham with Honey Apricot Glaze

Apricot Ginger Relish

Spicy Mashed Sweet Potatoes

Minted Peas

Sesame Waldorf Salad

Dinner Rolls

Chocolate Apricot Torte

Sugar Pecans

Mumm Cuvée Napa Brut Prestige

Watercress Soup

½ pound butter or margarine
2 medium onions, peeled and chopped
4 bunches watercress
½ cup flour

4 cups chicken broth
2 cups milk
Salt and freshly ground pepper

Melt butter in saucepan, add onion and cook gently for 10 minutes until soft. Set aside.

Wash and trim the watercress, removing most of the stems, but leaving a few. Chop coarsely. Add the watercress to the onions. Cover pan, and cook gently for 4 minutes.

Add flour, cook gently, stirring, for 2 minutes. Remove from heat and gradually add broth and milk. Bring to a boil, then simmer for 4 minutes. Add salt and pepper to taste.

Purée in a blender or food processor. This soup may be prepared a day or two ahead, and gently reheated when ready to serve.

Baked Ham with Honey Apricot Glaze

1 10-pound bone-in, fully cooked smoked ham (pre-sliced)

1 cup honey

1 6-ounce can frozen orange juice concentrate, thawed

2 tablespoons prepared mustard

⅔ cup apricot jam

½ teaspoon ground nutmeg

¼ teaspoon ground cloves

Preheat oven to 325 degrees. Place ham on rack in shallow roasting pan. Mix together remaining ingredients in medium bowl; set aside. Bake ham for 30 minutes. Pour glaze over ham and continue to bake until ham is heated through, about 1 to 1½ hours. Ham should be refrigerated within two hours of serving.

Apricot-Ginger Relish

1 cup dried apricots, chopped

½ cup golden raisins

1 tablespoon fresh ginger, minced

1 teaspoon fresh orange zest

1 teaspoon fresh lemon zest

¼ cup orange juice

1 tablespoon lemon juice

½ cup raspberry vinegar

1 cup apricot jam

Place chopped apricots in bowl. Cover with boiling water. Let stand 1 hour; drain. In a medium steel saucepan, combine soaked apricots, raisins, ginger, zests, orange juice, lemon juice and vinegar. Bring to a boil, stirring frequently, until apricots are tender, about 10 minutes. Add apricot jam to saucepan and combine well. Cook briefly to blend flavors and allow chutney to thicken.

Spicy Mashed Sweet Potatoes

6 to 8 large sweet potatoes, scrubbed
4 tablespoons butter, melted
½ teaspoon ground cinnamon
¼ teaspoon freshly ground nutmeg
1 cup coffee cream or whole milk

1 teaspoon salt
Black pepper to taste
2 teaspoons balsamic vinegar (raspberry
    vinegar may be substituted)

Preheat oven to 400 degrees. Bake sweet potatoes about 50 minutes, until soft when tested with a fork. Cool and peel. Place in pan and mash. Add melted butter, cinnamon and nutmeg. Stir in cream.

Return to medium heat and beat with spoon until creamy. Season with salt, pepper and vinegar.

Minted Peas

2 tablespoons butter
1 cup onion, diced
1½ teaspoons lemon zest, grated

2 (10-ounce) boxes frozen tiny peas, thawed
Salt and pepper to taste
1 tablespoon fresh mint, chopped

In a medium saucepan, melt butter over low heat. Add the onion and lemon zest; cook gently, stirring occasionally until onion is soft but not browned, about 4 minutes.

Add the peas to the pot; stir to combine thoroughly. Season with salt and pepper and cook for about 5 minutes, until peas are heated through. Stir in mint and serve.

Sesame Waldorf Salad

½ cup mayonnaise

¼ cup lemon juice

3 large apples, peeled and cut into slices

½ cup chopped walnuts

1 cup chopped celery

Salt and pepper to taste

Butter lettuce leaves, washed and dried

1 tablespoon toasted sesame seeds

In a large bowl, mix the mayonnaise and lemon juice. Add apples, walnuts and celery. Mix until everything is coated with the mayonnaise. Season with salt and pepper.

Arrange lettuce leaves on each plate. Divide salad between the plates, and sprinkle with the toasted sesame seeds.

Sugared Pecans

1 egg white

1 tablespoon water

1 cup sugar

1 teaspoon salt

1 teaspoon cinnamon

1 pound pecan halves

Beat egg white and water until frothy. Mix sugar, salt and cinnamon. Dip pecan halves into egg white mixture, roll in sugar mixture. Place in shallow pan. Bake at 300 degrees for 30 to 45 minutes, stirring every 15 minutes.

May be made ahead and warmed slightly before serving.

Chocolate Apricot Torte

Torte:
6 eggs, separated
½ cup plus 5 tablespoons sugar, divided   1 cup all-purpose flour

Chocolate buttercream:
¼ cup sugar   2 squares (1 ounce each) semi-sweet
3 eggs plus 2 egg yolks   chocolate
1 teaspoon vanilla extract   2 cups butter (no substitutes), softened
1 teaspoon instant coffee granules

Apricot filling:
2 cans (17 ounces each) apricot halves,   1 cup apricot preserves
   drained   Chocolate curls, optional

In a large mixing bowl, beat egg yolks and ½ cup sugar until thickened. In a small mixing bowl, beat egg whites until foamy. Gradually add remaining sugar, beating until stiff peaks form. Fold into yolk mixture. Gradually fold in flour. Divide batter between 3 greased and floured 9" round cake pans. Bake at 350 degrees for 15 minutes, or until golden. Cool in pans for 5 minutes; remove to wire racks to cool.

For buttercream, whisk sugar, egg, yolks, vanilla and coffee in a saucepan. Add chocolate; cook and stir over low heat until thickened (do not boil). Cool completely. In a mixing bowl, cream butter. Gradually add chocolate mixture; set aside.

Finely chop apricots; drain and place in bowl. Stir in preserves; set aside.

Split cakes into 2 horizontal layers each, place 1 on a serving plate. Spread with ⅔ cup buttercream. Top with another cake layer and ⅔ cup apricot filling. Repeat layers twice. Cover and refrigerate 3 hours before serving. Garnish with chocolate curls if desired.

Serving Sparkling Wine

Sparkling wine should be served in long-stemmed flutes or tulip-shaped glasses. They are designed to enhance the flow of bubbles and to concentrate the aromas of the wine. Crystal glassware is preferable to other glassware as the surface is rougher than ordinary glassware and more bubbles will form on these glasses. Do not chill glasses . . . it diminishes the enjoyment.

For many years, and still in use today, are hollow-stemmed, wide-mouthed glasses, which are also acceptable but not as satisfactory as flutes for several reasons. First, the hollow stem is quite difficult to clean properly and soap sediment will definitely impair the taste of the wine. Second, the wide mouth of the glass dissipates the bubbles more quickly than the flute or tulip-shaped glass.

Sparkling wine should be served cold at about 43 to 48 degrees Fahrenheit. This is easily achieved by placing the unopened bottle in an ice bucket containing one half ice and one half water for 20 to 30 minutes, or by placing it in a refrigerator for three to four hours.

Because a bottle of sparkling wine has a pressure of 70 pounds per square inch behind the cork, it should be removed carefully. Remove the foil and place a napkin over the wire hood and cork. (This will stop a "runaway" cork.) Hold the bottle at a 45 degree angle, and be sure it is not pointed at anyone. Then loosen the wire hood, and twist the bottle, *not the cork*, gently and slowly until the cork has been removed.

Wipe the neck of the bottle, and gently pour about an inch into each glass, allowing the mousse or froth to settle. Then return to fill each glass to two-thirds. This will prevent frothing over. Be sure to place the bottle back in the ice bucket to keep it chilled. Now, sit back and enjoy yourself!

A Selection of Favorite Recipes

from

Napa Valley Chefs

Baccala, Parsley Salad, Marinated Olive Salsa

Codfish Preparation:

½ pound salt cod

1 onion

1 carrot

2 celery stalks

1 fennel bulb

1 ½ quarts milk

1 cup white wine

2 bay leaves

Cover dried cod with cold water and allow to soak in refrigerator for 1 ½ days. Change water once during this time. This will remove excess saltiness. Drain. Place all ingredients listed above in a saucepan over low heat. Simmer for 45 minutes or until cod is tender. Remove cod from poaching liquid and reserve.

Codfish Cakes (Baccala):

4 ounces cream

4 ounces olive oil

5 garlic cloves

1 teaspoon ground fennel

3 potatoes, peeled, coarsely chopped

¼ cup Panko crumbs

½ cup Semolina flour

Salt and pepper

Place potatoes in cold water and boil until tender. Separately, heat garlic cloves in the olive oil. In another pan, heat the cream. Using a mixer, or by hand, combine drained potatoes, crumbs, ¼ cup Semolina, garlic, olive oil, and cream. Season with fennel, salt, and pepper. Form into 6 cakes. Coat the cakes with the remaining Semolina. Refrigerate for an hour or overnight.

Olive Salsa:

½ cup olives, chopped
½ cup olive oil
1 shallot, minced

Zest of ½ lemon
Juice of 1 lemon

Mix together all ingredients above and season with salt and pepper.

Parsley Salad:

1 bunch parsley
½ bulb fennel

Juice of ½ lemon
Extra virgin olive oil

Pick parsley leaves. Shave fennel bulb very thin and place in a bowl with parsley leaves. Dress the parsley salad with lemon and olive oil to taste. Divide the salad onto 6 plates.

Heat a large sauté pan over medium heat. Add olive oil. When the oil is hot, add the baccala cakes. When they have browned on one side, flip them over and cook the other side until brown. Place a baccala cake on top of each salad and drizzle with the olive salsa.

Serves 6.

We recommend Mumm Cuvée Napa Brut Prestige to accompany this dish.

Bistro Don Giovanni
4110 St. Helena Highway
Napa, CA 94558-1635

Pan Roasted Petrale Sole with
Tangerine Caper Butter and Watercress

6 tangerines
½ pound butter

2 tablespoons capers
Salt and pepper

Squeeze the juice of 3 tangerines and place in a saucepan over medium heat to reduce. Cut the butter into squares. When the juice has reduced by three-quarters, turn down the heat and slowly whisk in the butter piece by piece. Add the capers and keep the sauce in a warm place.

4 large petrale filets

¼ cup canola oil

Heat two large sauté pans over a medium-high flame. Add the oil. When the oil is very hot, but not smoking, add the filets skin side up. It is important to shake the pan a little after each piece is added to ensure that they do not stick. Allow the fish to brown and then flip to finish cooking. Petrale cooks fairly quickly and will lose its moisture if overcooked.

¼ pound watercress

Dress the watercress with the juice of 1 tangerine, olive oil, salt and pepper. Place one filet onto each plate and cover with the butter sauce. Place a pile of the dressed watercress on each portion and garnish with a tangerine half. Note: For added effect the tangerine halves can be grilled and roasted prior to presentation.

Serves 4.

Mumm Cuvée Napa Blanc de Blancs pairs well with the sole and watercress.

Bistro Don Giovanni
4110 St. Helena Highway
Napa, CA 94558-1635

Chicken Stewed in Tomato Sauce
with Asparagus and Pearl Onions

For the tomato sauce:

6 medium-sized ripe tomatoes, cored

2 garlic cloves, peeled

1 small jalapeño pepper, stem off

½ cup chicken stock

2 tablespoons dry oregano

2 teaspoons salt

In a four-quart saucepan, boil 3 quarts water. Add tomatoes, garlic and jalapeño pepper; simmer for ten minutes and remove. Peel tomatoes. Combine tomatoes, garlic and pepper in a blender. Add chicken stock, oregano and salt. Purée and set aside.

For the chicken and vegetables:

1 4-pound chicken, cut in 8 pieces

1 cup all-purpose flour

2 tablespoons butter

1 tablespoon salad oil

1 carrot, peeled and medium-diced

12 small crimini mushrooms, halved

20 pearl onions, peeled

1 pound asparagus, cut in bite size pieces, diagonally and blanched al dente

1 cup Mumm Cuvée Napa Brut Prestige

Preheat oven to 350 degrees. Season chicken with salt and black pepper. Coat chicken with flour evenly and shake off excess flour. In a 12" round, 2" deep heavy-bottomed ovenproof pan, over medium high heat, melt butter and oil and add chicken. Brown each side for 3 minutes. Remove chicken from pan and add mushrooms, onions and carrots, and cook until golden brown for about 5 minutes, stirring frequently. Deglaze with sparkling wine and reduce until it is almost evaporated. Add tomato sauce and bring to a simmer. Add chicken and cook in the oven for 25 minutes. Add asparagus and cook for another 10-15 minutes. Serve over mashed potatoes.

Serves 4.

Enjoy this dish with Mumm Cuvée Napa Brut Prestige. Cheers!

Cole's Chop House
1122 Main Street
Napa, CA 94559

Seared Salmon with Plum Sauce, Baby Greens and Mango Avocado Salsa

For plum sauce:

¼ cup plum sauce
¼ cup sweet cooking rice wine
¼ cup water
1 tablespoon soy sauce
1 teaspoon sesame oil

1 tablespoon lime juice
1 tablespoon cilantro, chopped
   (fresh coriander)
Pinch of chile flakes

In a small bowl, combine all of the above ingredients and set aside.

For the salsa:

1 firm ripe mango, medium diced
1 ripe avocado, medium diced
1 green onion, chopped
3 tablespoons cilantro, chopped
1 orange, sectioned

1 teaspoon chili flakes
   (or pinch of cayenne)
1 tablespoon lime juice
Pinch of paprika
Salt to taste

In a medium bowl, very gently combine all ingredients and set aside.

For the greens:

¼ cup rice vinegar
3 tablespoons lime juice
½ cup salad oil
1 tablespoon honey

1 tablespoon shallot, finely chopped
Salt to taste
½ pound baby greens, washed and dried

In a small bowl, combine the first six ingredients and set aside.

For the salmon:

4-6 ounce salmon filets

Kosher salt (to taste)

Freshly ground black pepper (to taste)

1 tablespoon salad oil

Preheat oven to 500 degrees.

Season salmon with kosher salt and freshly ground black pepper. In a heavy bottom oven-proof 12" skillet, heat 1 tablespoon salad oil over medium-high heat. Sear belly side first for about 2 minutes. Turn over and add plum sauce, reserving enough sauce to use as garnish. Place in preheated oven for 6 to 8 minutes for medium doneness.

While the salmon is in the oven, place baby greens in a bowl and add enough dressing to coat the leaves. For each serving, on a 12" round plate, place ¼ of the greens. Place salmon filet on greens and add a large spoonful of salsa. Drizzle plum sauce over the top.

Serves 4.

Complement this dish with a glass of Mumm Cuvée Napa Blanc de Noirs.

Cole's Chop House
1122 Main Street
Napa, CA 94559

Chicken in Filo with Amaretto Lemon Cream

1 package phyllo dough, thawed if frozen
2 Granny Smith apples, peeled
  and sliced thin
8 thin slices Gruyere cheese
4 (5 to 6 ounce) boneless chicken breasts

¼ cup brandy
¼ cup sugar
4 tablespoons unsalted butter
  + ¼ cup melted butter
Pastry brush

Amaretto sauce:

½ cup + 2 tablespoons amaretto liquor
1 cup cream

1 tablespoon fresh lemon juice

In sauté pan, melt 2 tablespoons butter, sauté chicken until cooked. Do not overcook. Place cooked chicken on a plate and refrigerate until needed.

Sauté apples in 2 tablespoons butter until soft. Add brandy and sugar, cooking until slightly glazed and tender. Remove from pan and refrigerate until needed.

Melt the ¼ cup of butter. Remove the chicken, cooked apples, and phyllo dough from refrigerator. On a dry surface large enough to lay out the phyllo dough, unwrap and lay three sheets on your work surface. Working quickly, brush each sheet with melted butter, then lay each sheet on top of the other length wise. Place 1 slice of cheese on the phyllo about 6" in from the end closest to you, then on top of cheese place 3 slices of apple, then a chicken breast, 3 more slices of apple, then 1 more slice of the cheese.

Fold the front flap of phyllo over the chicken and apples, and brush sides with more of the butter (there should be no dry spots or the dough will crack). Fold in the sides as you would if wrapping a package. Roll the chicken and phyllo over until you come to the end. Brush a little more butter on the end and press the end against the package to seal.

Continue this process with the remaining chicken breasts, cheese, and apple so you end up with four packages. Cover with plastic wrap and refrigerate for about 1 hour or up to 2 days.

When ready to prepare, preheat oven to 450 degrees, place the chicken phyllo packages on a baking sheet, spray with a little pan spray and bake for approximately 20 to 25 minutes.

While baking prepare the sauce: In a medium sauce pan add the cream, amaretto and lemon juice and cook over medium-high heat being careful not to boil over. Reduce down until sauce is thickened slightly or coats the back of a wooden spoon. Remove chicken from oven when it is nice and golden brown.

Place on work surface and with a serrated knife slice in half, or you may serve it whole if you like. Place on plate. Pour sauce over bundles and serve with steamed broccoli or grilled asparagus.

Serves 4.

Mumm Cuvée Napa Brut Prestige (Excellent pairing)!

Tomas Wagstaff, Owner and Chef

Misto Restaurant
916 Franklin Street
Napa, CA 94558

Insalata Bresaola, Celery Root, Endive, Black Truffles

6 ounces Bresaola
1 small celery root
1 endive
1 bunch arugula
1 lemon, juiced

1 ounce Parmesan
Extra virgin olive oil
White truffle oil
Salt and pepper
1 small black truffle (optional)

Bresaola is an air-dried filet of beef that can be found in a good Italian food store. Its flavor and texture are divine.

Slice the beef as thin as possible and dress immediately with a drizzle of lemon and olive oil. Peel the celery root and julienne. Julienne the endive spears and place in ice water for 5 to 10 minutes. Drain and pat dry. Reserve.

In a small bowl toss the celery root, arugula and endive with lemon and olive oil to taste. Season with salt and pepper.

Divide the salad onto 4 chilled plates. Drape the Bresaola on top and drizzle with truffle oil. Garnish with thinly sliced Parmesan cheese and shaved truffle.

Serves 4.

Mumm Cuvée Napa Blanc de Noirs is suggested.

Bistro Don Giovanni
4110 St. Helena Highway
Napa, CA 94558-1635

Truffle Stuffed Salmon with Buerre Blanc and Fried Leeks

6 4-ounce medallions of salmon filet

12 to 18 paper thin slices of fresh truffle, black or white

½ ounce good quality truffle oil

2 tablespoons butter

1 recipe Buerre Blanc

Salt and pepper

Butterfly the salmon—slice open. Sprinkle with salt and pepper. Keep refrigerated. Heat butter and truffle oil in a large sauté pan. When butter gets foamy add truffle slices sautéing lightly on each side and season lightly with salt and pepper. When cool put inside each piece of salmon and fold to close. Season outside of salmon and brush lightly with butter truffle oil mix. Broil 2 minutes per side. Should be slightly rare. Place on Buerre Blanc. Sprinkle with crispy fried leeks.

Buerre Blanc:

8 tablespoons butter

1 shallot, thinly sliced

2 tablespoons vinegar

Place shallot slices in a saucepan with the vinegar and simmer until the vinegar is reduced by half. Add 4 tablespoons butter and stir over a saucepan of boiling water until the sauce becomes frothy. Add remaining butter in tiny pieces. Remove from heat.

Fried Leeks:

2 leeks, sliced hair-thin

1½ cups vegetable or peanut oil

Heat oil to 375 degrees in small batches. Deep-fry leeks for 30–40 seconds. Drain on paper towels, sprinkle with sea salt. Place on salmon.

Serves 6.

Mumm Cuvée Napa's Blanc de Noirs is recommended for this entrée.

Mustard's Grill
7399 St. Helena Highway
Napa, CA 94558

Duck Breast with Papaya Lime Chutney

4 pieces, 2 per bird, Moulard duck breasts. Remove skin and slice meat diagonaly into 2-ounce cutlets. Pound the cutlets between moistened (with water) plastic until thin and even.

10 cloves of garlic, mashed into a paste
3 tablespoons smashed green peppercorns
1 tablespoon cracked, white peppercorns
1 tablespoon sea salt
1 cup olive oil, approximate

Combine garlic, peppercorns and salt. Mix well and liberally season the duck cutlets. Brush with oil. If you desire you can skewer two cutlets on two bamboo skewers running parallel so they are easier on the grill. Grill over a hot fire for about 40 seconds to 1 minute per side. To serve, top with a spoonful of Papaya Lime Chutney.

Papaya Lime Chutney:

4 papayas, peeled and minced
½ tablespoon chili flakes
1 jalapeno, no seeds, minced fine

4 limes, fine grated zest and all juices
1 teaspoon white pepper

Mix all ingredients and spoon over duck. Note: It is important to use sweet, ripe papayas, or use mangos.

This dish is served as an appetizer at Mustard's in the winter when mangos are at their best.

Serves 6 to 8.

Brut Prestige by Mumm Cuvée Napa pairs well with the duck breasts and chutney.

Mustard's Grill
7399 St. Helena Highway
Napa, CA 94558

Green Onion Corn Cakes
with Smoked Salmon and Lemon Dill Cream

½ cup cornmeal
½ teaspoon kosher salt
½ cup boiling water
2 tablespoons butter
1 egg
½ cup milk
¼ cup all-purpose flour

1 teaspoon baking powder
½ cup chopped green onions
¼ cup fresh corn kernels
   (optional or in season)
1 teaspoon vegetable oil
8 ounces good quality smoked salmon,
   sliced very thin

For cream sauce, whisk together:

1 cup sour cream
¼ cup heavy whipping cream
2 teaspoons minced fresh dill
   (save some whole sprigs for garnish)

2 tablespoons fresh lemon juice
2 tablespoons lemon zest minced fine
Salt & pepper to taste

Combine the cornmeal, salt and boiling water in a mixing bowl and let stand for 10 minutes. Melt 1 tablespoon of the butter. Beat the melted butter with the egg and milk. Add to the cornmeal mixture. Combine the flour and baking powder and stir into the cornmeal mixture until smooth. Do not overmix. Stir in the green onions and corn. In a large skillet over high heat, melt together the vegetable oil and the remaining 1 tablespoon butter. For each corn cake, spoon about 2 tablespoons of batter into the pan and fry until the uncooked side starts to show bubbles. Turn and cook until golden. Lay smoked salmon on top of corn cakes. Drizzle with cream sauce. Garnish with fresh dill sprigs and lemon wedges.

Makes 8 corn cakes. Serves 8 as first course or 4 as light lunch.

We recommend Mumm Cuvée Napa Blanc de Noirs.

Chef Nickie Zeller
Pearl
1339 Pearl Street
Napa, CA 94559

Pan Roasted Ahi with Almond/Pepper Crust and Wasabi Vinaigrette

4 5-ounce pieces of number 1 or
   number 2 ahi. Cut or have your fish
   purveyor cut these from the loin in a bar
   shape about 4" by 2" by 2"
1 cup Korean kogi sauce (recipe follows)

1 cup almond/pepper coating
   (recipe follows)
4 tablespoons or more wasabi vinaigrette
   (recipe follows)

For the ahi:
Preheat oven to 450 degrees. Put ahi in shallow dish with kogi sauce. Turn and coat all pieces well with sauce. Pour half at a time of the almond/pepper mixture on a plate. Roll and press each piece of ahi in the almond mixture until coated on all sides. Place the ahi on a lightly oiled baking pan and bake at 450 degrees, 4 minutes for rare, 8 minutes for medium, 10 minutes or more for well done. Remove to cutting board and slice each piece in ¼" slices. Fan slices on a bed of thin noodles tossed in more of the kogi sauce. Serve with steamed asparagus with garlic butter.

Korean kogi sauce:
½ cup toasted sesame seeds
¾ teaspoon coarse ground black pepper
¼ cup chopped garlic

1½ teaspoons dry chili flakes
3 chopped green onions

Process all of the above in a blender or a processor until paste-like.

Additional ingredients for kogi sauce:
¼ cup olive oil
½ cup vegetable oil
¾ cup seasoned rice vinegar

¾ cup soy sauce
¾ cup water
¼ cup lemon juice

Add all of the above to blender with previous ingredients and process until well blended.

Almond/Pepper coating:

1 cup toasted whole almonds, cooled

1 tablespoon coarse ground black pepper

1 teaspoon white pepper

Process almonds in food processor until coarse ground. Add pepper and pulse until blended. May be made in advance. Keeps up to a month or more, tightly covered in the refrigerator.

Wasabi Vinaigrette:

⅛ cup soy sauce

¼ cup lemon juice

1 cup vegetable oil

¼ cup rice vinegar

2 cloves garlic, finely minced

⅛ cup extra virgin olive oil

4 tablespoons Wasabi powder, made into a paste with a little water

Place soy sauce, lemon juice, vegetable oil, vinegar and garlic into blender and blend until well mixed. Add olive oil and Wasabi paste. Blend again until well combined.

Serves 4.

Mumm Cuvée Brut Prestige is a perfect accompaniment!

Chef Nickie Zeller
Pearl
1339 Pearl Street
Napa, CA 94559

Smoked Salmon with Horseradish Potato Salad

1 ¼ pounds smoked salmon, minced

2 ½ pounds potatoes, peeled, diced ¼",
  blanched

5 bunches watercress, pick leaves

2 leeks, split in half

2 ½ teaspoons horseradish

¾ cup crème fraîche

3 ¾ tablespoons chives, chopped

2 ½ tablespoons shallots, minced

7 ½ ounces citrus vinaigrette, see recipe

Juice of 2 ½ lemons

⅓ cup toasted horseradish, to garnish

Sea salt, to taste

Freshly ground white pepper, to taste

Toss potatoes, horseradish, shallots, chives, crème fraîche, lemon juice, salt and pepper, and smoked salmon in large bowl.

To serve: Spoon mixture into ring mold and compress. Lift ring mold making sure to preserve the mold shape. Wrap leeks around mold. Toss watercress with citrus vinaigrette and place on top of mold. Sprinkle toasted horseradish for garnish.

Citrus Vinaigrette:

1 ½ teaspoons minced orange zest

6 tablespoons fresh orange juice
  or 3 tablespoons each orange and
  tangerine juice

3 tablespoons Champagne vinegar

¾ teaspoon salt

9 tablespoons light olive oil

Combine everything but the oil in a small bowl, then whisk in the oil.

Makes 10 servings.

Mumm Napa Cuvée Blanc de Blancs is suggested.

Sean S. Knight, Executive Chef/Partner
Pinot Blanc
641 Main St.
St. Helena, CA 94574

Endive Leaves with Smoked Salmon and Crème Fraîche

10 leaves endive, cleaned
2½ ounces smoked salmon, finely diced
1¼ tablespoons crème fraîche
⅝ teaspoon lemon juice
⅝ teaspoon chives, minced

⅝ teaspoon shallots, minced
⅝ ounce caviar
Sea salt, to taste
Freshly ground white pepper, to taste

Combine smoked salmon, crème fraîche, lemon juice, chives and shallots in a bowl. Season with salt and pepper. Spoon mixture onto endive leaves and garnish with caviar.

Makes 10 servings.

Mumm Cuvée Napa Blanc de Noirs or Brut Prestige accompanies this hors d'oeuvre well.

Sean S. Knight, Executive Chef/Partner
Pinot Blanc
641 Main St.
St. Helena, CA 94574

Lemon Grass Scallops & Prawn Skewers

2½ pounds Day Boat (large) scallops

The Marinade:
2 cups (1 can) coconut milk
3 tablespoons yellow curry paste
3 tablespoons fish sauce
3 tablespoons sugar
½ cup fresh ginger, grated

2½ pounds fresh Tiger prawns,
    deveined, with tails

1 to 2 jalapeño peppers, seeded
    and finely diced
½ cup lime juice
1 lemon grass stalk, peeled and
    finely minced (white part at base only)
Lemon grass stalks for skewers

Combine all marinade ingredients together and mix well. Add the scallops and prawns and marinade for at least 1 hour.

Cut lemon grass diagonally into 3 to 4" skewers; peel the outer layers if too large. Save the peelings for soup, etc.

Skewer one prawn and one scallop on each piece of lemon grass. Grill on a hot griddle or grill on each side. Serve charred, medium rare. Serve with green papaya salad with peanuts.

Serves 8.

Mumm Napa Cuvée Brut Prestige is suggested to accompany this dish.

Wappo Bar & Bistro
1226-B Washington Street
Calistoga, CA 94515

Accras Caribbean Baccalao Fritters

1 pound boneless salt cod
2 cups water
2 ounces butter
1 teaspoon garam masala spice
½ teaspoon chile flakes

¼ cup sliced green onions
2 cups all-purpose flour
7 whole eggs
Peanut oil for frying

Soak cod in water overnight, changing water 2 to 3 times to remove salt.

In a heavy-bottomed saucepan, bring water, butter and spice to boil. Remove from heat, add flour all at once, stirring with a wooden spoon to form a ball. Return to low heat and stir with a good amount of muscle to dry the "panade."

Remove from heat. Add green onion and chile flakes. Then add eggs one at a time, mixing until fully absorbed into the batter. This step is most easily done in an electric mixer with the paddle attachment.

Remove all bones and sinew from salt cod and flake apart with fingers. Add to batter in mixer and mix until homogenous.

Heat peanut oil in a deepfry or cast iron Dutch oven to 350 degrees. With two tablespoons, scoop the batter into oval shapes and slide into the hot oil. When the accras float and are golden in color, they are done. Remove from oil and drain on absorbent paper. Serve immediately while hot, accompanied by your favorite spicy aioli.

Serves 8.

Mumm Napa Cuvée Blanc de Blancs pairs well with this entrée.

Wappo Bar & Bistro
1226-B Washington Street
Calistoga, CA 94515

At Mumm Napa Valley, our hospitality is as welcoming and friendly as our sparkling wines.

Our tours are considered unrivaled in the Napa Valley, and our staff is always happy to help you savor and celebrate the finer things in life.

The spectacular view from our glass-walled salon and sunny terrace make the winery the ideal location for your special luncheon, evening receptions, and elegant dinners.

The Gift Shop presents an array of wine-related items that are ideal for home entertaining and gift giving.

The winery is located at 8445 Silverado Trail. The winery is open seven days a week, the year round, from 10 A.M. to 5 P.M. Guided tours are offered hourly from 10 A.M. to 3 P.M. Private tours and tastings are available by appointment.

The winery may be reached by phone at (800) MUM NAPA (800-686-6272) and at (707) 942-3359. Mail may be sent to Box 500, Rutherford, CA 94573. The fax number is (707) 942-3440.

THE ARMY-NAVY GAME

THE
ARMY-NAVY GAME
A Treasury of the Football Classic

EDITED BY GENE SCHOOR
Illustrated with Photographs

Dodd, Mead & Company · New York

ACKNOWLEDGMENTS

THE EDITOR wishes to express his gratitude to the following individuals and publishers for permission to include the material used in this volume:

Frank Conniff and Herbert Kamm of the *World Journal Tribune* for special permission to use selections from the New York *World-Telegram and Sun*, the New York *Herald-Tribune*, and the New York *Journal American*. Selections from the New York *Sun*: "Army Triumphs Over Navy, 17-7," 1931, and "Navy's All-Time Eleven," 1932, by George Trevor. Selections from the New York *Herald-Tribune*: "He Was There in 1890," 1935; "Navy Rises to the Occasion," 1939, and "Here's the Way It Was in 1905," 1953, by Red Smith; "A Military March Down Memory Lane," 1934, "A Sub Named Jim Craig," 1937, and "Tradition Is Broken," by Richards Vidmer; "No Upset?" 1950, by Jesse Abramson; "Navy Beats Army in Football—and Singing," 1920, by Heywood Broun; "Dietzel's Arrival at West Point Parallels Blaik's," 1962, by Al Laney; "A Marine Steals the Show as Navy Sinks Army," 1941, by Everett Morris; "Borries' Runs, Cutter's Kick Win for Navy, 3-0," 1934, by Stanley Woodward; " 'Monk' Meyer at the Front," 1944, by Homer Bigart. Selections from the New York *Journal American*: "Speaking of Great Athletes," 1954, "Fame Catches Up with Whitey Grove," 1936, "About Gar Davidson," 1937, "This Is the Navy Coach," 1946, and "Man on a Spot," 1959, by Frank Graham; "English Writer Finds Us Riotous Enthusiasts," 1931, by Margaret Lane.

Charles Hoerter for permission to use articles from the New York *Daily News*: "Army vs. Navy—More Than a Football Game," 1934, and "The Long Gray Line," 1934, by Paul Gallico; "Stichweh, One of Army's Best," 1965, and "Football Pays High Dividends in Battle," 1946, by Gene Ward.

The New York Times for use of the following selections: "Army 21, Navy 21," 1926, by Jim Harrison; "Biff Jones, Army Football Coach," 1929, by Vern Van Ness; "The Army's Football Coach," 1930, and "Men vs. Supermen," 1945, by Allison Danzig; "Old Rivals Stage Novel Broadcast," 1943; "Nautical But Nice," 1959, and "Anchors Aweigh and Away," 1964, by Arthur Daley; "New Navy Coach Plans to Beat Army without Fanfare," 1965, by Joe Sheehan; "A Daring Captain Saves a Company," 1966, by Charles Mohr; "Cahill Substitutes Hard Work for Gimmicks," 1966, by Robert Lipsyte. Copyright © 1926, 1929, 1930, 1943, 1945, 1959, 1964, 1965, 1966 by The New York Times Company. Reprinted by permission.

Fred Byrod of *The Philadelphia Inquirer* and John Wilson of *The Philadelphia Bulletin* for use of material from these newspapers. Selections from *The Philadelphia Inquirer*: "Reporting the Game—1890 Style," 1954; "The General and the Private," 1947; "Army Beats Navy in Sensational Game, 17-14," 1922, by Perry Lewis; "Navy Heads for the Sugar Bowl," 1954, by John Dell; "Army Stuns Favored Navy," 1966, by Fred Byrod; "The Last Game: Sweet, Yet Sad," 1966, by Frank Dolson; "Gloomy Gil," 1919, by Art Robinson; "Army Stages a Classy Show for the President," 1961, by Art Morrow; "A Team of Destiny," 1950, by John Webster. Selections from *The Philadelphia Bulletin*: "Navy Conquers Army, 21-15, for Five in a Row," 1963, by Ray Kelly; "Vow of POW's Comes True at Army-Navy Game," 1953.

The Washington Post for permission to use "Army Offers a Smooth Machine in Mastering Its Dearest Foe," 1914, by Stan Milliken; and "Fighting Middies Come from Behind to Tie Army, 21-21," 1948, by Shirley Povich.

Bill Stern for "The First Football Helmet," "A Substitute Wins for Navy," "Tom Trapnell, Hero," "Five Favorites from Stern," and "Two Kids from Kankakee," from *Bill Stern's Favorite Football Stories*, Pocket Book edition, 1948.

Tim Cohane for "Charlie Daly and Pot Graves," from his book *Gridiron Grenadiers*, G. P. Putnam's Sons, 1948, and "The Vindicators" by Earl Blaik and Tim Cohane, from *You Have to Pay the Price*, Holt, Rinehart & Winston, Inc., 1960.

"Paul Bunker, All-American" from *Men of West Point* by R. Ernest Dupuy, published by William Sloane Associates, Inc. Reprinted by permission of William Morrow and Company, Inc. Copyright © 1951 by R. Ernest Dupuy.

Sport magazine, by permission of Al Silverman, editor, for: "Chris Cagle—Eight Years a College Star," 1963, by Ed Linn; "Navy's Big Gun," 1958, by Al Silverman; "Navy's Ike," 1953, by Stuart McIver; "Sailor Zug Takes to the Air," 1951, by Harry Beaudouin; excerpts from "The Bouncer's Boy," 1950, by Bill Bailey.

Pete Martin for permission to use "Portrait of a Fullback," *Saturday Evening Post*, 1945.

Harold M. Martin for permission to use "My Life at West Point," by Pete Dawkins as told to Harold M. Martin, *Saturday Evening Post*, 1950.

Glenn Davis for "My Greatest Day in Football," from *My Greatest Day in Football*, G. P. Putnam's Sons, 1944.

Max Wilkinson for permission to use "Football's Greatest Father and Son Act" by Stanley Woodward. Copyright © 1950 The Curtis Publishing Company.

Life magazine for permission to use "Captain Pete Dawkins Keeps on Winning" by Sam Angeloff, Life Magazine © 1966, Time Inc.

Shirley Povich for permission to use "Dynamite Joe of the Navy," *Saturday Evening Post*, 1960.

Barry Gottehrer for permission to use "Sailor with a Future," excerpts from *Football Stars of 1963*, Pyramid Books.

The Associated Press for "The Lonely End," 1958, and "Report from Vietnam," 1966.

North American Newspaper Alliance, Inc. for permission to use "Garbisch Defeats Navy, 12-0," 1924, and "A Tribute," 1936, by Grantland Rice.

Jerry Nason for "Army's Best Quarterback," *The Boston Globe*, 1959.

The Boston Herald for "He Was Determined to Play for West Point" by Arthur Sampson, 1936.

The Baltimore *American* for "The Navy Captain" by Sam Crane, 1906.

"Buzz Borries, Navy's All-American, Never Made His High School Team," 1934, by Lawrence Perry, Hearst Corporation, by permission of Herbert Kamm.

Spencer Pearson for "Brothers Replay 1926 Game," *The Corpus Christi Caller-Times*, 1965.

Leon Bramlett for "A Magnificent Defeat," 1966.

Wallace C. Philoon for "The Game Won by Fight! Fight! Fight!"

Francis Stann for "Win, Lose, or Draw," *Washington Star*, 1945.

Don Hill for "News Extra," radio broadcast, June 13, 1942, Radio Station WAVE, Louisville, Kentucky.

Baltimore *Sun* for "Navy's One and Only," by William Stump, the Baltimore Sunday Sun Magazine, 1949.

R. J. Burt for "Army vs. Navy in 1893."

"The Press Covers the 1911 Game," *Philadelphia Herald*, 1911.

Oscar Hagberg for "A Pat on the Back," 1945.

"The Traditions of Annapolis" by H. A. R. Peyton.

"Fight! Fight! Fight!" by John C. H. Lee.

For special permission to use the photographs in this book, grateful acknowledgement is made to: Kenneth Rapp, Assistant Archivist, United States Military Academy, West Point; L. Budd Thalman, Sports Information Director, United States Naval Academy, Annapolis; Frank Walter, Sports Information Director, USMA; the *World Journal Tribune* Photo Library; the New York *Journal American* Photo Library; Culver Photo Service; Wide World Photos, Inc.; *The New York Times* Photo Service; the New York *Daily News* Photo Library; the dozens of individual players, coaches, and fans who have contributed to the photographic section of this volume.

The editor wishes to thank his editor at Dodd, Mead & Company for her kind indulgence, understanding patience, and meticulous efforts. A particular thank-you is due Kenneth Rapp and Frank Walter, USMA; Budd Thalman, USNA, and his assistant, Miss Norma Lucas. Special appreciation for the use of personal scrapbooks goes to Admiral Tom Hamilton, Major General W. R. Shuler, General Garrison H. Davidson, Tim Cohane, Captain Buzz Borries, General Charles "Monk" Meyer, General George Smythe, Captain Alan Bergner, General Omar Bradley, General Dwight D. Eisenhower, Captain Oscar Hagberg, Colonel Edgar Garbisch, Admiral Lou Kirn, Leon Bramlett, Arch Douglas, Captain George Dalton, Captain Percy Northcroft, Lawrence Reifsnyder. The assistance of all who helped make this volume possible is gratefully acknowledged.

To the memory of
PRESIDENT JOHN FITZGERALD KENNEDY
who first suggested the idea for this book

FOREWORD

THE EDITOR hopes that the stories, anecdotes, the great moments, the personal reminiscences of former Army and Navy football players, the color, excitement, and glamor of the annual Army-Navy game will in some measure contribute to the further glory of the service academies at West Point and Annapolis.

The editor further hopes that this volume with its heroic moments on the gridiron—and the more dramatic and glorious moments of Army and Navy men in the greater performance of their duty to their country in moments of great stress—will serve as a source of inspiration to future officers and men of West Point and Annapolis.

General Douglas MacArthur noted:

"Upon the fields of friendly strife are sown the seeds that, upon other fields, on other days, will bear the fruits of victory!"

General Dwight D. Eisenhower, in a letter to the editor, spoke of his experiences during his war days and said: "I noted with satisfaction how well ex-footballers seemed to fulfill leadership qualifications. . . . Personally, I think this was more than coincidental. I believe that football, almost more than any other sport, tends to instill into men the feeling that victory comes through hard—almost slavish—work, team play, self-confidence and an enthusiasm that amounts to dedication."

Gene Schoor

CONTENTS

1. THE BEGINNING

2. THE BIG GAMES

5. THE COACHES

6. THE RIVALS: VIGNETTES

7. FROM GRIDIRON TO BATTLEFIELD

1
THE
BEGINNING

The first Army-Navy game, played at West Point in 1890. The Army team in black caps is defending the goal, while Navy in the striped hats is on the offense. Navy won, 24-0.

This is the story of how football came to Annapolis and West Point, and includes a colorful account by Gen. Harvey Jablonsky of that first Army-Navy game, the beginning of the greatest rivalry in the history of football. Jablonsky captained the 1933 Army team that defeated Navy, 12-7. An All-American selection that year, he was an assistant football coach under Gar Davidson. Today, as Maj. Gen. Harvey Jablonsky, he is Military Advisor to the Iranian Government.

Football Comes to Annapolis and West Point

GENE SCHOOR

WHEN AMERICA'S FIRST MIDSHIPMEN WERE ESTABLISHED IN 1794 BY Presidential Order, they occupied a position unique in the college world. They had come into existence fifty-one years before the founding of their alma mater.

There were but forty-eight Midshipmen in that first group, but having no course of instruction, they were free from the worries of becoming unsatisfactory sailors— at the time of their appointment, education was considered rather a liability, for the service at large felt strongly suspicious of educated young men interested in the sea. A sailor needed no education.

On March 4, 1845, George Bancroft became Secretary of the Navy, and seeing the sad state of Midshipman training and education, determined to take affairs into his own hands. He took over the abandoned Army post at Fort Severn, Annapolis, and here the Naval School was formally opened on October 10, 1845.

On July 1, 1850, with Comdr. Franklin Buchanan as the first superintendent and with a class body of fifty Midshipmen, the Naval School became the United States Naval Academy.

By 1865, Adm. David D. Porter, Superintendent of the Naval Academy, alarmed and disturbed by reports of drinking and carousing in the taverns at Annapolis, decided that the Naval Cadets needed a more wholesome diversion and a different type of leisure-time activity after a hard day in classes and the rigorous drills, and so he established a system of sports activities and athletic competitions.

By 1867, a series of Thanksgiving Day carnivals featuring track events, foot racing, swimming, wrestling, baseball, and other sporting events had begun at the Academy.

Comdr. Hawley Rittenhouse, who attended the Academy from 1866 to 1870, describes what is believed to be the beginning of football at the Naval Academy. In 1869 a Midshipman returning from leave appeared on the drill field with a football under his arm. He dropped the ball as he was tossing it to another Midshipman, and immediately there was a mad rush for the pigskin. A dozen eager Cadets bore down on the ball, scuffing at it and kicking it from one group to another. Before long, sides were chosen and the two teams battled each other up and down the field, until a tremendous kick by one of the Middies, probably Rittenhouse, drove the ball out of the field into the Severn River and the first football game at Annapolis was over. It was William Maxwell, a Naval Cadet from Washington, D.C., who organized the first Navy football team, was its coach, manager, and trainer, and arranged for a game with the Baltimore Athletic Club on December 11, 1879.

Maxwell, upon learning that his Navy team would be outweighed by ten pounds per man by a Baltimore club composed of former Princeton, Yale, Hopkins, and Pennsylvania stars, decided upon a bit of strategy that would later affect the gridiron uniform.

"Our men went to Bellis, the tailor," said Maxwell, "and he made us sleeveless jackets of canvas, laced in front and drawn tightly to fit the body. Walter Camp said I invented it, but I did not know there was anything original in the idea. All I knew was that canvas wet from sweat or water was mighty slippery to hold on to. I had learned this from furling sails, especially in cold weather."

The first Naval Academy football game ended in a 0-0 tie, but the game was, according to the Baltimore *News-American's* account, "a battle from beginning to end, a regular knock-down and drag-out fight. The scrimmages were something awful to witness. Living, kicking, scrambling masses of humanity chasing the ball to and fro."

Bill Maxwell was graduated in June of 1880, and it wasn't until Vaux Carter entered Annapolis in 1882 that the school competed once more in a football match. Cadet Carter organized a team that year that registered the first official football victory for Navy, defeating a team composed of former Harvard, Princeton, Pennsylvania stars playing under the banner of Johns Hopkins University. The boys from Johns Hopkins pushed the smaller Navy team up and down the field, but never were able to score against the determined Midshipmen.

To George Washington Street went the honor of scoring the first touchdown in Navy's football history. The following year, 1883, the Johns Hopkins team defeated Navy, 2-0, in the annual Thanksgiving Carnival at Annapolis. Star of the Hopkins team was Paul Dashiel, who became, first, a chemistry professor at the Naval Academy, and then in 1904 its football coach. A year later in 1905, under Dashiel's guidance, Navy was to compile the most successful season to date, and for the first time gain national recognition as a possible future football power with ten victories —one tie and one defeat.

In 1884, the Naval Cadets turned the tables on their local rivals, Johns Hopkins, defeating them 9-6, and by the next year, 1885, football had become one of the more important activities at the Academy, with the faculty reluctantly admitting that football "was mighty interesting and good for the young Naval Cadets." That year Navy defeated Hopkins, 46-10, but lost to Hopkins in a return game, 12-8, and then was beaten by the Princeton University Freshmen, 10-0.

John B. Patton, who played for Navy in those pionering days, wrote:

"The enrollment at Annapolis was then less than 200, the entrance age being from fourteen to eighteen years of age. It was really just a boys' school. No wonder our regular college opponents looked like old men to us. We were compelled to spend the Saturday morning preceding a football game at sail drill aboard the frigate, *Wyoming*, in Chesapeake Bay. We players would put in four hours furling and unreefing sails, scampering up and down the top gallant yard. This strenuous exercise was topped by a roast beef dinner and followed by two 45-minute halves of football."

Between 1886 and 1890 the Naval Cadets played a total of twenty-one football games, winning twelve while losing nine games, but it was not until Army accepted a Navy challenge in the autumn of 1890 that this awesome rivalry began.

Physical training at West Point had begun as early as 1817. In 1839, Cadet Abner Doubleday, "the Father of Baseball," outlined a baseball diamond and a set of rules, and organized team sports at the Academy were under way.

The Cadets also displayed interest in football and occasionally were "gigged" or disciplined for kicking a ball around the barracks field. A class "gig" sheet of 1850 records that Cadet Phillip H. Sheridan was disciplined for kicking a football near his barracks. Cadet Jerome Napoleon Bonaparte, Jr., class of 1852, grandnephew of Napoleon, wrote his father on May 5, 1850, "The officers have presented a football to the Corps and you may depend on the Cadets taking plenty of exercise."

But American football, despite its popularity at Harvard, Yale, Rutgers, and Princeton, was slow coming to West Point. In 1890 only three Cadets had ever played the

Dennis Mahon Michie, who organized, coached, and managed Army's first football team is known as the "Father of West Point football." Michie Stadium at West Point is named in his honor.

Naval Cadet Bill Maxwell (extreme left) organized, coached, and managed the Navy football team which played its first match in history on December 11, 1879, against the Baltimore Athletic Club. The score: Navy 0, Baltimore 0.

game: Leonard Prince, Butler Ames, and Dennis Mahon Michie. Young Michie had been born at West Point, the son of Lt. Peter Smith Michie, who had served with distinction during the Civil War, and had been stationed at West Point to teach Philosophy. Lieutenant Michie was one of the most conservative and one of the most powerful men on the Academic Board, but Dennis was able to get his way, more often than not.

It was young Dennis who arranged for a Midshipman from Annapolis to send a challenge to West Point for a football match. It was young Michie who promptly took the challenge to his father, argued that a challenge from Navy could not be ignored. And the tough old professor could do nothing but agree, and he even secured final approval for the game from Col. John Wilson, Superintendent of the Academy.

The United States Corps of Cadets today number over 3,500. In the fall of 1890, it numbered only 271.

"As I recall it," says Gen. John M. Palmer, reporting the event, "there was plenty of promising material in the Corps, but among those cadets who were physically qualified, only three men had any experience."

Young Dennis Michie had a bit of a problem. He was all at once captain, coach, trainer, and business manager of a nonexistent team scheduled to play a championship game in eight weeks. There wasn't the time, under normal circumstances, for Michie and his two assistants, Ames and Prince, to teach the mere fundamentals to the eager but raw recruits. And at West Point, the only time they had for their practice sessions was the short intervals of time between drills and other military duties.

It was only on Saturday afternoons, when the weather was too bad for drill and dress parade, that Dennis and his two aides could count on any time for continuous practice. But he did get his teammates up at 5:30 A.M., half an hour before reveille, for a jog around the Plains, down and back Flirtation Walk, over past the old Thayer hotel, around the superintendent's quarters, and then back to the barracks.

The great day of the game, Saturday, November 29, 1890, was a cold autumn day, and the clouds hovered over the Plains as the special ferryboat chugged to a stop at the Point, and a happy spirited group of Naval Cadets stepped briskly ashore and began the uphill walk to the gridiron. On their way a group of Naval Cadets passed the home of a noncommissioned officer, where a scrawny but spirited goat blinked at the antics of the happy Navy men, kicked up his heels, and walked away.

"Hey, that goat would make a good mascot," said a cadet.

"Let's take him. He ought to bring us good luck." Quickly the goat was commandeered and taken to the game. Navy has never been without a goat mascot since that day.

Maj. Gen. Harvey Jablonsky, now serving as military adviser to the Iranian Government, an All-American star and captain of the team at Army in 1933, describes the first Army-Navy game from actual reports of that day:

"The scene when the game began was a magnificent one, the sides of the field lined with hundreds of uniformed officers and cadets, with their wives and sweethearts wearing the maroon and white of the Naval Academy or the orange and black of West Point; the armed guards patrolling the boundary lines while the teams struggled for supremacy inside, and, above all, the magnificent scenery. On the north, grim old Crow's Nest, with a great black cloud hanging over, seemed to frown down upon the animated field. While Break Neck, across the Hudson, lighted up by the western sun, seemed to cheer up the throng. Old Fort Putnam, now falling in ruins, looked down from the hill in the west, while the solid stone buildings of the Academy closed out the view of the river on the south.

"But when the teams trotted out on the field, people forgot the beauty of the surroundings and cheered their favorites as college men cheer their athletic pets. What giants they were in the West Point rush line! Think of it! They averaged ten pounds more than did the Yale forwards and eighteen pounds more than the Princeton 'Tigers'; 184 pounds was the average of the team that lined up against the 175-pounders from Annapolis. And they were quick and active in spite of their bulk. Such players as these need only the practice to make them equal to a first-rate college eleven. Colleges have more men to choose from than the 250 who attend West Point and Annapolis. But don't forget that these 250 are picked men; each has passed a most searching physical exam before admission to either place.

"Time is called. The West Point Military Band starts up 'Annie Laurie.' Annapolis, having won the toss, takes the ball. She guards the north goal, a strong wind blowing somewhat against her. The game is begun with a V and before it is demolished by the military heavyweights the ball has been carried 20 yards. Then Emrich is pulled down and about a dozen young giants pile on top of him, while the pretty girls outside the roped area exclaim 'How cute' or 'Horrid,' according as they sympathize with the soldier or sailor boys. Hartung follows with a good run and then Michie makes another. He loses the ball, however, and then West Point begins to rush the ball up the field and Annapolis is placed on the defensive by the brilliant individual work of the West Pointers.

"The latter, however, don't know how to play the game very well. There is no semblance of team work. Michie makes a good run and then Timberlake dodges and squirms for 5 yards. But they do it all by themselves, while the rushers look on without knowing that they ought to interfere in behalf of their runners. Big Murphy hardly knows on which side of the line to push with his 200 pounds, and the Cadets guy him good naturedly.

"Soon the ball goes to Annapolis on four downs and six minutes from the opening of the game, Emrich is pushed and dragged over West Point's line with the ball. He fails to kick the goal though, but makes up for it a few minutes later by scoring another touchdown. Again he fails to kick a goal. West Point again does good individual work, but when Annapolis gets the ball she puts the soldier on the defensive. Plebe Johnson, the only freshman on the Annapolis team, makes a good run and the third touchdown. The wind is blowing too hard to kick a goal, and the half ends with the score 12-0 in Annapolis' favor.

"West Point has learned a little more about the game when the second half begins and, in consequence, Annapolis scored but twice; each touchdown, however, yielding a goal. The signals by which the Annapolis captain directs his team are something appalling. 'Clear ship for action!' he yells. But the girls who looked on and who feared

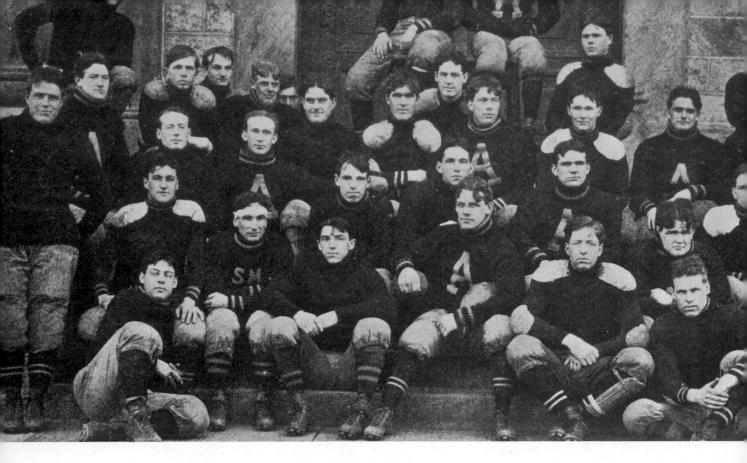

Army fielded a great team in 1903 and romped over Navy, 40-5. Captain Clyde Farnsworth (with ball) led the Cadets to a victorious season.

that blood was surely to be spilled, only saw the ball sent far down the field by a well-directed kick. Even the Military Cadets, brave though they are, looked frightened when 'Fire to the front, change front to the rear for the left piece,' was signaled. But all this meant only that the right guard was to try to run around the left end of West Point's line.

"Young Walker, the West Point quarterback, had the wind knocked out of him early in the game. He recovered and a few minutes later was walked upon by Annapolis men and hurt again. Still he played on. The second half began and a hard tackle of Althouse stretched him out limp as a rag, on the hard ground. When he recovered, after a pail of water had been poured on his head, he refused to heed the cries of Cadets that he should give way. Ten minutes before the game ended he was again stretched out, and was this time carried off the field. The final score: Navy: 24; Army: 0.

"One thing that was shown very clearly during the game was that both elevens have splendid material. Every man in the two teams played hard during the two 45-minute halves, and was in good condition at the end of the game. For Annapolis, the best work was done by Emrich, Laws, Irwin, French, and Lane; for West Point, by Walker, Michie, Prince, Adams, and Ames. Annapolis interfered well; both teams tackled hard and low; the backs kicked and dodged well, but both teams were weak in backing up their men and following the ball.

"Outstanding player for Navy was Halfback Charles Emrich, who scored four touchdowns, worth four points each, and kicked four extra points. It is a feat that has to this day never been equaled. Quarterback Moulton Johnson scored the other Navy touchdown.

"Dennis Michie, Ed Timberlake, Butler Ames, and Taurus Murphy were standouts for Army.

"The Army players understood the rules better than the Army supporters. When Emrich faked a kick and ran the length of the field for a touchdown, the Cadet rooting section seethed indignant at the officials because they did not call the ball back. But Dennis Michie laughed and slapped Emrich on the back.

"Another time Emrich was topped by Taurus Murphy, who spun him around 360 degrees and then released him. Duly appreciative, Emrich sped on for a touchdown. When Murphy was asked why in the world he had ever done such a thing, he said:

"'When I stopped him, I heard a lot of yelling from the sidelines. I thought I had done something wrong, so I let him go.'

"All during the game, a rather stately lady on the Army side kept exhorting the Cadets in a distinctly foreign gutteral:

"'Ghhhuard your man! Ghhuard your man!'

"But it was Navy's day. To climax it, the Cadets threw a hop for the visitors. Frank Schoeffel, the Army right tackle, attended it wearing a spectacular black eye.

"'I got it in the first five minutes,' Colonel Schoeffel recalls, 'when an opponent fetched me an uppercut. I thought it was a pretty low-down trick, and while I might have retaliated in kind, I didn't. I used a little strategy, and the next time he came to me, I arranged to grip him by the neck and scraped his nose in the ground. I did that four times hand-running.'

"Kirby Walker, the Cadet quarterback, didn't get to the hop at all. He was knocked out three times during the game. The third time, five minutes from the end, they carried him to the cadet infirmary, where he remained for thirteen days, recovering from a concussion.

"So ended the first Army-Navy game.

"The game was officiated by only a referee and an umpire.

"It is interesting to note that one of the officials was a Midshipman, as Belknap was of the class of '91, at Annapolis.

"At one time in the game, an Army man is said to have tackled Emrich of the Navy as he ran with the ball. The spectators voiced so much enthusiasm, however, that the Army player feared he had erred and released his grip. Whereupon, Emrich galloped for a touchdown.

"Imagine if you can, the Navy cheerleaders then leading this cheer:

"'Rah, rah, rah
Hi, ho, ha!
U. S. N. A.
Boom, s-s-s-s, bah!
Navy! Navy! Navy!'"

The first clash between Army and Navy in 1890 inspired some vivid prose. This story from The Philadelphia Inquirer *in 1954 recounts the flights of fancy of reporters of an earlier day.*

Reporting the Game – 1890 Style

THE PHILADELPHIA INQUIRER

If you could turn back the clock to a saturday afternoon in late November, 1890, and be on the Plains of the U. S. Military Academy at West Point, and then live to be among the 102,000 crowding Municipal Stadium today, you would be an eyewitness of a startling contrast.

That initial game of the great Army-Navy series was played before fewer than 2,000 spectators. But if the game itself matched the write-ups, it was truly a classic.

The newspapermen wrote their accounts for posterity in wild, tragic, and highly emotional language.

When Navy challenged the West Pointers the only cadet who had ever played the game before was Dennis Mahon Michie.

Navy was seasoned. Back in 1879, when the Midshipmen were known as Naval Cadets, William John Maxwell had organized a team playing under Rugby rules which tied the Baltimore Athletic Club, 0 to 0. Maxwell is also given credit for invention of the sleeveless jacket of canvas. This when wet was very difficult to grip.

By 1882, Navy was winging it, and defeated the Cliftons, also of Baltimore, 8 to 0. The Cliftons turned out to be Johns Hopkins University boys who adopted this *nom de combat* because the Hopkins authorities frowned on their participation in such a rough and rowdy sport as football.

Navy in 1889 had played six games, winning four, losing one, and tying the other. It had won five and lost one in 1890 when it challenged Army. Only powerful Lehigh had defeated the sailors.

Army was justifiably amazed at Navy's proposal, but the Graylegs immediately organized a team, received permission to practice in a curtailed period, and purchased one football.

Michie, a versatile cadet who was to die heroically at San Juan Hill in the Spanish-American War of '98, took charge at once as captain, coach, manager, and trainer. His young soldiers were eager, aggressive, and willing but completely green. A few simple formations were all they dared attempt.

Army came bounding through the ropes on the auspicious afternoon, wearing (amid other toggery) black stockings and black-and-orange caps, while Navy donned red stockings and red-and-white caps.

What a tug-of-war then ensued before Navy had its expected victory, 24 to 0, can be gleaned from the lurid accounts of contemporary writers.

One inspired newshawk wrote: "The flower of the United States Navy invaded the classic precincts of the National Military Academy and captured the flower of the Army.

"It was the greatest victory Navy has achieved since Decatur and John Paul Jones, and it has reason to be proud! The Army, however, was not disgraced."

Navy led, 12 to 0, at the close of the first half, and another enthusiast wrote: "The second half was even more ferocious than the first." He added: "In the grand collision of the sides nearly every man on the field is laid out, and four of them cannot rise. One is having his arm jerked into place, another is having his leg pulled, and a third is having his lung pumped. The fourth, Cadet Walker, is unconscious, and even the surgeon cannot revive him. He is carried to the hospital and the game goes on to the end."

Sensing the fierce mood of the rivals, still a third reporter wrote, "Blood on both sides is now hot. The Navy is ferocious and the Army reckless. They come together with a great crash and the Navy is HIT ON THE NOSE!

"The Navy is now like a wild beast that has tasted blood. It leaps against the throat of poor, confused Army, and in a little while Johnson is forced over the line for another touchdown."

One scribe wired his paper from the small and overworked telegraph office that the final score was 32 to 0, crediting Navy with eight phantom points.

When the final horn sounded, the young fellows immediately forgot their enmity on the field, hugged each other, exchanged mutual congratulations for plucky and courageous work, and went off to mess arm in arm and singing.

How *The New York Times* treated the first Army-Navy game.

Army chalks up its first win against Navy, and the big names are Michie and Bagley, two names that will always be remembered at West Point and Annapolis. Heroes in war, heroes in peace, no men have given more of themselves to their schools, the gridiron, and their country.

The First Army Win

GENE SCHOOR

NOVEMBER 27, 1891. THE DAY BROKE SHARP AND CLEAR, BUT THE EARLY morning mist that enveloped the Plains at West Point Military Academy seemed to indicate a portent of things to come.

There was an ominous quiet that was most unusual in the dining hall as the 273 cadets sat down for breakfast. The constant hum of conversation was missing. There was a strange feeling—a strange uneasy feeling that suddenly erupted into a roar as Cadet Capt. Dennis Michie left his detail to gather his teammates.

"Mr. Moore," called Michie.

"Here, sir," called Left End Lieutenant Moore.

"Mr. Haule."

"Here, sir."

Gleason, Adams, Clark, Smith, Prince, Walker, Dawson, Timberlake—

One by one, as the members of Army's football eleven rose to their feet, and smartly saluted, the Cadets roared with anticipation, for this was a historic hour in the epochal football story of West Point.

To avenge the 24-0 defeat by Navy the year before, seventeen Cadets, led by Lt. Daniel Tate, Coach Harry Williams, and Capt. Dennis Michie, were leaving West Point, for their second encounter with the Navy football team. Army had lost the first game, the first ever played between the two service schools, but Michie, Prince, Butler Ames, and Ed Timberlake, as well as the others, vowed vengeance. To back up that vow, officers at the Academy and at Army installations all over the world had sent in their financial contributions to defray the cost of the 1891 season.

Michie, who had devoted countless hours in first organizing, then coaching the Army team, realized his own knowledge of football was limited, and so, early in the fall of 1891, he approached Lt. Dan Tate, officer in charge of football.

"If we're going to have a try at beating the Navy, we need somebody to help the team—somebody who knows more football than I do," he said.

"There's nobody on the post here to fill the bill," said Tate.

"I think that we can get Harry Williams. He was a great star at Yale. He's teaching here at Newburgh. Maybe if you talked with him, he could help us out. And I think we can get him to help without pay, 'cause we really don't have any money for him."

Lieutenant Tate promptly contacted Williams, and Harry agreed to spend two afternoons a week with Army's football team. Williams, a football and track star at Yale, later became famous as coach at the University of Minnesota and created the Minnesota shift, a forerunner of the famous Notre Dame shift. Under Williams' more expert tutelage, the Army slowly emerged as a team. They moved as a unit on set signals, with previously arranged plays. As a further test for the big Navy game. Williams suggested the possibility of several preliminary games, and Lieutenant Tate and Michie arranged a schedule.

Army opened the 1891 season by defeating St. John's College, 10-6. Later, St. John's would be known as Fordham. Then, in rapid succession, Army was tied by the Princeton Reserves, 12-12; won a 14-12 victory over Stephens School; lost to Rutgers, 27-6; and scored a 6-0 victory over Schuylkill Navy.

Navy started the season with several startling victories, defeating St. John's, 28-6; then went on to triumph over Rutgers, 21-12; then defeated Gallaudet College, 6-0; drubbed Georgetown, 16-4. Three days after the Georgetown game, Navy ran over Dickinson, 34-4. Feature of the game was Quarterback Worth Bagley's spectacular play. The lithe 156-pound Bagley caught a punt and raced 60 yards through the entire Dickinson team for a touchdown. Then, in a never-to-be-forgotten football week, Navy took on its third opponent within seven days, and lost to Lafayette, 4-0.

Having learned that Army had a professional coach in Williams of Yale, the Navy called on the great Princeton star, Edgar Allan Poe, to coach the Navy eleven. Poe, a

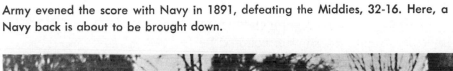

Army evened the score with Navy in 1891, defeating the Middies, 32-16. Here, a Navy back is about to be brought down.

descendant of the great author, had been a student for several weeks at West Point, had transferred to Princeton, and was an All-American quarterback for the Tigers in 1898. He came to Annapolis the day before the Army-Navy game and supervised the Navy practice, but an Army team thirsting for revenge, was not to be denied.

The Army team stayed in Baltimore on Friday and then traveled by train to Annapolis Saturday morning, arriving at 10:15. The Naval Cadets who met the boys from Army took them on a tour of the Academy and then sat down to lunch with them.

Meanwhile, special trains brought hundreds of rooters from Baltimore, Washington, and nearby posts, and by two o'clock, the crowd had swelled to more than 3,000 persons, including hundreds of Army and Navy officers.

The West Point team, clad in gray suits with black stockings and black-and-gray caps, moved onto the field, led by Dennis Michie. The Army band broke out into a rousing song. A moment later, the Captain of the Naval Cadets, Charlie Macklin, trotted onto the field, followed by Quarterback Worth Bagley and the rest of the team. The Navy players wore red-and-white caps and red stockings. The crowd roared at the colorful spectacle and there was a great cheer as the referee, Mr. Vail, called out Captains Michie and Macklin for the choice of goal. Army won the toss and took possession of the ball.

Navy was an odds-on favorite to win the game, but the Middies were in for a surprise.

Army put the ball into play with a series of powerful, well-organized drives with Dennis Michie, Ed Timberlake, and Ed Clark advancing the ball through the fighting, stubborn Navy team. Then suddenly, Ed Clark, the burly 200-pound guard, dropped back in a "guards back" play, caught Navy off balance, and crashed through the Middies from the 5-yard line for the first score of the game and Army's first touchdown in history against Navy.

Michie's goal after the touchdown by Clark put the score at 6-0 (touchdowns were four points, and a goal after counted for two points).

But now the Navy team came alive and started to move the ball. Navy's star quarterback, Worth Bagley, tore up the field in a brilliant display of rushing and was stopped just short of the Army 10-yard line. And it was Army's Dennis Michie who

Navy's first great football star was a 155-pound dynamo, Worth Bagley. His outstanding play during three years, 1891-1893, earned him the title of Navy's "superstar."

stopped Bagley. Once again Bagley carried the ball to Army's 5-yard line, and once again Michie and Timberlake stopped Bagley. Then it was Martin Trench powering through the line for a Navy touchdown and the score was tied, 6-6.

Army took over, moved the ball up the field, with Michie and Timberlake crashing through for long runs, but Michie was stopped on the 10-yard line by Bagley. By this time, the game had resolved itself into a personal duel between Capt. Dennis Michie and Worth Bagley of Navy.

Navy failed to move the ball and Bagley attempted a punt. The kick was blocked. Army's Bill Smith fell on the ball in the end zone. It was Army 12, Navy 6.

Clark scored for Army once again and the West Pointers led, 18-6. By this time the field was a bedlam—the players on both teams battered, bleeding, and groggy.

Stockings were torn off, five noses were bleeding, one man's ear was split, two Midshipmen were knocked unconscious, recovered, and along with Army's Smith and Prince, managed to stagger and crawl along the edge of the game, until Timberlake's final touchdown put Army ahead, 32-16, and the match was over.

Army went absolutely wild with joy. The Cadets dashed out onto the field and carried off the victorious players, singing, dancing, and shouting, as they marched off the field with a tired but happy Army squad.

That night both teams attended a dance at the Navy boathouse and the players from both squads danced with all the frenzy and ferocity they had displayed on the gridiron. Before the evening was over, each Army player and each Navy player personally congratulated the other on the fine game, and when the final number of the evening waltzed its slow rhythmic beat across the Severn River, Capt. Dennis Michie, Army's star, and Worth Bagley, Navy's great quarterback, shook hands. "Till we meet again."

Worth Bagley and Dennis Michie met three times after that savage game of 1891. They met in 1892 when Michie was the coach of the Army squad that lost to Navy, 12-4, and it was Worth Bagley who was the Navy's outstanding player. Bagley scored a touchdown and kicked two goals as Navy completely dominated this game.

In 1893 Army again was defeated by a Bagley score as Navy triumphed, 6-4, and once again Bagley's kick was the deciding factor, and again Bagley was congratulated by his former rival, now Lt. Dennis Michie, U.S. Army, on duty at Fort Russell, Wyoming.

"We'll get together for a beer real soon, Worth," said Michie.

"Be my pleasure to drink to your health, Lieutenant," said Bagley.

But that toast and the meeting never came to pass, for both Ens. Worth Bagley and Lt. Dennis Michie gave their lives for their country in the war against Spain. Both men died at their battle stations in 1898.

Ens. Worth Bagley, executive officer of the U.S.S. *Winslow*, was on duty patrolling the waters off Cuba. Suddenly and without warning, hidden Spanish guns opened up with a thunderous barrage of fire. A boiler on the *Winslow* was blown up; another shell poured onto the ship, destroying the steering engine.

Acting without a moment's hesitation, Ensign Bagley immediately took over the exposed position on the deck of the engineroom. Desperately he tried to direct the steering of the stricken ship by its propeller—Bagley was quarterback again in the biggest game of his life, this time in defense of his ship and his country. Once more the hidden Spanish guns blasted into the *Winslow*. A shell crashed directly on the exposed deck. Bagley and five other seamen, who were assisting him were killed.

Naval Ensign Worth Bagley was the first and only United States Navy officer killed in the Spanish American War. The date—May 11, 1898.

Army star Dennis Michie, who organized, originated and developed Army's first football team in 1890, and then went on to Captain and star in the 1891 victory over Navy, graduated in 1892.

As a second Lieutenant he coached the football team in the fall of 1892, and then served in the 17th U.S. Infantry for a five-year period. Lieutenant Michie served two years at Fort Russell, Wyoming and three years at Columbus Barracks, Ohio.

At the outbreak of the war with Spain in 1898, Dennis, now a Captain, was stationed at Fort Leavenworth, and was appointed aide-de-camp to his old friend, the West Point Commandant, General Hamilton Hawkins. Shortly thereafter, the regiment embarked for the invasion of Cuba.

Captain Michie was in the middle of the battle of Santiago in Cuba. Shortly before noon on July 1, 1898, he returned from a patrol along the front lines during an action at the San Juan River.

"I can see them up there on the hill," he said to his old teammate, Lt. Harry Patterson, "and in a few minutes will give them hell."

Then, gathering his men of the 16th and 6th Infantry, he led the assault on the hill, when a bullet from a Spanish gun killed him. The date—July 1, 1898.

He was only twenty-eight, the same age as his friend, Worth Bagley. His name and Bagley's will live forever in the treasured annals of Army-Navy history.

In the first Army-Navy game, in 1890, Navy defeated Army, 24-0. The victorious Navy team was captained by Charles Emrich, who scored four touchdowns and kicked four field goals. Navy players included: (Back row, l. to r.) Charles Macklin, RT; Martin Trench, RG; Noble Irwin, C; Rufus Lane, LG; Henry Ward, LT; Harry Smith, substitute. (Center row, l. to r.) Powers Symington, substitute; Charles Emrich, RHB and captain; Moulton Johnson, QB; Renwick Hartung, LHB. (Bottom row, l. to r.) Henry Person, substitute; George Lans, RE; Adelbert Althouse, FB; John Beuret, LE.

General Malone, class of '94, was at that first Army-Navy game in 1890. This news story, from the New York Herald-Tribune in 1935, records his recollections.

He Was There in 1890

NEW YORK HERALD-TRIBUNE

MAJ. GEN. PAUL MALONE WILL BE OUT AT FRANKLIN FIELD TODAY, ROOT-ing for the Army football team against Navy, just as he did at that first Army-Navy game forty-five years ago.

Only then he wasn't a major general. He was just a brand-new freshman cadet in 1890, when the Cadets and the Middies collided on the football field for the first time.

Today he is 65, Commander of the 9th Corps Area on the Pacific Coast. He is a short, stocky man, with silver-gray hair, ruddy complexion, and a jovial smile. He is also due to retire next year.

"I expect the Army will win today, but the game will be hard fought and the score close," he said. "I'm not saying that because I'm an Army man, for last year I picked the Navy and then won."

"But what a contrast between the game today, and that first game at the Point. I guess there's not many of the fellows left, who saw that first game, if that is what you would call it. You see, football was unknown at the point until Dennis Michie came from a prep school, where they played a little football.

"Now West Point at the time was under the command of Gen. Hamilton Hawkins, and when he heard that the boys at Navy challenged us at the Point, he promptly told us to get ready for battle. Believe me, it was a battle. There were more fists brought into play than you can count. As a matter of fact, before we could play, we had to have uniforms. Well, a number of girls who lived near the post heard about our need for uniforms, and they volunteered to make them. They did. The suits were so tight the players could hardly wiggle, once they got into them.

"I didn't play with the team. I was a little squirt. I weighed a little more than 119 pounds."

General Malone, who was graduated from West Point in 1894, was in charge of training American soldiers in France during World War I and commanded the 2nd Infantry.

Charles Macklin, who later married "Cadet" Emmie Stewart, led the Navy team in 1891 when Army, thirsting for revenge after its defeat the previous year, ran over the Annapolis team, 32-16.

Her husband was Adm. Charles F. Macklin, Navy '92, captain of his football team. Her two sons were graduated from the Academy. She is the only woman to hold a diploma from Annapolis. This is an interview with that grand old lady, Mrs. Charles F. Macklin, who, as Miss Emmie Stewart, won the hearts of the Midshipmen all. It is from the Baltimore Sun *in 1949.*

Navy's One and Only

WILLIAM STUMP

MRS. CHARLES F. MACKLIN HAS THE DISTINCTION OF BEING THE ONLY woman to hold a diploma from the United States Naval Academy. When she went there, she was called Cadet Emmie Stewart, '92, and she wore a long-skirted blue uniform decorated with gold braid.

She never had to march in formation. She never barked an order. She never attended a class in navigation. But she did do such things as receive at parties, ring in the New Year on the boathouse bell, and serve the athletic teams as a special sideline mascot.

In such roles, she made herself so generally indispensable and so generally liked that the Class of 1892 adopted her as the only class girl in academy history, and on its graduation day gave her a diploma, too.

The men certified that she had passed with "honorable distinction" the prescribed course in Friendship and Good Fellowship. And every one of them signed this testimonial.

Then, on top of that, the regimental commanders picked her as color girl that year —she ditched the uniform, and wore a flowing white and yellow dress for that thrilling occasion.

All this came about quite spontaneously, Mrs. Macklin says now, in her home on Bolton street, where the walls hold pictures of two generations of navy men—she married a member of that Class of 1892, who became an admiral. Admiral Macklin was senior naval officer of the Baltimore area during the last war. He died in 1945.

The first time she visited the Naval Academy, Mrs. Macklin recalls, was the spring of 1890. She was invited as the weekend guest of Yates Stirling, Jr., a childhood friend from Baltimore and another '92 man who was destined to become an admiral.

"Yates met us at the station—my mother went with me—and you might have thought he was greeting the President. He was standing at attention and there wasn't a smile on his face. Maybe his age accounted for his bearing; he was only 18—had been ony 16 when he entered the academy.

"For that matter, all my 'classmates' were in their teens; 1892 was often called the Kid Class. But all the cadets were younger then; it was customary to enter Annapolis at an early age, for the four years of study brought only the grade of 'past midshipman'; two more years had to be served at sea before a man became an ensign.

"On Saturday night that first weekend, there was a hop in the drill hall. Charles A. Zimmerman, who composed the music of 'Anchors Aweigh,' directed the orchestra, and it played waltzes and polkas."

On Sunday afternoon, the cadets and their girls strolled through the elm-shaded academy grounds to listen to the band.

"Perhaps it was the combination of early spring and the band music," Mrs. Macklin thinks now. "But whatever it was, I was very much impressed with the United States Naval Academy."

The Academy was evidently impressed with her, too, for, she was invited back the next weekend, and then practically every weekend for two years.

"Always," she says, "I was the 'date' of a '92 man. The class was small and its members were all great friends. I spent most of my time with them, and soon they were referring to me as Cadet Emmie Stewart."

Then someone in the class thought she ought to have a uniform, and so she had one made. "The boys made me wear it to football and baseball games and around the grounds. I'm sure some of the other visitors thought I was a genuine Cadet. And I know I felt like one."

Although the social life was formal, it was pleasant and friendly, Mrs. Macklin says.

One party is recalled by an account in a Cadet's scrapbook. "The New Year's hop was held in the boathouse on Thursday night," this reads. "Mrs. Craig and Cadet Myers received. Eight bells rang out, the bell being struck by Miss Emmie Stewart, the bugles struck up reveille, and the New Year was duly ushered in. The class dispersed and sought their partners to be the first to exchange the season's greetings."

The Cadets played football and baseball, too.

Many of Mrs. Macklin's friends played in the first Army-Navy game, and she remembers the excitement that ran through Annapolis when the team was given permission to go to West Point. Navy won the game, 24-0.

Naval Academy sports have always had a warm place in Mrs. Macklin's heart—she married the man who was the only one in academy history to captain both the football and the baseball teams. This wasn't the reason Charles Macklin won her hand, however, although the rest of the class jokingly charged that it was.

"Charles proposed to me aboard ship," she says. "It happened in the aftercabin of the *Santee*. The other men wanted to give me a miniature class ring to commemorate the occasion—the first such ring ever seen at the academy—but Charles wouldn't hear of it."

Instead, then, the class gave her a leather-bound autograph book with "EMMIE S. STEWART, '92" inscribed on the cover. It is filled with drawings, jokes, autographs, and songs.

The three old watchmen on the academy grounds were just as sentimental about Miss Stewart as the young fellows. When graduation neared, they presented her with a silver bonbon dish.

The day when four years of academy work and play came to a close for the class of '92 was bright and hot. The Severn sparkled in the sun as the battalion, in white uniforms, marched over the green parade ground. The competition for the best drilled company was held and Cadet Lieutenant Ferguson's company won.

That company formed a hollow square facing the reviewing stand. Miss Stewart, chosen color girl by the four company commanders, presented the flag to its commander.

When they left to serve their two years with the fleet, the men made Miss Stewart promise to wait for them. "Mr. Macklin said he didn't see how any girl could wait around for two years, but I did.

"I met them when they came back to Annapolis to take their final examinations," Mrs. Macklin says. "They had attained beards and mustaches of every description, not to mention an air of maturity and capability."

Soon after they were commissioned, the officers scattered, and Miss Stewart married Ensign Macklin. But she didn't lose touch with her other classmates. Many of them became admirals, and those who are living, still drop by Bolton street when they are in Baltimore.

Mrs. Macklin has returned to the academy on many occasions, the proudest of which were the graduation days of her two sons. Both of these served at sea during the last war. One is now retired as an admiral. The other, a captain, is on duty at Norfolk.

This is one out of the "old album." Brig. Gen. R. J. Burt (Ret.), author and composer of West Point's alumni marching song, "West Point, Thy Sons Salute Thee," recalls the last Army-Navy game played at Annapolis. That was in 1893.

Army vs. Navy in 1893

R. J. BURT

THE SQUAD TRAVELED BY RAIL OF COURSE. CONSISTED OF THE TEAM—THE only team, mind you. Each chosen member expected to, and was expected to, play the whole game. Substitutes were little thought of. Only a broken bone or cracked head (no helmets!) gave them a chance.

An old, old man's estimate is that there were, perhaps, fifteen or sixteen players taken along. On the fringe there, one or two Cadets—travel manager—liaison with the Naval Academy team management, et cetera. Possibly a medic, of such I have no recollection.

One civilian, however, was a curiosity, to us, a "trainer." He was sent over from Yale, probably by Lowrie Bliss, just for this important Army-Navy game. His badge of office was a bucket of water and in it a sponge—with which to revivify in case of any possible unexpected exhaustions. More of him anon.

Then above all was His Majesty the Tac! Lieut. Amos W. Dunning. (Strange how the name ripples up from the subconscious after sixty years in quietude!)

Turly Amos (I will not write what the Cadets really called him) was a majestic figure on our sideline—over six feet—over 200 pounds. Such as to put the fear of Heaven into younger Cadets.

I felt that he was there to protect us from all possible trickery by the Middies. He strolled up and down the sideline, fidgety as any substitute. Even called occasionally to our team captain suggestions for play! There was no real team coach.

The game: 4-6 Navy! I do not remember how promptly they made their touchdown and kicked their goal, but it was early in the game and thereafter we moved back and forth, forward and back, until finally our quarterback, Sammy Creden, so fired up the team that they marched down the field, in the ground—no passing—to cross the Middies' goal line. We breathed easier. Then! Some ten-thousand-more-or-less breaths were held while Abe Lott held the ball and Kit Carson, team captain, kicked, and missed.

There was no further scoring!

Enough said! We held no converse with each other back to our dormitory. Later, the Middies voraciously invited us to attend their, what they now styled, "Victory Ball."

I was the only Cadet to attend. It being my duty as a hop-manager at West Point, to pick up any worthwhile hop pointers. One point I did pick up in twenty minutes, was that no girl in the hall wished to dance with Army. And so—back to barracks—and so to bed!

In the train next day there was less than "joy and laughter." In sullen silence I crouched in the back corner of the railway coach. Sammy Creden's brother who had come all the way from Boston to see his brother play, tried to be sociable, but I would have none of it. Remember, I was just a kid, barely eighteen years. Out of the true "Wild and Woolly West!"

Then the "Trainer" from Yale, full of personal anecdotes, also strolled by but stopped when he sized me up as a listener. Now, looking back, I see him as "In the corner of a score of prizefighters." I write this for climaxing. He proudly stated that he had a silver plate in his skull. Cause—unknown! But it penetrated my kid astonished mind, to remain there until now.

Our train was late showing into the West Point station—after dusk—the Corps had finished supper but Shurge had had a "spread-out" for the squad in the mess hall. Note: A terrific dispensation had been passed out by the top brass. The Corps was free to go off limits to the station to welcome the Team! And this they did with much noise and forced hilarity—back slapping, et cetera, et cetera, but 6-4 was a dimming symbol that remained with all West Point until "Wait until next Time" began to awaken.

P.S. Team instructions—En masse by a few of the older fellows, knowing not much more than we football beginners did.

Basically:

(1) Don't get caught off side.
(2) Don't tackle around the neck or below the knees.
(3) Spot the enemy carrying the ball and "get" him.

The Navy team of 1892. Led by Captain Martin Trench (with ball), they beat Army, 12-4. Worth Bagley, Walter Izard, Art Kavanaugh, Charles Bookwalter, and Joe Reeves were among those still with the team in 1893, and they and their teammates again triumphed over Army, 6-4.

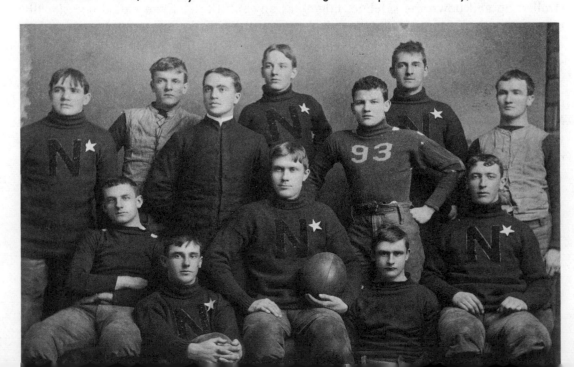

The 1893 Navy team featured a striking head guard worn by Joe Reeves. An outstanding tackle, Reeves was frequently kicked in the head when he dived headlong into a mass of players. So he used a crude protective device shaped like a beehive, which became the first football helmet.

Back in 1893, it was a little old lady, believe it or not, who produced the first football helmet. She didn't want to see her Navy men hurt. This is sportswriter Bill Stern's account.

The First Football Helmet

BILL STERN

ONE WINTRY DAY IN THE FOOTBALL SEASON OF 1893, A GENTLE LITTLE OLD lady went to see the Annapolis football team play a game, because she had become acquainted with Navy's right tackle—a youngster named Reeves. (Incidentally, that youngster, Reeves, in time, went on to become Admiral

Reeves, Fleet Commander in Chief of the United States Navy.) Well, back in the football season of 1893, that little old lady saw young Reeves accidentally hit in the head during a fierce scrimmage. Even after the game, she couldn't quite forget how her young friend had suffered a blow on the skull while playing football—and she began to worry about him and all football players who engaged in the grueling sport.

And so she decided to do something about the welfare and safety of her young football-playing friend from Annapolis. She went home and designed a moleskin contraption for the Midshipman which he could wear to protect his skull when playing football. And football-star, Reeves, wore that moleskin contraption in the next football game he played. It created a sensation. The fans as well as the rival football players laughed at Midshipman Reeves and his funny headgear. But it set a new fashion in football and revolutionized the wearing apparel of players everywhere. For the moleskin headgear, which a gentle, little old lady from Annapolis devised for that Navy football star, Reeves, back in 1893, was THE FIRST GRIDIRON HELMET ever used—a helmet that was destined to become part of every football player's equipment—a headgear to protect football players from injury and possible death.

Members of the 1901 Army team that defeated Navy, 11-5. (Top row, l. to r.) Charlie Daly and Pot Graves. (Center) E. E. Farnsworth. (Bottom row, l. to r.) J. A. McAndrews and F. H. Phipps. (In uniform) H. C. Smithers, assistant coach (above) and L. B. Kromer, coach.

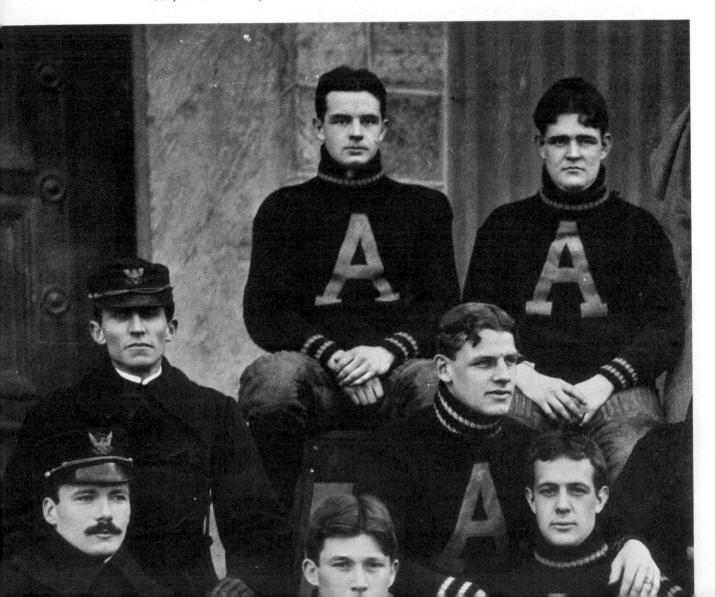

Tim Cohane, former editor of Look magazine, looks back to Army football at the turn of the century and vividly recalls the great gridiron exploits of some of Army's greatest, including the fabulous Charlie Daly and the powerful Pot Graves. Those were the days when gridders wore their hair long, and when such men as Vinegar Joe Stilwell and Adm. William (Bull) Halsey went all out for their service squads. It was at this time, too, that the great pomp and ceremony began to lend that bit of extra to the Army-Navy clashes. Sometimes the drama took place outside the gridiron limits and Tim Cohane's story of the bloody fistfight between Pot Graves and Tom Doe, another Army great, is a classic. This is excerpted from his book, Gridiron Grenadiers.

Charlie Daly and Pot Graves

TIM COHANE

TIM DALY KEPT A SALOON AT 760 WASHINGTON STREET IN BOSTON. JUST before closing up one night, the story goes, he caught one of his bartenders with a hand in the till.

"What do you think you're doing?" Tim asked.

The bartender was quick on the trigger.

"Sure now, Tim," he explained, "I was only after taking a little carfare home."

"Is that so?" said Tim. "Where do you live, in Honolulu?"

Even if some of Tim Daly's bartenders were tapping the till, his saloon prospered. Along around 1890 he moved his wife and six children, four boys and two girls, from the Cove, a district between Boston and South Boston, to a big, elegant house at 561 Massachusetts Avenue near Chester Park.

The Daly boys attended nearby Dwight School. Charlie Daly played quarterback, and older brother David, halfback, on a neighborhood kids' football team called "The Wellingtons."

Charlie, who was born on October 31, 1880, was the youngest and smallest player on the team. He was smart, brave, fast, and wiry. And he had an air about him. When he got to know people, Charlie could unbend. At Boston Latin School, where he was a 125-pound quarterback in 1895 and '96, he was called "Dan" Daley by his teammates after a popular comedian of the day. After two years at Boston Latin he was able, by native brightness and extra study, to pass the entrance examination for Harvard. James L. Knox tells in the Harvard H Book how the 1898 team, with eighteen-year-old, 142-pound Daly quarterback, stayed in Meriden, Connecticut, the night before the Yale game.

Far Left: Army's great quarter-back, Charlie Daly, was head coach, 1913 to 1916. Daly turned out two undefeated and untied teams, in 1914 and again in 1916.

Left: Ernest "Pot" Graves captained the 1904 Army team and later became an outstanding coach. His book on football strategy is a classic still referred to today.

"Parading the streets to the great amusement of the natives," he says, "were the great, big-hearted giant, Percy Jaffray, '99, and little Charlie Daly, '01. Percy had found a hat that accentuated his great height and Charlie another in which his active brain was lost. Percy led Charlie by the hand through the public streets, Charlie walking bowlegged to diminish his size, so that the picture was, for all the world, like an organ grinder and his monkey. And that carefree byplay was on the eve of the Yale game. Verily, a great change had come over the Harvard football player as viewed by old standards."

The change didn't hurt Harvard any. They beat Yale, 17-0, on a rain-swept, mud-logged field in New Haven the next day, and Daly excelled in field generalship, ball handling, and return of punts. In his three years as varsity quarterback, Charlie played in only one losing game. That was a 28-to-0 defeat by Gordon Brown's Yale team in the finale of his senior year. Walter Camp named Daly to his All-America first team in 1898 and '99 and to his second team in 1900.

Daly felt he had still to reach his peak. He got his chance to play more football when Congressman John F. (Honey) Fitzgerald appointed him to West Point. He passed the examinations and arrived on the Plain in the summer of 1901. One of Daly's fellow plebes had been a fullback for three years at the University of North Carolina. His name was Ernest Graves, but the nickname "Pot" followed him from Chapel Hill.

Pot Graves played fullback at Army in 1901 and was then shifted to tackle, where he became one of the best of his time. Graves was large and strong with especially powerful, long arms. And he brought to football one of the best minds in West Point history. As a player and later as a coach, Graves developed a concept of line-play strategy and technique far beyond most of his contemporaries. Much of what he taught forty years ago is still sound today.

Pot Graves would have titillated Jack London. His mind was as tough as it was brilliant. The *Howitzer*, West Point yearbook, describes him as:

"... a gentle, graceful, winsome lad, who never knew a harsher tone than a flute note and who runs amazingly to neck. In football, he stands high, plays low, slugs hard, and never gets caught. He made an annual habit of eating young Navies alive until they begged to have him muzzled. He doesn't give an ogee-faced damn for anybody that he ranks. He can jump the highest, fall the hardest, yell the loudest, and eat more railroad iron and more spikes than any man in the class. . . ."

Graves learned considerable about line play in the Army-Yale games of 1902, '03, and '04 from three harsh but thorough Yale pedagogues: Tom Shevlin, end; Jim Hogan, tackle; and Ed Glass, guard; all All-Americas. Pot was a willing, if unruly pupil. Shevlin, Hogan, and Glass believed firmly in the adage: Spare the rod and spoil the child. They tried to dissect Graves, and he reciprocated.

In one of the games Graves and Hogan got into a fight. Walter Camp is supposed to have disapproved of Graves for this incident. At any rate, he consistently overlooked him at All-America time. He was not overlooked at Army. When he was slow rounding into form early in the 1902 season, Charlie Daly remarked to Capt. Dennis Nolan, coach that year:

"I'm afraid Graves is slowing up. He's heading for the sidelines, sure."

"Don't worry, Daly," Nolan said. "When Graves is on the second team, we'll have quite a first team here."

That passage suggests Daly enjoyed rather a special relationship with the Army head coaches he played under: Leon Kromer, Nolan, and Ed King. He did. They not only recognized the 5 foot 7, 150-pound, dynamo as the greatest player by far West Point had ever seen, but conceded his superior knowledge of the game. Looking back, Gen. Dennis Nolan says of him:

You would have to pick Daly on any team for any one of four attributes. First, at calling the right play he was infallible. Second, as a runner he was very shifty and had that extra burst of speed like Glenn Davis. He could run faster with a football than without one; it was as if you had handed him an electric battery. Third, as a dropkicker he could aim the ball between onrushing tacklers. Fourth, as a punter he could average 40 yards beyond the line of scrimmage and aim the ball out of bounds near the corner of the field.

Football in 1901 was just as rough as it had been in Dennis Michie's day, but the Cadets carried more protection. They wore rubber nose guards, shin guards, shoulder and elbow pads. The average pants were padded enough to have stood erect at inspection with nobody in them. Equipment was not streamlined; each player was, in a sense, his own outfitter. Head protection later provided by helmets was supposed to be furnished by letting the hair grow to leonine length.

Army players were permitted to wear long hair at inspection during football season. They had their training table. They got no other concessions. Head Coach Lt. Leon B. Kromer had them for practice in uniform for two hours only on Wednesday afternoons (Herman Koehler, now commissioned a first lieutenant, was concentrating on his Master of the Sword duties). The other four days they ran through signals in their Cadet uniforms for a half hour after supper under a few electric lights strung along the trees near barracks. To improve their wind and stamina, they galloped around the Plains before reveille and again at 9:30 in the evening.

Interest in the climactic game with Navy reached a new high. Franklin Field's 25,000 seats were scarcely enough. Ticket speculators bobbed up for the first time in the series. They secured some of the invitation cards and sold them for as high as $40 each. The game also had begun to take on its traditional trappings. The Military Cadets and the Naval Cadets made their colorful, stirring march onto the field. The high-brass and Washington officials present were headed by President Theodore Roosevelt. He was surrounded by several hundred police and secret-service men; William McKinley had been assassinated in September. Roosevelt sat on the Navy side for the first half and crossed the field to the Army side for the second half. The Navy goat was on hand, as redolent as ever, but the Army mule, which the Cadets had adopted earlier as a mascot, was temporarily absent. After Navy's victory in 1900, Army had sold him for $42.

West Point sent its strongest team, up to that time, into action. Charlie Daly at quarterback was supported by Ed Farnsworth and Joe McAndrews, ends; Tom Doe and Paul Bunker, tackles; Napoleon Riley and Nelson Goodspeed, guards; Robert (King) Boyers, center; Capt. Adam Swattsy Casad and Horatio (Dumpty) Hackett, halfbacks; and Pot Graves, fullback.

Camp and Whitney both placed Daly and Bunker on their All-America first teams. And in subsequent years they were to select Boyers, Riley, Doe, and Farnsworth for honors.

For all the excellent players on his own side and a Navy team that was one of the strongest turned out by Annapolis, Charlie Daly dominated the game. He drop-kicked a 35-yard field goal to give Army a 5-to-0 lead. Before the first half was over, Navy drove to a touchdown, but missed the extra point, leaving the score tied—the value of the touchdown had been increased from four points to five in 1897. When the Naval Cadets scored, President Roosevelt forgot all about police protection and assassins. He leaped over the rail separating the stands from the field and, with a wild Comanche yell, ran to the Navy bench. For a moment it looked as if he intended to get into the game itself. The Cohoes *New York Republican* reported that the crowd went wild over the President.

Not even T.R. could steal the show from Charlie Daly. At the beginning of the second half, he delivered the sensation of the game and perhaps the most talked-of single play in Army-Navy history. Navy lined up to kick off. Charlie Belknap, Navy's kicker, had been instructed to be sure to keep the ball away from Daly. When Belknap was subsequently removed from the game, he was found to be suffering from a concussion received in the first half.

The Navy team in 1902. Charles Belknap was captain that year, as Army defeated Navy by a score of 22-8. Navy's stars were Bill Halsey and Ralph Strassburger, while Captain Charles Daly and Paul Bunker were standouts for Army.

That may have been the reason he kicked the ball straight down the middle of the field. Daly was standing on the goal line between the goalposts. He came up about 10 yards to take the ball on the Army ten, 100 yards from the Navy goal. Army had practiced a kick-off return play based on Daly getting the ball. Now the blueprints were put into operation. Daly headed straight up the field for a few yards, then veered for the right sidelines, with his blockers operating according to diagram. Harry (Sheep) Nelly, a sub halfback, who started the second half, threw the key block that eradicated two Navy players and sprung Daly into the clear.

Before the roaring crowd understood fully what was happening, Charlie had outflanked Fred McNair, the last Navy man with a shot at him, and was racing in the open. As he put the ball down in the end zone, his eardrums were threatened by the noise from the Army stands. Teddy Roosevelt was bursting with joy.

With his customary *savoir-faire*, Daly drop kicked the extra point. He had accounted for all eleven of Army's points. And now he excelled at protecting them. Time after time his deadly punts rolled Navy back. Twice he made open-field tackles that cut off touchdowns. He had been right in thinking he had not reached his peak at Harvard. He reached it that day against Navy in Franklin Field.

The final score was Army 11, Navy 5. Navy thought it should have been Daly 11, Navy 5, Army 0. At the end of the game, President Roosevelt shook hands with Colonel Mills.

"Extend my congratulations to your boys," he said, "and particularly to Daly. And tell Daly I said this was a great day for the Irish."

In the school year of 1901-02, Pot Graves roomed with two other plebes: Tom Doe and Pat Winston. Like Graves, Doe was from North Carolina and tough. He had

29

moved into a regular-tackle berth just before the Princeton game, when a horse kicked and broke the leg of John Munroe, the regular center, necessitating a shift in the line-up. Except for the 1902 Navy game, which he missed because of a broken arm, Tom Doe played regularly for four years, either in the line or the backfield.

On a winter Saturday afternoon after inspection, Graves, Doe, and Winston returned to their room. After a short time, Winston left. Graves and Doe had been getting on each other's nerves for weeks. What preliminary remarks passed in their room that afternoon are long forgotten, but they were soon swinging lustily.

The room was outfitted with three beds, three lockers, a washstand, three laundry bags, two tables, and three water buckets. Graves and Doe thrashed among these articles like two angry young bulls. They decorated each other with enough contusions to make a Dali mural. They splashed the walls and furniture with their blood.

They began fighting sometime after 2:30. Supper was at 6:00. Cadet Charlie Eby, a first classman, passing the embattled room on his way to eat, heard a smashing of furniture and glass. He rushed into the room and pried apart the two thoroughly tattered and torn plebes. He ordered them to wash and make themselves as presentable as possible, which was not presentable at all. They went to supper but had trouble chewing their food.

After supper, by tacit agreement, they set busily to work scraping the blood off the furniture and walls. But they could do little about their faces. On Sunday morning Col. Charles Gould Treat inspected their quarters. When he saw their faces, he put his hand up to his mouth and coughed.

"Cadet Graves," he said sternly, "report to my office at three this afternoon."

"Yes, sir."

"Cadet Doe, you report to me at 3:15."

"Yes, sir."

"Cadet Graves," said Colonel Treat, when Pot reported, "did you and Cadet Doe have a fight?"

"Yes, sir."

"Was it prearranged?"

"No, sir."

After the 1901 game, Navy had claimed Army was a one-man football team: by name, Daly. This irritated the Corps. Some Cadets talked about "beating them without Daly." Daly heard it and was sensitive to it. He went to see Capt. Dennis Nolan, who was to succeed Lieutenant Kromer as head coach in 1902.

"I had two years of high school football at Boston Latin, Captain," he said. "I played a year of freshman and three years of varsity at Harvard. I've played a year here. I'm getting a little tired of football. A little stale. I don't think I should play anymore."

"All right, Daly," Nolan said. "But wait until next fall before you make a final decision."

In the fall Daly decided not to play. He helped out as a Cadet coach. Nolan assigned him to putting in the "Harvard offense," a modification of the tackle-back formation to be used only in the Navy game. Army always put in two offenses in those years. They used one, usually the basic T (without any modern man in motion, or flanker), for the early-season games, and prepared a special formation for Navy.

Even with Daly on the sidelines, the 1902 team was too strong for most opposition. Jimmy Shannon proved a good quarterback. Paul Bunker was shifted from tackle to halfback. He had power, speed, and a flaming competitive spirit. Pot Graves was moved from fullback to tackle. His place at fullback went to Harry Torney. Besides Daly, only Adam Casad and Nelson Goodspeed were missing from the team that had started against Navy in 1901.

In the pre-Navy games the Cadets lost only to their nemesis, Harvard, 14-6. They beat everybody else and tied Yale, 6-6. Pot Gaves slammed in to block and kick that set up the Army touchdown. One charge by Bunker and another by Torney, and the ball was over.

Meanwhile, Coach Dennis Nolan was hoping Daly would change his mind about playing.

"I felt that Daly's inability to get anybody to quarterback the 'Harvard offense' as well as he could himself," recalls General Nolan, "would make him want to get back into action. Whether that was the reason, he finally did tell me he wanted to play against Navy. Of course, I was very glad to have him."

A committee from the three upper classes waited on Daly and persuaded him to play against Navy. He said he would, if they would let him alone the next year. With Daly running the team again, the Cadets reached a seasonal peak and beat Navy, 22-8. Bunker scored two touchdowns; Daly and Hackett, one each. Navy trailed at the half by only 10-8. Ralph Strassburger, star back of the Midshipmen, as they were now called in preference to Naval Cadets, ran 60 yards for a touchdown. On the way he stiff-armed Bunker and eluded Daly. Strassburger and Bunker spent much of the game punishing each other. Years later they met in the Philippines.

"Bunker," Strassburger said, "I hate you. Let's have a drink."

Army played with such purposeful drive, seven Midshipmen were carried off the field. Pot Graves was having a field day. He dished it out and he took it. During the first half he got kicked in the head.

"I can't focus my eyes," he told Nolan between halves of the game.

But he came out of it and played the full forty-five minutes of the second half.

Bunker was placed at halfback by Camp on his first team. Capt. King Boyers was center on the second team. Charlie Daly was at quarterback, and Harry Torney at fullback on the third. Playing only part of the season undoubtedly hurt Daly's chances of making Camp's first team for the fourth time in five years.

Early in the 1903 season Navy suggested to Army that only those Cadets and Midshipmen should be eligible for the service game who had not played more than four years, including any years they might have played on the first team at a college giving an A.B. degree. Navy claimed Army's older-age limit for entrance, 21 years to 20, gave her an advantage in accepting players from other colleges. Army countered that Annapolis had twice as many men from which to draw a football squad.

Navy replied numerical superiority could not neutralize such players as Daly, with his three varsity years at Harvard; Graves, who had played three at North Carolina;

31

Boyers, then completing his sixth year at West Point, and Captain-elect Farnsworth, who would be playing against Navy for the fifth season.

Nevertheless, Colonel Mills stood firm.

"I am glad to say," he wired the adjutant general, who had asked if Army would accept a compromise, "that the Military Academy will be willing to arbitrate any athletic differences that may exist between the two national academies, provided that the right of any Cadet not debarred by studies or conduct to play in any athletic contest or sport be not questioned."

Charlie Daly settled the controversy. He realized he was the cause of it. He announced he would play no more football, and this time he meant it. Navy was satisfied temporarily, since the major menace had removed himself. And West Point was satisfied, since she was conceding nothing in principle.

But for a while it had appeared there might not be any 1903 Army-Navy game. To insure an important climactic contest, Army had scheduled a mid-November game

Holding the ball is A. F. Casad, captain of the 1901 Army team. (Top row, l. to r.) Tom Doe, Paul Bunker, Ken Boyers. (Bottom row, l. to r.) H. M. Nelly and N. A. Goodspeed. (Far right) Dennis Nolan, assistant coach.

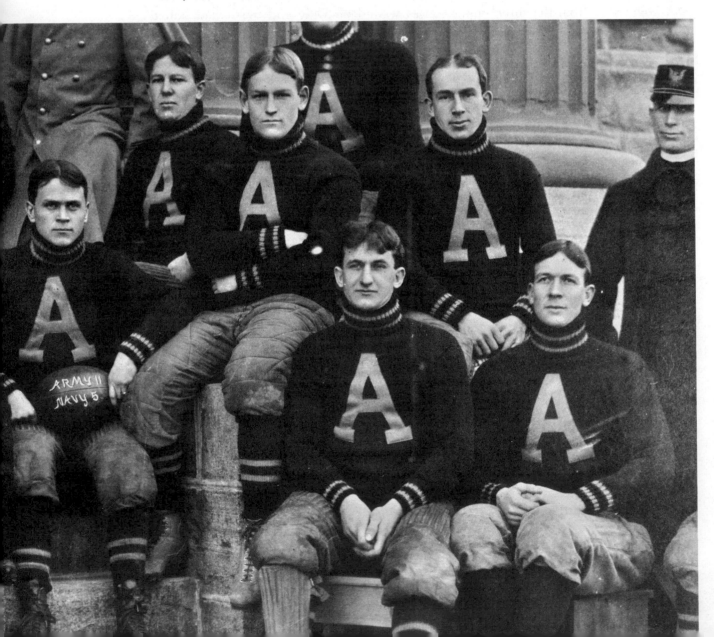

with the University of Chicago. Chicago, who plays no football at all these days, then featured long hair on the gridiron as well as off it. Amos Alonzo Stagg's team played a fourteen-game schedule in 1903 and ranked second in the West only to Fielding (Hurry Up) Yost's "Point-a-Minute" Michigans.

Chicago's strength was appreciated by Capt. Dennis Nolan's successor as head coach, Lt. Ed King, the former left-footed kicking star and captain in 1894 and '95. King had a powerful team. He had lost Bunker and Boyers, besides Daly. But some lively new blood filled in: Arthur (Bull) Tipton, Fred Prince, Russ Davis, and Ray Hill, backs; and Alex Gillespie and Charlie Rockwell, ends. Tipton, Prince, and Gillespie were to earn All-America honors from Whitney and Camp.

Daly was out every day helping with the team. Chicago had a prodigious freshman quarterback, Walter Eckersall. Among other things, he was dangerous running back punts. To prepare the Cadets, Daly simulated Eckersall in practice. Charlie tried his stop-and-start technique on Tom Doe one day. Doe refused to be feinted out of position. Daly laid down the ball.

"You're learning, too." He laughed.

A crowd of 12,000 came by train, wagon, and boat to watch Army's first intersectional game. There were 3,800 seats. Those without seats did the best they could. Marty Maher rented out stepladders at thirty-five dollars each.

"And the party who bought one," Marty recalls, "had to move it himself."

Army led at the half, 5-0, scoring a touchdown but missing the point. Eckersall was dangerous. He gave the Cadets heart failure running back punts, but they always managed to pull him down at the last second. And when he got close enough to try a field goal, Tom Hammond and Alex Gillespie, the Amy ends, swarmed through on him.

Early in the second half, Chicago turned on a relentless touchdown drive and kicked goal to lead, 6-5. That was how it stood until, with time for only one play in the game, the visitors lined up to punt in front of their own goal line. Back around midfield, a skinny little quarterback waited for the kick.

He was just a substitute quarterback, a little guy with a good head on his shoulders and plenty of guts and enthusiasm. He started Army's first basketball team, that year. After graduation he returned as an assistant coach and started the forerunner of the valuable Army "B" squad, the Cullum Hall squad, so called because they practiced over on the east side of the Plain in front of the building by that name. But Joe Stilwell is best remembered by his fellow cadets for what happened after Chicago kicked the ball to him with time for only one play that November Saturday back in 1903.

The Chicago kicker got the ball off. As it soared down the field, the final whistle blew. But the play had to be finished. Stilwell got set to catch the ball. A burly Chicago tackler bore down on him. Stilwell thought fast. Judging the course of the ball and the Chicago player, he saw the ball would hit the Chicagoan right in front of him. It did, and just as it did, Stilwell raised his right hand, signaling a fair catch.

The referee called interference and walked off the 15-yard penalty, putting the ball on Chicago's 35-yard line. Time had run out, but under the rules Army was allowed one more play after a penalty. There was only one possible play to try. A field goal.

When Daly had retired, Tom Doe had come into the picture as a place kicker. He had booted a 40-yard field goal for Army's only points in the 17-to-5 loss to Yale that year. Now he got ready to try his luck. A silence fell over the field, reminiscent of the day Captain Samuel's bugler had blown recall. Stilwell set the ball down. The Chicago line charged through. Doe swung his right foot in a cool, careful arc. The ball rose, turned over and over, and sailed directly between the goalposts, with the five points that gave Army a 10-to-6 victory. The Corps gave out a roar and rushed for Doe.

Army went on from the Chicago game to drub Navy, 40-5, the most one-sided beating in the history of the series. Hill, Davis, and Prince led the backfield charge. Up front, Hammond, Doe, Riley, Tipton, Thompson, Graves, Rockwell, and Gillespie ground the Midshipmen to bits. The Middies in the stands sang valiantly but pointlessly:

"Army, what makes you feel so badly?"

And the Cadets sang back, more *ad punctum:*

"We'll keep your little graves green."

The 40-to-5 holocaust was followed by more eligibility discussions. Colonel Mills relented on his former stand, influenced, perhaps, by the one-sidedness of the 1903 game. On the following April 15 he signed a three-year agreement with Capt. Willard H. Brownson, Annapolis superintendent. The document limited participation in the Army-Navy game to those who had not played more than four years of college football, including any years as a first-team member at any one of forty listed colleges.

In June of 1905, Daly and Pot Graves were graduated and commissioned second lieutenants. Their four years had coincided with Army's first football era. In the fall of 1905 they assisted Lt. King Boyers, who had succeeded Lt. Ed King as head coach in 1904. The 1905 team won four, lost four, and was tied by Navy, 6-6. Once again Casper Whitney put Harry Torrey at fullback on his first team.

In 1906 Daly resigned his commission. Graves assisted Capt. Henry C. Smithers with the team that year, until Smithers was suddenly called to Cuba. Then Graves took over as head coach. The Cadets won three, tied one, and lost five, including a 10-to-0 defeat by Navy. The 1907 team, under Smithers, did better, winning six, losing two, and playing Yale a scoreless tie. But one of the defeats was by Navy, 6-0.

Pot Graves left West Point after the 1906 season. In 1912 he returned as head coach. But it was not until 1913 that Daly and Graves were together again in West Point football.

And West Point missed them in the years between.

There are few writers who can match the wit and humor of Red Smith. Here he gives us, on the eve of the 1953 Army-Navy game, a letter from Brig. Gen. Alexander G. Gillespie (Ret.), captain of the 1905 Army team, with some notes on the way the game used to be played. Red spices the communication with some notes on the survival rate of the service gridders, both in war and on the gridiron.

Here's the Way It Was in 1905

RED SMITH

IN ALEX GILLESPIE'S DAY ARMY HAD A SKINNY LITTLE SUBSTITUTE QUARTER-back named Stilwell. One gets the idea that he grew up moderately tough, because later on when they asked Lt. Gen. Vinegar Joe Stilwell about the part horses had played in the China-Burma-India war theatre, he replied: "They were good to eat."

There was another Army player named Thompo Thompson, and Navy's fullback was Bull Halsey. They also won some distinction afterward, and when they met again, Admiral Halsey said, "Last time I saw you, you were rubbing my nose all over Franklin Field."

Maj. General Thompson spread his hands. "How was I to know you were going to be commander of the fleet in the South Pacific?"

Happily, this week, there came a letter. It was signed simply: "Alexander G. Gillespie, Brigadier General, U.S.A. (Ret.)." The writer did not mention that Alex Gillespie, end, was captain of the Army football team of 1905. He did not identify himself as the man who made Walter Camp's second All-American team in 1904. He wrote simply: "On Dec. 2, 1905, there was played at Princeton, N.J., the last football game of the old era. A description of that game as reported by Langdon Smith in the Chicago *Record-Herald* was as follows:

" 'In that grueling contest President [Theodore] Roosevelt had seen players writhing on the ground as though in the agonies of death. He had seen them lying prone and senseless, with eyes staring skyward, devoid of reason. He had seen sweaters ripped from players' backs and the raw, rasped skin exposed, soon to grow black with mud and bruises, and never before had a President of the United States seen a more brutal game.

" 'There was no slugging, and but few displays of temper. It was the dull, insensate grind of a mass of brawn and muscle, where arms were wrenched, necks twisted,

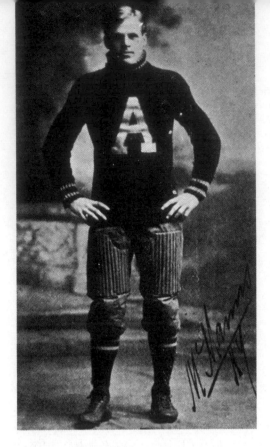

In 1905, Alex Gillespie, a three-year veteran, was elected captain of the football team and led Army to a 6-6 tie with Navy in what was described as "one of the most hard fought football games ever seen."

breath knocked from bodies, heels planted on necks and faces, and at least 11 players temporarily disabled.

" 'It was an eloquent sermon, not on the game itself but on the way it is played. It may well afford a text to President Roosevelt, who likes the sport, to interfere in the interest of the game . . .'

"President Teddy Roosevelt's remarks after the game, as reported by Smith, were: 'By George! It's a great game, but it should be materially amended so as to avoid such injuries. It is deplorable.' Other observers included ex-President [Grover] Cleveland and future Presidents [Howard A.] Taft and [Woodrow] Wilson, but what they thought of it, if anything, is not recorded.

"Teddy, though, had the rules changed the following winter. In the old game we played 70 minutes with a 10-minute interim at the half. This was changed to four 15-minute quarters with a 15-minute rest at the half.

"The length of the field was cut 10 yards, which made those long touchdown runs not quite so difficult. A neutral zone was established, probably so a lineman's teeth would not be quite so close to his opponent's ear. And the forward pass was permitted, with restrictions.

"All this was designed to open up the game so the spectators could see the ball once in a while. Formerly one never saw it except at the kickoff and during punts, dropkicks, and placekicks. Its progress, normally, was marked by the pyramidal piles of players, all supposed to be 'in on every play.'

"The man at the bottom of the pile was not comfortable, especially if one of his opponents happened to be inclined to a bit of mayhem. The ball itself was not exempt, either. In this 1905 game it collapsed and a new one had to be brought in.

"The writer, who played in every minute of the game, can testify that the carnage as described by Mr. Smith was not really so bad. Tackling, of course, was deadly, as it was supposed to be, and when a man went down he stayed down.

"He didn't crawl ahead any, for he had nothing to crawl with; his knees were pinned down. There was none of this bunny-hug and piggyback type of tackling.

"Further evidence that this 1905 game was not so devastating is that of the fourteen men (eleven regulars and three subs) who played on the Army side that day, nine are still alive after forty-eight years. What the Navy mortality rate is, we have no present information."

Those encouraging vital statistics are commended to the special attention of the young men scheduled to participate in tomorrow's entertainment here. Alex Gillespie and his colleagues not only went up against the Navy blockers and tacklers, but also against enemy bullets in at least two wars. Still they survived.

Football can't be so bad after all. The only thing to fear in Municipal Stadium tomorrow is fear itself. The joint's full of Roosevelts.

Army football captains. (By rows, from top, l. to r.) E. L. King, 1894 and 1895; W. D. Connor, 1896; W. F. Nesbitt, 1897; L. B. Kromer, 1898; Dennis Michie (Father of Army Football), 1890; W. D. Smith, 1899 and 1900; A. F. Casad, 1901; Bill Boyers, 1902; E. E. Farnsworth, 1903; Ernest "Pot" Graves, 1904; A. G. Gillespie, 1905; Rodney Smith, 1907; R. C. Hill, 1906.

Gen. John C. H. Lee, recalling the football heroics of his era at West Point, 1909, writes a pep letter to the Army cheerleaders of 1926, and calls on them to inspire their gridders to bigger and better victories over Navy.

Fight! Fight! Fight!

JOHN C. H. LEE

WAR DEPARTMENT
MISSISSIPPI RIVER COMMISSION
Third District
Vicksburg, Mississippi

October 27, 1926

TABLE COMMANDMENT:— PLEASE HOLD THESE COPIES UNTIL CORPS IS CALLED TO ATTENTION, NEAR CLOSE OF MEAL.

Memorandum for the Cadet Cheer Leader:

Having had your job eighteen years ago, am coming to Chicago a month from today to see how the Corps backs what seems to be one of the strongest teams we have ever had. I predict either a great victory—one to comfort ardent men like Nelly of '02, who, when asked if he preferred to see a "good close game," replied "close h--l! I hope to see the game when we beat 'em a hundred and fifty to nothin'!" —Yes, I predict either a great victory resulting from strength, skill, and MORALE—or else a bitter, humiliating defeat.

Do you know the Academy's football history for the years 1905-1908? If not, let me urge you to study it. Ask Colonel Koehler about it, or Major Stearns. It has a close analogy to your situation, only reversed.

In 1905 the teams tied. Next year the Navy won over what was considered a stronger Army team. Again, in 1907, our powerful and almost confident team went down in defeat. With 1908's Graduation, departed over half the first team, leaving no class at West Point with a football victory over the Navy to its credit. The Navy on the other hand retained practically its entire team—a machine seasoned with the habit of victory, confident, sure. In the face of these odds, in the face of apparently poor prospects among the plebes, but in the face of having to graduate otherwise without a victory, the class of 1909 pledged itself to "Lick the Navy." Under that inspiration, the Corps as a unit backed that team with a morale of never-say-die determination which could have only one result—a clean sweep over the Navy, not only in the desperate 6-to-4 fight in Philadephia but in all other sports as well—why? Because the Army was heavier? No, we were far lighter. Because we had more stars? No, we had but one crippled star, Pullen, while the Navy had an All-American captain heading a veteran team. Because we had good substitutes? No, we had practically an eleven-man team and prayed daily that no one would be hurt before the game. No, the reason was, as the great soldier Bonaparte said, morale was to the physical as three is to one—that team won on courage, guts, determination, and a fighting fury that surged in the breast of every man in the Corps. That was the origin of "Fight! Fight! Fight!"—it burst spontaneously from the Army stands and throbbed for that long, grim hour, till the whistle blew and out battered, bleeding, but conquering team was carried cramped and crippled into the old Quaker Gym. Stearns will tell you how the trainers worked to bring them round—they had given all they had—and it was enough to win. That team had to *win*—it was hypnotized with the grim viciousness of Joe Beacham, the irrepressible drive of Henry Nelly, the death-gripping mastery of Cope Philoon, and the deep, unceasing, pulsing roar of a Corps aroused, single-minded and militant, to carry its team to the victory it had to win.

Lad, with spirit like that, and the team you've got, God! what a victory you can see! Have you the Corps inspired? Does the first class silence the knocker before he knocks? Is the team a solid unit and an integral pulsing part of the Corps? Does every Cadet WANT to turn out each day to encourage the squad? Frankly, I fear not. The Corps for the past three years has failed to convince me at the game that they really, deeply, desperately cared.

Do I make you angry? I hope so, for I want now to tell you why.

Down at Annapolis is a blue-clad brigade, with no class having seen a football victory over the Army—one tie—two defeats. Do you get the analogy? They have beaten Princeton. Our team in 1908 held Princeton to a tie score—it was blood and wine to our hungry yearning craving for victory. We then *knew* our team could fight. The Navy now knows its team can win. But can they do as Cope Philoon's team did in 1908—beat a proud confident veteran team of their ancient foe? I wonder. The whole Army wonders—will the country wonder when the last whistle sounds on November 27? Do you wonder—or are you confident?

I shall always remember how cheerfully confident and magnanimous the Navy's cheerleader was to me before the Game—almost pitying. "I'll tell you, old chap, you fellows sing a little song, and we'll do ours. No good to work against each other, you know. People like to hear our cheers and songs—really all right they are, too"—He was told we didn't expect to hear them—we didn't—nor did our team. Nor did our team hear the screaming siren which had wailed disappointment and defeat in deafening waves for three bitter games. But they heard our "charge" which brought every soldier —old and young—to his feet—raised his blood to fever height and kept it there.

Do you get this, old man? Does it find response? Are you burning with the will to win, yet humbly praying that you may be worthy of your crushing task of leadership? Your responsibilities are second only to Hewitts', and it's not to be discharged by

Cadet Pullen, right tackle, 1907.

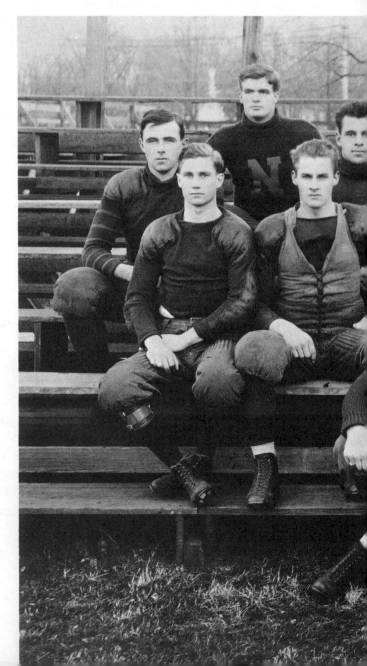

The Navy football squad in 1909. Ralph Meyer was captain. Army cancelled the traditional game with Navy because of Eugene Byrne's fatal inury in a game with Harvard.

handsprings and cartwheels. The fire in your eye—the challenge of your commands —the mastery with which you lift out from that glorious fighting symphony, the Corps, the battle cry of its very soul—these things will tell if you are worthy.

Some of us there will know—we shall follow you with hungry eyes to catch the spark of leadership, and we will rise to the heights of frenzied fighting zeal with your roaring deep-voiced Corps if you will only lead it, arouse it, inspire it, inflame it to the white heat of fighting passions which will throb in the subconscious minds of our team and carry them to the greatest victory in West Point history. Forty to five is the record— give us 80 to 0! Crush the backfire the Navy is starting, to burn over our team in terrible unexpected defeat. Prove that this is the Corps' greatest year—it's up to you, Soldier. I pray you may be worthy of the Corps. Here's to you. I know not your name, but I look to you for leadership. True leadership and Victory.

John C. H. Lee
1909

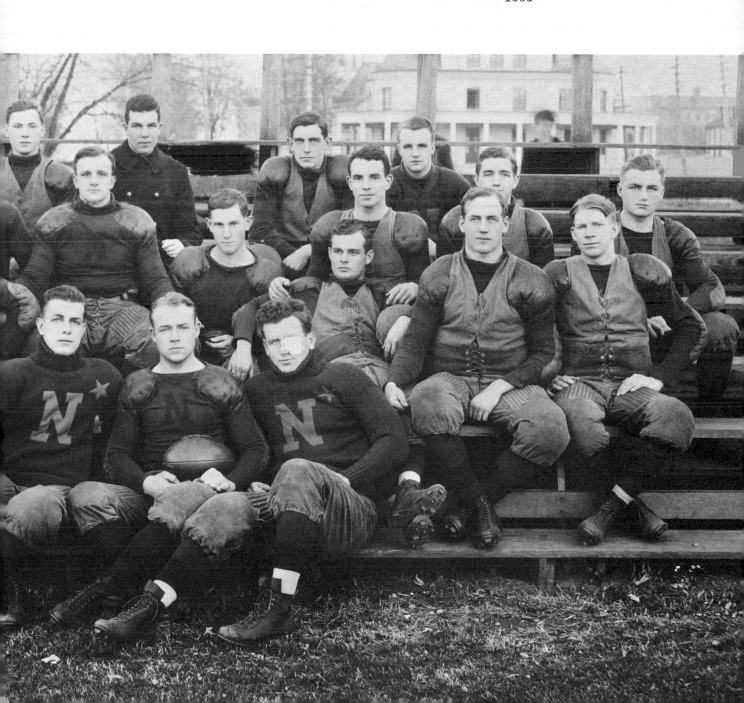

The most unhappy young men were at Annapolis and West Point during the 1928-32 years, for it was during this period that the Army mule and the Navy goat had their major disagreement over the eligibility of Army players, and the two schools called off their traditional interservice game. The games were resumed in 1930 and 1931, but only as benefit postseason matches, with the proceeds going to charity in the midst of the Depression. Finally, in 1932, the superintendents of the service schools, Maj. Gen. William D. Connor and Rear Adm. Charles Hart, agreed to resume their traditional schedule, and the Army-Navy game has had an uninterrupted run since that date. You can follow the events in these news stories from the New York Herald-Tribune.

Tradition Is Broken

RICHARDS VIDMER

ARMY BREAKS OFF GRID RELATIONS WITH NAVY

The annual football classic of the Army and Navy, most colorful of the seasonal pigskin dramas over a period of thirty-eight years, apparently came to an end today.

The definite break in athletic relations, considered inevitable now by Army men, appeared in publication of a series of letters between Adm. L. M. Nulton, superintendent of the Naval Academy, and Maj. Gen. Edwin Winans, head of West Point.

Although a four-year contract for the annual football clashes, entered into October 1926, still has three years to run. Admiral Nulton requested on December 3, that Army add to the individual contract a clause stipulating that: "No contestant shall take part in this game between the two service schools, who has had three years' experience in intercollegiate football." Refusal to accede to this request would be considered: "Rejection of the contract and the Naval Academy will consider itself free to schedule another game on November 24, 1928."

In his reply, published today, General Winans said, "It is obvious that the Navy wishes to withdraw from football competition with Army." General Winans said, "I wish to fully assure you, that the authorities of the Military Academy will not oppose your wishes."

Admiral Nulton of the Naval Academy said that he would issue a statement within a day. Comdr. Jonas Ingram, Director of Athletics at Navy, also said that he would withhold any statement.

There was considerable surprise at Navy, when General Winans made his first statement. However, the feeling is that the action of the general simply forecasted the action of the Naval Academy and that the statement of the latter would have accomplished the same end.

While it is felt that the heads of the War and Navy departments may take some action looking toward continuation of relations, no step in that direction will be taken immediately. . . .

CONGRESSMAN FISH HAS NEW ARMY PLAN

A compromise of the differences between the West Point and Annapolis academies which resulted in a suspension of athletic relations between these two military institutions is suggested in a letter sent to Secretary of War Good today by Representative Hamilton Fish, Jr., of New York.

West Point and Annapolis fell out over eligibility rules two years ago, the Navy Academy authorities insisting that West Point asserted its rights to play men on its team who had already seen three years of football service in colleges.

In his letter, Mr. Fish suggested that the Government institutions compromise on a four-year rule and expressed the opinion that if West Point accepted this, Annapolis would readily acquiesce.

Efforts were made during the Coolidge Administration to compromise the troubles between West Point and Annapolis, but proved futile. Among those who took steps in this direction was Representative Britten of Illinois, Chairman of the House Committee on Naval Affairs.

Mr. Fish forwarded to Secretary Good a copy of a letter written by Horatio S. White of Cambridge, Massachusetts, who, as chairman of the Harvard Athletic Committee in 1903-07, had a part in arranging with Princeton and Yale the three-year regulation. "This regulation," Mr. White wrote, "is a very valuable rule for preserving the amateur spirit and checking the migratory athlete.

The fact that such colleges as Harvard, Yale, Notre Dame, Nebraska, and Stanford continue to play West Point, does not mean that these colleges condone or accept the present West Point eligibility rules as being fair or consistent with the amateur regulations governing college football, but because the Army eleven is a big attraction to the public, especially when the Cadet Corps is permitted to accompany the team.

"There are very few college graduates who enter West Point except well-known football players. The last four West Point football captains have all been former college stars. It is much more important to maintain the principle of equal opportunity for the youngsters entering West Point and the amateur standing of American football than winning victories.

"Any team composed of former football stars can win. What chance has the average boy of eighteen, who enters the military academy, to make the Army team his second year in competition with a lot of older and experienced players?

"My main objection to the present West Point policy is that it is unsportsmanlike to turn out teams composed largely of former college stars. Representing the congres-

Ray Stecker races fifty-two yards for Army's winning touchdown in 1930.

A charging Navy line blocked the kick after touchdown, to make the final score, Army 6, Navy 0.

sional district in which West Point is located, I have always wanted to see West Point win, but not under the existing six-year rule which, in my opinion, is undemocratic, as it permits Cadets to play three years on the Army team, who have already played three years on other college teams.

"Every other large college in the country has adopted a three-year rule, including the Naval Academy, which last year was able to defeat both Princeton and Pennsylvania, two of the strongest teams in the East.

"Neither the Army nor the Navy permits freshmen to play on the varsity, but as long as the Army insists on the six-year rule there can be no resumption of football relations on a friendly basis.

"My compromise proposal is that the Army should adopt a four-year rule, which would permit a Cadet who has only played one year at college, to play all three years at West Point, and if he had played two years on a college varsity, to play two years at West Point, or if he had played three years at college, he would be only allowed to play one year at West Point.

"I am confident that the Navy football authorities would agree to play West Point if the Army will adopt a four-year rule, even though it does not affect any West Point player who has already made the team. This will still leave a big advantage to the Army, as the Navy would continue to abide by the three-year rule, but it is a compromise that could be effected without loss of dignity or prestige by either academy.

"The Navy is not at all free from blame in backing out of the contract before its termination, which called for a certain number of games between the two academies, but if football relations between the Army and Navy are to be resumed, it must be on a practicable and equitable basis, and it seems to me, in view of the willingness of the Navy coach last year to accept a compromise along the lines I have suggested, that it still could be made the basis for a mutual understanding as regards to eligibility rules.

"The Army and Navy are natural and logical rivals, and it is hoped that through the efforts of the Secretaries of War and Navy that the service teams will soon meet again on the grid-iron, and carry on the high ideals and traditions of that famous game, and of the outstanding football stars produced by both academies in the past."

ARMY AND NAVY AGREE TO MEET IN FOOTBALL NEXT 3 YEARS PACT ENDS DISPUTE OVER ELIGIBILITY THAT BEGAN AFTER 1927 GAME

Army and Navy will resume athletic relations. The first game under a three-year agreement adopted here today, will be played here [Philadelphia], on December 3, 1932. Football games will also be played in 1933 and 1934.

The new accord, which closed a breach opened in 1927, was adopted at a meeting in the Bellevue-Stratford Hotel, Philadelphia, this noon, between Maj. Gen. William D. Connor, Superintendent of the Military Academy, and Rear Adm. Charles Hart, Superintendent of the Naval Academy.

The agreement was precipitated by the fact that Army and Navy have been forced by official and popular pressure to meet in benefit football games during the past two years.

The question of eligibility, which forced the original break after the game of 1927, does not figure in the new agreement. Each school is to determine its own eligibility rules. Neither school has yielded on the original issue, which was Navy's objection to Army's use of athletes who had played in collegiate varsity games during three previous years, and the Army's insistence that any Cadet in good standing was eligible to participate.

Theoretically the breach is closed, therefore, only for that period, as it was closed for a day on the occasions of the two benefit games last fall and the previous year. Actually, however, the Army-Navy disagreement seems to be at an end. It seems unlikely that the difficulties will be revived.

The announcement of the renewed relations between the two service schools, was received with great enthusiasm at both academies.

The plebe class at Annapolis received the news at mess, and responded by holding the first rally ever held in the mess hall. The rest of the Midshipmen are either at home on leave or cruising between the Azores and Halifax on the battleship, *Wyoming*.

Graduates of both academies were elated when told of the new accord and all seemed to believe that the breach had been closed for all time.

At West Point, cheering Cadets greeted General Connor's announcement with cheers and then listened to the General's sober words: "In the excitement of a great football game with Navy, it is easy to forget the long, tedious hours that our players have to endure, to insure a victorious team, but our fellows must also have your support when things are not going our way. It's quite easy to support a winning team. It's more difficult to buck up the boys, when the going gets tough. Your continuous support is most important."

During the evening at West Point a great football rally was held; old songs, cheers, and slogans were revived and applauded. The meeting was addressed by Maj. Ralph Sasse, Football Coach; Lt. Col. Robert Richardson, Commandant of Cadets; and Cadet Milton Summerfelt, Captain of the Army Football Team.

If newspapermen had a Hall of Fame, Heywood Broun would be sitting high in it. Here is how he covered Navy's 7-0 victory over Army in 1920. The game is there, with all its dramatics. So is General Pershing, saluting a program hawker "who wore a red hat and undoubtedly was mistaken by the general for a Rumanian field marshal." Only Broun could report a football game the way Broun reported it.

Navy Beats Army in Football—and Singing

HEYWOOD BROUN

PROBABLY IT WILL BE JUST AS WELL TO GET RIGHT DOWN TO THE FEATURE of the Navy's 7-0 victory over the Army at the Polo Grounds yesterday.

The most surprising event of the afternoon was the discourtesy of the two service teams to General Nivelle. In a field box sat the French leader who helped to establish at Verdun the slogan, "They shall not pass," and both Army and Navy tried it continuously. However, nothing much came of it. Neither line smashing nor forward passes availed. The Navy won the game by deception.

It is also traditional that a distinct point shall be made of the fact that a large crowd was present. Of course, by this time there is probably no great element of surprise in that. If it were possible to say "only ten persons witnessed the game between the Army and the Navy yesterday," that would be news and worthy of note. Still, there was a large crowd present. We counted up to 50,000 before the game began, but a few may have come in later.

We distinctly recognized Secretary Baker, who sat in a box on the Army side, and Secretary Daniels on the Navy side. This imparted a rather pathetic touch to the afternoon, for this was the last year in which either gentleman will see the game from a good seat. Mr. Berleson was engaged in speeding up last week's special-delivery letters and could not attend. The day was so bad that it seemed as if Mr. Palmer must have had something to do with it, but he was not visible.

In accordance with custom it should be stated that among the 50,000 spectators were hosts of pretty girls. Beauty, to be sure, is relative, and we don't want to make the statement too positive. It's just one of those shrewd guesses which the trained newspaper observer chances now and again. It should be qualified by the information that the Ziegfeld Follies was out of town and that *Tip Top* was playing a matinee. At any rate, there were a lot of girls present, and undoubtedly a great many of them were pretty.

Personally, we didn't see Helen of Troy or anybody who looked much like her.

We know that Helen launched a thousand ships, but we are also told that she burned the topless towers of Ilium. And it is also noteworthy that in the launching of those ships there was not even a hint of scandal, at least no scandal of a financial nature.

Be that as it may, General Pershing was present and in his bluff and democratic way he was observed to salute one of Harry Stevens' program sellers who wore a red hat and undoubtedly was mistaken by the general for a Rumanian field marshal.

General Pershing sat next to Nivelle and explained the fine points of the game to him. At first this was easy enough, as there weren't any fine points, but, after the final whistle had blown, the general was observed to be having a little difficulty to think of the French equivalent for "moral victory."

The Cadets and the Midshipmen came in late, as did almost everybody else. The crowd was handled badly and each ticket holder was made to feel that the Polo Grounds was the eye of a needle and that he was a rich man or a camel. Once inside there was ample evidence that the simile about the camel was not holding up any too well.

The delegations from the two academies arrived in time to do a little preliminary singing, and the Navy had a bit the best of it. These young men will someday shout orders in the teeth of typhoons and above the roar of guns. They sang very loudly. The cheering honors were even. No rooters in the world cheer so enthusiastically as Cadets and Midshipmen. If a runner were thrown for a 10-yard loss, an equal volume of cheers came from each side.

The Navy, however, gave more advice, shouting in unison, again and again, "Block that kick!" and "Fight like hell!" Maybe the first injunction was not heard, for the Navy didn't block any kicks, but it fought like hell, as did the Army, and both were liberally penalized for it. Service games are apt to be rough, though not dirty.

Most of the heavy work was candid and frank. Whenever a prone player wanted to get up he helped himself to his feet by resting an elbow on the back of some foeman's neck and putting a knee in the small of his back. These, however, were pleasantries, for there were no injuries of moment and time out was called infrequently.

The first period gave promise, or perhaps threat is better, of a nothing-to-nothing game. Neither side could gain, and in the first quarter, indeed, both actually lost ground by rushing. The Army had three rather difficult shots for field goals in the first half, but French missed them all by wide margins.

Let us trust that there will be no more wars, and that if there are, French will not be in the artillery. His infantry would suffer. All his barrages were short.

The first half disclosed little advantage for either side. Both lines sifted through fast and spilled most of the plays before they could get started. French made a few short dashes for the Army but was never able to get started on a long run. Interference was crude, and neither team played keen football, except in the simplest elements of line defense.

Late in the third period the Navy had its first real chance. A poor kick by French sent the ball out of bounds on the Army's 46-yard line, and from this point the Navy took the ball over after a steady and brilliant advance. The Army line had shown its

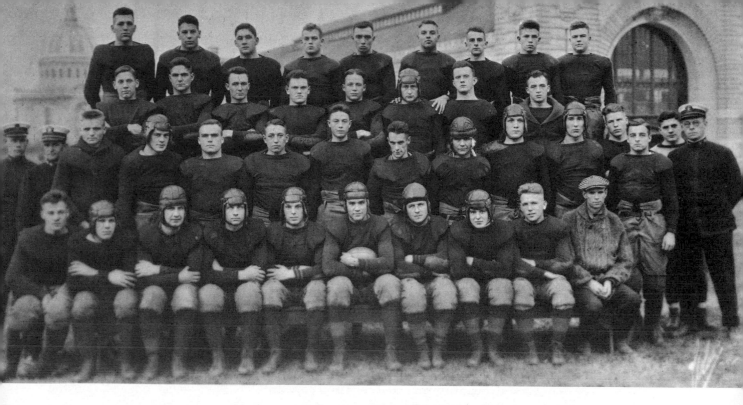

This 1919 Navy squad beat Army, 6-0. Clyde King kicked two field goals and Ed Willkie, brother of Wendell L. Willkie, the 1940 candidate for president, was one of the stars. Eddie Ewen (center, with ball) was captain. At extreme right, on bench, is Coach Gil Dobie.

Army's 1920 team lost only two games all season long, but they were the two big games of the year —Notre Dame and Navy. Outstanding members of the 1920 Army squad included Gar Davidson, Fritz Breidster, George Smythe, and Larry French.

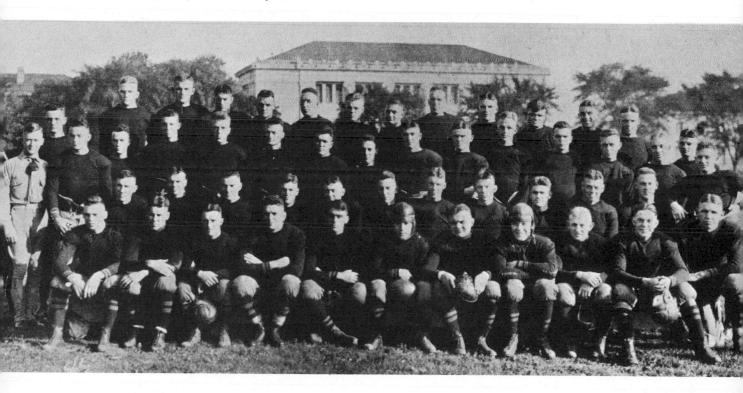

Edward Cole Ewen is probably the only Army-Navy football player to compete for five years. He is also the only two-time Navy football captain in history, leading the 1919 and 1920 Navy teams.

strength defensively against mere power, but the Navy suddenly switched to deception. Most of it was rather simple deception, but it served to fuddle a line which, although strong, was not very smart.

The beginning of the fourth period found the Navy attack in full swing. Only one forward pass was thrown, and that was a short one, but all sorts of double and delayed passes worked beautifully, and the Army forwards charged ahead doggedly to the wrong point and Navy backs skipped by them.

It was a curious accession of power which came to the Navy, a team which had previously shown absolutely nothing on attack. It seemed to find itself suddenly when the opportunity offered. It was inspired. In its own territory and in midfield it had been able to gain nothing, but with a goal line in sight it was full speed ahead.

The last yards, which are generally the most difficult, were surprisingly easy. From the 7-yard line Koehler shook himself free on a double pass and came over for a touchdown with hardly a hand laid upon him. Later in the period the Navy made another brilliant advance, but lost the ball on a fumble on the Army 12-yard line.

The closing minutes of the game were devoted to the wild and rather aimless forward-passing game which has featured the last attack of most of the losing teams this season.

The whistle blew and the Midshipmen came swarming onto the field, but Nivelle kept his seat. Seemingly, he had not altogether understood the fine points which had been explained to him. He watched the Annapolis men throwing their hats over the goalposts eagerly and with great interest. It is possible that he thought of these as field goals and all an integral part of the Navy's attack.

"How shall I tell him that the game is all over?" asked Pershing. "Is 'fineesh' the word? My French is getting dreadfully rusty."

"I'm not sure," said the aide. "But you might just sort of poke him in the ribs."

But it was Nivelle who did the poking. He turned and thrust a thumb into the side of the leader of the American Expeditionary Forces.

"*Chapeaux*," said Nivelle.

"*Ah, oui*," said Pershing, without a moment's hesitation, but he stuck a moment in trying to think up the French for "subway." Finally he rendered it freely as "*le Métro*." Nivelle said something that sounded like "*say toot*" and got up to go.

Another Army and Navy game had gone down into history.

2
THE
BIG GAMES

THE WHITE HOUSE

WASHINGTON

December 2, 1961

TO THE CORPS OF CADETS AND THE BRIGADE
OF MIDSHIPMEN

It is easy to pick the real winner of the annual
Army-Navy football game: the people of the United
States. For the outcome is certain from the great
spirit of competition, the lessons of good sportsmanship, and the skill and perfection with which
the players of both teams perform, all of which
bring to the Officer Corps of our Armed Forces
lasting benefit in terms of leadership. From this
leadership, our nation is stronger, and the cause
of freedom in the world is safer from encroachment.

A less serious benefit, of course, is what the
Army-Navy football game brings to intercollegiate
football, and to the world of sports. The game
sets a fine example of hardhitting fair play that I
hope will inspire Americans, young and old, in
the world of sports.

My greetings and warm good wishes go to all of
you who support the West Point and Annapolis teams
today.

John F. Kennedy

A long-standing Army-Navy tradition each year is the message from the Commander in Chief to the Corps of Cadets and the Brigade of Midshipmen. Here are the words of the late President John F. Kennedy issued prior to the Army-Navy game in 1961.

"Not a mere football game, but something vital, alive, and wholly thrilling!" That is how one of America's top writers, Paul Gallico, viewed the Army-Navy classic in his column in the New York Daily News in 1934.

Army vs. Navy—More Than a Football Game

PAUL GALLICO

ARMY-NAVY GAME. . . . ELEVEN KIDS AGAINST ELEVEN OTHERS. BANDS, crowds, spectacles, chevrons, and gold lace, brass hats, officials, politicians, and dignitaries, and still, just a football game. But, of all the thousands of football games played all over the country from October to December, this is the one game that really matters, the only one at some later day, many, many years hence, might still exert its influence in some way that might affect the millions of people who inhabit this country. To me this adds spine-chilling thrills to that annual encounter. I look forward to it as I do to few others. The Army-Navy game is the yearly parade of the future commanders of the armed defenders of the United States. This is serious business. Watch these boys play. Watch them think. Watch their moves. Our lives may some day be in their hands.

As the lives of all of us are reckoned, football games are written on waters—a few hours' entertainment, a story in a newspaper, a few minutes' idle gossip, and Monday-morning quarterbacking. A lot of the youngsters who play football are profoundly impressed by the game, often to their own detriment, but that hardly affects us. But these players on the field at Philadelphia today will some day be in charge of our line of defense at sea, on land, in the air. These are their habit-forming years. The lessons learned, the habits formed, the friendships made, every element that goes in their making as soldiers and gentlemen may some day be our concern.

To begin with, these twenty-two boys who face one another on Franklin Field today are successful boys. They have achieved a goal. With intelligence, self-denial, courage, and fine bodies, they have won the right to represent the Service of the United States. They are fine physical specimens or they could not play the game. They are not brainless physical hulks or they wouldn't be in either Academy. They have maintained fine scholastic standing in two of the most difficult curricula in the country. There isn't a speck of yellow in a single body. They are all gallant, honest, and fair, and have learned the lessons of sportsmanship and playing the game within the rules. These are twenty-two important men who will be on the field today. They have begun to make a habit of success.

On the average, the West Point and the Annapolis football player represents the highest type of officer material. In war, a rugged, splendid physique animated by a good mind, is paramount. These Army and Navy athletes, and by athletes I do not limit it to football, will all make splendid leaders. Take a look at Midshipman Borries today as he fades back to throw a pass. Note how cool and unflustered he is, how, with a quick glance, he takes in the situation and adapts himself to it immediately. Ten years from now, Borries will be a commander, perhaps in charge of a destroyer, or a sub, or a nest of war birds. Wherever he is, you won't worry about him. You'll be glad to know that he is there if there should be trouble.

The men who play in this Army-Navy game form friendships and associations that they never forget. It is almost like a great fraternity. They must make good in after-life, far and above football, but, unquestionably, the records they make on the football field are remembered and help them in their service career, socially as well as in the military sense. One would imagine that if there were two officers of equal ability, length of service, talent, etc., from which to pick for promotion, the superiors would be inclined to lean toward "Babe" this and "Biff" that or "Spike" Whosis who made the winning points in the Army-Navy game. There is a camaraderie about this service football that never ends. The players who bring honor to their schools are never forgotten. For, unlike a college football team which disbands when the season is over and scatters to the four winds, these boys will always be united by the bond of the oath to the United States, and, in one way or another, if they stay in the service, will continue to be associated with one another.

And so as you sit in the stands today—if you are one of the lucky ones—you will not be watching just an ordinary game. You will be looking at something that some day may turn into history, at men whose names a hundred years from now may be written alongside of Sampson and Dewey and Schley and Pershing, Wood, Lejeune, Schafter, and others. There they are in the incubators, these Martians of tomorrow. Perhaps the hero isn't on the field, but in the blue or gray crops in the stands. But those men you will see in action represent all that is the best and the most admirable and the most capable perhaps of both the schools. That is why this is not a mere football game, seen today and forgotten tomorrow, but rather something vital, alive, and wholly thrilling.

Cadet Wally Philoon captained the Army team in 1908, a team that defeated Navy in a bruising, no-quarter-asked game. An outstanding center for Army in 1907, '08, and '09, Philoon was justly proud of the 1908 win, for it was Army's first victory over the Middies since 1904. Here is his account.

The Game Won by Fight! Fight! Fight!

WALLACE C. PHILOON

IN 1908, THE "EXPERTS" GAVE US NO CHANCE. NAVY CLAIMED THE BEST team in its history. At West Point, 1908 graduation had almost cleaned us out. "Red" Pullen, a great tackle, handicapped by a bad knee, was about our only standout remaining. The squad was thin and light. We averaged 169 pounds against Navy. Our heaviest man, a guard, weighed 193, and our lightest, an end, 152. The pre-Navy season had been only fair with small scores by both West Point and its opponents.

Our class had few good football players. Devers, Eichelberger, Emmons, Lee, Patton, Simpson, and many others destined to play major parts in future wars were there, but only a few were varsity football material. However, 1909 did have something that usually brings results—fighting spirit—the will to win. And, of course, the corps followed such leadership.

Head Coach "Sheep" Nelly had the same fighting spirit. Capitalize on the breaks you get and avoid giving any to your opponents was the policy of head field coach, Capt. Joe Beacham. Small scores were the result. With no backfield stars, a light, green line—no wonder the experts passed us up.

But in various games, although we messed things up, we did show a spirit that made us hard to beat. Yale, outweighing us twenty pounds per man, had been held to one touchdown made possible by a penalty. Princeton, sixteen pounds per man heavier, could not score even though she had had sixteen downs inside our 20-yard line. In another bumbling game our opponents finally scored in the closing minutes. This was the spark we needed. In six plays we had tied the score.

We went to Philadelphia knowing we were the underdogs, but we knew also that we were not going to let the corps down. We were going to win. In the words of "Sheep" Nelly, every time we hit a Navy man we were going to give him something to put in his "Lucky Bag." We were thoroughly keyed to Joe Beacham's slogan that we'd heard so often through his clenched teeth: "Viciousness! Speed and Fight will win! Viciousness."

In 1908, Wallace Philoon, captain and center, led the Army to one of its finest football seasons, winning six games and losing but once, to Yale.

HEADQUARTERS U. S. MILITARY ACADEMY.

WEST POINT. N. Y., December 1, 1908.

GENERAL ORDERS,
No. 42.

The Superintendent desires to congratulate the officers and cadets, as well as the Army at large, upon the splendid victory obtained by West Point at Philadelphia against what seemed to many to be overwhelming odds.

This was accomplished by a wise selection of and subordination to the coaches, a complete support by officers and cadets of the coaches and team, and by the supreme efforts of all concerned, which brought us to Philadelphia with a well trained team, a solid front, and that spirit of fight, fight, fight — "That spirit of old West Point" — which has led our armies to many victories in the past and if carried out as exemplified at Philadelphia will win many for us in the future.

BY ORDER OF COLONEL SCOTT:

Captain, 2d Cavalry,
Adjutant.

Congratulations from the Superintendent for a West Point victory in 1908.

The game in those days consisted of two 35-minute halves—no quarters—and a player once taken out could not return. The forward pass was in its infancy—if incomplete, the ball went to the opponents. The New York *Sun* report of the game states: "The game was remarkable for the fact that the ball was punted almost incessantly." Neither side could gain consistently by rushing. Scarcely three minutes after the kick-off our break came. Navy's star quarterback, Ed Lange, missed a punt and Harry Chamberlain, our 156-pound fullback, taking the chance that our line and the other backs would give the kicker adequate protection, was on the spot to grab the ball and set sail for the Navy goal. A desperate tackle stopped him on the 4-yard line. But in two plays Bill Dean scored and then promptly kicked the goal. We had capitalized on a break. Now could we hold off powerful, confident Navy for another thirty minutes and then the long 35-minute second half? Some fifteen minutes after our score Navy advanced to our 6-yard line. It was during those anxious minutes that "Fight! Fight! Fight!" was born. As Navy forced us back, some cadet began yelling: "Fight! Fight! Fight!" Those around him at once took it up and presently it swelled to a chant by the entire corps.

We on the playing field may not have been conscious of the words but we certainly knew the fighting spirit behind us. We knew that every cadet looked to us to make this "Big Navy Day" an Army victory. We didn't let them down. The middies were forced to try for a field goal. It was successful but we still led—6 to 4. The first half was scarcely half over. Could we hold them off until that final whistle?

Well, we did. Navy never got a real break or again seriously threatened. Again quoting the New York *Sun:* "The Army eleven—showed a vast improvement over its previous games this fall and never lost a trick. The rush line was on tiptoe at all times, breaking through quickly and blocking with remarkable strength. The backfield worked like a piece of well-oiled machinery and during the second half did so much effective battering that the Annapolis eleven was literally cut to pieces, so that before the game ended the Navy had six substitutes in the lineup."

We made three substitutions, one to strengthen a position and two near the close of the game due to the absolute exhaustion of a 179-pound tackle and a 152-pound end.

A large part of the corps missed their train back to West Point because they insisted in escorting their team back to the hotel. But a new special was promptly arranged for them and a sympathetic Supe forgave them their breach of discipline.

A sore but happy squad was drawn up the hill on Sunday afternoon by a jubilant corps; 1908 had seen a victory over Navy. The corps and its team had certainly put a bitter pill in the Navy's "Lucky Bag." The Navy song, "It Looks to Me Like a Big Navy Day," had boomeranged. "Fight! Fight! Fight!" had done the trick.

The Army-Navy game eats up a lot of space in the sport pages around the country. Here is how the story took shape for the Philadelphia fans in 1911, from the Saturday before the big battle, right through the game, and after. Predictions, preparations, player portraits and, finally, the game itself—and the aftermath. Live the week of the 1911 Army-Navy game, with the sports staff of the Philadelphia Herald.

The Press Covers the 1911 Game

PHILADELPHIA HERALD

NAVY ON THE HOMESTRETCH

ANNAPOLIS, MD., Sunday—The Naval Academy coaches will tomorrow start on their last week of work before the final struggle against the Army team next Saturday.

Those close to the team are satisfied with its condition at this time and confident that it will reach its highest point of efficiency on the day of the game. There will be hard scrimmages on the early days of the week, but great care will be taken with the men in order to avoid injury. The last practice will be held here Thursday, and the team will leave early enough on Friday to practice on Franklin Field, Philadelphia, that afternoon.

Lieutenant Howard and Ensign Ingram, the regular Navy coaches, and Frank Wheaton of Yale, the field coach, will be assisted during the closing week by Herman Olcott and Weymouth, one-time noted Yale players, and by a number of old Navy stars. All of the Yale men have had notable success as coaches since they left New Haven, and particular benefit is expected from the instruction of Olcott.

FINAL WORK BY NAVY

ANNAPOLIS, MD., Monday—The Naval Academy football squad started its last week of preparation for the West Point game with much spirit this afternoon. There is a general feeling that the team is strong enough to win this year and thereby win the rubber of the series, each team having seven victories to its credit.

The work this afternoon consisted of a long signal drill, some kicking, and a short scrimmage. There is much satisfaction over the physical condition of the squad, the trainer, "Jim" McMasters, having done his work so well that all the members are available, with the possible exception of Leonard, a fast substitute back. It was thought that Leonard's wrenched knee would surely keep him from playing but it is now thought that he will be back in the game by Saturday.

Herman Olcutt, the old Yale linesman, who has been coaching New York University this season, joined the staff of Navy coaches this afternoon and will stay with the team during the week.

ORDER ISSUED TO FORBID NAVAL CADETS TO BET ON ARMY GAME

Annapolis, Md., Monday—An order was issued today at the Naval Academy forbidding the Midshipmen to enter a betting pool or to make individual bets on the Army-Navy football game next Saturday. It is understood that West Point cadets sent $5,000 to Annapolis to wager on the Army eleven.

FULL NAVY SQUAD IS IN FINE TRIM

"Scotty" McMasters Has Every "Middie" in Condition for Football Game with Army

Annapolis, Md., Tuesday—It was announced today that the friends of the Naval Academy team had seen it in action for the last time before it lined up against the military Academy eleven on Franklin Field, Philadelphia, next Saturday. The contemplated open practice on Thursday will not be held, and the team will practice in secret on that day, just as on the other days of the week. There was a long signal drill this afternoon, using a number of men in the backfield, and various trick formations were tried, though there was no regular scrimmage.

The full squad was on the field this afternoon. "Scotty" McMasters, the trainer, having achieved quite a triumph in bringing the squad to such a high degree of physical excellence at this point of the season. Leonard, the fast substitute back, who wrenched his knee so badly more than a week ago, appeared on the field, and completed the squad. He is a valuable man, having done good work at both halfback and quarterback. There will be no regular practice games this week, and there is every reason to believe that the full strength will be available next Saturday.

It was noticed today that the full team will be drawn from two classes—the first and third—the third class alone furnishing seven of the team men, an unprecedented number to come from one class in the history of football at the Academy. The third class men who are to be in the final lineup are: Brown, Howe, Redman, McReavey, Gilchrist, Nichols, and Rhodes. The first class men are: Captain Dalton, Hamilton, Wakeman, and Weems.

PRESIDENT TAFT NOT TO ATTEND GAME

Philadelphia, Pa., Thursday—Although President Taft has practically decided not to attend the game, it is more than likely that Mrs. Taft and Miss Helen Taft will represent the White House at this struggle between the generals and admirals. The President's wife and daughter, if they do decide to come, will make the trip on a special car attached to one of the special trains being run up from Washington and will bring a party of friends with them. All will lunch on their car, which will be sidetracked on the South Street siding, and go direct from there to the field. After the game they will return to their car and go directly back to the national capital.

But even if the President will not be on hand there will be a host of eminent men from all walks of life, political, social, Army and Navy. Secretary of the Navy George Von L. Meyer will bring a large party of friends; Secretary Stimson, of the War Department, will also act as host to a big party. Admirals, senators, congressmen, governors of states, Atty. Gen. Wickersham, and scores of others will be among those present when the big contest is on.

SERIES EVEN TO DATE

PHILADELPHIA, PA., Friday—A feature which will make tomorrow's game of more than ordinary interest, is the fact that in the series to date, the two teams have won the same number of games. All told, there have been fifteen games played since the series was started in 1890. Of this number, each eleven has won seven games, there having been one tie.

A quiet air of confidence of victory hangs over the rival camps, the Navy at the Hotel Walton and the Army under the watchful eyes of trainers and coaches in the Waynewood, at Wayne.

Following them came an invading army of generals and admirals and officers of every rank in both branches of the service, as well as government officials. Tonight

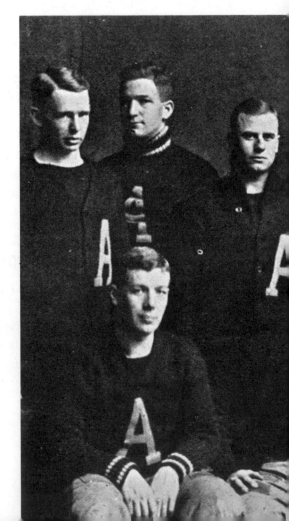

Army's 1911 team lost to Navy, 3-0, for the second straight year. A field goal by Jack Dalton, Navy's great kicker, won the game. (First row, l. to r.) Huston, Wood, Hyatt (captain, with ball), Walmsley, Devore, Keyes. (Second row, l. to r.) Littlejohn, Dean, Gillespie, McDonald, Browne, Cook, Arnold, Hoge. (Third row, l. to r.) Rowley, Weyand, Lee (manager), Sibert.

60

the corridors of the Bellevue-Stratford and the Hotel Walton were thronged with men resplendent in glittering uniforms with gold lace and brass buttons and women in gorgeous gowns.

DALTON'S GOAL FROM FIELD GIVES NAVY VICTORY BY 3-0

Brilliant Punting of Retiring Captain Brings a Repetition of Last Year's Triumph and Wins "Rubber" Game with Army

PHILADELPHIA, PA., Saturday—The superb punting of John Patrick Dalton, captain and left halfback of the Annapolis team, gave the Navy a victory over the Army here today in one of the finest exhibitions of the new football that has been seen in the East this season. The score was Navy 3; Army 0, the score being made in the second half after the Navy, using Dalton persistently, had rushed the ball from her own 25-yard line to the Army's 23-yard line, a distance of 62 yards.

The Navy forwards opened great holes in the Army line at this period of the game, through which Dalton was shoved for big gains. Dalton alternated his line plunges with dazzling runs around the Army ends until he got the ball exactly where he wanted it. Then on the 35-yard line he gave the signal for a kick from placement behind scrimmage. This is a particularly hard way to kick a goal, for not only must the pass be perfect, but the man receiving it must get in position for the punter instantly.

In this instance the play worked like a charm. Weems, the Navy center, made a

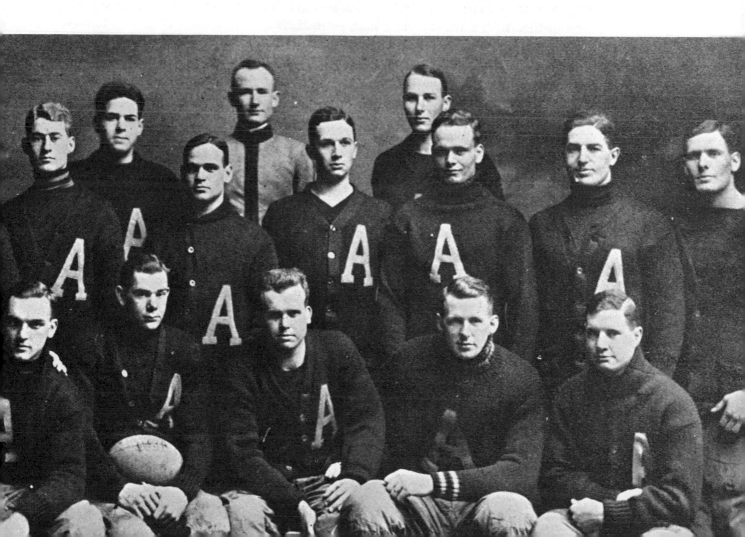

perfect pass to the kneeling Gilchrist, and before the Army ends could get down on the play Dalton had booted the ball squarely between the goalposts for the only score made in the game. It was a beautiful play, beautifully executed and the Navy stand went wild with enthusiasm over it. It was the play that won the victory and Dalton was entitled to all the credit of it, for it was his splendid offensive work alone that made the opportunity.

Hopelessly outplayed in both offensive and defensive work in the first period, and barely holding their own through the early part of the second period, the Navy became so heartened after this score that the Army could do nothing with them. They made many substantial gains around the Navy ends and twice got in position where field goals were possible. But the Army, without Dean, had no one to offset the fine work of Dalton.

They couldn't get the ball between the bars, and when they got close to the goal line and the range of play closed in, the Navy defensive would tighten and hold. Then Dalton would not only recover all that Army had gained in straight football, but some besides, with one of his wonderful punts. One of Dalton's punts went 72 yards from the toe of his boot to the point where it struck the ground and several other of his punts went 60 yards.

Outside of the kicking there was little to choose between the two teams, but Dalton was so vastly superior in this department of the game to either Hyatt or Keyes, of the Army, that there was no comparison.

In offensive work the teams were about equal. Both the Army and Navy backs were able to gain at times. There wasn't much to choose between the ends, either, save that the Army ends were a bit surer in tackling. The Navy ends were fast, but frequently overran themselves, missing their man entirely.

Both teams used a quick wing shift, the quarterbacks giving the signal and getting the ball in play before the men were set. This enabled the backs to start with the whole team moving at the time the ball was put in play. It is a ruse that has been worked with varying success by many teams this year, and while it was worked with success by both sides today, no substantial gains were made.

In providing interference for the runners the Army was superior to the Navy, but the Middies made up for this by brilliant individual plays. The Army used the forward pass four times and the onside kick twice, but failed to work them successfully. That punting and ability to keep on top of the ball all the time are the most valuable assets in the new football was again proved in today's game. De Witt and Sam White proved it in the Yale-Princeton game a week ago and the Navy proved it again today.

Dalton is the big hero here tonight. It is his last year at the Naval Academy and he captained a victorious team which the football experts were so certain would be beaten that they were offering odds on the Army before the game began.

Thirty thousand people witnessed the game, among them officers of the Army and Navy. George Von L. Meyer was one of the early arrivals and took his place in a box in the Navy stand. He was greeted with great applause and was obliged to doff his hat repeatedly. A few minutes later Mr. Stimson, Secretary of War, walked across the field to the Army stand and was warmly greeted. Then a regular procession of generals, captains, admirals, commanders, and lesser officers of the Army and Navy came in and took their places.

At half-past one o'clock the West Point cadets, headed by their band, marched on the field. After they were seated the Annapolis cadets, about three times as many in number, came in and marched around the field. Passing the Army stand, the rear-guard stopped long enough to point the Navy goat at the cadets and then marched on. There was no Army mule to answer this challenge with this year. The old fellow that the Army used to use is reported to have died some time ago. At any rate he has been missing for two years, and the Army has not succeeded in digging up a mascot to take his place.

That the Middies were primed for vigorous action became apparent as soon as they took their seats. They began hurling their cheers and waving their flags of blue and gold at the Army stand at once, and they never let up once during the game or during the intermissions. There will be a lot of speechless young men at Annapolis tomorrow, that is certain.

There seemed to be something wrong with the Army cheering. Perhaps it was the absence of the mule. At any rate, it was completely drowned out by the exultant yells of the Middies, who showed surprising vocal energy and endurance. The Middies have a lot of new songs. One that was particularly popular with them was timed to the tune of "Anchors Aweigh," and ran:

> Stand Navy down the field,
> Sails set to the sky.
> We'll never change our course,
> So Army, you steer shy.
>
> Roll up the score, Navy,
> Anchors aweigh;
> Sail Navy down the field,
> And sink the Army, sink the Army gray.

The ripping up that the Army gave the Navy in the first period didn't discourage the Middies in the least. They just kept on cheering as though the game was as good as over, although it certainly did look ominous for the time. Just to show how much they thought about it they brought their band in front of the stand and sang the following verse the two minutes of intermission:

> Fight, you team in blue and gold;
> Fight to win this game;
> Fight your way through the Army gray,
> Fight with might and main.
> Fight, you men who wear the N,
> Fight for Navy's name;
> We'll fight to begin and we'll fight to the end—
> Fight, Navy team, FIGHT!

The playing of Dalton in the latter part of the second period sent the Navy stand into a frenzy of happiness. A Middy, like a Cadet, is supposed to guard his headgear and his other articles of clothing, but when Dalton began his plunge up the field the Middies forgot the regulations and hurled their hats in every direction.

When Dalton booted the ball between the bars for the score the Middies found it impossible to give adequate expression to their feelings with flags and hats, so they took their coats off and waved them in the air.

There was deep gloom in the Army stand after this score, but the Cadets did their best. But nothing they could do was enough to offset the work of Dalton, who had but to make a punt to regain in an instant all the gains that the plucky Army backs had made.

And when the whistle blew that sounded the end of the game, the Middies dashed onto the field and headed by their band began a snake dance around the gridiron, halting as usual before the Army stand to give the despondent Cadets a cheer. The Army boys tried to respond and did fairly well, but there was no denying they were heatbroken over the outcome.

If ever a team felt confident of victory, it was the Army team, when it went on the field today, and the confidence was shared by all its supporters. The Cadets were anxious to wipe out the Navy's 3-to-0 victory of last year, but the Navy just repeated and they can thank their captain, John Patrick Dalton, for it.

Including today's game the Army and Navy have played sixteen games. Seven games have been won by the Army and eight by the Navy, the 1905 game resulting in a tie. No game was played in 1909. Today's game was the rubber and curiously enough it was won under exactly the same condition, but the same score and by the individual work of the same man as last year, Dalton.

Coy, of Yale, never played a more beautiful individual game than Dalton did today. The doughty little Navy captain was in every play, tackling surely on defense, breaking through when necessary, catching punts and shooting them forward in a way which made the experienced spectators gasp.

The kicking was the decisive factor in the game. Had the Army had a punter anywhere near Dalton's class, the result is uncertain. Certainly the Army line played as well as the Navy line in both offense and defense and certainly the backs were as speedy.

ANNAPOLIS GAY AS NAVY RETURNS

Annapolis, Md., Sunday—The Naval Academy team which won from the Military Academy at Philadelphia yesterday, was given a glorious reception when it returned to Annapolis this afternoon. Because it was Sunday, Superintendent Gibbons ordered the enthusiasm to be restrained while the team and other members of the party were in the city, but when they arrived within the Academy gates, there was no limit to the exuberance of the Midshipmen in showing their delight over the result and their feelings toward the lads who had fought for the Navy and triumphed.

The second battalion, commanded by Midshipman John Wilbur, the cheer leader at

Franklin Field, was allowed to march to the West Street Station to meet the football party when it arrived at half-past five and act as its particular guard of honor.

The horses were taken out of the vehicles and the football men were drawn through the streets by their comrades. The first battalion, with the band and hundreds of the Naval Academy and Annapolis citizens, were just inside the gate and fell in line as the football party and the other battalion arrived.

Headed by the Academy band and with each Midshipman armed with a broom, which was set afire, the whole brigade escorted the warriors to Bancroft Hall. Just in front of the main entrance the Midshipmen had piled their wastebaskets and these were set aflame, the brooms also being thrown on the bonfire. The vehicles were stopped at the door and the players and coaches were called for. Beginning with Captain Dalton and the head coach, Lt. Douglas Howard, each one of the coaches and players mounted the top of a "bus" and spoke to the Midshipmen.

Captain Dalton said: "Boys, this is the proudest moment of my life, because I led a team of fighters to victory. It was a case of the best team in the country beating the second best. The big men on the team, such as Brown and Dalton, did not make the team; it was the little kids like Shaw, the 135-pound substitute back, who showed the real spirit that made us win. I also want to tell you that the real hero of the game was Gilchrist. In the third period, when things looked doubtful, he came to me and said that he thought the best interests of the team demanded that someone else should go in. I told him that it was necessary for him to play the game out, and he said that he would, and he played to the end." As Dalton closed by saying that he had played his last game for the Navy he was overcome with emotion.

Lieutenant Howard praised the manly way in which the Army coaches had accepted defeat and said that they had told him after the game that the Navy had the strongest team in the country and that the Army was the next best. Lieutenant Howard expressed the same belief and said that the Navy had been limited to four plays when they had opposed Princeton and that they would have beaten them on a try day. Lieutenant Howard praised the spirit of the team and of the brigade and said that if it was maintained, the Navy would keep on beating the Army.

Familiar names now—Omar Bradley, Jim Van Fleet, Paul Hobson, Bob Neyland, Paul Hodgson, Vern Prichard, Leland Hobbs—they led the Army to a stunning 20-0 victory over a determined Navy team that doggedly refused to admit defeat until the final whistle. Stan Milliken, The Washington Post's reporter, describes the Army victory in his column of November 29, 1914.

Army Offers a Smooth Machine in Mastering Its Dearest Foe

STAN MILLIKEN

ARMY'S POWERFUL AND SMOOTH-RUNNING FOOTBALL MACHINE REMAINS unconquered for 1914. The black, gold, and gray warriors from the banks of the Hudson hurled back and finally crushed beneath them the blue and gold of Navy inside the historic and battle-scarred walls of Franklin field this afternoon. The gridiron superiority of the Cadets over the Midshipmen was as marked as the 20-to-0 score would indicate.

Army came out of the fray victorious because her sons played better football. In every department save one—gameness—that well-balanced corps of cadets smashed, hammered, and literally tore its way to a victory that in one way will go down as one of the most decisive ever attained over the lads from the Potomac. Before the kickoff, West Point was conceded to have the advantage. Five minutes thereafter it was never in doubt.

Franklin Field never capitulated to a more wonderful scene than it did today. Everywhere the black, gold, and gray of the Army fluttered. Everywhere the blue and gold of the Middies flaunted itself. Upon thousands of pennants "Navy" or "Army" appeared, while to the ever increased patches of color upon the sides of the gray-hued field chrysanthemums of a rich gold were displayed in riotous profusion. Slowly but steadily the fortunate holders of tickets streamed through the gates until well after one o'clock when the real invasion of the holiday hosts began. As the turnstiles whirled and Argus-eyed ushers guided men and women to box or less pretentious seats, the broad field speedily lost its amber aspect.

The setting of the scene when once within the gates, will never be forgotten by the some odd-32,000 spectators; it was one of the most magnificent spectacles that one has ever witnessed at an annual clash between Uncle Sam's service elevens. Every bit of available space was taken in both permanent and temporary stands. Because of the cosmopolitan character of the gathering—and there were many notables from Washington—the competing colors of the two institutions were unusually prominent.

The supporters of the Army and Navy followed every cue given by cheer leaders of the sailors and soldiers, and as a result, the long oval-shaped stands surrounding the field was constantly aripple with the hues of either West Point or Annapolis.

The touch of real militarism as faint as it was before and after the contest caused those of the older generations to square their shoulders and enliven the scene. Age mingled with youth throughout and when the band broke into the Navy slogan to the air of "Tipperary," the vast assemblage rose en masse and cheered until it seemed as if the echo would never cease. One immediately thought of what this song meant to those who are fighting across the briny deep and to the lads who were making merry the day on Franklin field. The din had no longer ceased when the band struck up "The Star-Spangled Banner," and then pandemonium reigned. Secretary of War Garrison was the center of the Army's side of an assemblage of distinguished Washington folk, including many officers and their families. While the band played "Tipperary," which seems to have become as great a favorite with the men of either branch of Uncle Sam's service as it has with the British troops, the West Point cadets did their famous two-step into the west stands.

Navy put these words to "Tipperary":

It's a long way to Philadelphia.
It's a long way to go.
We have come to beat the Army
With the best old team we know.

But this song did not turn out very well for the Middies, so let's go back to the game itself. It was said in a preceding paragraph that Army won because its eleven played the better football. This is so, and the score really should have been larger, for Army twice lost touchdowns by fumbling after one of her men had carried the oval across the coveted chalk mark.

Army flung this back to Navy, also to the tune of "Tipperary":

It's a long way to Philadelphia
    For the Army to go;
But we don't mind a little travel
    When we lay the Navy low.
Good night, dear old Navy.
    This is Army day,
For our fight, fight, fight will win the battle
    For the black, gold, and gray.

The last two lines of the Army version also goes for the Navy, for when it comes to fighting, no football teams have ever engaged in a gamer struggle, a struggle to the last ditch, and when the referee's whistle sounded taps the lads from Annapolis still had their boots on and were firing as best they could into a victorious enemy.

Navy's defeat cannot be taken as a rout, although the score should have been larger. Army had the superior team, and that is all there is to it. Once the powerful Army ma-

Army's forward pass combination—Prichard to Merillat—was good enough for two touchdowns in the 1913 game with Navy and a 22-9 Army victory. In 1914, Prichard and Merillat connected for another Army win, 20-0.

chine got going, there was no stopping it. The Annapolis combination was outplayed and outgeneraled, and only the splendid fighting spirit of the Middies, in the face of certain defeat, saved them what was left after the wreckage had been cleared away.

The game lacked closeness 'tis true, but it furnished a splendid picture nevertheless. The ball had hardly been kicked off before Army showed its superiority. As is generally the case in these battles between Uncle Sam's men, punting was quite frequently resorted to, each team in the majority of cases kicking on the third down.

A punt, by the way, led to the first score of the game, and it remained for Blodgett, the Navy halfback, who played back on kick, to become a most important factor in the kicking end of the game. In the first quarter, Army took the ball to Navy's 40-yard line and then kicked. Navy attempted to return the kick, but it was blocked and Blodgett fell on it behind his own goal line for a safety, giving Army its first two points.

But Blodgett was to become a more prominent figure in the result. In the second period the Middies could not gain through the Army line. Then a punting duel was indulged in, Army gaining on every exchange. Finally Blodgett fumbled. This was just what the Cadets hoped would occur, and this error paved the way for Army's first touchdown. Merillat, who played a corking game at end for Army, fell on the ball, on Navy's 15-yard line. Prichard made a perfect forward pass to Merillat, who romped across the Navy's line. The trial at goal was a failure as were the other two attempts after Army touchdowns.

The second touchdown was made on a repetition of these plays, and also came in the first half. Navy kicked off, and on the second lineup Army booted back. Blodgett again fumbled, and again Merillat recovered the ball. Line plunges failed to net the necessary ground, and Prichard again shot the ball to Merillat, who was downed on Navy's 1-yard mark. On the very next play Hodgson plowed his way through Navy's line for a touchdown. This practically settled the contest, but still Navy fought on.

In the second half both teams went at it hammer-and-tongs fashion. Navy was determined to even up the count. Army was bent on preventing it scoring more points. The latter team accomplished its purpose. In the final period after a punting duel, Army got the ball on the 50-yard line.

Hodgson, Army's fleetest and most consistent ground-gainer, running from a fake kick formation—and there were many of them during the game—squirmed his way for a 35-yard run. Another forward pass, Prichard to Merillat, took the ball to the 5-yard mark. Van Fleet made 2 yards. Hodgson added the same number, and then Benedict shot over.

Navy was worn down by a veteran and superior machine—superior in every way save gameness. It looked to be the best team that has represented the Hudson River lads for many a day. The fighting spirit shown throughout by both teams resulted in several penalties and numerous injuries, none of which, as far as could be learned, was serious. Perry, the Navy center, was guilty of slugging and was ordered out of the game, the Middies suffering a penalty of half the distance to the goalposts.

Both offensively and defensively the Army proved too strong for the Navy eleven. The West Pointers' interference formed quickly and was deadly when it once got under way. Prichard's generalship was marked with every play. His judgment far outdid the Navy quarterbacks. In forward passing Army had all the better of the arguments. Prichard's shots in the majority of cases were true to their mark and Navy seemed unable to cover the receiver of the ball.

Navy attempted many forward passes but without much success. Only two worked successfully and these came during the dying moments of the game, but the Cadets would not be beaten this day and finished with a 20-to-0 victory for the first undefeated season. Army was chosen national champions by the All-America Coaches Committee and Center John McEwan was selected on the All-American team by Walter Camp.

George W. Smythe was one of West Point's great football stars. A smart, quick-thinking quarterback, Smythe's 1922 run that was the prelude to Army's winning touchdown is here recounted in thrilling fashion by The Philadelphia Inquirer's Perry Lewis. General Smythe retired in 1957 as one of the most decorated World War II officers in the history of the Army.

Army Beats Navy in Sensational Game, 17-14

PERRY LEWIS

LET THE ARMY MULE BE SHOWERED WITH GARLANDS, LET A WREATH OF laurel be hung about the neck of the noble beast, let it be fed with bay leaves, and let a Norristown, Pennsylvania, youth—one George Smythe—do the feeding. Let the mule be so honored in celebration of the Army's thrilling 17-14 triumph over the Navy in the annual service classic played on Franklin Field yesterday, and let Smythe be given a post of honor which he valiantly earned.

In plain United States English, the Army beat the Navy; the youths who court the mermaid were sent to their love by the brawny sons of Mother Earth. The Army scored two touchdowns and so did the Navy, but the men of West Point put over a field goal for three points and the men of Annapolis did not. That's why the score is 17-14.

The Army, in triumph, and the Navy in defeat, furnished to America, nay to the world of sport on which the sun never sets, the most dramatic of all pictures. In that limning was seen the flower of our youth in bloodless and clean competition traced before a colorful host representative of America, the young giant of all the nations.

There were few in that great multitude there by right of blood. Rather it was a conclave of those who achieve a fitting group to witness such a contest. Certainly it was martial in its coloring, for this was a martial picture. There was Gen. John J. "Blackjack" Pershing in the forefront of the victorious hosts and Admiral Wilson smiling in the face of defeat. There was Franklin D. Roosevelt, Assistant Secretary of the Navy and other military and naval dignitaries too numerous to mention.

Not in all the history of Army and Navy football classics can be found another such dazzling contest as that engaged in Penn's new stadium yesterday; and all the annals or the gridiron can be searched in vain for a record of individual achievement surpassing that furnished by the young Cadet Smythe, a Muhlenberg graduate.

Twice did the gritty and lightning-fast Navy team go into the lead and twice did a glorious Army team come from behind. The last time to ultimate and wonderful victory. A victory that will never be forgotten by victor or vanquished, or by the 60,000 who saw it achieved.

The Navy had scored a touchdown in the second period, and the skillful toe of Cadet Edgar Garbisch, Army's great center, had driven the ball straight between the uprights and over the crossbar from the 45-yard line in the same period, bringing the score at half time to 7-3 in favor of the Middies.

Early in the dramatic third period, West Point had swept into a 10-7 lead by scoring a touchdown and it looked like the Army's day until a brilliant forward passing attack led by Ed Norris, who replaced Steve Barchet at fullback for the Middies. Norris connected to Marvin Parr his left end; another pass Norris to Cullen, and then with the ball on Army's 1-yard line, Conroy scored for the Middies.

The end seemed to be at hand for Army. Navy had effectively bottled up the bull-like rushes of the Army's backs, Timberlake, Dodd, and Bill Wood. It had all the appearance of another Navy triumph. But they reckoned without George Smythe.

There was less than seven minutes to play, when Navy's Halfback Cullen punted to midfield. Smythe, back at safety, waited until he judged the ball correctly, babied the ball to his chest, and then realizing that he had no running room, for Navy tacklers were upon him, decided to scramble back towards his own goal line. He faded back, back, and Army's rooters screamed for him to cut away, and dash back upfield.

Then suddenly, he began to move upfield, slipping off one Navy tackler after another. Back and forth, he twisted and turned, and now he had room and he was out in the open and in the clear. Finally a desperate Navy tackle downed Smythe on the 12-yard line, while 60,000 fans screamed in excitement.

It was a brilliant run of 48 yards, the most exciting run on a football field this reporter has ever witnessed. It did not score, but Smythe's run put the ball in position for that last play.

With but minutes to play, Smythe coolly took a shovel-pass from Fullback Bill Wood, faked a run around his own end, and then out of the corner of his eye spotted Pat Timberlake sprinting into the end zone. Smythe on a dead run pitched a perfect strike to Timberlake for a touchdown. Ed Garbisch kicked the extra point and Army had snatched the game right out of a fighting Navy team's hand.

Left: George Smythe, Army's great halfback, whose touchdown pass in the closing minutes of the 1922 game turned a Navy lead into an Army win.   Right: Fritz Breidster, All-American and captain of the 1922 Army team that won a thriller over Navy, 17-14. Army went through a ten-game schedule without a defeat that season.

In 1924, sports headlines across the nation proclaimed the amazing story of Cadet Edgar Garbisch's spectacular one-man war against the Navy. Single-handedly, West Point's captain and All-American star kicked four goals from the field to defeat Navy, 12-0. Perhaps the most graphic description of this one-man blitz was the story written for the West Point Howitzer by one of the best of American sportswriters, Grantland Rice. It was used in the official Army-Navy program as follows.

Garbisch Defeats Navy, 12-0

GRANTLAND RICE

"ED GARBISCH, THE BIG ARMY CAPTAIN, USED HIS BIG RIGHT TOE AS A FLAMing howitzer today in the Baltimore Stadium and beat the Navy single-handed as 80,000 people looked down upon the field of war.

"Probably the greatest gathering that ever saw a football battle in the East surrounded the Maryland plain as the brilliant Army center drop-kicked four field goals and came within one shot of tying the five-goal record which Brickley and Eckersall had established in other years. Garbisch is through tonight, and the Navy isn't sorry. For it was Garbisch, 12, and Navy, 0, as the game ended under a gray, shadowy sky with a shrill wind singing its song of winter from the north.

"With two great forward lines locked in battle, where neither attack would make any notable headway against hard, clean tackling that never wavered, the tide of war veered in the direction of an accurate toe, and Garbisch in his final game rode this tide to his greatest triumph. It took the Army captain just one period to get this howitzer warmed up to its winning action. He missed three attempts before he got the range, but after this booted the ball across from varying ranges in the second, third, and fourth periods, netting four out of the last five salvos or salutes.

"But the field was fast, the air was keen; and everything was set for rapid action, which only two powerful defensive teams stood ready to roll back at almost every charge."

That action came in the first few minutes when Gillmore intercepted a Navy pass thrown by Hamilton, but Navy held and Garbisch missed his first field-goal try. He had another chance in this period, but missed again, and then Chillingsworth transferred play with a tremendous boot to the Army 5-yard line.

Rice continues: "But all this while Captain Garbisch had been warming up his famous toe. He had been adjusting it to the proper range with care and coolness. It was much after the manner of a sharpshooter adjusting his sights. He had barely missed

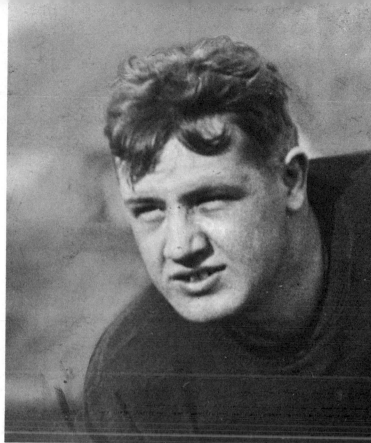

Left: Edgar Garbisch was a bulwark of the Army line for three years, from 1922 to 1924. He startled the world of football with his magnificent performance in the 1924 Army-Navy game, when he kicked four field goals to defeat Navy, 12-0. Right: Frank Wickhorst played in that 1924 game when Garbisch's kicking toe held the spotlight. In the memorable 1926 tie game he was captain of the Navy squad and was named All-American that year.

two goals in the first period which would have smashed all records. One had been blown just a foot off line against the wind. The other, from 40 yards, had fallen short of the bar by less than a yard.

"He was getting nearer and nearer to his mark, and when the alert Fraser blocked a Navy kick around midfield the proud citizens of Washington, Pennsylvania, where Garbisch lives, were about ready to light the old home bonfire in honor of the gallant deeds of a native son. The Navy fought off this rough break with unusual courage, but just a few plays later, Farwick, one of the greatest of all guards, blocked another Navy punt and the bounding Garbisch covered it on the 40-yard line. Gillmore and Wood drove through for a first down, and when the Navy braced and repelled the next attack, Garbisch, from the 32-yard line, sent a dropkick spinning on its way to Army glory.

"By this time the Army mule was beginning to look with envy upon a right foot of such power and precision. The Army mule couldn't have equaled the job, and the demonstration which broke out among the 1,200 Cadets came near shaking the big stadium loose from its mooring and caving down the concrete walls."

After another miss late in the quarter, Garbisch drop-kicked successfully from the 42 and 20 in the third period, and from the 30 in the final session.

Jim Harrison's story of the color, excitement, and sheer drama of the "greatest Army-Navy game of them all" ranks among the finest in the history of sports reporting. Harrison covered all the major sports for The New York Times *in the late 1920s and early 1930s.*

Army 21, Navy 21

JIM HARRISON

THE FOOTBALL GAME THE ARMY AND NAVY PLAYED ON THE WINDY SHORES of Lake Michigan this afternoon furnished the greatest contest, the fiercest warfare, and the largest crowd that football has ever seen.

Before many of the celebrities of this broad land, the teams struggled through to a 21-21 tie as 110,000 looked on with all the emotions that stir the human breast.

For three hours, twenty-two young giants fought back and forth on Chicago's Soldier Field. In the dusk of a late November afternoon they still were battling it out on the same line. When it was so dark that you could hardly tell the Army mule from the Navy goat, they were attacking and counterattacking in a contest that enthralled Vice-President Dawes, Cabinet members, mayors, governors, and gold-braided officers as much as it gripped the commonest of the football fans.

It was a football game that never will be forgotten—this twenty-ninth meeting of the lads from the Hudson and the boys from the Severn. If it was not the greatest of all football games, then there has never been a good football game played in this country.

Whether Chicago's Doric temple of football ever sees another Army-Navy game, the windy town always can remember that its service battle will never be forgotten. For who could forget any minute of it, from the first period to the last?

Who will not remember how the Navy ran up 14 points before the second period was very old, how the Army rushed back with the fury of a demon and tied the score, how the Cadets ran a third touchdown over in the third quarter, how it then was the Navy's turn to show a stout heart and a stiff punch and tie the score as the fourth period came rolling around?

Brave rallies and gallant stands, drama, suspense, thrills—all these were packed into the game until the senses were bewildered. Now it looked like the Navy's game sure, now as certainly the Army's. Just when you had the game charted and decided a rip-roaring back would go tearing through the line, passes would darken the sky and the nicest calculations went up in smoke.

In the early moments it looked like an overwhelming defeat for the Cadets. The

Navy, cruising from mid-field, rammed the ball down to the Army's 2-yard line and catapulted Caldwell over for a touchdown. Again in the early moments of the second period the Midshipmen scored on a march of 62 yards. Schuber dove off his right tackle for the touchdown.

At this pulsating juncture you would have rated the Army's chances as being worth something less than a plugged Mexican nickel, but up on the plains of the Hudson the spelling lessons do not include the word, "quit."

In shorter time than it takes to tell it, "Lighthorse Harry" Wilson and Chris Cagle and Wilson again, had flown like the wind, and in three mammoth jumps were over the Navy goal line, Wilson making the final incursion. A few minutes later Ransford dropped a punt on his 25-yard line. Harbold, the fine West Point end, picked it up and drove some 15 yards for a touchdown. Wilson kicked the goal and the game was just as even as four and four.

Between halves the Secretaries of War and the Navy exchanged salutations in mid-field and agreed that if they never saw another football game, they could still die happy. Vice President Dawes crossed from the Navy side to the Army, maintaining a benevolent neutrality on a day when to maintain any kind of neutrality was a feat deserving at least the D.S.C.

It appeared for a while that the Vice President had brought victory with him to the Army legion, for in the first few minutes of the half Wilson got loose for a 17-yard sortie, and Red Cagle followed immediately with a brilliant dash of 43 yards for a touchdown. But back came the gladiators from Annapolis. From their 44-yard line they pulled up anchor and they ran, plunged, and passed through an Army team which was fighting desperately, furiously, bitterly to finally score a touchdown on a superb 8-yard sprint by Shapley around the Army's left flank.

But wait! There was still one point to go. As Tom Hamilton fell back to try to drop-kick the goal, the field was almost as silent as a tomb. The Middies in the east stand held their breath. The Cadets were indulging in silent prayers, but Hamilton kicked his way into Navy immortality and the Navy thunder from the east was picked up by a wind from the lake and carried out over the land.

There was still one scene left in the drama. The Army rushed back to the attack and stormed down to the Navy's 16-yard line.

Here the Midshipmen's defense became as steel and concrete, and ultimately, Harry Wilson went back to try for a placement goal from the 25-yard line. In other moments and other scenes Lighthorse Harry has kicked many such goals, but it was the one tragic note of the day for the West Pointers, when the ball flew wide of the target.

So ended a game which moved 110,000 persons so powerfully that they forgot aching feet, frostbitten noses, and congealed ears. Two great football teams, evenly matched and perfectly conditioned, with ripping attacks and abundant stars, fought it out to a satisfactory tie. It was, as the French would say, a game without reproach.

The two corps—1,200 Cadets, 1,900 Midshipmen—marched back to the East tonight with banners flying high.

There was glory for all—for Harry Wilson and Red Cagle, and Murrell, Daly and Trapnell and Harbold, for Alan Shapley and Schuber, for Tommy Hamilton and Cald-

Navy's Tom Hamilton calmly kicked the extra point after Alan Shapely's touchdown in the closing minutes of the 1926 game to tie the score, 21-21.

well and Capt. Frank Wickhorst, and all the others of these serried ranks. When the irresistible meets the immovable there is always a fifty-fifty break.

For these were two of the greatest football teams ever turned out by Uncle Sam's academies—two teams with a wonderful record for the season, which had earned their championship laurels and now were staking everything on the fortunes of a single afternoon.

When Cadet meets Midshipman there is no quarter asked or given, no pain is too great to bear. In short it is no pink tea affair, yet in the clean, hard, football of today there was not one trace of unsportsmanlike behavior. They buried each other's noses in the mud, but it was all in fun. And incidentally, it was an excellent lesson for the civilian witnesses, in stamina, strength, self-sacrifice, and the other stalwart qualities.

If you imagine that this was only a football game, you have missed the point. It was a great national spectacle—watched by 110,000, followed by countless millions on radio from the rock-ribbed coast of Maine to the golden sands of California.

By land and by sea the Army-Navy game was fought out and followed. The news of it was flung by wireless and radio to all the Army and Navy posts, to the Marines and the foreign squadrons and the American outposts, even to the very outer fringes of civilization. All over the globe American Army and Navy officers and soldiers and sailors were cocking one ear toward Soldier Field, Chicago.

The celebrities were outnumbered and almost outshone at this first service game to be played in the West. In a box on the Navy side sat Secretary Curtis D. Wilbur.

76

Across the field was Secretary of War Dwight Davis. In another box was Mayor Jimmy Walker of New York. Governor Ritchie of Maryland cheered the boys from his state. Nicholas Longworth, Speaker of the House, was a neutral eyewitness, so was Mayor William Dever of Chicago, official host for the occasion.

There were a score of assistant secretaries and undersecretaries and a large delegation of braided generals and admirals, led by Gen. March B. Stewart, head of West Point; Adm. Louis Nulton, Superintendent of the Naval Academy; and Gen. John L. Hines of the War Department. All the sumptuous splendor of other service games was to be seen again—the pomp and panoply, the color and glamour, of the only football game in America, which has no twin.

With the sun still shining and the air clear, the Cadets and Midshipmen marched into Soldier Field before the game. Led by a band garbed in blue uniforms, with capes of gold, the Midshipmen paraded in columns of squads, then cut across the field and strode to their seats.

Twenty minutes later the Cadets came into sight, marching in a column of squads. There again was the old flawless rhythm, the faultless cadence, the perfect swing of the finest drilled body of soldiers in the world. In straight, unwavering lines—as even as if they had been cut out by some master hand—the West Pointers swung into a close line of companies and finally moved into their seats. The future generals, grouped in a solid segment, looked like a gray slab carved out against the more somber background of the arena.

It was a great picture that caught the eye—on each side in the middle of the stadium, the high Doric columns of this football temple; then the sweeping curves of the horse-shoe as they met toward the south; at the other extremity the closed end of the horse-shoe; and in the center the drab, brown turf of the gridiron, with marching troops, frisking players, bands playing, flags flying, cheer leaders tumbling and gyrating. It was a vast canvas for a great picture.

To the credit of Chicago, it was the best conducted Army-Navy game in history. The record-breaking crowd was handled without an iota of confusion or delay. The arrangements were letter perfect.

Between halves the proceedings were enlivened by a sham battle between a cruiser and a tank. The cruiser fired several mean broadsides and the tank retorted with several brisk volleys and barrages. They chased each other around the field and while this was going on, bombs were exploding freely on the greensward.

A great game, a great crowd, a great day—what more could a football fan ask?

Chris Cagle (far left, with ball) sprints for a 27-yard Army gain in the second quarter of the 1926 game at Soldier Field.

George Trevor's graphic description of the 1931 Army-Navy classic is one of the finest jobs of sports reporting that this reporter has ever read. It is one of my favorite stories of this great football rivalry.

Army Triumphs Over Navy, 17-7

GEORGE TREVOR

A SLATE-COLORED PHALANX IS MASSED ON THE FADED GREEN FIELD FACING twin-decked west stand of Yankee Stadium. Twelve hundred Cadets wearing the long gray coats and saucy bolero capes of the United States Military Academy form that solid square.

Their heads are bowed in mock sorrow as they stand like mourners before their friendly enemies, the Midshipmen from Annapolis. Figuratively speaking, these bare-headed Cadets, dabbing at their slyly twinkling eyes with handkerchiefs, are attending Navy's funeral. For the Army boys it is a sweetly solemn moment tinged with the sardonic irony that youngsters love. For Navy rooters, these sham burial rites constitute a collective jibe that, though all in good clean fun, is not without its sting.

Presently a bugler in Cadet gray steps to the front of the gloating mourners. There is silence for a moment. Then the haunting notes of taps, long drawn and lugubrious disturb the stillness, that peculiarly poignant call which tugs at heartstrings.

"Rest in peace," the sad, limpid notes of the bugle seem to say, "Rest in peace, Navy team, rest in peace." It is a requiem for Captain Tuttle's gallant men who, true to the Annapolis code, have gone down with colors lashed to the mast, scorning surrender.

The sham obsequies ended, a spontaneous cheer erupts from 1,200 Cadet throats and the Post band, unlimbering its most doleful brasses, breaks into the wailing melody beloved of Victorian serenaders.

"Good night, Navy,
Good night, Navy,
Good night, Navy—
We're going to leave you now.
Merrily we roll along, roll along, roll along,
Merrily we roll along to celebrate tonight!"

That defiant jingle finished, the West Point musicians, their white capes flung back, strike up "On Brave Old Army Team!" while the Cadets fall in behind and snake-dance jubilantly around the cleat-torn field, brandishing bits of the goalposts which have already been uprooted and broken into small pieces as souvenirs of victory.

This is the first time since 1927 that West Point has serenaded Annapolis, though defeat hasn't perched on Army banners for a decade. Last year there was no mock funeral when Army triumphed. The Cadets ignored the goalposts and snubbed the Middies, as they trooped out the gate in a sullen silence that bespoke their resentment at Navy's three-year-rule ultimatum.

Last Saturday's little "funeral ceremony" marked the end of that interservice apathy. It symbolized the rebirth of an age-old rivalry; it presaged perhaps a renewal of athletic relations between two academic bodies, which are at once each other's staunchest friends and fiercest foes.

This 1931 Army-Navy game was worthy of the traditions that cluster about the service series, as well as of the charitable cause which prompted it. For stark fury, it has had few counterparts. Both teams meant venom, yet the play was as clean at it was savage and relentless. No quarter was asked or given down there in the muck of the line where Captain Jack Price and his gold-crested comrades locked horns with Captain Magruder Tuttle and his black-helmeted colleagues.

Those Navy boys, obviously outmanned, took the field in a mood of exalted desperation. For sixty unforgiving minutes they played better than they knew how against an infinitely more powerful and polished foe. Spirit alone saved the Midshipmen from a humiliating rout. They took as their motto the flaming slogan of John Paul Jones, whose body lies in the crypt at Annapolis: "Surrender? We've only begun to fight!"

The West Pointers, with everything to lose and little to gain in the way of gridiron reputation, were no less determined. They matched the fanatical frenzy of the under-

Left: All-American tackle and captain, Jack Price played for Army with a broken nose during the 1931 game. The Cadets won it, 17-7, and Price and Milt Summerfelt were picked as the game's outstanding linemen.   Right: A pass from "Bullet" Lou Kirn, Navy halfback, set up the Middies' only touchdown in the 1931 game.

dog with a grim refusal to be thwarted of their just deserts. Repeatedly thrown back on the threshold of the enemy citadel, they rallied to the attack with the frenzy of a savage tribe of Indians.

What an example the rival captains set for their men! McGruder Tuttle, fiery Southerner from Lenoir, North Carolina, slashed like a catamount through the Cadet line to smear the ball carrier. Those Carolina boys go crazy on the football field. Like Lassiter of Yale, a brother Carolinian, "King Tut" is a berserker when the whistle blows. But for Tuttle, Tom Kilday would have rammed the Navy amidships and sunk it "without a trace," as our U-boat friends used to say.

Big John Price, Army militant leader, gave a Spartan display of gameness when he stuck to his guns despite a broken nose that had swelled up like a toy balloon. Price broke his nose in practice before the Notre Dame game. He went the route against the rugged Irish, suffering silently, and insisted on facing Navy. Late in the first half, Price got a crack on his tender beak and had to be relieved.

Sitting in the locker room during the intermission, Price was tortured by sinus pains which wracked his head. Coach Sasse urged him to let Lincoln start the second half. "This is my team and my last game," Price insisted. "My place is out there with the boys." Major Sasse called the team doctor aside. "If Price can stand the terrible pain, it won't do him any physical harm to play," said the surgeon in answer to Sasse's question. The latter is the type of coach who puts the players' welfare ahead of victory.

Price played! His rawboned frame opened the holes through which the shirtless Stecker—his jersey clawed to tatters by Navy tacklers—buzzed like a yellow-striped hornet. Not until Army had clinched the game, by scoring a second touchdown late in the final period, did Captain Price agree to leave the field. Incidentally, it was Price who made that touchdown possible by tearing a gap between guard and tackle after Navy had three times hurled back Army's power plunges on the 1-yard line, thus duplicating the Horation goal-line stand of Captain Mike Trench's 1892 Navy team. A stoic, that boy Price. Who says the human race is getting softer?

There were dramatic moments aplenty in Saturday's game, yet the impression that stayed with you as you filed down the somber ramps of the house that Ruth built was one of mettlesome tackling and lethal blocking. Somehow the zigzag dashes and soaring passes were forgotten, while the dull impact of bodies echoed in one's ears. Those teams were not playing tag football! You could hear the runner grunt clear up in the mezzanine tier when a tackler smeared him. It was "out cutlasses" and Army started its big push early in the second period, when, with Carver mixing up his plays like a Foch, the Cadets marched 63 yards. On that parade Stecker sliced off tackle, Kilday rammed through center, and when Navy's secondaries were lured too close Stecker whipped flat passes to Brown. Forced back to its goal line, Navy repelled a boarding party, led by Stecker, and punted out—but got out of danger.

On second down Stecker unleashed a beautiful 25-yard pass to Bob Carver who was stopped on the Navy 10-yard line. Then calmly, almost casually, Travis Brown stepped back to the 15-yard line and kicked a field goal for the first time in his career. The ball just cleared the crossbar only two minutes after the second period had begun to give Army a 3-to-0 lead.

Those three points broke the ice, though they didn't demoralize Navy. Major Sasse sent in his second-string backfield, and these fresh, eager subs proceeded to run Navy ragged. Ken Fields looked even faster than Stecker. After he had stabbed off tackle for a first down, Fields hoodwinked the Midshipmen via a nifty cross-over pass, on which the Army ends crossed each other's trails as they raced into Navy territory. Fields rifled the ball on a wide tangent to Peter Kopsak, who took it as Johnny Evers used to catch one of Kling's red-hot pegs to second base, and sprinted for Navy's goal. An Army touchdown was a mere formality after that. Ed Herb actually plunged over twice, but got credit for only one tally. An offside nullified his first scoring jab.

Navy came out for the second half full of fight. Those who anticipated a runaway got the shock of their lives. An Army punt was blocked; an Army fumble was recovered, but Kirn's aerials misfired. Then came a third chance. On a swinging end run Lou Kirn turned Army's left flank for 10 yards, reaching Navy's 43-yard stripe. Three Middies mopped up ahead of him on that sprint.

Army naturally anticipated another rush, since it was first down, but canny little Kirn reasoned that Navy lacked the power to parade, and decided that a surprise pass was the proper caper. For once, he caught Army's secondaries napping. Fading back behind air-tight blocking, Kirn cut loose a prodigious heave. The ball rode the air like a full-rigged clipper ship scudding before a following breeze.

Joe Tschirgi, called the "Swiss Admiral" by his mates, kept astride with the ball. Next to Waybright, Tschirgi is the fastest man on the Annapolis squad. He had to be fast to catch that 45-yard floater. By veering inside and then cutting back toward the boundary, Tschirgi shook off Kilday, who had been assigned to cover him.

On Army's 13-yard line Tschirgi and the ball made connections. Joe picked it out of the air and crowded on full steam. He could hear Kilday's cleats drumming the squashy turf behind him. Pursuer and pursued emerged from the shadow cast by the upper deck of the grandstand into a bright patch of sunshine. Too late, Kilday stretched out eager arms and flagged his man. Down went Cadet and Midshipman in a tangled skein of arms and legs, but the momentum coasted Tschirgi across the goal line.

It was then that 2,000 bluecoated Midshipmen reared up on their hind legs and chanted to the tune of the "Old Gray Mare":

> "We don't have to hike like the infantry,
> Ride like the cavalry, shoot like artillery
> We don't give a damn for the Army
> We are the old Nai-vee!"

And so they were, but Army had another shell in its caisson, and Gunner Ray Stecker touched it off. A less courageous if equally formidable team might have become panic-stricken when Kirn looped that touchdown ball through the murky air, but Army reacted like Napoleon's drummer boy at Austerlitz who, when ordered to sound a retreat, replied, "Sire, I know not how—but I can beat a charge that will wake the dead!"

81

For thirteen long years the Midshipmen returned to Annapolis after the Army-Navy game in a state of complete frustration. Once, in that interminable period, they had been able to hold West Point to a scoreless tie. And there was that memorable 21-21 standoff in 1926. But, finally, and only after the kind of drama Army and Navy can conjure up, the Middies poured out onto the field to mob the Navy gridders and to tear down goalposts. Sportswriter Stanley Woodward gives us his account of that exciting Navy victory of 1934.

Borries' Runs, Cutter's Kick Win for Navy, 3-0

STANLEY WOODWARD

THE FIFTY-TON ANCHOR WHICH THE NAVY FOOTBALL TEAM HAS BEEN dragging around in all its engagements with the Army for thirteen years was weighted, catted, and fished to the full satisfaction of 80,000 on muddy, slimy Franklin Field this afternoon.

The Navy football team, driven and inspired by that Kentucky racehorse of backfield men, Buzz Borries, knocked the Army back on the heels by controlled ferocity in the first few minutes, kicked a field goal before the teams changed goals, tied up the Cadets for the balance of the game, and won the thirty-fifth engagement of the service academies, 3 to 0.

It was the first time the Navy had won since 1921, when Steve Barchet broke away for a single touchdown at the Polo Grounds. The three latter-day points emanated from the toe of Slade Cutter, Navy's bruising right tackle and heavyweight boxing champion.

Navy had reached the 7-yard line through an amazing punt by Bill Clark and ensuing slashing assaults by Borries. On third down with a yard to go, Norman Edwards, Army's right end smashed in and dumped a Navy end run on the 12-yard line.

The Navy called time out. Cutter, knowing what was expected of him, took off his head guard, dropped behind the knot of his teammates, and took careful bearings on the goalposts. The whistle blew, Navy huddled, Army deployed, and Cutter still was back there studying the range.

Clark, kneeling in the mud on the 19-yard line, placed the ball for him. Cutter took a step and a half and hit it fairly. It rose over upstretched Army hands, cleared the east crossbar by six feet equidistant between the uprights, and scored three points which perhaps may be called the most significant in the athletic history of the service of the sea.

Fred "Buzz" Borries was everybody's All-American in 1934 and is still considered one of Navy's all-time great stars.

Navy's Buzz Borries takes off in the rain and mud of the 1934 game for a gain around end, led by blockers Dick Pratt and Bill Clark.

Slade Cutter's kick in the 1934 game that was played in a sea of mud seems to leave all the players stunned. It was Navy's first win in thirteen years.

It was the kick felt round the world. Army men in the Canal Zone and far-off Corregidor felt it, and Navy men at Pearl Harbor and the remote China station derived from it the most complete satisfaction since the lean destroyer fleet packed the German undersea craft back into Kiel and the North Sea.

Of course it happened early and there was much work to do to make it significant, but the men of the Navy set themselves in the Franklin Field morass and stopped the Army thenceforth. On one or two occasions the cadets were dangerous but they never got really close. The midshipmen tackled like furies, knocking the churning legs from under Jack Buckler and Maurice Simons, swarming in to smother the powerful drives of Joe Stancook.

In the end the Army was thoroughly beaten and the final whistle blew with the ball in Navy's possession 13 yards from the Army goal. The Navy players, plastered from head to foot with mud, trotted off, trying not to look self-conscious. The Navy noncombatants dressed in dark-blue service overcoats and white-topped caps, swarmed on the field like ants.

The Midshipmen didn't break down the goalposts. They pulled them up by the roots. They bore them to the Army side of the field and set them up again in front of the slate-blue Cadet corps. The whole regiment of Midshipmen massed in front of the Army stands, whooping and singing. An imaginative song leader led them in "The Service Boast." They played taps over the Army with unctious flourishes. Then Army and Navy mingled in the ooze of the playing surface and went away together.

The setting for this renewal of the ancient struggle was in spite of non-co-operation from the gods of wind and weather. Rain had been falling on Philadelphia for thirty-six hours before the game began. It slacked off for a while this morning, then started again and beat down with relentless persistence on the Cadets and the Midshipmen as they marched onto the field an hour before game time.

Despite the downpour the crowd came. Every seat in the huge double-decked stand was occupied. Umbrellas blew like mushrooms in the exposed seats, as the sodden crowd settled down to soak and to watch.

The rival cheering sections lifted the roof, disdaining the elements. Hardy aeronauts flew overhead under the low ceiling, devotedly advertising a popular brand of whiskey. Civilians draped with oilskins and blankets tipped up quarts with the idea of numbing themselves against the current meteorology.

But there was a slight relenting on the part of the gods of war or whatever divine subdivision had been assigned to allot the weather. Just before game time the rain stopped and the sun made a feeble effort to come out. It rained no more, but the field was lost beyond redemption. It was a soggy, oozing morass. Mud plastered the players from the first play on and the ball was as slippery and untenable as an enlarged oyster.

Navy was supposed to rely on finesse and chicanery for victory, but finding that these virtues were going to be inapplicable, it went in exclusively for power and hard-hitting. When you can't dodge and you can't pass you must, in necessity, drive.

There is no denying that the Navy in the first flurry of action knocked the Army back on its heels. The Navy line, which had nullified the power of Notre Dame and had taken the dreadful punishment which Pittsburgh can administer, charged a fraction ahead of the men in gold and black and gained a valuable primary advantage.

Navy's advance to its three points was relentless and marred by no mistakes. On the second play from scrimmage Navy blockers, already anonymous in mud-stained blue and gold, erased the left side of the Army line and the incomparable Borries, that longback who combined speed with drive and toughness, went 20 yards through the mud.

That's how Navy got the game in hand. It worked relentlessly into scoring position, beating the Army in the vital department of punting through Clark's accuracy and a favorable breeze, stopping the Army cold at the line of scrimmage and driving for valuable yards when in possession of the ball.

Clark's amazing punt led directly to the score. Stopped by the Army 31-yard line, Navy was confronted with the problem of giving up the ball and holding its tactical advantage. Clark was entrusted with the job. He dropped back 10 yards and kicked for the corner.

Bob Dornin, of San Francisco, the end whose pass catching helped Navy to victory over Notre Dame, furnished valuable co-operation. Clark's punt rolled toward the corner. It was a question whether it would go out of bounds or into the end zone, but Dornin settled the matter by overtaking it on the 1-yard line and batting it out of bounds.

Army was in desperate straits. Jack Buckler had to kick a slippery ball from the end zone. There was no assurance that the center's pass would get him or that he could handle it cleanly if it did. All went well, however, and Buckler hoisted the ball out to the 35-yard line. Army coverers held Borries to a runback of 3 yards.

Navy started from there. On the second play from scrimmage Borries gave Dick Pratt a shuttle forward pass and the latter ran behind great blocking to the Army 12-yard line. Two runs by Borries brought 9 more yards and the Army had been pushed to within 7 yards of its goal line.

It was at this juncture that Edwards, the Cadet right end, jammed through and halted Borries for a loss, that the Navy called time out and that Cutter kicked his epochal field goal. This department has never been very strong for sympathetic nature

—orange sunsets, purple shadows, and the like—but hard-bitten accuracy demands reporting that, as the ball went over the crossbar, the sun came out for the first time.

It was as if Providence approved of a Navy victory so long delayed. There was, of course, a most extraordinary vocal reaction in the dark-blue north stand. It is reliably reported that the Secretary of the Navy punched the Secretary of War in the ribs and said, "Ain't that something?" Maj. Phil Fleming, now a brainwielder in the Public Works Department, was inconsolable, and Babe Brown, the Navy director of athletics who used to kick goals every few minutes against Army, lost the stoop that he acquired through years and years in the submarine service.

Before the mud-soaked game had run its course, the Army made several bids to redeem the game and occasionally the Navy adherents were thrown into the most dire mental anguish by the actions of operatives in gold helmets.

On the last play of the third period, the entire north stand gasped when Simons, replacement for the damaged Buckler in the Army backfield, intercepted an ill-advised pass and would have got loose but for the tackling ministrations of this man Borries.

Halfway through the fourth period the defensive value of Borries was demonstrated again. Clark, handicapped by a dribble pass from center, failed to get his kick away on the Army 37-yard line. Bob Stillman, the guard, blocked it and Moose Miller, Army tackle who rose from the ranks, picked it up and set out for the Navy goal line.

Borries, the only Navy man in position to catch him, headed him off and brought him down. Miller isn't fast, but he would have been free except for that tackle.

This man Borries, supposed to be a veritable shadow of a back, was Navy's all-around man. He carried the ball thirty-six times out of forty-seven. He made tackles and he intercepted passes. He called the signals and, as far as I could ascertain, he made only one serious mistake—when he threw a pass on first down in his own territory on the last play of the third period.

Even that wasn't too bad in the opinion of Mr. Tommy Tomb, Columbia's good quarterback, who viewed the game from the press box. Said Tommy, "It was a good passing down. In a place like that, you might shake a man loose."

Bill Clark backed up the line tremendously and punted the soggy ball like a master. Other individuals in the Navy frontier played inspired football, and it is my opinion that the play of the Navy line actually determined the outcome. It had fire and drive on the offense when the chance came to score and a fierce lift on the defense when the time came to sit tight and hang on.

Navy dominated the game until after it had scored. Army was unable to move until the second period when it advanced into Navy territory and lost the ball through Borries' interception of a pass on his own 30-yard line.

The third period was played across midfield with Clark holding his own in a punting engagement with Simons despite a fresh adverse breeze. Just at the end Navy put the ball in play on its own 45-yard line and Borries elected to pass.

Simons took the ball out of the Navy receiver's hands near the north sideline and set out. He went 15 yards before Borries brought him down on Navy's 35.

The teams changed goals and Army made its bid. Running wide around left end

Navy fullback Bill Clark gets off a punt during practice for the 1934 season.

behind great blocking, Simons made 7 yards. Stancook, running twice in succession from double-wing formation, jammed through for a first down on the Navy 24-yard mark. Subsequently the Army stalled and on third down Clark intercepted a pass.

The Navy was deep in its own territory but Clark rectified this situation with the greatest punt of this day. Standing on his 11-yard line this invaluable operative hoisted the ball over the head of Grohs, the Army safety man. It bobbed and rolled to the Army 12-yard line, where Grohs picked it up and came back 10 yards.

A poor return punt gave Navy the ball almost immediately on the Army 32-yard mark, but the men of the sea couldn't gain and reverse English was applied when Clark's kick, an attempt to put the ball out of bounds again, was blocked.

Miller, who scooped the ball, got across midfield before Borries caught him. This gave Army an outside chance but a fumble on the first play spoiled it. Thenceforth the Navy sat on the ball game. At the very end Grohs fumbled a marine punt and Mandelkorn, Navy end, recovered 13 yards from the last line. Time was up before the men of Crabtown could do anything about it. At this juncture two queues of men in dark blue and white were sneaking up on the goalposts and biding the timer's signal.

There can be no denying that the Navy deserved to win this game on play. The men of the sea gained 82 yards by rushing to 56 for West Point. Each completed a pass, Navy for 11 yards, Army for 1. Navy had the better of the punting, the running back of punts and, to get the point, of the place-kicking.

Swede Larson throws a substitute back into the breach and a Navy team, which has lost five straight games, rises to glory in 1939, trouncing a highly favored Army eleven, 10-0. Red Smith tells the glorious Navy story.

Navy Rises to the Occasion

RED SMITH

NAVY MANNED THE LIFEBOATS YESTERDAY, ABANDONED THE WRECK OF A football season that foundered under the shock of five successive defeats, and cruised to the safe harbor of a 10-0 victory over Army—the only opponent that ever really counts at Annapolis.

In fog and rain and mud and a cold, clinging mist through which Municipal Stadium's host of 104,000 strained and squinted to make out the shadowy figures on the field, the Midshipmen of the United States Naval Academy charted an unwavering course.

Through the ranks of a favored Army team that hadn't even time to fling up its defenses, the sailors streamed 51 yards on their first fifteen offensive plays to set up a 35-yard field goal and a three-point lead.

Then, after hurling back West Point's best challenges with almost insolent ease through the second and third periods, they hastened downfield again. This time they traveled 47 yards in eight plays, sending a slender torpedo named Dick Shafer rifling through the line on a 22-yard touchdown dash.

Thus was accomplished, deftly and with altogether overwhelming conviction, Navy's first conquest of its dearest enemy in three years, the fifteenth triumph for Annapolis in the 40-game series that began at West Point in 1890.

Thus was won, too, undying fame for two obscure substitutes, who as recently as two weeks ago had reason to doubt they would even be in uniform for this struggle.

One is Shafer, frail-looking back from Oberlin, Ohio, whom Coach "Swede" Larson dug up out of the obscurity of Navy's B team no more than a fortnight ago.

The other is stubby, little Robert E. Leonard, a "youngster" (sophomore) from Gainesville, Texas, who cooled his heels on the Navy bench through 154 of the game's 156 plays.

Just twice Larson nodded his way, and Leonard flung off his sheepskin coat and racked onto the field. The first time he kicked a field goal, a placement of exquisite position steered from a difficult angle across almost the exact center of the crossbar.

Teed up by Monty Whitehead on the 25-yard line, the grimy ball traveled 35 yards to clear the posts set 10 yards back in the end zone.

Twenty-year-old Leonard trotted happily back to the bench then, and there he remained until Shafer ripped through for Navy's touchdown.

Once more Larson nodded. Once more Leonard raced out to report to Umpire Bill Crowell. Once more he kicked, and once more his aim was true, adding the extra point that completed the scoring.

There'll be other Army-Navy games for Leonard, but this was the first and the last for Shafer. He is a first classman, a senior. Every fall these last three years he has reported to the varsity coach, struggled with the others for a position on the squad, and wound up always with the scrubs.

If Larson, driven almost frantic by injuries to one after another of his regulars, hadn't brought him up from the B team, for the game with Princeton a week ago, the likelihood is Shafer would have been in the stands yesterday.

It wasn't that he couldn't play football. It wasn't that he lacked ambition. It was simply that coaches considered him too small.

Well, he's smaller than ever now. He weighed 155 pounds when Larson sent him in after Leonard's field goal to take the place of weary Cliff Lenz, who had led the Navy march into scoring position.

He weighed 153 pounds when he returned to the dressing room between halves. And when he came out of the game in the damp dusk his weight was 149.

Those figures tell better than words possibly could what kind of a game twenty-two-year-old Shafer played. While he was in there he did the kicking and carried the ball on fully 50 per cent of the plays. And if there was a single one of his withering rushes that Army halted short of the line of scrimmage, you couldn't detect it from the murky distance of the press box.

Navy left so little room for argument that the game wasn't especially exciting to the crowd that sat huddled under slickers and overcoats and parka hoods and newspapers folded hatwise, peering through the gray veil of rain and mist. The estimated total of spectators, by the way, was arrived at by adding press, police, Pinkerton agents, attendants, and such to the 101,610 who actually bought tickets.

Army never made a real scoring threat until the closing minutes of the game, when a passing attack sent the Cadets to Navy's 19-yard line. Bill Montgomery, Navy end recently graduated from the B squad like Shafer, literally stole the ball out of the hands of West Point's Herb Frawley to finish that advance.

Early in the third period, Army connected with a splendiferous 31-yard pass from John Hatch to Emory Adams for a first down on Navy's 35. But a pass interception by Ed Gillette took care of the situation, and a little later when a penalty for roughness put the Midshipmen back in their own territory again, Lenz intercepted another pass.

All told, Navy, whose pass defense was the weakest part of its game this season, grabbed five Army passes out of the air. Of thirteen forwards attempted, the Cadets completed only three.

On the ground, Army was hardly more effective. The Cadets gained only 86 yards by rushing compared with 207 for Navy, and although West Point had seven first downs to the Midshipmen's eight, only one of them was made in the first half. The six

There were many heroes in Navy's 1939 upset victory, but two substitutes, Bob Leonard and Dick Shafer, carried off the major share of glory. The Middies started this lineup: (Front row, l. to r.) Bill

in the second half were made with Navy out front and content to let Cadets advance as long as they didn't try to cross midfield.

So it wasn't close enough to be exactly thrilling, yet it was played with a ferocity that forced recognition of the ability of many individuals. For Navy, in addition to Shafer, Lenz and Leonard, Montgomery, and another end, Louis Burke, gave outstanding performances, and the big Annapolis captain and tackle, Al Bergner, was destruction personified.

Bergner's parents were in the stands, as were members of the family of Harry Stella, Army's All-American captain who played as Bergner's teammate in Kankakee (Ill.) High School. Papa Silvio Stella had occasion to admire not only his rugged son, but also Army's Hatch, Joe Grygiel, and Fred Yeager, ends.

Rated 18-to-5 favorite, Army seemed stunned when the first Navy bombardment started. It happened with such unexpected suddenness—a kickoff, two Army plays and a punt, and Navy was coming.

It was Lenz on a cutback over his left tackle; Lenz on a blast outside his right tackle; Phil Gutting (still another B-team graduate) on a wide reverse and Monty Whitehead charging through the middle. Then Lenz again, and again and again.

Out of fifteen plays, Lenz carried the ball on 11. He made a first down, Navy's fourth in a row, on the Army 20 and there for the first time the Cadets dug in. They yielded 3 yards to Lenz, flung him back a yard, grudgingly yielded the same yard back. Fourth down, seven to go. That's when Leonard arrived.

All through that first quarter Army never got past its 40-yard line. Indeed, the Cadets

90

Montgomery, Alan Bergner, Bex Trimble, Dave Wolfe, Hal Harwood, Tom McGrath, Dick Foster. (Back row, l. to r.) Phil Gutting, Ralph Boyer, Earl Rowse, Tom Blouet.

had the ball only three times, held it for only thirteen plays. But after the field goal they rallied their stricken defenses, and the second period saw neither team cross midfield.

The Hatch-to-Adams pass and subsequent Army forays by air kept the Middies on defense until a few minutes before the third quarter ended. Then Whitehead put Army smack-dab in the barrel with a tremendous punt that bounced out of bounds 2 yards from the West Point goal.

Shafer ran Army's return punt to the West Point 47. He passed to Dick Foster, left end, for a first down. He and Gutting and Whitehead banged out another on the 26. An end-around play by Foster added 4 yards more.

By this time the players were barely visible from the stands in the gathering dark. But no rain nor mist nor murk of night could stay these couriers from swift completion of their appointed round.

On the next play—the first of the fourth period—Shafer burst through a niche as Army's right guard was mouse-trapped out of commission. Once through the hole, he reversed his field sharply, cutting to his right and outrunning the Army secondaries, who'd been sucked over to stop his plunge. Not a hand touched him, although Frank Waddell's despairing dive just missed as he crossed the goal line.

Then, there came that Leonard once more.

That was all. There was a good deal of frantic passing by Army, a good deal of adroit defending by Navy, a great deal of floundering in the mud. But the ballgame really was over, and everyone knew it.

Comdr. Oscar E. (Swede) Hagberg, Navy coach, said, after the 1944 Army-Navy game, "Davis broke the game wide open for just about the best Army team that I have ever seen." Here is the story of that game as Glenn Davis, one of the most brilliant backs of all times, tells it.

My Greatest Day in Football

GLENN DAVIS

OF THE MANY THRILLS I'VE HAD, I SUPPOSE THE ARMY-NAVY GAME OF 1944 gave me my greatest. We at West Point considered that victory the best of our undefeated streak. Yes, I like that game-thrill but I can't help thinking of the time I flunked out of the Academy. I guess, whenever I think of it, that incident gives me my greatest chill.

Not many people are familiar with it, but I was dropped from West Point after my plebe year, in which I ran into scholastic trouble. Fortunately, the Academy enables you to take another exam—a makeup exam—if you desire to continue at the Point. All through the 1944 summer I crammed, and the tedious studying paid off when I passed the test and was readmitted to school. Otherwise I wouldn't be in a position today to relate the thrill I got out of the Army-Navy game in 1944.

That was a game played in Baltimore in which millions of dollars in war bonds were bought by a sellout crowd as the price of admission. Army won, 23 to 7, and there was more to it than just a victory; more to it than just a victory over Navy, too. You know what it means to a West Pointer to beat the Middies. Well, this game carried more than the regular traditional significance.

First of all, we had lost five straight games to the Tars. Rubbing salt in the deep wound was the fact that Army had scored but one touchdown in those games. And, most of all, we were on the threshold of the first unbeaten Army season since 1916. Navy was the only team standing in the way of our winning the intercollegiate football championship—and what an obstacle!

They were great. As Coach Earl Blaik said after the game:

"I think it was a case of the country's No. 1 team beating the country's No. 2 team."

Navy was considered to have the nation's best line—Bramlett, Whitmire, Carrington, J. Martin, Chase, Gilliam, and Hansen. But we had greater linemen that day in Pitzer, Arnold, Green, St. Onge, Stanowicz, Nemetz, Poole, Foldberg, and Coulter.

I don't remember when we worked so hard in preparation for a game. The two-weeks' practice period was spent in brisk, long drills, during which we had repeated scrimmages. Coaches Blaik, Herman Hickman, Andy Gustafson, and Stu Holcomb pounded us through offensive and defensive maneuvers, leaving no stones unturned. But as the game drew closer, it became more apparent to the players that if we could handle Don Whitmire, the mastodonic tackle who made All-America at Alabama and Navy, we would win.

That job of stopping Whitmire primarily belonged to Hank Foldberg and he proceeded to play one of the greatest games of his career. It was Hank's duty to throw the blocks on the huge Whitmire and nobody envied his position; Whitmire had been tossing opposing linemen around like spitballs. Foldberg's success now is history, but more about that later.

A couple of days before the game, Captain Dick Pitzer's fallen arches began kicking up. For a while—in fact, almost until we took the field—it looked as though Pitzer's bad feet would keep him benched. Coach Blaik finally decided to go along with the badly needed end as long as he could stand on his aching feet and Pitzer gamely put out all the way.

But it wasn't only Pitzer's feet that bothered Blaik. It was Navy's feats that had our worried coach nervously pacing back and forth like an expectant loser just before we prepared to take the field. Now, Blaik wasn't the type who went in for dramatic pre-game messages. He generally issued a few last-minute instructions and then sent us out. This time, however, he walked silently up and down as we sat waiting. Finally, Coach Blaik made an unprecedented talk—for him, that is. He reached into a pocket and pulled out a telegram. It was from a buddy of his, Gen. Robert Eichelberger, one of World War II's top generals. It asked us "to win for all the soldiers scattered throughout the world," or words to that effect. That's all Blaik said.

Well, we went out and won it "for all the soldiers, etc." But more so for ourselves because, as I've said, it earned Army the national championship and helped us beat Navy after five straight defeats.

We played great team ball. Our blocking was exceptionally fine. The way our big forwards cleared out and racked up those Navy tacklers made it simple for us backs. Not that fellows like Blanchard, Kenna, Hall, Lombardo, Minor, and Dobbs couldn't help themselves when the situation arose.

Our big break came when Whitmire hurt his knee on the opening kickoff. That was the start of a severe pounding from Foldberg that enabled the courageous linesman to stick it out only until late in the second period. Then he had to be helped off the field. When Don departed, he seemingly took Middie hopes for victory.

We were leading, 7 to 0, at the time on a 24-yard, second-period touchdown scored by Hall's dash through Whitmire's tackle post. When Don left the game, he carried many sensitive mementos on his body left by the shattering blocks Foldberg threw— like the one that shook Hall past the line of scrimmage for the first touchdown.

Navy fought back, though. After we had increased our lead to 9 to 0, when Stanowicz and Arnold teamed to block Hansen's third-period kick that became a safety as Hansen fell on it in the end zone, Navy started to roll.

Little Hal Hamberg took charge of the Middie attack. In the next few extremely rough moments, during which the play was furious but clean, Hamberg ran and passed to the Army one. Clyde Scott smacked over on the second try and Navy trailed, 9 to 7, after Finos' conversion.

That's the way it remained until the last quarter; until Bobby Jenkins, who had been benched by an early injury, came into the game. It was like a shot in the arm to the Navy rooters and players. Those Middie linesmen started hitting us like raging madmen. Scott, Jenkins, and Barron moved behind the aggressive line play into our territory. Just when it looked as though they were heading for a touchdown, the Middies got one of those tough, unpredictable breaks. Jenkins' pass sailed right into my hands.

It was Navy's last chance. Blanchard ran wild. There was no stopping him. He either picked up his interference or ran past it. From midfield, the ball was moved almost single-handedly by Doc to inside Navy's 10. There, Minor went off in motion to the left and Blanchard, on a quick-opening handoff from Lombardo, crashed over guard for the touchdown.

We got another score after that but it wasn't needed. We went 69 yards in five plays. Four of them and an offside put the ball at midfield. Blanchard took up a station as a wide flanker to the right and Minor headed the opposite way as the man-in-motion. With the defense split, Lombard flipped me a lateral and I followed Blanchard around right end and down the sidelines for a touchdown. Minor, by the way, cut across the secondary to wipe out two defensive backs. It was easy, with that kind of blocking, to finish off a play that the boys nicknamed "The California Special." It was the first time we had used the maneuver and it helped me get my 20th touchdown and clinch the title as the country's leading scorer.

(ED. NOTE: In the locker room, after the game, Davis was walking out and Army Backfield Coach Gustafson turned to reporters and said, "There goes one of the greatest ball carriers I have ever seen." That sentiment was echoed by the Navy coach, Cmdr. Oscar E. (Swede) Hagberg, who added: "Davis broke the game wide open for just about the best Army team that I have ever seen.")

Glenn Davis is recognized as one of Army's all-time stars. The combination of Davis and Felix "Doc" Blanchard accounted for more Army touchdowns than Navy cares to remember.

Army's Glenn Davis takes off on a pitchout that gained eighteen yards in the 1943 game. Navy won, but it was a portent of things to come.

This is sportswriter Allison Danzig's story of the 1945 Army win over Navy—the heroics of the Midshipmen and the awesome exploits of two all-time greats, Doc Blanchard and Glenn Davis. Danzig wrote it for The New York Times.

Men vs. Supermen

ALLISON DANZIG

ARMY CLOSED THE BOOK ON ONE OF THE UNFORGETTABLE CHAPTERS IN football history today as the West Point Cadets defeated Navy, 32-13, for their eighteenth victory in succession, marking the first time they have ever gone through two perfect seasons in a row.

The most distinguished gathering that has attended a sports event in this country in many years assembled in the Philadelphia Municipal Stadium, filled to its capacity of 100,000 for the forty-sixth meeting between the service Academy rivals.

This was the first time since the 1941 contest, played a week before the attack on Pearl Harbor, that the climactic spectacle of intercollegiate football returned to its pre-war setting, invested with all of its old glamour and glitter and the huge crowd able to enjoy the show unreservedly in the return to peacetime pursuits of pleasure.

In honor of the happy occasion, President Truman furnished an official note with his attendance as Commander in Chief of the Army and Navy, and a host of war leaders from both branches of the military whose names have become worldwide bywords during the past four years, as well as most of the President's Cabinet, were present.

Such glamorous figures as Generals George C. Marshall, Omar Bradley, Henry H. (Hap) Arnold, James Doolittle, Jacob L. Devers, and Carl Spaatz; Admirals Chester W. Nimitz, William F. (Bull) Halsey, and Ernest J. King and British Air Chief Marshall Sir Arthur Tedder and Fleet Admiral Sir James F. Somerville, all of them famous artisans in the winning of the Second World War, vied with the play on the field for the crowd's interest.

As a matter of fact, the outcome of the game was decided before the President changed his seat from the Army to the Navy side during the intermission between the halves. Indeed, the result was foregone by the time that the renowned Doc Blanchard and Glenn Davis, who scored all five Army touchdowns, had gone across three times for a 20-0 lead in the opening quarter.

The scene during the intermission, when the President left his family to transfer his allegiance to the Navy side, was one of the most impressive of the almost ideally perfect football afternoon.

A hundred bluecoats formed in two lines, to afford a protecting lane for Mr. Truman's march. Surrounded by Secret Service men and escorted by Secretary of War Robert P. Patterson, Maj. Gen. Maxwell D. Taylor, superintendent of the Military Academy, and Brig. Gen. George Honen, commandant of cadets at West Point, the nation's Chief Executive left his box in front of the cheering 2,400 Cadets.

As he walked out on the playing field, greeting service men and the wounded war veterans who were seated along the sideline, the police all came to a hand salute. Waiting in the center of the field for the President were Secretary of the Navy James V. Forrestal, Vice Admiral Aubrey W. Fitch, superintendent of the Naval Academy, and Rear Admiral S. H. Ingersoll, commandant of Midshipmen. Under their escort, Mr. Truman proceeded across the field, as the 2,700 Midshipmen cheered, and took his assigned place as a Navy rooter.

The President was backing a loser from then on, but a loser who was as game as Navy and Army are under all circumstances, on the football field and the fighting front.

Everyone knew that the Midshipmen were a hopelessly beaten team, that their line was not quite good enough to match the powerful forwards of Col. Earl Blaik and, above all, that they had no lasting, consistent answer to the depredations of the twin football scourges of modern times, Blanchard and Davis, who raced 46 and 48 yards, respectively, for two of the Cadet's touchdowns.

But if everyone else sensed the hopelessness of their plight, the white-shirted stalwarts of Comdr. Oscar Hagberg refused to accept the inevitable. The game had gone against them from the very outset, as everyone had predicted, with Army marching 56 yards to a touchdown on seven plays and two 5-yard penalties from the opening kickoff, and it soon seemed that they would be humiliated by a far greater margin than the twenty-seven points by which Army was generally favored to win, but they had entirely different ideas.

The fact is that, after that first period, Navy made a fight of it every inch of the way, and when it scored, six seconds before the end of the half, on a tremendous 61-yard pass from Quarterback Bruce Smith to the blazingly fast Clyde Scott, who raced the last 40 yards as Davis sought to cut him down from behind, an element of uncertainty developed for the first time of the afternoon, with the score, 20-7.

It was the only time, however, for forty-eight seconds after the second half got under way Blanchard was stampeding 46 yards with an intercepted pass for a touchdown, with blockers springing up all around him. That lightning bolt of heartbreaking adversity definitely sealed Navy's doom.

Though it came back to go 26 yards for a touchdown by Fullback Joe Bartos, after Smith had intercepted a pass by Davis, the breaks of the game went against it, as interference by Navy was ruled—questionably it seemed—on a pass, to give Army the ball on the Middies' 31-yard mark, and Davis went 27 yards for the final touchdown two plays later.

There was no question that the better team won, and won decisively; and Blanchard, Davis, Arnold Tucker, Bob Chabot, who started in place of Shorty McWilliams at right half, Capt. John Green, Art Gerometta, Tex Coulter, and the other members of the Cadet line will long be remembered and acclaimed for their deeds today and throughout the season. But not all the honors belonged to Army today, and Navy deserves a royal welcome with a twenty-four-gun salute when it returns to Annapolis for the grand fight it offered against almost insulting odds.

Navy did things to Blanchard and Davis today that no other team has done. Time and again it stopped the two terrors of the gridiron or threw them for losses, and Leon Bramlett, the best end on the field, gave Davis, the fastest back operating in football, scandalous treatment as he broke through to nail him 8 yards behind the line.

Army was able to put on only one really long-sustained advance—from the opening kickoff—until the middle of the final quarter, when a 15-yard penalty for roughness and the 30-yard infliction for interference with a pass contributed to a 71-yard march that ended with Davis' 27-yard touchdown run. In between those two scores, the cadets were finding it difficult to launch an offense of any continuity, so strong was Navy's defense.

The Middies were using practically an eight-man line and Army was not passing except when it had the wind behind it. With Center Dick Scott and Fullbacks Bartos or Bob Kelly playing only a step behind their six-man line, the men from the Severn were squelching most of Army's running plays from the T formation and Arnold Tucker was more conspicuous than Blanchard on the offense for a good part of the game.

But Blanchard and Davis might be checked again and again and still it was not enough. They had to be stopped every time. To miss them once was to invite disaster, for, with their power, speed, and elusiveness, they are backs who are likely to go all the way if given the chance to get started or allowed the slightest loophole.

It was beyond Navy's strength and capacity to meet so exacting a requirement. The Middies used few reserves, as did Army, and they made mistakes for which Blanch-

Army's starting lineup for the 1945 game. (Front row, l. to r.) Henry Foldberg, end; Al Nemetz, tackle; Arthur Gerometta, guard; Herschel Fuson, center; John F. Green, guard; Dewitt Coulter, tackle; Richard Pitzer, end. (Back row, l. to r.) Thomas McWilliams, halfback; Arnold Y. Tucker, quarterback; Felix "Doc" Blanchard, fullback; Glenn Davis, halfback.

ard and Davis made them pay dearly. The crowd would rub its eyes at the sight of the twin engines of destruction being manhandled like ordinary flesh-and-blood backs. It would rub them again and again, and then, suddenly, there was Doc or Junior streaking across the goal line.

In the second period Army made one first down and never threatened. In the third quarter it never got beyond its 31-yard mark after Blanchard had sprinted 46 yards with an intercepted pass in the first minute and again made only one first down. In the final period it got one first down on a 15-yard penalty, another on the pass interference ruling and only one other.

All of this is set down not to belittle Army but to give due credit to Navy. Possibly Army may have let down after running up twenty points in the opening quarter and had no disposition to pour it on, but there is seldom any mercy shown in these fierce service battles, nor any expected or wanted.

Commander Hagberg said yesterday that he expected Army to run up the score if it could and that Navy would do so if it was able to. That is the spirit in which the games are played. So it is not fair to the Middies to attribute the closeness of the play in the last three quarters to the kindness of the West Pointers.

This was not the most thrilling Army-Navy football game but it was a better fight than was generally expected and the conditions were the best that have been obtained within memory in the Philadelphia Stadium.

The weather was a little too chilly for the comfort of the spectators, but they came warmly clad and the temperature rose from a low of twenty-one in the early morning to just above freezing by game time. The sun shone most of the time, an unexpected blessing, to take the sting out of the brisk wind, and helped to dry out the field, which was in excellent condition, dry, firm, and offering safe footing.

Despite the cold, the crowd came early to see all the show, including the marching Midshipmen and Cadets, the Army mule and the Navy goat, and the unprecedented assemblage of brass. Generals' stars and admirals' braid seemed almost as common today as chicken eagles, silver and gold leaves, and lieutenants' bars.

Among the star wearers were Brigadier Generals Blondie Saunders, who lost a leg in the war, and Rosie O'Donnell. Both of them were football heroes at West Point and both of them had great records in the Pacific with the Twentieth Air Force, whose B-29 Superforts were the terror of Japan.

Seated up in the stands was one of the most brilliant young pilots in the command—Lt. Charles Bolton. Recently returned from Saipan, Bolton wears almost every decoration except the Congressional Medal, including two Presidential Citations won in bombing missions over Japan.

Captains Green and Dick Duden, who was to suffer a leg injury during the play, met in the center of the field with the officials for the toss of the coin. Army won and Green elected to defend the north goal, so as to have the wind at his back.

Navy elected to kick off, which was not to Army's liking. The Cadets prefer to kick off themselves. But Duden did them no harm. West Point took the kickoff and went 56 yards across the goal line after Quarterback Tucker had returned the ball 19 yards.

Tucker went 13 yards off left tackle, Davis sped around Navy's left end for 19, and

Blanchard bulled across from the 1-yard line. Bo Coppedge hit him, but that didn't stop Doc. Dick Walterhouse came in to kick the extra point but failed.

Navy now took the ball and made three successive first downs to midfield, with Smith, Bartos, and Scott carrying and Tony Minisi going in motion and blocking. Both teams were loath to use the pass. Army stopped Navy and then was stopped dead in turn.

A break paved the way for the Cadets' second score. Kelly got only 11 yards on a punt and Army took the ball on Navy's 37, going to the 32 on a penalty.

Bramlett then broke through to tackle Davis for a 9-yard loss, but Tucker, taking the ball from Center Ug Fuson, went 24 yards on a quarterback sneak. On the next play Blanchard plowed the remaining 17 yards for a touchdown. Smith hit him head on near the line and went down. Blanchard went on.

Army's third touchdown came the very next time it had possession. It gave Navy the Pennsylvania treatment thereby. Smith kicked to Chabot, who returned 13 yards to Navy's 48. On the next scrimmage Davis broke through Navy's left tackle and sped like a deer for the goal line, with Minisi futilely in pursuit of the wind down the sideline.

The second quarter belonged to Navy. The Middies reached Army's 34-yard mark and the 20, but could not score until six seconds before the end. Smith passed 24 yards to Bramlett on a screened aerial, with the other three backs out as flankers, to put the ball on the 34. That threat was stopped as Captain Green threw Smith back to the 45 as he tried to get off another pass.

A poor kick by Blanchard, who usually gets splendid distance on his punts and kick-offs both, went only 10 yards and gave Navy possession on Army's 27. The Middies got to the 20 and lost the ball on downs. It seemed that Navy would never score until, six seconds before the end of the half, Scott caught Smith's pass on the 40 and raced for the goal line. Davis, 6 or 7 yards back, set out in pursuit and got the mercury-footed Scott by the heels as he crossed the last line. That shows how fast Davis is.

The Navy stands cheered madly at this success. The score was 20-7 after Dick Currence had kicked the point, but the second half had hardly got under way when Blanchard was tearing 46 yards with an intercepted pass to make the score 26-7. Neither team threatened for the remaining fourteen minutes of the third period.

Early in the final quarter Blanchard fumbled and Clyde Scott recovered, but the mistake did no damage. A minute later Bruce Smith intercepted Davis' pass and ran back 7 yards to Army's 26. This was Navy's big break, and it went to work to exploit it at once.

In five plays the Middies had their second touchdown. A pass was grounded. Then Bill Barron, who was a fine halfback offensively and defensively as a replacement for Minisi, went through the middle for a first down on the 15. Big Bartos found a big hole at center and went to the 3 for another first down. The Army line was sagging surprisingly. Barron went to within less than a foot of the goal line and, from there, Bartos crashed through left guard to score.

Army, incensed and perhaps a bit alarmed, with the score now 26-13, took the next kickoff and went all the way. Breaks were a big help.

In 1946, Army reached the heights of its all-time greatness as co captains Doc Blanchard (35) and Glenn Davis (41) romped over all opposition to extend its three-year run of consecutive victories to twenty-five games with a thrilling 21-18 victory over Navy. Coach Earl Blaik is seen with his all-time, All-American stars.

First came a 15-yard penalty on Navy. A pass failed and then the cadets suffered two 5-yard penalties for illegal motion and delaying the game. It seemed that they were stalled. Then Davis passed. Blanchard went down to receive the aerial. The officials ruled interference and gave the ball to Army on Navy's 31, a 30-yard gain.

This was a critical spot for the ball and Navy should have remembered it. Against Notre Dame and Penn both, Army took over on the 31 and went the distance in two plays, the first by Blanchard and the second by Davis. That was it again. Blanchard got four, and then Davis sent inside left tackle 27 yards for the score. It was an old script replayed again.

Army had two more chances before the game ended. Bill Lamar recovered a fumble on the Navy 32 and Army went to the 30, but Bramlett smeared Bob Stuart on fourth down. Then Bob Richmond intercepted a pass and ran it back 13 yards to Navy's 17. On the next play Johnny Sauer was thrown back to Navy's 35—of course by Bramlett, a great end today and all season. That was the end.

In the dressing room Colonel Blaik finally broke down and admitted that Army is the greatest West Point team of all time—at least of all he has seen. He hasn't seen them all, but no one will probably challenge his statement.

It's going to be difficult for the colonel to say good-bye to this great team and begin all over again next year. Only eight members of the regular starting lineup will be back again, including Blanchard, Davis, Tucker, and Coulter—and Army's opponents thought these past two seasons that war was what Sherman said it is.

Army's great head coach, Earl Blaik, exposes his innermost thoughts as a raging Navy team seems about to destroy the Glenn Davis-Doc Blanchard-Arnie Tucker legend of invincibility in the 1946 game. It was a game that will go down in Army-Navy history as one of the most thrilling in the entire story of this annual classic. This is excerpted from the book, You Have to Pay the Price, *by Blaik and Tim Cohane.*

The Vindicators

EARL BLAIK *and* TIM COHANE

WE WENT DOWN TO THE FINALE WITH NAVY IN 1946, OWNING A TWENTY-seven game defeatless string that had begun with the opener against North Carolina in '44. Nobody gave Navy a chance except their coach, Comdr. Tom Hamilton, the Navy players, and the Army coaches. I don't mean the Army players were overconfident, but defeat was not part of their thinking.

We were a weary, used-up ball club. To his bad shoulder, and a knee, which he had hurt against Penn, Arnie Tucker added a turned ankle a few days before the game. Blanchard, whose normal playing weight for us was 207, had been drained down to 198. In the picture section, there is a shot in Philadelphia's Municipal Stadium the afternoon before the game, which shows how Doc's sunken cheeks made him look thinner than Davis, Tucker, and myself. We took no workout that day. The players just walked up and down the field a couple of times in their Cadet-gray overcoats. It was obvious to writers on hand, and even a Navy official remarked, that we looked washed out, peaked, strained. Well, we were.

It would be just hell, I thought, to have this gang come this far with the effort they've made and then have the three-year record spoiled in the last game—and by the Navy. We sure would never hear the end of that.

Get them down fast. Keep them there. That was our plan, as in 1945. We started well. Tucker passed to Davis for 30 yards. Then Glenn took a pitchout from Arnold and snaked his way 14 yards to a score. Jack Ray kicked the extra point. That first conversion was to prove vital, though nobody suspected it at the time. Navy reacted strongly. Sparked by an unsung quarterback, Reaves Baysinger, the Midshipmen marched 81 yards for a touchdown, but missed the point.

Fortunately for us, we were able to play about as well in the second period as we had at any time all year. Blanchard and Davis were in fine form. They alternated in moving the ball from our 19 to our 48. From there, Doc shot over the middle, veered by a linebacker to the outside and outraced all pursuers down the sidelines. On that run, Doc looked more like the Blanchard of '44 and '45 than he had at any time all fall.

Presently, Bill Yeoman intercepted a pass on their 38, and we went on to score on a 26-yard-pass play from Davis to Blanchard. This was a deep pass breaking out of a buttonhook fake. Doc executed the fake about 10 yards downfield. After luring the defender out of position, he whirled suddenly, broke downfield again and took the lead throw from Glenn, who had bluffed the shorter throw. This was the last scoring effort of Blanchard and Davis for Army, but nobody anticipated that at the time. To the stands, it looked as if we could call our shots.

On the bench, however, we were not feeling secure. An early block had aggravated Tucker's knee injury and we had to take him out while we were on defense. To keep the leg from stiffening on him, he had to keep walking up and down the sideline. He was in much pain.

Arnold's condition certainly contributed to our misadventures in the second half. We not only missed him defensively, but his leg prevented him from dropping back to pass. He had all he could do to get the ball away on hand-offs.

That was our side of it, but far from the whole story. Navy caught fire and threatened for a long time to run us out of the stadium and to run off with the game. They ran and blocked like furies and mixed in good passes. They went 79 yards for a second touchdown and 30 yards for a third. They were trailing only 21-18, when they took the ball on their 33-yard line with seven-and-a-half minutes to play.

The crowd of 100,000 had gone hysterical. They had come to sit in on a final Blanchard-Davis walkover. Now they were seeing what threatened to become the most dramatic upset of all the gridiron eras. The day was unseasonably warm and humid. For us now, on the Army bench, it began to turn gray and cold. Navy had been marching without letup. I sensed they would march some more, and I did not know what, if anything, we could do about it. They had wrested the momentum of the game away from us. We were fighting for our lives. Yet, our team, scorched by many fires that year, was concentrating on the job with all the poise the situation demanded. But they were stealing frequent looks at the clock.

It would be just like the Navy, I thought, to spoil everything, to make us swallow a bitter, almost poisonous ending. Then, much of all this courageous Army team had done would be forgotten.

And now they were down on our 24. And now Lynn Chewning, their big fullback, came charging around our left side for 23 yards. They were down on our 3, and there was a minute and a half left to play.

There was nothing I could do. On top of all else, I had lost phone connection with my press-box spotters, Andy Gustafson and Herman Hickman. I thought something was wrong mechanically. It was not until sometime later, that I learned from Gerry Counts, who was sitting near Gus and Herman, just what happened. There was nothing wrong with the phones. Gus and Herman were ignoring the plaintive ringing. Their emotional state had overcome them. Gus just sat there, staring blankly off into space, afraid to look down on the field, or maybe afraid to miss the space ship he was praying would come and take him away from the awful scene. Herman wasn't looking at the field, either. He had his head down on folded arms and he was softly moaning, "O God, don't let it happen! O God, please don't let it happen!"

It was here "the brave old Army team," the Vindicators of 1946, stood fast like the Federals of Gen. George Thomas at Chickamauga. Chewning drove at our right side, but Hank Foldberg and Goble Bryant met him head on. Chewning tried the other side. This time Barney Poole hurled him back. Navy was penalized 5 yards for taking a fifth time out for the half, which set them back to the 8. That was a break. But there was still time for one more play. It was third and goal to go.

Fringes of the half-crazed crowd, unable to restrain themselves, had come down out of the stands and pressed against the sidelines at the southwest corner of the field, to see at close hand the climax of the almost unbearable denouement.

Bill Hawkins, a stalwart for the Midshipmen all day, offense and defense both, took the snap from center, faked a buck into the line, and flipped a lateral out to halfback Pete Williams. Williams drove 4 yards around our left end, but he was still 4 yards from home when Barney Poole dragged him down. Barney never made a better tackle than that one, or one that meant as much.

There were seven seconds to play when Tom Hamilton sent in a substitute to stop

Left: Arnie Tucker, quarterback for the "touchdown twins," Blanchard and Davis. Right: Army's 1946 national championship lineup. (Back row, l. to r.) Doc Blanchard, Arnold Tucker, Rip Rowan,

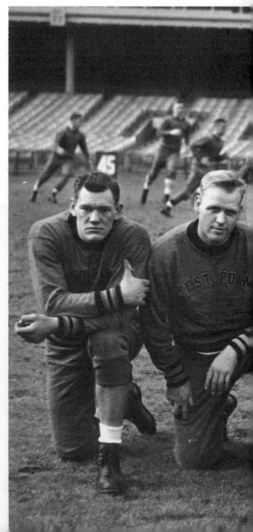

the clock. But before the officials saw the substitute, the clock ran out, and there was considerable argument at the time. Even had the officials seen the sub earlier, the clock would have been stopped only long enough to accept the substitution. It is doubtful there would have been time enough for Navy to run another play.

In the confusion and excitement of the last few seconds, in the traditional American eagerness to salute a gallant underdog which had come so close to achieving a tremendous upset, it was some time before there was full appreciation of what we had done. We had stopped them with the game on the line, after they had been marching unceasingly. We had stopped them twice on our 3-yard line and once on our 4. And that was the season-long story of that Army team of 1946; when the Cadets needed it most, they had it.

Willard Mullin did a typically humorous cartoon on the game. It shows atop the monument, a bronze foot symbolizing the three points' difference in our 21-18 victory, the three extra points kicked by Jack Ray. Inscribed on the base of the monument: "To commemorate West Point's great football teams. Unbeaten . . . 1944 . . . 1945 . . . 1946." Walking along, looking up at the bronze foot, are two Cadets. One says, "Weren't there a couple of other men on that team back there in 1946?"

"Yeah," replies the other Cadet. "Couple o' guys named Doc Davison and Glenn Blanchard, or something or other."

Glenn Davis. (Front row, l. to r.) Hank Foldberg, Goble Bryant, Art Gerometta, Jim Enos, Joe Steffy, Shelton Biles, Barney Poole.

Leon Bramlett was captain of the Navy team for the 1946 game. It ended up Army 21, Navy 18, but the Middies were beaten "not by the Cadets but by time." Here is the story of that thrilling game as the Navy captain tells it in his own words.

A Magnificent Defeat

LEON C. BRAMLETT

"I WISH TO STATE CLEARLY AND SINCERELY AT THIS TIME THAT THIS FOOTball team may have lost a number of football games, but they have never conceded defeat to any team; and furthermore, I believe that this Navy team can beat Army on the gridiron and we intend to do so."

Twenty years ago Navy's football coach, Capt. Tom Hamilton, spoke these words to the Brigade of Midshipmen on the eve of the 1946 Army-Navy game, which has long been remembered as the game when the clock ran out on an underdog Navy football team that had scoffed at the odds, ignored the sympathy and pity of the experts, thrown caution to the winds, and instead had staged a battle that would long be remembered by the Army, and the 102,000 spectators that witnessed it.

It was my privilege to serve as the team captain of this Navy squad and since that memorable day it has always been a source of pride to me that I was one of them. Over a span of twenty years, memory sometimes fails but with the indulgence of the reader, I will attempt to recall the incidents that preceded this traditional meeting, that was referred to by the immortal Grantland Rice as the game in which "a great Army team passed into history by beating an even greater Navy team by a score of 21 to 18."

It must be remembered that Navy had lost seven consecutive games and was faced with the hopeless task of meeting an Army team that was acclaimed as the greatest in football history—the Army with a Blanchard-Davis-Tucker combination had been undefeated in twenty-seven games over a period of three years, with only a scoreless tie with Notre Dame to mar an otherwise perfect record and by all reasonable standards of comparison Navy did not belong on the same field with them.

The details of the game itself have been discussed pro and con for many years by football enthusiasts the nation over. Nearly everyone remembers how Navy's bid for victory was snuffed out by lack of time on the 4-yard line after they had bounced back from a 21-to-6 deficit at half time and stormed the Army defenses with two touchdowns only to be beaten 21-18—a margin of three extra points. All of this is football history and, of course, Army won the game fairly and completely and kept intact a tre-

Leon Bramlett was captain for the Navy team that was up against the powerful Cadets in 1946.

Below: The Navy starting lineup for the 1946 battle that came within three points of one of the greatest upsets in Army-Navy history. (Front row, l. to r.) Leon Bramlett, Dick Shimshak, Jim Carrington, Dick Scott, Scott Emerson, Newbold Smith, Art Warket. (Back row, l. to r.) Robert Schwoeffermann, Reaves Baysinger, Myron Gerber, Ralph Peter Williams.

mendous win record. The outstanding recollection of this event to my mind was the magnitude of the job that Tom Hamilton did in getting us ready. After defeats on seven consecutive Saturday afternoons, his confidence in us never wavered and he flatly predicted to the sports world that we would win. As one sports writer so eloquently expressed it—"What he did will stand in history as a beacon to inspire every team weary of getting shoved around, and you can reduce that to individuals. The abandonment of hope never had a place in Hamilton's lexicon. He put to action what the cynics had regarded as worn-out platitudes about team spirit and good ole Navy fight. Here was a guy, you thought, who earnestly believed that if the Japs had had the atom bomb three years ago, it wouldn't have made any difference; America would still win the war on good ole Navy fight and spirit."

He bore down hard on us the entire week before the game on what we could achieve against the Army team if our determination was high enough. The day before the game he told us "we had it" and we believed him. The night before the game as the team gathered for the evening meal, he told us he would not trade us for any football team

in the country and we believed that, too, and we appreciated it. The entire squad to a man, loved and respected Tom Hamilton deeply and the attitude that prevailed was reminiscent of the old Notre Dame story of "winning one for the Gipper."

As we emerged from the tunnel onto the field the next day we were temporarily awed by the magnificence of the crowd and the splendor of the occasion. Tom said "Boys, this is a beautiful sight and one you will always remember. Now, take a long, hard look at 'em and forget 'em. Let's get down to the job at hand." During the first half we realized we could move the ball on Army. Even though we were behind 21 to 6 we had made 9 first downs to Army's 6 and we had scored on them, which Notre Dame had not been able to accomplish. The attitude that prevailed in the dressing room at half time was one of fiery enthusiasm. The fact that we were trailing by two touchdowns and three extra points seemed to be of little concern.

Adm. Aubrey Fitch who was Superintendent of the Naval Academy at the time, came into the dressing room and told us that President Truman sent his regards and congratulations on our spirited play. Tom Hamilton said, "Admiral, you go back and tell the President that 'he ain't seen nothing yet.' We're just getting ready to bust this game wide open." With that, Admiral Fitch grinned and said, "Tom, nothing would give me greater pleasure."

We quickly gained the necessary momentum to dominate the play in the second half by running up eleven first downs to Army's two, and two touchdowns to Army's none. In the final minutes we started a drive on our 20-yard line that carried 76 yards to the 4, only to fade as Army's fine line dug in and held until the time ran out.

There was considerable speculation after the game as to what would have happened had Navy been allowed one more play; or if the spectators had not crowded inside the sideline stripe preventing Navy's backs from running into the corner of the end zone. But all of this seems insignificant now. Army's greatness came to the front and their tremendous goal-line effort stopped us.

Being a part of Navy's valiant effort was a rewarding experience for all of us and therein lies the deep import of this particular game. The circumstances that were prevalent in this game and the final outcome serve to remind us that the American game of football is the finest sport of them all and that its lessons have a particular point in these times. These lessons are such things as sacrificing for an ideal, belief in one's self and confidence in one's ability, the physical and spiritual power to dig in and fight hardest when things look blackest, to play a hard game the fair way, to accept victory modestly and defeat gallantly, remembering always that the other fellow is trying to win, too, and that without co-operation and team work, the individual is help-less and doomed to fail. Football is built in large part upon these attributes and many more that no man can measure but that all can and should salute.

Much was said and written about the outcome but the one that was most appealing to me was expressed this way. "A legend was born in Philadelphia's Municipal Stadium on Saturday and unlike a lot of other legends, more than 102,000 witnesses were in on it. The Army-Navy game was one to remember. Of all the thrilling moments of sports, those dying seconds when the Middies stood around futilely and allowed them-selves to be whipped, not by the Cadets but by time, will never be forgotten."

History repeating itself all over again?

1926 — Army 21, Navy 21
1948 — Army 21, Navy 21

Here is The Washington Post's *fine sportswriter, Shirley Povich, and his outstanding story of the brilliant, bruising battle of 1948.*

Fighting Middies Come from Behind to Tie Army, 21-21

SHIRLEY POVICH

A SLIGHT, FOUR-EYED MAN STOOD TEETERING ON TIPTOE DOWN NEAR THE 40-yard line in Municipal Stadium, his pearl-gray hat bobbing like a floating cork as he craned and twisted and strained to see over the wall of blue Navy overcoats and white Navy caps whose owners towered in front of America's Commander in Chief.

Harry Truman, of Independence, Missouri, a former haberdasher and prominent fancier of hopeless causes, was struggling to focus his lenses on the hopeless Navy football team, a team that had lost thirteen successive games and now, with fifty-eight seconds of its season remaining, stood tied with undefeated Army, champion of the East, third-ranking power of the nation, and twenty-one-point favorite in the trustworthy Minneapolis line.

Fifty Secret Service men fidgeted, watching protocol go down the drain. For safety's sake, it has been their custom to get the President clear of the crowd two minutes before an Army-Navy game ends. Hot or cold, out he goes with two minutes to play.

But Harry Truman wouldn't budge. Like the 102,580 others present at the forty-ninth meeting of service academies, he simply had to see Navy fire the last shot in its locker.

Pete Williams took a pitchout and lost 3 yards. Bill Hawkins went twisting and wrestling through the line, gaining five. The clock showed thirty-three seconds left. Slats Baysinger, the quarterback, tried to sneak around end. He lost six. Navy huddled once more, rushed up to the line for one more play, but the referee stepped in, waving his arms.

The red hand of the clock stood at zero, and the best, most exhilarating and least plausible Army-Navy game in at least twenty years was over. The score, 21 to 21, was

Arnold Galiffa scored a touchdown for Army in the 1948 game, but the Middies were a match for the Cadets and the score was 21-21.

the same as that of 1926, the year historians always mention first when they try to name the finest of all Army-Navy games.

And even if you'd seen it, it was fearfully hard to believe. While the referee tossed a coin to decide on permanent possession of the ball, Baysinger walked around the periphery of huddled players, shook hands with Army's Tom Bullock and then with Arnold Galiffa. Army's guys walked off hurriedly, but Navy's froze to attention while the Midshipmen's band played, "Navy Blue and Gold."

Then all the players, save two, departed, as civilians and noncombatant Midshipmen and Cadets swarmed over the field. Dave Bannerman, Navy's substitute fullback, and Ted Carson, left end, just stayed there where the deed had been done. When small boys came asking for autographs, they signed abstractedly and kept rubbering around through the crowd. Maybe they were looking for a couple of peach cakes to share an evening's liberty. But it seemed more likely they were waiting in the hope that someone would give them one more crack at Army.

The great, sunswept crowd that paid six dollars a head hadn't expected anything like this. The customers had come to the show, the spectacle, the pageant of youth that always is about as thrilling as anything in American sports. They had thought to get their money's worth out of just being there; out of seeing the magnificent parade these kids always bring off superbly before the game; out of the shiver that scampers along the spine when the colors are brought to midfield and the band plays the national anthem and the packed stands are a frozen block of color, with the bright blue-gray of the Army on one side and the shimmering white of Navy caps on the other.

They figured to get a chuckle out of the kids' musty nonsense. And of course they did. There was a Navy dreadnought that rolled around the cinder track and shot off cannon and went down in flames. There was a huge papier-mâché goat and a huge papier-mâché mule. There were signs in the Navy stands: "Gallup Picks Army" (to which the Army stand replied with a cheer: "Gallup, Gallup, Gallup!") and a sly reference to the difference between Army and Navy schedules: "When do you play Vassar?" (Vassar, Vassar, Vassar!") and then after the Navy scored first: "Send in Alan Ladd" (no response to this).

But nobody expected a ball game, except the few people who bore in mind an old, old truth which the game restated dramatically. That is, that there never can be between undergraduate football teams of the same league a gap in ability too great to be bridged by spirit alone. Navy proved that beyond remotest doubt, and the guy who did most to prove it was a fellow playing on spirit and very little else. Bill Hawkins, ill a long while this season with a blood disorder that doctors called acute infectious mononucleosis, was entirely out of action for three weeks in midseason. Without preparation, he came back to play against Michigan on November 6. Then he played three minutes against Columbia and was hurt November 13. Since then he hadn't a minute of physical contact until today.

But today he was a bull, and mad bull into the bargain. He ran the ball fourteen times and made fifty important yards. He scored two touchdowns. He backed up the line, his blocking was like a crime of passion, and he played almost all afternoon.

It wasn't exactly a football game, it was an exhibition of pure, unbridled fury on both sides, for both sides persistently moved the ball against incredibly savage resistance. It was, altogether, as good a thing as could possibly happen to football.

Thirty-two Navy players got into the game, which means—if there is such a thing as justice—that the Navy added thirty-two full admirals today. For the guys down there on the field today were officer material, as ever was. It goes without saying that there are more than thirty-two full admirals in Philadelphia tonight.

Navy meets an Army team — which has played 28 games without a single defeat and only two ties, which has won 17 games in a row, which is favored to beat Annapolis by three touchdowns—and emerges victorious. Sportswriter Jessie Abramson gives us the story of the stunning 1950 upset.

No Upset?

JESSE ABRAMSON

NAVY DEFEATED ARMY, 14 TO 2, IN THEIR FIFTY-FIRST FOOTBALL GAME before President Truman and a capacity crowd of 100,000 who were shocked and dazed into disbelief or delirium by incredible events in Municipal Stadium today.

The unfathomable stalwarts from Annapolis marched 33 and 63 yards in the late second period to their touchdowns, scored by 209-pound Bobby Zastrow, quarterback from Algoma, Wisconsin, on a 7-yard sneak and his 30-yard pass to End Jim Baldinger.

They gave Army its only points in the middle of the third period on a safety when Zastrow, fading back to pass from his 13, was rushed all the way into the end zone and dumped there by End Bill Rowekamp and Guard Bob Velonnino. Roger Drew, Navy's place-kicking specialist, contributed both conversions.

Miracles such as this one are a dime a dozen in football history. It is frustrating to have to call it another miracle of football. A Navy team which had lost six of its eight games in one of its most disastrous seasons, had been beaten as badly as 22 to 0 by Northwestern and 27 to 0 by Tulane only a month ago, somehow managed to come up with a fantastic performance that no one believed possible.

But this one, of course, was against Army, which meant that Navy was starting a brand-new season from scratch. Forget the past. Against an Army team believed to be the finest team in the land, an all-conquering Army team which had won eight straight this year without being extended to its utmost; an Army team which had traveled twenty-eight games without defeat (two of them ties) and had won their last seventeen in a row; an Army team, favored by touchdowns, to conclude its second straight perfect season and its sixth unbeaten season in seven years. An Army team which had assailed its opposition for an average of 400 yards a game and whose wonderful defense had strangled the enemy all year and had permitted only twenty-six points.

How, then, could such an Army team, bursting with health, boasting advantages in every department of play, deeper in man power, lose to such a badly beaten Navy foe?

The answer, of course, is simple. Football is, as Red Blaik has said for everyone, a game of transcendent spirit played by American youth who will not concede anything in competition, no matter what the odds may be. Two teams of equal size and muscle met in a game and the team with the greatest emotional urge and drive came through with a victory it wanted more than anything on earth this day.

As President Truman, his guests, members of his Cabinet, generals and admirals by the bushelful, and the eyewitnesses of this thrilling game slowly started out of the Stadium in the semidarkness of a gray misty day, as the hysterical brigade of blue-coated Midshipmen swarmed onto the field of battle, as the winning players hoisted their new coach, Eddie Erdelatz, to their shoulders, a wild-eyed fan, obviously a Navy rooter, faced the press box and shouted: "Don't you dare call this an upset; Navy finally played the game it was capable of playing."

That was it, in a nutshell. Thank you, Navy fan. Navy hit and ran and drove with controlled fury that was overwhelming, churning the turf for two, three, four yards even after Army's fine defense had, to all purposes, stopped a play. Navy defended with eleven tacklers who swarmed over, ganged, and smothered Army swift runners, including even—and especially—the fullback, Al Pollard, who was rated the most unstoppable fullback in the country.

Navy's secondary covered Army pass receivers like leeches, so that even Captain Dan Foldberg, one of Army's greatest offensive ends in history, was restricted to two catches and was never for a moment unguarded.

The pattern of this game was established early, never varied, insofar as Navy's crushing superiority was concerned.

Zastrow, a quarterback who had been so often the goat in Navy defeat, played the sort of game a boy plays in his dreams. He directed Navy's T-formation attack, with its brand-new spread features, with boldness and with superb skill, deftly handling the ball to his backs, Dave Bannerman, Frankie Hauff, and Bill Powers, who rammed for short and consistent gains inside and outside Army's tackles and for short and consistent gains inside tackles and through the middle Zastrow ran for important yardage. Zastrow passed deftly.

In a duel of bruising, violent line impact, Navy in that decisive first half gained eight first downs to Army's one, and outpassed Army as well. Navy made its margin of superiority pay off for two touchdowns, Army could not mount an attack, rarely was across midfield, and could not break Navy down even when it recovered a fumble and had a first down on Navy's 22 in the early minutes. The Cadets had to give up the ball on the 15, and did not get inside the enemy 30 the rest of the half.

Between the halves everyone marveled at Navy's remarkable play that was almost foolproof and fumble-free, wondered whether Navy could maintain its burning flame against an aroused Army foe. Army did rouse itself in the second half, Navy made a few errors, including the third-down pass try that led to a safety. Those two points might have been decisive if Army could score two touchdowns. But Army, getting opportunities, attacking remorselessly, in the fourth period, could not shatter Navy's valorous defense. Navy never lost its poise, or its control.

Navy, which scored its first victory in the series since 1943, was backed up against its goal through all of the last period in defense of a 14-to-2 lead, with Army at the

20 or inside it three times, and passing with desperation. In these pinches, Navy was unbreakable, stopping the Cadets with an interception by John Gurski on the 17, another interception by Bill Powers on the 8, stopping Army again on the 15. The Cadets, under exquisite pressure against the clock, fumbled twice and lost the ball in the waning minutes, on the 28 and on the 5, then ran into a final interception on the final play after blocking a punt and reaching the 3.

So Army was balked to the bitter end, unable to score a touchdown for the first time since it went scoreless with Illinois early in 1947.

The final figures indicated, too, how richly Navy earned this triumph. It outgained Army, 13 to 5, in first downs, 200 to 77 yards in rushing, with Bannerman and double-duty Hauff leading the way with 67 and 61 yards each.

Zastrow completed five of ten passes for 68 yards, all in the first half, while Bobby Blaik was held to five completions in 22 for a mere 54 yards, and the other Army passers hit for only one in three. Pollard was held to 52 yards in twenty-one tries, was often smeared at the scrimmage line by Dritz Davis, a demon left tackle of six feet, four and 210 pounds, or Bob McDonald, his end neighbor. No other Army runner could dent Navy's ferocious line; the Cadets could not with all their vaunted speed, get around the ends. Army attacked virtually all the way on the first count, but Navy, with shifting lines in four- to eight-man alignments, was always ready for the Cadets. Army rarely changed direction on its plays, pounded Navy's left endlessly and fruitlessly.

Navy, for its part, came out with new stuff. Erdelatz installed a split end a halfback or fullback flanker. Often the split end and flanker were on the same side; sometimes spread on either side. They got good blocking angles. Navy had deception and change-of-direction plays, and pulled a fancy wide reverse, a naked reverse by Powers which went for 22 yards, the biggest run of the day that set up Navy's second score in the last minute before the half.

Though Francis Brady fumbled and recovered the opening kickoff, Navy wasn't a

Navy quarterback Bob Zastrow led his team to a 14-2 upset win over a favored Army eleven in 1950. Zastrow (16) bursts through a hole in Army's line to score one of his two touchdowns. Tom Bakke (86), Dave Bannerman (34), and Art Sundry (48) do the blocking.

John Trent, Army's 1949 football captain, congratulates newly elected 1950 captain, Dan Foldberg (right).

fumbling team today as it had been all year. Navy immediately began to move through Army. But on a fourth down at the Navy 35, Bob Cameron couldn't get his punt away, run instead and was knocked down. He fumbled. Army had the ball at the 22, but gave it up on the 15.

The decisive second quarter opened innocently enough with Navy halted at midfield and punting. The next time Navy moved up 26 yards with two first downs, before Hal Lochlein, of Army, intercepted on his 33 and came back to the 43. On the first down, Pollard, who came into the game for Gil Stephenson in the second period, fumbled a pitchout and McDonald recovered on the Army 27. An offside penalty set Navy back to the 33 (the referee was stepping off six 6 yards for 5 at this time), and Navy went for the score in four plays.

Zastrow, after a double fake into the line hit Art Sundry on an 18-yard pass on right sideline. Sundry made 2 yards. With the split end and halfback flanker to the right, Zastrow reached Hauff on the left with a 6-yard pass, Hauff sitting down on the catch.

On the next lineup, Zastrow burst through guard on a quarterback sneak, was stopped twice, but tore loose into the end zone. Drew kicked the point, and the Navy side, where the President sat (Navy was host), went crazy with excitement.

Army reacted vigorously to this challenge. Blaik hit Foldberg with a 26-yard pass to the 36, but Army kicked out on two more yards and, conservatively, punted. Blaik kicked out on the 4. This should have set up an Army chance. But Army, getting the return punt on Navys' 39, couldn't go anywhere. Army got reckless. It tried a fourth-down pass on the 37 and lost the ball.

Navy, on fire, took it and went 63 yards in five plays against the clock to its second touchdown. Zastrow started with an 11-yard burst on a sneak, threw an incomplete pass, then Powers, on the naked reverse, got loose around Army's left for 22 yards to the 30. Another incomplete Zastrow pass, then Zastrow faded to his left and threw to Baldinger in the end zone.

Coach Eddie Erdelatz talks strategy for the Army game with his two stars, quarterback George Welsh and end Ronnie Beagle.

1954 was Navy's year of triumph as the Middies ran over Army, 27-20. Here, quarterback George Welsh gets off a pass as Army's Arthur Johnson (83) rushes him.

Navy squad members, having completed final practice for the Army game, hurl Coach Eddie Erdelatz into the Severn River. It's all part of Naval Academy custom.

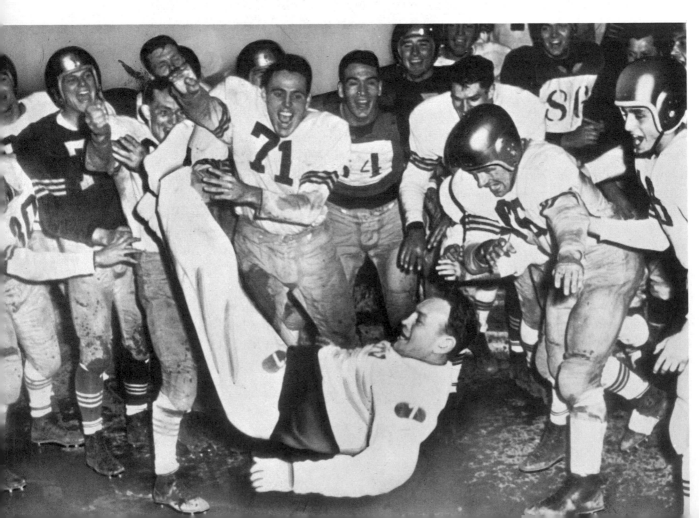

*Coach Eddie Erdelatz nicknamed his 1954 Navy team a "Team Named Desire."
They, in turn, praised Erdelatz as Navy's "greatest coach." The result—one of the
most thrilling wins over Army in a game that saw each team lead the other until
Navy, with its great quarterback, George Welsh, came from behind to defeat Army,
27-20. That year Navy voted to accept an offer to play Mississippi in the Sugar
Bowl. Once again the Middies romped home in front, defeating the "Ole Miss"
team, 21-0. Navy won the Lambert Trophy in 1954 as the "Best Team in the East,"
and after the victory in the Sugar Bowl was voted by many sportswriters as the "Best
Team in the Nation."*

Navy Heads for the Sugar Bowl

JOHN DELL

NAVY WON A TRIP TO THE SUGAR BOWL THIS COMING NEW YEAR'S DAY BY
beating a strong Army team in a game that was a thriller from start to
finish.

After the game, the Midshipmen voted to play the U of Mississippi at New Orleans,
when asked to express their desires by Secretary of the Navy Charles S. Thomas.

After congratulating the boys on gaining the greatest distinction any Navy team
can earn—i.e., beating Army—the Secretary asked them if they would like to play in
a postseason bowl game. They all shouted "Aye."

After the Secretary passed out voting slips, newsmen were barred from the dressing
room. When the doors were finally opened newsmen found Secretary Thomas, Coach
Eddie Erdelatz, Navy Superintendent Adm. Walter F. Boone, and Adm. William
F. "Bull" Halsey in the middle of a joyous group of Navy players. The players were
singing and Admiral Halsey was pounding the back of Phil Monahan who couldn't
play because of knee injuries that limited his action to about thirty minutes all season.

Naturally the Bowl game occupied much of the talk in the dressing room. But talk
now veered back to the thrilling win of the Middies as they simply would not be
beaten by Army.

All agreed that the turning point of the game was the short onside kickoff, late in
the second period. Army led 20-14 with less than a minute to play in the half.

The Cadets had scored at 12:05 in the period with comparative ease on a long forward pass, Quarterback Pete Vann to Bob Kyasky, to take the lead away from the
Middies.

Then came the onside kick. Navy regained possession of the ball on it's 47-yard line,
and in six plays—with but 47 seconds to go, scored to jump into a lead.

Navy's Joe Gattuso (with ball) makes a short gain in the third period of the 1954 game.

Col. Red Blaik commenting on the defeat, said, "To lose and to win is part of the game, and we lost. It was a fine Navy football team that beat us today. One of the finest I've ever seen and they deserve all the credit. Our boys played fine football, but a couple of mistakes—and that's that. But those Middies, I believe, were awfully smart." Blaik unhesitatingly named the Navy team as "the best that West Point had faced all year."

"I like the play of Navy's George Welsh. He was the outstanding Navy player on the field, and he's awfully quick." Blaik also singled out Navy tackles John Hopkins, Brooklyn, New York, and James Royer as "The men who stopped our drives all day."

Navy's Eddie Erdelatz commented, "Army is a great team, but ours is just a wee bit better. Our Quarterback George Welsh called a great game. I thought every player on the line was outstanding. Now I guess everyone will agree that our end, Ron Beagle, is a real All-American. He played a smashing game all afternoon."

Stressing the fact that he didn't want to single out any individual, in view of the Middies' great team effort, Coach Erdelatz admitted under questioning that Joe Gattuso's brilliant recovery of his own fumble and quick side-footed kick late in the fourth quarter was one of the key plays of the entire game.

While Erdelatz was wearing a permanent smile, he was asked if he intended to join former Navy Coach Tom Hamilton's staff at the University of Pittsburgh, which is looking for a new head coach. Erdelatz has been mentioned as a most likely candidate.

"There's no truth to it," he said, "I have another year to go on this contract at Navy and I'm very happy. Particularly with this, one of the greatest Navy teams I've ever coached."

Colonel Blaik called Pat N. Uebel, six-foot-one, 197-pound back from Bellevue, Kentucky, who led the Cadet ball-toters with 133 yards in twenty-seven tries as the Army's outstanding player, and he also spoke highly of Don Holleder of Webster, New York, an end.

Joe Bellino goes into action and wraps up a great win for Navy. Arthur Daley of The New York Times gives us an exciting account of the tremendous exploits of the great Navy back in the 1959 Army-Navy classic.

Nautical But Nice

ARTHUR DALEY

THE MIDSHIPMEN WHO HANDLED THE SIDE-SHOW GIMMICKS FOR THE Army-Navy game let themselves be carried away beforehand by a wave of optimism that seemed to border on the ridiculous. Their plans called for the release of a balloon whenever the future admirals scored a touchdown. And each balloon would waft with it into the atmosphere a West Point jacket.

If these nautical stage directors had listened to the experts, they would have made ready one or two jackets at most. But they let themselves be swept into the emotional tide of the "Beat Army" fervor that saturated Annapolis last week and rashly brought with them five coats of Cadet gray, a widely extravagant estimate.

Thereupon Navy scored six touchdowns in its rout of the Black Knights. What had appeared to be sheer presumption was nothing of the sort. So the last balloon arose without a cargo. By that time few noticed and none cared. The Middies had given the Kaydets a record trouncing, 43 to 12, as stunning a result as this old series had produced.

Once upon a time football was strictly a team game, with responsibility shared by each of eleven men. But the T formation had so distorted values that the quarterback now is two or three or ten times as important as anyone else. When the quarterback has a bad day, it invariably means trouble.

It isn't pleasant to point the finger at one young man and pin the blame on him, especially when he's an amateur who plays on one of the most amateur college teams in the land. But there is no way to avoid facts.

Joe Caldwell of Army is certain to get considerable mention for All-America honors this season and deservedly so. He has been one of the finest collegiate forward passers in the land. He went into his final game with a record of ninety-nine completions in 165 attempts for 1,228 yards and an efficiency mark of 60 per cent.

But he started in stumbling fashion against Navy and never regained his equilibrium until the last couple of minutes, when he completed four aerials for 69 yards. Toss that out of consideration. It was too little and too late. The true statistics and the ones that had direct bearing on the result were the ones that were compiled earlier.

All-American halfback Joe Bellino (27) drives through Army's line on his way to a Navy touchdown in the 1960 game. Navy won it, 17-12.

Here's the horror story in chronological detail: Six incompletions, a touchdown pass for 29 yards, five incompletions, a touchdown pass for 29 yards, five incompletions, an interception, an accidental completion for 18 yards after a Navy defender deflected the ball, an incompletion and an interception. This strains credulity.

Caldwell just had one of those incomprehensible days that will befall every football player. Cruel fate ordained that it would come against Navy. But Lady Luck buffeted Army all afternoon, especially Caldwell. He is a competent punter. On Saturday he uncorked one kick that skidded off his foot for 11 yards. He'd boot the ball and the playful pigskin would refuse to roll, but would stop dead or bounce backward. It was a day of almost total frustration.

Navy was no help to Army in its time of dire need. The Middies clamped on the pressure early and never relaxed it. Their line hounded Caldwell as he had not been hounded all season. The fleet backfield defenders convoyed the receivers so tightly that the Cadet passer had difficulty in finding targets. When he found them, his hurried throws invariably overshot their marks.

Not only were the sailors rock-ribbed on defense, but they also were afire in every direction. On the offense they tore and slashed almost at will. Joe Tranchini was the quarterback Caldwell was supposed to be but wasn't.

He was a sharpshooting passer and as mystifying as he was adroit as a ball-handler. For much of the game he didn't have a fullback but had three halfbacks behind the line with him. He exploited them shrewdly, especially Joe Bellino and Ronnie Brandquist.

When the Kaydets keyed two backers-up to halt Bellino, the alert Tranchini sprang Brandquist for big gains. Then he'd whipsaw Army, using one as a decoy, popping through the other. He faked beautifully on the ride series and Army would converge on a half back who didn't have the ball. Tranchini would be back to pass against confused defenses. Once he bootlegged for a touchdown.

It was a stunning exhibition of one team getting stronger as it progressed and the other crumbling before an inexorable pounding. The corps of Cadets watched with growing dismay and disbelief.

Wayne Hardin, the Navy coach, thus engineered one of the great upsets of the series. If he coaches at Annapolis for the next hundred years he's unlikely to have another as unlikely.

It was Roger Staubach and Pat Donnelly for Navy in the 1963 game. That was all that was necessary for an exciting 21-15 victory. Donnelly, a driving, crashing fullback, is shown as he scored the first of his three touchdowns to make it five in a row over Army.

"For want of a time-out a football game was lost . . ." That's how Ray Kelly of the Philadelphia Evening Bulletin *begins his dramatic story of Navy's 21-15 win over Army in 1963, a game which sent the huge crowd of fans into a state of frenzied tension, and left them limp when the final blast of the whistle announced that it was all over.*

Navy Conquers Army, 21-15, for Five in a Row

RAY KELLY

FOR THE WANT OF A TIME-OUT A FOOTBALL GAME WAS LOST BY THE ARMY yesterday.

On the way to what could have been a tying or winning touchdown the gallant Cadets, slow-pokey and confused, used up fifty-six seconds to get off one play and were two frustrating yards from glory when the gun ended their sixty-fourth annual service classic with Navy at Philadelphia Stadium.

Hence, with a trip to the Cotton Bowl hinging on the outcome, the Navy came off with a 21-15 victory as fullback Pat Donnelly scored three touchdowns to tie a record and Roger Staubach never stopped acting like the most exciting quarterback in the country.

It was Navy's fifth consecutive triumph in this end-of-season spectacular and it equaled a record set by the Midshipmen from 1939 through '43.

At the same time, Wayne Hardin extended his own victorious coaching streak over the Army to five in a row and his players hailed him as the "Coach of the Year."

The team captain, Tom Lynch, said: "If he isn't, there is something funny."

The Middies also accepted, by acclamation, an invitation to play Texas' National champions at Dallas on New Year's Day.

There were the usual 102,000 spectators in the South Philadelphia playpen and most of them were standing and wondering what was taking Army so long while the clock was running out of ticks at the strange finish.

By then, the onlookers were ready for almost anything on this ideal autumn afternoon. The Army, which went into the game a 12-point underdog, was the first to score and held the tars even, 7-7, in the first half.

Then after Navy went ahead on two scoring bursts by the talented Donnelly for a 21-7 lead, the Army regrouped. Paul Dietzel's soldiers, with masterful Carl Stichweh leading the fourth period charge, scored again, pulled off a two-point play and then unveiled the play of the day—an onside kick.

It worked, too. Stichweh himself pounced on the ball at the Middies' 49-yard line. There was a lot of time left—more than six minutes.

But it wasn't quite enough.

With Ken Waldrop and Ray Paske hammering away at off-tackle plays, the Cadets kept grinding out the yardage and twice they barely made the necessary yardage on fourth-down situations.

There was one point at the 23 when Dietzel sent in a replacement to use up Army's last time-out. Stichweh obliged the West Point cheering section with a pass in the flat to Don Parcells at the 7 for a first down with 1.38 to play.

It seemed ample. Hardin said it seemed like forever.

Now the audience was in a stand-up bedlam. Stichweh couldn't hear his own signals. He backed away and then resumed.

Parcells made two hard yards over left guard. The Navy was digging in and watching the clock, too. Only 1:22 to go.

Waldrop, who pounded off tackle like he invented the play, was hit all over while getting to the 4. There were 58 seconds left as he picked himself off the ground.

Army goes into a huddle. They come out and go into formation. But Stichweh backs away. Too much spectator noise. The referee, Barney Finn, stops the clock. And that's when Navy got a break.

The Army players didn't know the clock was started again as soon as order was restored. Hence, they went into another huddle which used up twelve more seconds.

Thus, only twenty-four seconds remained when Waldrop finally took a hand-off from Stichweh and went off tackle again—to the 2.

Now it was fourth and goal for the Cadets. Only they never came close to running off a play. Maybe those Middies took their time getting up from the ground, but there was a lot of blue-shirted soldiers running around trying to get in formation when the game ended.

The jubilant Middies jumped and danced in glee. The crestfallen Cadets trudged off the field. Some of them went into the clubhouse and cried—unashamedly.

Dietzel said: "Our boys couldn't hear the signals. There was too much racket and the clock ran out as we tried to get a little quiet."

Some of the Army players said they were not aware that the clock was restarted when they went back into that second—and useless—huddle.

Yet, as a local football official pointed out: "It took some guts for Ray Barbutti [field judge] to stop the clock in that kind of a situation—in an Army-Navy game."

Stichweh said he couldn't believe the game was over.

Recalling those last frantic seconds, he said: "We tried to yell out a play but our ends and tackles couldn't hear because of the noise. We tried to go to the referee, but either he didn't hear me or see me."

The slender 185-pounder from Williston Park, New York, at least had the satisfaction of stealing some of the individual thunder from the heralded Staubach and the brilliant Donnelly.

Dietzel praised Stichweh as "the outstanding player on the field, bar none."

While Stichweh was pounding out 103 yards for the Cadets, mostly on roll-outs and keeper plays, Staubach handled Navy's pro-type attack like an artist. Roger not only completed six of eleven passes but he caught one from Ed Orr besides picking up 20 running yards.

Donnelly's three touchdowns tied a Navy service game record set by Joe Bellino in 1959. He went over twice on short bursts and once from 20 yards out.

Fred Marlin, the surefoot from Woodbury, New Jersey, booted all three extra points for the winners.

Yet, while the backfielders attracted the most attention, this has to go down as one of the hardest-hitting games between the rivals. In fact, two 15-yard personal foul penalties against Army were wrapped up in the Navy's deciding third touchdown early in the fourth period. And on successive plays.

Moreover, the armchair strategists will have all winter to mull over a questionable decision by the Army before the Navy went on to post that six-pointer.

But that's the kind of a game it was.

Everybody knew it was going to be worth waiting an extra week (a seven-day postponement because of President Kennedy's assassination) after the preliminary skirmishes. The boys were hitting hard.

Lo and behold, Army wearing blue shirts and gold pants, displayed the best of intentions by scoring the first time it got hold of the ball. From their own 35, the Cadets, a possession outfit, strictly, kept pounding away. First Paske, then Waldrop, and then Stichweh..

The Cadets even fumbled a couple of times en route. But they also recovered and things looked good. Especially when Stichweh, on a third and nine countdown, went around his own left end 10 yards for the score. He carried Johnny Sai with him. Dick Heydt place-kicked the extra point.

"Now it'll be a ball game," the watchers decided.

The same watchers knew for sure shortly afterward. Navy took the ensuing kickoff and went all the way to the Army 3. It was first down and goal to go and here's what happened.

Sai made a yard off tackle. He lost two around end. Staubach went to the one-foot line on a keeper and then Roger was stopped for no gain off tackle. Army took the ball on downs.

The Cadets immediately added insult to injury. After two power plays gained 3 yards, Army got real tricky. After going into their regular T formation, the West Pointers started to shift for a punt. But as Kicker Ray Hawkins was moving into position, Stichweh took the snap from center and barreled off tackle for 8 yards and a first down.

"A well-executed play," Hardin admitted.

However, the Army eventually had to kick and it became a question of coping with Staubach, although the Cadets hurt themselves with a personal foul.

With the ball on the favorable side of midfield (in Army territory) Staubach took over. Twice he ran for big gains after being forced out of the pocket. And he also hit Sai for a 26-yard gain.

Finally, with the ball on the four, Donnelly went off tackle to score. Marlin kicked the point and the teams went into the dressing room with a 7-7 stalemate.

"That's when we changed around," said Hardin. "We went back to our basic stuff

Army's fine quarterback, Carl Stichweh (16), is virtually stopped in mid-air by Navy back, Pat Donnelly (38), after a 5-yard gain. Navy won, after a bruising battle.

Navy players congratulate one another on the field after beating Army in 1963.

after wasting a lot of time on special plays put in for the Army."

What he meant was—give the ball to Roger.

The third period was getting some age when the All-American and Heisman Trophy winner asserted himself. And he makes it electrifying merely by dropping back and taking it from there—on the hoof or with a throw.

He made it look easy, too. He connected on passes to Neil Henderson and Orr. There were a couple of runs up the middle after apparently being trapped and once, after being tackled, the quarterback threw a lateral to Donnelly.

"What can you do with a guy like that?" the soldiers seemed to be saying.

From the Army nine, Sai made four and Staubach took it to the one; Sai was stopped for no gain and again Army was making a stand. But Donnelly went off left tackle for the six-pointer. Marlin kicked straight and Navy was ahead, 14-7.

It stayed that way until the start of the final period and the budding generals made a wrong call that could have decided the game. It was like this:

With the ball on the Navy 17, Army sent Waldrop off tackle for a 7-yard gain. But Navy was off side on the play, so let's go down on the field:

Official: "You Army fellows can keep the ball where it is and have a second down and three to go—or you can take the penalty and have a first down and five to go. What'll it be?"

Army: "We decline the penalty."

Dietzel on the sideline:

This is what followed: Paske went up the middle for no gain. Paske went off right tackle for 2 yards and was inches short of a first down. Waldrop was thrown for a yard loss on fourth down and Navy took the ball at the eight.

Maybe the Cadets were burnt up. At any rate, Donnelly scooted for 13 yards and made four more. Somebody piled on him and it was a 15-yard penalty. Then one Army player hit a Navy player on the chops (out in the open, too) and it brought 15 more yards. This put the ball on Army's 28 and three plays later Donnelly went off tackle (he does that well), hightailed it for the sideline, and got away from Stichweh to score.

Now it was 21-7 and the Army sounded the famous cavalry charge.

Nothing fancy, mind you, simply power football. Slam-bang stuff. Stichweh and Waldrop took turns bruising the Navy line.

There was something awesome about it too—especially when Stichweh flipped the ball back to Waldrop and then led the interference off tackle. The leather was really crackling.

Stichweh ended a 52-yard drive by rounding his own right end for a touchdown after faking to Waldrop. Quarterback Carl stormed into the end zone for the two extra points.

Dietzel again reached into his bag of gridiron tricks. On the kickoff, Army lined up as usual, only Heydt was turned sideways near the ball as though he was going to give the "go" sign to his teammates. Only as Hawkins took his steps towards the ball, Heydt eased over and gave the ball a cross-field boot—and Stichweh grabbed the slick onside kick to give Army the ball on Navy's 49.

Six minutes and thirteen seconds remained in the game. It wasn't enough. . . .

Army sophomores Steve Lindell and Chuck Jarvis bring home a victory to Coach Tom Cahill in 1966. Fred Byrod of The Philadelphia Inquirer reports.

Army Stuns Favored Navy

FRED BYROD

BLOODIED IN BATTLE AND NEVER FOUND WANTING, SOPHOMORE BACKS STEVE Lindell and Chuck Jarvis spearheaded Army's football team to a 20-7 victory over favored Navy, Saturday, before 102,000 in John F. Kennedy Studium. Lindell, the first sophomore quarterback to start for Army in fourteen years against a Navy team, kept his coolness despite the vast crowd and a worrisome third quarter, then cracked a 7-7 deadlock with beautifully thrown scoring passes of 42 and 23 yards to Terry Young and Carl Woessner in the final period of a bitter struggle.

Jarvis, a nineteen-year-old fullback from Philadelphia's Father Judge High School, bolted 49 yards—the longest sprint of the day for Army's first touchdown and cracked out vital gains on plays preceding both of the Cadets' subsequent scores.

Each met the challenge in the game, which is the supreme goal for both teams, with their finest performances. Lindell ran the Army team with finesse and flourish—calling all the plays virtually himself—and connected on 12 of 17 passes.

Navy elected to kick off after winning the toss, and Army never relinquished the ball until they scored. The tally came after Jarvis took Lindell's shovel pass, tucked the ball under his arm, on Navy's 49-yard line—he got a tremendous block from Terry Young and went the rest of the way without a hand touching him. Lindell kicked the extra point that gave the Cadets a 7-0 lead.

Thus it stood until John Cartwright led Navy on its one sustained drive of the afternoon, 70 yards in eight plays, for the equalizing score early in the second quarter.

Through most of the third quarter Navy seemed to be churning up a storm, not so much by its own efforts as by taking advantage of the situation. Unable to advance the ball after receiving the kickoff, Army had to punt three times, and each time Ron Wasilewski's kick was shorter. Each time however, Navy's drive was shunted aside and stopped by a charging Army line that asked and gave no quarter.

Late in the quarter J. Church tried a field goal from the 37-yard line, but Cadet Captain Clarke drove through the Navy defense blocked the kick and teammate Bob Gora recovered for Army. Then Lindell pulled out his bag of tricks. With Navy expect-

Army's Chuck Jarvis (20) heads for a touchdown in the first period of the 1966 Army-Navy game, while Mark Hamilton blocks Navy's Rick Bayer and Don Downing out of action. Army won, 20-7.

A valued item in November, 1966.

ing a pass play, Lindell stuck to his ground game. In successive plays Jarvis blasted through for 5 yards—then Woessner went inside tackle for 9 and a first down and Army was on the move.

Then Lindell, with Navy shifting its defense to shore up its line, pulled another dandy. "Now we really had Navy jumpy. They were looking for us through the middle, so I promptly threw the ball to Terry Young." Young, the six-foot, three-inch junior end from Shillington, Pennsylvania, caught the ball while running at full tilt, and on his finger tips for the touchdown.

Army again scored five minutes later after forcing the Navy to punt. Seven plays later the Cadets were over for the third touchdown. The scoring pass went from Lindell to Woessner. Lindell's placement for the third extra point was blocked by Bernie DeGeorge. On paper Navy outgained Army in the air—215 yards to 164.

3
ARMY STARS

Charles Daly, class of 1905, Army's incomparable quarterback star and later head coach at West Point.

Jerry Nason, Boston sportswriter, believes that Charles Daly was one of the greatest quarterbacks in the history of football, and he tells us why. Well, Daly did beat Navy almost single-handed back in 1901, and that puts him right at the top for any Army man. This was written at the time of his death in 1959.

Army's Best Quarterback

JERRY NASON

ONE PRESIDENT (TEDDY ROOSEVELT) PUBLICLY APPLAUDED HIS PLAY ON THE football field.

He coached a second—a Cadet named Ike Eisenhower.

Three times he was Walter Camp's selection as All-America quarterback. Not even the great Walter Eckersall could match it.

He beat Army on the field as a Harvard opponent, later salvaged Army's causes as a partisan.

He belonged to the sports ages, and pages—but when Col. Charles D. Daly died, Thursday, in California, you discovered it in a remote typographical location.

This is not meant to be a personal genuflection to a bygone day. Charles Daly was a man grown, a career officer and a coach, before I was born.

But in my apprentice days around the old *Globe* sports office I got to know this amazing man, although I never met him . . . got to know him through Alec Gibson, and Walter Barnes, and Mel Webb.

One time, in greener years, we expressed a doubt in selecting a quarterback of cleverness, but unimpressive physical attributes, on the All-Scholastic football team.

And Alec Gibson replied, "Young man, let your conscience be your guide—but I will give you this:

"Charlie Daly of Harvard was one of the greatest college quarterbacks who ever lived. He weighed about 140 pounds!"

Off and on, in days to come, you learned more about this legendary Crimson immortal who came of the South End, prepped at Boston Latin, made All-America twice at Harvard, once at Army—and missed a four-year sweep because of a knee injury.

It rubbed off on you that here was an extraordinary player and individual who . . .

Called all the offensive shots for two (1898, 1899) undefeated Harvard teams . . .

Was a three-year key player over a stretch in which the Johns won 31 of 33 contests, tying the 32nd . . .

Was legendary John F. Fitzgerald's appointment to the Military Academy, upon graduation . . .

Scored all the Army points as a plebe quarterback in an 11-5 win in 1901 over Navy (28-yard field goal, 95-yard kickoff runback, point conversion) . . .

Kicked a 50-yard field goal against Yale, the same season . . .

Beat Navy in his first meeting (1901) as a player and in his last (1922) as a coach for Army . . .

Had a positive genius for making score-saving tackles of opponents loose in an open field . . .

Oddly enough, Army's only loss when Daly was its plebe quarterback was to his alma mater, Harvard.

Odder, still, was the fact that once in his brilliant career as a defensive safety man a ball carrier got past him: Bob Kernan (via a straightarm) in the 1901 Harvard game.

Kernan scored the winning points, and he was Daly's successor as the Crimson captain at the time.

That was one of the few fires, apparently, that Charlie Daly did not extinguish on the football field. (He later served as Boston fire commissioner, incidentally.)

He did, indeed, belong to the sports ages—and pages.

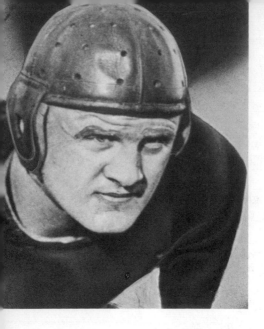

Elmer Oliphant ranks as one of the Cadets' all-time halfbacks. In the 1915 game, "Ollie" scored all fourteen points as Army won, 14-0. In 1916, Oliphant scored ten points to defeat Navy, 15-7.

Frank Graham gives us a quick sketch of the player who scored both touchdowns and kicked the two extra points to give Army a 14-0 victory over Navy in 1915. They called him Ollie and his name was Elmer Q. Oliphant. He was a star in baseball, football, track, and basketball, was heavyweight boxing champion of the Corps, and—quite rightfully—made the Hall of Fame. This was written in 1954, but no one will ever forget Elmer Q. Oliphant.

Speaking of Great Athletes

FRANK GRAHAM

THE NEXT TIME YOU HEAR ANYBODY SPEAKING OF GREAT ATHLETES HE HAS seen, ask him if he ever saw Elmer Oliphant. If he says "no," you can speak freely—and, if he says "yes," you'll both have something to talk about provided, of course, you know about Ollie. If you don't, but are interested, here's an outline of the man who too often is forgotten when great athletes are named. This, by the way, is more than a bit surprising because he is an important figure in insurance circles in this town and gets around considerably socially, too.

In his fifties now, he's still rugged and full of zing, as the result of the way he has lived, worked, and played through the years. Out of a mining town in southern Indiana, he worked in the mines during summer vacations when he was in high school and was a tough young hombre when he entered Purdue. There in three years of varsity competition, to which he applied himself between jobs he took on as a means of paying his way, he won three letters each in football, baseball, basketball, and track.

Some of his feats were almost incredible. Although he had suffered a broken ankle in a football game with Illinois, he kicked a field goal to defeat the Illini, 3 to 0. Knocked down or having fallen in the closing minutes of a basketball game with Wisconsin when Purdue was trailing, 20 to 21, he shot the winning basket while seated on the floor.

Art Nehf, the old Giant pitcher who, while at Rose Poly, played baseball and football against him, once said:

"Nobody ever can tell me there was a greater athlete than Ollie."

Those were the days of a freewheeling athletic policy at West Point, and Army football teams were loaded with huskies who had played well and, in some cases, four years on major college teams. And so, in 1914, no one so much as raised an eyebrow when Oliphant bobbed up at the Point.

There he became a legend. Plebes being eligible for the varsity teams, he won four letters each in baseball, football, track, and basketball and was heavyweight boxing champion of the Corps. His fourth letter in each sport posed a bit of a problem, since no provision had been made for such a symbol. As he once described it:

"My first letter was the 'A' itself. The second was indicated by a gold stripe placed above and below the crossbar of the letter and the third by a third gold stripe, this one across the middle of the letter. Seems no one ever had won more than three letters and they didn't know what to do about that. Since an Army regulation was involved, they took it up with Congress, believe it or not, and Congress advised sticking a gold star on the letter."

The only force that ever stopped Ollie was the Army itself. Graduated from the Academy in 1918 and commissioned as a lieutenant, he put in four years of soldiering. Then:

"After those four years, I was still a lieutenant. Maybe it was because I wasn't too bright, but I'll say in self-defense that, with the war over, the size of the Army was greatly reduced and promotions were slowed down. I liked the Army all right, but when I figured that if I was lucky I would be a major by the time I was forty-nine, I grew restless all of a sudden and decided to retire."

So he entered the insurance business and made a lot of money and has lived happily ever since.

Overlooked though he has been to some extent by those who talk loosely about great athletes of the past, he has received numerous and richly deserved honors.

He was, of course, on the late Walter Camp's All-America team. Knute Rockne placed him on his all-time All-America team, linking him with Jim Thorpe and Charley Brickley as the greatest drop-kickers. He was chosen overwhelmingly as the best amateur athlete ever born in Indiana.

Only last fall, he was selected as a member of the Helms Athletic Foundation Hall of Fame in Los Angeles. This seems to have pleased him more than any other form of recognition that has come his way.

"It was a wonderful surprise," he said. "I didn't think, especially after all these years, anybody away out there in California would remember me."

Richards Vidmer, sportswriter and fervent Army fan, remembers some of the names that made Cadet history on the playing field. It's an old-timer's dream, rich with memory of Army's gridiron greats.

A Military March Down Memory Lane

RICHARDS VIDMER

A BLARE OF BUGLES. . . . A ROLL OF DRUMS. . . . THE STEADY BEAT OF MARCH-ing feet. . . . A long, gray ribbon unrolls across the field as the corps cadets appears . . . it strides along . . . 1,200 strong . . . halts and explodes with a cheer that wakes the echoes from the past. . . . The rigid ranks break . . . scrambles to its seats . . . and forms again. . . . A solid square of gold and gray. . . . A long-eared mule and two long-legged riders gallop down the sidelines. . . . Gold-helmeted warriors dash onto the gridiron. . . . Scatter . . . then gather for final orders. . . . A sudden silence. . . . A roar like thunder. . . . A shrill whistle on the frosty air. . . . The Army is moving forward. . . . But thoughts go marching back. . . . Vernon Prichard's 1914 team. . . . The first in Army history to go through a season without a defeat or a tie. . . . Conquering Rutgers, Colgate and Holy Cross . . . Villanova, Notre Dame and Navy along the way. . . . Filling the air with bewildering passes all fall. . . . From Prichard to Merillatt . . . who learned their stuff the season before when Notre Dame made its first appearance in the East. . . . And beat the Army, 35 to 13. . . . The second-largest score ever made against the cadets. . . . Piled up principally by the passing from Gus Dorais to Eichenlaub and the late Knute Rockne. . . . A staggering defeat that started a beautiful friendship. . . . And a rivalry interrupted only by the World War. . . .

Bob Neyland, Bill Britton and Paul Parker playing side by side on that cadet line. . . . And for the last eight years working side by side as the Tennessee coaching staff. . . . Turning out five undefeated teams in their eight campaigns. . . .

Meecham, a big-hearted, broad-shouldered cowboy, who never saw a football until he reached West Point. . . . Unable to understand why it was against the rules to "slap a man down with your open fist" . . . Later an All-America guard. . . .

Big Jack McEwan in the center of the line. . . . A tank with wings . . . 220 pounds and first man down the field . . . Walter Camp's choice for top honors two years later. . . . Still later head coach at West Point and Holy Cross. . . . Now coach of Dan Topping's professional Brooklyn Dodgers. . . .

Woody Woodruff. . . . Too light for heavy duty, but a sharpshooter with a placement. . . . First of the Army's pinch kickers. . . . And the first Army man to score against the

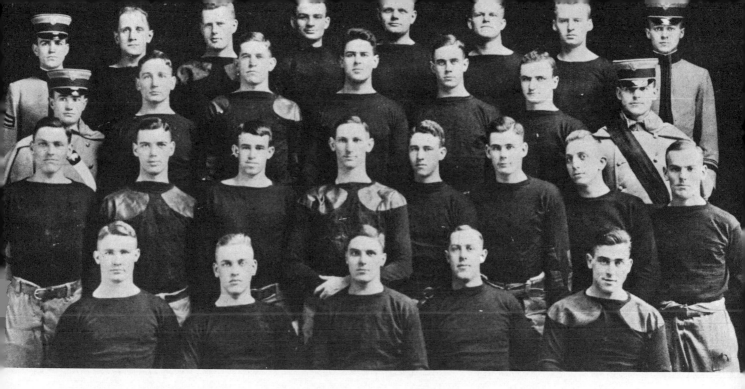

Climaxing the 1914 season with a smashing 20-0 win over Navy, the Army team, led by Captain Vern Prichard, had its first undefeated, untied season and with it—recognition as national champions. Coach Charley Daly and his assistants, Pot Graves and Ike Eisenhower, were delighted with the play of such stars as Bob Neyland, Paul Hodgson, All-American John McEwan, and the Vern Prichard-to Lou Merillat forward pass combination that won nine straight games.

Navy in four years. . . . With a 40-yard field goal in 1913. . . . The same year he beat Colgate after the final whistle. . . . Under circumstances even Ripley wouldn't believe. . . .

Leading, 6-0, in the last quarter, Colgate punted. . . . The timekeeper's whistle blew with the ball in midair. . . . But the play had to be completed . . . and Prichard took the punt down on his own 5-yard line. . . . Followed Walter Wynne, a giant tackle down the field. . . . Watch Wynne take out Ellery Huntington, Colgate's little blond quarterback. . . . And raced 95 yards for the tying touchdown. . . . Woodruff was summoned from the sidelines to kick the extra point. . . . And the Army tied the score, made a substitution and won the game after the final whistle. . . . Believe it or not.

Big Jack McEwan's 1916 team was the second and last to produce a perfect record at West Point. . . . With another great passing combination . . . Elmer Oliphant, star of all Army stars, on the throwing end. . . . Charlie Gerhardt at quarterback. . . . A gift from the gods. . . . Developed overnight when Charlie Daly, then coach, in desperation appealed to Sammy Strong, coach of the baseball team. . . . Did Sammy know of a single man who might be coaxed, coerced or cajoled into becoming a quarterback? . . . Sammy did . . . "Gerhardt. . . . He's light but he's fast. . . . He's little but he's game. . . . If he's inexperienced he will learn" . . . Gerhardt laughed when they told him to turn out. . . . He couldn't even make his prep-school team. . . . But he piloted the Army through nine straight victories. . . .

Oliphant (Ollie), a star in football, baseball, basketball, track, hockey, and swimming.

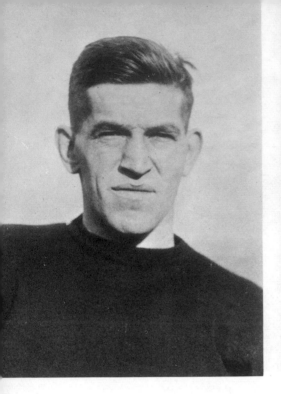

Left: John McEwan, All-American center, captained the 1916 Army team and was named head coach in 1923.   Right: McEwan receiving award "in recognition of his outstanding contribution to the advancement of the game of football."

. . . And heavyweight champion boxer of the corps . . . who never knew what it was to lose to the Navy . . . in any sport. . . . His farewell game when the Middies' one idea . . . their one aim was to "Stop Ollie" . . . And Ollie, catching the first kickoff, racing 93 yards to a touchdown. . . .

Time out for another game—the grim game of war, and then three straight defeats by the Navy in 1919, 1920, and 1921. . . . Followed by twelve straight seasons without a setback by the sister service. . . . With two ties and two blank years among the dozen. . . .

The game that started that string . . . at Philadelphia in 1922. . . . A seesaw score and the Navy leading, 14-10, in the twilight. . . . A dizzy run by George Smythe. . . . Half the length of the field and all the way from one sideline to the other. . . . The winning pass to Pat Timberlake . . . whose father and brother played before him . . . and two younger brothers followed after. . . .

The thrilling 21-21 tie on Soldiers Field at Chicago in 1926. . . . And the appearance of Christian Keener Cagle, the reckless redhead . . . first choice of the All-America Board of Catches four years in succession. . . .

A long line of great linesmen . . . Ed Garbisch . . . and the men who flanked him—Gus Farwick and Fats Ellinger . . . Buster Perry . . . Jack Price . . . Moe Daly . . . Milt Summerfelt. . . . And a battalion of brilliant backs . . . Lighthorse Harry Wilson . . . Bill Wood . . . Rosy Carver . . . Ray Stecker. . . . And Peck Vidal, Gene's kid brother.

D. M. Michie . . . captain, coach, and organizer of Army football in 1890. . . . They named the stadium after him thirty-five years later. . . . The worst defeat ever suffered . . . when Princeton conquered the cadets, 36 to 4 . . . With Doggie Trenchard, Phil

King and Langdon Lea stalking the plains. . . . Stars who later wore stars on their shoulder straps . . . Smedburg, Aultman, King, Lott, Dennis Nolan, W. D. Connor, Malin Craig, Stuart Heitzelman among them. . . .

W. D. Smith, the only man to captain two Army teams. . . . But they wouldn't let him coach. . . . Because he might expect the ends to smear the interference and make the tackle too. . . . And only Walter Smith ever had been able to do both at the same time. . . .

Bob Hyatt standing with his heels on his own goal line and tears in his eyes. . . . Crying that he'd rather be a plebe at West Point than admiral of the whole damn Navy. . . .

Pop Graves . . . Tom Hammond . . . Charlie Daly . . . Dan Sultan . . . Horace Hickam . . . Big Red Erwin . . . Ed Grebie . . . Dan Pullman . . . Archie Arnold . . . Leland Devore. . . .

> "E'er may that linc of gray
> Increase from day to day. . . ."

Members of Army's 1913 team included (l. to r.) Walter Wynne, Alexander Weyand, Alfred Forabee, Dwight Eisenhower, Charles Benedict, and Benny Hoge, captain. The boy between Benedict and Hoge is Richards Vidmer, son of the post adjutant, Capt. George Vidmer. He later became a sportswriter and editor.

All-American Glenn Davis said of him, "Where Red was unequalled—just tremendous —was going into a crowd of tacklers and picking his way—one by one—past all of them!" Chris "Red" Cagle was perhaps the greatest back in Army football history. Certainly he was the most colorful and most controversial player West Point ever trotted out on the gridiron. Here is his story, warmly and humanly related by Ed Linn and taken from his piece in Sport Magazine in 1963.

Chris Cagle: Eight Years a College Star

ED LINN

CHRISTIAN KEENER CAGLE RANKS WITH RED GRANGE, TOM HARMON, AND Glenn Davis as one of the four great halfbacks in collegiate history.

Cagle's great extra territorial fame, however, rests on the fact that, in strict noncompliance with the rule prohibiting a cadet from having "a dog, a wife, or a moustache," he was secretly married during his last two years at the Point. When the news broke, a month before he was scheduled to graduate, he was drummed out of the Academy without diploma or commission.

Keener Cagle was raised on a cattle ranch in Merryville, Texas, a little town just this side of the Mexican border. He always claimed that he had developed his passing eye by lassoing calves. ("Keener" was what he was called throughout his youth. It was only when he came to West Point that he began to be called "Chris" by the newspapers and "Red" by his friends.) As a boy, he wanted to become—of all things—a doctor. In his first year at Southern Louisiana Institute, he discovered that a pre-med course, mixed with football, basketball, track, and waiting on tables—was far beyond him. It was only the first of many ambitions that Chris Cagle put behind him.

Like many another athlete, he decided his best bet was to make use of his more obvious talents and become a coach. He was a good basketball player, a fine quarter-miler—and *great* in football. For four years, he ran wild. In his junior year, 1924, the first time SLI bothered to keep statistics, he set a national passing record by completing 67 out of 125 passes. He was also fifth nationally in scoring and, quite probably, the country's rushing leader with a 13.3 average. The following year, his statistics were almost as good.

The trouble was that no one was looking. He was then a 150-pound back playing for a tiny college, and little backs from little colleges have about the same chance of being picked on All-America teams as Jack Paar has of being drafted to play middle linebacker for the Chicago Bears. Keener Cagle wasn't even picked for the All-Southern teams.

138

If he had received any kind of recognition, Cagle quite probably would have married upon graduation and gone to work as an assistant coach in some equally small southern college. As it was, he had little reputation and no job offers.

For his own part, Cagle—always a modest, amiable, immensely popular boy—was not awfully upset. Even when he was assured of the appointment to West Point, however, Cagle was not sure he wanted to accept it. He was engaged to an SLI freshman, Marian Haile, and four years at West Point meant four years during which he could not get married. But his parents were very anxious for him to go. When, in the end, Marian told him to go, too, that was that. In the fall of 1926, Keener Cagle headed for West Point.

During his first two years, he was sure he had made a mistake. The West Point apparatus swallows up all incoming Cadets and sets them upon a long, gray, timetable. Chris was far from happy in such a rigid, regimented life; his letters to Marian reflected a homesickness rather astonishing in a man of voting age.

West Point's liberal rules made him eligible for the varsity from the start. But Chris had never been a man to rouse himself in practice, and, when the season opened, he was a substitute behind Tom Trapnell. The star of the team was Lighthorse Harry Wilson, who had previously been an All-America at Penn State. Gar Davidson, later both the football coach and the Superintendent of the Academy, was a substitute tackle. Chris spent the first two games on the bench. He got to play, finally, when Trapnell's nose was smashed in a bloody game against Syracuse.

Trapnell's nose was not the only one broken that day; a Syracuse back got himself thrown out for breaking the referee's nose with a crisp right hook. There were also periodic interruptions to allow the fans to riot a little and, as the game ended, at least one M.P. was out on the field with a drawn gun.

With such juicy items as these to report upon, it is little wonder that the newspapers tended to obscure the fact that a substitute freshman halfback, Chris Cagle, had scored the winning touchdown.

He was never a substitute again. In the Navy game, the boy from Merryville found himself performing before 110,000 spectators at Soldier Field, Chicago. He ran 43 yards for the final Army touchdown in a 21-21 tie.

By then, it had become obvious enough that the little redheaded plebe—built up by West Point chow to a solid 165 pounds—was the team's star. The following year, Coach Biff Jones rebuilt his offense to accommodate Red's talents, scrapping the Notre Dame box for a single-wing formation which would give Red the chance to run and pass out of a deep tailback position.

Harry Wilson, captain of the team, found himself completely overshadowed. There was no jealousy between the two great runners, though. In the Navy game—Wilson's farewell appearance—Chris refused to carry the ball once it had been brought into scoring position. "This is Harry's game," he told Quarterback Spike Nave. Wilson scored all the points and Army won, 14-9.

Chris might have felt a little different if he had known he would never get another chance to play against Navy. The Annapolis brass had adopted the conventional three-year varsity rule that season. Army flatly refused to go along. The following year, the Superintendent of the Naval Academy angrily canceled the game on the grounds that

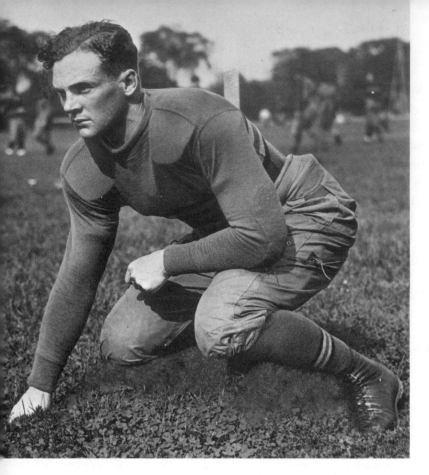

Christian Keener Cagle, better known as "Red" Cagle, one of the most sensational running stars West Point has ever had.

Halfback Red Cagle will ever be remembered for his outstanding play in the 1926 and 1927 Army-Navy battles.

Army was unwilling to compete on equal terms. The game was resumed in 1930 only because President Hoover ordered that it be played to raise money for charity. (And in 1930, plenty of charity was needed.) In 1938 Franklin D. Roosevelt, a onetime Undersecretary of Navy, issued a brief directive which read: "From now on West Point will abide by the three-year rule." Thus ended the era of the eight-year football player.

Cagle was worth watching. His Number 12 was as famous in his day as Red Grange's 77. An odd habit of wearing his chin strap over the back of his helmet seemed to lend a flourish to his running. A jolting tackle would send the helmet flying, and Cagle's red, curly hair would come suddenly and dramatically to view.

Red Blaik, who came to the Point as an assistant coach during Cagle's second year, is in a wonderful position to compare Chris with his own three-time All-America ace of the 1940s, Glenn Davis.

"Red," he says, "was very fast but he did not have Glenn's burning speed. He could pick up speed and power in the open but he did not have four or five gears like Davis. Where Red was unequaled—just tremendous—was at going into a crowd of tacklers and picking his way—one by one—past all of them! He was also, incidentally, one of the first backs—the first I ever saw, anyway—to throw long passes on the dead run."

Cagle could run equally well to either his left or right and he could cut on a poker chip. Most backs, in cutting, pivot exclusively off their inside foot, swinging a hip around in that classic newspaper pose. Red could also pivot off his outside foot, like a soldier doing a right or left flanking movement, an ability which permitted him to change directions in quick, darting 90-degree angles.

Generally, he would start wide out of a short kick formation. If he did not feel he had enough room on that side, he would swing around to see how the land lay on the other side of the field. It was not unusual for him to retreat up to 30 yards behind the line of scrimmage before he had the field spread out to his satisfaction.

This is what made Chris Cagle such a spectacular runner. He did not simply outrun everybody; first, he'd spread his field out, then he'd pick his way through it. A Cagle run left a pattern of sprawling bodies and clutching hands behind it. Since he sometimes ran 50 yards just to get back to the line of scrimmage, he could make an emotional experience out of a 3-yard gain.

His greatest run probably came against Stanford. Although he gained only 26 yards, the pictures showed that Red reversed his field seven times, eluded every man on the Stanford team at least once, and covered—in all probability—close to 200 yards. He was finally tackled from behind, just as he had maneuvered himself into the clear.

Doing for Army no more than he had done for SLI, Chris was an All-America in his sophomore year. He remained an All-America thereafter.

In June, 1928, after two solid years at the point, he finally went home on his first leave, an automatic two-month furlough which followed the completion of his yearling year. On the last day of the furlough, Red and Marian Haile were married.

Red, who had been scheduled to catch the nine o'clock train out of New Orleans, wired the Academy that he had missed his connection. When he did return, a day later, he was sentenced to walk the area for thirty-five days.

Four months later he got home again for the Christmas holidays, and once again he was a day late getting back. Once again he walked the area. These were the only two times Red got home during his entire stay at West Point. It was a year and a half before he saw his wife again.

For Red, the senior year was a rough one. As captain of the football team, he had his greatest season personally, and yet the team itself could not win a major game. Against Harvard, Cagle scored three touchdowns—two on runs of 20 and 45 yards—but a last-minute 50-yard pass thrown by a sophomore Barry Wood (a name to soothe the ulcers of all old Harvards) tied it up. The next week, Army scored two quick touchdowns against Yale, before coach Mal Stevens sent in a tiny sophomore named Albie Booth (this is for the tired old Yales). The littlest bulldog, having the greatest day he would ever have in his distinguished career, scored all Yale's 21 points, and Army lost.

The Notre Dame game was played on a day so cold and windy that not a pass was completed by either team. There was one intercepted. Cagle started wide to his right from the Notre Dame 11-yard line, then threw a long, diagonal pass to the other side of the field. It was not the best possible play under the circumstances, particularly since that area was being guarded by Jack Elder, the world record holder for the 60-yard dash. Elder took Cagle's pass and set a world record for the 95-yard dash with an intercepted pass. Another loss. There is the sense, sharpened by hindsight, that things had already begun to turn bad for Christian Keener Cagle.

With his eight-year education coming to an end, Chris had to begin to worry about making a living.

On April 18, two months before graduation, the Memphis *Commercial-Appeal* reported that Cagle had accepted a contract to coach Mississippi A&M (now Mississippi State). He was to get $3,500 for three months' work. Red also had an offer from a New Orleans bond house, anxious to pay him $5,000 for little more than the use of his name.

At this point there was no criticism whatsoever of Cagle's plan to take his diploma and resign. His resignation would have gone unmarked if he had not been persuaded to involve himself in a Congressional fight that was boiling up around a bill to increase Army pay.

The reaction was just about what any reasonable man might have expected. Cagle was blasted in both the sports pages and the editorial pages.

The worst was yet to come. Shortly after the statement was released, a Hearst newspaperman phoned Biff Jones to tell him: "There's talk around that your football captain is married." Jones immediately brought the rumor to General Smith, but both men assumed that the captain in question was the captain-elect, Polly Humber. Poor Humber, summoned on the spot, indignantly denied that he had taken unto himself a wife, or even a dog.

When the story of Humber's ordeal got around the campus, Cagle began to worry and announced his intention to resign. On May 13 the Hearst papers broke the story, complete with the date, the place, and the names of everyone involved. A half hour after Red admitted to the post surgeon that the story was true, the Academy had his resignation in the form of a certificate sworn before a notary public.

It was a grand day for all critics of West Point; those who disliked it because they

Red Cagle (with ball) drives for another first down in the first quarter of the 1927 game.

loved Annapolis more; those who disliked West Point, Annapolis, and any place else smacking of the military; and those graduates of other colleges who had never been able to forgive West Point the unpardonable sin of fielding a winning football team.

General Smith was no longer deploring the loss of Cagle's brilliant military mind. "This great Academy," he announced, "is not going to get excited over one little Cadet, at least not while I'm here. He is a foolish boy who has thrown away his prestige and his diploma."

There was no particular feeling against him at West Point, however. The Honor Board cleared him, presumably on the grounds that his attempt to get his commission, even after he had been married, had the approval of precedent. For rules or no rules, Cadets do get married. Red was deprived of the beautiful gold Edgerton Saber, which is traditionally presented to the outgoing captain, and also of the silver saber which goes to the most valuable player. His offer to turn in his class ring was waived aside, though, and he always wore it with great pride. His picture remained in the year book, too. Underneath it were the defiant words: Great in victory, but with that added characteristic that marks a real leader—greater still in defeat; modest and reticent almost to a fault; happy-go-lucky, but always sincere—that is "Red" Cagle."

The coaching career, after all the years of waiting, was short and sour. For reasons never fully explained, the other members of the Southern Association tried to get Mississippi A&M to back out of their agreement with him. Chris was signed anyway, but before the season was over he turned in his whistle and knickers and went back to New York to play for the Giants at $500 a game. Only Red Grange ($550) was getting more.

The biggest crowd of the year, 40,000 people, came to the Polo Grounds to watch him in his debut against the Green Bay Packers. Early in the game, Red took a short pass from Benny Friedman and was tackled so viciously by Packer end Tom Nash that both of them had to be helped off the field. Cagle had a gash alongside his eye that required four stitches. Nash had a broken nose that put him out of action for the rest of the season.

Chris returned to the game in the second half, with a bandage over the stitches. The first time he was hit, the helmet flew one way and the bandage another. He played out the game with blood running down his face.

Off the field, it was one disappointment after another. The stock-market break at the end of 1929 had not made it easy to step into a custom-made customer's man job. The New Orleans offer evaporated, and he had to start from the very bottom as a telephone clerk in a Wall Street firm. In 1932 he entered politics and backed Herbert Hoover—to show how bad things were going—against Franklin D. Roosevelt. After the election, he was sent to the Atlantic City Elks Club to help bind the wounds at a Republican rally. He found an audience of two Elks, one newspaperman, and no Republicans.

When he went to Hollywood to play himself in a movie called *All-American*, he fell in with another of the All-Americas, John Sims "Shipwreck" Kelly. The wild, fun-loving Kelly and the quiet, fun-loving Cagle hit it off so beautifully that they eventually scraped together $25,000 and bought the Brooklyn Dodgers, as ramshackle a pro football franchise as anyone could hope for.

It was a fruitful partnership if we're talking about laughs instead of money; the owners suffered from a chronic lack of funds, so much so that they were never more than one rainy Sunday away from bankruptcy. Capt. John McEwan, a West Point immortal, was hired as their coach. "It wasn't really a football team" McEwan says, "so much as a musical comedy."

McEwan, one of the best centers who ever lived, had been one of the real hell-raisers in West Point history. Obviously, he was a grand choice for the job.

Between halves, Kelly and Cagle would sometimes order McEwan to arouse the boys to dreams of glory with a Rockne-like pep talk. While their coach would be urging their employees onward and upward, the two owners would huddle together in a corner and roar.

In their second year, the two owners discovered that their star attractions—in short, Cagle and Kelly—were slowing down. Kelly had always been a wild runner. Like Cagle, he liked to retreat in a wide circle, look the situation over, and then come charging back up the field, streaking between tacklers. His favorite play was to run from deep in his own territory on fourth down with about 12 to go. In college, he had left them screaming with that one; in his first year with Cagle he had occasionally shaken loose. The next year, he was lucky to get back to the line of scrimmage.

Chris Cagle in 1942.

Red Blaik once stopped off in Dayton, on a cold, snowy day, to watch the Dodgers play an exhibition game. The owners, having decided to alternate during the game, spent more energy trying to coax each other onto the field than they spent on the game itself. At the end of the year, Chris—who hadn't made a dime to cut upon—sold his half of the club to Dan Topping.

His football days at an end, Red went to work for the Fidelity Phoenix Fire Insurance Co., where he eventually worked himself up to office manager.

The ties with the past were kept intact by frequent visits up to the Point. Chris loved to reminisce with Marty Maher, Gar Davidson, and the rest of the old-timers, and there was in him an increasing sense of regret that he had left the Army or, at any rate, that he had left the way he had. When war broke out, he hungered to get back in. He set his sights upon the Air Corps and knocked on every familiar door. When his overtures were coolly received, he even wrote to his old West Point buddy, Rosie O'Donnell, who was just beginning to make a reputation in the Philippines. In late October, 1942, he heard that his old roomie, J. A. K. Herbert—by then a lieutenant colonel in the Corps of Engineers—had returned from the Caribbean. Herbert—who came out of the war as a brigadier general—was shuttling between New York and Washington and was obviously not without influence at the Pentagon. Herbert was happy to do what he could, but just as he was starting to work on it in earnest, Chris died as the result of a fall down a steep flight of subway stairs. He was thirty-seven years old.

Cagle's friends from the Academy days believe that if he had lived, Chris would undoubtedly have got back in the Army, and that if he had got back he would undoubtedly have remained. They go even further than that, though, for a curious thing has happened. Since men tend to believe what it makes them most happy to believe, their attitude is that the Army lost "another Georgie Patton" because the stiff-backed, tape-bound Army brass kicked Cagle out of the Point on a purely technical charge. That Red wanted out, that he had not liked the military life, that he had shown nothing approaching a military mind—all that is forgotten.

But, after all, Red Cagle had learned early in life that he was living in a world where publicity triumphed after accomplishment had failed, where the fact could not stand against the myth.

It would not have surprised him that, in the end, it is the myth that remains.

He was just another Army back, playing with men like Jack Buckler, Joe Stancook, Monk Meyer, but in the Army-Navy game of 1935, an 80-yard run for a TD, a pass play for a TD, four perfectly executed punts for four extra points after touchdown, and "fame caught up with Whitey Grove." Frank Graham tells the story.

Fame Catches Up with Whitey Grove

FRANK GRAHAM

FAME CAUGHT UP WITH WHITEY GROVE IN HIS LAST GAME FOR ARMY. FOR two years Whitey's presence in Army's backfield was pretty well concealed from the general public by the glamorous forms of Jack Buckler and Joe Stancook, and this year Monk Meyer stepped out in front of him and took the spotlight away from him. Not that Whitey cared about that. Whitey is a smiling little guy from Glenwood, Minnesota, who, happy at being a West Pointer and being on the football team, didn't care whose names were in the headlines and whose pictures were in the paper.

He would block or carry the ball or receive passes and he always played a fine defensive game. But—take this season as an example—he wasn't as sensational as Meyer was at carrying the ball and when he caught a pass from Monk everybody talked about Monk's fine passing and paid no attention to the little guy who caught the ball and, maybe, ran with it for a touchdown. And, of course, nobody ever notices a blocker and only the linesmen ever got credit for defensive play.

So Whitey seemed in a fair way to wind up as a football player at West Point with only his teammates and his opponents knowing how good he was. Then came last Saturday's game with Navy in Philadelphia—the colorful climax to a dizzy season and the last fling for Whitey.

Lt. Gar Davidson had rigged up a couple of plays calculated to throw the Middies back on their heels and take the ball game away from them almost before it had begun, and it happened that in each of these plays the key man was Grove. These plays had been worked out carefully on the Plains for the past week and the Cadets had them whittled down to a point where they practically couldn't miss. Either one of them would do the trick. They would try one right off the bat and if that failed for some reason or other—as even the most carefully planned plays will fail now and then—they would come back with the other.

They talked it all over for the last time in the dressing room while the great crowd was gathering in Franklin Field. The first time they got the ball they'd feed it to Bill

Grohs and they counted on Navy being jittery about Meyer and watching him and waiting for him to get the ball. So then they'd give it to Grove and turn him loose along a route they had mapped out for him to the Navy goal line and see what happened. And if that play missed fire, they'd—

But Clifford kicked off and Navy couldn't gain and Schmidt punted. The ball rolled over Army's goal line and Army started from its 20-yard line. Grohs carried the ball on the first play and failed to gain. And now, while the Middies were watching Meyer and wondering when he was going to cut loose, the Army snapped into action again and Grove came up with the ball. The play was perfectly executed. Whitey was going full tilt when he hit the line of scrimmage. He slanted toward Navy's left end, cut back sharply and, in a twinkling, was in the clear. Navy's secondaries were trapped or blotted out. The only one who had a shot at Whitey was Case, but it was a thousand-to-one shot because Whitey had passed him and was on his way and all Case could do was to chase him over the goal line. Whitey kicked a goal placement to make the score 7 to 0 and that, if anybody wants to know, was the ball game.

Navy had a good team. Navy was courageous and full of fight. But that blow had been delivered so swiftly that Navy was bewildered and before it could gather its scattered wits, Army had struck again and again. Meyer threw a forward pass to Grove, who caught the ball in the clear on the 10-yard line and romped to a touchdown and then added another point with a placement kick. Meyer threw a pass to Clint True, who caught it and ran 35 yards for a touchdown and Grove added still another point with a placement kick.

In the second period Army got into scoring position with a trick play that startled the onlookers and completely dumbfounded the Middies. Meyer went back to punting position and the ball was passed to him. He went through all the motions of kicking, and the Middies began moving backward rapidly, but instead of kicking, he slipped the ball to Grove, who had come tearing around behind him and took it in a variation of the bewhiskered Statue of Liberty play. Whitey lugged it to the 7-yard line, and

Army's backfield in 1935: (l. to r.) Ed Grove, Joe Nazzaro, Clint True, and Ralph King.

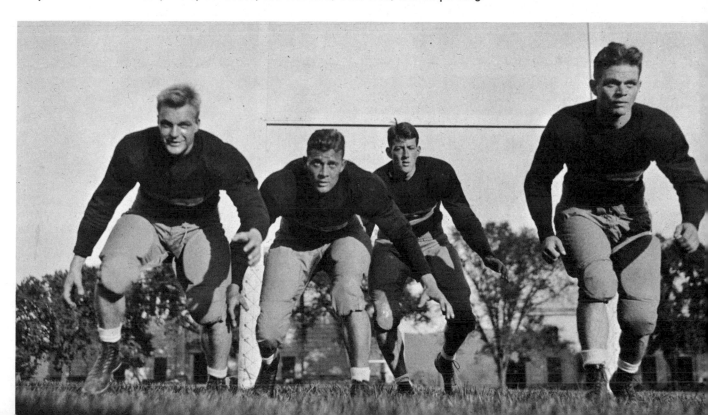

a couple of plunges, one by Meyer and the other by Grohs, netted the Cadets another touchdown. Then Grove, who apparently couldn't miss, split the bar with a placement kick.

Thus the half ended with the score 28 to 0 in Army's favor and up in the press box they were beginning to call him "Shut the Gates of Mercy" Davidson and wondering why he didn't have the decency to put the blankets on his regulars and throw his second- and third-string players into the gray to give the Middies a chance.

That was unfair to Davidson, however, and quite as unfair to Lt. Tom Hamilton and the Navy team. Davidson simply had sprung his trap with lightning speed in the first few minutes of play and was forcing legitimately the advantage he had gained. And Navy was looking for neither sympathy nor quarter. The Middies believed that if they could get themselves organized, they would give Army all the fight it could handle. Badly beaten as they were, they were in no mood to quit or to ask that the Cadets should pull their punches.

The second half gave a truer indication of the relative merits of the teams. Navy came surging out of its dressing room and, with John Schmidt in the van, launched a terrific attack. As the third period waned, Schmidt was hammering and battering his way to Armys goal line. A determined Army defense held him up as the period ended—held him up on the 2-foot line. But in the first play of the fourth period he found a spot inside left tackle and plunged over for a touchdown.

Navy kept trying, launching long thrusts at Army's goal line through the last period. But one drive was stopped when Schmidt fumbled and another when Vincent intercepted a pass, and when the game ended Army had the ball again and was puttering around with it on its own 35-yard line.

The crowd, trooping out of the stadium and gathering again in the hotels or the other hot spots, or rushing for the trains back to New York or Baltimore or Washington, was talking mostly about Whitey Grove. For fame had caught up with Whitey at last—which was more than the Middies could do.

Halfback Ed "Whitey" Grove, ripped Navy's line for two touchdowns in the 1935 game as Army trounced the Middies, 28-6.

Charles R. Meyer gave the impression of being slightly underweight and underfed, yet he was one of the greatest football players ever seen in action for West Point. His teammates nicknamed him "Monk," and he played football, basketball, baseball, and starred on the track squad. But it was on the gridiron that he achieved All-American recognition and led Army to a stunning 28-6 victory over Navy in 1935. Here is his story as reported by Art Sampson of the Boston Herald.

He Was Determined to Play for West Point

ARTHUR SAMPSON

HE IS A SLIM, ANEMIC-APPEARING YOUNG MAN AT FIRST GLANCE. UNTIL you shake his hand you wonder why his pals call him Monkey and then you figure that his vicelike grip gave him such a nickname.

You wonder how such a slight 147-pounder can stand the shock of sixty minutes of grueling football with rugged opponents who are from thirty to sixty pounds heavier until you hear the story of his career, which has the tinge of fiction. Then you understand why Cadet Charles R. Meyer is a great halfback.

When the thousands of spectators who sit in the stadium next Saturday afternoon rise to greet the Army team as it trots on the field they will see ten stalwart athletes, wearing gold helmets, and one little fellow. After the whistle blows and the black-shirted soldiers line up in offensive formation it will be the little fellow on whom the eyes will be focused.

Standing behind his ten rugged teammates, little Monk will do the running, the passing, and the kicking. To the majority, who watch the ball, he will be the center of attention on nearly every play. His running provides a thrill when you see him hurl his slight frame into the line. His kicking is not brilliant but effective. His passing is sensational.

And as the Army team advances, with little Monk as the spearhead of the offensive, you will admire the spunk and spirit of an enthusiastic American boy who pulled himself up by his own bootstraps over seemingly insurmountable obstacles.

There are countless gridiron stars in the country today. The nation is full of talented football players. But most of them possess the necessary physique, speed, and natural ability. All of them have had to work for perfection. The path to success in football, as in life, is not easy. It is not a game for the lazy or indifferent youth. But most of the outstanding performers had the necessary qualifications to start with. Meyer is an exception.

From the time he was old enough to know about football, Meyer wanted to play the game. From early youth he also wanted to be a cadet at the United States Military Academy. His big ambition was to wear one of those gold Army helmets.

When playing for his high school team at Allentown, Pennsylvania, he prevailed upon his school coach to take him to an Army game. The occasion came in his senior year. The time was late October. The place was the Yale Bowl.

Young Meyer was thrilled beyond words when he saw the Army team pound out the first touchdown that afternoon. His heart was shattered when Yale tied the score on the next play with Dud Parker returning a kickoff for a touchdown.

He was sad with thousands of others when Cadet Sheridan was fatally injured a moment later. But on the journey home after the game he made up his mind that some day he would be playing football in a West Point uniform.

Receiving an appointment from Congressman Doyle, Meyer entered the academy in 1933. Despite lack of weight he made his numerals in football, basketball, baseball, and track as a plebe.

He went out for the varsity football team the next season. He plugged on his fundamentals. As a reserve he scrimmaged against the varsity. He took his physical pounding with a grim determination. He kept trying to improve his technique.

Texas Jack Buckler was the spearhead of the Army attack that year. Meyer studied his every move. He copied Buckler in every way, with the hope that he would be ready to fill his shoes the next fall.

The 1935 season opened with Meyer on the sidelines. Due to the fact that little Monk looked frail and small, a sophomore named Jim Craig was given the regular tailback berth.

Meyer was disappointed but he didn't quit. All he waited for was a chance to prove that he could stand the battering that an Army spearhead had to take in major competition.

Craig started the first two early season games and looked good. He also started the Harvard contest, the first big game on the Army schedule.

But the Army attack sputtered and stuttered in the early moments against the Crimson. Sophomore Craig was still inexperienced. He couldn't set the cadets on fire.

At the start of the second period, Meyer was called upon. This was his chance. After all the years of work and preparation, little Monk wasn't going to miss his opportunity if he could help it. He went into that contest with fire in his eye and fast-pumping red blood in his veins.

The Army attack started to function smoother immediately. Little Meyer was the spark plug which ignited the power. Army started to roll and Meyer had successfully reached his goal.

Heralded as one of the great backs in the nation at the end of last season, Meyer didn't rest on his laurels. He had practised faithfully ever since the end of last season to improve his technique.

A visitor at the Plains will see little Monk lead all other Cadets to the practice field 'most any afternoon. Off by himself he will aim kicks for coffin corner. With a substitute or manager as a target, he will aim a barrage of bullet passes each day.

As a senior, Meyer is a finished football player. He can thread a needle with a football while running at top speed. He can take the shock of a fierce tackle with a minimum of punishment. He has realized his ambition by hurdling obstacles which would have discouraged a less courageous youth.

You simply have to admire such a boy as Charles R. Meyer.

Left: Monk Meyer, elusive halfback and great passer.   Right: In the first quarter of the 1935 game, Monk Meyer tossed a 40-yard pass to Whitey Grove for a touchdown. Minutes later Monk scored again by passing to Clint True.

Jim Craig warmed the bench for three years at Army. Once in a while he relieved Monk Meyer, Woody Wilson, Huey Long. Most of the time, he just sat and wondered when he could get into the game, do something which really counted for the Black Knights. The chance came in his last year. It was in the first quarter of the 1937 game against Navy. "Craig, get in there!" barked Coach Gar Davidson, and Craig was in there, carrying the ball on the first play, a play neither he nor Army is ever likely to forget. Richards Vidmer covered the game that day.

A Sub Named Jim Craig

RICHARDS VIDMER

FOR TWO SEASONS THE FARMER BOY FROM OKLAHOMA SAT ON THE SIDElines, his big, rawboned body draped in a gray Army blanket, and through game after game he gazed out onto the field, perhaps with envious and impatient eyes, at a scrawny little, narrow-chested lad playing the tailback position for the Cadets.

Once in a while the little fellow would get tired, or at least the coaches would think he was tired, and so once in a while Gar Davidson, the Army coach, would turn and look at the big farmer boy from Oklahoma and he would say: "Craig, go in for Meyer."

When he said that, big Jim Craig would bounce up from the bench, hurl his blanket aside, and go galloping onto the field, relieving little Monkey Meyer. But only once in a while, only for a few brief moments, for somehow the little Monkey never seemed to get very tired and somehow he never got hurt at all.

Yet these few times that big Jim Craig saw action, those few moments he had on the field of battle, gave him high hopes of future football. For little Monkey Meyer would graduate one year before big Jim Craig, and it was natural for big Jim Craig to feel that when the Monkey was gone he would take his place in the regular Army lineup.

But Monkey Meyer graduated last year and still Jim Craig spent most of the time sitting on the sidelines. He was on the sidelines again today, as 102,000 spectators peered down through the mist that hung above Philadelphia's Municipal Stadium and the Army and Navy teams met again in their traditional battle for the supremacy of the services. He sat there while Woody Wilson, Huey Long, Jim Schwenk, and Jack Ryan played in the Army backfield.

He sat there and fidgeted as neither team could gain a foot or an inch. And probably he thought to himself, but if they would just let him get out there on the field—if they just would give him that ball—he would lug it somewhere.

But back and forth the two teams battled through most of the first quarter, failing to gain, exchanging punts. Then suddenly the Army took to the air. A pass from Wilson to Schwenk took the ball deep into Navy's territory. Another from Long to Ryan put it on Navy's 3-yard line. Big Jim Craig's backfield mates were doing all right without him.

But it was then that Gar Davidson turned, as he has turned for three years, and the familiar words came again: "Craig, get in there."

So, big Jim Craig came bounding off the sidelines again, came galloping onto the field for the last time in his career, for this was his last game as a Cadet. And when his teammates found him in the backfield they knew what to do.

On the first play they gave Big Jim the ball and, just as he knew he could do, he took it somewhere. He took it across the goal line, and that was the ball game. It was the only score of the afternoon. Even the point after touchdown was missed. But the Army won, 6 to 0, and Jim Craig, the big farmer boy from Paul's Valley, Oklahoma, scored these six points, and in all likelihood he feels tonight that those three years of waiting and yearning, those three impatient years sitting on the sidelines most of the time, were well worth it.

After all, it isn't every man who can go through his military career, rising from a lieutenant to a captain, a captain to a major, a major to a colonel and, possibly, to a general, and always have the satisfaction through the years of knowing that he scored on the Navy.

That one plunge across the Middies' goal line is something that big Jim Craig can and probably will look back on the rest of his life and remember vividly. All the rest, the weary waiting and the hardships and the impatience of his three years, will be forgotten.

Jim Craig, who went in as substitute for Woody Wilson in the 1937 game and scored—to give Army a 6-0 win.

In 1945, Pete Martin gave his Saturday Evening Post readers a portrait of one of the greatest halfbacks in the history of football, Doc Blanchard. It moves through Blanchard's earliest experiences with the pigskin, his brilliant beginnings at West Point, and his even more brilliant feats that made him a superstar, if ever there was one. Incidentally, there is a good look at the everyday life of the cadet. You can share this life-sized story of a tremendous ball player, a story no one deserves more than the modest Doc Blanchard.

Portrait of a Fullback

PETE MARTIN

LAST FALL, WHEN ED MCKEEVER, NOTRE DAME'S COACH, TOOK A BUSMAN'S holiday to scout the Army team, he wired back to South Bend:

HAVE JUST SEEN SUPERMAN IN THE FLESH. HE WEARS NO. 35 ON HIS ARMY JERSEY. HIS NAME IS FELIX (DOC) BLANCHARD.

When Blanchard was a North Carolina freshman, Glenn Thistlewaite, former coach at Northwestern, saw him play. "I have seen all of the great fullbacks," Thistlewaite said, "but this boy will be the greatest." Clark Shaughnessy, Pittsburgh's coach, believes Blanchard "may be" the finest back football has ever known. "He isn't that now," Shaughnessy thinks. "Right now, such fullbacks as Nagurski and Standlee haven't been surpassed. But Blanchard is a prodigous player, a terrific ball carrier, a tremendous blocker. And he's football smart."

McKeever, Thistlewaite, and Shaughnessy were taking in a lot of territory—a territory on whose relief map loom such man-mountains as Nevers, Molenda, Joesting, Thorpe, Heston, Savoldi, Maulbetsch, Standlee, and Nagurski. It is hard to believe that any mere mortal constructed of the usual complement of flesh, blood, bones, and sinews can live up to Blanchard's advance billing.

Felix Blanchard, Sr., knew about those things. He had played for Tulane in the years between 1917 and 1920. He was a natural football player, and, although he weighed nearly 250 pounds and wore a size 12 shoe, he was as fast as a blooded race horse.

Leaving Tulane, Blanchard finished his medical education at Wake Forest, and settled down to practice medicine in Bishopville, South Carolina, a town with a population of 3,000. When a son was born to the Blanchards, he was named Felix Anthony Blanchard, Jr., but he was called Little Doc, since, with the easy informality of a small Southern community, his dad was called Doc.

The boyhood of Felix Anthony Blanchard, Jr., was as typically American as joining the Boy Scouts, playing mumble-the-peg or hooking school. At the age of four, he tried

154

his father's pipe and set the barn on fire. In the summertime, he earned pocket money as a delivery boy for the corner grocery. He had a brush with the law over a broken window, and the incident was settled with a ten-dollar bill contributed by his dad. When he was old enough to drive, he shared a stripped-down jalopy with his young sister.

Until Little Doc was old enough to go out for the Bishopville High team, his dad took him to see the home games. The first game in which Little Doc played was Bishopville's annual contest with its arch rival, Bennettsville. When the coach sent Little Doc in as sub fullback, a Bennettsville back carried the ball over him for a score on the first play. Little Doc thought seriously of quitting football, but after a heart-to-heart talk with his dad, he reversed his decision. The next time the Bishopville coach sent him into the game, he brought down a ball carrier with a bone-jarring tackle still remembered in South Carolina's Lee County.

A year later, when Big Doc entered him at St. Stanislaus College in Bay City, Mississippi, his letters home were as brief as the letters all sons away at school write to their parents. "Dear Mother and Daddy," he wrote, "I made a pretty good report this week. Thanks for the two dollars. Made first team. Will write later. Love, Anthony."

While at St. Stanislaus, he made the All-Gulf-Coast-Region Class A team, and played on the teams that appeared twice in New Orleans Toy Bowl as a curtain raiser for the Sugar Bowl game.

When he finished his St. Stanislaus career, in spite of the fact that Notre Dame's All-American Marchy Schwartz had preceded him at the Bay City school, the school paper printed the headline: BLANCHARD HAS RECORD AS GREATEST FOOTBALLER IN STANISLAUS' HISTORY. Colleges all over the country wanted Little Doc.

Felix "Doc" Blanchard, explosive fullback.

Blanchard driving for the first of his three touchdowns in the 1945 game. Army rode over Navy, 32-13.

Little Doc's first cousin, Jim Tatum, was responsible for his going to North Carolina. Tatum had returned to North Carolina in 1939 as director of freshman athletics and head freshman football coach. He used no high pressure on Doc, Jr., to enroll him at North Carolina. He had his cousin over to Chapel Hill for a few days, and he liked it there, so he stayed. That was all right with Big Doc. His son had considered only Tulane, Duke, and North Carolina, and, since Big Doc's health was bad, he hoped his boy would pick either North Carolina or Duke to make it easier for him to see him play. The relationship between father and son was a special one.

During his stay at Chapel Hill, Little Doc starred in every game the North Carolina freshmen played. The Tar Babies won the state title that year.

Little Doc was looked upon by the North Carolina coaching staff as the best fullback who had ever entered the university. He weighed 210, was six feet one and a half inches tall, ran the 100-yard dash in ten seconds, and cracked into the line like a locomotive. "There were several men on the varsity who got so they wouldn't try to tackle him," said R. A. White, who trained the North Carolina frosh. "Once he knocked out two would-be tacklers on the same play."

Bob Madry, who handles press relations for North Carolina recalls Blanchard's attitude about personal publicity with awe. Little Doc never came near his office or sought press clippings or photographs of himself. His lack of ego was unique in Madry's experience with a succession of scrapbook-happy athletes.

In 1943, at the close of his freshman year at North Carolina, he volunteered for the Army, after having been turned down by the naval unit at Chapel Hill because of defective sight; as a boy, one of his eyes had caught a mud pellet thrown by a playmate. Also, the Navy claimed that he was overweight for his size, a reason for his rejection that dumbfounded the Tar Babies' opponents, to whom Blanchard's weight had certainly seemed no handicap. In an effort to reduce his weight and have him accepted by the Navy V-12 course, Jim Tatum put Little Doc in a steam room and tried to sweat him down. "He was all muscle and concrete," Tatum said. "I could only cook about two pounds off of him."

The Army sent Blanchard first to Miami Beach for basic training, then to Clovis, New Mexico, where he served in the ground school of the Army Air Forces and specialized in chemical warfare. While he was at Clovis, Big Doc secured an appointment for his son at the United States Military Academy—he had been working on that appointment for a long time—and from Clovis, Little Doc joined 300 other appointees in the pre-West Point unit at Lafayette College.

When Doc Blanchard entered West Point on July 2, 1944, he had lost the diminutive "Little" in front of his name. Big Doc had died a few weeks before, but not until he knew his son would be a plebe.

Cadet Blanchard lives in No. 1, New North Barracks. He shares a room with two other Cadets. The room has two alcoves and contains two bunks a single one and a double one. It is also equipped with three study tables and three wall lockers. In addition to bunks, tables, and lockers, the room is supplied with a sink topped by a mirror. There is also a rifle rack that holds three rifles and three white dress-uniform belts.

"He is," one of Doc's roommates said, "easy to like. When he comes in, in the evening after football practice, he's bushed, and he has a hard time keeping awake over his lessons, such as engineering, which is tough."

Doc Blanchard (35) and Glenn Davis (41), Army's greatest backfield duo, were known as Mr. Inside and Mr. Outside.

This year he was made a cadet corporal. The appointment means much to a West Point second-year man, and any normal boy is bound to get a kick out of making several All-American teams, as Blanchard did at last season's end. Among them were the "All" selections of the Associated Press, the United Press, the All-America Board, INS, *The Sporting News*, and the *Daily News*. But Doc Blanchard doesn't talk about those honors. The two things that have meant most to him are the fact that he was chosen one of the West Pointers to form the guard of honor at President Roosevelt's funeral, and his sister's athletic success. Once started on his sister, he is eloquent.

Ralph Davis—Glenn Davis' twin brother—is Blanchard's best friend at the Point. They bunk together on team trips. His favorite gag is to dig up a D drag—deficient blind date—for Doc. "But," Davis hastens to add, "when Doc dates a girl himself, she is usually mighty attractive."

Blanchard has no particular formula for keeping himself fit. The Point routine takes care of that. Every Cadet participates in athletics, even if only intramural soccer. The various athletic squads—with the exception of the A and B footballers, who ride buses to practice—trot over the Point's paths on the double on their way to the athletic fields. Blanchard stands no chance to grow soft or short of wind, for his athletic program is a strenuous one, involving fall football, winter indoor track, spring football practice, and late-spring outdoor track.

Any Cadet's daily schedule is so chockablock that even a pause to pass the time of day cuts things dangerously fine. A typical Blanchard day goes like this:

5:50	Reveille
6:20	Assembly to breakfast
7:00	Back to room
7:45 to noon	Classes
12:15 to 12:45	Dinner
1 to 3	Afternoon classes
3:30	Football practice
5:50 to 6:00	Finish football practice
6:15	Dinner for rest of corps
6:30	Dinner for football squad
7:00	Finish dinner
7:15	Call to quarters; study
10:30	Taps

When a Cadet invites a drag to the Point for the weekend, it means that he expects to spend most of his Saturday and Sunday waking hours with her. But in the fall Blanchard takes part in football practice or a game on Saturday afternoons, and doesn't begin to act as a squire of dames until Saturday evening, when he can take his date to the movies before escorting her to the weekend hop. The Point's dance regulations specify that a Cadet must hold the girl with whom he is dancing at a "proper distance," which means that daylight must show between partners. Once at a hop, he can't leave the dance floor until he is ready to go home. Like other Army football players, Blanchard sleeps late on Sunday morning during the season, and wakes in time to have luncheon with his drag at the Thayer-West Point Hotel, after which he can take her for a walk or sit with her in the Thayer soda bar, where a mammoth scoop of ice cream dripping with hot fudge costs fifteen cents.

At St. Stanislaus, Blanchard devoured comic books, although officially they were frowned upon. At the Point, he has shown a weakness for Western fiction, his favorite authors being Zane Grey and Max Brand. His favorite movie star is Betty Hutton, but his Hutton fixation was somewhat dissipated by the star's recent marriage.

Those who know him say of him. "Outwardly, he's not nervous before a game, but he's mighty sincere about football." He talks in his sleep on the night before a game, and yells such things as "Get him! Get him!" while slumbering. Once, on a football trip, while still asleep in a lower berth, he began to move his legs as if running through and over tacklers on a broken field. A teammate in the berth above thought the train was coming apart.

Leo Novak, the Army's track coach, believes that with Blanchard's natural timing and co-ordination, he could excel at any sport.

"Blanchard is a tremendous man, and he's fast," said Novak. "He came out for track last December. At first, he did only thirty feet with the sixteen-pound shot. A month later he was hitting forty-one feet. Then, on March third, at the ICAAAA Indoor Championships in New York, he won the shot with a heave of forty-eight feet, three and a half inches."

On Saturday, May twenty-sixth, Plebe Blanchard won the shot in the Army-Navy dual meet with a distance of fifty-one feet, ten and three quarters inches, to establish a new meet record. Novak has seen men gain two feet with the sixteen-pound shot in a season, even five feet, but he had never seen an athlete lift his distance twenty feet in six months. Despite the fact that he must have known that he was tutoring his friend to replace him as the Army's No. 1 weight man, Ralph Davis had almost as much to do with making Doc a top-flight shot putter as did Coach Novak. "Ralph put him hep to the fine points," said a Cadet who knows them both, "and Doc did everything Ralph told him to do."

"The boy is well coupled," Novak explained. "And he's good for ten flat in the hundred." While ten flat is fast, it is no longer regarded as phenomenal. It's only phenomenal when a boy weighing more than 200 pounds does it. "Where Blanchard excels as a runner is on his getaway," Novak said. "He's ahead of everybody up to 50 yards, and that fast getaway helps him when he is lugging a football. He's popular and he's not conceited. He's always wrasslin' with Ralph Davis. They're like a couple of puppies."

Leo Novak and Ralph Davis, however, make it clear that Blanchard doesn't fool around when the chips are down. "In competition, he's a different man," Novak declared. "In practice, he'll get the shot out around forty-one or forty-two feet. Then, on Saturday, when it counts, he tosses it fifty."

"In football, you have to hit him low if you want to stop him," Ralph Davis said. It is an easy trick to prove that Blanchard plows into an opposing tackler with an impact of 6,750 foot-pounds, and as if this momentum were not enough, he has a habit of turning on an extra notch of speed in the split second before he hits an opponent—a device the most rugged tackler finds sharply disconcerting. Blanchard's natural color is florid, but his face grows even redder when he's excited or angry and his lips tighten into a straight line. He really hits for keeps then.

Lawson Robertson, coach of many American Olympic teams, thinks that the secret of Blanchard's success as a shot putter lies in his legs and thighs. "The impetus that sends the shot out beyond the fifty-foot mark starts in the legs and travels upward," Robertson said. No one who has seen Blanchard in a track suit will forget his thighs. Seeing them, it was easy to believe Novak when he said, "If that boy pulled a muscle, he wouldn't even know it."

Those legs may become as famous in time as the gams of Dietrich or Grable. Scarlett O'Hara's waist measured only seventeen inches when cinched in, but Blanchard's thigh bulges the tape measure at least eight inches more than Scarlett's waist, and his calf looks as if it had been removed from the statue of David by Michelangelo. Such underpinning contributes enormously to Blanchard's muzzle velocity when he cannonades into the line, just as the sixteen-inch calf and twenty-five-inch thigh of Jumping Joe Savoldi and the eighteen-inch calf and twenty-six-inch thigh of Bronko Nagurski made those human projectiles hard to stop.

Andy Bershak, end at North Carolina in 1937, and a member of the Tar Heel coaching staff while Blanchard was a freshman, once remarked to Jim Tatum, "Jim, I know some folks would rather see a pretty girl with a lovely figure than anything else. Personally, I'd rather look at Blanchard getting dressed for a game than any pretty girl I've ever seen! What a build!"

It is Army's policy to use Blanchard as a flanker in its T formation. "When Blanchard is out on the wing," said George Munger, the University of Pennsylvania coach, whose team lost to Army last fall, 62-7, "he's not only a good ball carrier—last year he gained 556 yards for an average of seven and one-tenth yards—but he's a hot pass receiver and blocker. He puts tremendous pressure on the end and the backer up. You never know whether he'll block the end, block the back, or keep on going and catch a pass, and that uncertainty helps open up things so All-American Glenn Davis can romp through."

Like a boxer, Blanchard possesses not only speed but timing. His blocks are razor-edge timed, so that the end can't get up and make the tackle after he's been blocked. An end must play Blanchard direct, instead of keeping one eye on the ball carrier. Doc is a vicious tackler. He moves in when he makes his contact and keeps driving with his legs. When he hits a ball carrier, that carrier is usually stopped or driven back.

One coach who scouted most of the Army's games last year says of him. "He's a better-than-average punter. When he warms up before a game, his punts average better than fifty yards. Some of them sail out as far as sixty-five or seventy yards. He kicks off for the Army, and 70 per cent of his kicks go over the goal line; many of them through the goalposts. His kickoffs average fifty-six and one-tenth yards per boot. Many times after kicking off, he gets down to make the tackle himself."

On pass defense, Blanchard is a ball hawk. He's a great pass receiver and takes them on the run out in the flat—a tough angle in which to catch a pass—as well as down the field. During a game he has composure. He enjoys every minute of it. He's not flighty or fidgety. He knows how to relax.

It is inevitable that Blanchard should be compared to the game's other great full-backs. Steve Owen, coach of the pro New York Giants, said of him, "He's as good as

Blanchard is given fine blocking by his teammates as he starts a 64-yard touchdown drive in the 1946 game.

Nagurski, only he has more finesse." Oscar Hagberg, coach of the United States Naval Academy, who has reason to know, said, "He reminds me of both Savoldi and Nagurski. He's terrific."

Clark Shaughnessy's estimate of Blanchard's place among fullback greats is more dispassionate, although Shaughnessy has a sentimental interest in him. For it was Shaughnessy who was coaching at Tulane when a young buck from the bayous named Blanchard played for the Green Wave under the name of Beaullieu.

In September, 1942, Shaughnessy was in a Durham, North Carolina, hotel room when a knock came at the door. "As the door opened, I saw a man filling it," he said. "His name was Felix Blanchard. I hadn't seen him for twenty years, when I coached him at Tulane. Right behind him, sort of jutting out all around his edges, was his son. He was a second edition of his dad, who was certainly proud of him. He'd done everything he could to develop the football ability that had been born in his son. He'd be even prouder now, if he were still alive. Big Doc Blanchard used to leave some mighty fast footsteps, but just as he seemed to jut out around the edges of his father that day I saw him in the doorway, Little Doc does everything his father did, and does it a little better."

With such tributes beating down on him like a hot white light, Blanchard was on the spot this fall. If he turned in a performance of merely All-American caliber, there was tongue clucking and head wagging in the press box. But when he took up this fall where he left off last year, there was no falling off in his stellar qualities. *The New York Times* compared him to a machine powered by atomic energy and—after the Michigan game—to a "charging wild buffalo." In the Army's opener, the P.D. Command game, he kicked off twice into the end zone, and on both occasions tackled the receiver. Against Michigan, he tallied twice, once on a line buck, and again burst through the line for 68 yards. On a 70-yard run by Davis, Blanchard helped throw one of the blocks that cleared the way.

After the Michigan game, one sports writer wrote, "Army won because of two reasons. One was Felix (Doc) Blanchard. The other was Glenn Davis. If one were to eliminate them, the fray would have been a toss-up." Blanchard and Davis would be the first to put the blast on such a statement. They would point out that, after all, there was a one-man task force named DeWitt Coulter in the Army line, and that there was a bullet back named Shorty McWilliams in the Army backfield, and that a number of other formidable characters such as Pitzer and Tucker helped out manfully. But they can't brush aside the fact that between them they scored three of Army's four touchdowns in the Michigan game—one paper called them the "twin high executioners"— and gained 370 of the 380 yards the Army made by rushing.

Early in this present season there was a tendency on the part of coaches to say that this year's Army team is the best collegiate one ever gathered together, and that it would be capable of standing toe to toe with the best the pro leagues have to offer. Almost in the same breath, the same coaches make the point, "Of course you can't tell really how good the Army is because they are playing against teams denuded of their natural strength and power by the loss of key men to the armed services." The size of last year's Army scores may well have reflected that situation. Despite the fact that

162

this year its opponents have been bolstered almost weekly by returnee stars, how well such players as Davis and Blanchard will do against a prewar type of opposition will not be revealed until next year—perhaps not until the year after. However, when Blanchard was acclaimed the greatest star St. Stanislaus ever had, and the finest full-back ever to enter North Carolina, the teams on which he played had no special advantages over the ones they met. And when he starred against Navy last year he was not playing against a team weakened by enlistments or inductions.

The official attendance at last year's Army-Navy game was 66,639. Unofficially, it was 66,640. Somewhere in the crowd was a huge block of a man with thinning hair and a soft Louisiana accent. Despite his bulk, he took up no room, for he wasn't there in the flesh. He had died seven months before. But a little thing like death wouldn't have kept Felix Anthony Blanchard away from the Baltimore Municipal Stadium, where his son was meeting his sternest test.

At least twice during each season while Little Doc played for St. Stanislaus, Big Doc made the trip from Lee County, all the way from Bay City, Mississippi, to see his son run with the ball. When Little Doc moved on to the University of North Carolina as a college freshman, Big Doc followed the Tar Babies even more faithfully. It is only natural, therefore, to suppose that he was among those present at the Baltimore Stadium last year when the Army and the Navy decided the 1944 national football championship.

In the third quarter Little Doc covered nine yards for the score that blew the game open. When he took the ball, veered slightly, and burst through the left side of the Navy line, the score stood Army 9, Navy 7. When he crossed the goal line carrying three frantic Navy hitchhikers with him, the game was Army's.

Before Little Doc reached that 9-yard line, Army Back Glenn Davis had intercepted a Navy pass and had downed it on the Army's 48-yard line. A Baltimore paper described the Army's march from that point: "Blanchard raced around Navy's right end to the Navy 32 . . . Blanchard hit left tackle for three . . . Davis added three at right end. . . . Blanchard hit the middle for a first down on the Navy 21 . . . Minor gained a yard at left guard . . . Blanchard bullied his own hole at right tackle to gain a first down on the Navy 9. . . . Blanchard ripped through the middle for Army's second touchdown. . . . Score: Army 15, Navy 7." Thereafter Doc and Glenn Davis brought the ball down the field for another score.

This year's Army-Navy game will be played on Saturday in Philadelphia's Municipal Stadium. Last year, the Blanchard clan was represented, for both mother and sister came North to see him play, and his cousin, Ed Tatum, Jim Tatum's brother, made the journey, too. Unless something unforeseen happens, they'll be in Philadelphia this December. And once more the official attendance figures will differ from the unofficial by one, for an invisible giant of a man who once put a football in his son's crib for luck will be on hand.

Last year after the game, Little Doc said to Ed Tatum, "He was there, Ed. I could feel him patting me on the back after each play and saying, 'Hit like your daddy did, son.'"

Pete Dawkins, captain of the Army football team, president of his class, Rhodes scholar, winner of the Heisman Trophy and the Maxwell Award, tells Harold M. Martin of the Saturday Evening Post about his football days at West Point. This is Pete's story, taken from the Post article of 1959.

My Life at West Point

PETE DAWKINS, *as told to* HAROLD M. MARTIN

My FOOTBALL COACH AT CRANBROOK, FRED CAMPBELL, KEPT URGING ME to apply for an appointment. He was an ex-Marine and seemed to think I'd fit in all right with the military life. He also knew how I loved football, and he thought I'd do all right as a football player at West Point. He wrote Col. Earl Blaik, the Army coach, and told him about my being a pretty good split-T quarterback who could pass left-handed and run pretty well. He even sent a picture of me. But Blaik wasn't bowled over, and I don't blame him, if it was the picture I remember. My 170 pounds, skimpily distributed over a gangly frame, wasn't an impressive sight. So Blaik wrote back that he thought I had better take another year of seasoning before I tried to come up there. I would be only seventeen years old when I got there, and he felt I needed a little more age and beef on me.

I think that's what made me determined to go to West Point. By the time I finally got an alternate appointment and took the exams, I was convinced that West Point would be the only school where I'd be satisfied. Late in June I got a telegram saying I had been accepted, and ordering me to report the first week in July. I threw the telegram up in the air and whooped.

Fred Campbell drove me up. We got there a day ahead of time, so I could register early and have the rest of the day to look over the place and get oriented. I got oriented all right. Like everybody else, I had a civilian slouch and an easygoing attitude. These faults are what West Point corrects first. Every time I looked up, some first classman had his nose up against mine, yelling at me to "brace"—to pull my chin in and pop my chest up and suck my gut in, and to wipe that silly smirk off my face.

Reporting for plebe football practice didn't do much to exalt my bruised ego. The plebe squad had more quarterbacks than we had players on the Cranbrook team, and that was discouraging. But I gave it all I had and got into nearly all the plebe games as the starting quarterback. I was pretty sad, though. My passes looked more like punts, end-over-end instead of spiraling. I also had trouble on defense, figuring out what the other team was going to do. I seemed to have an amazing consistency—I analyzed every play wrong! If I played back for a pass, they went into the line. If I played up close, they passed over my head. We had a good plebe team, though, and they made up for most of my errors. We lost one, tied one, and won the rest that year.

Spring football was worse. I was still playing quarterback and doing very poorly, and I ended up down in the deep depths of the scrubs. But a plebe gets a great lift from June Week. He loses his ignominious status then, and is "recognized" by the upperclassmen. So I got motivated again. I did a lot of practice on my passing during my month's leave at home, and in the two months of yearling training at Camp Buckner I fell in with a lot of fellows who liked to lift weights and do pushups and keep fit in general. We didn't have any weights, so we used big rocks, and I really felt good.

Maybe this is as good a place as any to explain why I'm sort of a nut about lifting weights. When I was eleven years old, I came down with high fever and headache; but it was at harvest time, and nobody could pay much attention to me. When the fever stayed high, though, the doctor gave me a shot of penicillin, and pretty soon I was all right.

The next year, though, my right arm and leg began to get weak, and I started carrying my head to one side and forward a little bit. My father noticed it first. We'd go out in the afternoons to a vacant lot so I could practice jump passing, throwing a football through a tire hanging from a tree, and he noticed my right arm didn't seem to have much strength. I was naturally a left-handed passer, but was trying to learn how to pass with either hand. So he took me to the hospital and they made a lot of tests, and the decision was that I had had a light attack of polio. My spine was beginning to curve, and my right arm and leg were weak.

There was a lot of talk about putting me in a brace, which upset me, for I knew I couldn't play football in a brace. Finally, however, it was decided not to put me in a brace, but to treat me at the Sister Kenny Clinic in Detroit. A wonderful lady doctor there named Dr. Calhoun gave me the treatments, and taught my father how to lay

Coach Earl Blaik talks over strategy with Army football captain, Pete Dawkins, before the annual clash with Navy in 1958.

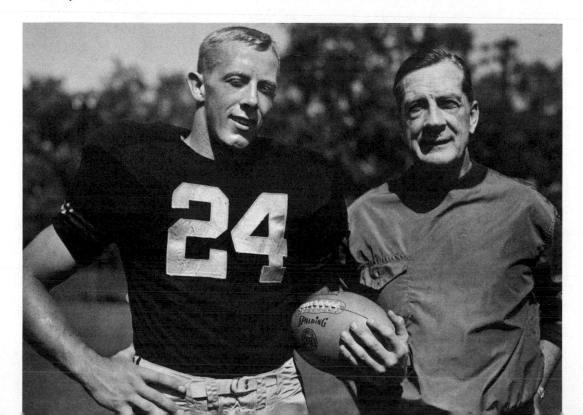

Pete Dawkins was named winner of the Heisman Trophy as the outstanding college football player of 1958.

me out on a table and exercise me by pushing on my legs and arms to stretch my muscles. She also encouraged me to use barbells to develop the weakened muscles, and I have worked with them ever since, even after I came to West Point. It is against regulations here to have weights in your room, but I sneaked some in anyway and used them at night after taps. Then I'd tape the bar to my bed rail and hide the flat weights under the mattress. I slept on that lumpy iron a year before an inspecting officer caught me. This year I'm allowed to keep them in my room—out of sight.

I came back for early football my yearling year in pretty good shape from lifting all those rocks during the summer. I figured I'd show those people who was going to play quarterback for Army the next three years. I showed them, all right; I showed them I couldn't block and I couldn't tackle. As a split-T quarterback I'd never had to do any blocking, and I just couldn't get the hang of it. Naturally, I ended up far down in the list of scrubs. I found out later that Coach Earl Blaik was thinking of dropping me off the squad, for an Army quarterback has to be a good blocker. Late one afternoon, though, the scrubs were doing a little head knocking and I was lucky enough to get off a couple of good long punt returns. The next day I wasn't a quarterback any more. I was a halfback.

I knew I'd have to concentrate on my blocking, which I did all through yearling year. I never quite came up to par, and I didn't get to play much. The highlights of the year for me came in the last minutes of the Michigan game when the score was about 48 to 7 against us. Michigan must have had the cheerleaders and the water boy in there by that time, for I managed to get away for a touchdown.

166

That encouraged me, and a year of hockey, at which I managed to do quite well, lifted my spirits still more. This new confidence reflected itself in spring football practice. By the end of it I was playing second-string halfback, along with Bob Anderson, who to my mind is one of the greatest backs West Point ever produced.

That year—1957—is not one I treasure in my memory. We lost the two big ones, Notre Dame and Navy, and my contribution to the Navy game is something I don't look back on with pride. I had a great deal of difficulty deciding which way to run. Three times I ran smack into Andy going in the opposite direction right behind the center, just about killing him. I did more damage that day than the Navy tacklers. The score was 14-0, Navy, and that was a long, miserable ride home on the train. And I can honestly say that nobody was more surprised than I when we took the vote for the next year's captain, and the team elected me. I figured after my performance that afternoon they'd do anything but choose me. But when they gave me the job, I resolved that next year things were going to be different.

Of course, there were a lot of tough people we had to beat before we got to Navy. And we were trying something new—the lonely end. Coach Blaik put Bill Carpenter out there by himself, about 15 to 20 yards from the center of the line. Bill was big and fast, and a good pass catcher, which made him a constant threat. At first Carpenter would huddle with us, then run out to his post, but after half a dozen plays he was pooped. So we devised a set of signals. He'd watch Quarterback Joe Caldwell's feet as we went into the huddle, to know whether it was a run or a pass. Then as we lined up I'd flash him the signal which way the play was going.

The first big test was the Notre Dame game. We were still sore about losing 23-21 the year before, so we were really going at it all afternoon. I've never been hit so hard and so continually in my life, and I think the Notre Dame fellows felt the same way. When I came off the field I was really beat—but happy. We won, 14-2. So one old score was settled.

The Pittsburgh game is one I'd like to forget. We were leading, 14-0, just before the end of the half, as I remember it, when Pitt got a drive going that looked as if it were going all the way. I'd been riding the bench with a charley horse, but it wasn't bothering me too much. So I figured that if I could go in there, fresh and rested, I might be able to stop this drive. I asked the colonel to let me go in, and he hesitated a moment; but I told him I was feeling good, so he waved me in. So there went old Dawkins, racing to the rescue! It was a miserable day, rainy and cold, and all the players were brown with mud, from cleats to helmet. Except me, in my fresh, clean uniform.

The Pittsburgh quarterback took one look at me and sent an end straight down the field. He didn't fake to the right. He didn't fake to the left. He came right at me, and I fell in step beside him, and he ran right off and left me, and over my head came this beautiful rippling pass, right into his arms for a touchdown.

I was so mad I couldn't speak for three days afterward. I think Pitt had a psychological block up to that point. They didn't really believe they could score on us, and this touchdown broke that mental block. They went on to tie us, 14-14.

So we came up to the Navy game with only that Pittsburgh tie to mar our record.

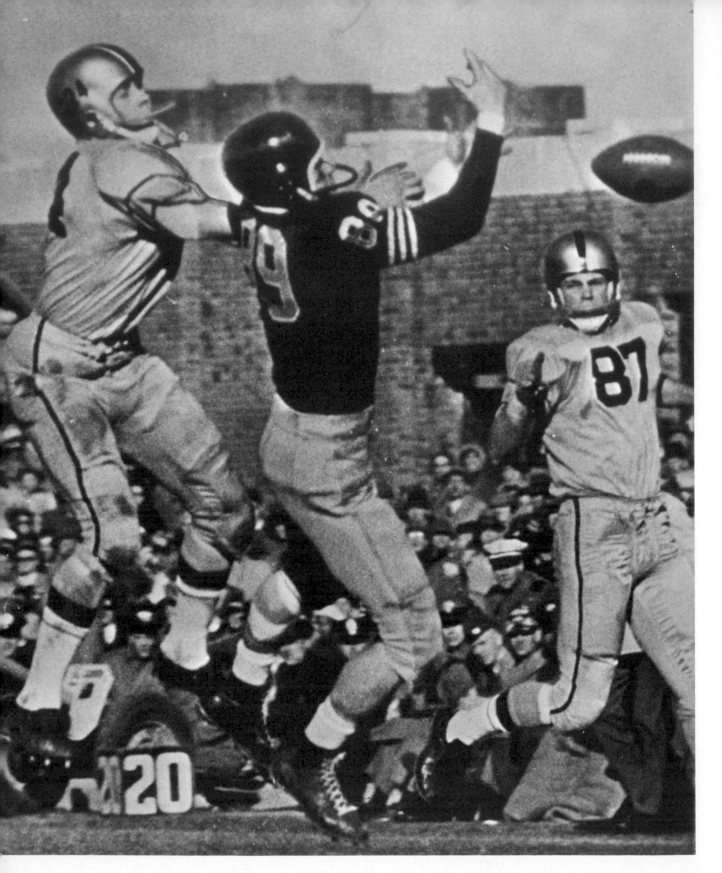

Army's Pete Dawkins breaks up a pass play to Navy's George Bezek (89) as Bill Carpenter (87) closes in to help in the second quarter of the 1958 service battle.

We had to beat Navy, though, or the year wouldn't be a success. Everything about the Navy game is important. The old graduates in the stands judge the whole corps by the way the cadets march when they come on the field between halves. If one man is bouncing in ranks, they feel that the place has gone to pot since their day. The big thing, though, is winning the ball game. Lose it, and a pall of gloom settles over Army installations around the world.

On the kickoff, because of a masterful play by me, it looked as if our chances were nil. I remember waiting for the whistle, just praying that they'd kick it to me, for if they did, I was going all the way. Well, there it came, right down to the goal line, and off I went, the happiest guy on the field. The blocking was good and I was beginning to move and things were opening up over toward the left—at least I sensed daylight over that way. So I cut to the left, with a Navy tackler bearing down on me from the right front, and Bill Rowe, our center, cut across to nail him. My elbow bumped Bill, and the ball squirted up in the air, and the whole Navy team fell on it.

But we still had a football game to play, so I called a quick huddle and said that we were in a hole, and it was my fault, but we could hold these people and beat them. And we held and we did beat them, 22-6. I didn't score, but it was the happiest day I ever knew, I guess—a fitting end to a wonderful season, and I had almost a feeling of reverence for having had the privilege of associating with such a group as that Army team.

Looking back to the football season and all my experiences in athletics, I realize how much they have done for me. I have been blessed with the physical ability to participate in athletics, and I'm grateful for that. I'm grateful, too, for the opportunity to enjoy a sense of teamwork, and sacrifice to an ideal, and the self-confidence a man gains from participation in sports.

I may have talked too much about football, but I recognize that all the publicity and the recognition that followed—about what I was doing at West Point—stemmed from the fact that I played football. A man could make first captain and stand high in his class academically for four years, and be class president and everything else, but it wouldn't attract attention outside of West Point if he weren't a football player. So, wherever I've gone, to dinners and banquets, I've tried to point out that there's a whole lot more to Cadet life than football.

I'm proud of being football captain, and grateful to those people who thought I was good enough to be rated All American. But I'm equally as proud of a lot of other things that West Point has done for me.

General MacArthur spoke for every Cadet, I think, when he wrote an open letter to the corps a dozen years ago. He spoke of the day he first joined The Long Gray Line, of the years of war that followed, and "the dreams that vanished with the passing years.

"But through the grime and murk of it all," he added, "the pride and thrill of being a West Pointer has never dimmed . . . I can still say that is my greatest honor."

I emphatically agree.

Here is a story about Bill Carpenter, the phenomenal "Lonely End" of Army's 1958 and 1959 elevens. As this story written in 1958 indicates, he wasn't always so lonely.

The "Lonely End"

ASSOCIATED PRESS

ABOUT THE LEAST LONELY MAN IN FOOTBALL IS ARMY'S FABLED "LONELY End," Bill Carpenter.

"Before this, nobody knew I was around," Carpenter said today while preparing for Saturday's game with Virginia. "Now I'm a marked man. I have to take a lot of ribbing. And I've started getting letters from strange people."

Carpenter, a towering 205-pounder from Springfield, Pennsylvania, is the key man in Coach Earl Blaik's new offensive which captured the imagination of the country.

He lines up 18 to 25 yards wide of the rest of his team, and just parks there as a pass-receiving threat and decoy. He never even goes into the huddle.

To the rival football coach, he poses a menace. But to his classmates and outsiders he is fair game for some friendly jibes.

At the Military Academy, the cadets have nicknamed Carpenter, "Lonesome George."

"What's the matter, Lonesome George," they'll say, "won't your best friends tell you?"

Jests follow him on and off the field, Carpenter said, and they've even started coming through the mail. He must be the No. 1 pinup boy of the Lonely Hearts Clubs. His fan mail is the heaviest on the team.

"Last week I got several letters from South Bend," he said. "They said I wouldn't be lonesome there; that there would be plenty of Fighting Irish to keep me company.

"I thought all this might subside after a while, but it seems to be getting worse."

Carpenter said he was constantly being asked what he thinks about while out in the flats. Does he dream about the evening date? Does he gaze at the spectators in the grandstand?

"The odd thing," Bill said, "is that with this formation I have to concentrate more than I ever did before. Because I don't get in the huddle, I must concentrate on the signals. I can't make a mistake.

"And it's tougher to catch a pass, too. They know I'm out there and they're always covering me. Lonesome? Heck, I never have time to get lonesome. The name is a big mistake."

Bill Carpenter, the "lonely end," was a constant threat to opponents.

Army's Carl Stichweh breaks loose for a 19-yard gain in the first quarter of the 1964 Army-Navy game. Army defeated Navy, 11-8, for its first victory over the Middies since 1958.

He scored two touchdowns for Army, ran for a two-point conversion after touchdown, almost upsetting Navy all on his own, in 1963. In 1964, he quarterbacked the West Point eleven to a brilliant 11-8 victory over the Midshipmen. This was a great quarterback, one of the greatest of all time, Carl (Rollie) Stichweh, and this is Gene Ward's story from his column in the New York Daily News.

Stichweh, One of Army's Best

GENE WARD

IN MODERN PROFESSIONAL FOOTBALL IT IS AXIOMATIC THAT REAL GREATness in a team is achieved only when there is a great quarterback at the helm, as witness the old Bears with Sid Luckman and the Browns with Otto Graham. The same holds true in modern college football, which is why there's more pre-season optimism on the plains of West Point than at any time since the era of Arnold Tucker, Doc Blanchard, and Glenn Davis.

Army is loaded with talent, and it has its great quarterback—Carl (Rollie) Stichweh.

He is, in fact, a most gifted and versatile athlete, who, two seasons ago, was playing left cornerback on the Chinese Bandits, which is Coach Paul Dietzel's all-defensive platoon.

The twenty-year-old from Williston Park, Long Island, out of Mineola High School, wasn't discovered by Dietzel or anybody else. He discovered himself. He is the first Cadet football player in the long and colorful gridiron history of the Academy ever to volunteer for a special assignment. He asked to play quarterback.

It was a Sunday, and Dietzel's first Army team, fresh from a 34-14 clobbering by Navy, had made a bus stop for lunch en route back to West Point. Stichweh approached the coach.

"Both our quarterbacks [Dick Eckert and Joe Blackgrove] are graduating, Coach," he said, "and I'd like to apply for the job."

It is Dietzel's contention that Stichweh "came of age as a quarterback" in those boiling moments when he fought the clock and the crowd noise, trying in vain for the winning points in last year's Navy game. But it is more than likely he came of age that Sunday when he volunteered for the assignment, because that took courage and confidence, particularly on the part of a sophomore defensive back.

Stichweh was the best football player in Philadelphia's Municipal Stadium at last year's squeaker defeat by Navy. Better than the touted Middie, Roger Staubach; better than anybody. He scored both Army touchdowns, was the ball-carrier on the two-point conversion play, and retrieved the onside kick which touched off the final drive.

Navy players voted him the best back they had played against all year.

Army had a good season last year, losing only to Minnesota and Pitt up to the Navy game. But for Stichweh it had been a great season, considering it was his first at quarterback. His over-all statistics showed him as the leading ground-gainer on 131 carries for 622 yards, or 4.1 average, while completing 46 of 94 passes for 454 yards.

Seldom does one hear a coach talk about a player as Dietzel does about Stichweh.

"He's our finest offensive man," Dietzel said, "and also our finest defensive player. In spring training he showed complete and utter confidence. He threw the ball with real authority and ran like a deer. But most important of all, his confidence infected our whole squad."

A boy with superb physical equipment—an even six feet and 186 pounds—he is a born leader with a talent for instant decision. While many of his upperclassmates were off in Europe as "third lieutenants" over this summer, Stichweh was assigned to Camp Buckner on the military reservation.

As an instructor of third classmen in field problems, he lived outdoors with the trainees. When the courses had been completed, Stichweh received the top honor of the rugged session—the award as the outstanding platoon leader at Buckner.

His tremendous athletic ability is hidden from the casual observer by his shyness and politeness and by the fact that, out of football gear, he appears much smaller.

Dietzel has a hunch Stichweh is the best athlete at West Point, and statistics bear him out. For instance, he twice has led his class in physical aptitude, a series of exercises and events designed to test the individual physical caliber of the Cadet.

There's rope-climbing, pullups, pushups, shuttle run, hop-skip-and-jump, etc. It's all a breeze for Stichweh. A week after he had quarterbacked the Regulars to a 14-6 victory over the Chinese Bandits-Go Team combination, the game which terminates spring practice, he won the broad jump in dual meet competition against Penn State.

Tates Locke, the basketball coach, says Stichweh would be a regular on his club if the conflict of football didn't prevent him from turning out for the hoop sport. He's also a tremendous lacrosse player. And he fools around with handball and squash, too, and holds his own with West Point's best players.

This could be one of the great Army football teams. It has the material and it has the testing schedule to bring out the best in that material—BC, Texas, Penn State, Virginia, Duke, Syracuse, Pitt, and Navy.

Most of all it has Carl (Rollie) Stichweh.

Townsend Clarke, Army's football captain in 1966, talks to a sportswriter about "playing the last game of varsity football." Frank Dolson of The Philadelphia Inquirer was the sportswriter.

The Last Game: Sweet, Yet Sad

FRANK DOLSON

THE BYWORD OF ALL WEST POINTERS IN VIETNAM IS "BEAT NAVY," BEST OF LUCK.

[SIGNED] GENERAL W. C. WESTMORELAND AND THE LONG GRAY LINE IN VIETNAM

Townsend Clarke, Army's football captain, received the above telegram before Saturday's game. He read it to his teammates—"in an informal way," he said—and put it in his locker room for safekeeping.

Some day, not too far away, Clarke expects to be in Vietnam leading an infantry company. "Everybody's going to the Far East, sir, in time," the young captain said quietly in the Army locker room at Kennedy Stadium. "I'm partial toward the infantry. I like rugged-type leadership."

Clarke had just provided the most rugged-type leadership imaginable in Army's 20-7 victory over Navy. But that was a football game, not a shooting war. It was important to these boys, very important, but it wasn't life and death.

"All the football players at West Point, they get carried away with football," Clarke said. "But they know it's a game."

The kind of game it is, the kind of emotions it arouses made Saturday a day the Army seniors had been eagerly awaiting, yet frankly dreading. There's something sad about playing the last game of varsity football. Nothing will quite ever be the same any more.

"You learn a lot of lessons in football," Clarke said. "You can apply them to lots of things. You get out there and lead ten, eleven football players, you can go out and lead an infantry company,"—the football captain hesitated a moment; then, a trace of a smile on his lips, he added—"Although there are complications leading an infantry company."

Leading this football team hadn't been easy, either. Paul Dietzel's sudden depar-

Quarterback Carl Stichweh tumbles head over heels through Navy defenders Ed Orr (33) and John Sai (48) for a touchdown in the 1963 game. Navy won, 21-15.

175

Army captain Townsend Clarke capped a three-year varsity career by blocking Navy's field goal attempt in the third quarter of the 1966 game with the score tied at 7-7. In the fourth period, Army battered Navy for two touchdowns and a 20-7 victory.

ture, just before spring practice, could have been disastrous if not for Clarke and his classmates.

"The seniors kind of carried us through," said Chuck Jarvis, who was recruited by Dietzel, but wound up playing for Tom Cahill. "Townsend Clarke is a real leader."

"We really felt lost, sir, really lost," said Clarke, thinking back to the dismal days when Dietzel had gone. Clarke filled the gap between the old coach and the new. Tom Cahill took it from there.

The contrast between coaches was marked. Dietzel was the personality-plus type who got more publicity than his players. Cahill ran the show firmly but quietly. Once Cahill got the job, Clarke said he had to fight for his. "Coach Cahill's staff, they let you know in no uncertain terms if we weren't doing our job. And the captain was no special person, either. I was playing on the second team for a while," smiled Clarke.

Today there isn't a college coach in the country who wouldn't play a man with the ability of Townsend Clarke. A standout throughout three varsity seasons, Clarke capped his college football career by making the pivotal play. Storming in from his linebacker's spot, he drove in and blocked a Navy field goal try on the last play of the third period. Four plays later, Army scored the go-ahead touchdown, ending the possibility of a second straight 7-7 tie with the Navy.

"I thought it would be another tie when I came in at halftime," said Clarke, labeled by Army coaches as the "finest linebacker seen at Army in the past ten years." "Then I just knew our guys would not settle for another tie. For a while, I got pretty discouraged, particularly when Navy started sending two men down with me on every play. I guess the fault was mine, I just wasn't getting downfield fast enough."

Too bad the fun and the games had to end.

4
NAVY STARS

One of Navy's all-time stars, Percy North-croft, was captain of the 1908 Middie squad.

Percy Northcroft booted the ball from the 43-yard line and Navy beat Army, 10-0. This was back in 1906, and Percy Northcroft made the Midshipmen's Hall of Fame with that field goal which brought Navy its first victory over Army in five long years. There's a story behind that long boot. It didn't come "easy." Nothing ever comes "easy" at Annapolis, as Sam Crane wrote for the Baltimore News American in those "good old days."

The Navy Captain

SAM CRANE

CAPTAIN OF THE NAVY FOOTBALL TEAM.

That is a title and an honor that many of the ambitious embryo admirals now going through their studies at the Annapolis Naval Academy would almost agree to forfeit all their high hopes of future promotion to secure.

To captain the Navy football team is considered the highest of athletic honors that can be earned at Annapolis. And, mind you, it has to be earned, too. There are no inside politics that secure that position at Annapolis, as has frequently been charged at some of our big universities. There are no secret societies to pull wires at either West Point or Annapolis.

Uncle Sam is the strictest of martinets where the future defenders of the country are concerned, and while he exerts a most fatherly and controlling interest over his wards, he exacts an honest, honorable, and manly return for his care.

And the return is accorded tenfold. What more brave, manly, and honorable lot of youths and young men can be found in the whole wide world than those who graduate from Annapolis and West Point? They cannot help but be manly men at everything they undertake. The service demands it, and the very atmosphere of the two academies brings out all that is best in a young man. If it does possibly fail, then good day and good-bye to the waverer.

In athletics at West Point and Annapolis the same spirit is shown. No unfair advantage is taken of an opponent and none of an individual who takes up athletics. The loyalty of college students to their alma maters is proverbial, but no undergraduate in any of our colleges was ever more loyal to his own than are the sailor and soldier boys of our naval and military academies.

The success of their football teams in strenuous struggles on the white-barred gridiron is the very life of the plucky youths who fight to the death for glorious victory; in either defeat or victory their flags are hauled to the mast. "Don't give up the ship" is the watchword—the slogan.

The annual football game between the Army and Navy has made that sport the most prominent and popular of any at both Annapolis and West Point; consequently, the captaincy of the eleven is the position most earnestly desired above all others.

The captain this year of the Navy football team is Cadet Northcroft, the famous left tackle of the eleven. Northcroft earned the captaincy, not alone by his ability as a player, but by his many other good qualities, mental as well as physical, that go to make a model cadet. He was elected to the position by his fellow players, and allow me to whisper that when that election took place the right man was chosen. No one can tell the characteristics of a man as well as his associates, particularly so when they are all young men.

Captain Northcroft is a model athlete. He stands six feet two inches in his stocking feet and is built in proportion. He is as strong as a bull, and is fast on his feet as well. Moreover, he knows the game thoroughly and is into every play. In fact, he is a born leader. His recent feat of kicking a goal from the field from the 45-yard line was a wonderful performance and a record for the Navy, if not for football. Christy Mathewson, the Giant's famous pitcher, is credited, I believe, with kicking a goal from the field from the 50-yard line when he was fullback for Bucknell, some ten or a dozen years ago, but Matty himself says he does not know the exact distance.

But there is a touch of real sentiment surrounding Captain Northcroft's entrance to the Naval Academy at Annapolis.

Young Northcroft's father is Wilfred North, the well-known actor, and there is no prouder father in the broad land than he today.

"I want my boy to be classy," was the remark Wilfred North invariably made to his friends when talking about "his boy." He could think of nothing "classier" than a naval officer—a graduate of Annapolis—and so the boy, after many complications, finally secured his appointment as a Naval Cadet. Wilfred North was the most pleased man in the country when "his boy" passed his examination and became a full-fledged Uncle Sam's boy. He had accomplished the object of his life, and sat back satisfied and complacent that "his boy" would make good. It mattered not that he had spent almost his last hard-earned dollar to furnish "his boy" tutors and teachers to prepare for the examination. "His boy" was to be "classy" and fixed for life. As for himself, he could struggle along as he always had, with his ups and downs.

But one day the proud and contented parent received a blow that "almost killed father." He received word from "his boy" that he had been suspended for one year for being behind in his studies. Possibly the youngster had paid too much attention to athletics and had neglected his routine duties. Anyway, the boy was turned back to the doting father. It was a sad day for both. But did either give up? Not on your life.

Wilfred North was game to the core, and his son was a chip off the old block. They got together and consulted as father and son should. It was decided that a new start should be made and that a year's study would put the youngster back on his feet again and in good standing at Annapolis.

And both father and son worked as a unit. Business was bad for Wilfred North just at that time, but by stinting himself to the limit, saving every cent, and often being obliged to live on the proverbial crust for days, the loving parent managed somehow or other to pay for more tutors for "his boy," so that at the end of the year's suspension young Northcroft went back to Annapolis and was reinstated with flying colors.

During the time of suspension, young Northcroft was in the daily habit of going up to Van Cortlandt Park and playing golf with pitchers Chesbro and Clarkson, of the Yankee ball team. It developed at that time that Northcroft was a pitcher of rare excellence and promise, and both Chesbro and Clarkson endeavored to induce the youngster to take up professional baseball, but he refused absolutely.

He said, "I owe it to my father to go back to Annapolis, and I am going to do so. He wants me to be classy, as he says, and I am going to show him that I can be." And he did.

Captain Northcroft, of the Navy football team, is the answer.

Does Wilfred North bewail the scrimping and stinting he has done to make a "classy" man of his dutiful and noble son, "his boy"?

I opine not.

Navy football history is replete with the names of illustrious sons who were standout performers on the gridiron. But no Navy footballer has ever been mentioned in the same breath as the immortal Jim Thorpe—that is, no one except the captain and star of the 1911 Navy team, All-American Jack "Dolly" Dalton. Dalton starred for the Navy in 1908, 1909, 1910, 1911. In the 1910 game against Army, with the score 0-0 in the fourth quarter, "Dolly" Dalton calmly kicked a 40-yard three-pointer to garner Navy's first victory over Army in four years. Once again, in 1911, Dalton booted one from the 30-yard line for the second 3-0 victory over Army. That year Dalton scored 14 touchdowns for Navy, was selected for Walter Camp's All-American team, and was captain of the track squad. Lt. Comdr. John Dalton died during World War I, after a sudden bronchial ailment. He was only twenty-nine.

Dalton Owed It All to Soccer

ANONYMOUS

It is a common occurrence that athletes who are proficient at college football enter and succeed in the soccer ranks. It is a very rare occasion where a proficient soccer player enters the college ranks. In the latter instance a most shining example is that of John P. Dalton, the star captain and halfback of the United States Naval Academy. He has developed into one of the greatest players the school has ever presented and his punting has been for the last three seasons a revelation to eastern circles.

Dalton received his preparatory schooling in St. Louis, Missouri, and was a student at the Christian Brothers College at the time of his appointment to the Navy. He was the leader in athletics at school and for three seasons was the star fullback on the soccer team. He passed his examination to the Naval Academy and gained the honor of becoming a regular on the Navy eleven, the first year at the Annapolis school.

When asked to what he attributed his success on the football field, Dalton is not the least backward in stating, as he has on numerous furloughs to St. Louis, that the early training he received in soccer has developed his kicking power, which has placed him among the leaders as a punter on the gridiron. This season he has the distinction of being captain of his team, and, as usual, is playing the same dashing and aggressive game which promises to place him on the All-American team—the goal to which every college football player aspires.

Jack Dalton, known to his mates at Christian Brothers Academy as "Dolly" Dalton, was perhaps the greatest athlete ever developed at the St. Louis School. During its heydey, Christian Brothers Academy was one of the leading schools in the Middle

West. The CBC, as it was popularly called in the early 1900s, won several National Championships in soccer, and it was natural that "Dolly" Dalton would turn out to be the finest soccer player in CBC history, hence his extreme skill in long-distance and accurate kicking.

Dalton attended CBC from 1905-08, and prior to leaving for his entrance into the Naval Academy, he set records in track and field as well as soccer and was one of the leading math students at the school. At CBC, Dalton was an active member of the school literary society and regularly appeared in plays staged at the downtown theatre.

In Middie football circles, Dalton is favorably thought of as the finest all-round football player in Navy history.

Jack Dalton, better known as "Three-to-Nothing" Dalton. His field goals gave the Middies 3 to 0 victories over Army in 1910 and 1911.

182

Navy hadn't won a game from Army in thirteen years and something drastic had to be done. So big "Babe" Brown, Navy's Director of Athletics, brought in an entire, new football coaching staff. One of Navys all-time stars, Tom Hamilton, became the new head coach. The result—a Navy win over Army, 3-0, in 1934. But the man behind the scenes was Brown. He had served his alma mater well, as he had so often done in the past.

The Man Behind the Drive—Babe Brown

GENE SCHOOR

THE NAVAL ACADEMY FIGURED THAT THIS HAD TO BE THE YEAR OF DESTINY, or maybe never. After all, the Middies had not won an Army game for thirteen big, long years. If a team that had such standout performers as Buzz Borries, Bill Clark, Slade Cutter, Capt. Dick Burns, Lou Robertshaw, Bob Dornin, and Jim Mini couldn't whip Army, the Navy's football future would have been two shades darker than indigo.

The man and the inspiration behind this great Navy team was the Middies ebullient director of athletics, one of the all-time football greats, John "Babe" Brown.

In the 1912 Army-Navy game the teams were locked in a scoreless tie, and a capacity crowd had cheered themselves hoarse, begging the Army or the Navy to score the decisive points.

There was but five minutes to play, when Brown and his teammate K. P. Gilchrist came up with a pretty bit of strategy. They worked the ball to Army's 30-yard line, and then Brown lined up for the kick. Gilchrist knelt to hold the ball, but lo and behold, to the amazement of the Army, Brown took a direct pass from his center Homer Ingram, and before Army could recover he was past the Army line—and on his way to a touchdown. He was on the 8-yard Army line before he was tackled. On the next play there was no fake. Brown calmly kicked the ball over for three points and Navy was out in front. There was but two minutes left, when Navy again tried a goal. Once again Brown kicked, and Navy within five minutes had six points by Brown and a 6-0 victory.

In the 1913 contest with Navy, Brown once again demonstrated his uncanny accuracy as he kicked Navy into a 9-9 tie at half time with a display of kicking accuracy that left the tremendous crowd limp with excitement. Babe booted field goals of 19 yards, 25 yards, and the last one from 29 yards out for a total of nine points.

But a fighting Army team desperately mixing a savage running game with a new

Left: John "Babe" Brown was the hero of the 1912 Army-Navy game as he booted two field goals in the last five minutes of play to defeat Army, 6-0.   Right: Brown, a vice admiral, was also superintendent of the Naval Academy.

forward-passing combination, Prichard to Merillat, scored two touchdowns in the second half, to win the annual battle, 22-9.

That year Babe Brown was named to the All-American football team. He also added to his laurels by winning letters in track and as a member of the Navy crew.

Graduating from the Academy, Babe Brown went on to greater fame and glory in the service of his country, as a leader of a submarine squadron during World Wars I and II, and he rose to the rank of vice admiral. Just prior to the outbreak of World War II, Brown served as Superintendent of the Naval Academy.

The number of Navy greats are legend. Who were the greatest of them all? George Trevor, of the old New York Sun, took a crack at naming the All-Time Navy Football Eleven in 1932. You may disagree with him, you may have your own favorite back, end, or tackle, but Trevor puts up a good argument for his men. It's a Navy squad that would be hard to beat.

Navy's All-Time Eleven

GEORGE TREVOR

FIRST TEAM			SECOND TEAM	
Magruder Tuttle	1931	Center	Frank Slingluff	1908
John Brown	1913	Guard	Art Carney	1923
John Halligan	1897	Guard	Charles Belknap	1902
Percy Northcroft	1908	Tackle	Frank Wickhorst	1926
Clyde King	1921	Tackle	Tom Eddy	1926
William Dague	1907	End	Walter Izard	1894
Wendell Taylor	1922	End	K. P. Gilchrist	1913
William Ingram	1918	Quarterback	John Whelchel	1919
Archie Douglas	1907	Back	Steve Barchet	1923
Fred Borries	1934	Back	Worth Bagley	1894
John Dalton	1911	Back	Jonas Ingram	1906

Palm trees nodding their plumelike fronds in the lazy tropics; Cuba's silver-black coast range etched in bold relief against a pearl horizon; a slim torpedo boat gliding stealthily shoreward; a gob whistling "There'll be a Hot Time in the Old Town Tonight"; a stalwart officer fearlessly exposed on the cambered deck; the hollow cough of a concealed battery off Cárdenas; the whir of a shell in flight; a rending of steel by high explosives; a widening patch of crimson on the commander's blue tunic; blurred words forced through pain-compressed lips—"Open fire, boys, they've got me."

Ens. Worth Bagley, the first and only American naval officer to be killed in the war with Spain, had met death unflinchingly while commanding the torpedo boat, *Winslow*, in a reconnaissance off Cárdenas. The same Worth Bagley, who only a few years before had matched 60-yard punts with George Brooks, Pennsylvania's human catapult. Old-timers never tire of recalling that Homeric kicking duel between Bagley and Brooks. Worth Bagley was the Dalton of the nineties. An oarsman and track athlete, Bagley found the rugged contact of football more congenial to his temperament. He was a bearcat in action, resolute in backing up a line, fearless in crashing through. And how he could boot that ball! It was Bagley's goal after touchdown that decided the 1893 Army game in Navy's favor, 6 to 5.

Bagley's name is coupled in Navy's football log with that of "Snake" Izard, joint hero of the '93 victory. Gray-bearded admirals will recall the then-current song:

> Rushing like a mighty blizzard
> Through the line went little Izard
> And when Bagley kicked the goal
> Terror seized on Army's soul.

While hardly worthy of a Byron, this poem sufficiently expresses the esteem in which Bagley and Izard were held at Annapolis. These legendary heroes flourished in the Gay Nineties, when sail drill on the frigate, *Wyoming*, was a daily feature of the curriculum. Nautical terms were substituted for signals. When the quarter shrilled: "Fore top gallant clew lines!", it was Izard's cue to turn the enemy flank. Any reference to an anchor meant a kick. Only a sailor could grasp the pilot's jargon. Izard could sweep around end as nimbly as he swarmed up a mast to stow the bunt. He was little, but tough as Navy bully beef. Izard ranks with the greatest of the Navy ends, a demon downfield, a Hinkey at knocking the runner cold. "Snake" was equally brilliant as a carrier, his twisting, sinuous runs explaining his nickname. He could go through, over, or around—you called his signal and you took your choice. Greased lightning in the clear.

Douglass and Dalton, the alliterative duo, will be toasted as long as congenial spirits (both kinds) make merry in the wardroom. Hugh Douglass pierced Army's mighty lines as a marlin spike penetrates manila rope. His ferocious plunges earned the touchdowns which tied West Point in 1905 and beat the soldiers in 1907. Army always respected Douglass. Not particularly fast, his lethal straight arm bowled over tacklers on end sweeps, while his sturdy legs withstood tremendous buffeting. Douglass was an all-round kicker, adept at getting off punts from under the shadow of his line. These quick kicks caught his foes off guard. One of Navy's unforgetables.

Jack Dalton, affectionately known as "Dolly," was Navy's greatest kicker and carrier. Dolly has been called Navy's "Oliphant," but it would be chronologically accurate to put it the other way around. Dalton antedated Oliphant by several years. The Navy goat didn't take any back talk from Army's mule, while Dalton wore Middy blue. A champion hurler, Dalton's high-flung knees ground tacklers into the sod. Weymouth, a Yale man who coached both Coy and Dalton, declared that Navy's star was the greater player. Weymouth's opinion will not be shared by many critics, but it indicates how impressive Dalton appeared.

Army has cause to remember Dalton's prowess as a kicker. His 35-yard goals from placement beat West Point in 1910 and 1911. It was Dolly's towering punts that held Princeton's 1911 champions to a draw. Sam White wasn't given a loose ball to run with that day. For the benefit of our feminine readers we might add that Dalton is hailed as the most accomplished dancer ever to earn an Ensign's commission. The kid was there with both feet.

"Navy Bill" Ingram, 185 pounds of cordite, rivaled Douglass and Dalton in all-round value. Under the modern Annapolis system, quarterbacks and halfbacks are interchangeable. Not since Chip Smith and Mustin has Navy had a quarterback in the precise sense of the word. Her pilots have really been halfbacks. You can shuffle 'em around to suit yourself. "Navy Bill" hit a line like a salvo from a triple-gunned turret. This buckaroo doubled the enemy's flank as easily as a destroyer "crosses the T" on a column of battleships. He punted magnificently and backed up his line in airtight fashion.

No Navy gunner ever got a six-inch piece on the target as speedily and accurately as Bill Ingram picked out uncovered receivers for his rifle-shot passes. In one Army game "Navy Bill" completed 18 forward passes. He could throw 'em or catch 'em with equal facility. Considerable football player, this bulky, brainy chap, who made a glowing reputation as a conference coach before being drafted by Annapolis. Critics agree that the 1926 Navy eleven was the smartest coached outfit ever produced on the banks of the Severn. As a cagey strategist, this cocky, chip-on-the-shoulder fighter deserves an admiral's stars.

Modest, unassuming Jonas Ingram feared nothing in human form. As the battle ram of Farragut's flagship sliced through Confederate cable booms off Mobile Bay, so Jonas tore enemy lines to shreds with his berserk plunges. Beyond all doubt he was the fiercest defensive tackler ever to back up an Annapolis line. Here was a take-out man of the Tack-Hardwick stripe, a fearless interferer who reveled in the shock of physical contact. They set 'em up in another alley for Jonas to knock down. It was Jonas Ingram who took the short over center pass on a fake kick from Norton to beat Army in 1906. That "mossback" was a new wrinkle then.

Bully Richardson had no superior at Annapolis when it came to line-breaking. His hammer blows carried the shock effect of a dreadnought's broadside. Neil Nichols, who played before the *Olympia's* guns thundered off Cavite, could hit a line himself. So could Bill Halsey, another Stone Age terror. Whelchel scintillated in a broken field. He could go up a mile to drag down passes or pick 'em off the clover tops while sitting down. Navy never has had a more talented pass receiver. It was Whelchel's amazing completions that almost enabled Navy to beat Werner's marvelous Pittsburgh machine in the 1916 seesaw battle, won by Pitt, 20 to 19.

Monty Nichols, fleet as a mustang, could turn an end faster than any other Navy carrier. He was another "Chet" Bowman in grid togs. Monty craved action. When America hesitated to get into the European free-for-all, Nichols joined the British Army and saw Flanders. Wounded in action, he went back for more and died, like Johnny Poe, advancing against the enemy. A short life but a vivid one.

McReavy's bull-like plunges won't soon be forgotten, nor will his acrobatic grabbing of passes while on the run. Steve Barchet, an artist at threading through a broken line, was an emotionally suppressed type—the sort of chap who gets keyed up to a fighting pitch under pressure. A stocky speed demon, hard to catch in the clear, Tom Hamilton plugged leaks in the line as a plumber solders a pipe. He piloted the 1926 champions, but his position was defense back. Hamilton stood in close when backing up, ready to hurl himself at any helmet which burst through his line. His diagnosis of rival plays appeared inspired. High-spirited, Tom mopped up for Schuber, Ransford, Hannegan, Caldwell, and Shapley. Unobtrusively he made vital contributions to Navy's triumphant 1926 campaign.

Roberts, a superb offensive back; Lange, dropkicker and defensive star; Rhodes, who later committed the unpardonable sin (in Navy eyes) of transferring to the Army; brilliant Alan Shapley, an individualist; Biff Long, punter and line rammer; cagey, fleet Taussig; chunky, determined Koehler; flashy Clark, Dobie's spearhead; Pete McKee, all-round dependable; Royce Flippen, who ran interference for Shapley; bullet Caldwell, and Butler were all high-grade backs. Shuffle them to suit yourself.

No discussion of Navy stars would be complete without mention of Carl Wilson, whose glittering career was cut short by a fatal neck injury. Wilson's vertebra was crushed making a flying tackle. His indomitable spirit enabled him to stave off death for six months. The end came in the Post Hospital, with his teammates at his bedside. This fleet Kentuckian might have become one of Navy's greatest quarterbacks. Old sea dogs will tell you that sandy-haired Mustin could get more out of a team than any subsequent Navy pilot. A flaming torch in action, Mustin had the inspirational fervor of an evangelist. Norton, the dropkicker, and Chip Smith, cagiest of Navy tacticians, were fine quarterbacks. Stringy, gawky Smith had a chess brain and a gob's nerve.

Coming to the ends, Izard has already been dealt with. If Princeton had her Sam White, Annapolis had her Cracky Dague—in fact, she had him first. Dague made it his personal business to convey any unescorted pigskin across the enemy goal. He had an uncanny nose for a loose ball. Let any rival fumble, and Dague was Johnny-on-the-spot to capitalize the break. "The goat maker" they called him, because of his habit of converting fumbles into touchdowns. His teeth-rattling tackles explain the nickname, Cracky. Dague was a demon at boxing the tackle as well as the fastest man downfield Navy has ever boasted.

Pugnacious Gilchrist may be preferred to Izard by many selectors. He hailed from the St. Louis waterfront, where only the fittest can survive. A hardy, virile type of natural leader, who inspired his men by precept. A brainy quarterback as well as a clinking end. His record was marred by Merillat's 60-yard run in the 1913 Army game, Gilchrist being neatly boxed on this play.

W. S. Taylor, rugged, fast and everlastingly dependable, is also remembered as a nifty pass receiver. Eddie Ewen wasn't big, but he couldn't be kept out of a rival's backfield. A crucifying tackler, Paddy Shay, fighting Irishman of the old sail reefing days, loved to hear their ribs crack as he tossed enemy carriers. A demon at paving the way for end runs, Hardwick, greatest of modern wings, always rose to the occasion. He played his greatest games when most was at stake. Remember his leaping catch of the pass that led to Navy's touchdown at Chicago last November? Parr, Overesch, Reifsnyder, and Howard were other crack wing men.

"Mammy" Weems, wildcat from the Tennessee backwoods, where babies cut their teeth on chewing tobacco, was the fightingest, wildest roving center the Navy ever produced. Rather light for a pivot, Weems was, nevertheless, heavyweight champion wrestler. Abnormally powerful legs and arms enabled him to outcharge and outrough his antagonists. A courteous, soft-spoken Southerner off the field, Weems became a raging whirlwind when the whistle blew. As hard as a belaying pin, Glendon picked "Mammy" for the all-time Navy crew. Weems had as much grit as a coal stoker.

"Sybil" Slingluff lacked Weems's range and scrappy disposition, but was bigger and technically more adept. A heady, cagey player, Slingluff never made a poor pass. He could beat the average end downfield. Slingluff had greater potentialities than any other Navy center, but one cannot forget how badly he was outplayed by Philoon of Army in 1908. Slingluff went stale that season. "Swede" Larson, unassuming and ubiquitous, was consistently strong. Goodstein, a Jewish comedian, would have gone over big on Broadway. This savage charger blocked an Army kick and recovered for a touchdown in 1916. In one Army game he faced Goodman, a West Pointer who hailed from a Southern district where Hebrews were not held in high regard. Turning to his team, Goodstein exclaimed "Oy, oy, oy! Goodstein and Goodman—two fine Jewish boys." The Navy jokesmith knew perfectly well that his opponent wasn't Jewish.

"Babe" Brown is a name to conjure with at Annapolis. The greatest forward ever to sport the midnight blue, Brown shared All-America laurels with Pennock of Harvard. Not as strong on his feet as the Harvard rock, Brown had greater speed and range. Plays could be built around this giant which few guards would have been nimble enough to handle. "Babe" loved to beat his ends downfield under punts. But Brown was more than a tower of strength in the line; he specialized at splitting the uprights from placement. From short ranges, Brown couldn't miss the target. His two field goals beat Army in 1912. A year later, "Babe" booted three over the bar, but West Point was inconsiderate enough to put on a catch-as-catch-can act by Prichard and Merillat which netted 22 points.

It's hard to choose between John Halligan and Bimbo Carney for the other guard

Left: Captain Archie Douglas dashed twenty yards for the only score of the 1907 game as Navy triumphed, 6-0. Center: Charles Belknap, captain of the 1902 Navy squad, is considered one of Navy's finest linesmen. He played from 1899 to 1902. Right: Magruder Tuttle, captain of the 1931 Navy eleven, was one of Navy's outstanding centers.

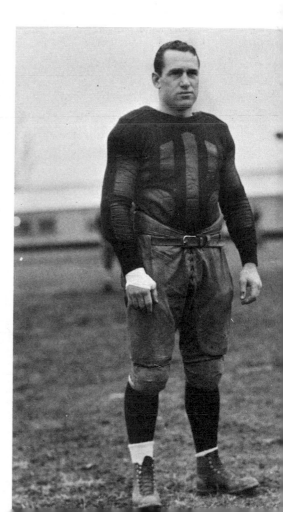

berth. Halligan, now a rear admiral, is a legendary hero at Annapolis. Roughhouse John never asked or gave quarter. His is the distinction of playing more years than any other Navy gridder. Navy didn't play Army from 1894 to '97, when Halligan starred, but the Middies thought so much of John that they rang him in for a fifth year. His name doesn't appear in the Navy records for that year, but Parke Davis and West Point both list Halligan as among those present. Halligan once played Big Bill Edwards to a standstill. His Navy followers christened him "the hub of the universe."

Of Bimbo Carney it has been said that he always did the right thing at the right time. This wide-awake, aggressive giant was a wizard at diagnosing plays. He led interference superbly. Carney's class was amply demonstrated after graduation against the keenest professional competition. Belknap, a combination punter-guard of the Hooks Burr type, ranks next to Halligan among the older generation. Denfield, a savage, penetrating charger; sturdy Perry and Big Willkie were other good ones.

Navy has produced four outstanding tackles, two of them playing on the present championship team. Percy Northcroft, a spectacular downfield tackler, always grabbed the limelight. A showy, slashing hole opener. His duel with Pullen of Army in 1908 is still a live topic in crow's nest, conning tower, and wardroom. Naval men love to retell the story of Northcroft's 48-yard goal from placement against West Point in 1906. Clyde King, a physical superman, was Navy's most powerful tackle. King knew how to make his weight count. He stroked the 1920 crew to an Olympic championship. An Atlas for strength.

Modernists can make out a strong case for Wickhorst and Eddy. Frank Wickhorst, the Illinois Thunderbolt, was a sensation as a freshman at Urbana before transferring to Annapolis. Zuppke will never forgive his defection, but Illinois' loss was assuredly Navy's gain. Wickhorst had the drive of a rhino and the endurance of a Missouri mule. He never let up. Tom Eddy had greater range. This beautifully proportioned tackle had few equals at knifing through to harass the punter or passer. Michigan blames the loss of the 1926 Navy game on Eddy, who punished Friedman unmercifully, thereby breaking up Yost's passing attack. Eddy shares with Weems and King the distinction of being Navy's finest stroke oar. Chunky Ward, a grim fighter, played with fanatical abandon. Grady, mighty hero of yesteryear; Murray, Scaffe, Bolles, and Redmond were superfine tackles. Only the graybeards will remember those two stalwarts—Reeves and Farley—who played when bicycles were built for two. And now, as the setting sun of memory limns, funnels and basket masts against the sky, we leave our Navy friends to their fond recollections.

Honorable Mention: Center—Causey, Whitlock, Kavanaugh, Tardy, and Ben Perry; Guard—C. Wright, Moore, Irwin, Trench, Kimball, Castleman, Landis, Marshall, Meyer, and Howe; Tackle—Macklin, Farley, Reeves, Bolles, Piersol, Edwards, and Redmond; End—Overesch, Reifsnyder, De Mott, McCauley, Howard, McCormack, Graves, Berrien, H. Ingram, and E. Taylor; Quarter—Norton, Conroy, Koehler, McCarthy, C. Wilson, and Bookwalter; Back—Long, Sowell, Shapley, Filippio, Clark, Martin, Butler, C. Mackim, Spencer, Caldwell, McKee, Asserson, Halsey, Craig, Neil Nichols, and Taussig.

Slade Cutter just watches the Middies play ball these days, but Army will never forget the field goal he kicked on that muddy afternoon in 1934 to beat the Cadets, 3-0.

Slade Cutter, Navy Hero

GENE SCHOOR

ARMY PLAYS NAVY IN FOOTBALL TWO SATURDAYS HENCE—AND SO FAR AS the Cadets are concerned, the best thing about the big spectacle is that Slade Deville Cutter will be watching from under a gold-braided cap instead of a football helmet.

Captain Cutter, born in Oswego, Illinois, forty-five years ago, is Navy's new director of athletics. Before that he was a wartime submarine commander with nineteen enemy ships and the equivalent of four Navy Crosses to his credit. And before that he was a Naval Academy star at lacrosse and an intercollegiate boxing champ who might have gone on to the world's heavyweight crown as a professional. But most of all, still blistering in the memory of the long gray line, Slade Cutter is the guy who kicked the field goal

THE field goal. That's how historic it was. The date was December 1, 1934. Not in thirteen years had Navy beaten Army, and on a rainswept, sloggy, muddy gridiron that had the Middies' razzle-dazzle offense slithering from sideline to sideline without any visible effect, it looked as if the Army was about to register Number 14 in the record books.

Suddenly Army's "Waco" Jack Buckler calls time, runs to the sidelines, and returns with a chunk of resin, which he hands to his center, John Clifford. Clifford hands the resin to Army's backfield stars, Joe Stancook, Grove, and Quarterback Grohs. The ball is on Armys 1-yard line, the result of a fine kick by Navy's Bill Clark.

Buckler boots the ball from his own end zone to Navy's Buzz Borries, who scoots to Army's 35-yard line before he is brought down. Buzz gets 5 yards on an off-tackle slant, then scoots for a couple more yards. A beautiful pass play, Borries to Dick Pratt, and Navy's left halfback Pratt zigzags past five Army tacklers to the Army 16-yard line.

The Navy side of the huge stadium is now screaming for a score and Navy sets to work. Borries again tries the Army line, gets five precious yards and is smothered by Army's Clifford on the next play.

Quarterback Dick Pratt, huddled with his Navy teammates, "Slade, we're gonna go for a field goal. Now let's go out there and get those three points." Pratt barked his signals as 80,000 frantic spectators held their breath, and then stopped breathing as big, blond Slade Cutter, Navy's All-American tackle, paced off his kicking area. He was calm and determined as he nodded to the rest of his teammates. The ball was centered to Bill Clark; Clark put the ball down and Cutter crashed into the ball, hitting it squarely up between the uprights for the precious three points.

Of Captain Cutter, his Navy intimates have said, "For Slade, the Army-Navy game is more than a contest. To him it is a way of life."

In Annapolis, Captain Cutter lives in the house reserved for the Academy's director of athletics, only 40 yards behind the goalposts in Thompson Stadium, which will be torn down at the end of this season and replaced by the new Navy-Marine Corps Memorial Stadium. Mrs. Cutter, when she does not choose to sit in the grandstands, watches Annapolis games from her second-story parlor.

"But only on Army-Navy day do we root against Army," says Slade. "That's tradition at the Naval Academy. We *want* Army to win all of its other games. We think it is important that the service academies get in the habit of winning."

Winning leadership is what comes out of Army *vs.* Navy, in Cutter's view. "There's a grapevine in the ranks of all the services, you know," he says, "and the men make it their business to find out quickly who their officers are, what they have done. There is a special respect for those officers who could carry the ball on a football field or throw a wicked block or make a dead-stop tackle."

As a submarine commander—the *Seahorse*—during World War II, Cutter said it another way: "After all, this war is like a game. Take a submarine crew. It's mostly a big team, each working together. Sports teach you to weigh each risk carefully. None of this suicide stuff the Japs are using, but an intelligent study of a situation to see whether a given objective is worth the risks."

The talk of the U.S. submarine fleet in the Pacific was Slade's wager with his old Annapolis teammate, Capt. Robert E. (Dusty) Dornin, also a sub commander, as to who would sink the most enemy ships. "They bet a suit of clothes, those two, and they gave me a headache," relates Adm. Charles Lockwood, Jr. "Each accused me of giving the other better hunting grounds in enemy waters."

Cutter added to the three letters he won in football the three varsity "Ns" he earned as Navy's undefeated heavyweight boxer. There was no intention by the blond, easy-moving chunk of brawn to attempt any boxing heroics at Annapolis, but in the gym he quickly caught the eye of Boxing Coach Spike Webb.

"I handled Gene Tunney when he started his ring career in France," Webb said, "and I can tell you frankly that Cutter can do everything better than Tunney did when he reached the same stage."

Cutter confesses that he did give a thought to turning professional. "Dad wasn't well," he says, "and the hospital bills were running up, and I was being offered big money to turn pro. But my father passed away a few months later and the insurance money eased the financial strain."

Football wasn't for Slade when he was a farm lad in Oswego. His parents counseled

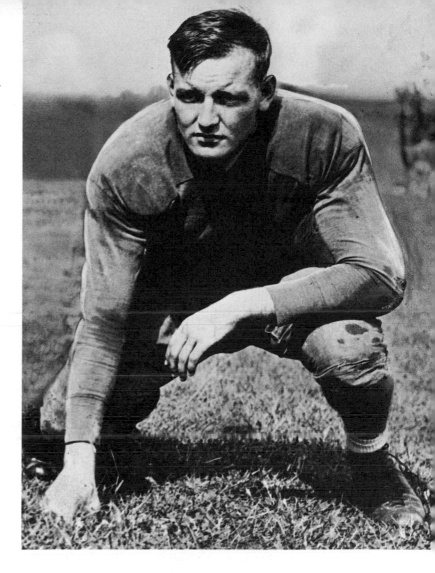

Slade Cutter, who gave Navy its first win over Army in thirteen years when he calmly kicked a field goal in the 1934 game, the only score.

him against it in high school and he didn't object. His interest then was music and with the Oswego High School band he was its Number One flute player. That talent led to his winning the interscholastic solo flute-playing championship, no less. Later he was offered an appointment to the Naval Academy.

There were more credits needed, though, and Cutter was enrolled at the Severn School, a Navy prep school near Annapolis. There his bulk came to the notice of the Severn backfield coach, later to win fame as Paul Brown, head coach of the Cleveland Browns. With parental permission he played fullback for Severn but a year later as a Navy plebe he was shifted to tackle.

Thus began Slade Cutter's interest in football at the Naval Academy which never slackened through three years as a varsity star, through four years as a submarine commander, through these recent years as vigorous leader in Navy's officer-fitness programs.

He'll be watching the Army-Navy game for the skills of Coach Eddie Erdelatz's Midshipmen on both attack and defense, but mostly he'll be watching for the signs of leadership that Captain Cutter's fellow officers call a near-religion with him.

And Army, we repeat, will be grateful that he's only watching.

How many times have you seen the famous star who comes into the game when all seems lost, and then goes on to win? Or the aspiring player who one day is noticed by the coach and then goes on to fame and glory? Well, that's the way it was in real life with the great "Buzz" Borries, Navy's All-American in 1934. Lawrence Perry penned this story.

Buzz Borries, Navy's All-American, Never Made His High School Team

LAWRENCE PERRY

LOTS OF TIMES IN THE PAST WEEK SOME MIDSHIPMAN OR CITIZEN OF Annapolis would say, "There goes Buzz Borries," wondering by what right or license the Navy's great ball player was walking the streets and the campus in civilian attire.

Well, it wasn't Buzz. It was Buzz's father, Fred Borries, Sr., of Louisville, Kentucky, who, trim, alert, and almost as young-looking as his son, "Buzz," was in Annapolis spending a glorious week celebrating Navy's first victory over Army in thirteen years, 3-0, a victory made possible by the magnificent all-round performance of Buzz Borries.

It is a curious fact as related by the senior Borries, that Buzz, while a student at high school, failed to win a varsity letter in football, baseball, or basketball. Yet at the Navy Academy, Buzz Borries went on to become perhaps the finest all-round back in Navy history, an All-American selection. And an outstanding performer in basketball and a star on the baseball team.

Borries has already participated in five victories over West Point in three major sports: football, baseball, and basketball. That is an accomplishment a few Midshipmen in history have accomplished. There is a good chance that Buzz could end his career with seven gold Navy stars, symbolizing a like number of Navy wins over the Army.

Buzz attended a small boarding school in Kentucky and played on the scrub team, but he never did blossom out as a potential varsity football player.

As a plebe at the Academy, Buzz went out for the team and was so awkward that he became the laughing target of the entire coaching squad.

Then, suddenly all the laughter stopped one afternoon, for in a practice session with the varsity, Buzz was given the ball and raced through the entire first team for 55 yards and a touchdown.

Buzz Borries, Navy All-American.

Of course, everybody thought it was a big joke—Borries scoring against the big team.

"Let's try that play again. Give Buzz the ball," said head coach Rip Miller. And once again on the very same play, Borries raced through the Navy varsity for a score.

"Okay, you big ——" said Miller. "Stop the horsing around. Let's see you get this guy."

But that day there was no stopping this fleeting son out of Louisville, Kentucky. He scored another touchdown before the afternoon was over, and from that day on, he was a varsity member.

A substitute sits on the bench and dreams of glory. This is an old story, but Dick Shafer, 155-pound Navy back, had something more than a dream; he had courage. All 155 pounds of him were in the game when Coach Swede Larson gave him the chance to play. The "skinny kid" made good—and in the biggest game of the 1939 season. Dick Shafer was only a sub, riding the bench, but his touchdown was enough to beat Army. Bill Stern tells about it.

A Substitute Wins for Navy

BILL STERN

SOME YEARS AGO DICK SHAFER PLAYED FOOTBALL FOR OBERLIN HIGH SCHOOL out Ohio way. When he graduated, young Dick figured himself some pumpkins as a football hero. He applied for admission to the Naval Academy. When his appointment came through, his joy knew no bounds. The idea of becoming an officer in the United States Navy was swell, sure. But even more than that, Dick Shafer saw himself as the star of the Navy football team, saw himself playing against Army, winning his letter with star as thousands cheered thunderous applause. The dream intoxicated him. Who could blame the fellow?

In his first year at Annapolis, Dick Shafer made the freshman team even though he was quite light. In spite of his weight, he managed to hold his own with bigger and heavier men. The following year, Shafer made the varsity squad and was issued the number "45" to put on his football jersey. Things seemed to be working out.

Dick fought his heart out to make the big team but he couldn't quite make it. He was still too light to play with the big men that made up the first team. He rode the bench game after game without ever getting into the lineup. He watched the Army-Navy game that year from a sideline seat, still a lowly substitute. "Well, maybe next year," he muttered to himself when the final gun went off. And so he waited patiently but with hope for the future.

Came the next season, Dick was still too light. Try as he would, he couldn't get over 155 pounds on his skinny frame. He continued to warm the bench, still hoping, still wishing. In practice he fought his heart out, ripping and tearing and smashing. At game time, Dick sat quietly on the bench on the sidelines. The season slipped by. The final gun sounded again and he had not been called on to play in a single game. Again

Dick Shafer, who made the game's only touchdown in 1939 as Navy defeated Army, 10-0.

Dick mumbled words of comfort to himself. "Maybe next year," he said. "They won't stop me then." But with the hope there was now a little pain in Dick Shafer's heart.

His last season rolled around. It was 1939. As usual, Dick reported for varsity football. Again they issued him his old number, "45." This would be the year. He couldn't miss. His scrub days were over for sure, he thought.

But it didn't turn out that way. He was still too light. Then they even took his number away. They sent him down to play with the "B" squad. No substitute could sink any lower. Dick was heartbroken. He felt that he was varsity material deep down inside. He was certain he could show them if they only gave him the chance. Instead, here he was, tugging and sweating with the "B" squad, completely forgotten by the coach, a lowly substitute playing out the string.

The weeks passed. As the season drew towards its inevitable close, Dick Shafer became painfully aware that his football-playing days were nearly over for good. But he didn't give up. The dream he had once had still clung to him. This time, though, there was a little voice that kept interrupting in a whisper: "Don't be a fool, Dick. It's only a pipe dream. June is coming and with it graduation. You're through, Dick. Forget it."

Three short weeks before the Army-Navy game, the "B" squad played a game. At its beginning, curiously enough, Dick was riding the bench. But he soon got into the game. As soon as he got on the field, all the pent-up ambition, disappointment, and rage exploded. So brilliantly did he play that the impressed coaches immediately gave him back his jersey and number "45." Back he went to the varsity squad and, what's more, he was taken along to Princeton for the final game before the contest with Army.

With Navy behind 20 to 0, Dick Shafer was sent in. The score meant nothing to him. He played as though there was every chance in the world to win. He tackled, blocked, did everything, and did them superlatively well. The result was that Coach Swede Larson took the skinny youngster along to Philadelphia when Navy left to play Army in the last game of the year.

There were 100,000 spectators at that game. At the start, Dick Shafer was in his usual place—the bench. There was still hope in his heart that he would be given a chance. This was his last Army-Navy game. He had to get his chance!

Suddenly the coach's voice barked out: "Shafer! Go in there!" Dick leaped to his feet. At last! His opportunity had come!

How he played that day! He tore off tackle. He punted long, booming spirals. He skirted the ends. He passed. He blocked like a demon. And to top it all, he suddenly broke loose to race for a touchdown with the wild cheers of the crowd dinning his name into his ears. Navy won that game 10 to 0. It was Dick Shafer's touchdown that made the triumph. Three years of trying, praying, and dreaming had at last come to pass. The lowly substitute had won an Army-Navy game. Dick Shafer's cup was filled to overflowing.

Sportswriters tabbed him the "Golden Boy" in 1945 when he captained a strong Navy football eleven and was named to the All-American team at an end position. Upon graduation, Dick Duden remained at Annapolis to assist Head Coach Oscar Hagberg. In 1951, he tried his hand at professional football with the New York Giants. Recently, Duden was named to coach the plebe teams at Navy. But you should have known him in his playing days. He was quite a guy.

Football Hero, 1945

GENE SCHOOR

THERE WAS NOTHING WRONG WITH COLLEGE FOOTBALL DURING THE WAR years that a few thousand football players couldn't fix. This has been amply demonstrated in the past two months. Able to tap once more hard-muscled young men for its lines and backfields, football has pulled itself together and taken off on a 79-yard run to reassert itself as America's top fall sport.

Brightest stars of the season, however, have been the service teams whose wartime holdovers have given them the edge in manpower and crowd appeal. Now Army and Navy will collide next Saturday at Philadelphia, and manpower is going to pay off in blue chips.

Navy's great expectations, for instance, will ride with one of the year's real Golden Boys—the brilliant captain and right end, Dick Duden.

He might spark the Middies to a victory at that. For around Annapolis they say that Dick Duden has the golden touch. Everything this Midshipman Midas does seems to pay off. Perhaps it's just as well that he's a large imposing youth. He needs his 205 pounds neatly hung on a six-foot, two-inch frame, to bear up under his accumulated distinctions.

He is, first of all, a happy combination as a college man, a fine scholar, a fine athlete, and a good Joe. He was the first Annapolis plebe to make the football, baseball, and basketball teams as a varsity regular. And when he is graduated in June he will join the memorable Tom Hamilton, Ira McKee, Buzz Borries, and Alan Bergner as a winner of nine major letters.

The affection and respect that his classmates have for Duden takes a less splendid, but no less appreciative turn. They simply call him "Monster." Duden has not only been a bearcat with his studies and a giant on the playing fields, but an officer and gentleman as well. He shared with a classmate the top undergraduate rank of Captain of the Brigade.

On the football field, where the greatest number of people know him best, the Monster is not spectacular. He never scored a point as quarterback during the past two years. But he's a workhorse and he's steady. He was probably the best collegiate blocking back in America, and in his new position at end this season, he continues to be a tower of defensive strength.

The reason for his shift, however, was to capitalize on his ability as a glue-fingered pass catcher. Comdr. Oscar Hagberg, Navy's Coach and a good ball player in his own day, says "Duden is the only man I've seen who can catch a ball thrown anywhere near him."

For all his honors, Duden has remained a relaxed and amiable fellow. He's headed for service with submarines, likes their easy informality. "I'm no spit-and-polish guy," he grins.

But as roommate Ed Deramee, a Louisiana boy, who plays a lot of football at guard will tell you, "Dick will be all right wherever he goes. He's so good-natured and friendly he can't miss. He's the kind of guy who can walk into a carnival and clean out all the prizes.

Next Saturday the prize he'll be after is Army.

A fine quarterback in 1944, Dick Duden was shifted to end for the 1945 season. He was elected team captain and selected on every All-American team.

Maybe Bob Reifsnyder couldn't tell you what ambidexterous meant, but he was All-American and one of the greatest linesmen to play for Navy. Al Silverman gives us a mighty pen sketch of a mighty Middie. This is from his article in Sport magazine in 1958.

Navy's Big Gun

AL SILVERMAN

REIFSNYDER IS THE GENUINE ARTICLE, AS THEY SAY IN THE PAWNSHOPS. Not only did he earn All-American in 1957 at two positions—center on some teams, tackle on others—he also won the coveted Maxwell Trophy as the college football player of the year. And this season, in the words of his appreciative coach, Eddie Erdelatz, "He is playing 20 per cent better than a year ago."

There may be better linesmen playing college football this season (a point that could be argued, futilely, from Annapolis to the West Coast), but Reifsnyder is just about the most spectacular linesman. Like an actor in the best Hollywood tradition, Bob has a splendid gift for stealing scenes from the more-publicized backfield corps. All it takes is a jarring tackle that separates ball from ball-carrier, a recovered fumble at a critical moment, a blocked try for extra point. Coach Erdelatz, who believes that Reifsnyder is the best tackle he's ever had at the Naval Academy, says, "He always comes up with the key play when needed. He's one of those fellows who just seems to be in the right place at the right time."

We could cite numerous examples of heroic Reifsnyderisms. In three of Navy's toughest games a year ago—Notre Dame, Duke, and Army—Bob was at his ferocious best. Against the Irish he went downfield on all punts and kickoffs to spill Notre Dame ball-carriers. Once in the game he managed to wrestle the ball away from Halfback Dick Lynch. The recovered fumble helped the Navy keep what turned out to be the final 20-6 edge. In the Duke game Bob broke up successive thrusts despite a sprained wrist on one hand and broken finger on the other. He maintains, incidentally, that that was his toughest game. "I never saw linesmen like that. Usually, I prefer playing against big guys because they're slow. But the Duke linesmen were big, fast, and rough. I really got a going-over."

Against Army, Bob played his finest football game. He was all over the field. At one crucial moment early in the battle, Army needed a yard for a first down. They sent Halfback Pete Dawkins into the middle. Reifsnyder hit Dawkins head on. The *"pop"* could be heard up in the stands. Dawkins was thrown for a 2-yard loss and that ended the Army drive. After it was all over, with Navy 14-0 victors, Bob was voted linesman of the game by the newspapermen, and he wasn't even around at the finish. He and an opposing tackle, Bill Melnik, were ordered to leave the field midway in the last period after a brief hand-to-hand skirmish.

That heave-ho was a source of embarrassment to a fellow who almost always looks to the bright side of life. Bob says, "I was rushing the passer. All of a sudden—*boom*—he hit me. He got me in the mouth and knocked out a front center tooth. I may have hit him with an elbow going in and he just got mad, but I never hit him deliberately."

The only other time in his college career that Reifsnyder was shown the door was in the 1957 Georgia game. He admits he deserved to be thrown out of that one, but claims good cause. "The Georgia middle guard was the dirtiest football player I ever went up against," Bob says. "He was throwing himself offbalance trying to do everything at once. I was bleeding from the nose like a stuck pig. I stood it as long as I could. Then, with about twelve seconds to go, I saw him giving it to our halfback, Harry Hurst. He had Harry on the ground and was punching away. I hauled off and let him have it from ten feet away. I guess I only got him with an elbow and a forearm. The funny thing was that my replacement, John Wetzman, came in for one play and the guy clobbered him and he had to come off with a bloody nose."

That game marked the fourteenth time (fourteen, that is) Reifsnyder had broken his nose. Bob's proboscis looks a little like a crumpled fender on the family jalopy. Football hasn't been the only culprit, either. As a baseball player in high school (and he was quite a ballplayer), errant ground balls often caused him and his nose untold misery. Bob has since undergone an operation in which most of the bone from the nose was removed, leaving only cartilage. The Navy has promised him a plastic job after this football season, so that he'll look like the officer on Navy recruiting posters.

Despite the pounding his nose had taken over the years, Reifsnyder refused to wear a nose guard until the 1957 Notre Dame game. Ask him why he waited so long and he just shrugs his shoulders. Last winter at the Maxwell Trophy dinner in Philadelphia, Reifsnyder was sitting beside Chuck Bednarik, the veteran Philadelphia Eagles' linebacker. Bednarik had, of course, noticed the condition of Bob's beak.

"How come you never wore a nose guard?" Bednarik asked.

"I just didn't like the idea," Bob answered bashfully.

"Listen, boy," Bednarik snorted, "don't ever be afraid of people talking about you, or calling you sissy. Us pros get the biggest bird cages available."

Reifsnyder mumbled an answer to the effect that, 'aw, that wasn't the reason at all.' The fact of the matter, it was. It was a matter of pride with Bob, and if he hadn't begun to get dizzy spells on the playing field last fall after getting bopped on the nose, he'd probably be still going without a nose guard today.

The twenty-one-year-old Midshipman from Rockville Center, Long Island, fancies himself, rightly, as a rugged customer out on the playing field. This is a boy who gets his kicks out of the rough-and-tumble contact that football provides. He is noted as a mean but clean tackler. And when he doesn't make the tackle, he clears interference like a bull stampeding through a crowd. "He just smells that ball," says line coach Ernie Jorge.

An indication of Bob's attitude towards contact sports is that one of his favorite pastimes at the Academy is field ball, a ghastly mixture of lacrosse and soccer that is played out of doors in all kinds of weather, fair or foul. "It's a lot of fun," Bob maintains. "It's good and rough. Lots of guys get hurt."

Bob didn't mean to imply that he takes a sadistic pleasure out of contact sport. It was simply a statement of fact that the rougher the game, the more fun it is for Reifsnyder. In high school he was an outstanding wrestler, once going to the finals of the Long Island high school tournament.

When not engaged in combat of one sort or another, Robert Harland Reifsnyder, who is called "Reef" and "Wimpy" by his teammates (the last for his record feat of eating ten hamburgers at one sitting), is an easygoing, genial guy who abhors violence everywhere except on a playing field. Navy Halfback Dick Zembruski, a close friend of Reifsnyder's, says, "Out of uniform Reef is quiet, almost retiring. But on the field he gets that light in his eye and turns into a real bull."

The Bull is very popular with his teammates, the coaching staff, and the entire brigade of Midshipmen. He is noted, among other things, for a quick sense of humor. Last year the team held a meeting before the California game. One of the coaches was talking about Cal's second-string quarterback, who, he said, was ambidextrous. Reifsnyder started to giggle.

"What are you laughing at?" the coach said. "You don't even know what the word means."

"Yes I do," Reifsnyder answered.

"All right," the coach asked wearily, "what?"

"It means a fellow who can run with both legs."

The quality among qualities that Ed Erdelatz admires most in Reifsnyder (and among the qualities he listed speed, good reaction, competitive heart, leadership, and desire a very important word to the Navy coach) is a willingness to do whatever necessary for the good of the team. As a sophomore, Reifsnyder played a full season at left tackle. Last year he played the first five games at center and then was switched to right tackle.

The sturdy "Reef" of the Naval Academy was born in Brooklyn on June 18, 1937, to Edythe and Harland Reifsnyder. Bob's dad was a football and baseball player at Brooklyn Tech High School.

As a boy, Bob got a kick out of playing touch football in the street. He was always big for his age and played with boys several years older than himself. When he was a freshman in high school, he was a stringbean six feet, one inch, and 150 pounds. By the time he was a senior, after summers working as a laborer to build himself up, his weight had shot up to a solid 200.

Bob's family moved to Long Island when he was very young and he attended the Wilson School in Rockville Center, where he played touch football, softball and basketball.

At Baldwin High School, Reifsnyder was a disappointment as a pitcher. He says that one day in his freshman year he found he couldn't get his fast ball going, that something had gone out of his arm. He never did regain the good speed and he wound up as a spot pitcher in high school, playing mostly in the outfield.

In football it was a different story. He was nothing short of sensational. As a sophomore and junior, he was a hard-charging fullback. In his junior year his team won the Long Island championship and Bob was named all-scholastic. A teammate, Chuck Gondoli, was named to the All-America high school team that same year and later played halfback behind Milt Campbell at Indiana.

Naturally, Reifsnyder was deluged with offers from colleges all over the country. At first he thought the choice lay between Iowa and Maryland, both of whom he figures were good football schools and both of whom had solicited him eagerly. But then his father stepped in.

"You want to get something more out of college than football, dont you?" he asked. Bob agreed, and so the choice narrowed down to either West Point or Annapolis.

It is a crowning irony, from Army's standpoint, to note that Reifsnyder was once on the verge of selecting West Point. He was wooed actively by Army's Doc Blanchard, then a member of the coaching staff. The great All-America fullback was one of Bob's earliest sports heroes. "Army really did more to get me than Navy," Bob says. "Doc came over to the house lots of times. I felt sorry I didn't go to Army because of Blanchard. He impressed me. But there was something about Army that had me worried."

Whatever it was, the same fear apparently didn't apply to Navy. Homer Hobbs, former line coach at Annapolis, visited Reifsnyder a couple of times and made it clear that Reef could expect no free ride. Despite this gloomy appraisal, Reifsnyder picked Navy, a choice he has never had cause to regret.

As a plebe in the fall of 1955, Reifsnyder played fullback for exactly one week. Then Eddie Erdelatz came over and gave the boy a long look. "I'm sorry, son," he said, "I'm shifting you to the line. We can't afford the luxury of a 230-pound fullback." So Reifsnyder became a tackle—one of the best in Navy history.

Bob Reifsnyder, Navy tackle.

"Right now, Ike is good enough to step right into pro ball," said Navy Coach Eddie Erdelatz of his All-American guard, and Eddie, who had been line coach for the San Francisco Forty-niners, could speak with authority. "Ike" Eisenhauer was the lad's name—not to be confused with President "Ike" Eisenhower, though each might have looked with satisfaction on the other's performance. This is taken from a piece by Stuart McIver, written for Sport magazine.

Navy's Ike

STUART McIVER

ALL IN ALL, 1952 WAS A BIG YEAR FOR IKE. THERE WAS MAGIC IN THE NAME as it swept across the country and no time was it mentioned more frequently than in the fall, a season traditionally given over to football and political elections.

At Annapolis, a stocky, 200-pound Midshipman named Stephen Swartz Eisenhauer was caught up in the infection. It was the year for people called Ike and he knew how to capitalize on it. With startling speed he advanced from the obscurity of a nonletter-winning sophomore in 1951 to All-America honors as a defensive guard a year later.

You might call it simply a spectacular case of Army-Navy co-operation. West Point's Ike put Annapolis' Ike in the spotlight. In return, Annapolis' Ike gave the Republican nominee free publicity all fall by keeping his name echoing through the public-address systems of many college football stadiums—"Tackle by Eisenhauer."

This fall both Eisenhower and Eisenhauer are firmly in office, endeavoring to live up to all the nice things said about them a year ago. Actually, Navy's Ike had plenty of opportunity to establish his All-America ranking last October and November. The expert job he did of selling himself as a class performer was best illustrated in the Duke game a year ago.

Injured in the Notre Dame game the previous Saturday, Ike was at first ruled out of action against Duke. The first diagnosis had been a broken rib. But the diagnosis became less and less alarming as the Duke game drew nearer. Still, as late as Friday night in Durham, North Carolina, Ike was a questionable starter. Dr. A. L. Gunderson, the Navy team's doctor, after careful observation, concluded no real damage had been done to Ike's ribs. It was just a matter of painfully bruised muscles and a touch of pleurisy had crept in to make the area all the more sensitive.

"If you want to play, you're in no danger of injuring yourself," said the doctor, who knew Ike was a hard man to keep down. "It could be very painful to you but nothing more serious than that."

Ike said he wanted to play, so the doctor and Trainer Billy Fallon went to work to fix up an "Ike jacket." The Navy version was a little different from the one the Army named after General Eisenhower. "It was like a straitjacket," said Dr. Gunderson. "Ike couldn't bend at the waist. It was made of fiberboard and lined with sponge rubber, about eight inches wide and twenty inches around from front to the middle of his back. The muscle hurt him as much as ever when he moved, but the padding prevented him from getting another bruising. He was a mighty plucky kid to play the way he felt."

Duke was a two-touchdown favorite. The Blue Devils' fast-striking, split-T attack sparked by Worth Lutz, the quarterback, had bowled over Tennessee and Southern Methodist and had been stopped only by mighty Georgia Tech.

But the Duke split-T sputtered when it collided with Ike. The Blue Devils couldn't gain through the middle, Ike's defensive responsibility. Their first drive into Navy territory halted abruptly when Ike snatched the ball out of Charlie Smith's hands.

Just before the half ended, Lutz began to click with his passes and Duke struck for a quick touchdown to lead, 6-0. That was all for the Blue Devils. In the second half, Navy stormed up and down the field with Fred Franco slamming across for a pair of touchdowns, moving the Middies in front, 14-6.

Ike, who had been tormenting Lutz all afternoon, chipped in with a scoring contribution in the final three minutes. He and Linebacker Charlie Sieber trapped the Duke quarterback in the end zone and dumped him to the turf for a safety. The final score was 16-6.

"The rib didn't give me much trouble," Ike said afterward. "I knew my limitations." Apparently there weren't too many. He was credited with fourteen tackles, eight assists, and he recovered a fumble and figured in a safety.

If there were any doubts left about whether or not Ike rated All-America honors, they melted that November afternoon in Durham. Playing under a severe handicap against a team that went on to win the Southern Conference championship, he led the Middies to one of their most surprising and most rewarding victories since the 1950 triumph over Army.

Still, that he should be chosen on anybody's All-America team is hard to believe under the circumstances.

Ike is a completely unsubsidized All-American. That just doesn't happen these days. But Ike got his own appointment to the Naval Academy without any help from the athletic office. As a plebe he attracted little or no attention. He was just a fourth-stringer lost in the shuffle of some 400 aspiring young footballers. At the start of his sophomore, or "youngster" year, he had advanced only as far as the junior varsity. In midseason, he was elevated to the varsity and even managed to start against Maryland's Sugar Bowl champions as offensive right guard. The result was anything but impressive. His assignment was to move Dick (Little Mo) Modzelewski out of the play. Little Mo stayed in. Later in the season, Ike hurt his shoulder. He played very little against Army in the 42-7 rout which saw the bench well cleared. So the result of his sophomore year was—no letter.

He showed little improvement in spring practice, 1952. Coach Eddie Erdelatz was switching from the T-formation to the Notre Dame box and his practice sessions were

Steve "Ike" Eisenhauer, Navy guard, had Navy supporters agreeing, "I like Ike."

concerned primarily with the change-over. On offense, Ike was developing slowly and his defensive talents had no chance to display themselves.

But when last September came, the time was right and the setup was right. All Ike had to do was deliver. He did.

For those who watched the story unfold it was hard to believe. As early as the second game of the season he was Associated Press "Linesman of the Week" off his great play against Cornell, which netted only two yards on the ground. He went on to lead Navy to its first winning season in seven years, a period of famine in which the Middies had won ten games, lost forty and tied four. The record for 1952 was six victories, losses to Maryland and Notre Dame, and a tie with Pennsylvania. A winning team never hurt anybody's chances of making All-America. Navy's Ike didn't need a campaign. He played superb football and, of course, he had that name. How does Ike feel about the coincidence that brought him fame?

"Why should I mind?" he says. "It gave me a break, didn't it? I did take a lot of kidding about my name, though. The only time it bothered me was just before election. There for a while, everybody I met went through the same routine. 'Nice to meet the next President.' . . . 'Where are you speaking tonight?' It got a little tiresome."

In the months preceding the election, Eisenhauer was bombarded with Ike buttons. Friends, casual acquaintances, and even total strangers sent them to him. One button, a king-size job with the word 'Ike' embroidered on it with beads, came all the way from India. It would have been an ironic twist if Eisenhauer had been descended from a long line of loyal Democrats. But his family is staunchly Republican.

The wonder of it all is how a player of Ike's caliber could have escaped notice for so long. And how he was able to make his move so quickly and surely when the break did come along. To understand both, let's go back to a little lumbering town in north-western Pennsylvania—and start Ike from the very beginning.

He was born in 1932 on the first day of December, the start of the deer season in Sheffield. Sheffield High School sits on a mountainside, overlooking the Tionesta River. Ike's father, Leiser O. Eisenhauer, is principal of the school, his mother the school math teacher. Leiser played guard and tackle at Bucknell, where he was a teammate of Lefty James, now head coach at Cornell.

During the war, high school coaches were hard to find for the small-town jobs, so Mike Cashmere, a townsman, and Leiser Eisenhauer pitched in to handle the Sheffield football team. So the first two years Ike was out for high school football his father was his coach. Football as played at Sheffield was somewhat different from the brand played in the city high schools. "My junior year we only had fifteen guys on the squad," says Ike. "We couldn't even scrimmage, not enough players for it."

Coaching a team like that consisted mostly of patient attention to fundamentals, including a lot of one-on-one work. In Ike's junior year he captained the team to a 7-1 season, a good record for a squad so limited in contact work under game conditions. Ike backed up the line and played running guard in the double-wingback formation.

Ike ran into trouble early in his senior year. On September 18, 1948, Sheffield was playing a traditional rival, nearby Ridgeway. On the opening kickoff young Eisenhauer injured his neck. It bothered him throughout the game, forcing him to play with great caution. "I avoided all head-on contact," he said. "Something told me to. It was the only time I ever dodged it."

After the game his parents noticed Ike was tilting his head at an odd angle. His neck wasn't hurting him; he just couldn't hold it in the proper position. He skipped practice the next week to see if that would help. On Friday, one week after the Ridgeway game, his parents decided to take Ike along for an X-ray examination at the Warren General Hospital. Doctors found his trouble was a broken neck. Hurt on the first play of the game, he had played almost the entire four quarters with a crushed fifth vertebra.

"The good Lord was looking after him," said Mr. Eisenhauer. "One more head-first play, one more snap, would have killed him."

That finished Ike as far as high school football was concerned but by January he was back in action as captain of the basketball team, to the surprise of everyone.

His broken neck was probably the reason no colleges were after him to play football. His last season, the one in which he figured to shine, was too abbreviated to attract anybody's notice. An old retired Navy yeoman, P. J. Finnerty, head of the branch bank in Sheffield, had been selling him on the advantages of the Navy. Ike did a little investigating. If he joined the Naval Reserve, studied a year at the Admiral Farragut Academy in New Jersey and attended 27 drill sessions at nearby Lakehurst Naval Air Station, he would then be eligible for a competitive exam. If he passed, he would be in. If he flunked, well, there was always the apprentice seaman's Navy.

At Farragut, Ike played football, basketball, and baseball. At the end of the year he won the medal as the Academy's outstanding athlete. But the important thing was that he took the competitive exam and passed it in fine style.

On July 3, 1950, he arrived at the picturesque, old colonial town of Annapolis on the Severn, ready to set the football world on fire and to prepare himself for his future career in the Navy. As a plebe he came out all right with the education end of it, but he didn't show much in football.

He was a jayvee in 1951 until coach Erdelatz ran into a shortage of able-bodied offensive guards and brought him up to the varsity. A year ago last spring he was still listed behind Joe Pertel and Alex Aronis, the regular starters in the offensive line. It was then that Erdelatz decided to make use of Ike's aggressiveness on defense.

At 200 pounds, Eisenhauer was one of the few heavyweights in the Midshipman's defensive lineup. Erdelatz helped overcome the size problem by giving the Middies some intricate defensive plans, based on those he had used with great effect as a line coach of the San Francisco Forty-niners when they were in the All-America Conference. Basically, Navy's defense lined up in the standard 5-3-2-1 but the linemen slanted in different directions, making it difficult for the opposition to put blocks on them. The key man in this defense is the center guard. He is supposed to slant through quickly between center and guard and break up as many plays as possible before they start. He must have good pursuit, enough weight to keep from getting crushed and ability to tackle well.

Ike was given this vital job and it didn't take Erdelatz long to find out that he had made a perfect choice. Navy's first two 1952 opponents, Yale and Cornell, gained a total of eight yards rushing. The Cornell game was the first Ike's father had seen him play since high school. Mr. Eisenhauer watched his son help rout the Big Red. He recovered two fumbles and blocked a kick which John Gurski fell on in the end zone for Navy's first touchdown.

Navy blanked William and Mary, tabbed as a high-scoring outfit, fell before Maryland's superior forces, and then tied Penn, 7-7, although the Quakers ran 20 plays from inside the Navy 20, and 14 more inside the ten.

The Notre Dame game proved how much Ike means to Navy. The Irish conscientiously ignored the center of the Middies' line in the first quarter but after an injury forced Eisenhauer out of the game, they pounded the line effectively and ran off with a 17-6 victory. After the game, Coach Frank Leahy said, "We just couldn't run through their middle with Eisenhauer in there."

When the final 1952 statistics were in, Navy ranked second in the nation on rushing defense, yielding an average of 93.7 yards a game.

Before the current season started, Erdelatz said of his star center guard: "Right now, Ike is good enough to step right into pro football. He's not big but he could play center guard for any team that used the same defense we have here."

There will be no pro football for Ike — not for some time, anyway. This fall he is busy putting offensive and defensive pressures on Navy's opponents. Then, next year, comes graduation and a career in the Navy.

And with his name, who knows?

"Nothing fazes that kid worth a damn!" It was Navy Coach Eddie Erdelatz speaking of his young quarterback, "Zug" Zastrow. The Middie could run, fake out his man, could pass that pigskin like a bullet, and as true, on a dead run. No one who saw him in action in the 1950 Army-Navy game will ever forget the brilliant performance of one of Navy's truly brilliant stars.

Sailor Zug Takes to the Air

HARRY BEAUDOUIN

THE NIGHT BEFORE FRANKIE ALBERT LEFT ANNAPOLIS, WHERE HE SPENT two weeks last spring instructing Navy quarterbacks in the sleight of hand that won him football fame with Stanford University and the San Francisco Forty-niners, Naval Academy athletic officials tendered him a farewell cocktail party. During the festivities, Capt. Howard Caldwell, Navy's athletic director, came alongside and said, "Well, Frank, did you find us any quarterbacks?"

Sipping his drink, Albert answered silently by raising a solitary finger.

He meant Robert Richard Zastrow, or, as he is known to his mates in the yard, "Zug" Zastrow. The hottest article to hit the Crabtown Brass Foundry since Buzz Borries, the rock-jawed twenty-one-year-old native of Algoma, Wisconsin, is being counted on to lead the Midshipmen to their most rewarding football season since the war.

Make no mistake about it, the curve on the Navy-gridiron graph slowly but surely is rising, and the feeling prevails that personable Eddie Erdelatz, who succeeded George Sauer, is walking into his first head-coaching assignment under pretty favorable circumstances. Navy had a crack plebe team last fall, and there are ten varsity lettermen returning, including Zug Zastrow, a guy who can fire deadly passes while running to his left, right, or backwards.

Sauer, who invested two years at Annapolis constructing a solid football foundation, quit last winter when Academy officials failed to renew the contracts of two assistants. Erdelatz, who coached Navy's end from '45 to '47 (under Tom Hamilton) and later served the pro Forty-niners in a similar capacity, is the man the Academy picked to succeed him.

Erdelatz arrived in time for spring practice, and in no time at all his eye was caught by the squat, seemingly indestructible 208-pounder from Wisconsin who is built so close to the ground that he looks more like a guard than a fancy-faking quarterback.

210

It wasn't just Zastrow's ability to hit a bull in the tail at 50 yards that struck Erdelatz. It was, as well, his consummate coolness under fire. "Nothing fazes that kid worth a damn," Eddie says. Rip Miller, the old Notre Damer who plays such a prominent part in Navy athletics, simply calls Zug "a pro," and by that he is in no way alluding to the $78 a month which Midshipman Zastrow receives from his benefactor, Uncle Sam.

Rating him off some of the stories told about him, one might easily take Zastrow for a pretty cocky character. Rather, his attitude towards football—or any competition, for that matter—is compounded of intensity, self-assurance, a high degree of conscientiousness, and immense pride.

His varsity debut, made last September against Southern California, offers an illustration. The Trojans won without undue travail, 42-20, but Zastrow was the whole Navy team and thrilled the multitude which jammed Memorial Coliseum with his sensational passing. He completed 17 heaves for 252 yards and a pair of touchdowns, in addition to authoring one personally on a sneak.

Los Angeles writers, departing from their usual chauvinism, called him the finest player on the field that day. Braven Dyer wrote: "In Zastrow, Navy introduced a player who gave one of the finest throwing exhibitions ever seen in this or any other town. . . . Given some help in the next two years, the Wisconsin whiz can be an All-American quarterback, for sure. . . ."

Immediately after the game, telecaster Cotton Warburton, an old Southern Cal hero, cornered Zastrow, George Sauer, and U.S.C. Coach Jeff Cravath. Sauer praised the Trojans highly and congratulated Cravath, who said it was an honor to have met the United States Naval Academy, and complimented the Midshipmen for having made such a "fine showing."

Warburton then turned to Zastrow and said, "Well, Bob, how about telling our television audience what *you* thought of this Southern Cal team?"

Dripping with perspiration, Navy's young quarterback—speaking for a ball club just clobbered by a margin of 22 points—looked him in the eye and said, "They didn't show me nuthin'."

Sauer later apologized to Cravath for "the kid's frankness."

But that's Zastrow. He may be down, but he's *never* out.

Zug sparkled just as brilliantly in the succeeding triumphs over Princeton and Duke, which marked the first time since '45 that Navy had won two football games in a row. The victory over Duke also was the first Navy ever scored against an eleven coached by the redoubtable Wallace Wade.

Duke, which had just licked a favored Tennessee team, came to Annapolis boasting a virtually impregnable pass defense. Its secondary had intercepted ten volunteer passes, just three less than had been completed against it. But Zug connected with ten of thirteen, netting the sailors three touchdowns. In the second half, he fired but three times, but one was good for 64 yards and the tying score, another for 36 yards and the tie-breaking touchdown. The Midshipmen went on to win breezing, 28-7.

Coming up to the fourth engagement on the Navy schedule, Zastrow possessed a three-game record unmatched by any back in the country. Columnists the nation over

Quarterback Bob Zastrow led the Middies to a 14-2 win over Army in the 1950 classic. Zastrow was responsible for all fourteen points as he scored one touchdown and passed for another score.

were calling him a sure-fire All-American and comparing him with the best in Tar history. But any dreams Zug himself may have entertained in this respect went up in smoke that day. And of all places for the Navy team as a whole to give its poorest performance of the year, it was at Madison, Wisconsin.

Fully a third of the Badger squad had played with or against Zug in high school days; his family and girl were in the stands; the local papers the week before had plastered his picture all over the sports pages. Half the people who wedged into the stadium that afternoon were there to see one boy—Bobby Zastrow, making his first collegiate appearance before the home folks.

It wound up 48-13, Wisconsin on the long end. Zug had four passes intercepted, two of which resulted directly in Badger touchdowns, the other two setting up scores. One Washington writer wired back this lead:

"Navy didn't bring its goat—Billy XI—to Wisconsin today, but Bob Zastrow proved a very able stand-in. . . ."

This was something less than square. Two Wisconsin touchdowns followed Navy fumbles. Also, the Navy line couldn't get out of its own way, much less flatten the opposition, with the result that Zastrow spent most of the afternoon with alien forms draped about his neck. Even so, he managed to get off a scoring beauty to Halfback Duff Arnold, an instant before being wrestled to the ground by two Badger linemen.

Zug, who quite understandably would just as soon forget it, simply says, "It was awful."

Navy owes Zastrow's presence on the banks of the Severn to a pause for refreshment made one hot summer day in 1947 by Comdr. Red Coward, plebe coach, who was visiting Green Bay, his wife's home. Coward stopped at a local drugstore for a Coke, and in walked Clark Hinkle, the old Packer star.

Hinkle said, "Navy interested in any football players?"

Coward said, "Are you kidding?"

Hinkle, who had refereed some high school games around the state, said, "Well, there's a kid named Zastrow over in Algoma—about 25 miles from here—who's really got it. Only I think Wisconsin's gonna get him."

"Full speed ahead," cried Coward, heading forthwith to Algoma, where he found the curly-haired youngster laboring in a foundry. At lunch, Red asked Zug, "How would you like to go to Annapolis?"

Zastrow looked up and said, "Where's Annapolis?"

Regaining his voice, the commander delivered the Blue and Gold fight talk, and Zastrow was sold. To prepare for Annapolis, he enrolled at Admiral Farragut Academy, in New Jersey, subsequently earning his appointment through competitive examination. As a Navy plebe, he led his team to eight straight victories.

From the day he came up from the plebes to win a varsity berth, Zastrow never has left any doubt as to who is running the outfit. In an early-season practice scrimmage last year, he called play 36-A. But just before the Midshipmen left the huddle, a first classman, or senior, said, "Check—better make it 42-A instead."

Zastrow looked at him and said, "Lookit, buddy, you may rank me in the yard, but out here I'm boss. It's 36-A."

Sauer once said, "The kid's a natural leader, that's all. I believe if he told the team to take off their pants in midfield, they'd do it."

Since Zug has become such a celebrity, of course, Annapolis has become better known along the shores of Lake Michigan, and the Dairy State delegation to the Academy is steadily increasing. As Coward says, "We're beginning to spread the gospel up that way."

"Ordinarily, I don't count on sophomores," said Eddie Erdelatz, "but I'm counting on this one." "This one" was Navy's Joe Bellino, and Joe paid off. He scored Navy's lone touchdown against Army in 1958. In 1959, he ran wild, scoring three TDs against the Black Knights, and establishing a Navy record. In 1960, his touchdown proved the winning margin in the annual classic. Bellino was just unbelievable, even when you saw him in action. Here are excerpts from award-winning Shirley Povich's story of "Dynamite Joe" written in 1960.

Dynamite Joe of the Navy

SHIRLEY POVICH

IN LATE NOVEMBER OF 1959, CONGRESSMEN WERE SPEAKING OUT AGAINST bickering in the armed forces. The charge was that interservice feuding was endangering the weapons race with Russia. On Monday morning, November thirtieth, a Pentagon colonel ruefully agreed that Army-Navy rivalry was indeed getting out of hand. "Now Navy has come up with an anti-Army missile. They call it their 'Bellino,'" he said.

The Navy Bellino had indeed visited havoc on Army personnel two days before. In a public demonstration before 98,618 in Philadelphia's Municipal Stadium—and millions of others in the television audiences—Navy unleashed its new projectile with a three-touchdown warhead and jubilantly watched it destroy the forces of the United States Military Academy, inducing depression among Army men everywhere.

That was the day Midshipman Joe Bellino of Winchester, Massachusetts, blasted off against an Army football team that was a seven-point favorite. Seven minutes after the opening kickoff, tracking stations caught Bellino looping into the Army end zone on a 16-yard caper. He achieved re-entry only two minutes and thirty-eight seconds later, on a 46-yard burst. The third time he did it with a 1-yard dive.

In becoming the first Annapolis man to score three touchdowns in a single contest in sixty Army-Navy games since 1890, Bellino not only spurred his team to a tremendous 43-12 win but also gave himself a headstart for All-American consideration during his final season this year.

His feats against Army were a sadly fulfilled prophecy for Dale Hall, West Point's head coach. One year before, with the 1958 Army-Navy game coming up, Hall had been an Army assistant in charge of scouting Navy. He told the New York football writers that Bellino, then the Annapolis equivalent of a college sophomore, was the man Army had to fear.

"He has the potential to be the best runner in America," Hall said. "Bellino is the explosive type. You have the feeling he is going to cut loose and go." Bellino was Navy's best rusher against Army in 1958, and scored the Middies' only touchdown, but the Cadets won, 22-6. It wasn't until 1959 that he created the utter devastation Hall had feared.

Bellino is a stumpy dervish of a halfback—five feet, nine inches, and 185 pounds— who does not propose to be stopped by anything in front, and in seven years of school and college football has never been caught by anything from behind. His Navy career has not, however, been without problems.

When Bellino first reported to the Annapolis varsity in 1958, there were no football stockings large enough to fit the biggest legs Navy coaches ever saw on a 185-pounder. With the help of Navy quartermasters, this difficulty was solved, but the coaches were left with a more vexing worry—how to keep their prize in school. Joe was flirting with disaster in some of his academic subjects and, worse for Navy, a half-dozen major-league baseball teams were flirting with him.

The baseball interest began when Joe was a catcher with the plebes. He had a .310 batting average, and seven of his thirteen hits were home runs. In his sophomore year, when he batted .428 in twenty-two games and led the Eastern Collegiate League in stolen bases, Bellino was told by the Annapolis sports publicist, John Cox, that fifteen major-league clubs—never previously interested in Naval Academy baseball—had written to ask for the Navy schedule.

As for the scholastic threat to his football future, this was sufficiently serious for Eddie Erdelatz, the Navy head coach when Bellino arrived, to shoo Joe away from spring practice. "Stay out of this until fall and put in some more study time. A flunking halfback is no good to me," Erdelatz told him.

To his intimates Erdelatz said, "Ordinarily, I don't count on sophomores, but I'm counting on this one." He knew Bellino's record with the plebes—ten touchdowns scored, and an average of 11.4 yards gained on ninety-one carries—and he had the testimony of the plebe coach, "This may be the finest football player Navy ever had."

If that be true, it will be no surprise to the citizens of Winchester, Massachusetts. They knew Joe Bellino as the best football, baseball, and basketball player in the history of the local high school. So did the fifty-two colleges which offered him athletic scholarships.

Joe was the third of four Bellino boys to play football for Winchester High. When Joe first put in his appearance, Coach Henry Knowlton jumped for joy. "I was dreaming of the day when I would get a big Bellino," Knowlton explained not long ago.

Big? Joe was then only 160 pounds.

"I know," said the coach, "but the other Bellinos—Sammy, Tony, and, later, Mike— began at 119 pounds. Joe looked big to me and, best of all, he was a Bellino. I knew how they could go.

"It always was impossible to anticipate Joe. I could have told Army as much. One day I told Joe he was carrying the ball in the wrong arm when he was trying to reverse his field. He said, 'Sorry, coach, but when I start running I don't know which way I'm gonna go.'"

That was the schoolboy Bellino. Navy coaches and opponents now testify that no matter how helter-skelter Joe's course may appear at times, his maneuvers are based on cold calculation of how to make the best use of his running room. "It helps," adds Bellino's present head coach at Navy, Wayne Hardin, "to have Joe's rare ability to stay on his feet. If he's blessed with a sixth sense, it's a sense of balance. He stays on his feet when he has no right to."

With six minutes left to play against the University of Maryland last November, Navy was bogged down in an unsatisfying 14-14 tie. Then Maryland fell into the error of booting the punt directly at safety-man Bellino on the Navy 41. Joe was hemmed in as he started up the sideline. In front of the Navy bench he could hear Coach Hardin screaming, "Run it out of bounds!"

Hardin had solid reasons for this order. He saw no chance for a long punt return, and was eager for a dead ball that would permit him to send offensive Quarterback Joe Tranchini back into the game without drawing—under last year's rules—a critical 5-yard penalty for a time out. Bellino willfully disobeyed. He danced away from a pinch of tacklers on the sideline, skipped back toward midfield, and went 59 yards for the winning touchdown.

"I heard coach," Bellino said later, "but I thought I could find daylight and we wouldn't need a quarterback if I did, except to hold for the extra point."

Hardin was forgiving. "When I saw Bellino going all the way on that play, I suddenly remembered what his high school coach told me about Joe," Hardin said.

Actually, the cards were stacked against every school bidding for Bellino except Annapolis. Navy never fully realized the luck it was playing in . . . for Navy already had

on its side the Italian doctor who, in 1939, delivered into the Bellino household the bouncing boy named Joe. This was Dr. William D. Barone, the greatest influence in steering Joe toward Annapolis—not quite from birth, but as soon as it was discovered that Joe could handle a football.

Although Dr. Barone's own service experience had been with the Air Force as a flight surgeon in World War II, he was Annapolis-minded for Bellino. He says, "It could have been vicarious. Perhaps I never got rid of the small-boy appeal Annapolis had for me. Perhaps I took advantage of my friendship with the family. But it was my ambition for Joe."

Dr. Barone's influence is apparent to all visitors to the Bellino household at 43 Swanton Street in Winchester. Papa Michael Bellino, who emigrated from Sicily at sixteen, calls the family doctor, "Mucha good boy."

At the time this writer visited the family, Michael Bellino was waiting out one of his periodic layoffs from the gelatin factory, where he worked. He was tending the little garden that is endemic to all the wooden frame houses in the Plains, Winchester's neat Italian section.

It was obvious that the rugged Navy halfback did not get his size from his father, a frail 120-pounder. "No, from me," said Mrs. Sarah Bellino when the point was brought up. Mamma Bellino, who more nearly approaches Joe's 185 pounds, coyly said to Dr. Barone, "Shall I show him Joe's legs?" Dr. Barone said, "Go ahead, Sarah." She drew up her skirt discreetly to reveal the sturdy Joe Bellino-type calves and said, "Look, Joe's legs."

In 1959, Navy romped over Army 43-12. Navy's Joe Bellino (27) outraces Army's Bob Anderson (right) and Joe Caldwell to score on a 45-yard run. Bellino accounted for two other touchdowns in the game.

As a member of the Navy plebe team in 1957, Bellino was sensational. In game after game he broke away for lengthy scoring dashes. Varsity Coach Eddie Erdelatz decided to test the plebe hotshots by sending a fourth unit of his varsity against them in a regulation game. The plebes won, 14-7. Bellino contributed both plebe touchdowns, one on an 85-yard run from a straight handoff.

As a sophomore in 1958, Bellino was disappointed not to find his picture in the Navy football brochure. Annapolis protocol, you know; only upperclassmen get their portraits in the booklet. "I didn't know that," Joe says now. "I just thought they didn't like me."

Bellino's sophomore year of football at Navy was a personal disappointment to him. He suffered a twisted knee while throwing a block against William and Mary in the first game, and was hampered the rest of the season. "For most of the year I couldn't cut on it, and if I can't cut, I'm dead," he says. "But I saw some action."

Even before Bellino made the varsity, the Naval Academy's physical-education department knew that Joe was very special. They tested and charted him—along with the rest of the 3,800 in the brigade—and found him to be a remarkable athletic specimen.

Joe romped through exercises he had never known before. He was marked for dips on the parallel bars, chin-ups, gymnastics, water ability, wall climbing, rope climbing, agility routines, and applied strength. Only two Midshipmen in the entire corps outranked him, and neither played football or baseball. On the summer cruise after his sophomore year, Joe got off the boat in Portugal, ran in a track meet for the first time in his life, and won the 100 meters from experienced sprinters in 10.9.

Wayne Hardin took over from Erdelatz as Navy's head coach in 1959 and immediately installed Bellino as the No. 1 left halfback.

Up to the time of last season's Army game, things were even more frustrating for Bellino than they had been in 1958. He twisted his knee again against Boston College, reinjured it in the Southern Methodist game, didn't play in the defeat by Syracuse, saw little duty against Notre Dame, and carried only seven times when Navy was held to an upset 22-22 tie by Penn.

In the Boston College game, however, Bellino gave the home folks a show before getting hurt. Winchester High had played its own game in the morning, so that local citizens could watch Joe in Boston that afternoon. The first thing he did was to dash to the Boston College six to set up a touchdown. On his next carry he went all the way, scrambling 50 yards with a pitchout.

Boston College Coach Mike Holovak called this "the greatest do-it-yourself run I ever saw." Bellino swept to the right, got rid of two tacklers, reversed his field twice and confused his own blockers, then threaded the last 40 yards without benefit of blocking. Unfortunately he pulled up lame.

Bellino remembers that three days before the Army game Coach Hardin told him sternly, "I want sixty minutes of football from you on Saturday." This was tantamount to giving a small boy the key to a candy store.

"Ever since I was in high school, I dreamed that someday a Navy coach would let me play sixty minutes against Army, and now Coach Hardin was making it an order,"

In 1960, Joe Bellino scored for Navy as George Kirschenbauer (45) and John Ellerson (87) of Army try to stop him.

Bellino relates. "I had some other dreams, too. I dreamed that first touchdown against Army, weeks before the game. I dreamed that I would get the ball on a handoff and cut around Bob Anderson, and I knew I could outrun him. That's what I did, with a hip fake, but I had to outrun Joe Caldwell, the safety man, too. That wasn't in the dream, but it came out all right."

This was a mere 16-yard touchdown play. When Navy next got the ball, Joe traveled 46 yards. He started through Army's right side, then slanted wide to the right. There he again faked past Anderson and outran Caldwell to score.

Bellino's third touchdown was a 1-yarder, but he set it up with a 42-yard carry on a pass interception. This made him the only Navy man ever to score three times in one game against Army. A quartet of Army backs have done the same—Prince in 1903, Doc Blanchard in 1945, Gil Stephenson in 1949, and Pat Uebel in 1953.

In the third quarter a record-breaking fourth touchdown was Joe's for the taking. In three plays Bellino bumped the ball from the Army, 11 to 1, and back in the huddle Quarterback Joe Tranchini was calling Bellino's signal again. If Hollywood scenarists had scripted what happened thereafter, it would have been scorned as pure cornball. Navy got the touchdown, but our good, kind, manly hero would seek no more glory for himself, and tapped another for the honor.

Tranchini told about it in the days following the game. "I was sending Joe at 'em again from the 1-yard line and called his signal, but the play never got off. Army jumped offside, and we had to go back in another huddle. This time Bellino said, 'I've

219

Halfback Bellino bolts through the Army line. This was in the 1960 game.

had my big day. How about giving it to Ronnie? He hasn't scored yet,' I said, 'Sure,' and Ronnie Brandquist got the ball and a touchdown against Army. As Joe said, Ronnie had been playing a great game."

Submarine service appeals most to Bellino. Last summer he was group captain of fifty midshipmen at the New London, Connecticut, sub base. They took off on an undersea cruise that ended just in time for him to get back to Annapolis for early football practice. If his knee stays strong all season, and likewise the Navy squad, it will be hard for All-America selectors to pass up Bellino this year.

Joe's personal forecast, made with tongue in cheek, was that he hoped to be Navy's No. 1 left halfback again. Bellino sometimes plays the pixy. At the annual awards dinner of the Washington Touchdown Club last winter, he received a massive trophy as the outstanding service-school player. Bellino spoke the customary thanks with a twist. "I want to thank the Touchdown Club," he said "and I want to thank the Navy coaches and my great Navy teammates. And I also want to thank the Army football team." Then he smiled, very slowly.

220

Roger Staubach was an All-American quarterback when he was only a sophomore at Annapolis. An elusive ball carrier, a dangerous runner, a sure-fire man with the forward pass, the football pros came to watch him play. Staubach was unquestionably one of Navy's all-time greats. This is taken from Barry Gottehrer's story.

Sailor with a Future

BARRY GOTTEHRER

SEATED HIGH IN THE STANDS AT MAMMOTH PHILADELPHIA STADIUM IN 1961, the slim, boyish plebe cheered and shouted as Navy rolled to its third straight victory over Army. "It was a great game," said the plebe, "but I had a lot of trouble concentrating. I kept imagining that it was me down there in the field running the team against Army. I dreamed of such a day, but honestly I never thought it would come true."

In 1962, before 100,000 wildly screaming fans at Philadelphia Stadium, Roger Staubach's dream came true in three dimensions and with stereophonic sound. It was one of the most complete and startling naval conquests in history. Against Paul Dietzel's highly publicized Chinese Bandits and Army Regulars, Staubach, a twenty-year-old sophomore, quickly passed 12 yards to end Neil Henderson for the first touchdown and sprinted 20 yards for another and a 15-0 lead. Before he was taken out of the game in the final quarter, Staubach knifed 2 yards for a third touchdown and passed 65 for a fourth as Navy routed Army, 34-14. For the afternoon, Staubach, a pinpoint passer and an elusive runner, completed 11 of 13 passes for 188 yards and rushed for 34 more. It was a brilliant performance, one of the most sensational in the service series, and it had been accomplished by a sophomore, playing in his first game against Army. "Sure I was nervous," said Staubach in the dressing room. "With your parents, 100,000 people, and the President of the United States in the stands, who wouldn't be nervous?"

To everyone else, Staubach, nicknamed "Jolly Roger" by the Annapolis publicity man, was the coolest man on the field. "He was great," said Dietzel. "When he's in there, he's in charge. All day long he turned potential losses into gains, with those passes and his runs. He's a real football player. Navy's not the same without him."

Navy Coach Wayne Hardin was even more enthusiastic about his naval hero. "Roger's fantastic," said Hardin, wiping sweat off his face in the now steaming, teeming dressing room. "But I've been saying that all year and nobody really believed me."

Staubach has been making believers out of football coaches and scouts since his senior year at Cincinnati's Purcell High School when he started playing offensive quarter-

Roger Staubach, Navy quarterback.

Opposite: Roger Staubach eludes Army tacklers to toss a touchdown pass to end Neil Henderson in the third quarter of the Army-Navy game in 1962. Navy won, 34-14.

back for the first time. Tall and rawboned (he is now 6-foot-2, and 193 pounds), he attracted scholarship offers from most of the Big Ten schools and Midwestern independents. At first, Staubach couldn't make up his mind.

At one point during his senior year, Staubach, who had once thought about becoming a priest, wanted to go to Notre Dame. "They told him they didn't have any quarterback scholarships left," says Hardin. "Then a Notre Dame coach saw him play in the Ohio All-Star Game and they told him a scholarship had opened up. He refused it. That's the kind of kid he is."

By rejecting Notre Dame, Staubach had merely narrowed the field. Finally, he signed a letter of intent with Purdue, but, at the last moment, changed his mind again, settling this time on the Naval Academy. There was only one drawback: though his grades were better than average, his math marks were low and he had to go to junior college for one year before entering the Academy.

Though he was outstanding as a plebe in 1961 (he also starred in basketball and baseball), he was still a third-string quarterback when the 1962 season began. "It wasn't that we didn't think he was good," said Hardin. "We knew he was a real good one, but we didn't think he was ready." In the first three games of 1962, Navy was no more ready than its young quarterback. The Middies lost to Penn State, 41-7, in the opener, staggered past William and Mary, 20-16, and then collapsed against Minnesota, 20-0. In the first three games, Staubach played a total of six minutes, threw four incompleted passes, and lost 14 yards rushing. A nervous youngster who occasionally tears away at his fingernails to relieve the tension, he rarely had enough time to warm up before being replaced. "I feel a little sick before every game, but after the first play I'm all right," he said. "I still thought that if I had the right chance, I could move in."

222

Staubach got the right chance in Navy's fourth game against Cornell and he stayed in for the rest of the season. When Staubach wasn't within hearing distance, Hardin and his assistants often paid glowing tribute to the youngster. "Roger not only can throw the ball, but when a team puts a big rush on us he has the speed and agility to move with the ball," said Hardin. "He also has the rare gift of looking over his receivers in only a second and picking out the one most open. I've been around for a while and I've seen very few with this sixth sense. Heck, he's already proven himself under fire more than any sophomore I ever coached."

In any year, the Army-Navy game is the premier event of the college football season, attracting more fans, more publicity, and more second-guessing than even the Rose Bowl. For any coach, victory in the Army-Navy game can turn a dismal season into a glowing one.

Preparing for the big one, both coaches couldn't stop thinking about the same athlete quarterback, Roger Staubach. He was the key to Hardin's attack and he was the key to Dietzel's defenses. "The best thing Navy does is to get you worried about Staubach and then hand the ball off to Johnny Sai or Pat Donnelly," said Dietzel. "Defending against Staubach is really a three-pronged affair. You worry about his long-passing game and then he drops little tosses to his backs, moving diagonally or just over the line. Get set for those and Staubach gives the ball to Donnelly or Sai on a draw. If you get all these covered, you open yourself up to the worst problem of all because now Staubach has run with the ball himself. And he is a very dangerous runner, especially when he drops back as if to pass and then breaks away. He's as elusive a ball-carrier as there is in the college game."

In his six full games, he had compiled a remarkable set of statistics—completing 56 of 85 passes for 778 yards and five touchdowns, and rushing for 231 yards and five more touchdowns. Dietzel, a defensive specialist, was counting on more than his defenses to stop Staubach. Playing before 100,000 fans in his first game against Army, the youngster figured to suffer from nervousness at least in the beginning, possibly making a mistake or two before regaining his poise. Any sophomore is a serious liability in an Army-Navy game—and a sophomore quarterback is usually courting disaster.

Yet Staubach, nervelessly picking the Army defenses apart by passing when the linesmen charged and by rushing when they held back, did not make a single mistake. His 222 yards gained against Army gave him 1,231 for seven games, only 117 yards short of the Navy-season record set by George Welsh playing nine games as a senior in 1955. Staubach also finished with 67 completions in 98 attempts for an extraordinary 68.4 per cent, the top average in the nation.

In the dressing room, a reporter asked Hardin if he felt there was a turning point to the game. Hardin looked at his young hero, grinned, and said, "Yep. When we showed up."

Staubach laughed easily. "It's still really hard for me to believe all this has happened," he said, wiping the burnt cork from under his eyes with a sweaty towel. "It will take a while for me to get used to it."

5
THE
COACHES

Gil Dobie, whose outstanding Navy team lost only three games in the three years he coached at Annapolis, 1917-1919.

Gil Dobie was one of the most successful football coaches in the fabled history of the gridiron. Yet it seemed to his fellow coaches and to sportswriters that as Gil gained in stature, turning out winning teams, he became more gloomy and pessimistic. Dobie turned out nine consecutive unbeaten teams at the University of Washington, and in 1917 took over the head coaching job at Annapolis, replacing the great Jonas Ingram. In this story the Dobie dourness is clearly felt as the team gets ready to play Army in the annual battle. Sportswriter Art Robinson wrote it in 1919.

Gloomy Gil

ART ROBINSON

THE MORBIDITY WHICH CONSUMED THE COACHES OF THE ARMY FOOTBALL team early in the season is as nothing compared with the depressions which seem to be taking the joy out of the lives of the Navy coaches. But the younger and optimistic men at Annapolis can see only the sun and a victory over the Army for the first time since 1912, when a field goal by Brown, the Navy's great guard of that year, defeated the Cadets.

They are preparing for just such a victory with practical foresight. They are diligently practicing a number of new cheers and songs, and when they sing "The Navy Brought Them Over and the Navy Brought Them Back," a singular significance makes itself manifest. They sing in a manner which maliciously seems to suggest that they were peculiarly selfish in making the return trip for the Army as safe as possible.

The Navy and the Army meet at the Polo Grounds on November 29, and the belief is general that the Navy will win. But the Navy coaches do not say so. As a matter of fact, they are looking forward to the Georgetown game a week from Saturday with a great deal of apprehension, and one of the attachés of the Navy staff expressed an opinion that Georgetown would win by at least 20 to 0.

There is, he said, a great poverty of material. The line, in his opinion, is passing fair, but the backfield is not quite that. He also said that the ability of the team is greatly exaggerated, because of the fact that the middies have scored a total of 136 points in the three games which they have played and won to date.

It was said that the team hasn't as many as five plays of more than a purely elementary character. It was said that the Army would win easily if the teams were to meet tomorrow, instead of next month, but when your correspondent requested an opinion on the probability of an Army victory on November 29, no reply was forthcoming.

In short, the sorrowful expressions of the Navy coaches were nothing more than an affectation for which football coaches are noted. It is an affectation carefully cultivated for the purpose of deception, but it is an affectation which is no longer as stylish as it used to be.

Nevertheless, it seems to have made serious young men of the Navy players, and their practice today was marked by an earnestness which reflected itself in the manner in which they ran off their plays in a signal drill, and later in a workout against the scrub team.

Oliver Alford, who is looked upon as the star of the backfield, did not take part in the practice, and it is feared that the injury which he sustained last week may prevent him from playing against the Army. Alford is a graduate of the Flushing High School, and in the early games of the season gave indications of developing into a player of all-American possibility.

The backfield of the Army game will probably be made up of Clark, Benoist, Watters, and Koehler, if they come out of the games which are to be played against West Virginia, Wesleyan, Georgetown, and Colby, in good shape. But the Navy coaches are in a state of mind sorrowfully receptive to all sorts of catastrophes, and they almost persuaded your correspondent to believe that fate and the Army have entered into a conspiracy to beat the Navy by almost any means.

Larson is the first choice for center, and Denfield and Moore are the guards. King and Murray are the tackles, and Graves and Ewen the ends. The line as a whole is admitted to be passing fair by the coaches, but students at the Academy believe that only a six-inch mortar will make it possible for the Army to open a hole in their line.

Clark and King do the punting, but Gil Dobie, the head coach, has been unable to discover a drop-kicker of any ability, but in this connection it was said that the Navy has not tried to score a field goal in three years.

Your correspondent was turned over to several members of the football council by Dobie, and he was told to ask as many questions as he desired; somehow, his curiosity on certain phases of the Navy defense and offense seemed to concern itself with none of the virtues of the team and with all of its defects.

He was told, first, that there is neither a good drop-kicker nor punter on the squad; that the offense is limited in scope; and that the forward pass has not been of any use because of a lack of skillful passers and receivers.

But Navy men have full confidence in Dobie, and, while they will not say so, they believe in their hearts that their team will score a victory over the Army for the first time in seven years.

Dobie's system has been definitely established, and the indications are that the success which he had at the University of Washington, where he turned out teams which went through nine consecutive seasons without a defeat will be duplicated to some extent here, so far as victories over the Army are concerned.

The candidates for the team have been divided into two squads, the first of which is composed of the first and second teams, the scrubs and substitutes. The other is made up mostly of first-year men who devote most of their time to fundamentals. It is from this squad that future Navy teams will be made, and against the future Dobie and his assistants are preparing and building now, carefully and systematically.

As a player during the 1914, 1915, and 1916 seasons, Biff Jones was a standout performer for Army. After World War I, he returned to West Point as head football coach and later as athletic director. Vern Van Ness, writing in 1929, recounts the highlights in the career of the "incomparable Jones."

Biff Jones, Army Football Coach

VERN VAN NESS

WHENEVER AND WHEREVER AN IMPORTANT SPORTING EVENT IS BEING staged, such as the intercollegiate games, the international polo matches, the Poughkeepsie regatta, and a big, brown-haired man rises to voice enthusiasm, displaying in doing so one of the most remarkable smiles you ever looked at, you can put that man down as Lawrence McCheny Jones, otherwise Capt. Biff Jones, Army football coach.

It is legend that he missed few of the outstanding events in sports, and during the last few years he has perforce added to his list such other spectacles as the Army-Yale, Army-Notre Dame, and Army-Navy gridiron struggles.

But last Saturday afternoon, when the Smiling Warrior brought his 1929 edition of the Army eleven to the Yankee Stadium and sent them after Knute Rockne's band of battlers from South Bend, Indiana, Capt. Biff Jones, West Point, '17, was marking the prelude to his swan song as an Army coach.

It is quite possible that in the impending future when highly specialized sporting events occur in this part of the world, Captain Jones will be a spectator. He is going back to school.

Of course there is a catch in that last statement. The Army football coach merely is departing for the Artillery School, but he will first lead his eleven westward for the Stanford game on December 28.

In the regular course of events, the United States Army being unsentimental in the matter, all West Point football coaches, no matter how good they may be, receive a detail after a while which takes them away from the Plains on the Hudson. So that Biff Jones's passing is nothing out of the ordinary.

There was one season, however, when he packed his kit and departed from the Point with mingled joy and regret, marking a period that he is not likely to forget. That was in 1917, and the young giant who slipped out of the reservation at West Point was Lt. L. M. Jones, bound for the World War, joy in his heart. His regret was due to the fact that he had been elected captain of the Army football team; he had won that cherished post but could never fill it.

Biff Jones turned out some of Army's greatest teams. He was coach of the 1926 thriller that ended in the 21-21 tie.

In 1914, which is quite a march back along the gridiron trail, the annual picture of the Army football team designated man No. 11 as Jones, left tackle. The next year it listed him the same way, but it might have prefixed the name by the symbol Biff.

Biff was a symbol richly earned by Cadet Jones by the very logical process of biffing opposing lines. While Left Tackle Jones was operating in the front line sector of the Army football maneuvers in 1914, 1915, 1916, Notre Dame and Navy were being trampled beneath Cadet feet.

Left Tackle Jones helped to beat Notre Dame in 1914, helped to hold Notre Dame to a 7-0 victory in 1915, and assisted in trouncing Notre Dame, 30 to 10, in 1916. In that same period Left Tackle Jones also aided Oliphant, McEwan, and Vidal to sink Navy three times in a row.

In fact, it was following the 1916 struggle with Navy at the Polo Grounds, when Oliphant, McEwan, and Vidal, the chief heroes, went back to West Point loaded down with such Navy trophies as fatigue caps, headgear, and sweat shirts, that the team got together and elected Jones captain for 1917.

Of course the football captain-elect was delighted at the prospect. But in August of 1917 he was graduated ahead of time, commissioned a second lieutenant, simultaneously commissioned a first lieutenant, and went off to war instead of football.

In 1920 he was commissioned captain, was mustered out in 1922, then appointed a first lieutenant, and in 1926 again was made captain. Also, in that year, he succeeded McEwan as coach at West Point and he has been on that job ever since.

He has been assisting also in building up athletics in general and polo in particular at West Point. He was one of the leading forces in creating a heavier Army football schedule, with more dates away from home. The impelling reason was that Army could make more money away from the Plains; this meant more money for the athletic fund and for the Army's new polo field.

Football is not Captain Jones's leading diversion, odd as that statement may sound. He is diverted by any athletic activity, for which reason he never kept his players from other sports just because they were primarily football men. If they wanted to play lacrosse, hockey, or anything else that might cause consternation on the part of most coaches, it was all right with Coach Jones.

That is one of many reasons why the football squad at West Point to the man will vote for Biff Jones on almost any proposition that can be imagined. The men regard him as a great leader, a fine teacher, a square shooter, a real friend, and a smiling taskmaster.

Captain Jones was born in Washington, D.C., on October 8, 1895, so that it will be seen he is thirty-four years old. This is an age that is too young to make an Army officer eligible for retirement. But Captain Jones is looking forward to that day.

"Then I can play squash all I want to," he exclaimed in confessing his secret desire the other day.

But as a matter of fact he plays plenty of squash as it is and he is a good player.

But the real ambition that he has in mind when he retires is to be a breeder of blooded horses. He wants to retire to raise horses and ride them and play them at polo.

"Now, that is what I call life," he declared, smiling his famed smile.

"Of course Army captains when they retire might find it a bit difficult to become breeders of blooded horses," he admitted. "But that is my ambition just the same—that and beating Stanford in my farewell game as coach."

Coach Biff Jones, with Major General W. R. Smith, superintendent of West Point, New York's Mayor Jimmy Walker, and Army star Red Cagle in 1929, one of the years without an Army-Navy game due to the dispute over eligibility rules.

Gen. Ben Lear said, "If Sasse had been given a chance to see overseas duty, he would have been as great a battlefield leader as George Patton." Ralph Sasse was not sent overseas. He was beyond the age limit for overseas duty when the shooting began. This story, by Allison Danzig of The New York Times, is an inspiring account of the man who coached Army's eleven to three straight wins over Navy—in 1930, 1931, 1932.

The Army's Football Coach

ALLISON DANZIG

A FEW WEEKS AGO A PEREGRINATING CORRESPONDENT STOPPED AT WEST Point to be taken in custody by Captain Wells and marched off to Army football headquarters in the gymnasium.

Three flights up, they entered a large, sunlit room, where their eyes fell upon a half-dozen officers in their shirt sleeves seated at desks, each of them absorbed in a mass of papers whose text might have been the diagrams of military maneuvres.

Around the walls of the room were blackboards covered with similar diagrams, copiously annotated, and the atmosphere of the whole place was one of strict business, though there was nothing rigid or formal about it.

Into this room there stepped shortly, from an inner sanctum, a stalwart, sandy-haired, blue-eyed officer, slightly older than the young aides at the desks. His firmly modeled, cleanly defined features relaxed into a cheery smile of greeting to his visitors. Maj. Ralph Irvine Sasse, Army's new head coach, was standing in the midst of his staff and one had only to be in his presence for a moment to feel the contagion of a vibrant personality that inspires confidence and implicit faith and commands respect and wholehearted loyalty.

When Capt. Lawrence M. (Biff) Jones completed his four-year detail at the Point and went to Fort Sill, Oklahoma, to pursue his military career, Army lost one of the most universally liked football coaches it has had. In Major Sasse, end coach at the Academy for seven years, Army has a successor who is held in the same high regard and whose enterprise and thoroughgoing efficiency in organizing and carrying out plans for a reformation of the Army system of attack have attracted public attention to his team in a year that has witnessed the exit of the most colorful player in West Point football history, Red Cagle.

This reformation has witnessed the scrapping of a close-order offense that has endured at the Academy like the Rock of Ages and the introduction of the Warner system of attack.

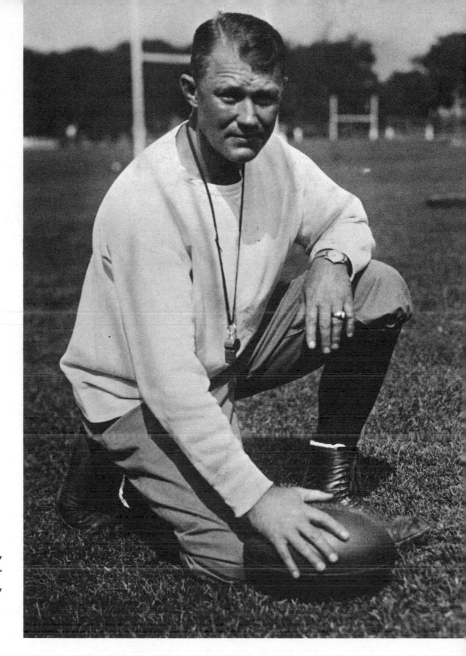

In his three years as head coach for Army, Ralph Sasse had the distinction of defeating Navy three times in a row—1930, 1931, 1932.

To appreciate properly how far-reaching has been this renovation, which marks the most drastic change in Army football since the Cadets got a glimpse of the Dorais-Rockne forward passing combination in 1913, one must be aware of the difference in temperament and training between Major Sasse and Captain Jones.

Captain Jones, an artillery man, was the conservative exponent of the Napoleonic school, which holds that the side with the heavier cannon wins. Straightforward power plays, simply designed and depending for their success upon sheer power, were the weapons with which he armed his team, though it was not lacking in aerial auxiliaries, and Cagle was an open-order attack in himself, with his lone dashes off the tackles and around the ends.

The steamroller has been the symbol of the Army teams of the past and there is a story that Col. Pot Graves, probably as brilliant a teacher of line play as the game has known, once pointed to one of these stone crushers, chugging along the Academy grounds, with the remark, "There's my team."

Major Sasse, trained in the cavalry school at Fort Riley, Kansas, and who, incidentally, commanded a tank battalion in the Twenty-seventh Division with distinction, comes to the game with altogether different conceptions of attack.

Like Jones, he is a stickler for detail, and has laid the groundwork of his system with Prussian efficiency. In addition, it is only natural that a man reared in a school that emphasizes the elements of deception and surprise and who thinks in terms of flanking movements should have been won over to the double-wingback formation.

There was nothing halfhearted about this conversation of Major Sasse. Once he had committed himself to the Warner methods, he left for Stanford with two of his assistants to spend six weeks as the guests of Glenn Warner, observing the spring practice and acquainting themselves with every detail of the system. Upon his return to the Academy, Major Sasse called out his candidates in the first spring practice Army has had, and so intensively were they grounded for eight days in the basic elements of the new attack that by the middle of September the squad was far advanced and had achieved finished execution in many plays.

Not content with revolutionizing Army's style of football, Major Sasse effected other changes. New paraphernalia, including scrimmage machines for six and seven man lines, such as Warner uses to perfect co-ordination, were introduced.

The color of the jerseys was changed, the weight of the uniforms and pads cut down, and, as an indication of the Army coach's consideration for the spectator, numbers were ordered to be sewn on both the fronts and backs of the jerseys.

An additional innovation was the inauguration of a daily session of Major Sasse and his quarterbacks and centers immediately after dinner and before the Academy study period, made possible by his arranging for these men to eat ahead of the other members of the Cadet corps.

All of this indicates the energy and enterprise with which Army's football destinies are being directed. How successful the new methods will be remains to be determined by the season's results. But if the team's showing in its first two games, in which it has rolled up close to a hundred points, is any criterion, the unbounded confidence that Major Sasse has inspired in every man on the Academy grounds has not been misplaced.

The record of the major as an end coach at West Point is an augury for success in his new post. During the seven years that he was working with the ends, Army's flanks were one unfailing source of strength. In 1928, when the situation on the wings looked to be acute after the loss of Born, Brentnall, and Harbold, Major Sasse relieved the stringency by developing Carlmark and Messinger, now in their third season as regulars and one of the best pairs of ends in Army football history.

One might expect that a coach who had stepped into his job right after such men as Cagle, Murrell, and Perry had wound up their careers and who was undertaking to install a new system would be noncommittal, if not dubious, about the outlook. This is not the attitude, however, of Major Sasse.

He has a proper appreciation for the line which he inherited intact with the excep-

Ralph Sasse and Jack Price, Army's team captain in 1931.

tion of one man and for the fine crop of backs who came up from the plebes. He has a high regard, too, for the efficiency of his assistants, Johnny Stokes, "Fats" Ellinger, Harry Wilson, "Red" Blaik, Charley Born, and "Red" Reeder, and he knows what an asset high morale is.

It is upon this morale, upon the spirited and enthusiastic co-operation he is receiving from his men that he is counting to offset what they may lack in technical experience in the new system he has given them, and the existence of this spirit is in itself a commentary on the character of the man who has inspired it.

235

A Marine Steals the Show as Navy Sinks Army

EVERETT MORRIS

THE BIG MARINE LANDED IN PHILADELPHIA'S MUNICIPAL STADIUM TODAY, and kept the situation well in hand, while 98,000 soldiers, sailors, marines, Army and Navy Officers political bigwigs and ordinary citizens thrilled to the pomp and pageantry, music and fun, which formed a glamorous background for the best Army-Navy football game in many a year.

The Marine was Maj. Emery E. Larson, the big, hearty Swede from Minnesota, whose combined six-year playing and coaching career at the Naval Academy came to a close with Navy's brilliant 14-6 conquest of the friendly enemy from the banks of the Hudson. Six times Larson has faced Army, three times a center on great Navy teams, and three times as head coach of the Middies' football squad.

Not once in those six years has he known defeat at the hands of the West Pointers. A month from now, he will bid farewell to Annapolis and begin studies in the Naval War College at Newport, Rhode Island. With him will go the big, blue and gold Navy blanket on which are inscribed the scores of his triumphs over Army. Already this bed coverlet bears the following lettering around the huge block N: 1919, Navy, 6-0; 1920, Navy, 7-0; 1921, Navy 7-0; 1939, Navy, 10-0; 1940, Navy, 14-0; This week Grandma, Swedes' wife, will attach: 1941, Navy, 14-6. Then the blanket and its mute story of Larson's success will be complete.

Thus it came to pass that for the third time in the fifty-one-year history of this service football classic, Navy had taken three decisions in a row from the Cadets. The first stretch was from 1910 through 1912. Next one was 1919 to 1921, when Larson played for Navy, and now Swede has wrapped up another skein of three in a row.

Larson agreed that the turning point in the game occurred in the third period, when Navy had the ball on the Army 16-yard line, fourth down and six yards to go.

"I sent in Wes Gebert with instructions to go around the end," said the Swede, "and, boy, didn't he carry out instructions. He gave the play to Bill Busick and Busick took the ball 15 yards to the Army 1-yard line. He was the real key play of the entire afternoon. Then I rushed in Phil Hurt with instructions to use our 37 buck, a short-side plunge, and over he went. It was wonderful to see those boys play."

Swede Larson (right) with John Whelchel, who succeeded Larson as coach for Navy.

"Howard Clark's 6-yard run for the second Navy score was supposed to be the same sort of play," said Larson, "but it didn't develop as we thought."

As he finished the interviews, Larson suddenly thumped his star Navy tackle across the back. Chewning grinned. Smeared with dirt, torn and tired. Chewning smiled and said, "Major, here's the game ball. You deserve it."

Larson's grin was a mile wide. "Thanks, Billy, I'll always remember this fine gesture of yours."

Garrison H. Davidson starred in two Army victories over Navy, coached the West Pointers to three wins over their traditional rivals from Annapolis, and became Superintendent of the Academy. Here is a story about the magnificent Gar Davidson written by Frank Graham.

About Gar Davidson

FRANK GRAHAM

THERE WAS A FOOTBALL RALLY AT WEST POINT THE OTHER NIGHT IN advance of the Navy game and in the course of the rally they called on Gar Davidson to speak, and Gar said:

"I don't know where I will be a year from tonight, but wherever I am I will have many happy memories of the experiences I have had as coach of the Army football team."

Nobody knows where Gar will be a year from now, because Gar is in the Army. That Navy game was his last game as coach of the Army team and he must go back to the troops. He may be in Hawaii or the Canal Zone . . . or some isolated post on the desert's edge in the Southwest. But wherever he is, he will have . . . as he said . . . many memories of the time he coached the Army.

They will not all be happy memories, for no coach, however able, can look back on any five-year span in his life and find all of it pleasant. Gar must have had moments of uncertainty and dread when first he took over the job at West Point. Because this is one of the biggest football coaching jobs in the country, and Gar was just a slim, blue-eyed, prematurely gray-haired young man, not yet ten years out of the academy, when he took over this job.

He followed some great fellows and great coaches into the job, too. Fellows like Ralph Sasse and Biff Jones. Fellows who had welded smashing Army teams. Good fellows, good mixers, fellows the public knew almost as well as the Army knew them. Fellows who weren't easy to follow, especially for a kid just out of the academy, and a lieutenant at that. A kid who wasn't used to the headlines and the crowds. A kid who knew how much was expected of him . . . and who must have sometimes wondered in those early days if he had all the stuff he needed.

He worked quietly, almost desperately, at times. He lost Red Blaik and Tubby Ellinger, assistant coaches, who had been credited with much of the success Army teams had had, and he went without them. He knew moments of bitterness over lost games Army should have won. And knew moments of elation over Army victories.

Army coach, Gar Davidson, talking things over with team captain Harvey Jablonsky during a practice session in 1933.

Memories of these moments will come crowding back to him wherever he is a year from now . . . or five years from now . . . or ten. And among the memories will be one of Philadelphia last Saturday, when the murk hung heavy over the Municipal Stadium and over 100,000 sat excitedly in a fine, drenching rain and saw Army beat Navy.

These wonderfully great teams, these Army and Navy teams that played at Philadelphia last Saturday, were not the greatest. Nor was this a great game. But it was hard and closely fought, as all Army-Navy games are. And, especially considering that it was played with a wet ball on a soggy gridiron, was well played.

The decisive action came in the first period when, following some exchanges of punts, Army passed its way to within striking range of Navy's goal line and then struck fiercely, so that at the end of the drive Jim Craig was catapulted over the line for a touchdown.

Navy was reaching almost frantically in this game for a smashing finish to a disappointing season. They thought at Annapolis in the early fall that this was the best Navy team in years. It was a fine-looking team, big and fast and powerful, and it was coached by Lt. Hank Hardwick, who had made a reputation first as an assistant coach at the

239

academy and later as coach of teams off the battle wagons of the Pacific fleet.

Navy won and lost. When it won, it won the hard way. When it lost, it missed scoring chances that would have enabled it to win easily. As the weeks rolled by, they said at Annapolis:

"Do not give up on our team. Some Saturday afternoon it will click, and when it does, it will blast the other team right out of sight."

Now it was in there with Army. Last chance, trailing by a touchdown . . . and time running out on the big clock on the east rim of the bowl.

Once it seemed as though Navy was going to click. As though the recollections of the defeats by Notre Dame and Penn and Princeton would pass away in a glorious victory over Army. That was at the outset of the second half. Navy was hot then. Lemuel Cook and Emmett Wood, behind a Navy line suddenly whipped into a fury, drove and smashed through Army's defense, and the Middies, sitting row on row, above the east side of the gridiron, clamored for a touchdown. Army reeled on its heels; through the huge crowd the excitement was terriffic. And then Army suddenly tightened. The Navy threat was beaten off. Army's line was pounding once more. Army backs were lunging through gaps in the Navy wall. . . . And on the big clock, time was running out.

So the game ended as dusk gathered over the field and floodlights blazed down and a fine rain slanted through the yellow haze from the lights. Army had won and the Cadets rushed across the field behind their band and gloated over the Middies, who sat row on row, and took it in the fashion that is traditional with the academies.

Gar Davidson had seen his career as Army's coach end in triumph. Twice before Army teams coached by him had beaten Navy. But twice Navy had beaten his teams. This was the game he had wanted most to win, his last game, the game he will think of most.

Gar went back to West Point with his players yesterday. The corps was waiting for him and dragged him and his players up the long hill from the depot to the Plains, in the coaches that have been used for this purpose since the long ago, when Benny Havens kept his pub in Highland Falls. The Cadets sang and danced and made the walls of the gaunt gray buildings rattle with their cheers.

That's another scene that Gar will remember, in all its vivid color, when Army and Navy meet again . . . a year from now . . . wherever he is.

How do you introduce a story on Navy's Eddie Erdelatz? A great football player, a great coach, a great man—it's all here in Bill Bailey's account of one of the finest coaches in the game, an inspiration to any man who ever played football under his tutelage. This is taken from his story written back in 1950.

The Bouncer's Boy

BILL BAILEY

JOE ERDELATZ CAME OVER TO THIS COUNTRY FROM AUSTRIA WHEN HE WAS fifteen. That was sixty years ago, and he didn't stop at the first place he got off, but he went right out to California. He did one thing and another for a while, and then he started tending bar on the waterfront in San Francisco.

There was a lot of what writers call life around there then, and Joe could handle any order you gave him. He was just under six feet tall, and was wide in the shoulders and went to 200 pounds. He could mix it any way you wanted it.

"I guess he could really go," his kid says now. "They tell me that in those days when something started, chairs, tables, and everything else went. Whatever it was, I guess he could take care of it."

After a while Joe got his own place. It was in the toughest section of the waterfront, and it was called Joe-the-Bouncer's. It's still there with the same name on it.

Joe married a girl who had come over from Germany. They were very happy and then the boy was born, and two weeks later Joe's wife died.

It was a tough spot for Joe. He was crazy about the kid, but a guy like Joe couldn't take care of a baby alone, and so he put the kid out with his wife's best friend. She and her husband took care of the kid until he was three, and then they turned him over to her father and mother, and every chance Joe got he would visit the kid and bring him things and spend the whole time down on the floor playing with him.

When the kid was seven, Joe put him in St. Joseph's Academy. It was a pretty strict school, and Joe knew it and so he never missed a Sunday. Sunday afternoons were when the parents were allowed to visit the kids, and every Sunday he'd be there no matter what the weather. In the summers he'd take the kid and they'd go up into the mountains or somewhere along the ocean and they'd fish and swim and talk together for almost the whole summer.

When you add up everything, Joe did all right for his kid. You see his kid's name in the papers now, particularly since late last December.

Late last December there were a lot of newspapermen—sports writers—sitting around the United States Naval Academy at Annapolis. The brass had just announced that they were getting a new football coach. Almost at the same time, they announced that they were asking Eddie Erdelatz—that's Joe's boy—if he'd take the job.

The newspapermen were sitting around and playing poker. They played poker for three days. They were waiting for Eddie Erdelatz to make up his mind. At the time they were waiting he was still the line coach of the San Francisco professional team, the Forty-niners, but when you are an assistant coach anywhere, the head coach always does the talking, and you never get to know the newspapermen and they never get to know you.

The newspapermen did know that Navy was going to go right on playing "teams of representative institutions from various sections of the country." That's the Navy's description of its suicide schedule, and they knew that if Eddie took the job, this is what he would be facing. They just didn't know Eddie, and they didn't know his private picture.

"In the first place," Eddie says now, "imagine having a job under a nice guy like Buck Shaw and with the Forty-niners. You go to work at ten in the morning and most of the time you're done by noon. You receive X number of dollars, which isn't bad. Before I made up my mind I came near having a breakdown."

Of course, Eddie was flattered to be asked to be the head coach of the Navy. The Navy was flattered, too, when he accepted, because he was the one man everybody at the place wanted.

Eddie started playing football at the age of nine. "In those days we all used to wear knickers and long, black stockings. I got chalk out of the classroom and I striped my stockings with it. Then I tried to stick acorns onto the bottom of my shoes—this sounds crazy now—with mud. Of course, they wouldn't stick, but then I found an old football with no air in it, and then I really went to town.

"I'd put the old, flat football down for the kickoff. I was all alone, but I'd line up the team. I'd go through all the motions of the game. I'd wave to the officials and then I'd kick off.

"Of course, the ball wouldn't go more than four or five feet. Then I'd imagine the whole game. We'd stop the other team, and then we'd take over. I'd shift into the Notre Dame box, and then the next thing you knew I'd have the ball and I'd be cutting and stiff-arming and, of course, I'd score the touchdown and we'd win the ball game."

When he got tired of this Eddie rounded up a few other kids in the school and they formed a team. They practiced for weeks until the others began to kick that there wasn't much fun in always practicing if they didn't play any games.

"There was one Brother there I will never forget," Eddie says. "His name was Brother Phelan and he was a nice old guy. I went to him and told him we had a football team, and that we'd like to get some games. He said: 'But first, we'll have to get you uniforms.'

"I said: 'But where will we get the money?' He said: 'We'll raffle off a gold watch.' Then I said: 'But where will we get the money to buy the watch?' and he said: 'Don't worry about that.'

"He told me to hitchhike down to the printing shop where the St. Mary's College paper was printed, and they printed the tickets for the raffle. After we'd sold enough tickets, Brother Phelan bought the watch, and we were completely outfitted, with the exception of shoes.

"But in college," Eddie says, "football was our main sport, and we were told that that was why we were in school."

That was at St. Mary's. He started playing freshman ball at end, under Red Strader, who later became head coach at St. Mary's and who is now coaching the professional New York Yanks. Red shifted him from end to the backfield, but when he moved up to the varsity he played end for three years and did the kicking. Slip Madigan coached St. Mary's then, and Slip put the school on the map. His big intersectional money-maker every year was with Fordham. Fordham was an Eastern powerhouse in those days, with Jimmy Crowley coaching them and Frank Leahy handling the line.

Eddie had a good afternoon against Fordham in his sophomore year. His best year was 1934, his junior year, though, and his best game was against Fordham. It almost cost him his life.

Fordham had a real club. They had Leo Paquin at end and Joe Maniaci at fullback

Navy coach Eddie Erdelatz discusses tactics with his varsity.

Navy coaching staff in 1946. (Front row, l. to r.) Ray Swartz, Johnny Wilson, Tom Hamilton, head coach, Rip Miller. (Back row, l. to r.) Ben Martin, Eddie Erdelatz, Lou Bryan.

and Amerino Sarno and Joe McArdle, among others in the line. All Eddie did was play his end and do all the kicking and catch the touchdown pass just as it was cutting the corner of the end zone. St. Mary's won, 14 to 9, and the play is remembered because in going for the ball Eddie banged into one of the officials and stiffened him.

"That," he says now, "was just about the end of my football."

When Eddie got back to the locker room after the game, his right shin hurt him where somebody had stepped on it. There was a radio announcer in the room, though, walking around with his microphone and his pear-shaped tones, and by the time he finnished interviewing Eddie all the medical supplies had been packed.

"So they slapped some cotton and tape on it," Eddie says, "and it still bothered me a little." When the kneecap began to swell and Eddie couldn't stand or bend the knee they got a doctor. The doctor found the infection from the shin had spread and worked into part of the lining of the kneecap and sections of a couple of cartilages.

They got Eddie's dad. It was a tough moment. Eddie's dad signed the papers, though, and they cut Eddie's leg open. At first they thought he was going to die, and then they thought he was going to lose his leg. After the operation the first thing he did was throw back the covers to see if he still had the leg.

He had it, but they told him he'd always be stiff-legged. They were wrong, because he worked the leg back into shape, and he played the next year wearing a brace and taking shots of Novocain. He was the old man's son.

During that last year he started helping Slip with the other ends. When he was graduated, in 1935, Slip took him on as an assistant.

Eddie worked under Slip in 1936 and 1937. In 1938 he married Agnes Connor, a nurse he met while he was in Providence Hospital in Oakland suffering with the leg, and that year he shifted to the University of San Francisco as end coach under George Malley.

When Strader took over at St. Mary's in place of Madigan he hired Eddie back, this time as line coach. In 1924 Eddie went into the Navy, as a lieutenant, j.g. He took his indoctrination course at Annapolis.

At Annapolis they started liking Eddie from the day he first came in to assist Hagberg. The kids who played under him liked him as a guy as well as an end coach, and three of the ends he coached—Dick Duden and Leon Bramlett and Phil Ryan—were the captains of their teams.

Navy's head coach, Eddie Erdelatz, points to blackboard on which play is diagrammed for members of the Navy squad as they hold skull practice for Army-Navy game. From left, the players are Joe Gattuso, Bob Cameron, John Weaver, Fred Franco, and Tony Correnti.

When Eddie came back this spring as head coach they were all new kids to him, of course. Working with the pros hadn't changed him, though, even if he had been a little worried about it.

"It's a little easier to keep close to pro players," he says. "College players are just that much younger than you are."

As soon as he took over, Eddie began applying a little practical psychology. When he was introduced to the 400 members of the incoming class in the auditorium in Mahan Hall he started to put himself in with them like this:

"We have at least one thing in common. We're all starting out as plebes. We've all got four years to do a job."

"He'll sell himself to the players, too," Red Strader said when he had heard that Eddie had accepted the job. "That's a coaching gift."

Eddie started his sales campaign in spring practice. Some of the oldest Navy brass say they don't remember a squad that had more enthusiasm than this one.

"I don't know whether they thought they were getting away with something," he says, "but they sure worked hard."

Another thing he did was abolish the annual spring practice game with an outside squad. This undoubtedly shocked some of the brass.

"If you win one of those games," he said, "everybody goes around talking about an undefeated season. If you lose, they all say: 'Well, the same old Navy team.' No matter what happens it doesn't help morale."

He started working on the morale problem in another way, too. He announced that while the Navy had been in the habit of carrying from forty-four to fifty men on its squad he'd cut the number to thirty-seven, and that it would be up to them to either carry the load or fail.

"Why carry players," he said, "that you wouldn't use in a ball game if it lasted three weeks? They're the guys who sit on the bench and when you make a substitution they turn to the ones next to them and they say: 'Why don't he use me? You saw what I did in scrimmage with that guy last week.'

"Those are also the ones," he said, "who are always complaining that the pillows are hard and that the steaks are tough and that the potatoes are lumpy. The ones who play say nothing."

Eddie also imported from the West Coast, for two weeks of the spring practice, Frankie Albert, the star quarterback and passer of the Forty-niners. Albert worked with the quarterbacks and he impressed the whole squad.

"The kids were crazy about him," a Navy man said, "and it was good psychology. He's only a little guy, and they all looked at him and they said to themselves: 'If a little guy like that can be a star playing with the big pros, what have we got to worry about?'"

There wasn't a lot for Eddie to cheer about when he took over, though. He is having his worries, but if you sit around and talk with him when he's off the field you never know how tough he is on himself when he's alone.

"I guess I do too much thinking," he says, "especially when I go to bed. I lie there and I say to myself: 'Why not let it go until tomorrow? You've got all day.' Then I say:

The Erdelatz squad beat Coach Earl Blaik's Army team in 1954, 27-20. Here, Blaik gives his varsity backfield a pep talk before that game. (From left) Tom Bell, Bob Farris, Pat Uebel, Pete Vann, Bob Kyasky.

'But I can work this out now, and improve on it tomorrow and then I'll be that much better off.' Then I don't get to sleep."

Eddie is having some sleepless nights. After all, Sauer signed for four years, too, and was gone after two, but if Eddie can make it go, he's made. If he can't make it go, he'll be just another victim of something that has already knocked off some other pretty capable football brains. If it gets Eddie, though, it won't get him backing off. He inherited a lot from his old man.

"My dad is going on seventy-five now," he says. "He lives at the Olympic Club and he walks five miles a day and then has a swim and his weight is still the same.

"He still owns a place in the Crystal Palace Market where they specialize in steam beer. One night he was in there and there was some big young guy about thirty who was getting obnoxious. My dad walked up to him and told him in a nice way that he didn't want any trouble, so the big guy took exception.

"Now all the time my dad was talking to him he had his left hand on the other guy's right arm. Most bar fighters and street fighters will swing first with their right, you know, and my dad knows that, so while he was talking he was holding the guy's right arm and just turning him a little.

"When the guy went to let a punch go he couldn't move his right, and when he swung his left my dad turned him and then turned him back and let him have it in the stomach. When the guy hit the floor my dad picked him up and tossed him out on the street.

"As you can see," Eddie says, "I'm very proud of my dad."

Earl "Red" Blaik starred for West Point as a Cadet and returned to the Academy to coach its gridders for eighteen glorious years. Here is a tale of "Red" Blaik and his son, Bob, a football star in his own right, as Stanley Woodward penned it in 1950 for the Saturday Evening Post. It is a story of a legendary figure at West Point and the son who played under him.

Football's Greatest Father and Son Act

STANLEY WOODWARD

THE FIRM OF BLAIK AND BLAIK, CURRENTLY COACH AND QUARTERBACK OF the Army football team, has been in existence for twenty-one years, but it never went into the athletic business as a unit until July, 1948, when the junior partner entered the United States Military Academy. Up to that time Red—Col. Earl Henry Blaik, the coach—had seen Bob—Robert McDowell Blaik, the quarterback—play only one half of one period of a football game.

To get this brief glimpse the colonel and Merle, Bob's mother, stood in the shrubbery at the end of the Highland Falls, New York, high school field and peeked through the wire fence. Subterfuge was necessary, for Bob was adamant in his decision that his parents, particularly his father, should not see him play football.

In effect, he said, "This is my own business. You stay over at West Point and coach the Army team. I'll take care of myself."

However, Blaik, senior's, business is football and he had convincing circumstantial evidence that Bob was playing it. The year before, Blaik, junior, had come home with his right arm in an airplane splint, and there still is a big bump on his right collarbone because he went back to playing football as soon as the splint was taken off.

So Blaik, senior's, curiosity became intense. One Friday afternoon in the fall of 1946 he and Mrs. Blaik got into the family car and drove the two miles to Highland Falls. They left the car some distance from the football field and approached it circuitously. They took their places in the shrubbery just after the game had started—an additional precaution to make it impossible for Bob to see them.

"I had to leave for Army practice before the first period was over," said the colonel, "but we stayed long enough to see that Bob's team was going to get a good licking."

This incident was typical of a relationship which Red Blaik has, until now, refused to discuss for publication. For two years he has been turning down writers who came to West Point eager for details on what was obviously a great human-interest story.

The next time Blaik saw his son play he was on the Army plebe team in 1948, having

248

Coach Earl Blaik with his son, Bob Blaik.

put in a year at Exeter getting additional preparation for West Point. He started like a house afire that fall, but wore out as the season advanced. A tendency toward tenseness is his greatest handicap.

Blaik never actually coached Bob until last fall, when the boy came up to the varsity as a yearling—the West Point term for a sophomore—and qualified as understudy for Arnold Galiffa as quarterback of the offensive team. The Army is one of the positive two-platoon teams in the nation, and young Blaik has yet to play on defense in action.

As coach and player, the relation between Blaik and Blaik is approximately the same as the relation between Blaik and any other member of the Army squad. They meet on the practice field, in the training room, at the squad conferences which occur Sundays after church and at the special football table in the mess hall. The military makes little allowance for family life of the cadets. They get up at 5:50 A.M. and almost every minute is occupied until taps at 10:20 P.M. The only time Blaik, the quarterback, goes home to the house by the stadium is when he shows up for dinner on Sunday at noon, generally bringing from one to thirty other cadets with him.

During the academic year the Blaiks never have a chance to talk privately except at quarterback meetings, when they consult on football strategy. In these sessions, Blaik advises Blaik and, conversely, Blaik sometimes questions Blaik about tactics. Ordinarily, however, if Blaik—meaning the quarterback—is bothered by a football question, he takes it to Vince Lombardi, the backfield coach, who has him in immediate charge.

There is no doubt that Blaik, senior, is delighted that the younger of his two sons turned out to be a football player, for he himself is completely devoted to the game and completely convinced that it is good for boys to play it. But he brought no influence to bear on either of his sons. Bill, the older, never took any interest in competing as an athlete. He went to Dartmouth, took two years out to serve as an enlisted man with the Occupation Army in Germany, and is now back at Dartmouth for his senior year. He is majoring in geology and plans to be a petroleum engineer.

Without any urging, Bob started to be an athlete at the age of six. His father encouraged him, not by harangue, but by buying him the athletic gear he needed and by listening when he wanted to talk about his exploits. Inasmuch as Bob's athletic interests ran to baseball, skiing, hockey, speed skating, and numerous other subdivisions, in addition to football, Mrs. Blaik has spent a good part of her life adjusting uniforms and sewing on letters and numbers.

Through most of his high school career Bob was a skinny, overgrown kid with two left feet. At one point he got a little help from his father. Blaik, senior, clandestinely watching as Bob fooled around the edges of Army football practice, passing and punting with other casuals, saw he had some ability in these departments. So one day he went over and showed him how to "pass over his toe"—that is, step in the exact direction of the throw—and how to follow through with his arm. He also asked Doug Kenna and Johnny Sauer, Army backs of the era, to help him with his punting.

When Bob went to Exeter, Colonel Blaik wrote Bill Clark, the football coach—Clark played for Red at Dartmouth—suggesting that Bob be spotted at quarterback in the Exeter T-formation attack because of his passing ability. That was the first time the boy had ever played T football—Highland Falls was singlewing—and he took to it so well that he won the traditional game with Andover virtually single-handed. He threw two passes for touchdowns and made the longest run of the game in leading Exeter to victory, 13 to 0.

Bob had no thought of going to the Military Academy until his father went back there to coach in 1941. Blaik, senior, had served three years in the cavalry following graduation in 1920, and then resigned. Later, he got into football coaching, and in 1934 he became a head coach at Dartmouth. He returned to the service when World War II began, and made an abortive attempt to get closer to warfare than West Point. The War Department vetoed his application and sentenced him to coaching for the duration. He was in uniform, and eventually won his silver eagles, but he did the same work he had done as a civilian; albeit for less money.

All this had an influence on Bob, who had hardly seen a military uniform all the time he was growing up in Dayton, Ohio, where he was born, and in Hanover, New Hampshire, where he went to grammar school while his father was coaching at Dartmouth. He decided, without urging, that he wanted to go to West Point.

Blaik, senior, is an indoctrinated Army man whose idol of idols is Gen. Douglas Mac-

Arthur. He was no doubt delighted when Bob announced his decision, but the Blaik family is run on a plan of self-determination. If Bob had changed his mind, there might have been an argument, but there would have been no countermand.

Bob had exercised self-determination before and got away with it, even when it was in opposition to the plans his father had made for him. In 1944, after Bob's freshman year in Highland Falls High School, the colonel and Mrs. Blaik decided that both boys should go to Kimball Union Academy in Meriden, New Hampshire. That was the year Glenn Davis and Doc Blanchard, Army's greatest backs, started streaking across the gridirons of the nation. Davis was Bob's great hero, and the thought that he was going away from West Point and would not see Glenn play began to depress him.

As the opening of school approached he became glummer and glummer, but his parents thought he would like the school, once he was established there. Mrs. Blaik drove the boys to New Hampshire. Bill was happy. Bob was silent and thoroughly depressed. He didn't say anything until half the distance had been covered.

Then he said, "I didn't bring my football shoes."

Mrs. Blaik recalls the incident. "That settled it. I knew he didn't intend to stay if he hadn't brought his football shoes. When we got to the school he didn't want to take his trunk out of the car. We stayed in a hotel that night and he didn't sleep at all. His father had told him he could come home if he didn't like the school. The next day when we drove back to the school he told me plainly he didn't want to stay. I told him to go in and explain his feelings to the headmaster.

"He must have had a sympathetic reception, for when he came running out to the car a few minutes later he was the happiest boy I've ever seen. He jumped in the back seat and immediately went to sleep. He didn't wake up until we were crossing Bear Mountain Bridge, two hundred and fifty miles from the school."

When he was a grammar-school boy in Hanover, Bob had aspirations to be a musician. The school taught music, and he took up, successively, the piano, the French horn, the cello, and finally the cornet. He showed promise on the cornet, and when the family moved to West Point he studied with M.Sgt. N. E. Fisher, one of the career musicians who play in the Army band. The sergeant noted that a certain muscle in Bob's upper lip, which is essential to cornetists, was exceptionally well developed, and foresaw a musical career for him. Bob was an enthusiastic pupil and used to shut himself in the Blaik bathroom and play over and over again a single tune, "I Don't Want to Set the World on Fire."

However, the sergeant made a serious strategic error. Noting one day that the junior Sousa seemed anxious to hurry through his lesson and get out, he said, "Bob, you've got to take your choice. You can either be a musician or a ballplayer, but not both."

The reaction in favor of the muse which the sergeant expected did not occur. Bob never returned for another lesson, and he has hardly played the cornet since.

There was no scene in the Blaik household. Bob had decided he didn't want to play the cornet. Period. No one mentioned it again.

Neither of his parents has ever made Bob practice music or study his schoolwork. Mrs. Blaik says that it has never been necessary to force him to do anything he obviously had to do, and she doesn't remember ever wakening him up in the morning.

Even when he's on leave and reveille doesn't sound, he is up before everyone else except his father.

Father and son are very much alike, tall—about six feet two—broad-shouldered, slim. Bob doesn't have his father's bronze hair. His is light brown and cut to the bone in a crew job that beats West Point regulation. His hands are large, capable of being wrapped around a football. He weighs 185 pounds and could carry ten pounds more. He would, too, except that he has a certain asceticism, also characteristic of his father, which causes him to believe that eating all he wants is sinful.

In the academic scale at West Point he stands almost exactly where his father did thirty years ago, just below the upper third of the second class—corresponding to the junior class in a civilian college—which comprises 608 cadets.

In meeting strangers, young Blaik is tight-lipped and apparently ingrown, but his classmates and his fellow football players seem to like him.

In addition to being the football quarterback, Bob is the baseball second baseman and the greatest hockey player who ever entered the Military Academy. If he were not committed to a career in the Army, he would be a red-hot prospect for professional hockey. Throughout his high school career he played on an independent hockey team in reasonably fast company. At Exeter he won the traditional Andover game, 3 to 2, with a thirty-foot shot down the center alley. Now he's the Army's hockey mainstay.

Hockey is probably a more natural sport for him than football, but his development as a football player has been phenomenal since he entered the Academy. Vince Lombardi, who handles the Army backs, is hopeful that he will be the greatest of all Army quarterbacks as a firstclassman in 1951.

"Bob doesn't make the same mistake twice," says Vince. "I regard him as an exceptionally intelligent football player. He knows the assignment of every man on every play. If any player, even a linesman, gets mixed up, Bob is capable of straightening him out. He took up golf during his leave last summer and I think it did him good. He was so tense last year that he sometimes did not execute properly. On plays requiring that he hand off the ball, then fake a pass, he was so stiff and hurried that he didn't fool anyone. Golf taught him the value of proper relaxation. Now, when he fakes a pass, he carries it out just as if he had the ball."

Colonel Blaik sat silent while Lombardi discussed Bob's progress. He interrupted once to say that Bob has made many mistakes in the past, and no doubt would make more.

"And I'm less charitable about his mistakes than others'—that is, if I'm charitable about mistakes. . . . What was the most serious one? Let's see. He made a bad one in the Virginia Military game last year. He went back to pass and the line rushed him. He threw the ball when he was pressed and off-balance, instead of eating it. They intercepted."

Did the colonel tell him about it at Sunday dinner?

"No. We never talk about things like that at home. I spoke to him about it when he came off the field and later I showed it to him in the movies."

Was he criticized in front of the squad?

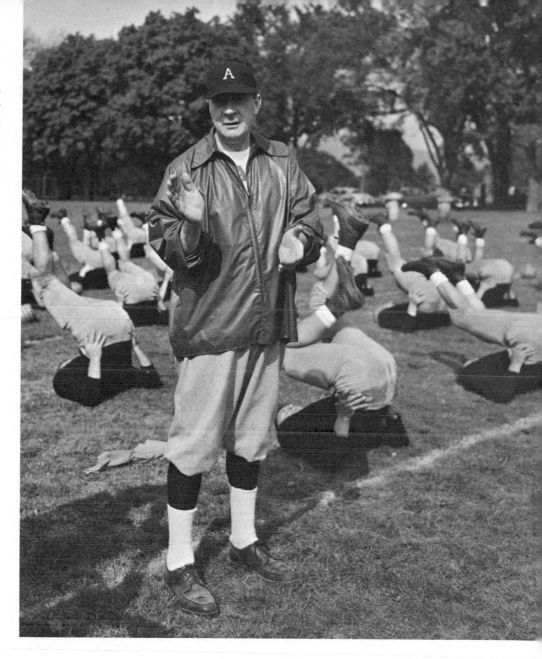

"Army's got to play at top speed sixty minutes of every game," said Coach Red Blaik. "A football player will not be subject to injury, if he's in good condition."

"No. I never criticize the quarterback in front of the squad. I go on the assumption that his mistakes are my mistakes."

The colonel made it clear that the father-and-son business doesn't influence this arrangement one way or the other.

"I talk to him just as I talked to Arnold Tucker and Galiffa in other years. . . . Yes, I watch him more closely when he is in the game than any other player. But that's only because he is the quarterback, the man who is running our attack. If he were the left guard I wouldn't watch him so closely."

When the other team has the ball, Bob sits on the bench, the Army being a two-platoon team. Occasionally, men shift from one platoon to the other and back again, but he plays only offense. The reason for this is that the colonel doesn't want him hurt.

The father-and-son relationship doesn't come into this, either. The reason he doesn't want Bob hurt is that Bob is the man who has been trained to run the attack, and if he were knocked out of the game, the coaching staff would have to start all over again with someone else.

Both of Bob's predecessors at quarterback were great defensive players. Tucker played all the time on the defense, but Galiffa almost never. Tucker was hurt three times playing defense in his last year, which was 1946. His resultant absence from the game, and his reduced effectiveness when he was in it, caused the colonel to conclude that the offensive quarterback should be out of harm's way when the other team has the ball.

There is some reason to believe that the father-son relationship did affect Bob Blaik's football career last fall, but adversely. Close followers of the Army believe that if Bob hadn't been the son of the coach he would have been the regular quarterback. He wouldn't have got in because he was better than Galiffa, the incumbent, but because the situation screamed for Galiffa's services in another spot.

Gil Stephenson, the fullback, had a leg operation to remove calcification. He got over it, but there was a hangover weakness, and he sustained another injury that rendered him virtually useless in the early season. In the Michigan game Colonel Blaik took him out after two plays. In fact, he didn't get going in true form until the last two games of the season, against Pennsylvania and Navy.

In Galiffa, Army had a tremendously powerful runner, and a fast one. The team had a fullback-pass series which it hadn't been able to use since 1947, because the fullbacks were either inept as passers or too stubby to see over the line. So Galliffa's great ability as a passer could have been used if he had been shifted to fullback. He certainly would have been a terror running the strong plays the Army T offense provides for the fullback. He was a running threat even from the quarterback position under center, in spite of the fact that he had only six dubious plays in which he carried the ball.

But shifting Galiffa to fullback would have necessitated putting Bob in at quarter. If the move were made, it might look as if Blaik were being overkind to Blaik. I might be bad for team morale. Anyway, Stephenson's leg might be better in a week or so. . . .

The colonel admits he nearly made the shift. He won't admit that if the second-string quarterback hadn't been his own son he would have made it, but close friends at the Academy admit it for him.

"That is eyewash," says the colonel. "I considered the move after the Michigan game. But the next week Stephenson seemed to be running better, so I put it off. I certainly would have liked to see Galiff run from fullback. He would have been great. . . . Bob? No. He wasn't ready."

Blaik, senior, is a conservative with an overexposed sense of fair play. His reluctance to change is illustrated by the fact that he still calls himself "Blaik," the name his father brought from Scotland, despite the fact that practically all his relatives have succumbed to the American insistence on spelling it "Blake."

However, the change from Stephenson to Galiffa and Galiffa to Blaik was so clearly indicated that friends and admirers of all those involved were amazed it wasn't made.

Coach Blaik and 1954 captain, Pat Uebel.

"What's the matter with Red?" they asked one another. "Is he mad at Bobby?"

You couldn't criticize the colonel too much, however, because Army won all its games. Stephenson came through in the Penn game with a burst of running that was instrumental in winning it, 14 to 13.

As for Bob, he sat on the bench and said nothing. He played in every game but one —Penn—and he drove the Army team to at least one touchdown in each of them, despite the fact that his longest tour of duty was fifteen minutes, in the Navy game. Against Columbia, he passed for two touchdowns and ran for another, all in the space of eleven minutes.

When the current season began, Galiffa had been graduated and was on the way to Korea as a second lieutenant. Blaik was so obviously the Army quarterback that he had to be put in. Vince Lombardi and the other assistants would have besieged the colonel in his office if any other move had been made.

Bob Blaik has understood the decision his father made about him because, essentially, he is the same kind of guy his father is—conservative, stubborn, sharp, intense.

All these facets of his character were discernible when he was a little boy around Hanover. In those days he was on the sideline every time any kind of Dartmouth team practiced or played. At the baseball games he doubled as a picker-up of soft-drink bottles. Each time a kid turned in seven empties he got a full one free.

After one ball game he sought the advice of his mother. "What would you do if you found a dollar?"

"Why, I'd look around to see if I could find out who lost it, and if I couldn't, I'd keep it, I guess."

"I found a dollar at the ball field today. I guess I'll go back and get it tomorrow."

"Why, it won't be there. It'll blow away or someone else will find it."

"It will be there," said Bob. "I put a brick on it."

The next day he and his father walked over to the ball field, and sure enough, there was the dollar under the stands. It was completely covered by a brick.

Bob Blaik was appointed to the Military Academy by Rep. Clarence J. Brown, of Ohio, who was campaign manager for Sen. Robert Taft in his last presidential-nomination campaign. The legal residence of the Blaik family is Dayton, Ohio, where the colonel operated in the building business for many years between football seasons.

The Blaik and Blaik football combination will be dissolved after the Navy game of next year. Some people think Blaik, senior, will quit coaching then. He is now fifty-three years old; he has been appointed permanent athletic director at West Point, and he has been heard to praise the action of his friend, Fritz Crisler, who turned over the Michigan football team to Benny Oosterbaan a couple of years ago to concentrate on directing the entire athletic plant. After all, coaching is a tough business, and not conducive to sleep. If Blaik, senior, doesn't quit coaching when Blaik, junior's, undergraduate career ends, everyone agrees that he will coach forever.

This year and next, however, should be great ones for America's No. 1 football family. It will be extraordinary if a certain quarterback named Blaik—spelled the same as the coach of that name—isn't high on various All-American rosters. Not this season, perhaps. But watch him in '51!

Coach Oscar Hagberg leaves his football post at the Naval Academy with a most creditable record, writes Francis Stann in the Washington Evening Star in 1945.

Win, Lose, or Draw

FRANCIS STANN

BARRING AN UNLIKELY CHANGE OF ORDERS, COMDR. OSCAR HAGBERG, U.S.N., has completed a phase of his naval career—that of coaching Navy over a two-year period. If he were a coach at a civilian college, the chances are that Hagberg would be signed again for 1946, providing a rival school did not lure him away. Which is to say he did a fine job.

That Navy team he placed on the field last week came close to being as good as any Annapolis eleven ever to play in the service classic. Possibly the 1926 team starring Tom Hamilton and Frank Wickhorst was better. That's the great eleven that tied a famed Army eleven, 21-21, in the greatest game ever played between the two service elevens.

Anyway if Commander Hagberg's team wasn't the absolute best, it may well have been the most dramatic. For the better part of two years the middies had been hearing stories of the great Army juggernaut. Experts claimed it was the best college team in history.

Army had the fabulous Glenn Davis, Doc Blanchard, Tex Coulter, Al Nemetz, Arnold Tucker, Green, Poole, Foldberg, and the rest. And then on Saturday this Army machine rolled up 20 points in less than fourteen minutes, and when the fellow sitting next to you predicted a score, 100-0, it didn't sound silly.

Teams of lesser caliber might well have folded under the great pressure, but not Navy. The Middies roared right back and actually outplayed Army the rest of the game. They outscored the Cadets, too, despite the fact that Army counted twice more, on an intercepted pass and with the help of a double-interference penalty.

And—Navy made its amazing showing with two of three great backfield stars on the bench with injuries. Bob (Hunchy) Hoernchemeyer, former Big Ten passing star; Bob Jenkins, a potential All-American fullback; and the former Notre Dame star, Bob Kelly.

Using reserve backs, Joe Bartos, Bill Barron, Bruce Smith, and Skippy Minisi, Navy made it a memorable game. After those first stunning moments, when it seemed that everything said about Army had been understated, the Middies were magnificent.

257

Oscar Hagberg (left), coach of the Navy team, and Middie captain Dick Duden discuss the big game coming up with Army in 1945.

All of those bouquets for Commander Hagberg are a bit belated. For a fellow whose coaching ability was questioned from time to time, mostly by outside-of-the-Navy people, Hagberg is leaving a very creditable record. He's won 13 games, tied 1, and lost 4.

In the won-and-lost columns, Hagberg's record at the Navy ranks with the best. Capt. Billick Whelchel won 13 and dropped 5, in 1942-43. The late Swede Larson won 16, lost 8 and tied 3 in three years, 1939-41. During his two-year stretch Hank Hardwick won only 8 games, lost 7, and tied 3, from 1937-38. Hardwick will always be remembered as the crack end of the 1924, '25, '26 Navy team. Tom Hamilton won 19 and lost 8 in the three years, 1934-37.

To those fans who argue that Navy needs a civilian coach there are rebuttals which suggest the change is unnecessary. Navy's last civilian-coached teams were the 1931-32-33 elevens under the capable leadership of E. E. "Rip" Miller, the former Notre Dame star, whose Navy teams won 12, lost 15, tied 1.

Before that, in 1925, Jack Owsley of Yale won 5 out of 8 games, including a loss to Navy. Bob Folwell, one of Pennsylvania's great linesman was named to the varsity coaching job at Navy in 1920, chalked up a fine record. His Navy teams won 24, lost 12, and tied 3 during a five-year reign. Gloomy Gil Dobie, whose coaching brought the University of Washington to the top of the Pacific Coast Conference, took over as head coach at Navy during the World War I period, and from 1916-19, Dobie's record was the finest in Naval Academy history. Gloomy Gil's 1916 team won 7 games while losing to West Virginia, 7-0. His 1917 record was 4 wins, 1 defeat. In 1919 Dobie's Middies compiled 6 wins to 1 defeat, including a 121-0 win over hapless Colby University.

Commander Hagberg operated during World War II years and he was supposed to have a tremendous advantage in the caliber of material available, but the way things turned out the submarine hero had to battle uphill all the way. And it's lucky for Navy it's the way he fights best.

Ingram is one of the most fabulous football names in the history of the Naval Academy. Jonas was the first of seven Navy athletes, a hard-driving fullback on the 1906 eleven that defeated Army, 10-0. In 1915-16 he was head football coach, later the director of athletics. A brother, Homer L. Ingram, was an outstanding linesman from 1910-13. A third brother, "Navy Bill" Ingram, was a great quarterback, captain of the 1918 team, and also coached the Middies. Jonas' son, Bill, was a fast and shifty halfback from 1935-37. In 1945, Admiral Ingram wrote some kind words to a harried Navy coach, Oscar Hagberg, whose team was up against Army's great Blanchard-Davis combination.

A Pat on the Back

JONAS H. INGRAM

3 December 1945

Commander Oscar E. Hagberg, U. S. Navy
Head Football Coach
U. S. Naval Academy
Annapolis, Maryland

Dear Hagberg:

Just a little "pat on the back" from one who knows about your job and what you went through this fall. You may step out with nothing to be ashamed of. Your boys had one swell opportunity Saturday for a big upset, and just a couple of good breaks might have brought it about.

This Army team is not as good as its press; yet it is considerably better than the wartime college league. Your boys gave them all they wanted. A break on the toss, a little better kicking, and if they had settled a bit sooner you might have banged them good. The team appeared to me to be both well coached and well handled on the field. That's about all you can do for them, boy—so cheer up!

This is to remind you that there are still a few old veterans who watch Navy athletics with interest and who know how the load is being carried and by whom.

Wishing you good luck, and with my best regards, I am

Faithfully and sincerely,
Jonas H. Ingram,
Admiral,
Commander in Chief,
United States Atlantic Fleet

Jonas Ingram, fullback on the 1906 Navy team, was later head football coach, and director of athletics.

Navy's coach Tom Hamilton (left) and 1935 football captain Lou Robertshaw.

Navy's quarterback, Tom Hamilton, in the closing minutes of the gruelling 1926 classic, calmly and efficiently kicked a wet and soggy pigskin for that extra point after touchdown, his third of the afternoon, and the Cadets were tied, 21-21. He coached the Middies to two victories over the Black Knights in his first three-year stint as head coach at the Academy. After a brilliant World War II career, he returned to coach at Annapolis in 1946 and 1947. This story by Frank Graham is our favorite Tom Hamilton yarn.

This Is the Navy Coach

FRANK GRAHAM

THIS IS BEING WRITTEN BEFORE THE ARMY-NAVY GAME. IT MAY BE THAT by the time you read it, the game will have been played and Army will have won in a romp. I don't think it will be that way—meaning, the outcome of the game. It would take at least a small miracle for Navy to win and, so far as I know, there haven't been any miracles, large or small, performed in the Municipal Stadium, unless you want to count the result of the first Dempsey-Tunney fight, which seemed, at the time, to have been something of the sort. But I do think that somewhere between the first whistle and the last, Army will know it is in there with a rugged foe and will be hurt . . . and shaken . . . and, maybe, even scared a little.

And at the moment, I am here thinking of a guy who believes in his heart that, somehow, Navy will win. His name is Tom Hamilton and he is a captain in the Navy and the head coach of the football team. I know he believes Navy will win because he keeps saying so and he is not the sort of guy that says things he doesn't believe.

There are coaches who, even when they know they are going to win, will tell you that all they can hope to do is to make a fair showing and pray they will not be humiliated.

But Tom Hamilton never has learned to talk like that.

Tom Hamilton is as typical of our Navy as John Paul Jones. He is a big, darkly handsome guy and is as rugged as the iron men who sailed the wooden ships in the days when our Navy was young. See him . . . talk to him . . . sit around with him . . . get to know him . . . and you couldn't possibly picture him as being anything but a Naval officer, although he was born and reared in the landlocked midlands and never saw a battle wagon until, as a Midshipman, he went on his first summer cruise. But he was born to sail the seven seas, this guy—and, when there was any fighting to be done, to fight like hell.

Left: Navy's R. J. Morrell and Coach Tom Hamilton.   Right: Hamilton, shown here in his playing days, replaced Rip Miller as head football coach at Annapolis.

He was a great athlete when he was here as a Midshipman. He won letters in football and baseball and basketball. He swam, wrestled, and boxed. In the years between he has learned to play golf and tennis, to ride horses—and to ride a surfboard like a native of the Islands. For a couple of years after he was graduated, he came back here as an assistant coach. Then he had three years as head coach.

When the war came, his assignment was that of physically training kids to man the planes in the rapidly expanding air arm of the Navy. He not only did that by organizing a program carried out by most of the first-rate college coaches in the country, by fighting off the tall brows and the muscle jerks who would have substituted setting-up exercises and hand drills for contact sports, he saved football.

Tell that to him and he will deny it because he doesn't believe it. But it's true. It was his insistence that football be a big part of the training in the preflight schools and that it be preserved in all the colleges where Navy trainees were sent that kept the sport alive.

Having put his plan in operation and supervised the training of 100,000 men, he almost literally fought his way back to the sea. The big brass in Washington wanted him to stay where he was, since he was doing such a magnificent job. He never stopped struggling until he convinced his superiors the program could go on without him, and that his place was on a fighting ship.

In the end, he was successful. When our war was at its toughest in the Pacific, he was executive officer of the *Enterprise*—when the Big E virtually was a one-ship Navy, roaming the seas . . . finding the trouble spots . . . blasting the Japs . . . cruising on in quest of more action. For a time, while waiting a command of his own, he was skipper of the Big E. That was the time when enlisted men were bragging to their mates:

"We were playing basketball on the deck this afternoon and do you know who barged into the game? The skipper! What a guy! It was a pleasure to get knocked down by him."

No more heartfelt tribute ever was paid by enlisted men to their skipper. Mind you, they were playing on a steel deck.

The war was over . . . Tom had got his own ship, a baby cruiser, but too late to get into any fighting with her. . . . He was asked to organize and coach a Navy team worth its salt, the big brass in the Pacific having grown tired of watching Navy teams mauled by teams from the Army and the Marines. So he put together a team that mopped up its opponents as efficiently as the Big E had mopped up the Japs.

Last spring, he was called back to Annapolis when Swede Hagberg was ordered to rejoin the submarine pack in the Pacific. The prospects seemed excellent for a first-rate team this fall. But a number of the players decided that, since the war was over, they didn't want to be sailors, and went back to Pennsylvania and Arkansas and such places. Tom struggled on, won his first game, then lost seven in a row.

Now he is about to send his team against Army and the odds are terrifically high against him. He doesn't like the idea of losing to Army. For one thing, he isn't used to it. Navy beat Army when he was playing on the team and, in two of his three years as head coach here in his first hitch, Navy beat Army.

He and his young men will give the Cadets a rumble today. Don't think they will not. It seems incredible that they will win—but Tom's the kind of guy who likes to throw punches at the incredible.

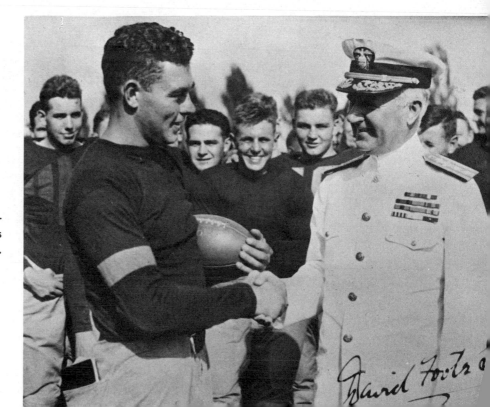

Admiral David Foote Sellers, superintendent of the Naval Academy, greets Tom Hamilton as head coach in 1934.

Army football players have a play diagrammed for them by Coach Dale Hall.

Dale Hall meets the press in New York City, as he takes over the most difficult job in the football world—replacing Earl Blaik at West Point. Frank Graham told the story in 1959.

Man on a Spot

FRANK GRAHAM

THIS WAS AT LEONE'S RESTAURANT WHERE DALE HALL WAS MAKING HIS first public appearance as the new head football coach at West Point.

Hall is thirty-six years old, tall, wide-shouldered, good-looking in a manly way, and out of Parsons, Kansas. As a halfback at Army, he was overshadowed by Doc Blanchard, Glenn Davis, Tucker, but so was every back in the country at that time.

He had taken on a rough assignment as successor to Earl Blaik, but he asked for it. Remember, here is what he said, when Blaik announced his retirement and somebody asked him if he would like the job.

"I've already applied for it," Dale said.

Dale, having been separated from the service after a tour of duty in Germany that ended in 1948, was an assistant coach at Purdue, University of New Hampshire, and University of Florida, before returning to West Point as defensive backfield coach in 1956.

He will start this year with a staff of assistants with whom he worked under Blaik . . . and with the remnants of the team that went to glory with a smashing 22-6 win over Navy.

"I told Colonel Blaik," he said, "that he was beginning to talk like a retired coach when he said we had good material already for next season."

Actually, Hall has about four regulars left over from 1958 and he's going to miss the seven others whom he helped to coach and who benefitted greatly by his scouting reports on Navy.

Army's new football coach was Navy-bound seventeen years ago until he was "intercepted and measured for the Army gray," and made to see the light by none other than Gen. Gar Davidson, the same man who named him to his present post at Army.

Col. Frank Roberts, Army's new athletic director, discussed this interesting tidbit in introducing Hall. In Hall's dossier at West Point, said Roberts, is a letter to the then Head Coach Red Blaik. Dated December 18, 1941.

"Dear Red, here's a boy who'd be well worth while getting [clipping enclosed of

Above: In the 1960 game, Army's Dick Eckert (10) was downed by Navy's Ron McKeown (36) but still tries to pass before Greg Mather (85) ends the play.

Army's football coach in 1959 was Dale Hall. Here he discusses a new play with key members of the team. Squad members include: Bill Carpenter (left), Bob Anderson (21), John Eielson (12), Steve Waldrop, and Joe Caldwell (30).

Hall's high school play]. He's not too keen about going to Annapolis, and just might be persuaded to go to West Point."

The letter was signed by Gen. Gar Davidson.

The record further disclosed a return letter from Blaik to General Davidson, dated December 20, 1941, indicating that "appropriate steps had been taken toward the measurement of Hall for a suit of Cadet grays." Thus began the unusual chain of events culminating in Hall's appointment as Army's Head Football Coach last Saturday by Gen. Garrison Davidson, Superintendent of the United States Military Academy.

On his own and under continued questioning, Hall pledged determined effort to continue the running tradition established by Colonel Blaik. "We do have some excellent players returning, but there aren't too many of them. I'd like to point out that Bill Carpenter (the "Lonely End"), Don Usry, Joe Caldwell (a fine quarterback), and Bob Anderson will be the nucleus of another fine Army team. I hope to continue the "Lonely End" formation devised by Colonel Blaik last year," said Hall. "It has unlimited possibilities and we intend to exploit them."

On paper, the appointment of Paul Dietzel as Army's new football coach in 1962 was as perfect as any sportswriter could imagine. He was one of the most successful coaches in the nation, and his "Chinese Bandits" were tough, cocky, and proud of their assignments. There was a curious parallel in the football careers of Dietzel and the great Earl Blaik of Army. Sports reporter Al Laney points it out in his story of Dietzel's arrival at West Point.

Dietzel's Arrival at West Point Parallels Blaik's

AL LANEY

THE HIGH, WOODED AREA ACROSS THE RESERVOIR FROM MICHIE STADIUM overlooking the Plains of West Point and offering a magnificent view of the Hudson Valley is known about the Military Academy as Snob Hill because most of the big brass lives there in houses specially built for them.

Into the pleasant deadened road up there called Patridge Drive, vans turned this week, loaded with crates, boxes, and all manner of household goods shipped all the way from Baton Rouge, the site of Louisiana State University, a territory known in football circles as the land of the Chinese Bandits.

These equipages drew up before one of the nicest houses on the hill. It was the House that Blaik Built and into it were carried the worldly possessions, goods, and chattels of Paul Dietzel, Army's new coach, his wife, Ann, and progeny, Steve, 13, Kathy 8. And then yesterday the little family itself came through the snow to the house where Earl Blaik, one of the greatest figures of Army's proud football tradition, lived for eighteen years.

For those who set store by signs there are plenty of them here. The parallel lines along which the football careers of Earl Blaik and Paul Dietzel have run may seem to the observant a little too constant for mere coincidence. Some will hold that it was not chance but destiny when Dietzel was called to the Point.

Exactly twenty-one years ago this snow-filled February week, Blaik, who had been both cadet and assistant coach, earlier, came to West Point for the third time to take over as head coach. Now Dietzel had done the same in strikingly similar circumstances. Army's football fortunes were very low in that pre-Pearl Harbor winter when Blaik, called to the rescue, moved his own little family down from Dartmouth, leaving there an outstanding coaching achievement.

There is a feeling among Army people that when the Academy fails to win at football, especially against Navy, it declines in virility. This is an assumption that may be challenged but Army prefers to remedy the situation rather than debate the proposition. So Blaik was hired in 1941 with the idea of bringing cheer to the Corps of Cadets and assuaging the suffering of the brass both along the Potomac and to the far-flung outposts of what used to be called empire.

So, too, are Army's fortunes low this winter and Dietzel has been called to the rescue from L.S.U., where he also leaves a lustrous record. And it also is for him the third time at the Point. He served Blaik as plebe coach in 1948 and as varsity assistant in 1953 after turns of duty elsewhere.

Blaik and Dietzel are natives of Ohio. Both graduated from Miami University, at Oxford in that state, where both played football and both married Miami co-eds, both of whom, naturally, were pretty girls. Blaik's co-ed was named Merle McDowell; Dietzel's was Ann Wilson. And both these mothers gave birth to sons while in residence at West Point while both fathers worked in minor coaching roles.

The Dietzels are moving into the House that Blaik Built, before it is quite ready for

Paul Dietzel (left) with Army's 1964 quarterback, Carl Stichweh.

them. Ann is going to be pretty busy these next weeks, what with things piled here and there and moving from room to room while paint goes onto the walls of one and paper comes down from the other. The Dietzels lived all on one floor in Baton Rouge and with three floors and a basement here she thinks her legs are going to be in fine shape come spring.

She won't be one bit busier than Merle was when the Blaiks moved in, though, if you want to push the parallel over a little more onto the distaff side. Because although Earl, who had been in the construction business with his father out in Ohio for a time, had everything to say about how the house was constructed, Merle had a few things to say about remedial measures and rearrangements.

But Merle and Earl were happy as could be in this house, just as Ann and Paul were yesterday. All the Dietzels are happy as can be. Young Stevie already is after his dad to put him in for an appointment to the Academy although he's only just going to be in the seventh grade at the Post school, and Kathy has found friends in the third.

Paul? Why, Paul is talking like he might be Kathy's age and it was the night before Christmas. He is acting as if he had come home at last. Paul is big, blond, handsome, and extremely cheerful and here you have to get right off the parallel track. In temperament he does not the least resemble his predecessor.

Where Blaik, most personable and kindly of men, was likely to be a bit withdrawn and inclined slightly toward the melancholic, Dietzel is outgoing, very friendly, and that rare thing among football coaches, a man of genuine sanguine temperament.

The coach rummaged around in various bags, drawers, and boxes and, having come up with a natty sports jacket and clean linen, declared himself ready to repair to the Bear Mountain Inn for some football talk over sustenance. He is a remarkably articulate man and he is so full of football it seems to pour out in a stream. A delightful stream since Dietzel is as full of humor as of hope.

His conversation is liberally sprinkled with references to the Chinese Bandits, that remarkable set of football defenders he invented at L.S.U. They seem very wild and very attractive the way he speaks of them and you may be very sure their counterparts will be roaming the plains above the Hudson when the haze of dying summer next mingles with the reek of autumn.

He will find them among the Cadet football candidates he is sure since, contrary to belief, they were born down South, not of plenty but from the necessity forced by famine. Anyhow, it's too good a gimmick to leave exclusively to the bayou country. Why, the coach has even brought along the orchestration of the Bandits' song for the Army band. Musically, the number is not overly difficult and he feels the Cadets will have little trouble learning it.

Dietzel brought something else along with him, too. A most attractive personality, the kind called winning. Now if somebody will only do for him, as was done for Blaik, deliver a couple of Blanchards and two or three Davises, he may turn out to be the most popular football coach in the country.

Wayne Hardin, who coached Navy to five straight victories over Army, resigns, and the football world is stunned. That's the way Arthur Daley put it in his column for The New York Times.

Anchors Aweigh and Away

ARTHUR DALEY

THE NORTH BEAT THE SOUTH IN A WINGDING FOOTBALL THRILLER AT Miami a week ago and there was an odd twist to it. At quarterback for the losers was Roger Staubach and in one of the two coaching posts for the losers was Wayne Hardin. Thus did their gridiron relationship end on the same unhappy note that had marked the end of their football careers at the Naval Academy a month earlier when Navy was upset by Army.

Everyone knew then that the superlative Staubach had completed his pigskin chores at Annapolis. Normal academic progression took care of that phase because this phenomenal young athlete will be commissioned next June. But few suspected then that Hardin was also on the verge of pulling up anchor and making a hasty departure.

However, not too long after the Navy coach had lost to the Cadets for the first time in six years, he was given clearance to head out to the open sea. Technically he resigned despite a four-year holdover clause in his contract. But that device fooled no one. He didn't fall. He was pushed.

Although Hardin was a winning coach—except for his final injury-laden season—and although he annually came through with the sine qua non of any successful Navy coach, victory over Army—again there was the same exception—his personality did not endear him to Navy brass. He antagonized many of those close to him at Annapolis while some of the things he did even irritated gruff admirals scattered all over the globe.

If the scuttlebutt is to be believed, the same fierce inner drive that lashed Hardin along the road to success was to prove his undoing. He finally overreached himself. The key position at the Naval Academy is that of assistant director of athletics. He has a permanence that the athletic directors lack because they are hauled in from sea duty, given a short term at Annapolis, and then returned to the fleet.

It is an exaggeration to say that Edgar (Rip) Miller has held the post of assistant athletic director ever since Admiral Farragut was Midshipman. It just seems that long. The old Ripper was one of the Seven Mules on the famed Four Horseman team at Notre Dame and has been at Annapolis for most of the time since, serving in many capacities

Wayne Hardin, who took over as Navy's coach in 1959.

including that of head football coach. On the banks of the Severn he is regarded as being as solid a fixture as the statue of Tecumseh.

Rip is a bluff, hearty, amiable man with a smile so winning and a personality so engaging that he has the ability to gain instant friendship. Uncanny is his knack of persuading schoolboy stars to embrace the rigors of Academy life and just as striking is his ability to persuade Congressmen to give them appointments. Herman Hickman, no mean charmer himself, made that discovery when he joined Red Blaik at West Point and was handed the recruiting chore.

"I'm in the big leagues now," said Herman with a rueful drawl. "Rip is the toughest competition there is. He knows where all the bodies are buried."

In a few years the Ripper will reach retirement age and Hardin, rumor says, couldn't wait to replace him. Since Miller is easily the most popular man at Annapolis, this impatience rubbed everyone in authority the wrong way—at the Academy, on the ships at sea, and in the halls of Congress. Rip has too many friends, including those in high places. Hardin had too few.

Hardin was a much harsher taskmaster than the man he succeeded, Eddie Erdelatz. The light-hearted Eddie believed in making practice fun. Hardin did not. It has been said that he grew so mad after a defeat that he ordered an unusual Monday scrimmage for his injury-riddled forces—and came up with more injuries. The top brass seethed.

Some of the Hardin statements didn't sit well with those who prefer graciousness from a Navy coach. Before the service classic this year he snapped at Paul Dietzel, his opposite number at West Point.

"He talks an awful lot," said Hardin, "for a fellow who never won an Army-Navy game."

Navy men all over the globe were ashamed at a happening in a game against Pitt a few years ago. The Middie flankerback jogged slowly toward the sidelines as if he were

272

heading for drydock. Suddenly he raced downfield and took a pass from Staubach for 66 yards and a touchdown. It was the ancient sandlot classic, the sleeper play. It was legal but it was roundly condemned as being perilously close to an infringement of the code of ethics. Navy men were embarrassed and Hardin finally offered formal apology.

As the Navy post is considered one of coaching's most prized and envied spots, the abrupt vacating of it by Hardin left the football world stunned. As any submarine commander would freely testify, most of an iceberg is below the surface of the water. This move also has extra depth. It sure is a strange one.

Wayne Hardin was one of Navy's most successful coaches. During a five-year period, Navy took five games in a row from Army. Here he congratulates Roger Staubach, his star quarterback.

As a seventeen-year-old high school football player, Bill Elias was a spectator at a Navy game in 1941. Turning to his friend Lou Groza, who was to win fame later on as one of the great kicking stars in professional football, Elias said, "I'd give anything in the world to be a football coach at Navy." Twenty-three years later, in 1964, Elias was appointed varsity football coach at Annapolis. This is Joe Sheehan's story that appeared in The New York Times.

New Navy Coach Plans to Beat Army without Fanfare

JOE SHEEHAN

BEING NAMED FOOTBALL COACH AT THE NAVY ACADEMY "FULFILLED A childhood dream" for Bill Elias, the new uncommissioned officer-in-charge of blocking and tackling at Annapolis revealed yesterday.

In town with Capt. Bill Busik, Navy's director of Athletics, to attend a Navy League dinner at the Brooklyn Navy Yard, Elias took time out to discuss his football plans and philosophy.

The forty-one-year-old coach, a stocky, handsome man with a strong jaw, deep-set, snapping dark eyes, grayish hair, and a mild manner of speaking showed himself to have been well indoctrinated in the Navy way of thinking in less than a month on station.

The first thing Elias said was, "I think you safely can say Navy will put continued emphasis on the Army game." He added, however, that he saw little reason to employ gimmicks to fire up Navy's team for its annual contest with Army.

Wayne Hardin, Elias's predecessor, went in strong for gimmickry. It was part of his gamesmanship—successful in five years of six—to send Navy's players against Army, wearing jerseys or helmets emblazoned with "BEAT ARMY" or "DRIVE FOR FIVE."

As Elias sees it, there's no real need to stoke Navy fires that already are blazing.

There's such wonderful *esprit de corps* at Navy, I feel all I have to do is know how to spell one four-letter word—"A-R-M-Y,", said Elias, whose Virginia team upset Army last fall, 35-14.

Though he has yet to see Navy's squad in action, Elias has had one moving exposure to the spirit at Annapolis. On January 19, the day he signed his contract, he was invited to have dinner with the brigade of Midshipmen.

He was introduced, said a few words, then spent the next twenty minutes being carried around in his chair, by a score of Midshipmen, while the rest of the brigade made Bancroft Hall's vast mess hall ring with the din of cheering.

"It was something that really hit you in the heart," said Busik.

"Coaching at Navy has been my ambition since I was seventeen," Elias said.

"As high school seniors at Martins Ferry in Ohio in 1941, Lou Groza, who was a teammate, and I were taken to our first college football game. It was between Navy and Notre Dame in Cleveland. Notre Dame won the game, I remember, but Navy won my heart.

"In fact, I turned to Groza and said, 'Someday I'm going to coach that Navy team.' As time went on, I began to think I'd never have the chance. When it finally came I didn't waste any time. Captain Busik offered me the job at 1:30 on January 19. I accepted it at 1:40."

Though he has talked to Navy's players individually and studied motion pictures of Navy's 1964 games, Elias has not made any decisions on 1965 personnel.

"We'll get to that in spring practice, which will start March 1, or the first day thereafter the weather lets us," he said.

The loss of Roger Staubach, Pat Donnelly, and many other key 1964 players by graduation doesn't perturb Elias.

"We may not have any super stars starting out," he said. "But they'll emerge. There's always a solid foundation of good material at the service academies. The coach at Navy never has any call to bring out the crying towel."

Bill Elias has some words of wisdom for his quarterback John Cartwright (15) and halfback Terry Murray (24).

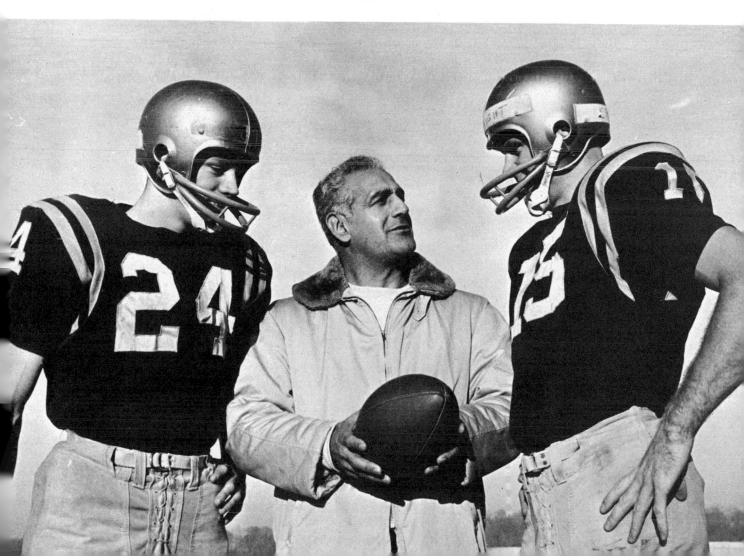

"Aggressiveness" is the keynote of Elias' football philosophy. He said: "We like to move the ball—and throw it—on offense. On defense, we like to stunt, loop, and slant in the line and fire the linebackers. Our aim is to keep maximum pressure on the other team both ways."

Navy coach Bill Elias discusses a new play with fullback Danny Wong before the 1965 game.

*One of the year's most dramatic stories of the 1966 season concerned Tom Cahill,
Army's head coach. Bob Lipsyte of The New York Times tells the once-in-a-lifetime
story of the "Cinderella" coach.*

Cahill Substitutes Hard Work for Gimmicks

ROBERT LIPSYTE

THEY SNARLED AND THEY GRUNTED THROUGH THIS MORNING'S MIST, 108 OF
them hurling themselves over the damp grass as assistant coaches bel-
lowed, "Faster, faster."

It was the first fall practice session of the West Point football team, and they strained
to get lower, hit harder, as a two-star general, whip lean in starched fatigues, danced
out of their gasping, heaving way.

Tom Cahill just watched and made notes. Sometimes he wondered which of them
would turn up blue chippers and help keep him in the colonel's house.

Cahill is a tall, forty-six-year-old with a long, tired face. For seven years he coached
the plebe football team and lived in a house on captains' row and worked late hours in
a bare, dingy cubicle, that was laughingly called his office. In 1956 Cahill was named
"Coach of the Year" in the central New York region. Yet here he was, ten years later, a
coach of the Army plebes.

Suddenly, last spring, Coach Paul Dietzel, left his post as Army's head coach to take
a similar position at South Carolina. Desperate, the authorities at West Point asked Cahill if he would conduct spring practice, and he said yes, squeezing in some time to
brief all the well-known coaching applicants they brought up to consider the coaching job at the Academy.

On May 11, three days before the end of spring practice, they announced that Cahill was the new head coach. It was thought to be an interim appointment, until some
big name was free, and they let Tom know that he could go back to work with the
plebes, he had a home forever.

And so they moved him into the splendid big house by the reservoir that had been
built for Earl Blaik and they let him do his homework in a carpeted and paneled office
that can be measured in yards.

"Life can change so quickly," said Cahill today. "For twenty years I put my shoes on
the same way, then all of a sudden people want to know, 'How does it look, Tom?'—people who never asked me anything before."

Army coach Tom Cahill (center), sophomore Steve Lindell (left), and Army's football captain, Townsend Clarke, get together for a last minute meeting before the big game.

The black helmets that Coach Dietzel made seniors wear ("you're the leaders") are gone. Everyone was wearing gold, with his name taped in black in front and back. The six different-colored jerseys showing a man's position in Dietzel's slamming order are gone, too.

"Today, everyone has an equal chance, they're only names and bodies," said Cahill. "There are no black helmets, because we're in this together. Everyone will be judged on what he does now, not what he did, and the coaches, who don't know any of them, will be unbiased."

Cahill knows every one of them, though. He coached them all as they moved up the plebe team to Dietzel, where they heard slogans and battle cries and then battled Dietzel's fierce Chinese Bandits.

Cahill is aware that his position, though tenuous, has advantages. "How well do I have to do? Must they have 10-0—is 5-5 enough for them to keep me?" asked Cahill. "I don't know."

There was appreciation at the Point when Cahill stepped in so quickly.

The big disadvantage for Cahill is that, as he concedes, he has to play for this year. "I can't look ahead at all. Most coaches come in with five-year contracts, and can afford to take a beating as they rebuild their squads and their recruitment programs. Cahill has only a year to make good.

"I feel the boys are with me and that this is my big chance. Most of the pressures are self-imposed. I've never had more than a one-year contract, not here, or at Manlius High, or at River Dell High School. So I've got nothing to lose, except the house, and the office and my pride."

6
THE RIVALS:
VIGNETTES

The scene in Philadelphia prior to the start of the 1962 Army-Navy game. Carolyn Bazydlo (left) and Linda Stelly pose as the brigade of Midshipmen take the field in ceremonies before the kickoff.

The International News Service assigned Miss Margaret Lane, a feature writer for the London Daily Express, to report her impressions of the Army-Navy benefit football game played in New York in 1931.

English Writer Finds Us Riotous Enthusiasts

MARGARET LANE

AN ARMY AND A NAVY PITCHED IN THE FIELD, THE MOST EXUBERANT SPORTS battle in the world.

Listen to eighty thousand shouting throats, look at the blue and gold, the sun and shadow on the torn field, the crowds on the rooftops, peering into the bowl, and the flying crowds cheering from the elevated train that rattles round the rim of the stadium.

Navy did themselves proud in the way of their mascot. Their honorable white goat turned up at the game with a pair of milk-white twins in blue-and-gold coats, to the utter chagrin of the Army mule, who has no family to boast of.

They were excused the duty of following Navy's ball up and down the sidelines, being too young and tender for the work of the big-time goat. He galloped up and down between two Middies, while the kids nibbled meekly at the sidelines and twitched their white ears.

Army's golden helmets gleamed in the sun like the helmets of Roman warriors. Navy's shone blue as the shells of lobsters. Fire and water hissing together over a trampled field.

Americans show a more riotous enthusiasm for her games than any other country in the world. Not even a Derby winner romps home to such a splitting cataract of cheers as Ed Herb scrambling to a touchdown. Only the bullfighters of Spain know in their heyday such tumult and glory as America accords her fighting Cadets matched on a civil field.

It was the most dramatic and emotional game of the year, because, while there are a score of college teams one doesn't give a hoot for, everyone has a passionate preference for either the Army or the Navy. It's a desperate matter who wins. Navy brightens the interval with colored card tricks and the Army mule gallops as absurdly as a circus, but underneath the frivolity, this afternoon's game had the grim intoxication of war.

The grueling game, Army points ahead until near the end of the third quarter, and then like a golden arrow from the tussle of bodies, Joe Tschirgi breaks away to the goal line and falls to the ground, with the ball gripped before him and his gold silk breeches muddied from the tackle that failed.

The stadium roars till our heads hum like a pain. The patron kids are raced up and down on their tethers. They have brought luck at last. A placement kick thrusts up the Navy's score. The little goats at last have won their horns.

And it might have been an even game, but, just in that last quarter, Army, massed like a battering ram on the Navy goal line, nagged the ball by yard and inch to a second triumphant touchdown.

The Army mule raced like a thoroughbred over the field, spreading a scornful nostril at the Navy goat and his presumptuous twins.

Ben Born (left) and his brother, Charles, recall their playing days when they were on opposing Army-Navy teams.

Ineligible receiver downfield? Or incomplete pass? The referee's ruling was critical in the Army-Navy game of 1926, which ended in a 21-21 tie. Two brothers who opposed each other on the gridiron that memorable afternoon, Rear Adm. Arthur S. (Ben) Born and Maj. Gen. Charles F. Born, join the battle once again. It's a short but great story, as reported in The Corpus Christi Caller-Times *in 1965.*

Brothers Replay 1926 Game

SPENCER PEARSON

TWO FORMER FOOTBALL STARS WHO OPPOSED EACH OTHER IN ONE OF THE great games of the 1920s are still arguing over what the outcome should have been.

They are Maj. Gen. Charles F. Born (U.S.A.F., Ret.) and his brother, Rear Adm. Arthur S. (Ben) Born (U.S.N., Ret.), who are here visiting their other brother, Capt. Howard E. (Marty) Born (U.S.N., Ret.).

The game in question was the Army-Navy game of 1926, which wound up in a 21-21 tie before an estimated crowd of 123,000 people at Soldier Field in Chicago.

"We should have won," General Born, an All-American end at West Point, remarked, He referred particularly to an incomplete pass "that should have been ruled as an ineligible receiver downfield."

The "ineligible receiver," was brother Ben, a guard who got hit in the head by the ball.

"I saw it hit him right smack on the head and bounce off," the general said.

When the referee ruled it an incomplete pass, Chuck grabbed his brother and dragged him over to the referee.

"Tell him it hit you in the head," he told Ben.

Ben said it didn't.

Chuck's explosive reaction to his brother's "lying" almost got him thrown out of the game.

Ben said yesterday he really didn't believe the ball hit him at the time but reflecting on it later in the dressing room, "I figured it must have hit me. But the game was over by then," he remarked, smiling at his brother.

Marty didn't enter into the argument yesterday, since he wasn't in the game. He came along a bit later, and Ben even coached him when he was a plebe at Annapolis.

"Marty was more of a lacrosse player," he said.

Both General Born, who was transferred to the Air Force after it was separated from the Army, and Admiral Born retired ten years ago.

This is the first time the three have gotten together in twenty years.

Here is another story about the Born brothers—at least about Midshipman Born—and a good-luck penny. It was written in 1954, but it goes back a long way—to that game in 1926.

The Lost Penny

ANONYMOUS

THIS STORY HAD ITS BEGINNING DURING THE FOOTBALL SEASON—TWENTY-eight years ago.

On November 27, 1926, the Army and Navy football teams met on Soldier Field, Chicago. Playing right guard for the Navy was Midshipman Arthur S. Born, today Senior Navy Officer attached to the Office of the Secretary of Defense. At right end for the Army was Arthur's brother Charles, now a major general and commanding officer of the Crew Training Command, U.S.A.F., San Antonio, Texas.

Taped to his skin under his jersey, Midshipman Born carried a good-luck penny engraved: "CARRIED BY A. S. BORN IN ARMY & NAVY GAME," and the date.

It was a tough battle, ending in a tie. During the ruckus, midshipman Born lost his penny.

After that day the Born brothers went their separate ways, and saw each other only occasionally during the intervening years. But not long ago Captain Born received a letter postmarked Racine, Wisconsin. He opened it. A penny dropped out—his lucky penny.

The letter read: "Dear Sir: I am sure you will be interested to know that the other night among my pennies I found your keepsake penny. I did not know of your whereabouts so I asked the local paper for assistance, which they gladly gave. Through the article in the paper, your aunt phoned and gave me your address.

"I am the mother of eight young sprouts who are very much interested in that penny. My 11-year-old Bob wants you to tell him about that game and if the penny brought you good luck. I'm sure that if the penny could talk, it might tell some interesting tales. If you would like to tell us, we would like to know where your brother is who played in that game also. I bet your Mom was hoping it would end in a tie. Now take good care of this little penny as we have done and we all hope it brings you lots of 'good luck.' Sincerely, The Charles Brunnelson Family."

And that is how Captain Born got his lucky penny back.

Grantland Rice, for years the dean of American sportswriters, penned a prose-poem in 1936 in praise of the Army-Navy game, which he finds "close to the final touch in amateur sport, amateur ideals, and the highest form of hardest-fighting sportsmanship." It is praise well earned, and well deserved.

A Tribute

GRANTLAND RICE

WIPING AWAY THE DUST FROM AN OLD FOOTBALL RECORD BOOK, I RAN across these figures . . . 1890—Navy 24, Army 0. That was forty-six years ago—the first Army-Navy game. At that date, they were the struggling striplings of football. Forty-six years later in the Sesquicentennial Stadium in Philadelphia, these same two Army-Navy teams put on the greatest combination of pageant and battle and attendance that football has ever known in all its extended, colorful history.

National championships are myths. Other old rivalries draw their quota of camp followers and hold their places on the football map. But from 1890, Army and Navy have moved forward with a public lure that now surpasses the field from Berkeley to Cambridge, from Minnesota to Tulane, from the Yale Bowl to Texas.

Why has this game between the two greatest service institutions in the world for land, water, and air defense reached such a peak? The answer is simple. Because it embodies all the elements or ingredients that make football what it is . . . spirit-sportsmanship-color-action . . . a rivalry that goes to the final ounce and the final inch of play . . . something beyond any mere championship—something that reaches the soul of every true American who understands what West Point and Annapolis mean.

I can look back and see their old stars swing into action again—Daley and Douglas, Oliphant, Howard, Ingram, Dalton, Garbisch, Prichard, Merillat, Hamilton, Cutter, Bunker, Born, McEwan, French, Smythe, Brown, the fleet and valiant Buzz Borries, Eddy, Wickhorst, Buckler, on and on through more names than I can mention here, until we come to 1936 with two outstanding stars.

Who are they? One, Monk Meyer, is the son of an Army colonel, a kid born at West Point. The others, Bill Ingram, is the son of Comdr. Jonas Ingram and the nephew of "Navy Bill" Ingram.

Here are two opposing stars born and reared in the traditions of West Point and Annapolis, two brilliant rivals who will carry into action all the heritage of Army and Navy forebears. Army and Navy teams do not represent any one section—East, West, North, or South. They represent the entire United States. They cover every section. They belong to all sections. And there is a general understanding everywhere that in a day when certain barriers have been lowered in so many places, there are no "tramp athletes" at West Point or Annapolis.

It has been said today that football of the modern era, as played down the stretch, belongs to the winning teams as far as crowds are concerned. Army and Navy have shot this theory or belief full of holes. Army has lost two games and Navy has lost three. And yet there is no other championship game that would attract such a following or create greater enthusiasm. These two have proved that it is the game that still counts, when the game is played at a high level of spirit, sportsmanship, and skill.

Football today is far different from what it used to be. Here is a Navy team that has lost to Yale, Princeton, and Pennsylvania. Yet in at least two of these games, Navy was never outplayed and the breaks, to my mind, were the winning factors. This 1936 Navy model has been one of the best Navy teams I've seen in years—a team capable of matching its ability against the best. The 1936 Army team started out with high hopes and then ran into an epidemic of injuries and influenza. But in the last week or ten days, Army has again come along to find its October condition. So on paper we again have two evenly matched teams keyed up to the last flick or flutter of flaming spirit where the entire season rides with victory or defeat.

The game is only part of this tremendous spectacle. This has been a season notable for its crowds from coast to coast. It has been a season of record attendance. Yet, this Army-Navy contest at Philadelphia will outdraw any other game played this year by more than 20,000 spectators. It will be one of the largest gatherings that ever looked at a sporting event in the country. It will include more notables from every walk of life than any sporting event has known in a decade.

These things are all interesting. But more interesting to me is the fair and fierce rivalry of the Cadets and the Midshipmen, from stand to field. They are the young and representative parts of an entire nation, not a single section. And they give something to a football game, even if it is not always the top flight in power and experience and skill, that no other rivals quite seem to match.

The nation at large senses the fact that an Army-Navy meeting is close to the final touch in amateur sport—amateur ideals—and the highest form of hard-fighting sportsmanship. That's what makes an Army-Navy game what it is today.

John Ryan, being tackled here as he catches a pass that led to a touchdown on the next play, quarterbacked the Army team in the 1936 game.

Alan Bergner, captain for Navy in 1939, with Coach Swede Larson.

Here is one of my favorite Army-Navy stories. In essence it demonstrates, dramatically, that an Army-Navy game is more than a game; it is a way of life. It is all of America's youth, marching up and down the gridiron of life. It is a story that could happen only in America. The story of Alan Bergner and Harry Stella is one of which all Americans can be proud.

Two Kids from Kankakee

BILL STERN

AMONG THE THOUSANDS UPON THOUSANDS WHO CAME POURING INTO THE United States on the flood tide of immigration years ago were two young men, one an Italian, the other a German. Poor and eager to make their mark in this new land, they settled, one as an engineer, the other as a carpenter, in the thriving Midwest city of Kankakee, Illinois.

Eventually they married. And each, in time, had a son. The engineer named his boy

288

Alan. The lad grew up to be a big husky chap. The carpenter named his boy Harry. He turned out to be a little shrimp of a guy.

The two boys, grown and eager to play football, came, at last, to Kankakee High School. When the coach laid eyes on burly Alan, he gleefully rubbed his hands and shouted for all to hear, "There's my new star!" When he saw little Harry, he sniffed in disgust and grumbled, "Too light, kid. You're not built for a football player."

Alan, with all his advantages of size and brawn, became a shining star. Harry, who worshiped the big fellow, was able, with his speed, courage, and determination, to make the team, too. The two boys became close friends. In the last year of high school football they were elected co-captains of the team.

Harry Stella, Army's football captain in 1939, with Coach Bill Wood.

Alan Bergner, captain for Navy in 1939, receiving awards from Rear Adm. Wilson Brown, superintendent of the Naval Academy. Bergner lettered in football, wrestling, boxing, and lacrosse.

Tackle Harry Stella (front row, second from left) and his Army teammates defeated Navy, 14-7, in 1938. Bergner and the Middies got revenge the following year with a 10-0 win.

After graduation, the two boys separated. Alan went to the Naval Academy at Annapolis. Harry was appointed to West Point. Both made their service teams. The city of Kankakee was happy enough to burst.

The years passed quickly. Freshman, sophomore, junior seasons went by. The trail of these two small-town friends crossed only at Army-Navy time.

One cold winter day at the end of the 1938 football season, sensational news came to the citizens of Kankakee. Harry had been elected captain of the Army team! The streets buzzed with excitement. And everyone began to speculate. "Those two boys are like two peas in a pod," they said. "Do you suppose, now that Harry's been made captain at West Point, Alan could make it at Annapolis?

In a few days, the news that sent Kankakee wild with joy and pride arrived. Alan had made it! He was to be captain of the Navy team in 1939!

The 1939 football season was a grueling and bitter campaign for both Army and Navy. Victories and defeats studded their records. Harry and Alan played their hearts out for their respective teams. Then came the great game of the year!

Before 80,000 hushed fans, including statesmen and diplomats, Cadets and Midshipmen, girls, dignitaries, and plain ordinary football fans, Harry and Alan, the two kids from Kankakee, walked out to the center of the gridiron and shook hands as is the custom for opposing football captains. Having reached the end of their golden football trail, they gripped hands and looked each other in the eye. Good luck, Harry!" murmured the Navy captain. "And good luck to you, Alan!" answered the Army leader.

The game was a thrilling, bruising battle. No quarter was asked or given. All over the world, Army and Navy officers took time from grim duty to listen to the shortwave account on the radio. In every part of the globe, men far from home sat entranced by the

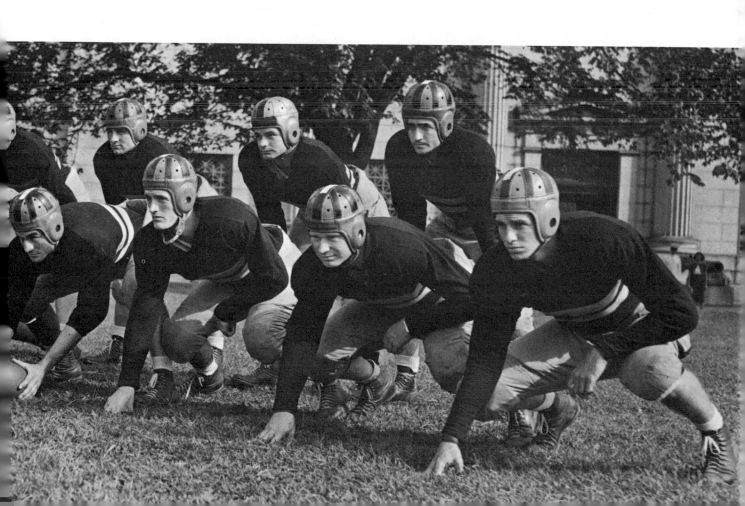

details of the contest in which two small-town friends, the sons of two immigrants, captained their teams through a fierce battle.

At last, the game was over. Delirious thousands flowed out of the stands on to Franklin Field in a wild celebration of victory for the Navy, 10-0. And, pushing through the dancing, wildly cheering Navy crowd, walked Harry to congratulate his Navy buddy, Alan Bergner. The two captains shook hands warmly, they had battered each other throughout the long day, but in the end it was Navy's day, and a tremendous victory.

It was the last outpost for the two friends from Kankakee. Schooldays and football were soon over and duty called. Off they went now, in the service of their country, one on land, the other at sea.

That isn't the end of the story—for actually it had just begun. Harry Stella served with great distinction in the South Pacific during World War II, earning numerous awards for his gallant service under enemy fire, including the Silver Star, Legion of Merit, two Bronze Star Medals. During the Korean War, Captain Stella further distinguished himself by winning another Legion of Merit Medal. Col. Harry Stella went on to serve his country with great honor and distinction as assistant chief of staff, G1, with the Eighth Army in Korea.

Ens. Alan Bergner was stationed at Pearl Harbor, when the Japs attacked in force on December 7, 1941. Ensign Bergner served more than three years on active submarine duty in Jap-infested waters. Decorated on numerous occasions and promoted several times, Lt. Comdr. Bergner was personally decorated by Secretary of Navy James Forrestal and awarded the coveted Navy and Marine Corps Medal. Commander Bergner voluntarily risked his life to transfer an injured sailor to another submarine in dangerous waters, using a rubber boat to row the man safely to the sub. Capt. Alan Bergner later returned to duty in the Pentagon in Washington, working in the Antisubmarine Warfare Program.

And so the story that began more than thirty years ago in the little city of Kankakee, Illinois, with the friendship of two boys who played football together, continues in the service of their country.

Col. Ed Garbisch, old Army great, and Capt. Steve Barchet, old Navy great, review the classic 1923 Army-Navy game between the halves of the 1943 clash of the two big squads. That would be interesting enough, but the colonel is flying a bomber as he talks into the microphone, and the captain is piloting a submarine in the Atlantic. It was a stunt, but it also gives us a good line on the character of the men who play for the service elevens, as well as a few amusing items. Bill Stern was the broadcaster.

Old Rivals Stage Novel Broadcast

THE NEW YORK TIMES

FROM HIGH UP IN THE CLOUDS YESTERDAY, FROM AN ARMY BOMBER IN flight over the eastern part of the country, Lt. Col. Ed Garbisch, former Army football star, spoke over the radio with Capt. Steve Barchet, former Navy star, in a submarine located in the waters off the eastern coast. And, as the Army went down, so did Colonel Garbisch. For he bet Army would beat Navy in his two way conversation with Captain Barchet and, if he pays off in the manner he promised, Colonel Garbisch is in for an interesting time.

Between the halves of the Army-Navy clash these two, who were rivals in the scoreless tie the service teams played twenty years ago at the Polo Grounds, penetrated the ether for contact in a novel radio stunt, and reviewed the game of 1923. They recalled how each missed a bid for a field goal in that memorable struggle and, when Captain Barchet offered to eat Colonel Garbisch's hat if Navy lost yesterday, the former Army star snapped at the bet, offering to take his place in front of the Navy Goat if Army lost.

Here is the transcript of the broadcast:

BILL STERN: Ladies and gentlemen of the radio audience. The National Broadcasting Company, in co-operation with the United States Army and the United States Navy, is about to bring you an unusual few minutes. High over the eastern part of the United States right at this very moment is an Army bomber. Also right at this very instant, somewhere off the eastern coast of America, is a Navy submarine. On board the Army bomber is Col. Ed Garbisch, former Army football star, while on board the Navy submarine is Capt. Steve Barchet, former Navy football star.

These two gentlemen played football against each other in the Army-Navy game of 1923. Hence, what could be more natural than that these two, Ed Garbisch of the Army and Steve Barchet of the Navy, should meet each other again on another Army-Navy football game day, exactly twenty years after they faced each other on the gridiron. So,

293

Ed Garbisch, who kicked the field goal following George Smythe's brilliant run and Timberlake's touchdown to give Army a thrilling 17-14 win in 1922.

in just a moment, Col. Ed Garbisch of the Army will be speaking from an Army bomber high over the land as he greets Capt. Steve Barchet of the Navy waiting to greet him in a Navy submarine. Let's listen in as these two old football adversaries meet once again.

We take you now to NBC announcer Bob Denton, who is flying somewhere over the eastern part of the United States in an Army bomber carrying Army's star of the 1923 game, Col. Ed Garbisch.

DENTON (*from plane*): Good afternoon. Right beside me up here in this Army bomber is Col. Ed Garbisch—so come on in, Ed, and take over.

GARBISCH: Thank you. It surely doesn't seem any twenty years since I played against Steve Barchet in the 1923 Army-Navy game. I haven't seen Steve for quite a while. And now they tell me he's down somewhere below in a Navy submarine. Can you hear me, Steve?

BARCHET (*from sub*): Yes, Ed, I can hear you fine. I'll bet I'm more comfortable down here in this submarine than you are up there in that plane.

GARBISCH (*from plane*): Oh, I don't know. But it surely does seem good to talk to you, Steve. You know we faced each other in another Army-Navy game exactly twenty years ago at the Polo Grounds in New York. Boy, did we take care of you guys that day!

BARCHET: As I remember it, we took pretty good care of Army that day.

GARBISCH: I'm doggone sure Navy didn't win.

BARCHET: And I know that Army didn't either. As a matter of fact, it ended in a nothing-to-nothing tie.

GARBISCH: Yes, that's right, but you know I seem to remember the headlines that night reading Steve Barchet tries field goal for Navy—and misses.

BARCHET: That's right, Ed, but now that you brought it up, didn't you also try a field goal that day for Army?

GARBISCH: I guess I did and before you can rub it in, I missed, too. So the game wound up in a nothing-to-nothing tie. We both tried field goals for our respective teams, and we both missed. Fine pair we were! Did you get a bawling out from the Navy Coach that night for missing your try?

BARCHET: Well, Ed, I wouldn't exactly say he kissed me. How about you? Did the Army coach lay it in to you for missing your try?

GARBISCH: I'll tell you this, Steve, he wasn't very happy about it. But to get back to the present, isn't it a wonderful age when, twenty years later, you and I meet, you in a submarine, me in a plane? Hey, what's it like in that submarine of yours?

BARCHET: This is the silent service, Ed, breaking silence for once, just for this special occasion. We in the submarines are called the silent service because we're never ashore long enough to talk. Maybe you read the Secretary of the Navy's box score on Japanese losses—506 Japanese ships sunk and 328 others damaged. Our submarines knocked off 355 of the 506. That means that the American subs sank two-thirds of all the Japanese ships sunk, and of the damaged vessels, we're responsible for more than a third. But, we're not bragging, there are still too many Jap ships afloat.

GARBISCH: Hey, Steve, don't forget the Army bombers have gotten a few, too. As a matter of fact, our problem is not getting planes, but rather fitting our men for flying. You know, if we could get the seventeen-year-old boys who want to become fliers into the Air Corps enlisted reserve, we'd save a lot of time. 'Cause then these seventeen-year-olds would soon come under the guidance of the C.A.P., Civilian Air Patrol, who are planning night classes while these youngsters are still in high school. These classes will be in navigation, map reading, special mathematics, all to prepare these seventeen-year-olds for the pre-flight schools. So, if any of these seventeen-year-old lads are listening in and want to join the Army Corps Enlisted Reserve, get in touch with your nearest Army enlistment office. And we need more women in the WAC, too.

BARCHET: Say, Ed Garbisch.

GARBISCH: Yes, Steve, what is it?

BARBHET: I suppose you think Army is going to win today?

GARBISCH: Of course I do. Want to make something of it?

BARCHET: Well, if Army wins, I'll eat your hat.

GARBISCH: And if Navy wins, I'll take my place in front of the Navy goat.

Steve Barchet (fourth row, sixth from left) and the Navy squad of 1922.

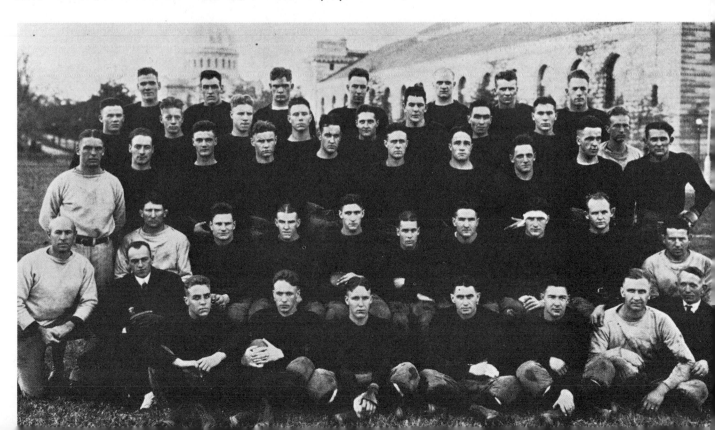

Tecumseh, the Japanese bell, the Navy goat—all are part and parcel of Annapolis football tradition. H. A. R. Peyton, a Midshipman in 1959, fills us in on Navy rituals that lend so much color to life and football at the Naval Academy.

The Traditions of Annapolis

H. A. R. PEYTON

TECUMSEH

One of the oldest and most famous of Naval Academy traditions is that of Tecumseh. Originally the figurehead of the U.S.S. *Delaware*, the likeness of this venerable old Indian chief is now the "God of 2.5" to the regiment of Midshipmen. Throughout the years he has received the offerings of prayers and pennies with which from many generations of Midshipmen have sought his aid in their eternal struggle with the academic departments. He has, doubtless, also received in disdainful silence the execrations of many Midshipmen leaving the Academy on "extended vacations." To his special care is entrusted the fate of the football team. As a special offering, when the regiment marches off to a football game it gives a left-hand salute and showers him with pennies. The $150 thus expended annually by the Midshipmen is a great source of income to the children of the officers on duty at the Academy, for the Navy juniors start gathering a rich harvest from the ground as soon as the regiment has passed.

Just before the game with Army, Tecumseh takes the warpath in brilliant war paint. When Christmas rolls around, Tecumseh dresses in Santa Claus style to comfort those unfortunate Midshipmen who have lost their Christmas leave through failure to meet the required academic standards or who have had serious "incidents" with the powers that be.

Another of Tecumseh's more pleasant duties is to keep watch upon the Midshipmen's drags, and tradition has it that he will reward with all his arrows a drag whom he finds true to her Midshipman. As yet his supply of arrows remains intact.

The original figurehead was wooden, and became so scarred and weatherbeaten that the Class of '91 donated a handsome bronze replica in which were hermetically sealed

Members of Navy's 1956 football team salute Tecumseh, the Naval Academy's figurehead mascot before the battle with Army.

a '91 class ring together with the heart, brain, arrows, pipe, and tomahawk of the original, thus transmitting its identity to its successor.

THE JAPANESE BELL

The ringing of the Japanese bell is the consummation of a football victory over the Graylegs. Immediately after the victory the "home guards" move the bell onto the steps of Bancroft Hall and start ringing it. When the regiment returns, the youngsters take over and keep the bell ringing until the team returns the next day. Then each member of the team strikes out the score. After the captain has struck out the score the bell is returned to its place in the yard to wait silently for another year and another victory over Army. In recent years the bell has been put to use with satisfying frequency, but Tecumseh can remember one period of almost fifteen years when the bell was silent. The bell, which was cast in the twelfth century, was presented to Commodore Perry during his visit to Japan in 1854.

THE NAVY GOAT

No college in the land has a mascot more famous than the Navy's goat. Through many football seasons, starting with the first Army-Navy game in 1890, the Navy team has had a goat for its mascot. Upon that occasion the Navy rooters borrowed one from a noncom's quarters on the reservation at West Point. The first mascot,

Coach Tom Hamilton and Midshipmen ringing the Japanese Bell in 1936 after victory over Army.

Navy's varsity backfield romps onto the field with the Naval Academy goat, Bill XV, to open the 1963 season. With Bill are (l. to r.) Dick Earnest, Roger Staubach, Pat Donnelly, and John Sai.

named "Galena Bill" after the mascot of the old gunboat *Galena*, once led a naval landing party to victory. Some of the most famous mascots are still in the trophy room at the Academy, stuffed in fighting poses. Among these is "Three-to-nothing Jack Dalton"; it was present at the football games in 1910 and 1911 when its famous namesake won for the Navy by one field goal on each occasion. Each goat has its own blanket on which is a huge block "N," with a gold star for each time it has lead the Blue and Gold to victory over the Army mule. Upon two occasions the Navy diverged from the traditional mascot. Once they used a six-foot colored man, and once a pair of homing pigeons. The fact that neither of them brought luck seated the goat's popularity even more securely.

The present goat is Bill the IX, who assumed his duties the day before the opening of the 1941 football season. He relieved Bill VIII, winner of two Navy stars, who was forced to retire from active duty due to the loss of a horn.

The care of the goat is entrusted to two football stars who are unable to play, either through injury or ineligibility. It is their task to keep Bill facing the opponent's goal from the opening kickoff to the final gun.

THE MACEDONIAN MONUMENT

At the opposite end of Stribling walk from Tecumseh stands one of his bitterest rivals, Old Schnoz. This monument, a reproduction of the figurehead of the H.M.S. *Macedonian*, has a typically Macedonian nose, hence the sobriquet. Almost invariably that organ of smell acquires a thick coat of red paint immediately preceding the Army game. In past years Schnoz, too, has come in for his share of pennies as the regiment swings down Stribling Walk on its way to away football games.

THE NAVY BLUE AND GOLD

Navy football teams first went into action against Army sporting red and white as its colors, but the following year the blue of the sailor's uniform and the gold of his buttons were appropriately adopted as Navy's colors. The words of the Naval Academy's alma matter song, "The Navy Blue and Gold," were written by an anonymous officer in the fleet and were set to music by Prof. J. W. Crosley, the Academy organist and choirmaster.

CAP AND FEMME

One of the most enjoyable of Naval Academy traditions is that of cap and femme. It is another custom whose origin is unknown; whose author is greatly to be praised. During the flapper decade it fell into disuse, but its popularity is once more on the increase. It is a custom which requires that when a girl puts a Midshipman's cap on her own head, she is liable to be kissed at once by the fortunate owner of the cap. The beauty of the custom is that Midshipmen never remove their caps on the streets and there is never any deterring publicity about this tradition. Therefore, let those who date Midshipmen after the game this afternoon be forewarned.

Paul Gallico attends a pre-game football rally at West Point and it raises the hair on his scalp. This was in 1934, but it holds true today.

The Long Gray Line

PAUL GALLICO

It would be hard to describe what it sounds like to hear the cadet Corps of the U.S. Military Academy at West Point giving mass cheers in their enormous mess hall, at a pre-game football rally; and I should have no intention of trying. It is something that should be experienced; and it *is* an experience. You have all heard them cheer at their football games out in the open. The small gray patch, stuck like a label onto the side of any stadium they happen to occupy, can give forth startling volumes of sound from their short, staccato, barks of encouragement to the truly startling roar that ensues when a touchdown is scored by their team. It seems as though the very sky were reverberating to it. The same sound, heard in the confines of even as large and roomy a mess hall as the one at the Point, simply raises your hair.

Cheers and football songs are rather disillusioning things, when seen on paper. The cheers are arrant gibberish and too absurd for words, and the lyrics of the songs are one and all trite poetry about fighting for the old school, or loving the old school, or never forgetting her or the colors, or doing something to the other school, such as tearing through their line, or rolling up the score, or smashing down the tacklers. You have heard or read dozens of them, and, I will warrant, never found an original line or idea in any of them. But, by George, you listen to that Cadets Corps shout one in that mess hall, and I want to tell you, the thing lives. It means something. The rollicking march music of the melody stirs your blood, of course; but even the old, well-worn words come to life, and take on meaning when the straight-backed kids, with clear eyes, cry out, or sing them at the top of their lungs.

At such times, the old songs are no longer old, but something new and stimulating, as each boy looks into his heart and finds there the primitives, so simple, and yet so wonderful to discover—this is my school; I love it! These are my companions! I would die for them! Together we stand against the world! Here, amongst us is safety! We are the salt of the earth! Nowhere else are there any such as we! How wonderful it is to be banded here together against whatever may come! Strength, strength, strength! Pour it out in song!

The occasion was the rally before the Army-Navy game tomorrow. And I envied those kids, because they were able really to care. They seemed to care terribly whether their team won or lost, and I, who perhaps never did, and certainly do not now, truly envied them. Sitting at the mess table with the Cadets and the cheerleaders, worrying over whether my talk was going to please the youngsters, I still found time to look back into my own life and wonder whether I had ever cared that much for victory or defeat. And for a moment, I caught a glimpse of a past, so long dead, that I shuddered at the dry rattle of it. There once was a boy who thought the sun rose and set on his boat, and whether it won or lost.

Why isn't it possible to hold that? The cheerleader who led the rally spoke to the corps with his eyes blazing and his body as taut as a bowstring with purpose, and he was saying that Army could win; that Army was a jinx buster, that Army would go down there to Philadelphia and knock the hell out of Navy; and the cadets got up on their hind legs, and yelled affirmation; and the great hall was alive and throbbing with the glory of youth. We can! We will! We've got the stuff! They can't beat us! Our team is the best team on earth! There is no defeat or sorrow! All things come to those who want it hard enough! Fight! Fight! Fight! Does it always work? I wish I knew. I wish

Send-off at West Point — the Military Academy band, a tank, and plenty of Cadets escort the buses

I were that lithe young cheerleader high on the platform, aflame with belief. I wish I didn't know what I know. I wish I weren't so damned smart and bitter. I wish that I could go to West Point, and believe, and struggle, and suffer, and rejoice. . . .

It is rather pleasant to walk up to the Point unannounced, and unexpected. My appointment was for six o'clock. I arrived two hours earlier, and wandered about. It was cold for the first time in the year, crisp and clear. The buildings and the embattlements were too lovely for words. I watched the football team struggling to learn its lessons. I watched the plebes play some freshman team. I caught a glimpse of a soccer game, and teams playing lacrosse, and I watched a lone Cadet studying a long putt on the campus golf course. I stood around and listened to the nonplaying cadets on the sidelines talk—bright, young, cheerful chatter. They were discussing their athletes and their strengths and weaknesses. They were so alive and interested in what was going on all about them. It all meant something and mattered to them. It was all seen through soft eyes. Well, I had something on them, at the end, I think. Twilight fell on the post with such beauty that it hurt to see it. They went to their quarters to do their duties and left to me the pain of inexpressible loveliness.

carrying the football team headed for Philadelphia in 1965.

There is no one who knows more Army-Navy stories—the men who coached and the men who played the game—than Bill Stern, whose colorful sportscasting filled the airwaves for more than thirty-five years. Here are five of his favorites—stories, sketches, and insights into some of the most glorious names in Army-Navy football.

Five Favorites from Stern

BILL STERN

MAN OF PROPHECIES (Ellsworth "Swede" Larson)

Ellsworth "Swede" Larson was a football man. He was also a curious gridiron warrior who made his prophecies come true!

It was in 1917, when an unknown, husky youngster enlisted in the U.S. Marines to fight for his country in the First World War. He was a scrappy American boy named Larson. By the time the war was over, the nineteen-year-old kid had decided to make the sea his career. So, he became a Midshipman at the United States Naval Academy at Annapolis.

Swede Larson went out for football. Cocky, courageous, husky, and tough, he made the team! And one day, while joshing with his teammates, he made his first prophecy.

Someone had said to Larson: "Well, Swede, now that you're on the football team, we can't lose to the Army!"

Swede Larson snapped back: "Mister, you can say that again. As long as I play Navy football, we'll never lose the Army game!"

Maybe that was said in jest, maybe it was spoken in earnest belief. But that crack made Swede Larson something of a marked man at Annapolis. His teammates began to tease him about it. Swede Larson stuck to his prophecy.

For three years, Swede Larson starred on the Navy football teams. For three years, underdog Navy teams met highly favored Army, and each of those three years, a Navy team never lost. Army could never even score a point against Navy while Swede Larson played on the team.

In 1919, at the end of the annual Army-Navy game, the score was Navy, 6; Army, 0. In 1920, Army was an odds-on favorite. But when the annual service game was over, Army's score was nothing, while Navy had 7 points. The same thing happened the following year, with the identical score. Swede Larson's prophecy had come true!

Years later, long after Midshipman Swede Larson had finished his studies at Annapolis, he returned to the football wars in a new role, as the head football coach of

Emery E. "Swede" Larson, Navy coach whose 1939-1941 years at Annapolis brought successive wins over Army.

the Navy team. Someone recalled his prophecy and teased him about it. Swede Larson replied:

"As long as I'm the Navy football coach, no Army team will ever lick us!"

And so it came to pass! Three times in all. On November 29, 1941, an average Navy team took the field against a mighty Army squad. The Cadets were heavy favorites. But true to Swede Larson's prophecy, Navy scored a sensational upset and licked Army for the third year in a row by a score of 14 to 6.

Immediately after that game, surrounded by his happy football players, Swede Larson spoke again.

"This will be the last football for me for quite a while. There's a bigger game coming up and I'm going to be in it."

Again his prophecy proved true. Eight days later, came Pearl Harbor! Swede Larson —the Marine whose Navy football teams never bowed to Army in three years as a player and three years as a coach—went off to the wars!

Asked whether he planned to return to football after the war, Swede Larson replied: "I'm afraid it'll be a long, long time. Maybe never again!"

His final prophecy came true with shocking truth. Swede Larson, the famous football warrior, holder of a perfect record over Army, died, at the age of only forty-six.

LaVerne "Blondie" Saunders in 1942.

Joe Stilwell as a Cadet.

PORTRAIT OF AN EX-GENERAL TO REMEMBER

Quite recently a general named Blondie Saunders left the United States Army. He left quietly without any fanfare and without benefit of any headlines. He left the Army, a one-legged man, to go back to his home town of Stratford, South Dakota, there to live with his memories of days gone by, and adventures lived through. For Gen. Blondie Saunders, there will be many memories, for he has packed a lot of living into his life.

Blondie Saunders really began his life on the windy plains of West Point. That was about a quarter of a century ago. At West Point, Saunders became a famous football player, and sparked an Army team that one season crushed a powerful Knute Rockne-coached Notre Dame team, crushed it with such overwhelming power, that after the game, Rockne faced his unhappy players and said: "Boys, don't feel too bad about taking a beating from this Army team. There's one consolation in defeat—it's good to know that if we should ever have a war, there'll be guys like Blondie Saunders and his teammates on hand to protect our country."

How right was the wise Bald Eagle of football! How well he could judge men, even if they were rival football players. For when war did come, it was Blondie Saunders,

All-America football player of the great Army football teams of the middle 1920s, who created an amazing story of courage and bravery.

Blondie Saunders and a small crew of men arrived at Guadalcanal when that historic spot had not yet become the focal point of military operations in the Solomon Islands. He didn't know how he and his men were going to get Flying Fortresses into the air from a base that was nothing better than just a thin sandy strip of swampland but it had to be done, and Blondie Saunders went about doing it.

Blondie Saunders was just as hard a man to stop in war as he had been on the football field. It was he who led the first B-17 raid on Guadalcanal. Once, on a mission, both the pilot and co-pilot were killed. Blondie Saunders took over the controls and landed the crippled bomber.

One day, flying on an important mission, Blondie Saunders crashed in the jungle near Piradoba, in India. For a night and a day, he lay in the twisted, tortured remains of his ship with a heavy airplane engine on his chest. But with those powerful hands of his, once the strongest pair of hands in football, he finally managed to pull himself away from the wreckage and save his life.

When Blondie Saunders, the once-famous All-American football player, came out of the hospital, he was minus a leg, minus one of the precious legs that had carried him to national fame as a football player.

By the time the war ended, Blondie Saunders was a brigadier general in the United States Army.

But now, his Army days are over, as are his football days, too.

Recently, General Saunders left the United States Army, left quietly without any fanfare and without any headlines, went home, a little gimpy, to his native South Dakota to live with his memories.

VINEGAR JOE

On November 14, 1903, the great Chicago University football team, with the immortal Walter Eckersall, came to West Point to play against an underdog Army team. The odds were 20 to 1 that Eckersall with his trip-hammer Chicago teammates would slaughter the Army team.

As the game opened, Chicago lived up to all advance notices. Their methods were revolutionary and revelationary, but by some miracle, the Army players managed to plow through for a touchdown. Whereupon, the enraged Eckersall and his equally angry teammates ripped through for a touchdown to tie the score at 6 to 6. And there it stood as the game moved foot by foot, yard by yard toward its finish. Suddenly, with very little time left in the game, the Army quarterback was hurt. And from the Army substitute bench came Joe!

And the guy named Joe found himself noseguard to noseguard with the famous Walter Eckersall, probably the greatest quarterback in gridiron history.

Well, Army started down the field with a touchdown glint in its eye. But there was a fumble on the 10-yard line and Chicago grabbed the ball. Eckersall fell back to his 5-yard line for a neat kick and the ball landed directly in Joe's hands on the 45-yard

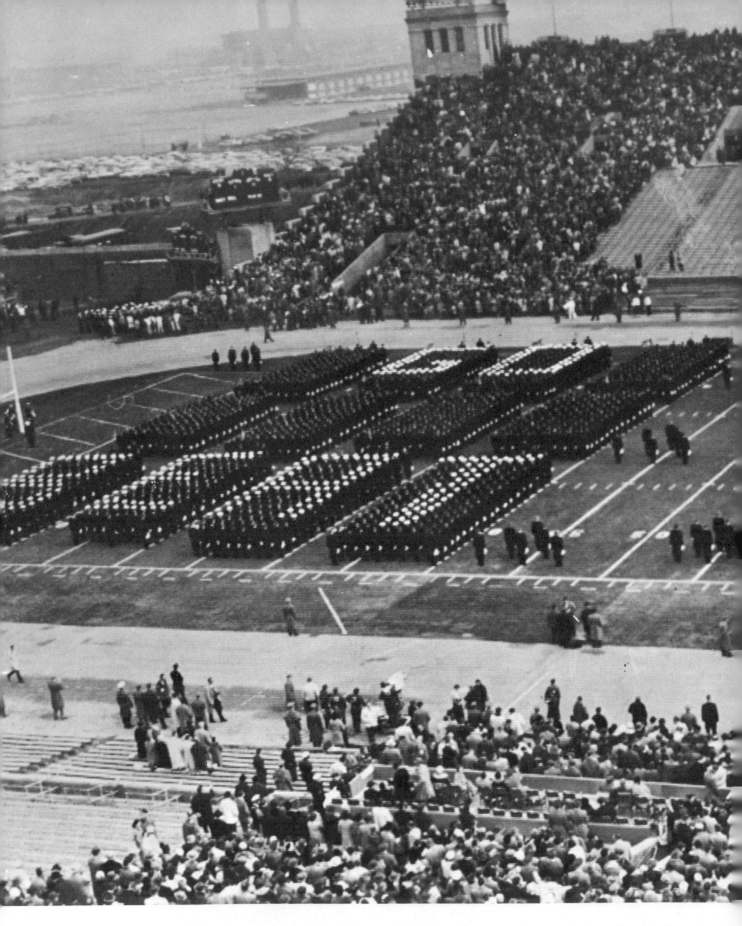

The Middies urge their team to victory by spelling out the slogan "Go Navy, Beat Army" prior to

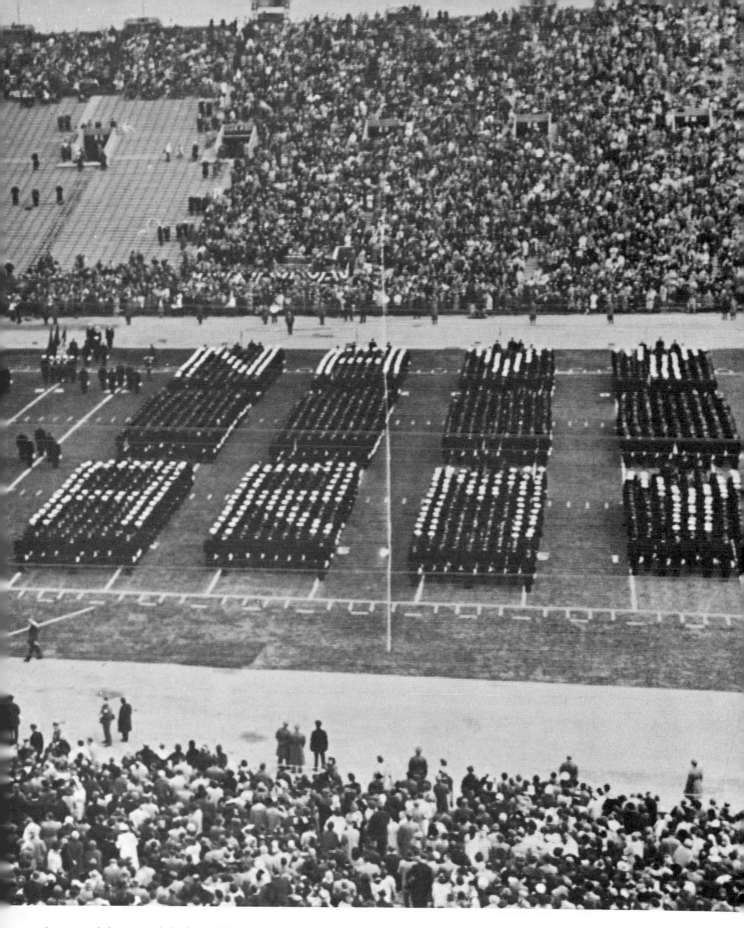

the start of the annual clash in 1961.

line. The substitute might have done the usual thing of trying to carry the ball. If he had done that, he might have been tackled and dropped in his tracks—for the great Eckersall was bearing down on him even while the punt was still in the air.

But substitute Joe was an unusual guy. Out of the corner of his eye he saw Eckersall charging down at him—so, he made a split-second decision. He simply decided to "hold." He was half crouched when the decision was reached, and it caught Eckersall completely off guard. The Chicagoan, expecting him to dash off, interfered. It was a costly blunder. Chicago was penalized 25 yards and the ball moved down to the 20-yard line. The substitute Joe, by deciding merely to hold, outfoxed the great Eckersall. And so, with a few minutes left to play, Army gambled on a field goal. They made it, and the game was won by Army, with a single field goal. It was one of the most stunning football upsets in gridiron history!

Substitute Joe became the hero of the hour—and all because he had made that split-second decision which brought a startling victory.

That substitute Joe who, many years ago, outfoxed the great Walter Eckersall and brought victory to the Army football team, went on to become a great football star. He went on to become a great leader of men, too. From West Point to China, he became known as "Vinegar Joe"—and his "holding" tactics became of vital importance to all United States in the past war. He amazed the world with his "holding" courage when he led a brave company of men sloshing through the steaming jungles of Burma under a rain of Jap bombs and bullets—and successfully completed a trek over perilous mountains from Tungoo, with thousands of half-starved refugees. From West Point to China, his "holding" tactics in the face of danger have become historic legends.

That was "Vinegar Joe"—a football hero from long ago—known the world over, until his death, as Gen. Joe Stilwell, who commanded the U.S. forces in the East and bedeviled the foe with the sledgehammer tactics he learned as a Number One football star at West Point.

1942 BROADCAST

It was Allen Walz, the famous crew coach at Yale who told me this curious football story.

One day in 1942, he was in the company of ten American sportsmen, in a private sailing boat, peacefully fishing off the coast of Newfoundland. However, those ten fishermen were mixing some football with their fishing. For they were listening to the broadcast of the annual Army-Navy game.

Suddenly, seemingly out of nowhere, came a cannon shot. Shocked and surprised, the ten American fishermen looked to see what had happened. To their amazement, they made a startling discovery. For, a couple of hundred yards away, loomed a submarine, flying a German flag.

A German officer with several armed sailors boarded the little fishing boat and angrily demanded to know what the Americans were doing in those waters. He threatened to blow their little boat to pieces, as he accused them of sending radio messages. The ten Americans protested, insisting that they had a right to be fishing in those wa-

Cadets decorate the barracks at West Point with "Sink Navy" displays in support of the team against their biggest rivals.

ters. Suddenly, from the radio, came the voice of the sports announcer:

"The moment has come! The Navy is taking to the air! The Navy receivers are coming out . . ."

The German officers and his crew heard no more. Quickly they left the little fishing boat and returned to their submarine. For several minutes, the ten Americans in that tiny fishing boat were too stunned to speak, as the German submarine submerged and disappeared. Then it suddenly dawned upon them why the Germans had fled in such a hurry. The German officer had mistaken the football broadcast for a genuine Navy message. When he heard the voice of a sports announcer shout: "The Navy is taking to the air—", it was enough for him. The radio broadcast of an Army-Navy football game had helped ten American fishermen out of a tight spot.

Allen Walz, the famous crew coach was one of those fishermen, and he told me that story because he thought I would get a kick out of knowing the name of the sports announcer broadcasting the Army-Navy game on that particular day in 1942. He was a sportscaster named Bill Stern.

FATS ELLINGER

In the cold record books of the game Fats Ellinger is listed merely as a once-famous football player and chief assistant to Red Blaik, noted Army football coach. But there's more to the man than that. Maybe he never made the headlines as a big-time successful coach but there wasn't a great Dartmouth or Army team during his day that wasn't moulded into invincibility by the sure hand of Fats Ellinger. Some of the greatest linesmen in gridiron history were taught, trained, and shaped by his capable hands.

Fats Ellinger was line coach in 1933 when this picture was taken. That year the West Point coaching staff consisted of (l. to r.) Art Meehan, Harley Trice, Red Reeder, Moe Daly, Gar Davidson (head coach), Earl Blaik, Fats Ellinger, Bill Wood.

The story of Fats Ellinger, as he was known to a host of friends, is the curious story of a great and courageous football heart that wasn't good enough to make a man a soldier. For that is what Fats Ellinger wanted most to be. For years he had yearned to serve his country as an Army man, but the big brave heart that made him the most feared man on a football field was the same organ that ruined him as a soldier.

Harry "Fats" Ellinger played at guard for West Point on the 1923 and 1924 elevens. He was a member of the famous center trio of Garbisch, Farwick, and Ellinger, heroes all, at the Point to this day. Fats was a glib, humorous talker, rated the best "jockey" on the Cadet eleven. His clever repartee kept his mates on their toes.

As much as Fats loved football—he made All American—more than anything else in the world he wanted to be an Army man. It was with ill-disguised impatience that he waited for graduation day when he would receive his commission in the United States Army.

The day came at last. Before he could receive his bars he went to be examined by the Army medical board, the usual procedure. They looked him over carefully and then the ceiling fell in on Fats Ellinger. The medics told him he had a bad heart. He was to avoid all violent exercise and undue excitement if he cared to go on living. With regrets they denied him what had been his goal all his life, a commission in the United States Army.

Fats Ellinger stood stunned only for a minute. Then he let out a roar. "You're crazy, gentlemen!" he shouted. "You can't bust me on the flimsy excuse of a bad heart! That's a laugh! Why, for three years I've been tearing up and down the football field with this same heart of mine. Don't you know I've gone through two long football campaigns without a minute's relief? You mean to say I've done that with a bad heart? I don't believe it, and I'll prove to you that you're dead wrong!"

Fats Ellinger tore out of the examining room, ran at top speed to the Hudson River, jumped in wearing full Cadet uniform, shoes and all, and swam as fast as he could to an island. Then he turned back without pausing for breath, swam to shore, rushed up a steep hill, and burst into the examining room where the medical board was still in session. In dripping uniform, and with water pouring all over the floor, Fats demanded another examination of his supposedly bad heart.

They looked him over again. And the verdict was the same. His heart was still bad and he had to be rejected for a commission. And, in spite of what he had done to prove his point, the doctor shrugged his shoulders and said, "Sorry, Ellinger. If you want to go on living at all, I advise you to avoid violent exercise and undue excitement. That's all."

Fats crept out of the examining room, a brokenhearted youngster. He disappeared for a couple of years to forget the whole business. Then, three years later, he showed up at the Point as one of the assistant football coaches. In time he became assistant to Earl "Red" Blaik, head football coach at Dartmouth. No matter what he did or where he went, Fats Ellinger completely ignored the warning that had once been given to him by the West Point medical examining board. He worked as hard as the most ambitious of the youngsters under his charge. He reveled in excitement and, during practice sessions, he mixed it vigorously with the healthy and husky young players in his charge.

After seven years at Dartmouth, Fats went with Red Blaik to West Point when the latter was named head coach there. Again Fats was more than happy. West Point had always been in his blood and here he was back at the Point! He scrimmaged on the gridiron. He played baseball. He played tennis, hunted, fished, swam, skied. He went into the woods, logging with the big woodsmen.

For seventeen years this went on. Then one day he went to sleep and never woke up. The death sentence handed down in a medical report in 1925 had finally caught up with him. So passed away Fats Ellinger, a colorful, hard-playing, vigorous personality in the world of football. He died young when he might perhaps have lived carefully to his three-score-and-ten. But he wouldn't have been Fats Ellinger if he had lived quietly and carefully. He would have been someone else.

President John F. Kennedy, a lifelong football buff, thoroughly enjoys the 1961 Army-Navy game, along with more than 100,000 fans. It was noted that the President, although maintaining an air of impartiality, was noticeably delighted with the result as Navy defeated the Cadets, 13-7.

Navy Stages a Classy Show for the President

ART MORROW

HISTORY CONTAINS NO RECORD OF WHAT THE PRESIDENT OF THE UNITED States said to the Governor of Pennsylvania during the first half, nor what he said to the Governor of Ohio during the second, but on his return to Washington, D.C., the wartime PT-boat skipper declared that he "greatly enjoyed the game."

So did approximately 101,000 others, especially those garbed in Navy blue. For the U.S. Naval Academy won the sixty-second football clash with the U.S. Military Academy at the Philadelphia Stadium, 13 to 7, December 2.

For a man who ranked as a mere junior-grade lieutenant, John F. Kennedy had a pretty good seat. He viewed the first half from a box on the 40-yard line along the west side—the Army, or home side—of the field, and the second half from a similar position on the east, or Navy, side.

He saw his own former branch of service literally kick the Army into defeat. Greg Mather, Navy, talented end, place-kicked a 32-yard field goal in the second quarter to put the Midshipmen ahead; then, after fleet Bill Ulrich had matched Army's third-period touchdown, he converted the extra point and, finally, booted a fourth-chukker three-pointer from 36 yards out.

Mather's toe thus spelled the final difference, the first time a field goal has resolved the Army-Navy game since Slade Cutter kicked one out of the mud of Franklin Field in 1934 for a 3-to-0 Annapolis triumph.

Mr. Kennedy, the first Chief Executive to attend the game since Harry S Truman, saw Navy roll to a 7-to-0 victory in 1952, witnessed a hard-hitting, clean-fought battle. The Midshipmen had to come from behind to win, but they actually dominated most of the action. Army did not ring up a first down until the latter stages of the second period. Navy simply packed too much speed and savoir faire for the Cadets, and save for the West Pointers' grim determination, the outcome could have been much more decisive.

Hardy as they were, the players were rivaled by the President. Brilliant sunshine flooded the field, and the air was crisp. Still, everyone wore an overcoat, even the gold-braided generals and the brass-buttoned admirals; everyone, that is, except the President.

Mr. Kennedy did not even wear a hat and sat through the first half and most of the second without donning a topcoat. He missed much of the pre-game show. His silver DC-6B airplane did not arrive at the Philadelphia Navy Yard port until 12:55 P.M., and by that time the brigade of Cadets and the regiment of Midshipmen had marched to their seats.

At precisely 1:30 P.M., kickoff time, the two team captains entered the stand where the President was sitting and asked him to toss up the coin. The President had already lighted a cigar and obviously was enjoying himself.

He had come well prepared—with two silver dollars.

The first he tossed into the air and Mike Casp, the Army captain, correctly called the turn of the coin.

Mr. Kennedy immediately gave him the silver dollar, minted in Philadelphia, 1935.

As consolation, Navy's captain, John F. Hewitt, also received a silver dollar minted in 1935, the last year the United States turned out such coinage.

Mr. Kennedy spent most of the first period in conversation with Governor Lawrence.

Army received the kickoff but could not get anywhere. Navy, thanks principally to a pass from Ron Klemick to Mather, made a first down but then had to kick. Mather's kick bounced dead on the 1-yard line.

An exchange of punts followed and it wound up with Army in possession as a result of an interception by Harry McMillan on the Navy's 28.

Piling on cost Navy 15 yards on the ensuing punt and, from their own 34, the Middies marched to Army's 11 before the first period closed.

On third down, with seven to go, Klemick lost eight yards on an attempted pass and Mather had to drop back for a field goal. With 1:46 of the second period gone he made it and the score became 3 to 0.

Army received the ensuing kickoff with Tom Culver returning Mather's boot 29 yards, but Steve Hoy intercepted a pass by Dick Eckert two plays later and Navy was on the prowl again. From Army's 41, Navy moved to Army's 19 with the help of two passes. From there, Mather dropped back to the 27 and tried another field goal.

He missed—wide to the left and Army took over on its 20. Now the Cadets made their initial first down. Jim Beierschmitt sparked this drive. He and Army's fastest back, Ken Waldrop, carried out to the 47. Then Cammy Lewis, son of the old West Virginia coach, came in as Army quarterback. With the help of one offside penalty, the Cadets moved to the Middies' 19.

Here Dick Heydt dropped back to the 29 and attempted a field goal, which fell short.

During the intermission, the President went down to the mayor's private clubhouse and had a bowl of Philadelphia's famous pepperpot soup.

As a result, the second half was somewhat late in starting but, when it did start, Army struck quickly. Navy pounded out a first down but finally surrendered possession of the ball on its 37 after an incomplete pass by Klemick. Mather kicked and, after Lloyd

President John F. Kennedy is an interested spectator at the sixty-third Army-Navy game.

Army quarterback Dick Eckert is all action as he drives for a gain in the first quarter of the 1961 Army-Navy game. Bob Sutton (16) and Vern Von Sydow of Navy move in to stop him.

Asbury's return, Army was in possession on its own 31. Beierschmitt ran one play, then gave way to Dick Eckert; Eckert, throwing to his left, arched a pass over John Sai's head and Culver caught it. Sai caught him at the 13.

Rushes by Al Rushatz and Eckert produced a first down on the three. Rushatz plunged for another yard and a half, then dove over for an Army touchdown at 6:19 of the third period.

Heydt's conversion—succeeding in 26 of 28 attempts this year—made the score, 7 to 3, in favor of Army.

But Navy bounced back. An exchange of punts followed the touchdown and, with Jim Stewart's punt return, Navy wound up in possession on its own 49. Here Bob Hecht tossed a downfield pass to Stewart and it was good for 38 yards and a first down at Army's 13. Ulrich raced around his right for a touchdown on the next play.

With Mather's conversion point, that made the score, 10 to 7, and Navy was ahead to stay. With three and a half minutes of the game remaining, Mather place-kicked his second field goal and that was it.

It was obvious that two big breaks hurt the Army team. "I said before that the breaks would probably decide this game and the breaks certainly had a great bearing on it," said Dale Hall, the Army coach.

"The first break came when Mather's punt rolled dead on the 1-yard line.

"The second major break came when our Joe Blackgrove fumbled early in the fourth period. I think we would have gone on for a touchdown if that had not happened. As game developments proved, Navy went on to Mather's second field goal, and that was the game."

So now the President of the United States, an ex-Navy man himself, left the game happily. He then went to board a train to return to Washington, D.C., his first train ride since he became President.

7

FROM GRIDIRON TO BATTLEFIELD

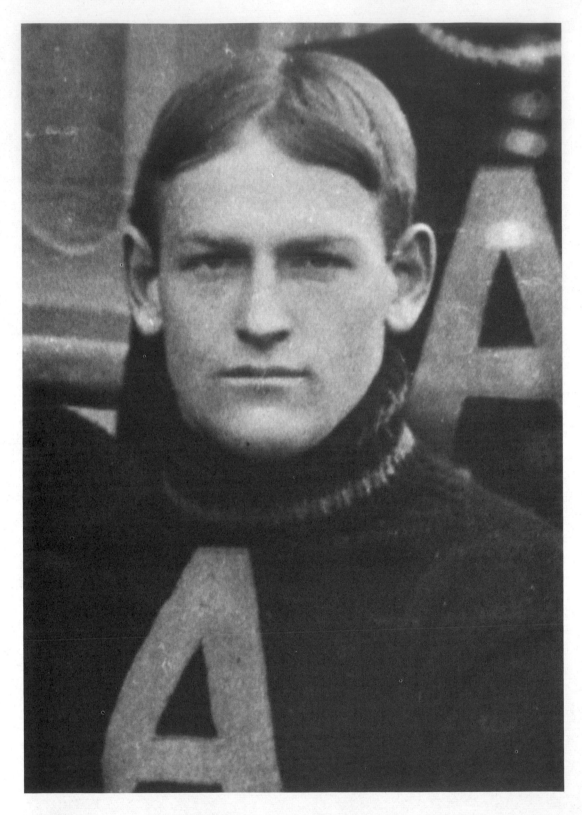

Paul Bunker, the only player in Army history to win All-American honors at two different positions — as tackle in 1901 and as halfback in 1902.

Paul Bunker, twice All-American tackle and fullback for Army, ordered the burning of the Stars and Stripes, as the Japanese closed in on his untenable position at Corregidor. But he saved a piece of that flag and sewed it under his cotton shirt. Paul Bunker gave his life for his country, but that piece of flag he sewed into his shirt lives on, enshrined in the museum of the Military Academy. No man brought greater honor to West Point, or to his country. R. Ernest Dupuy told the story in his book, Men of West Point.

Paul Bunker, All-American

R. ERNEST DUPUY

It's just a tiny piece of ragged bunting, resting today safe in West Point's custody in the Museum of the Military Academy. Until you know its story, you don't realize that interwoven in its shreds are the hopes, the prayers, the travail of American soldiers fighting and dying to keep their country safe; that it symbolizes the agony of the Bataan Death March; the murders, lashings, disease, filth, and starvation of Nip prison camps; deferred hopes, indomitable courage, accomplishment of duty.

It is particularly sacred to the memory of fifty-eight West Point graduates who died while in Nip hands, of seventeen more summarily executed or murdered by the Japanese, and of 153 others who succumbed to Allied air and submarine attack upon the hell-ships carrying them from the Philippines to Japan. Many of these died of thirst and general exhaustion before the Allied planes discovered the ships. Survivors declare that well over half of the deaths occurred in that category.

For this is Corregidor's flag; all that is left of the Stars and Stripes that floated over Fort Mills on the "Rock" until the end. It is Paul Bunker's message to the people of the United States. It is the Battle Hymn of the Republic. It is Corregidor *invictus*; no Nipponese hand ever defiled it.

Paul Delmont Bunker, class of 1903, born in Michigan, at West Point a classmate of Gen. Douglas MacArthur, won fame as one of Army's all-time football greats. The first Army player to make Walter Camp's immortal All-American team for his outstanding play at tackle during the 1901 season, he made Camp's team again the following year, 1902, as a halfback, scoring two touchdowns during the first half of the Army-Navy game, sparking the Army team to a glorious 22-8 victory. Bunker's flashy running and great defensive play dominated the day, marked by an individual dual between Bunker and Navy's inspirational fullback, Bull Halsey.

Bunker fought overseas in World War I. He was in the Philippines when Pearl Harbor was struck.

All hell was boiling on Corregidor's blasted rock at eleven o'clock on the morning of May 6, 1942, when to Col. Paul Bunker, Coast Artillery Corps, who had directed the long 155s of his 59th Artillery throughout the tragedy of Luzon, and commanded Fort Mills itself, came one of those orders which break men's hearts. At noon, he would personally lower the American flag, hoist the white flag of surrender, and then burn the standard under which he had fought.

Col. Paul Bunker obeyed that order. But before he gave the big flag to the flames he clipped off a huge piece of it. And in the soul-searing period of waiting until the Nip commander took over, found time to sew the flag, with nervous and trembling fingers under a patch upon his cotton suntan shirt.

Sick, emaciated, Paul Bunker was herded with the other prisoners from Corregidor into a barge on May 24; with them he later stumbled through three feet of water off Pasay Beach and waded ashore under the bayonets and gun butts of their guards. Then he collapsed.

Perhaps because he was a high-ranking officer, he was not clubbed to death as the other gaunt survivors were being paraded in infamy into Manilla and through its streets to Bilibid Prison's dank walls.

Instead, the Nips put him into a sort of improvised hospital at Pasay, operated by captive Navy medical personnel. He did not enter Bilibid until June 1, when, with both feet infected and one leg badly inflamed from blood poisoning, he was thrust into the prison hospital to a stinking cot beside Col. Delbert Ausmus, brother coast artilleryman.

Bunker felt sure he would not survive. But he had something important on his mind. Swearing Ausmus to secrecy, he whispered of the precious bit of the flag under that patch. That emblem, he said, he wished to carry to the Secretary of War. Would Ausmus share in the effort? Follow through if he, Bunker, died?

Ausmus agreed. Cautiously, warily, lest some guard espy them, their feeble fingers plucked upon the patch; the bit of bunting was then equally divided, the patch sewn up again. Ausmus tucked his portion into the frayed edge of the cuff off his own shirt, resewed the hem. And then there was nothing to do but wait. A prisoner's wait is long drawn out.

Bunker survived for a time. He survived the horrors of Bilibid, of Tarlac, of transportation in the suffocating stench of a prison-ship hold to Formosa. Above all, his remarkable spirit survived. As a Japanese inspecting officer remarked, looking at that living skeleton in the prison camp of Karenko, on November 27, 1942: "Very old, but looks very brave."

His was but a tenuous hold on life, however, and on March 11, 1943, sixty-two-year-old Paul Bunker died quietly in his sleep. Ausmus saw his body laid out later, could envisage the bit of flag still upon that torn, ragged shirt before the dead soldier was cremated.

Now it was up to him.

Inspected time and again by his jailers, Ausmus yet preserved his own precious shirt, patched and repatched, under their searching eyes. And he resisted all temptation to

Thirteen members of the 1935 Navy team gave their lives for their country in World War II. Captain that year was Lou Robertshaw, who went on to command a Marine unit in Vietnam.

share his secret with fellow prisoners. Strange things happen to men immured behind barbed wire and bayonets. Some of them unravel spiritually in that decay, in the canker of despair. So Ausmus kept his mouth shut—and survived.

On November 9, 1945, Colonel Ausmus, freed from his captivity, arrived in Washington to present to Secretary of War Robert P. Patterson that cherished shred of Corregidor's battle flag. And that was as Paul Bunker wished it to be.

Sportswriter Gene Ward calls the roll of Army and Navy gridiron stars who went on to achieve immortality in the lists of those who serve their country, both in peace and in war. This was back in 1946. The list would be much longer today.

Football Pays High Dividends in Battle

GENE WARD

"Upon the fields of friendly strife,
    Are sown the seeds
That, upon other fields, on other days,
    Will bear the fruits of victory."

—Douglas MacArthur

EISENHOWER . . . MARSHALL . . . PATTON . . . STILWELL . . . BRADLEY . . . OF the Army! Halsey . . . Ingram . . . King . . . Land . . . Ghormley . . . of the Navy! Call the roll of the top generals and admirals of World War II and at the same time you will be intoning names from football lineups of the past, thus proving beyond all doubt that the body and spirit building qualities of the American sport of football pays dividends in battle, that Douglas MacArthur, the nation's No. 1 football fan and a player himself as a youth, was making the greatest prediction of all time when he penned those words now immortal in the sports world.

The proof is buried deep in the musty archives at West Point and Annapolis—in the yellowed pages of the yearbooks, the *Lucky Bags* and the *Howitzers*, and among faded photographs in tucked-away files where you find ancient scenes of "guards back, first down, 5-yards-to-go" days. And as you dig into their athletic pasts you discover that a startling number of this nation's leading generals and admirals, who now have made this whole broad land of ours secure, first learned to defend their land on a tiny patch of gridiron turf.

And this defense of America which they chose was strictly according to the best American tradition that a good offense is the best defense, nowhere more aptly exhibited than in the game of football. And one who learned that lesson well on the gridiron as a Cadet went on to become the most offensive-minded general of all—George Smith Patton, the two-gun, two-fisted fighter who mounted the armored assaults which outblitzed Hitler's blitz boys.

Col. Meade Wildrick, West Point's present public relations officer, remembers Patton's athletic exploits well.

324

"He used to play football like he did everything else later in life—with a rambunctious aggressiveness. Even as a plebe he had a commanding appearance and he always was the most aggressive, if not the best player on the field. He loved the game and played the full four years."

Wildrick, who ran against him in hurdle races at that time, remembers when Patton set a record of 25:4 for the 220 lows (run on grass and in spikeless shoes in those days). Later, Patton became America's first pentathlon entrant in the Olympic Games at Stockholm.

The *Howitzer* of 1909 has this to say about America's future knight-of-the-armor— "two broken arms bear witness to his zeal, as well as to his misfortune, on the football field, but misfortune could not run fast enough to catch up with him on the track."

During the bitter European campaigns Patton had the penchant for surrounding

The class of 1915 at West Point produced some fine football stars, many of whom went on to distinguished military careers. Seen here are (First row, seated, l. to r.) R. B. Woodruff, L. S. Hobbs, V. E. Prichard. (Second row, l. to r.) J. S. MacTaggart, L. A. Merillat, D. D. Eisenhower, T. B. Larkin, P. A. Hodgson, C. C. Benedict, H. R. Harmon. (Back row, l. to r.) J. A. Van Fleet, C. E. Hocker, C. C. Herrick, O. N. Bradley, F. J. Dunigan, W. W. Hess.

Left: Gen. Vernon E. Prichard was commander of the First Armored Division in Italy in 1944.   Right: Emmett "Rosie" O'Donnell, Jr. was a hard hitting member of the 1926 Army team that tied Navy, 21-21. During World War II, O'Donnell was head of the Strategic Bombing Command in the Far East.

himself with football men in staff jobs. He made "Jeff" Keyes his aid; Lieut. Gen. Geoffrey Keyes, now commanding the 7th Army in Europe and the same who was a great back on the 1911 and 1912 teams. "Jeff" was with Patton when he died, rode with him on the last ride George Patton took with his armor.

What an all-general backfield this would make: "Blood 'n' Guts" Patton, "Ike" Eisenhower, "Vinegar Joe" Stilwell, and "Girtz" Craig, ex-Chief of Staff, colorful nicknames and all. And "Bull" Halsey, Jonas Ingram, Emory (Jerry) Land, and Bullet Bob Ghormley all were pile-driving backs for Navy in their day.

Like Patton, Ike's aggressive, daredevil play put him out of action on the gridiron. He broke his leg in his second varsity game. Stilwell and Craig both made grandstand plays in the big games that are remembered by oldtime fans to this day. And Bradley, the same who was to become conqueror of Bizerte and leader of all U. S. ground forces in the final smashing of the Nazis, was a vicious tackler, one of Army's best ends.

For Navy, Jonas H. Ingram, commander in chief-to-be of the Atlantic Fleet, clipped a long Army winning streak when he caught the first forward pass ever thrown successfully in this pigskin classic, running it to a touchdown. He was filling the fullback brogans of another big fellow, Admiral-to-be Ghormley, who in turn, had taken over the job after graduation in 1904 of another chap nicknamed Pudge—last name, Halsey. Before that, at right halfback on the 1901 team, was a fast leather-lugger, Emory S. Land, retiring head of the Maritime Commission; and the year before Ernest J. King was one of the "Hustlers," as Annapolis called its second team.

You might very well make General MacArthur the coach of this mythical all-general, all-admiral eleven of ours. He would be a great one. And contrary to popular opinion, MacArthur did play football. There's an early picture of young Doug taken when he played end for the West Texas Military Academy eleven, taken just a few days before he received word of his appointment to West Point.

While he wasn't a varsity man up the Hudson, he did become manager of the Army team of 1902, and donned an athletic hero's mantle on the diamond when he scored the first run of the first Army-Navy ball game.

Later he was in charge of the U. S. Olympic team at Berlin and when he finally returned to the Hudson Highlands, he was one of the most heated sports enthusiasts ever to do a tour of duty (1919-22) as West Point's superintendent, leaving a mark that has governed the sports policy of the Army to this day.

Pudge Halsey was the starting Navy fullback in the Army-Navy game in 1902 as the team MacArthur managed scored a 22-8 triumph on Franklin Field, Philadelphia.

The very top man of the Army board of strategy, boss of MacArthur and Eisenhower and all the other stars, was a football man himself. Calm, quiet George Catlett Marshall, who often has likened the planning of war to quarterback on a football field, was not a West Point graduate, being the sixth chief of staff to make the grade without the U. S. Military Academy "stamp of approval." But he had his pigskin training just the same, and played a terrific tackle.

Having tried in vain for an appointment to the Point, he entered Virginia Military Institute as, in his own words, "a clumsy, unpromising recruit, ill looked upon by the faculty of that ancient institution." But he graduated with the highest military rank in the Cadet Corps and won outstanding honors as an all-southern tackle. He calls this early football training the finest preparation he could have had for the job he just has done well.

West Point figures disclose there have been 513 cadets to win the varsity football "A" since 1890 and no less than eighty-nine have risen to the rank of brigadier general or higher. One of them—a boy from the big wheat fields of Kansas with a big smile to match—went to the top—General of the Armies!

And there's a story from the early football career of this lad from Kansas, of a long-ago day when two high schools, bitter rivals, battled it out on the gridiron. Salina and Abilene both had fine teams, but Salina was rated the better of the two. Its coach had developed a powerful play, a delayed smash through tackle largely responsible for its long string of victories.

The Salina quarterback called this play in the early moments of the game and, sure

A star football player, head coach for Army, and superintendent of West Point, Gar Davidson served in a score of command posts during World War II and the Korean War. Here, he is congratulated on his appointment as superintendent by Lt. Gen. Blackshear M. Bryan, whom he succeeded.

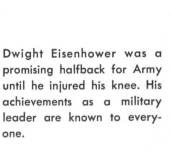
Dwight Eisenhower was a promising halfback for Army until he injured his knee. His achievements as a military leader are known to everyone.

enough, it produced a touchdown as the slender Abilene tackle was sucked out of position, hurled aside by two fierce blocks.

The Salina quarterback enthusiastically barked the signals for the same play again as soon as his side regained the ball. But this time that young Abilene tackle bounced the ball carrier for a 4-yard loss. And he repeated the spine-tingling defensive play again and again. Salina gained no more ground over Dwight D. Eisenhower.

When Ike first entered high school he was many pounds lighter than the average of his classmates, but he became, in the words of his old mentor, "the most outstanding tackle in the valley." His special talents were speed and ability to diagnose plays, the same speed of judgment and ability to call plays which took us into Berlin.

He carried that pigskin prowess on to West Point where he was shifted to the backfield on the plebe eleven. His brilliant ball-toting won him a starting berth on the varsity the following year, 1912.

In the opening game Colgate couldn't stop him. In the second, against Tufts, Ike broke his leg.

But that didn't finish his football, for he was on that field, once his leg permitted it, for every game as—a cheerleader! Later he took over extracurricular duties as freshman coach, staying as close to the sport he loved as possible.

That football pays dividends in battle is nowhere proven with greater force than by checking the year 1915 at West Point. That was Ike Eisenhower's graduating year.

On the walls of the red brick gymnasium is a row of plaques, each hung in honor of the member of the particular graduating classes who received the coveted "A" in a major sport. There are twenty names on the 1915 plaque and, of these, sixteen have served in two World Wars as colonels or higher. Ike is a quarter of the way down the list and just a bit below the name of Omar N. Bradley.

"Brad" developed into a sensational football man, but for the first two years he was held down to the "B" squad by his youth, inexperience, and slight stature. But above all Cadet Bradley had the same guts and stick-to-itiveness as Patton before him.

He set his goal on a varsity end position and in his third and final year that's where he played. His tackling and offensive play were terrific, so he wound up with the "hard-to-get A," more difficult to win in those days, plus a gold football. Bradley also possessed a powerful throwing arm (they say at the Point he tossed a baseball 400 feet, an Academy record) and this together with an ability to hammer the old apple made him a fine ballplayer. His three-year BA on the varsity was .383, a commendable record in any league.

Also on that 1915 plaque is the name Vernon Prichard, captain of the football team and only yesterday the major general and commander of the First Armored Division of the Fifth Army, blasters of Italy. Prichard had learned about the forward pass from Notre Dame's Knute Rockne and Gus Dorais in 1913 and had employed it in 1914 to whip Navy and complete an undefeated season.

And to continue along that 1915 list of football stars and generals-to-be: Hubert R. Harmon, later to command the 6th and 13th Air Forces; Roscoe B. Woodruff, commander-to-be of the 84th Infantry Division; James Van Fleet, who led the Fourth Division onto the beaches of Normandy; Leland S. Hobbs, to lead the 30th Infantry

Division; Thomas B. Larkin, to go up and become commanding general of services and supply in the Mediterranean and North Africa; Brig. General-to-be Walter W. Hess . . . proofs on a plaque that football pays dividends in battle.

Also on the 1914 club (the 1915 plaque including letter-winners of the '14 season), but not to graduate until '16, was Bob Neyland, later to be Tennessee's renowned coach and then a brigadier general and chief of engineers in the CBI theatre.

Opposite him at end in the Navy lineup was one of Navy's great athletes, Rear-Admiral-to-be Harvey E. Overesch. Charley Gerdardt, the same who commanded the 29th Infantry of the Ninth Army group, was on the Army squad in '14 and became first-string quarterback in '15.

Go back a few years before that and you find evidence of the athletic swath which Vinegar Joe Stilwell cut at West Point. Weighing slightly more than 145 pounds, a lightweight like Bradley, he turned out for practically every sport on the calendar. Because of his small build and the sledgehammer type of football played in that day, Vinegar Joe was on the second team a good deal of the time, but there came a day, November 14, 1903, when young Stilwell got his chance.

It was in an all-important game against Chicago, then a grid power. That team's great Walter Eckersall attempted a field goal that missed the uprights and an alert West Point halfback toted the ball for an Army touchdown. The aroused Chicago team charged down the field to knot the count a few moments later and there the score stood, 6-6, until Stilwell galloped onto the field as a replacement for his injured quarterback.

Three minutes to play!—and every play counted.

Army was on the march to pay dirt when an overanxious back fumbled on the Chicago 10. Sensing a punt by Eckersall, Stilwell dropped back and, sure enough, the ball came spiralling directly into his hands on the 45. Glimpsing a Chicago player ready to smack him, young Joe signaled for a "hold" or "fair catch," and the Chicago tackler couldn't check himself in time. He interfered and the resulting penalty gave Army the ball on the 20, the winning field goal coming a few moments later.

Just as an example of split-second thinking, of the sharp, decisive military mind-to-be.

About this time Navy was packing a terrific wallop from the fullback slot. First there was Pudge Halsey, a small, unwrinkled edition of the crusty task-force commander who was to carry the ball in those shattering raids from the Solomons to Japan itself. The *Lucky Bag* of 1904 has him looking "like a figurehead of Neptune"; mentions the fact he was president of the athletic association and played two years of varsity football.

Recently, Pudge, rechristened the Bull in later years, returned to Annapolis to watch Navy practice for the 1945 Army game. He remarked that he probably was the worst fullback in Annapolis history, which, as it turns out, was hardly the case, Halsey having operated as a first-stringer in this heavy-duty spot for two years, 1902, '03.

Bob Ghormley, another task-force admiral-to-be, took over in 1904 and '05, helping Navy gain a 6-6 tie with Army in his second year. And who should be the assistant coach of that club but Midshipman Halsey, a graduate but not yet commissioned an ensign.

Next came one of Navy's really great fullbacks of the old days, Jonas Ingram. That was a memorable era in Annapolis football and one of those afternoons in the fall of 1907, the team was stirred by the strains of what was to become one of the most popular of all sports songs—"Anchors Aweigh."

Ingram later was named a member of Grantland Rice's all-time Navy football team and in 1915 he returned to Annapolis as coach; again in 1926 as director of athletics and football. He's known as the one-armed admiral because of his old and oft-repeated saying, "I'd give my right arm to win this ball game."

The old lineup of that 1906 game in which Ingram starred discloses a fellow named Sultan playing center for Army, the same Lieut. Gen. Daniel I. Sultan who was deputy commander to Vinegar Joe in the CBI theatre. Dan Sultan won "all" honors at the pivot position that year.

Both before and after these great years of the fullback admirals there were many who played football and went on to stars and stardom in the grimmer game of war. They include William V. Pratt, former chief of Naval Operations; Curtis D. Wilbur, ex-Secretary of the Navy; Sam Robinson, former Commander-in-Chief of U. S. Fleet and teammate of Wilbur's; Joe Reeves, another ex-C-in-C, credited with the introduction of the football headguard and later a Navy coach; Joe Taussig, who commanded the first division of destroyers to cross the Atlantic in World War I and, in World War II, Commandant of the Fifth Naval District; James O. Richardson, still another ex-C-in-C who was a great "rusher-of the-line"; Rear Adm. John Halligan, captain of the Navy team in '97 . . .

1897—that was the year William D. Leahy, the so-familiar admiral seen at the right hand of the President, graduated. Admiral Leahy never made the varsity, but he played class football.

In later years there were many others who went up to become admirals in this last war, including Vice Adm. Aubrey Fitch, now superintendent at Annapolis and first airman to head the institution. He graduated in 1906 after playing four years of class football and starring as an all-around athlete. Admiral Fitch, in his final year at Annapolis, watched a young fellow named John F. Shafroth play a lot of football at right guard, the Rear Adm. J. F. Shafroth who led our warships in the first sea bombardment of the Japanese homeland.

There were six full generals on active duty in the U. S. Army a little over a year ago —Marshall, MacArthur, Eisenhower, Stilwell, and Arnold were five, all but "Hap" having played football. The sixth wasn't as well known at the time and has since died— Malin (Girtz) Craig who succeeded MacArthur as chief of staff. But aside from a distinguished military career he is revered at West Point because, as an undergraduate, he kicked a field goal from midfield and later pitched a no-hit, no-run baseball game. The Chicago Orphans (the Cubs of that time) attempted to get his name on the dotted line.

Like Vinegar Joe, Craig was a quick thinker on the gridiron. In one game against the

Seventh Regiment he was going hell-for-leather downfield when he suddenly found himself penned in. So he stopped dead and booted the pigskin square between the goal posts. The play was unplanned and was the first time a West Point player ever had pulled such a moleskin maneuver.

Recently, Brig. Gen. Emmett (Rosie) O'Donnell, one of the great airmen of World War II, made a surprise visit to the Metropolitan Football Writers' luncheon to tell a touching story of what a certain group of Army football men had done in battle. A brilliant halfback himself on the '28 eleven, Rosie returned as assistant coach in '34, remaining until 1937. It was of the men on the coaching staff of that period about whom he spoke.

Of the dozen who comprised Brig. Gen. Gar Davidson's staff, eleven saw service in World War II and only four came through unscathed: Davidson, Col. Tom Trapnell —greater hero on Bataan—Col. Bill Wood, and Rosie himself.

The five who gave their lives from that little batch were: Col. Moe Daly, Col. Ed Doyle, Col. Art Meehan, Maj. Bob Stillman, and Maj. Jerry Burlingame. Two others are alive but have suffered leg amputations—Brig. Gen. LaVerne (Blondie) Saunders and Col. Red Reeder, both outstanding on the football field.

The President honors a teammate. President Dwight D. Eisenhower presents the Distinguished Service Medal to Gen. James A. Van Fleet in a 1953 White House ceremony. Interested onlookers include Secretary of Defense Charles Wilson, Gen. Omar Bradley, and Gen. George Marshall. Eisenhower, Van Fleet, and Bradley all played football at West Point. Marshall was tackle for the Virginia Military Institute.

Daly, who had been center on the '26 and '27 clubs before turning to coaching, was captured at Bataan and died of exposure after the prison ship on which he was held was torpedoed. Trapnell, on the same ship, survived. Doyle's life ebbed out on the red sands of Casablanca in the original African invasion. Meehan, the backfield coach, was killed in the Solomons and both Burlingame and Stillman were lost in planes.

As MacArthur, in letters on file at the Military Academy, points out many times in referring to his now famous lines of prediction, it isn't always the actual playing of the game, but just as often it is the being close to the thing that is its spirit. Like MacArthur, Jacob L. (Jake) Devers, Class of '09, Patton's graduating year, and Robert P. Eichelberger, just back from Japan, never played varsity football, but they participated in the intramural pigskin program. Devers won his "A" in basketball, played lacrosse, and later was graduate manager of athletics.

Robert P. Eichelberger gets an assist for the last two terrific Army elevens. It happened this way: In his tenure as superintendent of the Military Academy, Penn Walloped the Army, 48-0, and right then and there General Bob decided to bring Earl Blaik back as coach, definitely feeling such beatings were not good for the Academy. With Blaik as coach and a revision of the physical standards of admission, the scores the past two years vs. Penn were: 62-7, 61-0, in favor of Army.

There is a great reservoir of confidence in the future to be gained from a look at these athletic pasts of our generals and our admirals of World War II.

On the football "fields of friendly strife" a tremendous Army eleven has just completed its second undefeated campaign in a row, led by its Touchdown Twins, Doc Blanchard and Glenn Davis.

And Navy, too, with its touted stars like Dick Duden, Clyde (Smackover) Scott, Dick Scott, and the others, has had a record almost as fine.

Perhaps these players won't be the Eisenhowers and the Halseys of tomorrow (let's hope they won't have to be), but history itself and all the odds as turned up by the archives say that some day some members of these 1944-45 Army and Navy elevens will be wearing stars on their shoulders and collars as battle leaders of another American fight for survival—and they'll be making football pay dividends in that battle.

And so the private said to the general, "Sir, about those Army-Navy tickets you promised me at Anzio . . ."

The General and the Private

THE PHILADELPHIA INQUIRER

BECAUSE GEN. MARK CLARK HAS MADE GOOD ON A PROMISE HE MADE TO A tank battalion private while touring the Anzio beachhead in February, 1944, the private, Dan W. Kerwin, and his wife will attend the Army-Navy football game in Philadelphia this Saturday.

General Clark's promise that when the war was won he would try to get tickets for the private was fulfilled yesterday, when Mr. Kerwin received a letter from the U. S. Military Academy at West Point containing two tickets for the game.

Mr. Kerwin recalled that when the general was making an inspection tour of the Anzio Beachhead in the rough days, for no apparent reason, Clark singled out Private Kerwin for questioning concerning the progress on the Anzio Beach landings. Mr. Kerwin recalled that during the conversation he made some cutting remarks about the Germans entrenched in the mountains nearby.

"You smiled, sir, and made some remark about what I'd be doing soon enough after the struggle was over," Kerwin wrote. "I told you that I'd probably be trying to get tickets for the Army-Navy game. I had tried for six years and never got tickets.

"You smiled, sir, and then said, 'Maybe when we clean up this war and everything is back to normal, write me and I'll see that you get tickets.'"

Mr. Kerwin, who now works for the American Brass Shipping Company, told the general that he had been home for more than two years.

"I didn't want to bother you right off the bat, so I waited," Mr. Kerwin wrote. "I've been talking with my wife and told her the entire story. She suggested that I write you for the tickets to this year's game in Philadelphia."

General Clark wrote to Col. Biff Jones, graduate manager of athletics at West Point, requesting that "Biff" send two tickets to the Kerwins. General Clark then wrote to Mr. Kerwin.

"I hope," he said, "that you and Mrs. Kerwin will enjoy the game and that the Army will win as it did at Anzio as a result of the magnificent fighting ability of men like yourself."

Mr. Kerwin said he is sending General Clark a check for the tickets, so that another lucky serviceman can see next year's game.

Left: In the early 1930's, Lou Kirn earned the nickname "Bullet Lou" with his accurate passes. In World War II, he commanded a bomber squadron based at Guadalcanal and hit the Japs with the same kind of accuracy.   Right: George Smythe, outstanding player in the 1922 game which Army won, 17-14, was a major general commanding the Third Infantry Division during the Korean War.

Navy Lt. T. C. Roberts pays off a wager on the 1964 Army-Navy game in Frankfurt, West Germany—washing the "dirtiest, grubbiest goat available" in public. If Brig. Gen. Fillmore Mearns had lost the bet, he would have been required to ride to work on an Army mule.

Bill Stern recounts Tom Trapnell's touchdown for Army in the waning moments of
the 1926 Army-Navy game; then turns the spotlight on Major Trapnell, soldier, and
the feat that earned him that most coveted combat decoration, the Distinguished
Service Cross for action in Bataan.

Tom Trapnell, Hero

BILL STERN

FOOTBALL PLAYERS, LIKE SHOOTING STARS, COME AND GO, BRILLIANT DURING
their season in the gridiron sky, obscure and forgotten when their pigskin days are over. But sometimes they get bigger headlines long after
their careers as players have closed. Take Tom Trapnell, for instance.

The 1926 Army-Navy football game was one of the most bitter in the long series of
clashes between the two services. Again and again the favored Navy team smashed its
way down the field to score, only to be countered by a savagely fighting Army team
that tied the score on every occasion. A youngster who played an important part in
nearly every play was Tom Trapnell. He was taking the field for the last time since
this was his last year of football. He had never been a great star but he was making up
for all the past seasons, today. A raging tornado of action, he simply did not seem to
know the meaning of defeat or quit. With the clock running out, and Army trailing by
a touchdown, it was Tom Trapnell, in the dying moments of the game, who speared
a long pass that led to a surprising touchdown that saved his team from defeat. The
final score was 21 to 21.

It was a happy youngster who plodded wearily back to the Army locker room when
the final whistle blew. He plopped down on a bench and let out a shout. "It's the last
of football for me, fellows!" he cried. "Guess I'll never see my name in the papers
again!" And everybody joined Tom Trapnell in the laugh that followed.

It seemed that Tom Trapnell was mistaken. True, the game was in time forgotten.
The players left West Point and scattered to all points of the compass. After all, they
were Army men and their duty was to follow the flag wherever it waved. And Tom
Trapnell, too, went his way into what he thought would be obscurity, happy in the
knowledge that he had closed his football career in a burst of glory.

Years passed. If possible, Tom Trapnell and his feats on the gridiron of Chicago's
Municipal Stadium were more forgotten than ever. Then, suddenly, Tom's name
flashed across the headlines bigger and blacker than ever. The story that went with
the headline made the 1926 business look pretty small indeed.

Tom Trapnell was an All-American Army player. During World War II, the Korean War, and in Vietnam, Trapnell again displayed outstanding leadership ability.

On a truck on a bridge that led out of besieged Bataan stood, all alone, a major in the United States Army. Japanese soldiers by the hundred bore down on him and his position on the bridge. The major held his ground calmly and bravely. Bullets couldn't stop him. Superbly cool under fire, the major set fire to his truck, watched the blaze spread to the bridge itself. The advance of the oncoming Japanese column was halted in its tracks. The major's act had saved a company of Americans. It had been a dangerous trick, but it had worked!

They gave Maj. Tom Trapnell the Distinguished Service Cross for that heroic feat. And all the papers in the land told the story. It was 1926 all over again. And again the name of Tom Trapnell showed big and black in all the headlines. Football hero to national hero, Tom Trapnell was in there fighting all the way.

What Army fan can forget the exploits of "Monk" Meyer, the 140 pound All-American back on the gridiron. Here is a great story of that illustrious "Monk" Meyer, a colonel—and a hero—at Leyte, as told in 1944 by war correspondent Homer Bigart.

"Monk" Meyer at the Front

HOMER BIGART

A SMALL GROUP OF JAPANESE, PROBARLY FEWER THAN SIXTY, INFILTRATED the American lines Sunday night and, crossing a mountain wilderness, reached the main supply route skirting Carigara Bay, six miles behind the front.

Seizing a roadside ammunition dump, they erected a roadblock with cases of shells, and wired them with dynamite. Then they struck eastward along the road, where they shot up five jeeps, one truck, and two ambulances. Fortunately, the ambulances were heading toward the front, but one contained a litter patient. The Japanese shot the wounded soldier and threw the litter into a ditch. They also shot two drivers. The others in the convoy apparently escaped.

For twenty-eight hours I was on the wrong side of the Japanese roadblock. I had spent Sunday night in a foxhole fifty yards from the spot where the Japanese had come out of the woods. At seven o'clock I hailed a passing truck and hitchhiked to the front. Our truck was the last to get through.

It was about noon when I got back to the base of Breakneck Ridge. There were two tanks in the road. A slim, bespectacled lieutenant colonel, straight as a ramrod and smoking a long cigar, was organizing a column of mud-spattered infantrymen behind them. He introduced himself as Charles R. Meyer, who will be remembered as "Monk" Meyer, All-American West Point football player. He inquired after Stanley Woodward (sports editor of the New York *Herald Tribune*) and then barked at the infantrymen: "Two cans of beer to the first man who returns with a Jap alive."

"To hell with taking them alive," one of the men growled.

The tanks started down the road escorted by a company of infantry, while another company cut off through dense woods covering the steep slope at the right of the road. Progress was very slow. Nobody knew the strength of the raiding party and, besides, the infantry could not see two feet ahead in the dripping underbrush.

We followed the tanks in a half-track, crouching behind the armored sides. There

Reunion in Vietnam, as two of West Point's illustrious graduates meet in 1966—Charles "Monk" Meyer (right) and Pete Dawkins, both former All-American football stars.

was a brief burst of small-arm fire on the forested slope and we heard the measured clatter of a Japanese heavy machine gun somewhere ahead.

But the road was deserted. The tanks reached the roadblock without drawing a shot. One blast from the lead tank shattered the barricade. The palm grove where the ammunition was cached seemed deserted.

Colonel Meyer drew his pistol and, jumping over the scattered ammunition cases, ran ahead fifty yards to where the ambulances had been stopped. Both ambulances, their windshields punctured by bullets, were empty. Inside, blankets and first-aid equipment were strewn on the floor.

Behind the second ambulance Meyer found the litter patient. Evidently he had been dragged from the ambulance and shot through the head and chest. This war isn't being played according to the Geneva Convention.

On opposite sides of the road were two more dead men. One was sitting in a ditch with his back against the slope, his eyes fixed on the ambulance. He looked so much alive that Meyer paused and spoke to him.

We got no farther that day. A hundred yards an hour was the best Meyer's men could do through the tangled vines and stunted palms. The tanks were already far ahead of the infantry, easy prey for Japanese grenadiers who might be sitting on the overhanging ledges. We went back and passed the night in a battalion bivouac.

The push was resumed at daybreak. We reached the ambushed convoy without incident and Meyer got out of his jeep to shout an order to a company commander up the slope. As he stepped off the road, somebody hollered: "Look out, Colonel! He's alive."

Meyer looked down and found himself straddling a Japanese playing possum. Meyer jumped clear, yanked out his pistol, and shot the Japanese in the back. The Japanese didn't whimper, but stirred slightly and we saw his hands. There was a grenade in each. Quickly, Meyer shot him again, this time in the head.

We went on past the shot-up vehicles. After a short, sharp fight in the hills, Meyer's men broke through to join a force moving westward from the opposite end of the roadblock.

There were still some snipers in huts along the shore. Meyer sent a squad down through some rice paddies to rout them out. Tank crews sprayed adjacent thickets with machine-gun bullets.

We passed the hole where I had hidden on Sunday night. Two M.P.s assigned to guard the road had shared the hole, which ran beneath a ragged native hut, offering some shelter from a downpour. Mosquitoes helped us to stay awake. I remembered that we had put in half the night arguing what day it was. One of the M.P.s clinched the debate with the remark: "It must be Sunday because the chaplain went past hitchhiking."

There was no trace of the M.P.s. I hope they got out all right. At noon the road was cleared. The Japanese had done surprisingly little damage, failing to reach the artillery emplacements which were their obvious objective. But they had blocked an essential supply road for several hours.

The gap which the Japanese found in the line had been plugged and all the high ground overlooking the road is firmly secured. Slowly we are learning the importance of protecting the flanks.

The aircraft carrier was down in the Battle of the Coral Sea. Buzz Borries, Navy All-American, was on that carrier. This short newscast out of "Buzz's" hometown, Louisville, Kentucky, was good news indeed in 1942. Don Hill was the announcer.

News Extra

DON HILL and Radio Station WAVE, Louisville

HERE IS A GREAT STORY WHICH WE JUST RECEIVED. "BUZZ" BORRIES . . . Louisville boy . . . son of Mr. and Mrs. Fred Borries . . . All-American football player at Navy . . . who was attached to the aircraft carrier, *Lexington*, which was sunk in the battle of the Coral Sea . . . saw action in that great battle, had a hand in the sinking of the many Japanese boats . . . and survived the battle. Borries was one of the members of the crew of the *Lexington* who were saved when the giant boat went to the bottom. Buzz was landed safely by a rescue ship in an unnamed West Coast city. He has talked with his mother and father here in Louisville by long-distance telephone twice, and both times assured them of his safety. Borries was pilot of a Navy fighter airplane which saw action in the Coral Sea battle. Exactly how many Jap planes he shot down is not known, but it has been definitely established that Buzz was one of the heroes who helped shell the Jap fleet from his plane. The only details he gave, in his conversation with his parents, were that the Japs missed him three times. He probably meant that he made at least three dive bombings at the Jap ships who had had any chances to shoot him down and failed. . . . Or he possibly meant that he was aboard the *Lexington* when the Japs bombed and torpedoed it, and that he survived three Jap bombings of the American carrier. The exact manner in which he escaped was not made clear. However, it was probable that his airplane was in the air at the time the *Lexington* went down, and he then made a landing in the water near a rescue ship. His parents have been besieged with calls, since the sinking of the *Lexington*, from friends all over the country who knew he was attached to that ship. His wife, who was in Honolulu, is now with him in the West Coast city from where Buzz telephoned his parents. So . . . Buzz Borries, one of the heroes of the Coral Sea battle, is safe. . . .

Slade Cutter gave Navy its first victory over Army in thirteen years. In World War II, Lieutenant Commander Cutter was one of the Navy's outstanding submarine commanders.

Buzz Borries receives the coveted Naval Academy Athletic Association Sword as the outstanding athlete of 1935 from Rear Adm. David F. Sellers, superintendent of Annapolis.

There isn't very much one can do, if you're a prisoner of war, far away from your country and your loved ones. About all you can do is dream and pray and hope to get back home. One of the things servicemen talk about is what they would like to do when hostilities are ended. This is a story of fifty men—our men—in a prison camp in Korea, way back in November, 1953, and their dream realization as reported by the Philadelphia Bulletin.

Vow of POW's Comes True at Army-Navy Game

PHILADELPHIA BULLETIN

Just two Army-Navy games ago, two groups of American servicemen made a vow. It was more of a dream, really, for the men were prisoners of war in Korea and had learned the future was not too bright, and not to expect too much of the future.

They needed dreams though, in the misery and squalor of the most dreary, God-forsaken Chinese Communist prison camps in North Korea.

Their vow was a simple one. If they could ever get through this bitter ordeal, this hell on earth, they would all try to get together and meet in Philadelphia at the first Army-Navy game held after their release.

Today the vows the men so solemnly made—their dreams—came true. For meet they did, each group in its own little section of Philadelphia's vast Municipal Stadium, and there were more than fifty men in all. It was a never-to-be-forgotten day.

Both groups sat on the Navy side, soldiers, sailors, and Marines alike. But there the solid good-will front ended. The soldiers carried pennants of Army gray, black, and gold for Army, while the other buddies waved pennants spelling Navy in gold on blue.

One of those who sat there was D. P. Shipes, Columbia, South Carolina. He joked about being once again in "enemy territory," for he was a soldier rooting hard for Army. Shipes and his buddies had the Navy outnumbered in their own tight little group.

It was during their long months of imprisonment that Shipes and his immediate friends in the Navy-rooting section made plans to attend an Army-Navy game . . . if they ever left the prison camp alive.

Only one man in the imprisoned group had ever seen Army *vs.* Navy and he regaled them over and over again with the color, excitement, and enthusiasm that they would find at the game, if they went.

So the group gave Marine Lt. (now Captain) Robert J. O'Shea of Valley View Road,

In Korea, two former Army football stars discuss the strategy of Army's famous "sucker" or "mouse-trap" play. Lt. Goble Bryant (left) played during the Davis-Blanchard era, while Gen. B. M. Bryan played in the 1920's.

Merion, the job of carrying out the future get-together.

O'Shea, the son of retired Marine Corps Gen. George O'Shea of Fort Lauderdale, Florida, said that thirty-six men made up their prison-camp group.

The twenty who planned to attend the game, he said, came from east of the Mississippi River. All were prisoners of war at least eighteen months.

Of the first twelve to arrive at the Warwick Hotel, only O'Shea and Maj. Walter R. Harris of Birmingham, Alabama, are Marines. Lester A. Ribbeck, Lockport, New York, is an ex-corporal.

George Wedsworth, one of the majority of Air Force men in the group, is a Canadian who joined the Air Force to become an American citizen.

When John Rambo turned up for the party, Lloyd Larkin, sales manager for the hotel, recognized him as the only man in Larkin's medical unit in Korea to be captured. Larkin didn't know until he talked to O'Shea that Rambo was alive.

The other group numbering thirty men gathered last night at the Naval Air Station, Willow Grove, with their wives.

The unofficial chairman was Navy Lt. J. W. Thornton, of Van Kirk St., Philadelphia, who returned home from Korea just two months ago.

The men, all still in service, came from all parts of the country. There were a number of men who made plans to attend but couldn't make it. Their recovery has been slower than expected and they are still hospitalized.

Sportswriter John Webster, as he watches Navy upset Army on the gridiron, recalls 2nd Lt. John C. Trent, captain of Army's undefeated 1949 eleven, and Lt. Thomas A. Lombardo, great Army quarterback, both killed in the fighting in Korea.

A Team of Destiny

JOHN WEBSTER

ANNUALLY, THE MEETING OF THE UNITED STATES MILITARY AND NAVAL Academies' football teams—the star-spangled Army-Navy game—has been heralded as one of America's greatest sports events. This is, of course, an understatement—its significance actually extends far beyond the boundaries of sports competition. While that may not be considered at all times, it certainly is in moments of crisis, as now when the world totters precariously on the jagged rim of war's flaming cauldron.

Quite a number among the 103,000 eyewitnesses to the fifty-first clash of the Cadets and the Midshipmen yesterday at our Municipal Stadium must have given it grim thought. More than a century has passed since the Duke of Wellington made his deathless comment. But time hasn't outmoded it: "Waterloo was won on the playing fields of Eton."

Warfare's style and methods have been vastly altered since that day. Its scope is now worldwide. Man's ingenuity not only made conflict infinitely more terrible but also incredibly more extensive than it was when Napoleon sought to dominate Europe. But the basic pattern doesn't change, as men fight, and die, for God, for country, for obligations, and for a way of life.

If you don't think so, you must not have been reading dispatches . . . tragic dispatches . . . from Korea in recent days. One of the more recent told of the death of 2d Lt. John C. Trent, twenty-four, of Memphis . . . great end and captain of West Point's unbeaten 1949 football team. That Army squad, red hot on last year's frozen November 26, routed the outmanned, but not outgamed, Annapolis team, 38-0, in the vast, sprawling saucer. The 1949 program's sketch on the West Point leader remarked that he "now looks forward to joining the infantry as a shavetail after graduation in June."

Trent arrived at Wonsan on November 12. He was a casualty three days later. He was the second West Point football captain to die in the Korean War. The first was Lt. Thomas A. Lombardo, who quarterbacked the Black Knights of the Hudson, and who was graduated in 1945.

John Trent, Army's 1949 football captain and an outstanding end for three years, was killed in action in Korea in November, 1950.

A half-dozen more football players of the Classes of 1949 at West Point and Annapolis are now serving Uncle Sam in the Far East. The Navy graduate who went on to the bigger arena is Elvis Purvis, the back from Glenville, Georgia. The five men from Col. Earl Blaik's West Point squad are Arnold Galiffa, the great quarterback from Donora, Pennsylvania; William R. Henn, tackle, Drexel Hill, Pennsylvania; Paul B. McDaniel, tackle, Leitchfield, Kentucky; William H. Kellum, end, Haynesville, Louisiana, and Raymond Maladowitz, center, Garfield, New Jersey.

With the United States, and the rest of the world, in perilous position, yesterday's football players who are to be graduated in June, could have no idea where they may be in another autumn. Nor has anybody else any idea of what a year may bring. However, the Cadets' inspiration for making this fifty-first game a memorial to fallen Army heroes was waffled in the fury of the Navy surge.

Those Middies, laughing at odds and points, hammered out a storybook upset to electrify Navy men the world over. Rank underdogs, they outdid the performance of any Annapolis eleven since 1943; they topped the Midshipmen's explosion of 1948 that held favored West Pointers to a 21-21 deadlock. They overshadowed the 1946 Navy squad, which was on the short end of a 21-18 score when time ran out as the blue-shirted men from the banks of the Severn had penetrated to proud Army's 4-yard line.

When the last gun checked the Navy charge four years ago, Army's record of twenty-eight games without defeat stood up against an old enemy's better blows. But Army, with a like mark of unbeaten showings, saw it shattered yesterday as President Truman, the service brass and gold braid, and the multitude looked on.

Maybe the story would have been different if Galiffa, last year's quarterback, had been at the helm for Army, and not in far-off Korea. But maybe it wouldn't, either. If you observed the ruthless manner with which the brusque Navy defenders smothered Galiffa's talented successor, Bobby Blaik, in his passing attempts, you might have wondered whether even the superb Galiffa could have done much better.

Last autumn, there was no argument about the respective quarterbacking—Galiffa stood out over the Navy's Bob (Zug) Zastrow, and there was no occasion for surprise when the Black Knights of the Hudson wound up with a hands-down, 38-0 victory. At yesterday's kickoff, it was probably a toss-up which team possessed the better signal caller—the Army with Bobby Blaik, the battle-tested son of West Point's Head Coach Earl Blaik, or Zastrow, the Algoma, Wisconsin, youth, who wishes to be a Marine when he is graduated in '52.

As the battle was waged, however, there was no argument: Blaik's punting was excellent, but in other respects he wasn't in the same league with the Navy man. Navy's airtight pass defense militated against Blaik completions, and through interceptions, profited from his vain tries. Zastrow and his backfield mates, Frank Hauff, Dave Bannerman, and Bill Powers, had the Cadets groggy from the short punches through the line and the more showy drives around the wings. Zastrow figured in every scoring play.

In the second period, Zastrow sneaked through from the 7, and never stopped until he'd hit the end zone; later in the same period, he rifled a pass from the 31 to Jim Baldinger, who shook defender Gene Gribble off his back in the end zone for the second Navy TD. Zastrow held as Roger Drew added two placement points. He was trapped, vainly seeking to pass in the end zone in the third quarter, for West Point's only points. So, from early until late it was Navy's Zastrow who was largely responsible for one of football's all-time upsets in the game that is something.

Here is a story that appeared in Life magazine in 1966 about Pete Dawkins—who took all West Point honors, as well as the Heisman Trophy and the Maxwell Award —serving his country in war.

Captain Pete Dawkins Keeps on Winning

SAM ANGELOFF

THE FIRST TIME YOU SEE PETE DAWKINS STANDING ON A DISTANT HILLSIDE with a dozen or so small figures gathered around him, you're reminded of the days outside the stadium locker rooms when he towered over a knot of kids, signing the slips of paper they shoved at him. But as you draw nearer, these small "fans" become in fact tough, leathery little men, soldiers of the Vietnamese airborne whose pleasure is killing all of the enemy they can find. Dawkins is their adviser.

The role of an American adviser in Vietnam is left carefully undefined. There are as many different twists and techniques as there are advisers and Vietnamese. Basically, an American adviser is assigned to a counterpart. In Dawkins' case this is the commander of the 1st Vietnamese Airborne Battalion, Maj. Le Van Dang. It is Dawkins' job to advise the commander, not command the battalion.

It is a tough, punishing, and often dangerous assignment, but Pete Dawkins asked for it. More than a year ago in the U.S., Dawkins began taking Army courses in battalion leadership, advising techniques and foreign languages—notably Vietnamese. His orders to report to Vietnam for duty therefore came as no surprise. Ten days after he arrived in the theater last September he was on his way to Kontum, where his battalion was protecting a nervous city from the Vietcong. The troops addressed him with careful correctness as "*Dai Uy* [Captain] Dawkins."

A new officer anywhere is a bit of a sore thumb. But an American officer in a Vietnamese unit is inevitably watched, studied, and tested by the men.

"It's a perfectly natural reaction," Dawkins says. "Here are some people who've been fighting this war for a long time, and suddenly here comes a relatively wet-eared officer. You try not to sweat it. But you're cetainly aware that every step is being observed."

There were local customs and manners to get used to. Vietnamese food can be braised chicken joints and duck-egg omelets, or beef and cabbage, both of which are excellent. But it can also be *nuoc mam* (rotten fish sauce) and half-hatched chicken embryos, which are something else again. All are washed down with sweet tea, or occa-

Capt. Pete Dawkins with a Vietnamese paratrooper during a break in the warfare in Vietnam.

sionally with *by xy de*, a rice whisky that tastes the way some model airplane glues smell.

"When you're used to beef and potatoes, and suddenly you're eating pigs' intestines and pigeon beaks and fish heads—well, anybody who says that doesn't take some doing has a lot tougher stomach than I have," says Dawkins. "Or else he's a bloody damn liar."

Dawkins never even considered avoiding Vietnamese food—even when the *nuoc mam* was overpowering and the *ba xy de* made his eyes water. "If you show a willingness to take Vietnamese standards at face value, they'll be more apt to take an honest look at yours."

Dawkins often spent his evenings in old-fashioned Army bull sessions, swapping phrases with men of the battalion in an amiable scramble of English, Vietnamese, and spirited sign language.

The battalion commander spoke not a word of English at the outset, putting the burden of communications on Dawkins' rudimentary Vietnamese. Whenever he had a free moment, the young captain would stop to chat with civilians. The Vietnamese, who had learned French for the French and are now learning English for the Americans, are almost invariable delighted to have an American jabbering at them in their own tongue.

"At first, right when you get off the plane, it all seems very strange," says Dawkins. "The Vietnamese do odd things—they urinate on the sidewalks and spit chicken bones on the floor and the men hold hands as a sign of friendship. It's very different. Later, as you wear through this surface glaze, they become human beings. They get angry and disappointed and happy at the same things we do.

"And then finally you really begin to understand them, and you realize it's a huge mistake to pretend they're just Americans on the other side of the world. On some vital matters they base their decisions on different things than we do. They have a different outlook, and you've got to be aware of it."

There is, for instance, the business of simply getting one's point across. Dawkins is a direct young man who likes to lay his shoulders into a problem the moment it appears. This is not the way things are done in Vietnam.

"They're not devious people—they're Oriental," Dawkins observes. "Part of their culture is that they attack a problem indirectly—they sneak up on an issue."

At the dinner table, between bites of fishheads and pigs' intestines, Dawkins at length began painstakingly to master this roundabout diplomacy. "It comes as a big surprise to most Americans that the Vietnamese don't just gobble up all this advice we give them. We find it bloody annoying, after giving eight or fifteen good reasons for an idea, to have our counterpart simply say 'no.' No reasons, no counterargument—just 'no.'"

Dawkins found that his purely military suggestions—i.e., the calling of air strikes and artillery support—were usually well received. Otherwise the Vietnamese tended to drag their feet. They balked, for example, at Dawkins' endless suggestions that they train when not in active battle. In the field they were tough and professional, but once off the field, Dawkins wryly observes, "they like to rest a lot." Much of the time, he found, it is best to bite one's tongue at moments when advice seems most urgently called for.

350

"Take this whole business of military punishment," he says. "It's quite startling to Westerners. A battalion commander might walk up to a young soldier and kick him, and then get a big stick and hit him with that. That is hardly within our concept of military justice and dignity.

"But our goal here is not to build the world in the image of America, or to take over the Vietnamese army. Beating a subordinate is shocking to us. But it's also shocking to that Vietnamese commander to find that we think it's wrong.

"It's awfully frustrating, spending a lot of effort and seemingly getting nothing done. And then you'll find that a suggestion you made three weeks ago—the one that was met with total indifference—is suddenly, mysteriously being used." His battalion has at last begun training, not so regularly as he would like but with more frequency than he had expected.

In the six months Dawkins has been with the 1st battalion, he has seen action in three major battles and a number of lesser fire fights. In that time he has earned three Gallantry Crosses—Vietnam's second-highest military honor. The U.S. Army also has recommended Dawkins for two Bronze Stars with V (for valor).

Dawkins describes the battles almost casually:

"The first really big action was in Hau Nghia province. We landed very close to the [Cambodian] border, thinking we'd cut the bad guys off. That's where they were, all right, and that's just what happened. We went in on December 31, and got the V.C. between us and the Fifth Airborne. They were shooting back pretty good, and that night there were a whole lot of tracers and air strikes and flares. It was a fine way to spend New Year's Eve."

In mid-January the battalion joined up with the American First Cavalry Division and other Vietnamese units in Operation White Wing. Dawkins' battalion was working east of Highway 1, sweeping toward the sea, when they ran smack into "the base area of a North Vietnamese battalion—mess halls, class areas, volleyball courts, and all."

The day-long battle was fierce, and toward nightfall when the battalion radioed that it wanted more ammunition, the enemy picked up the radio signals. Assuming the battalion was nearly out of bullets, they attacked.

"Well, we weren't all *that* low on ammo," says Dawkins cheerily. "We always keep a pretty good reserve. They were awfully sorry they had decided to attack."

After a brief rest the battalion was fighting again, this time near Quang Ngai. Intelligence sources said an enemy regiment was in the area, and almost immediately a joint attack was launched by Dawkins' airborne troopers and U. S. Marines.

"The idea was to land as close to this suspected regimental command post as we possibly could," says Dawkins. "We landed right in the midst of the scoundrels."

During the all-night fighting the Marines poured 1,200 rounds of artillery into the area. The enemy melted into the brush at dawn, leaving behind some 300 dead.

"The artillery sure helped us," Dawkins said. "But those Vietnamese troopers were just great. When they were out of ammo and grenades, they would stand up and throw rocks."

In all the battle action Dawkins hasn't suffered so much as a hangnail. He broke his shoulder, however, in a jeep accident back in the relative safety of Saigon. The medics strapped up the shoulder and told Dawkins to take it easy. He obeyed for ten days, then took off to rejoin his troops in the field. The shoulder healed up fine.

Dawkins' one-year tour of duty in Vietnam is half over, and accordingly he changed assignments last week. Most officers spend six months in combat positions, the other six in staff jobs. Headquartered in Saigon, Dawkins is now in the military liaison and co-ordination office dealing with the Vietnam rebuilding program known as Revolutionary Development. It's less dangerous than combat, but no less exciting to Dawkins.

"We're engaged in a lot more here than killing the enemy," he says. "The crucial question is whether all of us—Vietnamese and Americans—can grasp the essential peculiarity of this war. For the Vietnamese the goal has to be to end up with a nation that can survive in the twentieth century. We have to help them build it."

Pete's wife, Judi, and his son, Sean (who will be two years old this month), are back in the States, waiting out his tour. Although he misses them, they are safe, and he considers himself the most fortunate of men.

"I've chosen to be a professional soldier," he says. "My responsibility is to go wherever the military is most involved, namely Vietnam. This is just what I wanted."

"Lighthorse Harry" Wilson (right), captain of the 1927 Army football team, smiles as Lt. Gen. Charles Stone awards him the Air Force commendation medal.

Dick Eckert says that there is a lot in common in playing sports and being in battle. And he should know. He received the Purple Heart for wounds received in service in Vietnam.

Report from Vietnam

ASSOCIATED PRESS

"WHEN THE GOING GETS TOUGH, THE TOUGH GET GOING."

Quarterback Dick Eckert picked up the football battle cry at West Point during his playing days. Former Coach Dale Hall had it posted all over the locker room.

First Lt. Dick Eckert, who graduated from the Military Academy in 1963, never has forgotten the motto in the tough war against the Vietcong.

Eckert, who received the Purple Heart after being slightly wounded by a hand grenade, and three other former West Point football players are stationed here with the 173rd Airborne Brigade.

The others are Capt. Tom Blanda, class of 1961 and brother of veteran professional star George Blanda; Capt. Dick Bruckner, class of 1961; and 2nd Lt. Jim Koster, class of 1964.

All have the same fighting spirit here as they did on the football field. And the grim war, which Bruckner calls a "dirty war," has not dampened their sense of humor.

Blanda, twenty-five, also a former quarterback, often joked through an interview.

Once, when asked how he met his wife, he replied, with tongue in check: "She happened to be at the right place at the right time."

Eckert, Blanda, Bruckner, and Koster have been at this air base, located about twelve miles north of Saigon, since May 12, when the 173rd was deployed here from Okinawa.

Blanda said that in 1963, just before he left for Okinawa, the St. Louis Cardinals of the National League made him an offer.

He turned it down, he said, because, "I enjoyed being with the 173rd and what I was doing."

Eckert is in command of a weapons platoon in the 2nd Battalion, 503rd Infantry. Blanda and Bruckner are battery artillery commanders and Koster is a fire direction officer.

At least two other former West Point athletes, 1st Lt. Ronald Zinn and 1st Lt. Bob Fuellhart have been killed in action in Vietnam.

Zinn, also a member of the 173rd, was killed in a battle with the Vietcong in Zone

D, July 7. Fuellhart, a football teammate of both Eckert and Blanda, was killed less than two weeks ago while directing a helicopter attack near the village of Phung Heip.

Fuellhart played the lonely end position in the football offense directed by Blanda and Eckert. Zinn finished sixth in the 20-kilometer walk in the 1964 Olympics, the best an American ever has done in a walking event.

Eckert, twenty-four, who volunteered for duty in Vietnam last January before it was known the 173rd would be moved here, recalled the big battle when American, Vietnamese, and Australian troops ran into a well-fortified Vietcong village.

"We had four killed and eleven wounded," said Eckert. "We estimated that we killed around twenty Vietcong. We pushed the Vietcong unit out of the village.

"The village had a lot of tunnels and trenches and blood trails leading out of all of them. The Vietcong dragged out their wounded and dead.

"I shot one sniper in a tree. He fell out of the tree but we never found him later. Twice the Vietcong came out of the trenches and assaulted us. We threw grenades. We saw people drop. Again they pulled them back into the trenches.

"Zinn was the platoon leader of the lead rifle platoon.

"We were right behind them. When all the firing opened up, we couldn't figure what it was. So we went forward and came to within ten feet of Zinn. He was already dead.

"He was hit with the initial fire. The Vietcong kept hitting him with machine-gun bullets. Snipers were up in the trees. While we were organizing, there was sniper fire

and sporadic machine-gun fire from the enemy.

"The company commander moved the left platoon around to try to get around to the rear of the village. They ran into a machine gun. They put heavy fire on it and knocked this machine gun out. Armed helicopters put on heavy fire. Then we attacked and swept through the village."

Eckert and Zinn were personal friends.

"It [Zinn's death] is one of those things you expect to happen but you never expect it to be the person next to you. I really didn't think or comprehend it until it was all over and I had a chance to relax.

"After it was all over I started to think about his family. He had just gotten married. While it [the battle] is going on, you just accept it as part of the battle."

Eckert received his Purple Heart for being wounded in the upper part of his leg during an earlier operation, also in Zone D. He was interrogating one of the villagers, when another man came up behind him and flipped a hand grenade. The grenade turned out to be sort of a dud. Eckert hit the ground and the men escaped into the woods.

Eckert, who succeeded Blanda as first-string quarterback in 1961, said that actually there is a lot in common in playing sports and being here in battle.

"There's the same tension," he explained, "the same feeling. All the training is like practicing in sports. You've got to train. You develop the same type of team work that you do in battle. When the going gets tough, the tough get going."

Quarterback Dick Eckert (10) cracks through Navy's line for a 10-yard gain in the first period of the 1961 classic. Captain Eckert went on to quarterback a bigger team in Vietnam.

Navy's number one foe is Army. The submarine USS *Grouper* maneuvers in the Atlantic with a "Beat Army" sign in 1965.

Bill Carpenter, Army's famous "lonely end."

DATELINE: *South Vietnam.* SUBJECT: *Capt. William S. Carpenter, Jr., better known as West Point's "lonely end." Gen. William C. Westmoreland presented a Silver Star to Captain Carpenter for displaying "raw courage" in this particular action.*

A Daring Captain Saves a Company

CHARLES MOHR

A FORMER WEST POINT FOOTBALL STAR, CAPT. WILLIAM S. CARPENTER, JR., called for bombing and napalm raids almost on top of his own troops to save them from annihilation by North Vietnamese troops today. He and a handful of his men survived.

The boldness of Captain Carpenter, the "lonely end" of West Point football in the late 1950s and 1960, was a highlight of the third day of bitter combat in what appeared to be developing into one of the biggest battles of the war.

The arena was Kontum, a mountainous province a few miles from the Laotian border and about 200 miles northeast of Saigon.

The opposing forces were the First Brigade of the United States Army's 101st Airborne Division and the 24th Regiment of the North Vietnamese Army.

In most of the fighting since Tuesday morning the United States troops have been outnumbered, but they have inflicted heavy losses while sustaining relatively light casualties.

This afternoon Captain Carpenter, commander of C Company of the Second Battalion, 502d Infantry Regiment, ran into North Vietnamese, estimated at battalion strength, a few miles north of this little outpost. One of the two platoons with Captain Carpenter was almost immediately overrun and lost radio contact.

As North Vietnamese troops swarmed in on Captain Carpenter's position, he radioed: "Bring air strikes in on top of me. We are being overrun. We might as well take some of them with us."

Captain Carpenter was directing the hacking out of a helicopter landing zone at the battle site, United Press International reported.

Captain Carpenter won the name, "lonely end," when Army originated the formation of a flanking end who operated on his own without ever entering a huddle.

He was terribly alone for hours today until two other paratroop units reached him and helped relieve the pressure tonight.

The survivors of Captain Carpenter's missing platoon had made their way back and linked up with other platoons in a defensive position. His losses were not immediately known.

His battalion commander, Lt. Col. Henry Emerson of Milford, Pennsylvania, said he was recommending Captain Carpenter for the Medal of Honor.

Captain Carpenter's action in calling air strikes on his own was meant to hurt the enemy as much as possible before the large number of North Vietnamese troops destroyed C Company.

Although Captain Carpenter risked the destruction of his own unit, brigade officers said tonight that the air strikes had actually saved the situation, stopping the North Vietnamese attack before it could overwhelm the company.

While Captain Carpenter's company was fighting its desperate battle, B Company of the same battalion was fighting a North Vietnamese force estimated at battalion strength several hundred yards to the north.

Captain Carpenter's Third Platoon was also in a battle of its own nearby, and two other airborne companies moved up to the rescue.

A Company of the First Battalion, 327th Regiment, ran into North Vietnamese troops and broke through them as it hurried to Captain Carpenter's rescue.

Army's Joe Caldwell (12) heaves a long pass to teammate Bill Carpenter (87) in the 1958 Army-Navy game. In 1966, in Vietnam, Capt. Bill Carpenter further distinguished himself under Vietcong fire.

8
AS THEY
SAW IT

Who knows what Army-Navy football is really like better than the men who played it? In putting together this word-picture of the game and the players, a number of men who participated in the annual rivalry between the service academies graciously consented to set down their personal reminiscences of the days when they were members of the football teams.

Here, in their own words, are the anecdotes, actual feelings, and thoughts of former stars of the gridiron at West Point and Annapolis as they look back to the glory of their playing days. We are delighted to be able to share them with you.

The Editor

Midshipman R. L. Reasonover shakes hands with Cadet M. F. Meador before the start of the traditional Army-Navy classic.

John W. Heavey, class of '91, played in that very first Army-Navy game in 1890. His son, also a West Point graduate, relates a rare story about how his father made the team and an amusing incident concerning his father's retirement. Brig. Gen. John W. Heavey, who died in 1941 just before Pearl Harbor, saw service in the Spanish-American war, under Pershing in the Philippines in 1902, and in World War I.

Letter from William F. Heavey

Thought you might like to hear how my father (USMA 1891) made the *first* Army team, as he told me:

At noon the Cadet Adjutant read in the Mess Hall that Annapolis had challenged West Point to a game of football, to be played at West Point. An order followed that all cadets weighing over 180 would report to try out for the team. My father had come from Illinois, had never even seen a football, but weighed 198. He reported and was told the idea of the game was to stop the man with the ball. No instruction was given that first day in tackling. The coach lined up two scrub teams. All who had played *any* football were on the 1st team; all others on the 2nd team. My father was assigned Right Guard. At the very first scrimmage, the man with the ball charged right at Right Guard Heavey. Remembering he must stop that man, father grabbed him around the waist, threw him up in the air several feet. Still clutching the ball, he fell on his head unconscious. The coach rushed in and said, "Who did that?" Father kept quiet but several on the first team shouted "Heavey did it" and pointed him out.

The coach shouted to him, "Get over on the 1st team at Right Guard." That is how Heavey made the team.

Incidentally, someone in the bottom of the pile at the 2nd or 3rd scimmage of the game sunk his teeth into one of father's ears. Years later he proudly showed the scar to his sons, all of whom went on to West Point.

I suppose you know the Army team wore hockey stocking caps that first game. Father said he lost his in the 1st scrimmage and played all the game without ever seeing it again.

* * *

Another episode that may be of interest. When Teddy Roosevelt was Pres. all "obese" officers were ordered before a Retiring Board. Father weighed 201 so was ordered to appear. President of the Board asked my father if he wanted a Counsel to assist him. My father replied No, that he merely wanted to present one paper. Told to proceed, he handed the Board a copy of the program of the first A-N football game, which showed the weights of the players. The President of the Board read: RIGHT

GUARD HEAVEY 198 whereupon father looked along the line of the nine members of the Board and said, "Gentlemen, how many of you have added only three pounds since you entered the Army?" The nine members slouched down behind the long table, all of them. Father was NOT retired for obesity—he retired for AGE at 64.

Best regards,
W. F. Heavey

Navy back Jim Campbell (88) snags a pass to score for the Middies in 1962.

Emory Land scored the only touchdown in the 1900 Army-Navy game, to win it for Navy, 11-7. During World War II, Admiral Land was Director of the U. S. Maritime Commission. An ardent football fan, he holds a unique record for attending the classic rivalry, and chuckles as he recalls how he overcame President Franklin D. Roosevelt's wartime travel restrictions and got an OK to attend the 1942 game from FDR himself.

Letter from Emory S. Land

Many times over the years some of my sports writing friends here in Washington have written up the 1900 Army-Navy game frequently called "The Crap Game" as the score was Army 7 and Navy 11. As I made the only touchdown in that game, the scoring elements have been confusing. They consisted of a field goal (5 points) and a safety (2 points) for Army; a field goal (5 points) by Long of Navy, a touchdown (5 points) by Land of Navy and one point for goal after touchdown. Navy 11-Army 7.

I have attended every Army-Navy game except two, (when I was on the Asiatic Station), since 1898 and claim a record unequalled by anyone else in this regard. I even held the sticks at Annapolis and West Point in games played in WW II. I was a football official for 27 years, 1905-1932, and was once given the accolade of "All-American Linesman." In 1963 I was given an "Award for Distinguished Service" by "The Washington District Football Officials Association" which hangs in my office.

When the Navy-Marine Corps Memorial Stadium was built at Annapolis, I had the pleasure of furnishing the home team's dressing room. There is a large plaque at the entrance alley of this room indicating my gift. I also gave a trophy mountain goat, (which I killed in British Columbia), which is on the wall of the dressing room, a symbol, of course, of the Navy's mascot.

* * *

The only thing I can add to my previous letter is that during World War II, the President of the U.S. forbade any attendance for the games at West Point and Annapolis to those outside a 10 mile limit. This was done for travel restriction purposes. I got around this by getting the football officials concerned (all of them Army-Navy and game officials) to make me one holder of the linesman's sticks. Took it up with the President in a memo and he wrote on it, "Tell the damn fool if he wants to go that badly, to go ahead!" F.D.R.

Emory S. Land
Vice Admiral, USN (Ret.)

Letter from Wallace C. Philoon

Our 1908 team was very light but we did have "fight." I weighed 169 pounds for the Navy game—hardly the weight of a center now.

I believe our game against Princeton in 1908 was the finest example of "fighting" defense I have ever seen. . . .

During the years I was at West Point we were strong defensively but very weak on offense.

* * *

The attached copy of "The Game Won by Fight! Fight! Fight!" was written by me a few years ago at the request of the editor of the West Point cadet paper one football season when he thought that the team and the corps needed a boost in corps spirit to win the Navy game.

The article was published but, I regret to say, it failed to give the team and the corps the necessary punch to bring off a victory over Navy.

Sincerely,
Wallace C. Philoon

John Markoe entered West Point in 1910 and without previous experience made the football team as the regular end. In 1912 and 1913 Markoe was prominently mentioned on a number of All-American teams. His teammates included such Army players as Dwight Eisenhower, Leland Hobbs, Vern Prichard, Tommy Doe, Captain Benny Hoge, Lou Merrilat, and Babe Weyand. Today, as Father John Markoe, the former footballer is at Creighton University—and wants to set the record straight.

Letter from John P. Markoe

I entered West Point in March, 1910 and during my plebe year did not turn out for the football squad or team as I never played high school or college football. But as there were only about 600 cadets in the Corps at that time I was persuaded by upper-classmen to try for the squad. This I did during the football season of 1911, trying for a place in the backfield. After the season was over a member of the Class of 1912, Gilbert Cook, told me I was no backfield man but should try for end. This I did and immediately things began to click. I not only made the squad but left end on the first team in 1912. The roughest and toughest full game I ever played during my career at the Academy was against the Carlisle Indians with Jim Thorpe leading the Carlisle attack. As you know, Carlisle won. This game was featured in the press—the Indians against the Soldiers—the first Army-Carlisle game. I rate Jim Thorpe, with whom I took a shower after game, as the greatest all-around football player I ever played against or know of. Walter Camp gave me an honorable mention as a possible All-American end in the football guide for 1912. This same season, to the best of my memory, I played in all the games on the schedule, sometimes starting, sometimes subbing.

I forgot to mention above that, as nearly as I can recall, I was sent into the Army-Navy game as a sub in 1911, the game being played at Franklin Field, Philadelphia, thus winning my "A."

The season of 1913 (my last) was my best, I was first-string left end. Merillat (All-American on Walter Camp team) was right end, Benny Hoge, a right end, was captain, John McEwan was at center, also a Walter Camp All-American. Omar Bradley (now a five-star general) was a linesman, etc. I forgot to mention above when speaking of the Army-Carlisle game above that, as far as I can recall, it was in this game that Ike Eisenhower so injured his knee that he had to give up playing but continued to help out with the coaching of the Cullom Hall squad, as it was called, made up of possible first squad members.

Now comes the first Army-Notre Dame game in 1913. It was supposed to be a practice, warm-up game for the Army-Navy game to be played at the Polo Grounds, N. Y.,

Left: John P. Markoe, class of 1914, when he played for Army. Right: The Reverend John P. Markoe, S.J., of Creighton University, Omaha, Nebraska.

a few weeks hence. I was to be starting left end in this game and sports writers, in announcing the line-up, had me as left end. But, in scrimmage a few days before this historic game, I injured my back so Harry Tuttle, the trainer, pulled me out and Jack Jouett played left end. As a consolation prize I was made head linesman and thus watched the game from the side-lines. But for many years after I was mentioned in sports write-ups as having played left end in this game. This is one of the inaccuracies that still persists. I get tired explaining it so let it go.

Notre Dame opened the eyes of Charlie Daly, head coach, to the possibilities of the forward pass and began drilling us in the same. Two weeks later the Army team beat Navy on the Polo Grounds, N. Y., 22-9, mainly by using the forward pass. I played left end in this game.

This was the first victory and only victory of Army over Navy during my career as a cadet. Dalton of the Navy defeated Army in 1910, 1911, 1912 by his ability to kick field goals.

In this 1913 victory of Army over Navy I made the tackle after Army kicked off. As I still lay on the ground a Navy man fell hard on my left knee, badly spraining it. Time was taken out during which I cautioned Prichard, the quarterback, against throwing passes to me. He did, however, and somehow I managed to catch a few but could not run after the catch.

Between halves, Harry Tuttle (former trainer for the Detroit Tigers), taped up my knee, gave me a glass of whiskey and sent me into the second half. How I made it, I don't know, but I played the full game. But as soon as I stopped using my knee it began to swell like a balloon and I was hospitalized for several weeks after returning to West Point. Merrilat, right end in this game, made All-American (Walter Camp) that year, 1913.

Now here comes another thing I would like to get straight. In sports articles, the remarks of others down through the years, etc., I have been referred to as an All-American left end. Here is the straight dope on this.

Never have I referred to myself as an All-American nor have I ever claimed to be one. But at the time I was playing football on the Army team Walter Camp was the one recognized authority for picking All-American teams and during my four years at the Academy he began to lose his grip. His teams were picked almost invariably from Harvard, Yale and Princeton. They had a monopoly. Things began to change. Coaches began to pick their own All-American teams. *Colliers Weekly* had its own. Other publications got into the game and finally, Walter Camp died.

During this time of transition Walter Camp gave me an honorable mention in 1912. In 1913 some sports writers referred to me as an All-American. I have read this in a book on football, have been introduced to audiences many times as a former All-American Army left end, etc., etc. It is hard to stop a rumor once it gets going.

Years ago, in the N. Y. *Herald*, I believe, Dick Vidmer, a kid at West Point when I was playing, wrote a column headed: "What Happened to the Other End?" In it he described my career as a cadet and then my hectic career as a 2nd Lt. in the old 10th U. S. Cavalry stationed at Ft. Huachuca, Ariz., with all our duty along the Mexican Border (1914-15), and, later as a Capt. of Co. F, 2nd Minn. Inf. along the Texas Border (1916-17) and ended by stating that I had joined the Jesuits to study for the Priesthood. This may be the best way to end this report. I am still a member of the Jesuit Order, passed 75 years in age . . .

I have enjoyed writing the above and hope I have not unduly burdened you in the reading of it.

Sincerely,
(*Rev.*) *John P. Markoe, S. J.*

Dwight D. Eisenhower made the Army team in 1912, his second year at the Point. Unfortunately, his football career was cut short before that season was over by a serious leg injury received during a game. He later coached the Cullum Hall squad, watched the Varsity games from the bench, and never lost his love and respect for the game. Even during his brilliant military career, football had a special meaning. Here he talks about his gridiron experiences.

Letter from Dwight D. Eisenhower

Regarding any football incidents during the years I was at West Point you understand, of course, that my own active career in West Point athletics was not quite one full season in length. I made the first string as a plunging back and line backer in 1912 but just prior to the Navy game I received an injury that has kept me out of strenuous athletics ever since.

During my first year as a Plebe (at that time Plebes were eligible for the Varsity team) I weighed something on the order of 155 pounds. However, I was big-boned and was strong and had average speed. I was a member of Cullum Hall Squad which was comparable to a Junior Varsity at other schools. I showed up fairly well in the games we played and two or three times during the season was moved intermittently to the Varsity squad, but, within two or three days, would be sent back as "too light." In high school I had played at end and tackle but was converted by the picturesque Cullum Hall Coach, Toby Zell, to a back field position. At the season's end I was still a Cullum Hall player.

During the succeeding year I worked hard at running (particularly at starting) and indulged in every kind of gymnastic exercise that would strengthen leg and arm muscles. As a consequence I started the season of 1912 weighing about 174 and participated in West Point's first practice game, against a soldier team. In the latter half of the game, partially by good luck and partly by burning desire I showed up quite well and for the first time attracted some attention from the Varsity coaches, then headed by Captain Ernest Graves.

After completing several post-game laps around the field, I trotted toward the gymnasium, overtaking and passing the coaching group. I was some 15 or 20 yards beyond it when Captain Graves called sharply, "Eisenhower!" I stopped, ran back and saluted and, of course, said, "Yes, Sir." He looked at me and asked, "Where did you get those pants?" They were hanging around my ankles. I replied, "From the manager." He said, "Look at those shoes—can't you get anything better than that?" Again I said, "I am just wearing what I was issued." It happened that the Cadet Manager, named Perkins, was

Dwight D. Eisenhower as a
West Point Cadet.

in the group with Captain Graves and the latter turned to Perkins to say, "Get this man completely outfitted with new and properly fitting equipment." He went on to say a couple of other things but actually I scarcely heard him; I was walking on air, because this was my first intimation that I would probably become a member of the Varsity Squad.

Being dismissed by the Captain I raced to the Club House at a ten-second gait and refused to leave until the manager came in and had me completely outfitted for the next day's practice. I think that that particular evening provided me the greatest personal thrill of my brief football career at West Point.

369

One amusing incident: While, at 174 pounds, I was fairly light for line plunging and line backing I so loved the fierce bodily contact of football that I suppose my enthusiasm made up somewhat for my lack of size. In any event, always playing as hard as I knew how, in one game an opposing player made a protest. He turned to the referee who was standing close by my side and said, "Watch that man!" The referee with some astonishment said, "Why, has he slugged you or roughed you up in any way?" The man, who was probably green and over-excited said, "NO! But he is going to!" I think this was the oddest thing that happened to me on a football field.

* * *

During the following season the new head coach, Captain Charley Daly of Harvard and West Point, asked me to take over the active coaching of the Cullum Hall Squad. As such I was invited to sit on the bench at Varsity games.

The most thrilling game I ever saw was Army's victory over Navy in the fall of 1913. During the course of that season Army had taken on Notre Dame and ran into an unexpected reverse from the passing combination of Dorais and Rockne. They bewildered our defense. Sitting on the bench we got the full impact of the Notre Dame passing game, which, incidentally, featured what is now called the "option play."

Promptly after that game Daly changed some of his tactics and soon developed a fine passing combination of "Prichard to Merrilat." Heavily favored Navy of course expected us to play traditional football but found themselves slightly behind at half time. Nevertheless, such was the general confidence in their team's superiority that a Navy officer came over and visited a group of cadets with whom I was sitting; my leg was in a plaster cast. He said he would like to bet even money on Navy. Among a dozen of us cadets we collected $65.00. He promptly took out an equal amount and left it with us saying, "If I win I will be back for the money and if you win, of course, keep it." We went on to win by 22 to 9. I think it was the first Army victory in something like four years and you can imagine the scene among Army cadets when we finally got back to West Point to rehash every play of the game.

* * *

One sequel to my football experience: thirty years after those days, I found myself in the midst of war. I had occasion, because of my position, to be on the constant lookout for natural leaders. I noted with great satisfaction how well ex-footballers seemed to fulfill leadership qualifications: among others, Bradley, Keyes, Patton, Simpson, Van Fleet, Harmon, Hobbs, Jouett, Patch and Prichard, and many others, measured up. I cannot recall a single ex-footballer with whom I came in contact, who failed to meet every requirement. Personally, I think this was more than coincidental. I believe that football, almost more than any other sport, tends to instill into men the feeling that victory comes through hard—almost slavish—work, team play, self-confidence and an enthusiasm that amounts to dedication.

Sincerely,
Dwight D. Eisenhower

Elmer Q. Oliphant, who first played for Army in 1915, was an outstanding athlete in anybody's book. He won varsity letters in football, baseball, basketball, and track, made All-American, and the Hall of Fame. In a letter to a friend Max Kase, former sports editor of the New York Journal American, Ollie Oliphant discusses the amazing string of records he set—records that are still on the books after 50 years.

Letter from Elmer Q. Oliphant

I had 8 records not broken until Glenn Davis broke my season's yardage by 5. I had 927—his 932. But he didn't approach my 400 yards in one game with 5 touchdown runs of 65 yds or more. I think Red Grange had 5, but one was 40 yds.

So I had 7 records that haven't been touched in 50 years. One was broken by Bob Griese, QB of Purdue, to beat Notre Dame. Mine was 12 completed passes in a row. Bob beat me by 1-13. That leaves me 6 in 50 years still standing.

Last night I thought Larry Conjar was going to take one. I took the ball against Notre Dame down the field 16 times in a row. In Rock's book he says it was the greatest individual performance on a football field that he had ever seen. Larry, a Notre Dame back, did 8 times in a row last night—only half of mine. So my 6 records in 50 years still stand. . . .

Wishing you continued success, and with warmest personal regards,

I am as ever,
"Ollie"

John A. Stewart, a guard for Army, played four years at the University of California before his appointment to West Point where he played four more years of varsity football from 1920-1923. Colonel Stewart recalls a number of his teammates and relates an amusing incident.

Letter from John A. Stewart

So often in writing books where military rank is concerned the author or authors get carried away and make athletic heroes out of bums, because they played football, baseball, basketball, etc. and later became generals. In the meantime the men who were really good were passed over. I have read of certain generals and admirals being extolled as great athletes and I know damned well that they were no good. I won't call names because that is dirty pool, but I saw and played against some of them. A good High School player could have knocked one cabinet officer on his ass and he was made a star by one writer.

I played four years at the Univ. of California (Berkeley) before entering the Academy. 1915 as a frosh, 1917, 1918 and 1919 on the Varsity and at W. P. in 1920, 1921, 1922, and 1923. Storch and French my roommates had played two years each at Rutgers before entering the Academy, Georgie Smythe at Muhlenberg for two or three years, Mulligan at Columbia (Capt. Army in 1923), Strobecker at Oregon State College and against whom I had played on the West Coast. Oh! I'll set them all down if you are interested. . . .

I might add something else. Fire Chief William K. Blaisdell of Honolulu, Hawaii played at West Point in 1923, flunked out and then continued at Bucknell College or Univ. (I am not sure which) in Pennsylvania. His brother Neal now Mayor of Honolulu was already at Bucknell. . . .

I have been retired for twenty years come April—arthritis due to football injuries. Saw Stanford shellac the Army because the Army line was not alert and had lard where it shouldn't be. I played two years of soldier football and at the same time was a pro. I officiated for 18 years and still love the game. Also coached about six years during my active period.

In 1943 Breidster, Army captain in 1922, and I officiated a game between two Negro teams (U. S. Army) in Assam, India. It damned near killed both of us but we got the job done. Temperature 99° in the sun.

Sincerely
John A. Stewart
Col. U.S.A. (Ret.)

P. S. Breidster now is a retired Maj. General Natl. Guard of Wisconsin and lives in Milwaukee.

Walter French was one of West Point's finest all-around athletes in the early 1920's. As an Army halfback, he was a constant threat in any game, and after leaving the Academy he earned a spot for himself in major league baseball with the Philadelphia Athletics. A great many sportswriters have erroneously called "Larry" French. His real name is Walter. Recently Lt. Col. French, U.S.A.F. (Ret.) penned this note to a close friend, Major Gen. Charles G. Stevenson (Ret.).

Letter from Walter French

After 45 years my recollections of the Navy game are just about nil—I only remember 3 or four things and they are not worth recounting. I doubt if I tried 2 field goals. I used to kick pts. after TD's and did manage to kick a field goal in N. D. game but we never had kicking toes on our shoes and seldom spent more than 5 mins. practicing each night. It seems to be S.O.P. for all writers to use the wrong nickname. My baseball book has me listed as "Piggy" and I don't know how or where they came up with that.

The one sad incident I remember in the A & N games was when I was running from kick formation and was about to break thru the secondary when "Woppy" White ran into me and knocked me down. I believe I would have gone all the way—80-90 yrds.

Sincerely,
Walter

Note the words on Roger Staubach's helmet. He is calling signals in the 1963 game, and Navy did "Beat Army" that year.

"Lighthorse Harry" Wilson's exploits on the gridiron won't soon be forgotten. An All-American at Penn State before going to West Point, he was one of Army's great stars from 1924-1927. It was four years of famine for Navy as Wilson led the Cadets to three victories and a tie. During World War II, Colonel Wilson won the Distinguished Flying Cross and five air medals. He writes from Florida where he now lives.

Letter from Harry E. Wilson

The coaches and their assistants down thru the years. . . . "Biff" Jones, Earl Blaik, Bob Neyland, McEwan, Gene Vidal, Paul Parker (who went to Tennessee with Neyland), Ralph Sasse (deceased), Bill Woods (player and coach now at Norwich University), these are the ones I remember most during my time at the Academy. The trainers I think deserve a word for example Frank Wandel of my time. Sgt. Marty Maher a fixture at USMA since time began took care of the gym and helped the trainer by rubbing the boys down and working out the "charlie horses." He was full of West Point tradition and was actually a part of it.

I can remember the first time I reported to the gym for physical training Marty got ahold of me and took me all around the place giving me all the physical tests he could devise. The further we went the more mournful he became. After each test he would shake his head and tell me how much better Oliphant or McEwan or other Army athlete had done. I later found out who "Marty" was and that it was his habit to put the "Bee" onto any cadet who had a shred of athletic reputation before coming to West Point.

Names that stand out particularly during my years either for ability or personality are Harry Ellinger (later a coach) and Gus Farwick, guards in 1924, Garbisch at center, Bill Woods and Bill Gilmore, backs and the hardest working backs you ever saw on a football field, Tiny Hewitt whom I played against when he played for Pitt, Moe Daly a center, class of 1927. Later he was captured in the Philippines. He refused to try to escape on the march from Bataan because he had a company of men to take care of and he thought that more important. Trapnell, a back who was with Daly when he died in a Jap troop ship (prison ship), Bosko Schmidt, '26, a guard who played his heart out and later died in an aircraft accident. Rosey O'Donnell, '28, a back—later flew the last B-18 greatly overweight out of the Philippines, Blondy Saunders, '28, a tackle, was my room-mate for 4 years. His name was George and I always said he could hit you 3 times before you hit the ground. He was shot down in the Pacific in Jap territory and had to sit on the pilot's lap to land it (B-17) in the water. He was in command of the mission and Group C.O. at the time. Having gone out thru the window he had to go back in after the co-pilot whom he had thought dead. While he was doing this the airplane sank and the Lord knows how they got out. They—the ones still alive—got to shore in a rubber boat and the "coast watchers" took care of them until they could get a Navy "Dumbo" (rescue plane) in to pick them up. Later in China Saunders crashed in a B-25 and lay pinned in the wreck all night. As a result of his injuries his leg had to be amputated. He is retired now, lives in Aberdeen, S. D.

Skipper Seaman, Charlie Born, Harbold, "Chick" Harding, Bud Sprague, Johnny Murrell and Red Cagle were outstanding players in anyone's book, as the Navy will verify. Of course there are many others that deserve to be mentioned.

One thing I might comment on—it is a question I have been asked several times. Is there any difference between an Army-Navy game and, say, a Penn State-Navy game? Well, I couldn't see how there could be too much. I had played against Navy and with some success 3 times before going to West Point. As for rivalry we had had a pretty good thing going with the University of Pittsburgh at which we had *not* been too successful thanks to Tiny Hewitt, Davies, Peck, Frank and a few others (like Pop Warner). Anyhow come my first Army game with the Navy in 1924 and I was due for a distinct surprise. Evidently I should have studied up on the statistics of Army-Navy games. Previous records for the year should really count for something. Well of course they do—some—but far less than in any other rivalry I know of. Mediocre players become stars for a day and a more brilliant player may find himself handcuffed unless he can work himself up to the spirit of the occasion. I would say that the intense spirit which goes into this game does not increase the finesse of the play, for subtlety and strategy can be lost on someone too blind to see and all powerful with an overflow of adrenaline or whatever it is. However if you are looking for spirit, heart, and do-or-die rock 'em, sock 'em, clean football with great uncertainty as to the results—you got it! My answer to the question is Yes. It is hardly necessary to add that the color that is part of this occasion surpasses that of any other athletic event of the year.

Sincerely,
Harry E. Wilson
Col. U.S.A.F. (Ret).

Sports headlines throughout the land hailed Cadet Ed Garbisch after the Army-Navy game of 1924, for it was the strong right foot and stout heart of Garbisch that won the game for Army, 12-0. He kicked four big field goals to score all the points. Garbisch made additional headlines when it was discovered that he led his squad in a prayer in the dressing room before going out on the field. Here is that prayer.

Letter from Edgar Garbisch

I finally have found the verbatim version of the prayer I offered with the football squad in the dressing rooms just before going out to play the game. Here it is:

"O God, help us to play the game today in the spirit of clean sportsmanship and with no malice towards our opponent. Help us, also, to play our best and to acquit ourselves like men. Amen."

This prayer was offered for the first time just before the team went out on the field to play Yale in the Bowl, and it was repeated before all of our remaining games.

I want to repeat that the 1924 football team did not suffer any penalties beyond holding and off-sides all season; that is, there were no clipping, unsportsmanlike conduct, roughing the kicker, etc. penalties.

Sincerely,
Ed

Tom Hamilton is probably best recalled as the Navy player who drop-kicked the extra point in 1926 to tie Army 21-21 in what was perhaps the most exciting game in the history of this inter-service rivalry. In 1934, Hamilton returned to his alma mater as head football coach, holding that position until 1936 and returning for two more seasons in 1946 and 1947 as head coach and director of athletics. During World War II, he was awarded numerous honors and awards while on active duty. Today, Tom Hamilton is Commissioner of college football on the West Coast. Here is his personal story in his own words, taken from a tape recording he contributed in place of a letter.

Letter from Tom Hamilton

I feel that there is one man who has not been given his just dues by the historians of football. That man is Capt. Paul Dashiel who was one of the pioneers of the game. He played at Lehigh University and then came to the Naval Academy about the turn of the century as a coach. He had a very successful career as head coach at the Naval Academy and was a top official for many years. He was on the football rules committee for many years and had much to do with the formation of the game. He was one of the few men who was called in by President Theodore Roosevelt to revise the rules of the game to eliminate the serious injuries that were taking place about 1905. Dashiel was head of the chemistry department for many years and was revered by the midshipmen at the Naval Academy. He was a sort of Mr. Chips type: a most dignified and honored Naval officer but when he would come onto the practice field, the Midshipmen had a yell for him which they would chant out, which went something like this, "You can't imagine how proud we feel, our Paul, skinny Paul, Paul Dashiel." "Skinny" was the nickname for chemistry so that accounts for that word in the yell. He was a devoted student of football. I can remember when I was coaching there in the '30's, after the game on Saturday he would drive up the driveway of our house and come in and always say the right thing whether you won or lost and you knew that he was with you all the way.

Of course, there are so many other men who meant so much to Navy football, including Jonas Ingram and Doug Howard and, of course, Bill Ingram. Each has a great history and story to be told. Also Babe Brown who was the first Navy man to be voted into football's Hall of Fame and was probably one of the greatest football players of all time. He certainly was one of the greatest guards in history and also an outstanding place kicker. He had great influence upon his teammates, later as an assistant coach and as Director of Athletics. He was really a fine inspirational football man.

I'll go now to a recounting of the Army-Navy games that I know about. The first one in my plebe year was in the fall of 1923, played in the Polo Grounds in New York. It was a muddy field and the game was quite thrilling, at least to a plebe, and was evenly matched. I think the best play of the game was when the Army blocked Carl Cullen's punt on the third down and luckily so because Cullen nudged out an Army player to gain possession of the ball, and then was able on the fourth down to punt the ball out safely from his goal line. The final score was a tie 0-0. In 1924, the game was played in Baltimore and the Army won 12-0 on the strength of four drop kicks by Ed Garbisch, the Army center. The game was fairly even throughout the day but whenever Army got within range Garbisch was successful with his drop kicks for the only scores of the game. The 1925 game was a good one and the Army won 10 to 3. We scored first on a long pass from Alan Shapely to Harry Hardwick to Army's 10-yard line, but when we could not make the touchdown, I drop kicked the field goal. Army came back and scored a touchdown and late in the game Army's field goal star, Red Reeder, booted the ball for 3 points and the game ended 10-3.

In 1926, Bill Ingram was our coach and probably this game was the one with the greatest buildup of any of the whole series. It was the first time the Army-Navy game was to be played in Chicago where the crowd of 100,000 was the largest ever to witness a football game. Navy was undefeated in 9 games and Army was also unbeaten, although tied by Notre Dame, so this was certainly a game for the national championship. The weather was very cold and there had been a snow storm the night before. The field was covered by a tarp which was peeled off the next day. Just before the team left the dressing room, Bill Ingram, our coach, said that this would be the largest crowd that any of us had ever seen and he suggested that as we left the runway that leads to the field that we stop and have a good look at the vast crowd and drink in the significance of the interest in the game and then try to forget the scene. It made a tremendous impression on me that I've never forgotten.

The game turned out to be a ding-dong offensive struggle. Bill Ingram had installed a double-wing attack with wingbacks going in motion. It was deceptive and generated good power and also good passing. In the first period the Navy scored twice. We had a pass from Schubert to Hardwick which took the ball to the one-yard line and Howard Caldwell drove it over. In the second quarter the Navy made a good drive and scored a touchdown. This drive started with the ball on the two-yard line and on the third down we ran an off tackle play. Hank Hardwick, the end, and I as the wingback were to double team and block out Army's Sprague, but Army stopped us cold. The same play was called in the huddle for the fourth down and Hank Hardwick said to me that he would take Sprague himself and release me to block out the line backer. This time we scored the touchdown. Army also scored twice in the first half.

As the half opened Cagle broke loose for a 45-yard run and a touchdown. This was a very fine run by a dazzling star who was always a threat. One of the other Army touchdowns was scored by Harry Wilson who was one of the greatest backs Army ever had. In the fourth quarter with the Army leading 21-14, Frank Wickhorst, our captain, called time out. The ball was on our own 30-yard line and Frank said, "Do you guys see that goal line down there? We are going across it and we are not going to lose the ball until we put it across." This was a fine bit of leadership, and we were successful in doing it, the final play being a double reverse with Shapely carrying the ball around right end for the score.

Much has been said of me about what I was thinking when I had to kick the drop kick for the extra point—with Navy behind by one point. Wickhorst drew me out of the huddle and I cleaned the mud off my shoes while the team talked to one another about blocking out the Army team. I was more concerned about getting the mud off my shoe than anything else and when I had to kick it, it was more a matter of practice—it was the same as practice rather in an impending moment. I had practiced so long in my room in the Naval academy and the practice field that the actions were second nature and actually I did not think too much about it. More significant to me about this game is that I had a chance to play a whole game and did the line backing.

This game was certainly the highlight of my playing career, and I think it was one of the best games that I have ever had a chance to be a part of. I think it is significant that the players on both teams went on to Naval and military careers, and all of them were prominent in service in World War II. Ask any Marine about Tom Trapnell, the Army halfback. He was one of the early heroes in the Philippines when he blocked a bridge from being crossed by the Japanese by his personal bravery. I think that Blondie Saunders, one of the Army's tackles, lost a leg in the fighting early in the war. One of the stories I heard about him is that he had to be transported by air back to Hawaii for surgery to save his life. They did not have blood and plasma for him to give him transfusions, so a coach by the name of Shooty who has been the high school coach at Santa Barbara High School in California made the trip with him and they took the transfusion directly from Shooty's body into Saunders to keep Saunders alive.

This relationship between the Army and Navy on the football field and in other Army-Navy contests to me is quite important. Many times critics of sports have indicated that the intense rivalry between the Army and the Navy is not good and engenders bad feelings between the services for the rest of their careers. In my opinion, the very opposite is true. The best friends that I have in the Army were all people that I played against in football, basketball, or baseball, and I think while one competed as well as one could, the respect and admiration one had for this opponent gave you a proper outlook toward the other service and, indeed, practically the only friends I had in the Army were those I played against.

An interesting relationship for me has been with General Gar Davidson who was on this Army team and we played against each other in Chicago. Later on he was the head coach at the Military Academy when I returned to coach at the Naval Academy and we coached against each other in '34, '35, and '36. I believe that he had another year at West Point or maybe two more. Following those years of deadly rivalry we had a tour of duty in Washington where our wives and families became really good friends. We were able to play golf and meet together socially. Later on, after World War II, Gar and Verone were stationed at the Presidio when I coached the Navy team that came to Berkeley to play the University of California. It was very nice for us to have Gar Davidson and his wife to dinner with our staff and team after the game.

This was in 1947. Gar then went to West Point as Superintendent. I was athletic director at Pittsburgh. We had occasion to play the Army at West Point and our meeting with General Davidson was again most pleasant.

Another incident along this line is when I was the Air Officer of the USS *Enterprise* in the South Pacific in 1943 or 1944. We came into the Fiji Islands and I went ashore at Nandio to look at the airfield to see if it was suitable for the land operations of our air group, should they have an opportunity to train ashore for a period of time. I flew into Nandio and asked who was the commanding officer. They said that Colonel Wilson was in command. He was over in a hut on the opposite side of the field with a thatched roof over it. I went into the hut and, sure enough, there was Colonel Harry Wilson. We spent the rest of the day together and it was most enjoyable, talking about the Army-Navy games of yesteryear.

In this "new era," I guess we could call it, while being in the fleet after graduation I did have contact as an assistant coach under Bill Ingram for the game of 1927 which Army won 14-7. This was the year Ned Hannigan was captain and the last year Harry Wilson and Chris Cagle played. After this game, the series was called off until 1930 due to eligibility differences. In 1930, the game was highlighted by Ray Stecker's amazing 60-yard sprint, with the entire Navy team spread behind him for the only score as Army won 7-0. The Navy team played a fine game and they had some very fine ball players on its squad. Magruder Tuttle, the center, Lou Bryan, the tackle, Lou Kirn in the backfield, Gordon Chung-Hoon, a fine back, Oscar Hagberg, an end, and both Dale and Joe Bauer.

In 1934, after coaching the U.S. fleet team for three years on the west coast, I was called to the Naval Academy as head football coach. We had a most interesting season. Our squad was small but spirited and bright and they had tremendous confidence in themselves and above all had two great players which we were able to capitalize on a great deal. The first was Buzz Borries who, in my opinion still, is the finest football player I've ever seen. This squad, although it had spirit and great moxie, was not a great physical squad and had they been able to give the type of blocking on equal physical strength with opponents most of the time, I think Borries would have made a name as an open field runner that even exceeds what he actually did, which was plenty. He had an amazing style of running in a relaxed manner and then he still had a little reserve open to give him more speed when needed. He had tremendous ability to feint a would-be tackler. No one ever hit him square. The other great player was Bill Clark. He was the best punter that I have ever seen. His ability to not only kick long but play them very accurately meant a great deal to his team. We never covered both sides of the field. He would tell his teammates where he was going to kick it and he never let them down with a slip. This restricted the amount of area that we had to cover and we were able to utilize the kicking game very well. Our ends were Mantle, Corn, and Doran; the tackles, Cutter and George Lambert; the guards, Captain Dick Burns and Schaffer; the center, Robertshaw. There was also David Zbitzky, a great guard. The backfield consisted of Borries, Clark, Dick Pratt, and Tommy King. There were some excellent replacements—notably Smith in the backfield and Cole and Buggle as guards, Jim Mini, an end, and Carl Fellows, a back, and Rivers Morelle, a guard.

Tom Hamilton, when he was athletic director of the Naval Academy.

The Navy, not having beaten the Army for 13 years, came into this game with only one loss—that to Pittsburgh in the game just before the Army game. The Army had a fine squad—a back named Jack Buckler, also Monk Myer, and their captain, a boy named Joe Stancook, an excellent ballplayer. The game was played in a sea of mud on Franklin Field and our strategy was to try to score as fast as we could before the ball and everybody got too muddy. Borries was able to make about a 20-yard gain early in the first quarter and this gave us field position. Bill Clark took advantage of that position and finally kicked one which Dusty Dornin knocked out of bounds on the Army one-yard line. When the Army punted out, Borries made a nice punt return. We made a few first downs, one as the result of a shovel pass from Borries to Pratt. When we couldn't make the touchdown Slade Cutter kicked a place kick from the 20-yard line which turned out to be the only score of the day. The game was very exciting throughout. The Army quick-kicked on us once and Buzz Borries picked it up on the Navy 15 and ran it back about another 15 more; he almost broke loose. The Army threatened several times. One time King intercepted a pass and Clark really saved the day when he punted 68 yards over the safety man's head late in the game. Naturally this meant a great deal to the Navy Academy after being without an Army victory for so long, and this was a team of which I was very proud. They were not very big, but they certainly believed in themselves and played to the limit at all times.

The game of 1935 was played in Franklin Field in Philadelphia. The teams seemed pretty well matched. It was really quite a blow to lose this game 28-6 and perhaps it was the first time as a coach that I had ever seen a team freeze. In the first series of plays, immediately after receiving the kick-off on the first play of the game, the Army halfback Grove took the ball on a reverse play and went 80 yards for a touchdown. This seemed to throw our team into a state of shock, and, although we replaced several of the players, they seemingly were in a trance the rest of the day. The Army ran up 28 points in the first half. In the second half we out-played Army completely but were only able to score six points. Sneed Smith especially did a very fine job and we had Bill Ingram who played fine ball in the backfield. Pratt and King and Fellows were in the backfield. Our center and captain was Lou Robertshaw. His substitute was Hutchins who had a most interesting experience during the war as a skipper of a destroyer. He rammed a German submarine and kept his destroyer on top of the sub. The Germans came on deck and were firing anything they could get their hands on up at the bridge of the ship; likewise the blue jackets on Hutchins' destroyer picked up anything from potatoes to ink bottles or anything else to throw at the Germans until the German sub sank. It is quite an epic in destroyer history.

The Army star halfback, Monk Myer, is a flag officer in the Army and is now serving in Vietnam. We'll hear more from him I'm sure.

Tom Hamilton

When Lou Kirn arrived at Annapolis in 1929, Army and Navy had severed athletic relations, but he hoped and prayed that the "big day" would once again arrive. It did, in those post-season games of 1930 and 1931, and "Bullet Lou," as the sportswriters called him, did his part to try to put Navy ahead on the scoreboard. From the Pentagon, Rear Admiral Kirn writes of his gridiron days at Annapolis and tells of the unusual way he got started playing football.

Letter from Lou Kirn

First, and this should not be a surprise to anyone, the ambition of all football players at the Naval Academy and West Point is to play in the Army-Navy game. I was no exception. Both games I played in (1930 and 1931), you may recall, were post-season games scheduled for the benefit of charity.

In 1930, my principal and unhappy recollection is that of seeing Ray Stecker of Army go for about 50 yards for the only score of the game. Otherwise, it was a close and vigorous contested game all the way. I don't recall any particular incidents of consequence. I found it to be an exhilarating experience and I was pleased to have played almost the entire game.

In 1931 we lost again. This was a much more open game. Navy scored only once and that was on a pass that I threw to our wingback, Joe Tschirgi. This was recorded as one of the longest passes through the air of that period (about 50 yards as I recall) and resulted in our score. Spalding's Football Rules Book carried the pass as a record but I don't know for how long. After throwing the ball, and while I was wide open, I was tackled about as hard as I ever was in my life by Army's All-American tackle, Jack Price. He drove his 200-plus pound frame into my 155 pounds, and I felt as though a steamroller had hit me. As he was getting up he said, "Are you hurt, son?" Under other circumstances, I probably would not have gotten off the ground but this remark aroused anew the flow of adrenalin. I couldn't let him know he had been so effective. I replied, "Hell no, you big ox, get off!" Years later, I met Jack in an officers club and we had a friendly drink together, reminiscing about this game.

Another recollection is that I was pretty badly beaten up including a broken nose. Sam Moncure, who was our quarterback, and I were both taken to the Brooklyn Naval Hospital for x-rays and treatment. The doctors had decided to keep me there over the weekend but I insisted I had to keep a long arranged-for date in New York City that night. When our squad doctor interceded on my behalf and assured the hospital medics that he would look out for me, they agreed to let me go. Sam, however, was somewhat more battered than I and he had to remain in the hospital.

After the 1931 game, the football was auctioned off for about $10,000 and the proceeds given to the Salvation Army. This ball was autographed by the players on both teams and when I last saw it, was reposing in a trophy case at the Naval Academy.

Something I might have started this letter with is the manner in which I started to play football. The city of Milwaukee, where I lived, sponsored football leagues made up of teams of various weights. The lightest was the 120 pound league, which meant that the team on the field could not average more than 120 pounds. This required the officials to recompute the average weight every time a substitution was made. (Today, with the platoon system, it would take a computer!) Individual players, however, could weigh 135 pounds. I was about thirteen when I approached the coach of a team I was interested in and asked to join. He asked what my experience was, and my reply was "none." I weighed about 108 pounds at that point and obviously could not make much of a contribution. However, he must have been impressed with my strong plea to play because he worked out an unique solution. He said that if I would *lose* some weight he might be able to use me in a situation which called for several 135 pounders in the lineup and he would put me in to bring the team average down to the official limit. I then asked how I might lose this weight since I hardly had any to spare. This is when I first learned about a Turkish bath. He explained what it was and where I could get one. Since I was willing to do anything to get on the squad, one day after school I ventured forth to get my Turkish bath. The attendant asked me why I came and I responded, "To lose some weight." I spent about an hour and a half in the steam and dry rooms and then hurried over to the official weight recording office, where I weighed in at about 102 pounds. I had not eaten or taken on any liquids all day. Also, I did this on my own without the knowledge or consent of my family.

When I reported back to the coach he allowed me to join the squad. This gave me the "privilege" to practice with the team two or three nights a week and then sit on the bench on Sunday afternoons. I thought this was quite rewarding in itself. My big moment came one day toward the end of the season. The coach, in using more than the usual number of heavy players, and needing to bring the weight average down, called on me to play—tackle! I lasted about two minutes and after the offensive team had run roughshod over me a couple of times, the coach decided I wasn't quite ready, at least not as a tackle. This was the beginning, however, and without it I might not have pursued the sport.

The discipline, the competition, and the inculcated desire to win developed in competitive sports have stood me in good stead in later years.

Sincerely,
L. J. Kirn
Rear Admiral, USN

Fred Borries finds teaching mathematics these days a good bit calmer than the roaring excitement of being "Buzz" Borries, Navy All-American and standout performer from 1932-1934, especially in 1934 when he and his teammates defeated Army 3-0 for the first time in thirteen long years. Of course there was plenty of excitement for Commander Borries during World War II, but here he recalls in these notes some of the highlights in his career as one of Navy's greatest running backs of all time.

Letter from Fred Borries

Here are some recollections of my Army-Navy game experiences.

1932

I played about three-quarters of the game and on defense, which we were on most of the game. I went wherever Felix Vidal went and I remember he went lots of places.

1933

. I missed blocking the end on Baumberger's touchdown run but he slipped through the tackle.

I remember vividly how many times I was, and the other receivers were, open for passes and the passer didn't spot us.

1934

The tension in the dressing room before the game.

When I made that 20-yard plus run the second play of the game, how cramped my legs were. I couldn't make the cut back down field. After being knocked out of bounds, how they kept piling on. I slugged the last one. How the cadets roared.

How the Army kept punting to me, expecting a fumble. When I made about 20 yards on the punt return that helped set up our field goal, they punted away.

When Army blocked the punt and the end scooped it up and headed goalward, I took up the chase. I knew I had him so as I tackled him I hit the ball out of his arms. Unfortunately the referee thought he fumbled it after he hit the ground.

I remember missing someone on Cutter's field goal kick. Fortunately Cutter kicked the ball under the man.

Wiping my hands on the Army substitute's jerseys. We only had four substitutes the whole game. Remember we only had one ball and one towel per half in that sea of mud.

Monk Meyer playing one play and fumbling.

Buzz Borries

John Lawlor is a retired general and now Executive Vice President of the National Safety Council in Chicago, but in 1931 the most important thing in the world to him was for the West Point football team to "Beat Navy." They did, 17-7. Lawlor has an interesting story about an incident before the 1932 game.

Letter from John Lawlor

One story that I remember offhand was the pre-game setting of the 1932 game. The team stayed at the Valley Forge Military Academy outside Philadelphia and bedded down early on Thursday night in order to make up for all the lost hours of sleep that a cadet suffers during the normal routine at West Point. Unfortunately, Ralph Sasse, who was the Coach, had forgotten to tell the Superintendent of the Academy not to have his Drum and Bugle Corps play as usual at 6 o'clock in the morning. Hence, the Valley Forge "Hellcats" disturbed the quiet morning and the players' sleep to such an extent that Major Sasse vowed never to return to the premises under any condition. To say the least, he was quite disturbed about the whole situation.

Sincerely,
John Lawlor

Norman Edwards played for Army in the 1930's and vividly remembers the games —particularly the one during which he got slugged by the coach for his over-exuberance. Here are his comments about his days with the Army squad.

Letter from Norman B. Edwards

In my day, the "B" teams learned the plays of the next opponent from scouting reports and we usually had a couple of days of scrimmage against our opponent's offense before each game. Among the "scrubs" of my day were Westmoreland, now General in Vietnam; Abrams, now Vice Chief of Staff of the Army (I believe Abe later made the varsity as a substitute guard), Throckmorton, who was Westmoreland's Deputy in Vietnam, and others who have gone on to great heights.

Red Blaik, who was our backfield coach before going to Dartmouth as head coach, was the finest technician I have ever seen but Ralph Sasse, our head coach in 1931 and 32, had the greatest ability for bringing a team to fighting pitch before a game and during a half that I have ever seen. In 1932, before the Harvard game, Sasse had Milt Summerfelt, our Captain, read a letter to the squad immediately before leaving the dressing room to begin the game. The letter was from a young invalid boy in Vermont (I suspect Sasse wrote the letter) and the lad went into detail how the Army was his greatest inspiration and the best team in the country. The letter described the lad's afflictions and requested one of the team's practice footballs if it could be spared. It was a masterpiece of writing; a tear jerker and heart wringer, and so inspired us that we tore out of the dressing room and made four touchdowns in the first half of what was supposed to be a close game. In the second half of that game, I had just come out of the fracas and was sitting on the bench behind Sasse when one of our safety men returned a punt for a touchdown. In my excitement, I jumped up and slapped the coach on the back. Whereupon Sasse turned around and slugged me, knocking me completely backwards over the bench. Guess he was excited too. Anyhow, I had a sore jaw to add to my other aches and pains.

With respect to an Army-Navy game in 1934 in the mud at Franklin Field, when Army lost 3 to 0 for the first time in 13 (?) years, Slade Cutter, the Navy tackle, thought Moose Stillman, one of our guards, was holding him and invited Moose out behind the stands after the game. Stillman, knowing that Cutter was intercollegiate heavyweight boxing champion, replied rather sensibly, I thought, "What do you think I am, a G.D. fool?" Incidentally, that game was the only game, high school or college, that my parents ever came to see me play and it was so muddy that after the first play even the numerals on our jerseys were obliterated. So, although in the stands, my parents never saw me play a game of football.

Sincerely,
Norman B. Edwards
Major General, USA
Deputy Chief of Personnel Operations

Gar Davidson (right) and Harvey Jablonsky in 1933. Davidson was head coach for Army and Jablonsky was team captain.

Gar Davidson was a member of the Army team in that classic battle with Navy in 1926 which ended in the 21-21 tie. When he was appointed head football coach at West Point in 1933, he was the youngest one they had ever had. After military service that included numerous campaigns, honors, and awards, he became Superintendent of the Academy. Now retired, General Davidson recounts the high spots of his days as both player and coach.

Letter from Garrison H. Davidson

First, a few personal comments. On the train back from the Chicago game in 1926 (incidentally, I was listed as a tackle instead of an end in the newspaper accounts of that game), Ralph Sasse who coached the ends, with Biff Jones' concurrence, invited me to come back the following fall as end coach of the Plebes. I served three seasons in that capacity before becoming the head scout and coach of the "B" squad for two years and head coach of the Plebes for one. It was also Ralph Sasse who, in the summer of 1932, recommended me to succeed him when he departed the following January. There was quite an exodus of football players at graduation in June of 1933, and the prospects were not bright.

In September of '33, we really only had a few college-size players but the fifteen cadets who bore the brunt of the season had a tremendous spirit and a firm determination to live down the forecasts. As you know, we went undefeated until the last two or three minutes of the season when the old machine just wore out and several players made a mistake on a punt, any one of which, had it not occurred, would have made the play a success. In retrospect I often wonder how bad a mistake I made in not having the team take deliberate safety, but we had never had a punt blocked all year. It was many years later when we both were officers before I could disabuse Ozzie Simons, our kicker, of his worry that he had been at fault, which was not the case. It was the protection. However, I lay a great deal of the cause to our first major game against Illinois. It was a hot day and the evening before Bob Zuppke, in an address to the Illinois Alumni, had waxed extremely confident. We scored a touchdown and later kicked a field goal which was disallowed "because the holder of the ball touched his knee to the ground." It was not until the half that I was able to collar the Referee and have him read the rule. He admitted his mistake, said he was sorry, but there was nothing he could do. This meant that a greatly outmanned team had to play practically the entire game under sweltering conditions. It took a great deal out of them and each succeeding Saturday they came back a little more short of their capacity at the start of the Illinois game. By the time we reached the Navy game the smaller members of our team were playing pretty much on their nerve. Nevertheless we were able to hang on, as newspaper accounts show, on the strength of Beanie Johnson's fine punt return and Jack Buckler's nice run on our cutback play off tackle.

The next year was an in and outer, and of course we lost to the Navy for the first time in a long time under impossible conditions. As I remember it, the total number of first downs was five. Navy scored early and that was it. Despite the going, at one point in the game we again broke our cutback inside tackle clean through the line and had every Navy man taken care of. It would have produced a long run for a score had not Borries gotten up off his back and slithered across the field in the mud to drag down our ball carrier from behind just as he was in the clear. Monk Meyer, whom I saw off to Vietnam last week, got his first crack at the Navy in this game. He fumbled at a critical stage for which I did not blame him a bit, but he took it greatly to heart and swore he would never do so again. I don't remember him fumbling during his next two years despite the fact that he bore the brunt of our offense, handling the ball on two-thirds to three-fourths of the plays.

The Army-Navy game in 1935 was a Coach's dream. The newspaper account could have been written prior to the game from our written quarterback instructions. I wish I could find them and send them along. Red Reeder, with the able assistance of Blondie Saunders, who lost a leg during the War, and Eddie Doyle, who was killed in the North African landings at Algiers, did a superb job so that we knew just about what every member of the Navy team had for breakfast. Consequently, everything we attempted turned to gold and we scored twenty-one points in the first sixteen minutes of what was expected to be a tight ball game. We managed to get every cadet on the squad who made the trip into the game as well as one who didn't but left his seat in the stands and got dressed to sit on the bench.

Monk Meyer was our threat and we had rarely run to the weak side when he received the ball. My instructions to the quarterback were the first time he had the ball if he was in position to call a reverse in which Monk handed the ball to Whitey Grove on first down, or if he wasn't in position, to get in position and call the play on the second down. Billy Grohs did the latter and Grove went over eighty yards for a touchdown. He had also been instructed the first time he got a first down near mid-field to throw a special pass to Whitey Grove from formation left which we had not used a great deal. He did, and in a few minutes we had a second score. We instructed him the next time he got in Navy territory to throw a running pass to Clint True, our fullback. This also worked for a long score and a happy day was well begun. This pleasant victory was in no small degree due to the superb leadership of Bill Shuler who took advantage of proximity of the Navy goat to the sideline during the game to pluck some of his whiskers for a souvenir.

1936 was a nightmare for us. A very severe epidemic of the flu hit our squad about mid-season. For a couple of weeks the players dropped literally like flies and our team never recovered. I had a particular problem throughout the year with the quarterbacks. Finally, for the Navy game I decided to select the player with the most poise, experience, and leadership and instruct him intently and in detail for ten days before the game and rest our hopes on him. I selected Stan Smith, a guard, who is now the

Academic Dean of the Coast Guard Academy at New London, and he called a practically perfect game, his first and only effort at quarterbacking. Another difficulty we had to overcome was the lack of a competent wing-back and we converted an end, Riggs Sullivan, later Commandant of Cadets at the Air Force Academy and now a Major or Lieutenant General in the Air Force, into a halfback for that game, and he did a very superior job. It is still my opinion that there was absolutely no interference when he was called for that penalty which gave the Navy possession of the ball near our goal (incidentally, to this day I am still convinced that neither was there any interference against Milner in the Notre Dame game of the previous year).

1937 was my swan song and the Navy game loomed as an exceedingly tough one. We weren't sure how well we could run against them inside the twenty or twenty-five yard line; therefore, we cooked up a special reverse pass in which our spinning back, Jack Ryan, now Commanding General of the Strategic Air Force, spun, gave the ball to Huey Long, a lefthand passer we had not used very much, who faked a reverse play and then turned and threw diagonally back across the field to Ryan. We instructed the quarterback to use this play when he got in the vicinity of the Navy 25-yard line. He did, and Jack carried the ball to the Navy 3. To get added power, we had adopted also for this game the two old Howard Jones, U.S.C., and Ted Jones, Yale (Albie Booth) inside and outside tackle plays from a 5-1 unbalanced line and the quarterback was told to use them in succession close to the goal. This he did and Jim Craig scored the only touchdown of the game.

Best regards.

Sincerely,
Garrison H. Davidson

Harvey Jablonsky was one of the most aggressive linemen in Army's football history. He won All-American honors and was captain of the West Point eleven in 1933. Upon graduation, Jablonsky remained at the Academy for ten years as an assistant coach. He is now serving as Chief Military Advisor to the Iranian government and found time to set down these incidents and anecdotes about Army football.

Letter from Harvey Jablonsky

I have often been asked what I remember most about my playing days. I guess the thing that sticks in my mind the most was the season of 1933. We were a very small team with very limited experience, playing a 10 game schedule. Grantland Rice, in pre-season predictions, indicated that we would not win a major game. The best any expert would predict was perhaps two major victories. . . .

*   *   *

We were playing Yale and Harvard on successive weekends after the Illinois game and due to our very thin and light squad, Gar Davidson was unable to give us much rest. To further complicate matters the medics decided that our right halfback, Travis T. Brown, had an enlarged heart. They therefore ruled he could no longer participate in athletics as a cadet. He was also our place kicker. We went on to defeat Harvard and Yale, which was a pretty good accomplishment in those days and moved through to a victory against Navy, 12 to 7. At this point we had 9 straight wins with Notre Dame to go. Due to scheduling difficulties, we had played Navy before Notre Dame in 1933. . . .

*   *   *

You probably remember Monk Meyer who never did weigh more than about 137 pounds soaking wet. In 1936, his last season, Gar Davidson was determined to beef up Monk a little bit. The trainer prescribed a malted milk every evening after practice and toward this end a Hamilton Beach milkshake machine was procured for the training room. I can still see Monk downing these rich malted milks with egg every night for the month of September. By the end of the month he had lost 3 pounds. Incidentally, Monk is a brigadier general now and and has just received orders to Vietnam.

*   *   *

I think one of the greatest thrills I had was being on the coaching staff in 1946 under Earl Blaik when we had an undefeated season. This was Doc Blanchard's and Glenn Davis' last year. The Notre Dame game that year ended in a nothing-to-nothing tie with a great duel between Johnny Lujac and Arnold Tucker, our quarterback.

I guess one of the fondest memories I have of football is coaching at the Academy for 10 seasons. I was one of the assistant coaches from 1934-1942 inclusive and then again in 1946 after the war.

As you know, I played eight years of college football. I played for Washington University in St. Louis when we were in the old Missouri Valley Conference. In those days Washington University was on the fringes of big time football. I played one year under Bob Higgins, who later went to Penn State, and 2 years under Dr. Al Sharp of Yale. I was captain of that team in 1929 . . . when we played such teams as Kansas, Carnegie Tech, Haskell Institute, etc. This was pretty good opposition in those days.

In 1933 or 1934 I remember a Ripley Believe-It-or-Not Cartoon which featured the fact that I had been the captain of two college football teams, Washington University and West Point.

✿   ✿   ✿

I will never forget in 1941, Blaik's first year as head coach at the Academy. Jess Neeley called from Texas to indicate there was a good football player in the Port Arthur area. This kid, Bobby Vinson, had made all state, and Rice had offered him a scholarship. I went down to see Bobby in Nederland, Texas. There was no doubt about him wanting to go to the Academy as a first choice. Jess Neeley's position was if he couldn't get him to go to Rice the next best thing was to get him out of Texas. Bobby played great football for us in the next few years.

✿   ✿   ✿

Red Reeder was one of our most versatile coaches. He was known as the dean of the scouts and I remember one of my first scouting assignments with him. He remarked prior to going to the game that the tendency in a new scout would be to take too much detail. He told me to watch the guards and tackles and all he cared about was not whether a defensive man would go around or through a block, but whether the guards and tackles bulldozed their way straight ahead.

H. J. Jablonsky
Major General, U.S. Army
Chief ARMISH MAAG

Harvey Jablonsky when he played for West Point.

In 1934 Midshipman Dick Burns was captain of that glorious Navy team that defeated Army 3-0, by virtue of Slade Cutter's trusty right foot and the brilliant running and passing of Buzz Borries. Let Captain Burns tell the story of that 1934 season as he actually lived it on the playing field.

Letter from Dick Burns

That '34 season remains the biggest thing in my life—well, one of them. Led by Tommy Hamilton in his first year and Rip Miller—both recent Hall of Famers the team and the entire squad was truly dedicated; there was no dissension anywhere. I was most proud to have been elected team captain after the 12-7 game in '33.

Leading up to the '34 Army game we had won our first seven games, the 7th being our second straight over Notre Dame. In addition to the team's dedication I believe its aggressiveness and Borries' running, Bill Clark's highly developed punting, Cutter's field goals and Dornin's end play were highlights.

We were perhaps slightly bitten by "Rose Bowl-itus" after the 7th but Pitt's thorough shellac job they laid on us in the 8th ended that. The night after that our coaches gave us a relaxation party which most of us little appreciated in the forthcoming toughest, meanest preparation we'd known before the Army game. Before the game I'd have welcomed both Summerfelt and Jablonsky—All-Americans in '32 and '33 seasons —opposite me in the guard slot. There was no doubt that we should win and we still feel that the slop and slime of the game only held down the score. Cutter's kick, we felt, was only the start of the scoring but that was it.

I remember one play in the closing minutes. Bill Clark, as usual, got off one of his superb kicks to Grohs on the 13, high and long. It was easy to be waiting for it with Grohs. My thoughts were conflicting—steal the ball from him and go 13 yards for my first Navy touchdown?—Hit him high and lard for a fumble?—Or hit him low and insure we keep them in the hole? I chose the second—he fumbled, Tommy King recovered and we had the ball down there 'til the game ended. Philadelphia couldn't do too much for us that night.

It was a good season. Undefeated Minnesota was first in the ratings; Pitt, losing only to Minn., was second, and Navy, loser only to Pitt, was third. But we could have lost them all and the A-N win would have made the season.

Sincerely,
Dick Burns
Capt. USN (Ret.)

"You're too small for Army football, son. Better try the Cullum squad." Those were the first words that Charles Meyer, pint-sized cadet heard from an Army football coach when he reported for football at West Point in 1934, and small he was. But when Coach Gar Davidson saw little "Monk" Meyer in action he told the equipment manager to "get a special uniform for Meyer."

Meyer went on to become one of Army's finest running and passing backs and his spectacular play in the 1935 Army-Navy game won All-American honors for the little scatback. As Brigadier General Charles R. Meyer, he writes from Vietnam.

Letter from Charles R. Meyer

I would like now to go on record that I was probably the lightest individual who has ever participated in the Army Navy contest, weighing in at approximately 139 pounds. This, I am sure, you will find unique in your run down of Army-Navy football statistics.

Perhaps being such a lightweight and born at West Point was a natural sportswriter's delight and resulted in my getting much more credit as a football player than I duly deserved. The whole situation, I suppose, lent itself to good copy, and I often hear in reflection a well-worn line of many years ago which went something like this: "A spindle-legged son of an Army Colonel, born at West Point . . ."

I am very proud to say that my son, a third generation West Pointer, earned his letter this past fall by playing second-string linebacker. I hope he will do better next year.

Very sincerely,
Charles R. Meyer
Brigadier General, General Staff
Chief of Staff

A guard on the 1934, 1935, and 1936 Army teams, Major General Nils O. Ohman now is Vice Commander at Randolph Air Force Base in Texas. General Ohman's favorite football story concerns an incident connected with the 1935 Army-Navy game.

Letter from Nils O. Ohman

The one Army-Navy game that I remember best (since we won) was that of 1935. The team was advised shortly before the game that Moe Daley was failing rapidly in West Point Hospital, and his deathbed request was to have the radio turned to the Army-Navy game so he could go to his reward happy, provided Army won. Since we greatly loved and admired Moe, this provided an incentive for us to play possibly well beyond our normal capability with the result that at the end of the first half the score was twenty-eight to nothing. During the half, we learned that Moe Daley wasn't so sick after all. The second half, we played more our normal game with the result that Navy scored one touchdown, the final score being Army 28-Navy 6.

Sincerely,
Nils O. Ohman
Major General, USAF

LaVerne G. "Blondie" Saunders was an outstanding lineman on the West Point squads during a three-year period—1924-1926—that saw two wins over Navy and that classic tie of '26. "Blondie" later coached at West Point and is credited with discovering the abilities of "Monk" Meyer. Here he talks about the 1926 game in which he played and the 1935 game when he was line coach.

Letter from L. G. Saunders

These are two games that stand out in my mind one as a player and one as a coach. The 21-21 tie at Chicago in 1926. Navy had a fine team that year and was undefeated. We were beaten once by Notre Dame 7-0 on Flannagan's long run. (We were not up for that game and thought all we had to do was suit up and the game was ours.)

The 1926 was a close one all the way. Navy got two quick TD's on long passes to start the game and it was a hard lead to overcome. We drove to the 15 yard line in the closing minutes (stopped by a couple of offside plays) and Harry Wilson barely missed a field goal.

The 1935 game was exceptional in that our game strategy worked out perfectly. I was line coach then and had scouted the Navy once with the regularly assigned scout. Because of the defensive distribution in certain situations we designed certain plays to cope with their defensive distribution. Fortunately in the first quarter of the game four of these situations were presented to the Army team and they all went for TD's. The first quarter ended Army 27-Navy 0. The final score, Army 27-Navy 6 (I believe), This game stood out as a perfectly prepared game combined with good scouting. The Army scouts did a fine job. Col. Red Reeder now assistant Athletic Director at West Point was the head Navy scout for that year, I believe. We lost both centers in that game, which handicapped us in the 2nd half. "Jock" Clifford who was killed in the invasion of the Celebes and the late Casey Vincent both received shoulder dislocations. All the other games from 1924 thru 1939 that I was associated with either as a player or coach were typical hard fought games.

Sincerely,
L. G. Saunders
Brig. Gen., USAF (Ret.)

Halfback Woody Wilson was in the Army lineup in the 1937 game when Coach Gar Davidson's strategy and planning paid off. From the Philippines he shares his comments about the 1937 and 1938 Army-Navy clashes.

Letter from W. W. Wilson

My most vivid personal reminiscences of the two games in which I participated—those of 1937 and 1938—concern three subjects:

Prior to the 1937 game, Gar Davidson planned a complete series of plays to begin when we reached the vicinity of the Navy 40-yard line and to culminate with a pass from Huey Long to Jack Ryan off of a fake reverse play into the right sideline. Gar briefed the quarterbacks, and the others who might be calling signals, on this sequence of plays and walked through the series with us on the field. He drilled and redrilled us on the plan. During the game, the plan was implemented to perfection; the records will show that the touchdown scored on the culminating play was the only one scored in the game that day.

Two incidents stand out concerning the 1938 game—Huey Long's one-handed interception of a Navy pass in the end zone (when it appeared that possibly use of two hands would have been more sure, although Huey apparently did not feel that way!) and Harry Stella's hard tackle of a Navy back (whose name I do not recall) which caused the back to fumble. At the time, which was near the end of the game, the Navy was driving hard and the situation did not look too favorable for the Army team.

Sincerely,
W. W. Wilson

Allen Feldmeier joins his teammates in expressing their feelings about Army. Navy players are (l. to r.) Robert Froude, Eugene Flathmann, Vito Vitucci, Feldmeier, Bill Chewning, and Richard Foster.

Lt. Col. Allen Feldmeier, U.S.M.C. (Ret.) was a hard-running guard on the Navy teams of 1939, 1940, and 1941. He remembers those years when he and his teammates romped to three victories in a row over Army. Colonel Feldmeier fondly recalls an anecdote about coaches Swede Larson and Rip Miller.

Letter from Allen Feldmeier

Probably the most interesting facet of Naval Academy football in 1939-40 and '41 was the personalities of the Head Coach E. E. "Swede" Larson and the line coach Rip Miller. These two, as you probably know, were (and Rip still is) scarcely ever at a lack of words—both of them glib of tongue and humorous too. I saw the two of them one day in the Philadelphia hotel the evening before the game and they had some congressman backed into a corner and it was something to see!

Yours truly
A. *Feldmeier*
Lt. Col. (Ret.)

Oscar Hagberg was on the great 1928 Navy eleven. When he returned to Annapolis as coach in 1944 he faced the most difficult job in college football—that of meeting the most powerful team in Army history. Undefeated Army, with Glenn Davis, Doc Blanchard & company, were beating every opponent they met. Discussing that amazing era of Army-Navy football, Coach Hagberg reminisces.

Letter from Oscar Hagberg

In that era (if such a short period could be called an era) experimentation was the order of the day. Army had gone to the "T" formation the year before, and remnants of teams around the country were doing the same. Hard-nosed Navy single-wing football was going out of style simply because defenses were complicating this offense too much. In 1944 we decided to concentrate on a so-called weak side attack, with All America Bobby Jenkins at the tail-back position to keep the defenses honest. We saw no radical defenses during the progress of the season, and our estimates were that Colonel Blaik at Army was generally too conservative to stack the defense against us. In Baltimore, as a climax to our season, we saw Army come out with one of the most radically undershifted defenses to meet our weak-side attack we could hardly believe it possible. We lost Jenkins early in the game and Army went on to a well-deserved victory.

For the 1945 season Navy abandoned the single-wing and adopted the "T" formation. We anticipated troubles, as we had reared a particular brand of offensive linemen and the blocking would be foreign to them. We paid the penalty for relative inexperience in this form of attack, while Army, of course was improving on their performance with it, and Davis and Blanchard were having a banner year. Nevertheless we were the one team to push the great Army line around in the last quarter of the season 1945. We were the first college team to ever "blitz," that is, have the linebackers rush the passer in the 1945 Army game.

The odds on winning two Army-Navy football games in succession are big enough, but Navy had won 5 in a row up to 1944, a really remarkable feat. The Army teams of '44 and '45 were principally known for the Davis-Blanchard combination, but these teams had exceptional lines as well. Meanwhile the Navy line sparkled with players like Dick Scott and Don Whitmire, Deramee and Chase. Our "T" offense never really jelled, but we too had some fine backs in Jenkins, Ben Martin, Clyde Scott, Billy Barron, and Bartos.

Some short observations on Navy football prior to 1945:

(1) In my opinion, one of the greatest of Navy teams with which I was associated was that of 1934. They were not very big as football teams go, and not a rough and ready outfit in general. But they were smart—as heady a bunch of football students as I have seen. They had the great Buster Borries (the best I have seen in Navy uniform) and the punting artist Bill Clark; in the line were Slade Cutter, Lou Robertshaw, Dusty Dornin and Dick Lambert. Pittsburgh proved that they could be beaten convincingly, but nobody else could.

(2) The best of the graduate coaches at Navy was Tom Hamilton, a real innovator and student of the game. Tom coached the 1934-35-36 Navy teams and logged two wins out of three.

(3) I don't think anyone can fully understand the tension, the anticipation, and the utter determination of players and coaches faced with an Army-Navy game, unless they have been one. That spine-tingling hour when the two student bodies march on the field before the game is as much a part of it as the game itself. Nowhere do players react so much to the tenor of the student body.

Sincerely,
Capt. Oscar E. Hagberg, USN

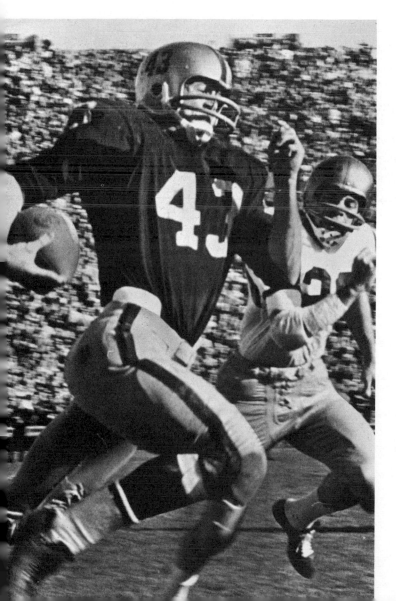

Army's Sonny Stowers is chased by Navy's Duncan Ingraham as he heads for a touchdown in 1965. It all ended in a 7-7 tie.

Leon Bramlett captained the Navy team in 1946 when time literally ran out for the Middies. Elsewhere he has given his account of that memorable day. Here he adds a few comments about old football friendships.

Letter from Leon Bramlett

I saw Tom Hamilton in New York at the Hall of Fame banquet. He and I had a great time together recalling old times. Also saw Rip Miller, Don Whitmire, Dick Duden, Ben Martin, Doc Blanchard, Glen Davis, Doug Kenna, Arnold Tucker and quite a few others. We had quite a get-together and spent much time talking over the Army-Navy games of the early forties.

Everyone agreed, including the Army people, that Army was "saved by the bell" in 1946.

Tom Hamilton has told me many times and he repeated it when we were together last week that the 1946 Navy squad had the finest team spirit and determination to overcome the staggering odds of any team he had ever coached. In his words and he told us this after the game—I can still remember it—"You are the greatest bunch of guys I have ever known. You took it on the chin week after week and you kept coming back for more. You were down but never out and you never let your flag down. The Navy will always remember what you did today. . . ."

Of course to me what I remember and cherish most from these Army-Navy games was the company and companionship of some great men—opponents and teammates alike. As with most old football players, those joining together in these great struggles enjoy the firm and solid bonds of friendship and mutual respect that the years never seem to dim.

Sincerely yours,
Leon Bramlett

The 1966 season at West Point provided sportswriters with the most unusual sports story of the year in Tom Cahill, who rose from the ranks as a plebe coach to head football coach and then in tribute to his magnificent season was named "Football Coach of the Year" for 1966. Here are his comments about the job and about Army-Navy rivalry.

Letter from Tom Cahill

The opportunity to assume the position of Head Coach of Football at the U. S. Military Academy is, of course, a great thrill for me. The circumstances surrounding my appointment are too well known to include in this, but basically it was being available at the proper time. Of the many awards that I have received as a result of our '66 season I must confess that probably the greatest accolade for me was the action on the part of our squad in requesting that I be their coach. In my opinion, working with the cadet football team as head coach and associating myself with the Corps of Cadets is the ultimate in the coaching profession. Those problems which exist for us on the coaching staff here at the Military Academy represent a challenge which we face with enthusiasm. The term challenge is often included in numerous conversations, but to face one and to see the collective effort of our squad and coaches overcome obstacles is a reward, in itself, for the long hours and hard work which we were called upon to expend.

It is our hope that the '66 season and its outcome will provide a lasting memory for our football squad. My own personal reflection on the season is one of deep gratitude to the squad, the Corps of Cadets, and all those with whom we associated. It is our sincere hope that we may continue to produce teams which reflect great credit upon the U. S. Military Academy.

The Army-Navy game in particular climaxed a season, which I suspect was a surprise to me. The experience of coaching the cadets against the Naval Academy was one that would be difficult to surpass. As is normally the case, past records mean very little in this contest, and regardless of the ultimate winner, it is my strong feeling that both institutions can be and should be extremely proud of the teams that represent them. In this one the normal problems of one school are identified with those of the other. As a consequence, it generally means that the intangibles necessary to the preparation of the squad must be emphasized. By intangibles, of course, I have reference to the mental preparation to include willingness to pay the price, dedication, and desire to be the winner. These attributes become all the more important, not only because of the game, but as a part of the continued drilling of these young players toward their ultimate goal as officers in the service of their country.

It seems to me that upon the completion of each of the Army-Navy games over the past, the feeling of accomplishment as enjoyed by the winner may be only equalled by the determination on the part of the loser to make amends. Tradition has shown that each game in itself is different than all others, because it is presently the one that counts. No question in my mind that the annual Army-Navy classic has to rank as the outstanding football game of each football season.

Sincerely,
Thomas B. Cahill
Head Football Coach

As a youngster playing high school football, Bill Elias dreamed that one day he would coach football at Navy. That dream came true in 1964 when he was appointed varsity football coach at Annapolis. His enthusiasm for Army-Navy football is revealed in his words here.

Letter from Bill Elias

There is no experience in football, and few in life, that can quite match it! That's the only way I can describe the Army-Navy football game.

People talk of Texas-Oklahoma, Michigan State-Notre Dame, California-Stanford, Harvard-Yale, as significant rivalries. The Army-Navy game dwarfs them all.

Lt. Comdr. Thomas J. Wadsworth looks out over the stadium as the Midshipmen take the field in pre-game ceremonies.

It's the one autumn afternoon when everyone takes a side.

The gas station attendant in Scranton, who helped to liberate Paris two decades ago, feels his old Army ties stir anew. The Kansas City attorney, a former PT boat commander in the Pacific, has the entire household behind "his" Navy team.

The rawest recruit at Fort Dix, New Jersey, and the newest seaman at Great Lakes, Illinois, are as ardent antagonists as the highest ranking Generals and Admirals at the Pentagon.

The impact of the game, as one must imagine, extends far beyond the geographical limits of the continental United States. There are 100,000 in the stands at Philadelphia, millions watching on television, and millions more rooting next to radio sets in all corners of the world. Many fans get up in the middle of the night to hear the action from a field thousands of miles away.

"Beat Navy" banners wave from North Barracks near the Plain at West Point and a headquarters hut near the 38th parallel in Korea. "Beat Army" artwork adorns the facade of Bancroft Hall and the hull of a nuclear submarine in the North Atlantic.

Inside Kennedy Stadium and on the field of play, the atmosphere is electric. Before the kickoff, the coaches and players are literally numb with excitement and anticipation. As the game unfolds, the numbness gradually disappears but it will return later, in the locker room, when the decision has been rendered and victory or defeat played their respective roles.

One hundred and twenty minutes of Army-Navy football, my entire experience in this service classic, flashes past as quickly as a second. I have spent most of my life in football. An Army-Navy game far outdistances any thrill I may have had as a player or a coach.

Thank you for soliciting my reactions on this greatest of all football games.

Sincerely,
Bill Elias
Head Football Coach

APPENDIX AND INDEX

Appendix

Army's All-Americans
(First-team Selections Only)

Year	Name and Position	Year	Name and Position	Year	Name and Position
1898	Charles Romeyn (B)	1928	Chris Cagle (HB)		Albert Nemetz (T)
1900	Walter Smith (E)	1929	Chris Cagle (HB)	1946	Doc Blanchard (FB)
1901	Paul Bunker (T)	1930	Jack Price (T)		Glenn Davis (HB)
	Charles Daly (QB)	1931	Jack Price (T)		Henry Foldberg (E)
1902	Paul Bunker (HB)	1932	Milt Summerfelt (G)		Arnold Tucker (QB)
	Robert Boyers (C)	1933	Jack Buckler (B)	1947	Joe Steffy (G)
1904	Arthur Tipton (C)	1935	Bill Shuler (E)	1948	Joe Henry (G)
	Henry Torney (B)	1939	Harry Stella (T)		Bobby Stuart (HB)
1905	Henry Torney (B)	1942	Robin Olds (T)	1949	Arnold Galiffa (QB)
1907	William Erwin (G)		Frank Merritt (T)	1950	Dan Foldberg (E)
1911	Leland Devore (T)	1943	Casimir Myslinski (C)		Elmer Stout (C)
1913	Louis Merillat (E)		Frank Merritt (T)		Charles Shira (T)
1914	John McEwan (C)	1944	Doc Blanchard (FB)		J. D. Kimmel (T)
1916	Elmer Oliphant (HB)		Glenn Davis (HB)	1954	Don Holleder (E)
1917	Elmer Oliphant (HB)		Joe Stanowicz (G)		Tom Bell (HB)
1922	Edgar Garbisch (C)		John Green (G)		Ralph Chesnauskas (G)
1924	Edgar Garbisch (C)		Doug Kenna (QB)	1957	Bob Anderson (HB)
	Gus Farwick (G)		Barney Poole (E)	1958	Bob Anderson (HB)
1925	Charles Born (E)	1945	Glenn Davis (HB)		Pete Dawkins (HB)
1926	Bud Sprague (T)		Dewitt Coulter (T)		Bob Novogratz (G)
	Harry Wilson (HB)		Doc Blanchard (FB)	1959	Bill Carpenter (E)
1927	Bud Sprague (T)		John Green (G)		
	Chris Cagle (HB)		Henry Foldberg (E)		

Navy's All-Americans
(First-team Selections Only)

Year	Name and Position	Year	Name and Position	Year	Name and Position
1907	Bill Dague (E)	1926	Tom Hamilton (HB)		Dick Scott (C)
1908	Ed Lange (QB)		Frank Wickhorst (T)	1947	Dick Scott (C)
	Percy Northcroft (T)	1928	Eddie Burke (G)	1952	Steve Eisenhauer (G)
1911	Jack Dalton (FB)	1934	Buzz Borries (HB)	1953	Steve Eisenhauer (G)
1913	John (Babe) Brown (T)		Slade Cutter (T)	1954	Ronnie Beagle (E)
1917	Ernest Von Heimberg (E)	1943	George Brown (G)	1955	Ronnie Beagle (E)
1918	Lyman (Pop) Perry (G)		Don Whitmire (T)	1957	Bob Reifsnyder (T)
	Wolcott Roberts (HB)	1944	Ben Chase (G)		Tom Forrestal (QB)
1922	Wendell Taylor (E)		Bobby Jenkins (HB)	1960	Joe Bellino (HB)
	Frank Wickhorst (T)		Don Whitmire (T)	1961	Greg Mather (E)
		1945	Dick Duden (E)	1963	Roger Staubach (QB)

The Games: Statistics

THE 1ST GAME

November 29, 1890 — West Point, New York

Lineup:

		Navy		Army
	Beuret	LE		Moore
	Ward	LT		Crabbs
	Lane	LG		Murphy
	Irwin	C		Adams
	Trench	RG		Heavey
	Macklin	RT		Schoeffel
	Laws	RE		Prince
	Johnson	QB		Walker
	Hartung	LH		Timberlake
	Emrich (Capt.)	RH	(Capt.)	Michie
	Althouse	FB		Ames

Summary: Score by halves:

Navy   12   12 — 24
Army   0   0 — 0

Coaches: Navy   none
Army   D. M. Michie

THE 2ND GAME

November 29, 1891 — Annapolis, Maryland

Lineup:

		Army		Navy
	Moore	LE		Symington
	Houle	LT		Beuret
	Gleason	LG		Pearson
	Adams	C		Holsinger
	Clark	RG		Trench
	Smith	RT	(Capt.)	Macklin
	Prince	RE		Ferguson
	Walker	QB		Bagley
	Davison	HB		Hasbrouck
	Timberlake	HB		Johnson
	Michie (Capt.)	FB		Webster

Summary: Score by halves:

Army   18   14 — 32
Navy   6   10 — 16

Coaches: Army   Dr. H. H. Williams
Navy   Edgar A. Poe

THE 3RD GAME

November 26, 1892 — West Point, New York

Lineup:

		Navy		Army
	McCauley	LE		B. Ames
	Lang	LT		Houle
	Wells	LG		Laws
	Kavanaugh	C		T. Ames
	Trench (Capt.)	RG	(Capt.)	Clark
	Reeves	RT		Smith
	McCormack	RE		Stacy
	Bookwalter	QB		Stout
	Izard	LH		Timberlake
	Johnson	RH		King
	Bagley	FB		Pattison

Summary: Score by halves:

Navy   0   12 — 12
Army   0   4 — 4

Coaches: Navy   Ben Crosby
Army   D. M. Michie

THE 4TH GAME

November 27, 1893 — Annapolis, Maryland

Lineup:

		Navy		Army
	McCauley	LE		Nolan
	Moody	LT		Lott
	Morris	LG		Battle
	Kavanaugh (Capt.)	C		T. Ames
	Karns	RG		F. Smith
	Reeves	RT		Aultman
	Dennett	RE		Harbeson
	Bookwalter	QB		Creden
	Davidson	LH		Shelton
	Kimball	RH		Stacy
	Bagley	FB	(Capt.)	Carson

Summary: Score by halves:

Navy   0   6 — 6
Army   0   4 — 4

Coaches: Navy   Josh Hartwell
Army   L. T. Bliss

1894-1898 — Army-Navy football competition prohibited by presidential cabinet action for these five years.

THE 5TH GAME

December 2, 1899 — Philadelphia, Pa.

Lineup:	*Army*		*Navy*
	Smith (Capt.)	LE	Long
	Farnsworth	LT	(Capt.) Wortman
	Hopkins	LG	Halligan
	Bettison	C	Adams
	Burnett	RG	Belknap
	Bunker	RT	Nichols
	Boyers	RE	Berrian
	Wesson	QB	Osterhaus
	Casad	HB	Fowler
	Clark	HB	Gannon
	Jackson	FB	Wade

Summary: Score by halves:

Army	5	12 —	17
Navy	0	5 —	5

Coaches:	Army	H. J. Koehler
	Navy	Bill Armstrong

THE 6TH GAME

December 1, 1900 — Philadelphia, Pa.

Lineup:	*Navy*		*Army*
	Read	LE	(Capt.) Smith
	Adams	LT	Farnsworth
	Fremont	LG	Boyer
	Whitlock	C	Bettison
	Belknap	RG	Goodspeed
	Williams	RT	Bunker
	Nichols	RE	Burnett
	Long	QB	Lahm
	Fowler (Capt.)	HB	Casad
	Land	HB	Clark
	C. E. Smith	FB	Phillips

Summary: Score by halves:

Navy	0	11 —	11
Army	5	2 —	7

Coaches:	Navy	Garrett Cochran
	Army	H. J. Koehler

THE 7TH GAME

November 30, 1901 — Philadelphia, Pa.

Lineup:	*Army*		*Navy*
	Farnsworth	LE	Whiting
	Doe	LT	Read
	Riley	LG	Carpenter
	Boyers	C	Fretz
	Goodspeed	RG	Belknap
	Bunker	RT	Adams
	McAndrews	RE	Soule
	Daly	QB	McNair
	Casad (Capt.)	LH	Freyer
	Hacket	RH	Land
	Graves	FB	(Capt.) Nichols

Summary: Score by halves:

Army	5	6 —	11
Navy	5	0 —	5

Coaches:	Army	L. B. Kromer
	Navy	Doc Hillebrand

THE 8TH GAME

November 29, 1902 — Philadelphia, Pa.

Lineup:	*Army*		*Navy*
	Farnsworth	LE	Whiting
	Hammond	LT	Rogers
	Riley	LG	Grady
	Boyers (Capt.)	C	Fretz
	Thompson	RG	(Capt.) Belknap
	Graves	RT	Farley
	McAndrews	RE	Soule
	Daly	QB	Smith
	Hackett	LH	Root
	Bunker	RH	Strassburger
	Torney	FB	Halsey

Summary: Score by halves:

Army	10	12 —	22
Navy	8	0 —	8

Coaches:	Army	D. E. Nolan
	Navy	Doc Hillebrand

THE 9TH GAME

November 29, 1903 — Philadelphia, Pa.

Lineup:	*Army*		*Navy*
	Hammond	LE	Howard
	Doe	LT	Grady
	Riley	LG	Chambers
	Tipton	C	Rees
	Thompson	RG	Oak
	Graves	RT	Doherty
	Rockwell	RE	(Capt.) Soule
	Hackett	QB	Strassburger
	Prince	LH	Root
	Farnsworth (Capt.)	RH	Becker
	Davis	FB	Halsey

Summary: Score by halves:

Army	12	28 —	40
Navy	5	0 —	5

Coaches:	Army	E. L. King
	Navy	Burr Chamberlain

THE 10TH GAME

November 26, 1904 — Philadelphia, Pa.

Lineup:

		Army		*Navy*
Hammond	LE			Howard
Doe (Capt.)	LT		(Capt.) Farley
Erwin	LG			Goss
Tipton	c			McClintic
Seagrave	RG			Piersol
Mettler	RT			Grady
Gillespie	RE			Whitney
Garey	QB			Norton
Prince	HB			Spenser
Hill	HB			Doherty
Torney	FB			Smith

Summary: Score by halves:

Army	11	0 —	11
Navy	0	0 —	0

Coaches: Army   R. E. Boyers
         Navy   Paul Dashiell

THE 11TH GAME

December 2, 1905 — Princeton, New Jersey

Lineup:

		Army	*Navy*
Rockwell	LE	(Capt.)	Howard
Erwin	LT		Piersol
Weeks	LG		O'Brien
Abraham	c		Causey
Christy	RG		Shafroth
Mettler	RT		Grady
Gillespie (Capt.)	RE		Woodworth
Johnson	QB		Decker
Smith	HB		Spencer
Hill	HB		Doherty
Torney	FB		Ghormley

Summary: Score by halves:

Army	6	0 —	6
Navy	0	6 —	6

Coaches: Army   R. E. Boyers
         Navy   Paul Dashiell

THE 12TH GAME

December 1, 1906 — Philadelphia, Pa.

Lineup:

		Navy	*Army*
Bernard	LE		Hickam
Piersol	LT		Weeks
Meyer	LG		Erwin
Slingluff	c		Sultan
Wright	RG		Christy
Northcroft	RT		Fowler
Dague	RE		Stearnes

Norton	QB		Johnson
Spencer (Capt.)	LH		(Capt.) Hill
Douglas	RH		Beavers
Ingram	FB		Smith

Summary: Score by halves:

Navy	0	10 —	10
Army	0	0 —	0

Coaches: Navy   Paul Dashiell
         Army   H. C. Smithers & E. Graves

THE 13TH GAME

November 29, 1907 — Philadelphia, Pa.

Lineup:

		Navy	*Army*
DeMott	LE		Besson
Northcroft	LT		Weeks
Myer	LG		Erwin
Slingluff	c		Philoon
Wright	RG		Moss
Leighton	RT		Pullen
Dague	RE		Stearns
Lange	QB		Mountford
Douglas (Capt.)	HB		Surles
Reifsnyder	HB		(Capt.) Smith
Jones	FB		Beavers

Summary: Score by halves:

Navy	6	0 —	6
Army	0	0 —	0

Coaches: Navy   Joe Reeves
         Army   H. C. Smithers

THE 14TH GAME

November 28, 1908 — Philadelphia, Pa.

Lineup:

		Army	*Navy*
Johnson	LE		Reifsnider
Byrne	LT		Leighton
Wier	LG		Wright
Philoon (Capt.)	c		Slingluff
Moss	RG		Meyer
Pullen	RT		(Capt.) Northcroft
Stearns	RE		Jones
Hyatt	QB		Lange
Dean	LH		Dalton
Greble	RH		Clay
Chamberlin	FB		Richardson

Summary: Score by halves:

Army	6	0 —	6
Navy	4	0 —	4

Coaches: Army   H. M. Nelly
         Navy   Frank Berrien

1909 — Game cancelled because of death of Army tackle, Eugene Byrne.

THE 15TH GAME

November 26, 1910 — Philadelphia, Pa.

Lineup:	Navy		Army
	Hamilton	LE	Wood
	Merritt	LT	Devore
	Wright	LG	Huston
	Weems	C	Arnold
	Brown	RG	(Capt.) Wier
	Loftin	RT	Littlejohn
	Gilchrist	RE	Gillespie
	Sowell	QB	Hyatt
	Clay	LH	Dean
	Dalton	RH	Browne
	Rhodes	FB	Surles
	King (Capt.) was ill.		

Summary: Score by halves:

Navy	0	3	— 3
Army	0	0	— 0

Coaches: Navy   Frank Berrien
         Army   H. M. Nelly

THE 16TH GAME

November 25, 1911 — Philadelphia, Pa.

Lineup:	Navy		Army
	Hamilton	LE	Wood
	Ralston	LT	Devore
	Wakeman	LG	Arnold
	Weems	C	Sibert
	Howe	RG	Walmsley
	Brown	RT	Littlejohn
	McReavy	RE	Cook
	Gilchrist	QB	(Capt.) Hyatt
	Nichols	HB	Browne
	Dalton (Capt.)	HB	MacDonald
	Rhodes	FB	Keyes

Summary: Score by quarters:

Navy	0	3	0	0	— 3
Army	0	0	0	0	— 0

Coaches: Navy   Doug Howard
         Army   J. W. Beacham

THE 17TH GAME

November 30, 1912 — Philadelphia, Pa.

Lineup:	Navy		Army
	Ingram	LE	Merillat
	Hall	LT	Wynne
	Howe	LG	Weyand
	Perry	C	Purnell
	Brown	RG	Huston
	Ralston	RT	(Capt.) Devore
	Gilchrist	RE	Markoe

Rhodes (Capt.)	QB	Prichard
Leonard	HB	Benedict
McReavy	HB	Hobbs
Harrison	FB	Keyes

Summary: Score by quarters:

Navy	0	0	0	6	— 6
Army	0	0	0	0	— 0

Coaches: Navy   Doug Howard
         Army   E. Graves

THE 18TH GAME

November 29, 1913 — New York (Polo Grounds), New York

Lineup:	Army		Navy
	Markoe	LE	Ingram
	Wynne	LT	Ralston
	Huston	LG	Howe
	McEwan	C	Perry
	Jones	RG	Brown
	Weyand	RT	Vaughan
	Merillat	RE	(Capt.) Gilchrist
	Prichard	QB	Nicholls
	Hoge (Capt.)	HB	McReavy
	Jouett	HB	Leonard
	Benedict	FB	Harrison

Summary: Score by quarters:

Army	0	9	7	6	— 22
Navy	3	3	3	0	— 9

Coaches: Army   C. D. Daly
         Navy   Doug Howard

THE 19TH GAME

November 28, 1914 — Philadelphia, Pa.

Lineup:	Army		Navy
	Neyland	LE	(Capt.) Overesch
	Butler	LT	McCroach
	Meacham	LG	Mills
	McEwan	C	Perry
	O'Hare	RG	R. Jones
	Weyand	RT	De Roode
	Merillat	RE	T. Harrison
	Prichard (Capt.)	QB	Mitchell
	Hodgson	LH	Blodgett
	Van Fleet	RH	Failing
	Coffin	FB	Bates

Summary: Score by quarters:

Army	2	12	0	6	— 20
Navy	0	0	0	0	— 0

Coaches: Army   C. D. Daly
         Navy   Doug Howard

THE 20TH GAME

November 27, 1915 — New York (Polo Grounds), New York

Lineup:

Army		Navy
Redfield	LE	Heimburg
Jones	LT	Ward
O'Hare	LG	Kercher
McEwan	C	Goodstein
Meacham	RG	Smith
Weyand (Capt.)	RT	Gilman
Neyland	RE	Johnson
Gerhardt	QB	Craig
Ford	LH	Davis
Oliphant	RH	Orr
Coffin	FB	Martin
		Sub. (Capt.) Miles

Summary: Score by quarters:

Army	7	0	7	0 —	14
Navy	0	0	0	0 —	0

Coaches: Army   C. D. Daly
          Navy   Jonas Ingram

THE 21ST GAME

November 25, 1916 — New York (Polo Grounds), New York

Lineup:

Army		Navy
House	LE	Jackson
Jones	LT	Clark
Knight	LG	Gilman
McEwan (Capt.)	C	Goodstein
Meacham	RG	Reifel
Butler	RT	(Capt.) Ward
Shrader	RE	Fisher
Gerhardt	QB	Whelchel
Place	LH	Perry
Oliphant	RH	Ingram
Vidal	FB	Roberts

Summary: Score by quarters:

Army	9	6	0	0 —	15
Navy	0	0	7	0 —	7

Coaches: Army   C. D. Daly
          Navy   Jonas Ingram

1917-1918 — War time: series suspended two years

THE 22ND GAME

November 29, 1919 — New York (Polo Grounds), New York

Lineup:

Navy		Army
Woodruff	LE	Kieffer
Murray	LT	Travis
Denfield	LG	Vogel
Larson	C	Greene
Moore	RG	Breidster
King	RT	Daniel
Ewen (Capt.)	RE	Blaik
Koehler	QB	Wilhide
Cruise	LH	Schabacker
Benoist	RH	Lystad
Clark	FB	McQuarrie
		Sub. (Capt.) George

Summary: Score by quarters:

Navy	0	3	0	3 —	6
Army	0	0	0	0 —	0

Coaches: Navy   Gil Dobie
          Army   C. D. Daly

THE 23RD GAME

November 27, 1920 — New York (Polo Grounds), New York

Lineup:

Navy		Army
Parr	LE	Storck
Bolles	LT	Mulligan
Wilkie	LG	Clark
Larson	C	Greene
Moore	RG	Breidster
King	RT	Davidson
Ewen (Capt.)	RE	White
Conroy	QB	(Capt.) Wilhide
Koehler	LB	Smythe
Hamilton	RB	Lawrence
McKee	FB	French

Summary: Score by quarters:

Navy	0	0	0	7 —	7
Army	0	0	0	0 —	0

Coaches: Navy   Bob Folwell
          Army   C. D. Daly

THE 24TH GAME

November 26, 1921 — New York (Polo Grounds), New York

Lineup:

Navy		Army
Parr	LE	D. Storck
Wiedorn	LT	Mulligan
Carney	LG	Breidster
Larson (Capt.)	C	(Capt.) Green
Frawley	RG	Garbisch
King	RT	Davidson
Taylor	RE	Meyers
Conroy	QB	Lawrence
Barchet	LB	Wood
Koehler	RB	French
Cruise	FB	Smythe

Summary: Score by quarters:

Navy	0	7	0	0 —	7
Army	0	0	0	0 —	0

Coaches: Navy   Bob Folwell
          Army   C. D. Daly

414

THE 25TH GAME

November 25, 1922 — Philadelphia, Pa.

Lineup:

Army		Navy
D. Storck	LE	Parr
Mulligan	LT	Bolles
Breidster (Capt.)	LG	Carney
Garbisch	C	Mathews
Farwick	RG	Winkjer
Goodman	RT	Clyde
White	RE	Taylor
Smythe	QB	(Capt.) Conroy
Timberlake	LB	Cullen
Dodd	RB	McKee
Wood	FB	Barchet

Summary: Score by quarters:

Army	0	3	7	7 —	17
Navy	0	7	0	7 —	14

Coaches: Army   C. D. Daly
Navy   Bob Folwell

THE 26TH GAME

November 24, 1923 — New York (Polo Grounds),
New York

Lineup:

Army		Navy
Baxter	LE	Taylor
Goodman	LT	Clyde
Farwick	LG	(Capt.) Carney
Garbisch	C	Mathews
Ellinger	RG	Swensky
Henney	RT	Shewell
Doyle	RE	Brown
Smythe	QB	McKee
Hewitt	LB	Devens
Gillmore	RB	Cullen
Wood	FB	Shapley
Mulligan (Capt.) Sub.		

Summary: Score by quarters:

Army	0	0	0	0 —	0
Navy	0	0	0	0 —	0

Coaches: Army   J. J. McEwan
Navy   Bob Folwell

THE 27TH GAME

November 29, 1924 — Baltimore, Maryland

Lineup:

Army		Navy
Fraser	LE	(Capt.) Taylor
Griffith	LT	Wickhorst
Farwick	LG	Lentz
Garbisch (Capt.)	C	Osborn
Ellinger	RG	Chillingsworth
Saunders	RT	Stolz
Davidson	RE	Caldwell
Harding	QB	Shapley
Wilson	LH	Flippin
Gillmore	RH	Hamilton
Wood	FB	Wellings

Summary: Score by quarters:

Army	0	3	6	3 —	12
Navy	0	0	0	0 —	0

Coaches: Army   J. J. McEwan
Navy   Bob Folwell

THE 28TH GAME

November 28, 1925 — New York (Polo Grounds),
New York

Lineup:

Army		Navy
Baxter (Capt.)	LE	Hardwick
Sprague	LT	Wickhorst
Schmidt	LG	(Capt.) Lentz
Daly	C	Hutchins
Seeman	RG	Edwards
Saunders	RT	Eddy
Born	RE	Bernet
Harding	QB	Hamilton
Trapnell	LH	Caldwell
Wilson	RH	Flippin
Hewitt	FB	Shapley

Summary: Score by quarters:

Army	0	7	0	3 —	10
Navy	0	3	0	0 —	3

Coaches: Army   J. J. McEwan
Navy   Jack Owsley

THE 29TH GAME

November 27, 1926 — Chicago (Soldier Field),
Illinois

Lineup:

Army		Navy
Sprague	LE	Lloyd
Davidson	LT	(Capt.) Wickhorst
Schmidt	LG	Cross
Daly	C	Hoerner
Seeman	RG	A. Born
Saunders	RT	Eddy
Brentnall	RE	Hardwick
Meehan	QB	Hannegan
Trapnell	LB	Hamilton
Gilbreth	RB	Schuber
Dahl	FB	Caldwell
Hewitt (Capt.) Sub.		

Summary: Score by quarters:

Army	0	14	7	0 —	21
Navy	7	7	0	7 —	21

Coaches: Army   L. McC. Jones
Navy   Bill Ingram

THE 30TH GAME

November 26, 1927 — New York (Polo Grounds), New York

Lineup:	*Army*		*Navy*
	Harbold	LE	Sloane
	Sprague	LT	Bagdanovitch
	Hammock	LG	Burke
	Hall	C	Hardin
	Seeman	RG	Woerner
	Perry	RT	Giese
	Born	RE	Smith
	Nave	QB (Capt.)	Hannegan
	Cagle	LB	Lloyd
	Wilson (Capt.)	RB	Clifton
	Murrell	FB	Hansford

Summary: Score by quarters:

Army	0	0	14	0	—	14
Navy	0	2	0	7	—	9

Coaches: Army   L. McC. Jones
          Navy   Bill Ingram

1928-1929 — During these two years, games not played because of quarrels over eligibility requirements.

THE 31ST GAME

December 13, 1930 — New York (Yankee Stadium), New York

Lineup:	*Army*		*Navy*
	Carlmark	LE	Steffonides
	Price	LT (Capt.)	Bowstrom
	Humber (Capt.)	LG	Underwood
	Miller	C	Tuttle
	Trice	RG	Gray
	Suarez	RT	Bryan
	Messinger	RE	Byng
	Bowman	QB	Bauer
	Kilday	LB	Gannon
	Frentzel	RB	Kirn
	Stecker	FB	Hagberg

Summary: Score by quarters:

Army	0	0	0	6	—	6
Navy	0	0	0	0	—	0

Coaches: Army   R. I. Sasse
          Navy   Bill Ingram

THE 32ND GAME

December 14, 1931 — New York (Yankee Stadium), New York

Lineup:	*Army*		*Navy*
	King	LE	Smith
	Price (Capt.)	LT	James
	Summerfelt	LG	Reedy
	Evans	C	(Capt.) Tuttle
	Trice	RG	Underwood
	Suarez	RT	Bryan
	Kopscak	RE	Elliott
	Carver	QB	Moncure
	Stecker	LH	Kirn
	Brown	RH	Tschirgi
	Kilday	FB	Hurley

Summary: Score by quarters:

Army	0	10	0	7	—	17
Navy	0	0	7	0	—	7

Coaches: Army   R. I. Sasse
          Navy   Rip Miller

THE 33RD GAME

December 3, 1932 — Philadelphia, Pa.

Lineup:	*Army*		*Navy*
	Edwards	LE	Murray
	Lincoln	LT	Brooks
	Summerfelt (Capt.)	LG (Capt.)	Reedy
	Evans	C	Harbold
	Jablonsky	RG	Burns
	Armstrong	RT	Kane
	Kopscak	RE	Miller
	MacWilliam	QB	Slack
	Fields	LH	Clark
	Brown	RH	Walkup
	Kilday	FB	Campbell

Summary: Score by quarters:

Army	0	7	0	13	—	20
Navy	0	0	0	0	—	0

Coaches: Army   R. I. Sasse
          Navy   Rip Miller

THE 34TH GAME

November 25, 1933 — Philadelphia, Pa.

Lineup:	*Army*		*Navy*
	Kopscak	LE (Capt.)	Murray
	Hutchinson	LT	Lambert
	Jablonsky (Capt.)	LG	Zabriskie
	Bucknam	C	Harbold
	Gooch	RG	Johnson
	Beall	RT	Cutter
	Burlingame	RE	Fulp
	Johnson	QB	Becht
	Buckler	LH	Rankin
	Sebastian	RH	Walkup
	Stancook	FB	W. Clark

Summary: Score by quarters:

Army	6	6	0	0	—	12
Navy	7	0	0	0	—	7

Coaches: Army   G. H. Davidson
          Navy   Rip Miller

THE 35TH GAME

December 1, 1934 — Philadelphia, Pa.

Lineup:

Navy		Army
Dornin	LE	Shuler
Lambert	LT	Miller
Burns (Capt.)	LG	Brearley
Robertshaw	C	Clifford
Morrell	RG	Stillman
Cutter	RT	Beall
Mandelkorn	RE	Edwards
Borries	QB	Grohs
Pratt	LB	Buckler
King	RB	Grove
Clark	FB	(Capt.)Stancook

Summary: Score by quarters:

Navy	3	0	0	0 — 3
Army	0	0	0	0 — 0

Coaches: Navy   Tom Hamilton
Army   G. H. Davidson

THE 36TH GAME

November 30, 1935 — Philadelphia, Pa.

Lineup:

Army		Navy
Shuler (Capt.)	LE	Fike
Eriksen	LT	Ferrara
Smith	LG	Zabriskie
Clifford	C (Capt.)	Robertshaw
Necrason	RG	Morrell
Wolf	RT	M. Miller
Stromborg	RE	Soucek
Grohs	QB	Pratt
Meyer	LB	King
Grove	RB	Schmidt
True	FB	Case

Summary: Score by quarters:

Army	21	7	0	0 — 28
Navy	0	0	0	6 — 6

Coaches: Army   G. H. Davidson
Navy   Tom Hamilton

THE 37TH GAME

November 27, 1936 — Philadelphia, Pa.

Lineup:

Navy		Army
Soucek	LE	Preston
Ferrara	LT	Eriksen
Dubois	LG	Smith
Miller	C	Hartline
Morrell (Capt.)	RG	Ohman
Hysong	RT	Isbell
Fike	RE (Capt.)	Stromberg
Case	QB	Ryan
Ingram	LB	Craig
Antrim	RB	Sullivan
Schmidt	FB	Schwenk

Summary: Score by quarters:

Navy	0	0	0	7 — 7
Army	0	0	0	0 — 0

Coaches: Navy   Tom Hamilton
Army   G. H. Davidson

THE 38TH GAME

November 27, 1937 — Philadelphia, Pa.

Lineup:

Army		Navy
Rogner	LE	Powell
Stella	LT	Lynch
Little	LG	Player
Hartline	C	Wallace
Skoer	RG (Capt.)	Dubois
Isbell (Capt.)	RT	Hysong
Sullivan	RE	Fike
Schwenk	QB	Franks
Wilson	LH	Cooke
Long	RH	Antrim
Ryan	FB	Wood

Summary: Score by quarters:

Army	6	0	0	0 — 6
Navy	0	0	0	0 — 0

Coaches: Army   G. H. Davidson
Navy   Hank Hardwick

THE 39TH GAME

November 26, 1938 — Philadelphia, Pa.

Lineup:

Army		Navy
Dobson	LE	(Capt.) Powell
Stella	LT	Bergner
Miller	LG	McGrath
Gillis	C	Wallace
Davis	RG	Spector
Mather	RT	Hysong
Samuel	RE	Boughman
Sullivan	QB	Gillette
Wilson	LH	Cooke
Long	RH	Hansen
Frontczak	FB	Wood
Schwenk (Capt.) Sub.		

Summary: Score by quarters:

Army	7	0	7	0 — 14
Navy	0	7	0	0 — 7

Coaches: Army   W. H. Wood
Navy   Hank Hardwick

THE 40TH GAME

December 2, 1939 — Philadelphia, Pa.

Lineup:

Navy		Army
Foster	LE	Yeager
Bergner (Capt.)	LT	Michel
McGrath	LG	Murphy
Sims	C	Gillis
Wolfe	RG	Rooney
Trimble	RT	(Capt.) Stella
Montgomery	RE	Helmstetter
Gillette	QB	R. Evans
Lenz	LH	Hatch
Gutting	RH	Dubuisson
Whitehead	FB	Frontczak

Summary: Score by quarters:

Navy	3	0	0	7 —	10
Army	0	0	0	0 —	0

Coaches:

Navy	Swede Larson
Army	W. H. Wood

THE 41ST GAME

November 30, 1940 — Philadelphia, Pa.

Lineup:

Navy		Army
Foster (Capt.)	LE	Seith
Flathmann	LT	R. White
Vitucci	LG	McKinney
Harwood	C	(Capt.) Gillis
Feldmeier	RG	Weidner
Chewning	RT	Harris
Froude	RE	Fenni
Chip	QB	Jarrell
Busik	LH	Mazer
Malcolm	RH	Johnson
Werner	FB	Hatch

Summary: Score by quarters:

Navy	7	0	7	0 —	14
Army	0	0	0	0 —	0

Coaches:

Navy	Swede Larson
Army	W. H. Wood

THE 42ND GAME

November 29, 1941 — Philadelphia, Pa.

Lineup:

Navy		Army
Froude (Capt.)	LE	Farrel
Flathmann	LT	R. White
Vitucci	LG	(Capt.) Murphy
Donaldson	C	Evans
J. Hill	RG	Wilson
Chewning	RT	Whitlow
Wanggaard	RE	Seip
Harrell	QB	Roberts
Busik	LH	Mazur
Woods	RH	R. Hill
Cameron	FB	J. Hatch

Summary: Score by quarters:

Navy	0	0	14	0 —	14
Army	0	6	0	0 —	6

Coaches:

Navy	Swede Larson
Army	E. H. Blaik

THE 43RD GAME

November 28, 1942 — Annapolis, Maryland

Lineup:

Navy		Army
Channel	LE	Kelleher
Montgomery	LT	Merrit
Collins	LG	Mesereau
Fedon	C	Myslinski
Chose	RG	Wilson
Schnurr	RT	Olds
Fowler	RE	Hennessey
Barksdale	QB	Roberts
Cameron (Capt.)	LH	(Capt.) Mazur
Martin	RH	Hill
Hume	FB	Troxell

Summary: Score by quarters:

Navy	0	7	7	0 —	14
Army	0	0	0	0 —	0

Coaches:

Navy	John Whelchel
Army	E. H. Blaik

THE 44TH GAME

November 27, 1943 — West Point, New York

Lineup:

Navy		Army
Channel (Capt.)	LE	McKinnon
Whitmire	LT	Merritt
Brown	LG	Murphy
J. Martin	C	(Capt.) Myslinski
Chase	RG	McCorkle
Sprinkle	RT	Stanowicz
Johnson	RE	Hennessey
Nelson	QB	Lombardo
Jenkins	LH	Anderson
B. Martin	RH	Davis
Hume	FB	Maxon
		Sub. (Capt.) Olds

Summary: Score by quarters:

Navy	0	0	7	6 —	13
Army	0	0	0	0 —	0

Coaches:

Navy	John Whelchel
Army	E. H. Blaik

THE 45TH GAME

December 2, 1944 — Baltimore, Maryland

Lineup:

Army		Navy
Pitzer	LE	Bramlett
Arnold	LT	Whitmire
Green	LG	Carrington
St. Onge	C	J. Martin
Stanowicz	RG	(Capt.) Chase
Nemetaz	RT	Gilliam
Rafalko	RE	Hansen
Kenna	QB	Duden
Hall	LB	Jenkins
Minor	RB	Barron
Blanchard	FB	Scott
Lombardo (Capt.) Sub.		

Summary: Score by quarters:

Army	0	7	2	14	—	23
Navy	0	0	7	0	—	7

Coaches: Army   E. H. Blaik
          Navy   Oscar Hagberg

THE 46TH GAME

December 1, 1945 — Philadelphia, Pa.

Lineup:

Army		Navy
Pitzer	LE	(Capt.) Duden
Coulter	LT	Kiser
Green (Capt.)	LG	Carrington
Fuson	C	R. Scott
Gerometta	RG	Deramee
Nemetz	RT	Coppedge
Foldberg	RE	Bramlett
Tucker	QB	B. Smith
G. Davis	LB	C. Scott
Chabot	RB	Minisi
Blanchard	FB	Bartos

Summary: Score by quarters:

Army	20	0	6	6	—	32
Navy	0	7	0	6	—	13

Coaches: Army   E. H. Blaik
          Navy   Oscar Hagberg

THE 47TH GAME

November 30, 1946 — Philadelphia, Pa.

Lineup:

Army		Navy
Poole	LE	Markel
Biles	LT	N. Smith
Steffy	LG	Emerson
Enos	C	R. Scott
Gerometta	RG	Carrington
Bryant	RT	Shimshak
Foldberg	RE	(Capt.) Bramlett
Tucker	QB	Baysinger
Davis (Capt.)	LH	Williams
Rowan	RH	Schwoeffermann
Blanchard (Capt.)	FB	Gerber

Summary: Score by quarters:

Army	7	14	0	0	—	21
Navy	0	6	6	6	—	18

Coaches: Army   E. H. Blaik
          Navy   Tom Hamilton

THE 48TH GAME

November 29, 1947 — Philadelphia, Pa.

Lineup:

Army		Navy
Rawers	LE	Markel
Davis	LT	Strahley
Steffy (Capt.)	LG	Emerson
Yeoman	C	(Capt.) Scott
Henry	RG	Schwieck
Bryant	RT	Shimshak
Trent	RE	Ryan
Bullock	QB	Horne
Mackmull	LH	McCully
Stuart	RH	Schwoeffermann
Shelley	FB	Hawkins

Summary: Score by quarters:

Army	7	7	7	0	—	21
Navy	0	0	0	0	—	0

Coaches: Army   E. H. Blaik
          Navy   Tom Hamilton

THE 49TH GAME

November 27, 1948 — Philadelphia, Pa.

Lineup:

Army		Navy
Trent	LE	Frasier
Feir	LT	(Capt.) Emerson
Lunn	LG	Schwieck
Yeoman (Capt.)	C	Lawrence
Irons	RG	Hunt
Davis	RT	Beeler
Parrish	RE	Ryan
Galiffa	QB	Baysinger
Stuart	LH	(Capt.) Williams
Scott	RH	McCully
Stephenson	FB	Hawkins

Summary: Score by quarters:

Army	0	14	0	7	—	21
Navy	7	0	7	7	—	21

Coaches: Army   E. H. Blaik
          Navy   George Sauer

THE 50TH GAME

November 26, 1949 — Philadelphia, Pa.

Lineup:

	Army		*Navy*
	Loehlein	LE	Andresen
	Shira	LT	Tetreault
	Ackerson	LG	Mahoney
	Stout	C	Owens
	Galloway	RG	Ridderhof
	Kimmel	RT	Hunt
	Trent (Capt.)	RE	(Capt.) Ryan
	Vinson	QB	Zastrow
	Shultz	LH	Hauff
	Abelman	RH	Powers
	Kuckhahn	FB	Bannerman

Summary: Score by quarters:

Army	7	6	12	13 —	38
Navy	0	0	0	0 —	0

Coaches: Army   E. H. Blaik
Navy   George Sauer

THE 51ST GAME

December 2, 1950 — Philadelphia, Pa.

Lineup:

	Navy		*Army*
	Treadwell	LE	(Capt.) Foldberg
	Tetreault	LT	Zeigler
	Denfeld	LG	Elmblad
	Bryson	C	Orders
	Lowell	RG	Roberts
	Hunt	RT	Ackerson
	Bakke (Capt.)	RE	Weaver
	Zastrow	QB	Blaik
	Hauff	LH	Cain
	Powers	RH	Martin
	Bannerman	FB	Stephenson

Summary: Score by quarters:

Navy	0	14	0	0 —	14
Army	0	0	2	0 —	2

Coaches: Navy   Eddie Erdelatz
Army   E. H. Blaik

THE 52ND GAME

December 1, 1951 — Philadelphia, Pa.

Lineup:

	Navy		*Army*
	Sieber	LE	Lincoln
	Tetreault	LT	Glock
	Fischer	LG	Lunn
	Bryson	C	Kramer
	McGowan	RG	Paulekas
	Gragg	RT	Krause
	Tiede	RE	Chamberlin
	Smith	QB	Fuqua
	Vine	LH	Inman
	Brady	RH	Mischak
	Wilmer	FB	Rogers
	Hauff (Capt.)	Sub. (Capt.)	Williams

Summary: Score by quarters:

Navy	21	7	0	14 —	42
Army	0	0	7	0 —	7

Coaches: Navy   Eddie Erdelatz
Army   E. H. Blaik

THE 53RD GAME

November 29, 1952 — Philadelphia, Pa.

Lineup:

	Navy		*Army*
	Gurski (Capt.)	LE	Sisson
	Fullam	LT	Guidera
	Pertel	LG	Lunn
	Olson	C	Ordway
	Lowell	RG	Ziegler
	Leach	RT	Doremus
	Anderson	RE	Mischak
	Cameron	QB	Vann
	Fisher	LH	Attaya
	Monahan	RH	Purdue
	Franco	FB	DeLucia
		Sub (Capt.)	Paulekas

Summary: Score by quarters:

Navy	7	0	0	0 —	7
Army	0	0	0	0 —	0

Coaches: Navy   Eddie Erdelatz
Army   E. H. Blaik

THE 54TH GAME

November 28, 1953 — Philadelphia, Pa.

Lineup:

	Army		*Navy*
	Mischak	LE	Riester
	Glock	LT	Perkins
	Lunn (Capt.)	LG	Textor
	Stephen	C	(Capt.) Olson
	Chesnauskas	RG	Eisenhauer
	Farris	RT	Webster
	Sisson	RE	Fullam
	Vann	QB	Welsh
	Uebel	LH	Hepworth
	Bell	RH	Monahan
	Lodge	FB	Gatuso

Summary: Score by quarters:

Army	7	6	7	0 —	20
Navy	0	0	0	7 —	7

Coaches: Army   E. H. Blaik
Navy   Eddie Erdelatz

THE 55TH GAME
November 27, 1954 — Philadelphia, Pa.

Lineup:

Navy		Army
Beagle	LE	Johnson
Hopkins	LT	Stephenson
Benzi	LG	Goodwin
Whitmire	C	Chance
Aronis	RG	Chesnauskas
Royer	RT	Ordway
Smith	RE	Holleder
Welsh	QB	Vann
Weaver	LH	Kyasky
Craig	RH	Bell
Guest	FB	Uebel
Monahan (Capt.)	Sub.	(Capt.) Farris

Summary: Score by quarters:

Navy	7	14	6	0 —	27
Army	6	14	0	0 —	20

Coaches: Navy   Eddie Erdelatz
          Army   E. H. Blaik

THE 56TH GAME
November 26, 1955 — Philadelphia, Pa.

Lineup:

Army		Navy
Johnson	LE	Beagle
Reid	LT	(Capt.) Hopkins
Slater	LG	Dander
Szyetecz	C	Whitmire
Goodwin	RG	Hower
Stephenson	RT	McCool
Chesnauskas	RE	Owen
Holleder	QB	Welsh
Kyasky	LH	Oldham
Lash	RH	Gober
Uebel (Capt.)	FB	Guest

Summary: Score by quarters:

Army	0	0	7	7 —	14
Navy	6	0	0	0 —	6

Coaches: Army   E. H. Blaik
          Navy   Eddie Erdelatz

THE 57TH GAME
December 1, 1956 — Philadelphia, Pa.

Lineup:

Army		Navy
Johnson	LE	Jokanovich
Reid	LT	Anthony
Fadel	LG	Stremic
Kernan	C	Whitmire
Slater	RG	Hower
Goodwin	RT	Reifsnyder
Stephenson	RE	(Capt.) Smith
Bourland	QB	Forrestal
Murtland	LH	Oldham
Morales	RH	Burchett
Kyasky	FB	Dagampat
Szvetecz (Capt.)	Sub.	

Summary: Score by quarters:

Army	0	0	7	0 —	7
Navy	0	0	0	7 —	7

Coaches: Army   E. H. Blaik
          Navy   Eddie Erdelatz

THE 58TH GAME
December 1, 1957 — Philadelphia, Pa.

Lineup:

Navy		Army
Jokanovich	LE	Warner
Anthony	LT	Melnik
Stremic	LG	Novogratz
Moncilovich	C	(Capt.) Kernan
Fritzinger	RG	Slater
Reifsnyder	RT	Wilmoth
McKee	RE	Graf
Forrestal	QB	Bourland
Oldham (Capt.)	LH	Anderson
Hurst	RH	Dawkins
Wellborn	FB	Barta

Summary: Score by quarters:

Navy	7	0	0	7 —	14
Army	0	0	0	0 —	0

Coaches: Navy   Eddie Erdelatz
          Army   E. H. Blaik

THE 59TH GAME
November 30, 1958 — Philadelphia, Pa.

Lineup:

Army		Navy
Usry	LE	Albershat
Bagdonis	LT	Thomas
Novogratz	LG	Fritzinger
Rowe	C	Dunn
Lytle	RG	Chomicz
Hilliard	RT	Boyer
Carpenter	RE	Kanuch
Caldwell	QB	Tranchini
Anderson	LH	Bellino
Dawkins (Capt.)	RH	(Capt.) Dagampat
Walters	FB	Matalavage

Summary: Score by quarters:

Army	0	7	0	15 —	22
Navy	6	0	0	0 —	6

Coaches: Army   E. H. Blaik
          Navy   Eddie Erdelatz

THE 60TH GAME

November 29, 1959 — Philadelphia, Pa.

Lineup:

Navy		Army
Dattilo	LE	Usry
Boyer	LT	Kuhns
Thomas	LG	Jezior
Visted	C	Oswandel
Hewitt	RG	Vanderbush
Erchul	T	McCarthy
Hyde	RE	(Capt.) Carpenter
Tranchini	QB	Caldwell
Bellino	LH	Anderson
Brandquist	RH	Kirschenbauer
Matalavage	FB	Rushatz
Dunn (Capt.) Sub.		

Summary: Score by quarters:

Navy	13	8	8	14 —	43
Army	0	12	0	0 —	12

Coaches: Navy   Wayne Hardin
Army   D. S. Hall

THE 61ST GAME

November 26, 1960 — Philadelphia, Pa.

Lineup:

Navy		Army
Dattilo	LE	Ellerson
Driscoll	LT	Kuhns
Hoy	LG	Casp
Visted	C	Joulwan
Hewitt	RG	(Capt.) Vanderbush
Erchul	RT	McCarthy
Luper	RE	Zmuida
Spooner	QB	Blanda
Bellino	LH	Kirschenbauer
Pritchard	RH	Adams
Matalavage (Capt.)	FB	Rushatz
Sub.		(Capt.) Gibson

Summary: Score by quarters:

Navy	6	11	0	0 —	17
Army	0	0	6	6 —	12

Coaches: Navy   Wayne Hardin
Army   D. S. Hall

THE 62ND GAME

December 2, 1961 — Philadelphia, Pa.

Lineup:

Navy		Army
Gill	LE	Ellerson
Testa	LT	Kuhns
Optekar	LG	(Capt.) Casp
Hoy	C	Miller
Krekich	RG	Butzer
Fitzgerald	RT	Kempinski

Mather	RE	Zmuida
Klemick	QB	Eckert
Fink	LH	Blackgrove
Stewart	RH	Culver
Merritt	FB	Rushatz
Hewitt (Capt.) Sub.		

Summary: Score by quarters:

Navy	0	3	7	3 —	13
Army	0	0	7	0 —	7

Coaches: Navy   Wayne Hardin
Army   D. S. Hall

THE 63RD GAME

December 1, 1962 — Philadelphia, Pa.

Lineup:

Navy		Army
Campbell	LE	McMillan
Testa	LT	Hawkins
Hoy (Capt.)	LG	Schillo
Pierce	C	Grasfeder
Von Sydow	RG	Vaughan
Gersham	RT	Saran
Sjuggerud	RE	(Capt.) Ellerson
Staubach	QB	Blackgrove
Sai	LH	Waldrop
Earnest	RH	Stanley
Donnelly	FB	Paske

Summary: Score by quarters:

Navy	8	7	7	12 —	34
Army	0	6	0	8 —	14

Coaches: Navy   Wayne Hardin
Army   P. F. Dietzel

THE 64TH GAME

December 7, 1963 — Philadelphia, Pa.

Lineup:

Navy		Army
Campbell	LE	Champi
Philbin	LT	Carber
Krekich	LG	Cunningham
Lynch (Capt.)	C	Grasfeder
Marlin	RG	(Capt.) Nowak
Freeman	RT	Zadel
Sjuggerud	RE	Chescavage
Staubach	QB	Stichweh
Sai	LH	Waldrop
Orr	RH	Parcells
Donnelly	FB	Paske

Summary: Score by quarters:

Navy	0	7	7	7 —	21
Army	7	0	0	8 —	15

Coaches: Navy   Wayne Hardin
Army   P. F. Dietzel

THE 65TH GAME

November 28, 1964 — Philadelphia, Pa.

Lineup:

Army		Navy
Schwartz	E	Ryan
Zadel	T	Philbin
Stowers	G	Connolly
Clarke	C	Kenton
Berdy	G	(Capt.) Marlin
Carber	T	Freeman
Champie	E	Norton
Stichweh (Capt.)	QB	Staubach
Johnson	LH	Leiser
Noble	RH	Calvin
Parcells	FB	Wong

Summary: Score by quarters:

Army	2	6	0	3 — 11
Navy	0	8	0	0 — 8

Coaches: Army   P. F. Dietzel
          Navy   Wayne Hardin

THE 66TH GAME

November 27, 1965 — Philadelphia, Pa.

Lineup:

Navy		Army
Norton	LE	Young
Wittenberg (Capt.)	LT	Ray
Connolly	LG	Braun
Dittmann	C	Dusel
Hartnett	RG	Carber
Taylor	RT	Roberts
Hester	RE	Champi
Cartwright	QB	Cook
Roodhouse	LH	(Capt.) Stowers
Taylor	RH	Barofsky
Wong	FB	Hamilton

Summary: Score by quarters:

Navy	0	7	0	0 — 7
Army	7	0	0	0 — 7

Coaches: Navy   Bill Elias
          Army   P. F. Dietzel

THE 67TH GAME

November 26, 1966 — Philadelphia, Pa.

Lineup:

Army		Navy
Young	E	Taylor
Steele	E	Clark
Harrelson	T	Ruland
Neuman	T	Redd
Montanaro	G	Cocozza
Nerdahl	G	Speers
D. Roberts	C	Dittman
Jarvis	B	Murray
Lindell	QB	Cartwright
Peduto	B	Wong
Woessner	B	Bassi
Clarke (Capt.)	Sub.	(Capt.) Downing

Summary: Score by quarters:

Army	7	0	0	13 — 20
Navy	0	7	0	0 — 7

Coaches: Army   Tom Cahill
          Navy   Bill Elias

Index

UA
10
M36
1973

Martin, Laurence W.

Arms and strategy;
the world power
structure today

21301 -2

Arms and Strategy
**The World
Power Structure Today**

Arms and Strategy

The World Power Structure Today

Laurence Martin

David McKay Company, Inc.
New York

Contents

Acknowledgments

The information in Appendix iii appears by kind permission of the Institute for Strategic Studies, 18 Adam Street WC20.

The publishers would like to thank Mr Denis Archer and Mr John Taylor for the help they have given in the collection of illustrations.

Photographs were supplied by, or are reproduced by kind permission of the following. Aerospatiale: 121, 135; African National Congress: 226, 228; Associated Press: 33, 46, 111, 112, 152, 168, 177, 190, 191, 194, 211/1, 256, 260; BPC: 142; British Aircraft Corporation: 71, 102–3, 258/1, 268; British Hovercraft Corporation: 258/2; Bundesministerium der Verteidigung, Bonn: 58, 173; Camera Press: 144–5, 149, 155, 200; Central Office of Information: 60/1, 60/2; Flight: 86, 105; Fotolink: 10, 156–7, 166, 169; General Dynamics: 99; Hawker Siddeley Aviation: 96; Israel Press and Photo Agency, Tel Aviv: 186, 189; Janes: 63, 64, 66, 133, 257; Keystone Press: 239; Los Alamos Scientific Laboratory: 132; McDonnell Douglas: 82; Ministry of Defence (Crown Copyright): 37, 38/1, 38/2, 92, 122, 127, 182–3, 184–5, 202; NATO, Bureau Photo: 180; Novosti: 98, 99, 118, 130, 211/2; Pilkington Brothers: 75; Revolution Newspaper: 150; Serab-Do/Photothèque: 34, 40; S.I.A.S. Service Presse: 95; South African Embassy: 218–19, 222–3, 225, 230, 231, 232–3; John Taylor; 15/1, 115, 262; Tass: 44, 115, 138–9; Thornycroft & Co: 252; United Press International: 198, 207, 210; US Army: 27, 76; US Air Force: 15/2, 94, 100; US Navy: 31, 107, 110.

Preface

This book is intended as an introduction and guide to the contemporary military scene. It is not a study of strategic theory but it is impossible to present and discuss the facts without an implicit theory. Consequently I have not hesitated to decide which interpretation of particular facts is most valid, or to enter into brief discussions of theoretical questions where this is necessary to understand a situation. The book makes no claim to break new theoretical ground but I do believe it is unusually comprehensive and that the reader will emerge well equipped to observe and make his own judgment of strategic happenings.

The overall organization of the book is very simple. There are four sections. The first discusses the balance of nuclear power and the prospects for proliferation, the second surveys the instruments of armed conflicts – the weapons; the third section surveys the areas of the world where the military balance is most important or where conflict has been sharp; a fourth section deals with certain special analytical problems. Because the subject is vast a great deal of information is presented in tabular or graphic form and the text is intended to be read in close conjunction with this material. A large amount of other frequently useful but by no means readily available information will be found in the appendices.

I would like to acknowledge the great debt which all who study such matters owe to organizations like the International Institute for Strategic Studies, the Stockholm International Peace Research Institute, and the Institute for the Study of Conflict, London, for the work they do in collating and disseminating a mass of information never available to students in earlier times. On a more personal level I must thank Mr Simon Lunn who has contributed much energy and his own considerable knowledge of military affairs to helping me collect the facts and in particular to helping to interpret them to those responsible for the diagrams. Finally, I thank my secretary, Sylvia Smither, for her usual skill and her relative tolerance of a few months even more disrupted than usual.

The Nuclear Powers

The Central Nuclear Balance

The strategic nuclear balance between the two Superpowers, the United States and the Soviet Union, dominates, directly or indirectly, all other contemporary military affairs. With the nuclear arsenals they have created, these two powers could virtually destroy each other as modern industrial societies and, in doing so, inflict immense damage on the whole world environment. Avoiding such a catastrophe has become the overriding strategic and diplomatic consideration for the Superpowers. All other nations are inescapably caught up in this balance, not merely because all would suffer if the ultimate catastrophe occurred, but also because, given their global interests and influence, the Superpowers watch over and may intervene in conflicts anywhere. Thus, to one degree or another, military events all over the world are linked to the great nuclear issues at the centre of the modern international system.

The Power of Nuclear Weapons

The explosive force of a nuclear weapon is usually known as its 'yield'. Yields of nuclear weapons are measured by reference to the amount of the chemical explosive TNT required to provide an explosion of similar force. The equivalent of a thousand tons is expressed as a kiloton (KT) and of a million tons as a megaton (MT). The bombs dropped on Hiroshima and Nagasaki were so-called fission weapons designed to yield 20 KT, although the actual yield may have been somewhat less. Weapons of this yield are now regarded as a standard of comparison and are sometimes referred to as 'nominal' bombs.

Nuclear weapons derive their force from the energy released when the nuclei of certain atoms are divided or fused. Among the very heavy elements, the atoms of which contain large numbers of protons and neutrons, bombardment with neutrons may produce atomic fission, creating new atoms and releasing spare neutrons to continue the chain reaction. This produces energy millions of times greater than that produced by the rearrangements of electrons involved in chemical reactions. The only natural element capable of sustaining a nuclear chain reaction is the isotope of uranium U235 which forms about 0·7 per cent of natural uranium, the rest being U238. Under controlled bombardment in a reactor U235 will release neutrons to sustain the process and also to combine with atoms of the U238 to produce a new element, plutonium (P239), which will also sustain a chain reaction. If thorium is introduced U233 may also be produced. U235 and P239 are extensively used to make nuclear weapons. So far as is publicly known U233 has not been so used.

At the other end of the spectrum of elements, the very light nuclei of certain isotopes of hydrogen, containing only a few particles, can be made to fuse if subjected to very high temperatures. This 'thermonuclear' reaction is produced in weapons by employing a fission bomb as a trigger. The two most suitable forms of hydrogen are deuterium and tritium.

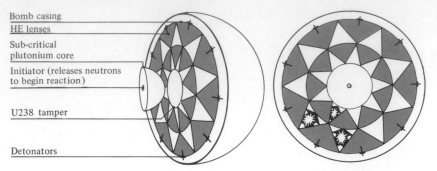

Bomb casing
HE lenses
Sub-critical
plutonium core
Initiator (releases neutrons
to begin reaction)

U238 tamper

Detonators

A simplified diagram of a nuclear bomb, based on unofficial French and American sources. Simultaneous detonation of the high-explosive charges compresses the plutonium core into a super-critical mass to sustain a chain reaction initiated by neutrons generated at the centre.

To sustain a fission reaction requires a minimum 'critical mass' of fissionable material. If this is assembled, the reaction may be begun by stray neutrons. A weapon therefore involves assembling less than critical masses which can be suddenly brought together and compressed by shaped charges of chemical explosive so that they become 'supercritical', and simultaneously generating an ample supply of neutrons, to guarantee a reaction. This sets upper limits on the size of fission weapons, as large amounts of fissionable material would explode spontaneously. Fission yields therefore rarely exceed 500 KT. No such limit exists with fusion weapons and the hydrogen isotopes are also much cheaper to manufacture than the fissile materials. Thus, despite the fact that more energy is released per atom in fission (which is of importance in making very small weapons), fusion reactions are the source of large cheap explosions. Yields are virtually unlimited; the Russians have tested a 57 MT device and yields of 5–20 MT are commonplace in the stockpiles of the Superpowers.

In addition to heat and blast, nuclear weapons yield various forms of immediate and longer term nuclear radiation. A weapon detonated in the air up to about one hundred thousand feet releases energy roughly in the proportions 50 per cent blast or shock, 35 per cent thermal radiation, and 15 per cent nuclear radiation. The thermal radiation travels at the speed of light over distances limited by the atmospheric conditions affecting visibility. Simple shelters offer substantial protection. The nuclear radiation released is comprised of about one third immediate or initial radiation emitted within about a minute of the explosion. This travels considerable distances and, unlike the thermal radiation, readily penetrates intervening materials; at about a mile from a 1 MT explosion humans would need some fifty inches of concrete for shelter. Residual radiation arises chiefly from the debris of the weapon, but if the explosion sucks up amounts of other matter, this will become radioactive as a result of neutron capture. Depending on the height of the explosion and the weight of the particles, the latter will either enter the upper atmosphere, to descend much later, or may be carried downwind over some hours or days. This initial, local fallout may be extensive; 10 MT exploded on the surface may produce severe fallout four or five hundred miles downwind.

Sophisticated designers of weapons can create weapons that yield a great deal of long-term radiation – 'dirty' weapons – or very little – 'clean' weapons. One way of obtaining great power cheaply is to jacket a fusion weapon with ordinary uranium which, though not normally fissile, will undergo fission by the high energy neutrons released by an H-bomb. This produces a very dirty weapon indeed. It is also possible to alter the spectrum of radiation yielded: for instance, to increase the proportion of 'hard' (high frequency) X-rays in the total yield of radiation. This achievement is important for various offensive and defensive purposes. Jacketing an H-bomb with cobalt would produce

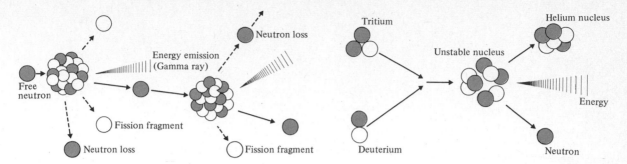

Two simplified diagrams showing fission (**left**) in which a free neutron strikes an atom of a heavy element (P239 or U235) and sets up a chain reaction; and a typical fusion reaction (**right**) in which atoms of light isotopes of hydrogen (deuterium, tritium) combine under intense heat. Both types of reaction release great amounts of energy.

particularly intense gamma radiation and could, theoretically, result in a weapon sufficiently dirty to induce radiation deaths on a hemispheric scale.

The damage that an offensive nuclear weapon may do obviously depends very much upon the nature of the target – is it concentrated or dispersed, strong or weak structurally?; on where the weapon is exploded – above, on, or below the surface; on the yield of the weapon; and, most important of all, on the accuracy with which it is delivered. If the weapon is dirty or if the fireball touches the ground and irradiates large masses of soil and other material, the resultant fallout may inflict many casualties both locally and at a distance over varying periods. Under any assumption, the large weapons in the megaton range would do almost inconceivable damage. One megaton airburst at, say, 10,000 feet, would knock down large brick buildings up to a radius of 3·5 miles, thus flattening an area of some 40 sq miles. Heat radiation would, according to conditions of terrain, weather and type of building, cause fires up to a radius of some 6 miles, or over 130 sq miles. This leaves out of account the immediate and delayed effects of radiation and the consequences of the disruption of all services that might contribute to relief and rehabilitation.

The Strategies

The delivery of large numbers of weapons of this kind would obviously constitute a catastrophe quite out of proportion to any conceivable rational purpose. Even one or two megaton explosions in densely populated areas would be a disaster of unprecedented magnitude. It is for this reason that securing immunity from nuclear attack takes first priority in the policy of the Superpowers. To do this without merely relying upon the goodwill of the potential opponent or upon the possibility of appeasing his demands, requires either a capacity to defend oneself against attack, or the ability to deter the opponent from attacking. Because a known capability for defence reduces an enemy's hope that his attack may succeed, defence can itself contribute to deterrence.

Defence entails physically blunting the enemy attack and minimizing its effects on oneself. Deterrence entails working on the psychology of the enemy so that he will not decide to attack. He must be convinced that the retaliatory damage or punishment he would inevitably receive for attacking outweighs, preferably by a great deal, the advantage he might hope to gain from the attack. It is a vexed question how much prospective destruction is enough to deter. At a time of great American strategic superiority, the former Secretary of Defense, Robert McNamara, suggested the ability to kill seventy-four million Russians (or 30 per cent of the population) and to destroy 76 per cent of Russian industrial capacity. This very high figure seems to have been arrived at, not by any calculation of what would be politically effective, but by recognizing the fact that after that level of destruction had been reached, the effectiveness of additional attacks would rapidly decline simply because all the worthwhile targets would already be destroyed. No one would dispute, however, that such a level of destruction would be regarded as unacceptable by a Soviet Government and that, consequently, a credible capacity to achieve such a result would be an adequate deterrent. In practice even the risk of much lower levels of destruction would doubtless be enough to deter.

For a deterrent policy to be effective it must not only threaten more destruction than the enemy cares to incur, but also do so with credibility. Credibility involves both intention and capacity. Whether you *would* execute your threat depends on what is at stake and how far you can limit the damage that will be done to you. Whether you *could* execute the threat depends on the ability of your forces to survive any attacks and to penetrate the enemy's defences.

If a deterrent is to threaten retaliation against a nuclear attack, the incentive to retaliate will be highly credible but the retaliation will have to be carried out with forces that have survived a 'first strike'. The capacity to retaliate under such circumstances is known as a 'secure second strike'. The capacity to wreak unacceptable damage with such a surviving force is known in American parlance as 'assured destruction'. If all that is required is to deter an all-out nuclear attack on one's own cities, then a capacity to retaliate against enemy cities in a 'counter-value' attack may be adequate. A nation that wants to use its nuclear forces not merely to deter all-out attacks on itself but also to deter other forms of aggression, such as conventional attacks or nuclear attacks on allies, must threaten to initiate strategic nuclear strikes. To do this credibly implies an ability to prevent the enemy succeeding in his own retaliatory strike. The capacity to do this is known as 'damage limitation', the reciprocal concept to assured destruction.

Damage limitation can be regarded as the remaining element of defence in the age of deterrence. Defences in the narrower sense can be divided into two forms, passive and active. Passive defence may involve measures to protect civil society – civil defence, shelters, evacuation, duplication of essential facilities, and provision for post-attack recovery – and measures to protect retaliatory forces – sheltering, concealment, dispersal and mobility. Active defences may include anti-aircraft artillery, missiles, and interceptors, anti-missile forces and anti-submarine warfare (ASW) to combat missile-firing submarines.

In addition there is the possibility of destroying enemy retaliatory forces before they can be launched. This would involve 'counterforce' as distinguished from countervalue strikes. If a state had a high capacity to destroy enemy retaliatory forces, it might enjoy the ability to launch a first strike with impunity. In other words, its damage limitation would negate its opponent's second strike. In that case there might indeed be no need for a first strike to hit enemy cities at all; instead the enemy's retaliatory force could be eliminated and the enemy cities preserved as hostages to a residual offensive force retained for bargaining purposes.

As we shall see, it is in practice today highly unlikely that a major nuclear power could be completely disarmed in a first strike. It is, however, possible to imagine counterforce 'exchanges' in which cities were spared and residual forces were retained for bargaining purposes. Indeed there might be a sequence of counterforce attacks. This is the concept of 'controlled response' and 'intrawar deterrence'. Such restraint may be unlikely in practice, given the emotions and degree of chaos implied by a state of nuclear war, but in theory at

Left The Russian Myasis-chev M5 strategic bomber (NATO code name *Bear*) carrying a 'Kangaroo' stand-off bomb.

Below The Boeing B52, mainstay of the US strategic bomber force for more than fifteen years.

least it is not enough to think only of precipitate, all-out mutual countervalue attacks in a 'spasm' war. If deterrence were to fail, the anxiety to postpone catastrophe might spur national leaders to attempt a controlled response. This is presumably the contingency President Nixon had in mind when, in his famous policy manifesto of February 1970, he asked: 'Should a President, in the event of a nuclear attack, be left with the single option of ordering the mass destruction of enemy civilians, in the face of the certainty that it would be followed by the mass slaughter of Americans?'

The concept of controlled response complicates the criteria for an adequate deterrent force; for this reason the concept is unpopular with some who seek to stabilize the strategic balance at low levels. While the minimum requirement for deterrence is the capacity to retain a secure second strike measured against the task of assured destruction of the enemy in an assumed simple attack and response, the possibility of a bargaining situation suggests that one cannot be completely indifferent to the relative superiority or inferiority of one force to the other and that this ratio must be calculated in terms of the situation after, as well as before, a first strike.

How much the question is complicated depends to a large degree on the state of technology. Thinking about first and second strikes, assured destruction and damage limitation, counterforce and countervalue, has evolved rapidly over

Some important possible sequences of nuclear 'exchange'.

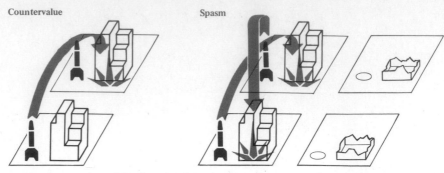

Countervalue   Spasm

recent years, hand in hand with the development of strategic systems. The adequacy of Superpower stocks of nuclear explosive to do unacceptable damage if delivered has not been doubted for decades. Providing 'delivery systems' that can survive attack and penetrate defences has, however, posed very difficult technical problems.

Efforts to solve these problems have produced several generations of delivery systems. It would be possible to deliver nuclear weapons under some circumstances by rather simple methods. Bombs could be placed in merchant ships sailed into foreign harbours, for instance, or conveyed by other apparently innocent vehicles. But while such methods are technically practicable, they are unlikely to appeal to major military powers, though the possibility of such action by lesser nuclear powers in the future cannot be excluded. The chief objection to such methods of delivery is the political and strategic risk involved. Such a plan would take a long time to execute and it would be hazardous to initiate it, with all the attendant risks of premature discovery, especially as political circumstances might change in the meantime. Consequently all known nuclear delivery systems are designed with a capability to strike quickly once the final decision for nuclear action has been taken.

So long as delivery depended solely on aircraft, there was some hope of mounting an active air defence that could impose heavy attrition on the attacking force. Even so, as soon as reasonable numbers of bombs were available, the chance of staving off catastrophe by defence was slight, simply because a very low rate of failure by the defenders would still result in tremendous destruction. The real dawn of the nuclear strategic balance as we know it, however, came with the advent of the long-range ballistic missile. In its perfected form, the ballistic missile combines the formidable properties of readiness, range, speed and substantial payload. The combination of these qualities with fusion warheads creates that possibility of almost instantaneous annihilation, without pause for reflection or negotiation, which gives the nuclear balance its peculiar nature.

The missile did not produce its full potential immediately. In their early forms, ballistic missiles were powered by rocket motors burning a liquid mixture which, because of its corrosive and volatile properties, could not be kept permanently in the missile. This greatly reduced the readiness of the missile and extended the time required to fire it. Moreover, the process of fuelling was difficult and this tended to dictate positioning the missile on the surface on a 'soft site'. Like aircraft, such missiles were therefore very vulnerable on the ground; indeed, small-arms fire could easily disable them. For many years, however, there was no defence against such missiles once they were fired. The early missile age was therefore one in which a great premium would accrue to the side that fired first, especially as the missiles travelled much faster, and thus gave

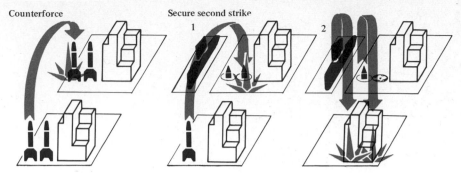

less warning, than aircraft. It was consequently an era in which fears of surprise attack were rife and in which the temptation to launch one's missiles at the first sign of attack was great. Large investments were made in radar warning chains and in satellite systems to detect missile launchings early.

Since the late fifties, however, rapid progress has been made in the development of both storable liquid fuels, which can be kept in the missile for extended periods, and solid fuels composed of materials that can be left in the missile indefinitely. The chief technical problem with solids was to devise ways of packing and forming the fuel to burn evenly. In recent years the United States has moved almost exclusively to solids but the Soviet Union continues to make much use of storable liquids which, if a little more troublesome in handling, do perform with high efficiency.

The adoption of storable fuels has facilitated the emplacement of missiles in underground silos, 'hardened' against the shock of explosion. In the early seventies silos are typically hardened to withstand an overpressure of 300 pounds per square inch (300 p.s.i.) but projects are on foot to 'superharden' emplacements. The development of hardened sites and the parallel deployment of missiles in elusive nuclear-propelled submarines greatly increased the chance of retaliatory forces surviving a first strike. This meant that the chances of a successful counterforce strike to disarm an enemy were equally diminished. Thus, with counterforce impracticable and no method of active defence feasible once offensive missiles were launched, no effective form of defence against nuclear attack was available. The nuclear powers therefore had to place their reliance primarily on deterrence by the threat of retaliation. With counterforce and active defence ruled out, it seemed quite possible to maintain a credible retaliatory deterrent which could 'ride out' a hostile first strike and therefore be free of the compulsion to react precipitately. The influential American Secretary of Defense, Robert McNamara, elevated this prospect of mutual vulnerability to assured destruction into a doctrine as the best basis for strategic stability. While the idea of willing vulnerability apparently had much less appeal to Russian strategists, who were more reluctant to abandon the pursuit of security through defence, a state of mutual vulnerability is what in fact emerged from the military policies of the Superpowers in the sixties.

The Weapons

Looked at in the simplest way, strategic nuclear delivery systems are either 'freefall' bombs carried on aircraft, or are some form of unmanned missile. The missiles may be either 'cruise missiles', which are virtually unmanned jet aircraft, depending on aerodynamic lift and usually powered by air-breathing engines, or 'ballistic missiles' which travel on predetermined trajectories for most of their course, having been launched by a brief burst of rocket power.

Missiles can be launched from the land, from vessels on or under the sea, or from aircraft. Each delivery system carries one or more nuclear warheads. On long-range ballistic missiles, the warhead is packaged in a 're-entry vehicle' (RV), which is shaped and shielded to protect the weapon from the temperatures generated upon high speed re-entry to the atmosphere.

Manned bombers retain a place in the inventory of both Superpowers. The United States operates over 350 B52 bombers which carry up to four bombs in the 1–24 MT range. Over 200 of these aircraft are B52 G/H which can carry two air to surface (ASM) cruise missiles, Hounddog, with a warhead of 5 MT. In addition, seventy of the swing-wing medium bomber, FB111, may be assigned to the strategic strike role. The United States also possesses a large force of short- and medium-range aircraft on its aircraft carriers with some strategic nuclear capability, but these aircraft are no longer primarily assigned to the strategic strike. The Soviet Union maintains a much smaller number of long-range bombers, of which about 100 are TU20 *Bears* and forty are Mya 4 *Bisons*. Some of the *Bears* carry an ASM, *Kangaroo*. (The names given to Soviet weapons are almost always NATO attributions.)

Bombers are vulnerable to active defensive countermeasures but they are likely to remain in Superpower inventories. Certain recent developments, mentioned later, reinforce this probability. The bomber has several merits as a delivery system. It can carry a very large weapon load and, if it survives, attack several targets. Moreover, it can reconnoitre, avoid already devastated targets, and observe the result of its own attack. It can be put conspicuously on alert – possibly a useful political gesture – and can be recalled after launch. Furthermore, even a small bomber force can impose heavy defensive costs and anxieties on its opponent.

The mainstay of a modern strategic nuclear strike force is the ballistic missile. Western analysts usually divide ballistic missiles into three classifications according to range. Those with a range of about 1000–1500 miles are designated medium range ballistic missiles (MRBM), those with a range of 1500–4000 miles are referred to as intermediate range ballistic missiles (IRBM) and those of longer range are the intercontinental ballistic missiles (ICBM). In addition, submarine-launched missiles, so far all of medium or intermediate range, are known as submarine-launched ballistic missiles (SLBM).

A ballistic missile system consists of a rocket or 'booster' to launch a re-entry vehicle containing the nuclear warhead. In an ICBM, the booster burns for some three to five minutes. After the booster, which usually contains three stages, has fallen away, most re-entry vehicles continue on a simple ballistic trajectory. Assuming a range of five thousand miles, the RV, having achieved a maximum velocity of about four miles a second, coasts for some twenty-five minutes, reaches an apogee of about seven hundred miles above the earth's surface and begins to fall back towards the target. This is the mid-course phase. Finally the RV enters the atmosphere at an altitude of about eighty miles and decelerates rapidly during the minute or so required to reach the ground or the height at which it is to detonate. To render all this possible, the missile must be provided with an accurate guidance and steering mechanism for use during the boost phase and the warhead must have some kind of fusing to ensure detonation at the appropriate moment.

Shorter range missiles, including all existing SLBMs, have similar characteristics, except that they reach lower altitudes and speeds. Like bombers, the SLBMs have the advantage of coming in from less-predictable directions than most of the land-based variety.

As the tables on pages 24 and 25 show, both Superpowers have accumulated a formidable inventory of these weapons. During the Kennedy and Johnson administrations, using missiles developed by the previous Eisenhower administration, the United States rapidly built up to a number of strategic missiles which it has maintained unchanged since 1967. After a period of very slow procurement under Chairman N. S. Khruschev, the Soviet Union, prompted perhaps by its diplomatic failure in the war of nerves over Berlin and Cuba, 1958–62, began a very energetic programme of procurement which continued until the strategic arms limitation agreement of 1972.

In 1972 the American strategic missile force consisted of one thousand solid-fuelled ICBMs, various marks of Minuteman, in hardened silos, and fifty-four large liquid-fuelled Titan 2 missiles, also hardened and retained for the sake of their high payload, permitting warheads of 5–10 MT. In addition the United States operates forty-one nuclear-powered missile-firing submarines (SSBN) armed with A2 and A3 versions of the solid-fuelled IRBM Polaris. All but ten of the SSBN are gradually re-equipping with the larger IRBM Poseidon. The Poseidon and Minuteman 3 can carry multiple and separately targeted re-entry vehicles (see below), while the A3 Polaris carries three re-entry vehicles which achieve a shotgun-type scatter.

The Soviet strategic missile force consists of a large number of ICBMs, many of them recently acquired. All but one, the SS13 with a 1 MT warhead, are fuelled by storable liquid. Most destructive of the Russian ICBMs is the SS9, which can carry a warhead of over 20 MT or three warheads of 5 MT. Another special feature of the Russian arsenal, arising quite naturally from the proximity of the Soviet Union to several of its potential enemies, is a large force of IRBMs and MRBMs. Russia possesses about 100 of the IRBM SS5, and 600 of the MRBM SS4. Some 630 of these are believed to be targeted on Western Europe and the rest on Far Eastern targets including Japan and China. The warheads of these missiles are thought to be about 1 MT.

For many years submarine-mounted missiles did not play a large part in the Russian strategic forces. A few medium- or short-range ballistic missiles have been in service for some time, together with a large number of cruise missiles. The latter are thought to be chiefly intended for use against Western aircraft carriers. Since 1969, however, the Soviet Union has rapidly introduced the SSN6, a missile comparable to the earlier Polaris, with a range of 1700 miles. This has been installed, sixteen to a boat, on a new SSBN known in the West as the *Yankee* class. A new SLBM of 3–4000 mile range has also been reported under development, probably for a *Yankee*-type boat with twelve missile tubes.

Technology and Strategic Stability

With the deployment of SLBMs and hardened ICBMs of the Polaris/Minuteman generation, many Western strategists hoped that military technology had reached a 'plateau' and that a period of stability might follow. As these weapons were thought to be unanswerable, it seemed reasonable to assume that once each Superpower had obtained the absolute number required to wreak the required amount of 'unacceptable damage' on the other, there would be no incentive to acquire more. There being no defence against the missile, an adequate arsenal could be calculated against the static standard of the enemy's society as a target, rather than, as in previous technological periods, against the dynamic standard of the enemy's defensive and offensive strength. Moreover, as retaliation was inescapable, there would be no temptation to attack. Thus strategic stability might be achieved in two senses; first, there

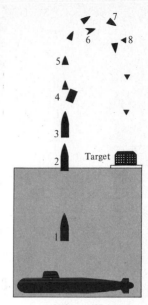

Target

The submarine-launched ballistic missile.
1. The missile is fired under water by compressed gases.
2. As it emerges from the water the first stage ignites. 3. The guidance system turns the missile on to target trajectory.
4. The first stage burns out and is jettisoned.
5. The second stage motor fires. 6. The nose fairing is jettisoned.
7. The guidance system sends a 'safe-to-arm' signal to the warhead.
8. The re-entry body containing warheads separates from the guidance system and follows a free-flight trajectory to the target.

Overleaf A comparison of the strategic weapon delivery systems of the two nuclear superpowers.

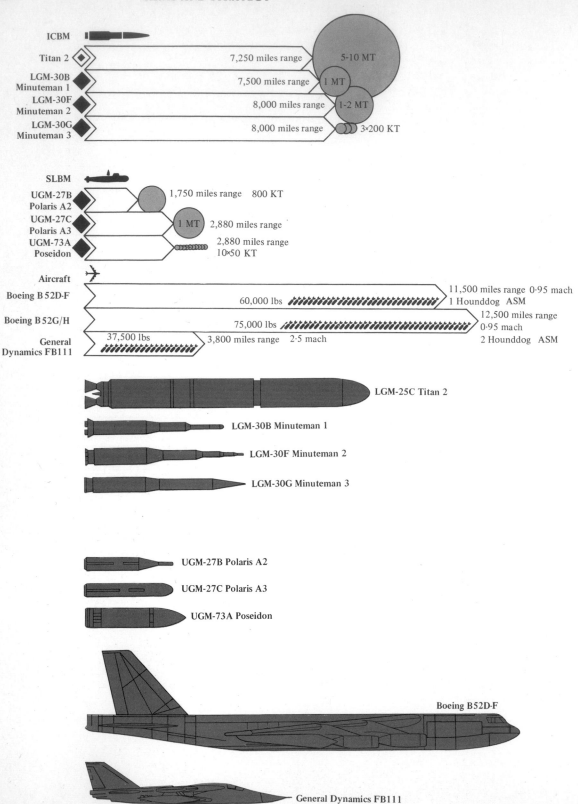

ICBM

Titan 2   7,250 miles range   5-10 MT

LGM-30B Minuteman 1   7,500 miles range   1 MT

LGM-30F Minuteman 2   8,000 miles range   1-2 MT

LGM-30G Minuteman 3   8,000 miles range   3×200 KT

SLBM

UGM-27B Polaris A2   1,750 miles range   800 KT

UGM-27C Polaris A3   1 MT   2,880 miles range

UGM-73A Poseidon   2,880 miles range   10×50 KT

Aircraft

Boeing B 52D-F   60,000 lbs   11,500 miles range 0·95 mach
1 Hounddog ASM

Boeing B 52G/H   75,000 lbs   12,500 miles range
0·95 mach

General Dynamics FB111   37,500 lbs   3,800 miles range   2·5 mach   2 Hounddog ASM

LGM-25C Titan 2

LGM-30B Minuteman 1

LGM-30F Minuteman 2

LGM-30G Minuteman 3

UGM-27B Polaris A2

UGM-27C Polaris A3

UGM-73A Poseidon

Boeing B52D-F

General Dynamics FB111

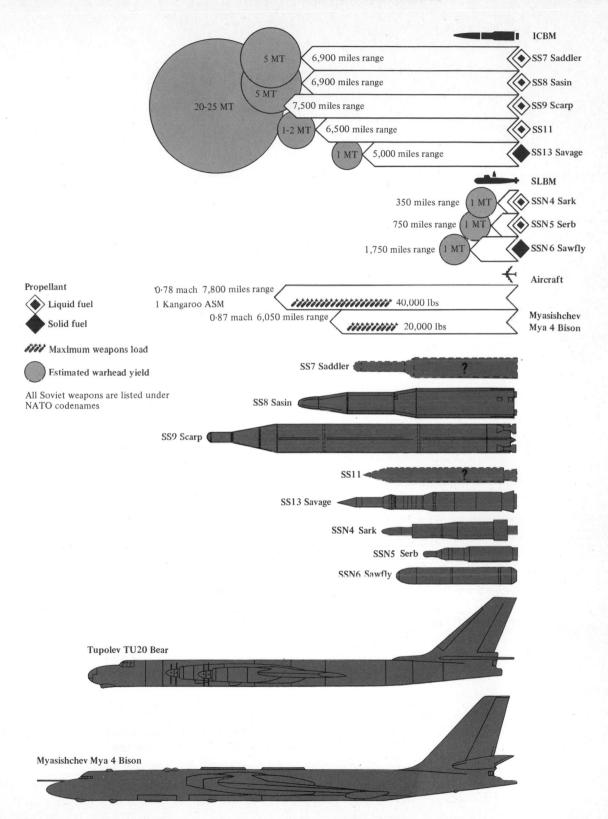

ICBM

5 MT	6,900 miles range	SS7 Saddler
5 MT	6,900 miles range	SS8 Sasin
20-25 MT	7,500 miles range	SS9 Scarp
1-2 MT	6,500 miles range	SS11
1 MT	5,000 miles range	SS13 Savage

SLBM

350 miles range	1 MT	SSN4 Sark
750 miles range	1 MT	SSN5 Serb
1,750 miles range	1 MT	SSN6 Sawfly

Aircraft

0·78 mach 7,800 miles range
1 Kangaroo ASM   40,000 lbs

0·87 mach 6,050 miles range   20,000 lbs   Myasishchev Mya 4 Bison

Propellant

◈ Liquid fuel

◆ Solid fuel

𝔐 Maximum weapons load

⬤ Estimated warhead yield

All Soviet weapons are listed under
NATO codenames

SS7 Saddler   ?

SS8 Sasin

SS9 Scarp

SS11   ?

SS13 Savage

SSN4 Sark

SSN5 Serb

SSN6 Sawfly

Tupolev TU20 Bear

Myasishchev Mya 4 Bison

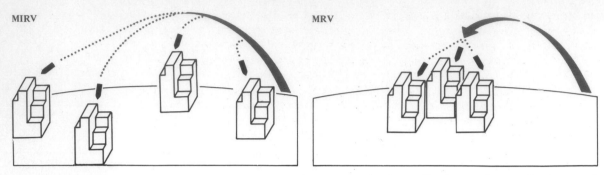

MIRV   MRV

The difference between MIRV, in which each warhead can be independently targeted on to a completely separate target, greatly complicating the problem of defence, and MRV in which the warheads simply fall in a wider 'footprint' on the same target, thus increasing the destructive effect.

would be an end to the arms race both qualitative and quantitative; and, second, there would be no strategic nuclear hostilities.

Events have shown this analysis to be faulty, for, in two important respects, technology was still on the move. In the first place, great improvements were about to be made in the guidance of missiles and hence the accuracy with which they could hit their targets. The accuracy of a missile is expressed as 'circular error probable' (CEP); that is, the radius of a circle within which a re-entry vehicle has a 50 per cent chance of falling. The CEP of early, prototype long-range missiles of the mid-fifties was about five miles at intercontinental ranges. A decade later, missiles like Minuteman were expected to have a CEP of less than half a mile and it was confidently predicted that this error could, if desired, be reduced to tens of feet by the late seventies.

The great significance of this improvement is that the effectiveness of weapons for destroying a small, well protected target like a missile silo, is much more sensitive to accuracy than to the size of the warhead. The blast, measured as overpressure (p.s.i.), from a nuclear explosion attenuates in proportion to the cube of the distance from the centre of the explosion. Consequently, doubling the size of warhead will increase the p.s.i. at one mile from an explosion by 60 per cent; doubling the accuracy (i.e. hitting within half a mile of the target) will increase the p.s.i. by nearly 500 per cent. In other words, increased accuracy is nearly ten times as effective as increased yield (see diagram on page 29). The implication of greatly increased accuracies is small for large, soft targets like cities, but is very great indeed for hardened targets like missile silos. Increased accuracy is therefore a step towards counterforce capability and throws into question the assumption that the hardened Minuteman-type missile is an invulnerable and reliable second strike weapon.

This tendency has been compounded by the invention of multiple re-entry vehicles (MRV) for missiles. A simple multiple warhead is made possible by modern improvements in weight-to-yield ratios for re-entry vehicles. The American Polaris A3 has long had three separate warheads and the Russian SS9 is being equipped with triple heads also. Such MRV can be designed to fall in a pattern (the 'footprint') to improve coverage of small areas. A further step is to provide the separate warheads with individual guidance so as to engage several widely separated targets or to improve the pattern of attack on a single area. A device of this kind, which steers and controls a warhead-carrying 'bus' after booster separation to achieve sequential release of a number of re-entry vehicles so that they are placed on ballistic trajectories towards separate aiming points, is incorporated, usually with ten RVs, in the new American Poseidon SLBM. A three-RV version is being fitted to the Minuteman 3.

These weapons are known as 'multiple independently targetable re-entry vehicles' (MIRV). Their counterforce potential depends, of course, primarily on accuracy; multiplication is a useful refinement. But multiplication has another disturbing implication for those who fear a counterforce strategy; this is that accurate MIRVs could attack more than one missile site, while a MIRved missile on the ground still only constitutes a single target. Thus the exchange ratio could once again come to favour the side that strikes first. It must be realized, however, that until accuracies become very high, a large warhead is still needed to knock out a missile silo and MIRVing imposes a weight penalty on RVs that reduces total megatonnage. Thus the SS9 is thought to be capable of carrying 25 MT in a single warhead, but only 5 MT in each of three MRVs. Nevertheless, current yields and accuracies cast real doubt on the safety of hardened missiles from counterforce attack. A 5 MT warhead with the supposed CEP of the SS9, half a mile, would have a 67 per cent chance of destroying a 300 p.s.i. silo (the reputed hardness of the Minuteman silo). If the accuracy could rise to a quarter of a mile, the chance would rise to 99 per cent. Any greater accuracy than a quarter of a mile would probably require the introduction of some terminal guidance and steering capability by which the RV could correct its course in the final minute. Such systems may well be practicable, but none are yet in service. But in any case, it must be realized that once a 1 MT warhead explodes within a quarter of a mile of a target, that target is likely to be covered with debris, regardless of whether it has been hardened to withstand the effect of shock.

The advent of multiple warheads, with their potential for ending the supposed invulnerability of the land-based strategic missile, undermines the assumption that counterforce cannot contribute to damage limitation. Thus, it goes some way to restoring the familiar military situation in which the adequacy of one power's forces must be weighed against the military capability of the possible adversary. At the same time another technological development has been having a similar effect. This is the appearance of practical systems for intercepting offensive missiles in flight. Ballistic missile defence (BMD) has restored the possibility of an active defence against missiles and therefore undermined the assumption that the only way to security is deterrence based on vulnerability.

Both Russia and the United States have long worked on the task of solving the problem of missile interception. There is some reason to believe that Soviet military doctrine, which has a strong defensive component and a long historic concern with the defence of the motherland, was never very willing to accept the concept of mutual vulnerability as the basis of security. Certainly no strategist can fail to realize that security through deterrence requires great faith in the rationality of the adversary, whereas defence, if practicable, offers the hope that one's own efforts will ensure safety whatever others may do. In any case, the mere possibility that BMD might prove practicable compelled both Superpowers to explore the necessary technology. Even a power content with deterrence through offensive forces must keep up with defensive technology, if only to appreciate the problems of penetrating defences should the opponent achieve a defensive breakthrough.

The task of building a missile defence is a formidable one. It requires securing prompt warning of attack, identification and tracking of incoming re-entry vehicles, and then their ultimate interception and destruction. An offensive missile passes through three distinguishable stages of flight: an initial, slow but accelerating ascent phase, a long mid-course trajectory and a terminal re-entry phase, during which the warhead re-enters the atmosphere and rapidly decelerates. In the first stage the boosters are very vulnerable but no system for intercepting them has yet proved practicable. It would obviously be difficult to obtain warning and to act with sufficient speed. Projects for early interception from satellites have not seemed cost effective. Instead, all existing systems concentrate on the terminal stages of flight and seek to destroy the re-entry vehicle in its late mid-course or re-entry phases. While speculation and research proceed on such expedients as performing the destruction with laser beams – which would permit repeated firings (shoot-look-shoot) – existing systems all depend on firing an anti-ballistic missile (ABM) to detonate a nuclear charge near the incoming warhead.

Early American efforts to design a BMD system foundered on the problem of tracking and intercepting numerous attacking vehicles. By combining radar and computers it was found possible, by 1959, to intercept single RVs reliably. But in

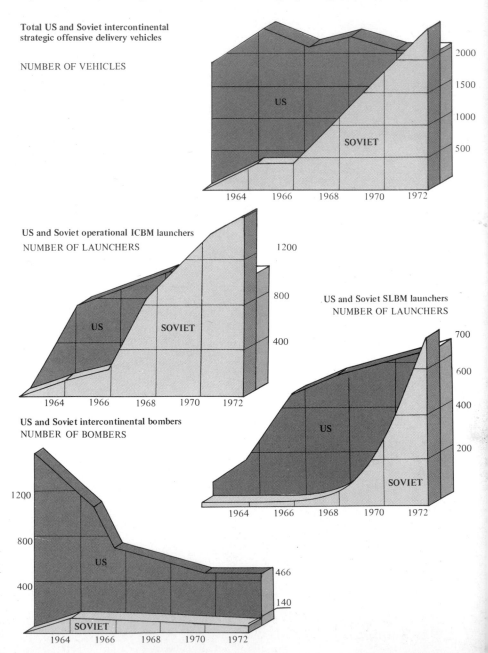

Right The nuclear race: the massive increase in strategic delivery systems up to the 1972 SAL Treaty which put formal limits on further growth.

Opposite A diagram showing the difficulty of comparing nuclear forces. Under the SAL agreement the US has a smaller number of launch vehicles, but due to her greater sophistication in putting multiple independently targeted warheads on these, the US can strike at far more separate targets. However, the Russian rockets have much larger payload. They therefore carry a much larger total gross megatonnage and *could* carry far more separate warheads than the American force.

Total US and Soviet intercontinental strategic offensive delivery vehicles

NUMBER OF VEHICLES

US and Soviet operational ICBM launchers
NUMBER OF LAUNCHERS

US and Soviet SLBM launchers
NUMBER OF LAUNCHERS

US and Soviet intercontinental bombers
NUMBER OF BOMBERS

a real attack there might be many RVs close together. Moreover, the attacker might design his weapons so as to disperse a great mass of metal 'chaff' to confuse the radar or even to eject lightweight, perhaps inflatable, simulations of RVs or 'decoys' which, in space, would behave like the real thing and result in the confusion and exhaustion of the defence.

Several technological conceptions have contributed to the partial solution of this problem. In the first place, great advances in both radar and computers have provided much-improved capacity to discriminate and track RVs. Most important here has been the replacement of mechanically steered antennae by 'phased array' radars in which the signal is passed electronically across a large

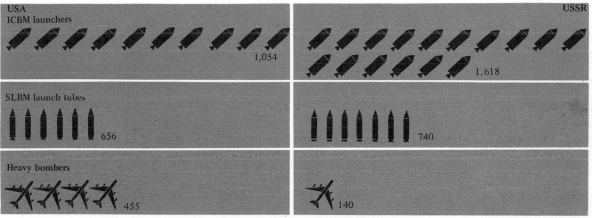

US — USSR missile balance under SAL agreement

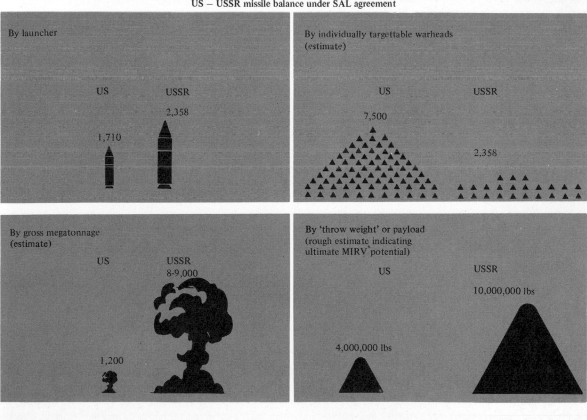

number of facets of a fixed surface. This permits the simultaneous handling of many targets.

A second source of optimism has been the realization that, in space, the radiation of a nuclear burst would not, as within the atmosphere, be transmuted into short-range forms of energy like heat and blast, but would travel for great distances attenuated only as the surface of the sphere of energy expands. Deposited on an RV, this radiation, particularly hard X-rays, would release highly destructive energy, especially on some of the more impermeable components of an incoming warhead. Defensive warheads can be designed to emit a spectrum of radiation specially matched to this task. In this way 1 MT might give good 'kill' capability over tens of miles. This would make it possible to eliminate the whole cluster of decoys and real warheads with one detonation, and thereby increase the tolerance acceptable for discrimination of targets and accuracy of interception.

Finally, an effort has been made to exploit the fact that, once light decoys enter the atmosphere, they become much more readily distinguishable from the heavier real warheads. Very late interception would thus facilitate discrimination as well as give a possible second chance to shoot at targets missed in the 'exoatmospheric' stage. To intercept late requires very rapid reaction and high acceleration in the interceptor. The American answer has been a high-acceleration ABM, Sprint, ejected by compressed air from its emplacement.

The Soviet Union began to deploy a long-range, exoatmospheric ABM, *Galosh*, around Moscow about 1965 and has completed a modest network of about sixty-five missiles. So far as is known the Russians have not taken the approach represented by Sprint but they have been developing a new long-range ABM and appropriate radars. Under Secretary of Defense McNamara, the United States government resisted BMD for several years, preferring mutual vulnerability as a basis for strategic stability. By 1967, however, McNamara was compelled to initiate a system (Sentinel) of long-range ABMs (Spartan) to give protection for the whole United States against a light attack, and of Sprints to protect the BMD network itself. This was said to be a useful defence against the kind of attack China might be able to make in the near future, but not so effective as to undermine the Soviet Union's confidence in its deterrent. A new round in the Soviet–American arms race might thus be avoided.

Under the Nixon Administration this decision was revised, and Sentinel was replaced by Safeguard. This system, using the same components, had as its first priority the defence of Minuteman sites against counterforce, though it would inevitably have provided some coverage for the American population as well if the full network, which was to be built site by site, had been completed. The second projected phase of Safeguard envisaged providing a defence for Washington, D.C. as the 'national command centre', to parallel the Russian provision for Moscow.

By the early seventies BMD still could not purchase anything like immunity for a population attacked by a large offensive nuclear force. The cost of saturating the defence with offensive RVs and of bypassing it by aircraft or very short range SLBMs from offshore was still much less than that of achieving a perfect defence and, as always with nuclear weapons, anything short of perfection is disaster. On the other hand, the thwarting of small-scale attacks that might be launched by lesser powers was practicable at tolerable cost and BMD had also become a cost-effective way of defending ICBMs against counterforce as compared, for instance, to multiplying the number of ICBMs. Moreover, it could be argued that such a measure was less likely to stimulate anxieties about a first strike in the mind of the opponent. Thus, in a few short years intercepting strategic missiles has moved from a science fiction dream to a practicable possibility that must be taken seriously in strategic calculations.

Implications for the Future Balance

The development of more accurate missiles, of MIRV and of BMD, presented here in highly condensed form, has prompted and been influenced by a complex strategic debate. Whatever their military value, these technical achievements have proved conclusively that there is no natural technological plateau on which strategy may rest. Instead it has become clear that if each Superpower follows

The American Spartan anti-missile missile. This is the long-range weapon of the US Safeguard anti-missile system.

A Russian SS9 intercontinental ballistic missile photographed during a parade in Red Square. This liquid-fuelled missile has a range of 6000 miles and is the largest military rocket in service.

a cautious policy of insuring against the technical potential of the other, offence and defence can pursue the same dialectic in the strategic nuclear field as that which has fuelled qualitative arms races in the past.

At present no BMD system, even if used in conjunction with a preliminary counterforce strike to weaken the enemy's offensive power, can purchase a reliable immunity from catastrophic retaliation. The SLBM systems, for instance, are immune to counterforce fire, and antisubmarine warfare (ASW) is far from able to counter the missile-firing submarine. Stability, in the sense that a first strike cannot seem a rational act, remains secure for the moment. But this will only continue to be the case if each Superpower keeps pace with the quality and quantity of the other's strategic arsenal. Stability in the second sense, that there is no incentive for competition in arms, is therefore no longer to be relied upon. An action and reaction process is still underway. The MIRV, for example, forms a useful part of the technology for penetrating a BMD system protecting populations, and therefore for keeping alive deterrence by threat of retaliation. It constitutes part of the whole business of penetration aids (PENAIDS) which is itself the response to BMD. Yet, as we have seen, the MIRV can contribute to counterforce action, and, by its threat to the missile silo, has stimulated the use of BMD to protect missiles. Moreover, although these systems cannot purchase immunity to retaliation, and therefore do not make it rational to seek a nuclear war, they may make it very advantageous to strike first if a war seems inevitable. For a BMD system will obviously work better against a second strike than against a first strike that has suffered no attrition and disruption.

These technological developments have been accompanied by, and helped to stimulate, a new acceleration of missile procurement. The growth of Soviet forces in recent years has already been mentioned. The rate at which the new Polaris-type SSBNs have been added to the Soviet fleet has been particularly noticeable and must, one supposes, represent Soviet recognition of the new doubts surrounding land-based missiles. As a further answer to this problem, the Russians have developed mobile missiles for use on land but no ICBM version of this is known to have been brought into serial production. A distinctive feature of Russian efforts has been experimentation with a fractional orbital bomb system (FOBS), an RV that goes into partial orbit and is then called back down on to target. Although this entails a loss of payload and accuracy, it makes possible globe-circling ranges and hence attack from virtually any direction. The FOB system can also be used to achieve a 'depressed trajectory' which significantly reduces warning time. To respond to this danger the United States has extended the arc of its radar coverage and pressed forward with the development of over-the-horizon radars (OTH) which can detect missiles much earlier than the conventional type.

Partly under pressure from the Russian build-up and partly, perhaps, simply

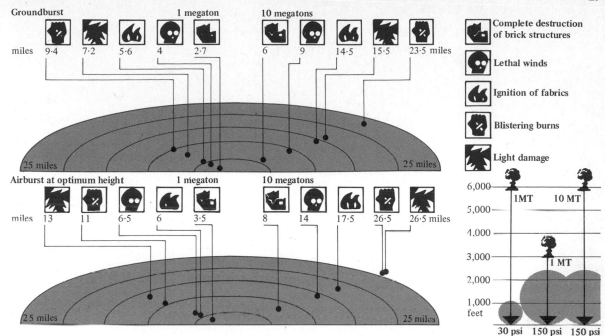

Groundburst   **1 megaton**   **10 megatons**

miles   9·4   7·2   5·6   4   2·7   6   9   14·5   15·5   23·5 miles

25 miles   25 miles

Airburst at optimum height   **1 megaton**   **10 megatons**

miles   13   11   6·5   6   3·5   8   14   17·5   26·5   26·5 miles

25 miles   25 miles

Complete destruction of brick structures

Lethal winds

Ignition of fabrics

Blistering burns

Light damage

6,000
5,000   1MT   10 MT
4,000
3,000   1 MT
2,000
1,000
feet
              30 psi   150 psi   150 psi

A comparison of the effect of one- and ten-megaton weapons detonated at optimal heights, and a diagram showing how improvements in accuracy bring a proportionally far greater effect than increases in yield. Twice the accuracy increases the blast effects fivefold.

as a result of the attractiveness of available technology, the United States has moved decisively toward the MIRV. Thus, without multiplying the number of its ICBMs and SLBMs, the United States is in the process of greatly increasing the number of its deliverable warheads or 'force loading'. The Minuteman 3, ultimately to replace 500 earlier Minutemen, carries three MIRVs of 200 KT, while the Poseidon, to replace the Polaris on thirty-one boats, carries ten MIRVs of about 50 KT. A new American SLBM, the undersea long range missile (ULMS) now named Trident, would be carried, twenty-four to a boat, and be capable of striking the Soviet Union immediately after leaving US ports.

Another form of multiplication has been the development of a short range attack missile (SRAM) for carriage by bombers. The B52G will be able to carry twenty-four of these, each with a range of 60–75 miles and a warhead of 200 KT. Stimulated in part by the new doubts about the invulnerability of missiles to BMD and counterforce, the concept of the bomber has, indeed, gained renewed life and the United States is developing a new version, the B1, capable of carrying thirty-two SRAMs. Russia is testing a large swing-wing bomber that may also be intended for strategic use (*Backfire*).

One sign of the increasing complexity of the strategic balance has been a resulting controversy as to what is the most significant measure of strategic power. Where it was once thought enough to count missiles, it is now possible to calculate by total megatonnage, by missiles or by warheads. Because, as we have seen, accuracy is more important for many purposes than size of warhead and because, consequently, several well-spaced small warheads will even destroy cities more completely than a single large bomb, the process of reckoning now raises controversial theoretical questions to compound the usual uncertainties of intelligence and the fact that some of the more crucial modern variables, such as CEP and number of RVs per missile, are peculiarly easy to conceal.

Strategic Arms Agreements

It is within this context that the Superpowers began, in 1969, to hold the Strategic Arms Limitation Talks (SALT) to explore the possibility of damping

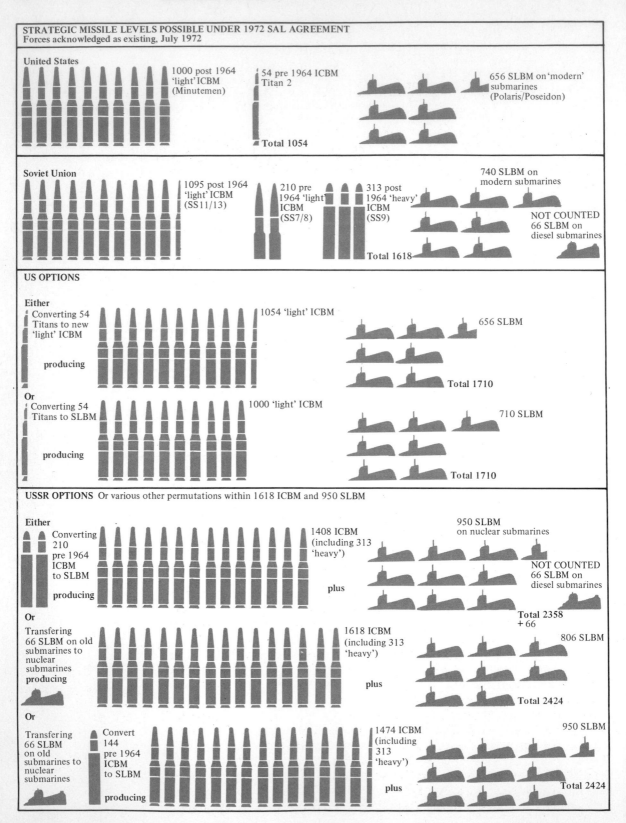

STRATEGIC MISSILE LEVELS POSSIBLE UNDER 1972 SAL AGREEMENT
Forces acknowledged as existing, July 1972

United States

1000 post 1964 'light' ICBM (Minutemen)

54 pre 1964 ICBM Titan 2

Total 1054

656 SLBM on 'modern' submarines (Polaris/Poseidon)

Soviet Union

1095 post 1964 'light' ICBM (SS11/13)

210 pre 1964 'light' ICBM (SS7/8)

313 post 1964 'heavy' ICBM (SS9)

Total 1618

740 SLBM on modern submarines

NOT COUNTED 66 SLBM on diesel submarines

US OPTIONS

Either
Converting 54 Titans to new 'light' ICBM

producing

1054 'light' ICBM

656 SLBM

Total 1710

Or
Converting 54 Titans to SLBM

producing

1000 'light' ICBM

710 SLBM

Total 1710

USSR OPTIONS Or various other permutations within 1618 ICBM and 950 SLBM

Either
Converting 210 pre 1964 ICBM to SLBM

producing

1408 ICBM (including 313 'heavy')

plus

950 SLBM on nuclear submarines

NOT COUNTED 66 SLBM on diesel submarines

Total 2358 + 66

Or
Transfering 66 SLBM on old submarines to nuclear submarines
producing

1618 ICBM (including 313 'heavy')

plus

806 SLBM

Total 2424

Or
Transfering 66 SLBM on old submarines to nuclear submarines

Convert 144 pre 1964 ICBM to SLBM

producing

1474 ICBM (including 313 'heavy')

plus

950 SLBM

Total 2424

A test firing of the US Poseidon submarine-launched missile. The missile is ejected at depth by compressed gas and its motor ignites once it is clear of the water.

down by agreement the arms race that technology would not stabilize spontaneously. (*See* Chapter 12:) Many political and military motives doubtless contributed to this mutual approach. Years before, by the establishment of the Hot Line crisis communication system in 1963, the two Superpowers had testified to their mutual interest in avoiding actual nuclear war. It is in the same spirit that much attention has been given to the command and control of nuclear weapons to ensure technical safety and to preclude unauthorized use.

While the new round that has begun in the strategic arms race may carry some increased risk of war, the more powerful anxieties leading to SALT are economic. There seems no reason to doubt that the Superpowers could keep each other deterred merely by unilateral efforts to compete in strategic technology. But this security would be bought at great cost. SALT represents recognition that all that would be purchased in this way would be mutual deterrence and is therefore an effort to see whether the same result can be frozen at a lower level by an act of political will.

The difficulties are, however, great. Although the Soviet Union has now achieved a closer strategic 'parity' to the United States than ever before (doubtless a precondition to Russian willingness to negotiate), the balance is still asymmetrical in many respects so that no neat package of even numbers can emerge. Moreover, this is only to be expected in view of the very different geographic and consequently strategic positions of the two powers. Nor can any agreed level of armaments be very low, for low levels of arms are very sensitive to surprises arising from cheating or technological breakthrough. Moreover, no one expects 'on-the-spot' inspection of an arms agreement, and verification of compliance will be dependent on 'unilateral means', which means chiefly satellite photography. Satellite surveillance is now maintained by both Superpowers and cameras are said to be capable of discerning objects no larger than one square foot from orbital heights. Yet interpretation is open to dispute and many of the most important characteristics of weapons, such as accuracy, can only be indirectly deduced.

In May 1972 the United States and the Soviet Union signed the first strategic arms limitation agreement, the details of which are also briefly discussed in the later chapter on disarmament. If the agreement is sustained it will terminate the competitive multiplication of missiles and restrict BMD to two sites for each nation, one to protect an ICBM field, on the American pattern, and one to protect the national capital, on the Soviet pattern. The agreements on offensive weapons concede the Soviet Union a numerical superiority in both ICBMS and SLBMS. The number of SLBMS is explicitly set forth in a protocol as a maximum of 710 for the United States, on 44 submarines, and 950 for the Soviet Union, on 62 submarines. The number of ICBMS is merely agreed to be the stock on 1 July 1972 but, in a unilateral declaration of its understanding, the United States has

Opposite The options which are open to the US and the Russians to improve their nuclear missile forces under the SAL agreement. Both can replace certain outdated equipment while keeping within agreed total figures, but the US has far fewer possibilities.

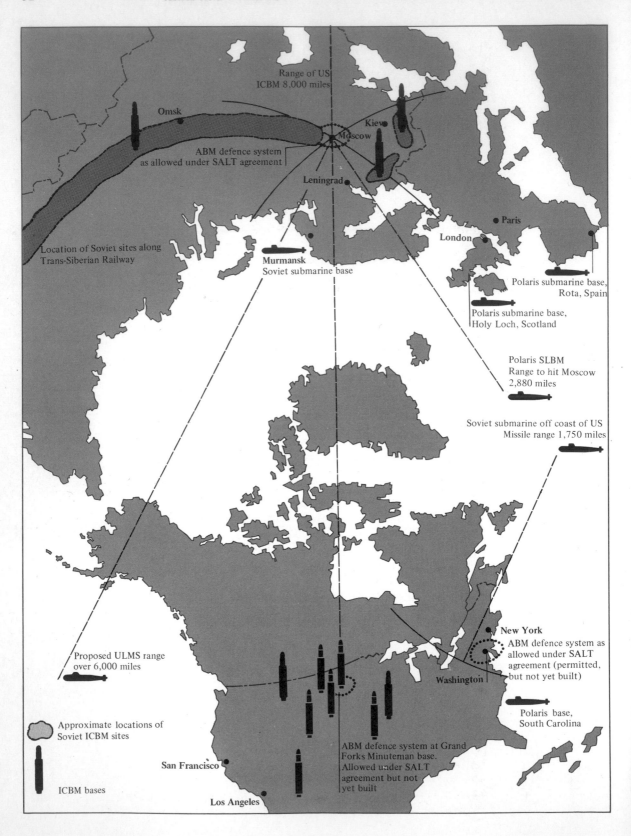

Range of US
ICBM 8.000 miles

Omsk

Kiev

Moscow

ABM defence system
as allowed under SALT agreement

Leningrad

Paris

London

Location of Soviet sites along
Trans-Siberian Railway

Murmansk
Soviet submarine base

Polaris submarine base,
Rota, Spain

Polaris submarine base,
Holy Loch, Scotland

Polaris SLBM
Range to hit Moscow
2,880 miles

Soviet submarine off coast of US
Missile range 1,750 miles

New York

ABM defence system as
allowed under SALT
agreement (permitted,
but not yet built)

Proposed ULMS range
over 6,000 miles

Washington

Polaris base,
South Carolina

Approximate locations of
Soviet ICBM sites

ABM defence system at Grand
Forks Minuteman base.
Allowed under SALT
agreement but not
yet built

San Francisco

ICBM bases

Los Angeles

held this to mean 1054 for itself and 1618 for the Soviet Union. By an agreement not to increase the number of 'heavy' missiles, the Soviet Union has restricted the number of SS9s (or their successors) within its arsenal. Bombers are excluded from the agreement, as are all tactical and intermediate range weapons. No restrictions are placed on technological development of such devices as MIRVs.

Spokesmen for the Nixon Administration have argued that the agreements are a good bargain for the United States despite the apparent numerical concessions to the Soviet Union. They point out that the agreement is initially for five years and that current rates of deployment made it inevitable that the Soviet Union would outstrip the United States by even more in the restricted categories. Meanwhile, the areas in which the United States excels, bombers and warheads, are left unconstrained. Critics, however, have suggested that this is precisely the danger: that the Soviet Union, having negotiated a ceiling on boosters affording them a perhaps fourfold advantage in payload or 'throw weight', are now free to exploit this with new warhead technology, while the United States is prevented from competing in numbers of missiles. Moreover, the Russians could, if they wished, turn to bombers.

Certainly, with all the exclusions, the agreements do not in themselves put a stop to the rapid technological innovation that has exploded the easy assumption of a technologically inevitable strategic stability. It remains to be seen whether the agreements testify to a political will to slow the pace of innovation and procurement. It also remains to be seen whether any such efforts to engineer a stable strategic relationship between the Superpowers will serve the wider cause of diplomatic *détente*.

There remains a deeper question as to whether any lasting sense of security can be based on policies of mutual and undisguised vulnerability. Vulnerability has been with us for some years as the unavoidable result of the state of military technology. It is, however, a rather different matter to codify and explicitly establish vulnerability as an apparent long term goal of policy. It is possible that the effort to replace deterrence by defence has been abandoned for ever, but it seems unlikely.

CHAPTER TWO

Lesser Nuclear Forces and Nuclear Proliferation

The two Superpowers have not enjoyed a monopoly of nuclear weapons for more than twenty years. Today there are three additional nuclear powers – Britain, France and China – while some suspect that Israel should be added to the list. These smaller nuclear forces are of great strategic interest in their own right. They also raise two important and more general questions: the first concerns the rate at which other nations may acquire nuclear weapons and the possible consequences; the second involves the extent to which the theory and practice of mutual deterrence worked out between the Superpowers in what has been a virtually bilateral relationship will require modification as the nuclear world becomes 'multipolar'.

The United States acquired and used nuclear weapons in 1945. Four years later the Soviet Union carried out its first test explosion. The United Kingdom reached this stage in 1952, France in 1960, and China in 1964. All of the lesser nuclear powers have now produced thermonuclear explosions, though France will have no operational thermonuclear weapons until about 1975. The Chinese situation in this respect is uncertain.

The British Force

Despite the much greater publicity accorded to the French and Chinese nuclear efforts, there can be no doubt that in the mid-seventies the British is the most formidable of the lesser nuclear forces. The British decision to acquire nuclear weapons was taken under circumstances very different from those attending all subsequent national decisions. Having participated with the United States in the Manhattan Project leading to the American bombs of 1945, and having a tradition of acquiring, as a Great Power, the most advanced weapons available, the British undertook to develop their own nuclear bombs as a matter of course. This decision was taken before the revolutionary strategic implications of nuclear weapons were fully appreciated, and several years before the thermonuclear weapon, which completed that revolution, had been proved practicable.

The first British strategic force consisted of free-fall bombs carried by the medium-range, transonic jet V-bombers – Victor, Valiant and Vulcan. Later, some of these aircraft were equipped with a 'stand-off' glide bomb, Blue Steel. After a period in which the Royal Air Force also operated American Thor IRBMs under joint arrangements involving an American veto over use (the 'two-key' system), the British planned to reorganize their own national force around a liquid-fuelled IRBM of British manufacture, Blue Streak. Escalating costs and appreciation of the vulnerability of such a soft-based missile to pre-emptive attack led to cancellation of the programme and British planning turned to joint procurement with the USAF of an airborne MRBM, Skybolt, which could be fitted to the Vulcan bombers.

After an American decision not to continue developing Skybolt for American

Opposite One of the French SSBS strategic missiles in its underground silo.

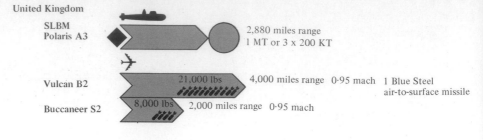

United Kingdom

SLBM
Polaris A3 — 2,880 miles range
1 MT or 3 x 200 KT

Vulcan B2 — 21,000 lbs — 4,000 miles range   0·95 mach   1 Blue Steel
air-to-surface missile

Buccaneer S2 — 8,000 lbs — 2,000 miles range   0·95 mach

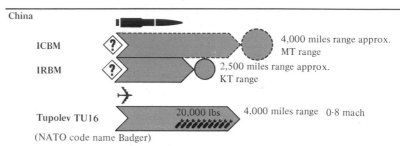

France

IRBM
SSBS S2 — 1,875 miles range
150 KT

SLBM
MSBS M1 — 1,380 miles range
500 KT

Solid fuel ◆
Liquid fuel ⬦?
Maximum weapons load

Mirage IVA — 8,000 lbs — 2,000 miles range   2·2 mach

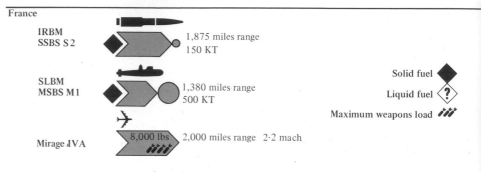

China

ICBM — 4,000 miles range approx.
MT range

IRBM — 2,500 miles range approx.
KT range

Tupolev TU16 — 20,000 lbs — 4,000 miles range   0·8 mach
(NATO code name Badger)

forces, Great Britain decided that the expense of developing the missile solely for British use would be prohibitive. It was at this point, in 1962, that the famous Nassau agreement was concluded whereby the United States undertook to provide Britain with Polaris missiles (without the warheads) and with assistance in building the necessary submarines in which to put them. To allay criticism that this constituted a dangerous dissemination of American nuclear knowledge, the British Government agreed to assign its submarines for use under the NATO Supreme Commander, Europe (SACEUR); an agreement that was almost completely vitiated by a reservation of the right to unilateral use in circumstances where an issue of supreme British national interest had arisen. It is, of course, impossible to imagine use under any less urgent circumstances.

The important question is whether the United Kingdom has the physical capacity to use the force independently. Over the long term, the British force is dependent on the logistical chain which provides both the British and American Polaris forces with technical support and replacement for the missiles. The warheads are of wholly British manufacture, though some important technical advice has been afforded by the United States, nuclear tests are conducted in America on behalf of Britain, and practice firings are conducted on US ranges. But in the short term the British have enough missiles and spares to carry them through a period of crisis or strained relations with the United States and the British government maintains that it has the physical capacity to communicate with and to launch the force unilaterally. While the British force is targeted in

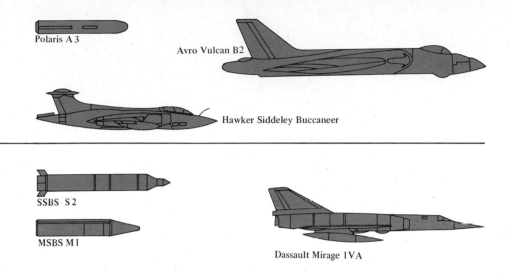

Polaris A 3

Avro Vulcan B2

Hawker Siddeley Buccaneer

SSBS S 2

MSBS M 1

Dassault Mirage 1VA

Tupolev TU16

The strategic weapon delivery systems of the three lesser nuclear powers.

Below HMS *Revenge*, one of Britain's four Polaris-armed submarines.

Left A British bomber being loaded with a Blue Steel stand-off bomb.
Below A Vulcan bomber over Niagara Falls. This with Victor formed the mainstay of the British deterrent until replaced by Polaris-armed submarines at the end of the 1960s.

conjunction with the United States force, provision for national targeting also exists.

There are a great many factors to take into consideration when judging the adequacy of the British deterrent. Many of the most important questions concern the political credibility of a small force opposed to a potential enemy of Superpower proportions. To a large extent these questions are special cases of the considerations affecting the more general determinants of nuclear proliferation discussed later. It is clear that a variety of motives have supported British determination to have a nuclear force and several of these coexist simultaneously without necessarily having been marshalled into a clear order of priorities by any one government.

Once it had become clear, in the fifties, that nuclear weapons raised very special theoretical questions, one justification advanced for a British force, and one never wholly abandoned, was that such a force provided insurance against a divergence of American and British interests. This argument was put forward in the general form that the United States might not support Britain in a crisis, an argument much to the fore after Suez, or on the narrower ground that there might be damage limitation targets (Russian MRBM sites or submarine bases for example) to which United States forces would assign a lower priority than British interests required. Other justifications of the British force have been based on broader diplomatic grounds: that it contributes to British prestige, partly by testifying to technological prowess; that it secures a place at the 'Top Table' of both interallied and wider diplomatic dealings; that it secures a foremost hearing at disarmament negotiations; and that only by having first-hand and partly autonomous familiarity with nuclear weapons can Britain uphold its position as a primary ally of the United States.

It is clear that the British nuclear force may be justified either as a supplement to allied forces – what has been officially called 'an independent contribution to the Western deterrent' or as a force for truly independent use in the event of a failure of the American guarantee. Critics of the latter conception argue that it is not easy to conceive of situations in which Britain could credibly threaten to launch what would presumably be a suicidal attack on the Soviet Union. Advocates of the force argue that possession of a national second strike force at the very least affords some assurance against nuclear blackmail and thereby stiffens British diplomatic will. Moreover, they argue, with some reason, that the whole business of nuclear deterrence, even between the Superpowers, is one of exploiting uncertainties, and that the mere possession of a physical capacity to wreak severe destruction must impose considerable caution on Russian decisions, whatever coldblooded and abstract analysis of political possibilities suggests. Finally, it must be remembered that the British nuclear force can be valued not only for its present utility but also as an option on an uncertain future in which other nuclear powers may emerge and in which there is every reason to believe that at least one other Western European power, France, intends to maintain what would be, in the absence of the British force, a local monopoly of nuclear weapons.

The merits of many of these arguments will be very largely determined by the technical efficiency of the British force. Perhaps the most conspicuous feature of the force is its small size, consisting as it does of only four Polaris submarines, each carrying, like the American boats, sixteen missiles. These missiles are the A3 type and, like their American equivalent, possess an MRV of three warheads. Taking into account refits, the British force, which employs the American practice of double-crewing to extract maximum use from the vessels, ought to be

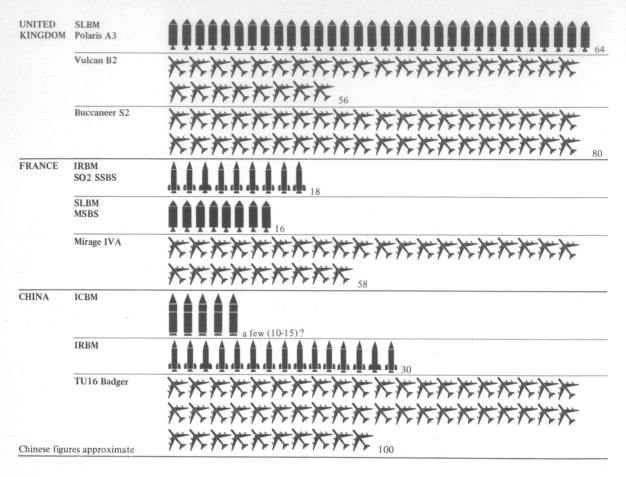

UNITED KINGDOM	SLBM Polaris A3	64
Vulcan B2		56
Buccaneer S2		80
FRANCE	IRBM SO2 SSBS	18
SLBM MSBS		16
Mirage IVA		58
CHINA	ICBM	a few (10-15)?
IRBM		30
TU16 Badger		100

Chinese figures approximate

Above Force strengths of the lesser nuclear powers.

A French ssbs being loaded into its underground silo.

able to have at least two boats on station at all times. In practice it seems that there will be short periods when only one boat will be on patrol. This raises two serious doubts: would such a small number of boats be very vulnerable to Russian ASW and could such a small number of missiles penetrate Russian BMD and do adequate damage?

The penetration problem does not appear serious for the moment. Russia's BMD system only exists in the Moscow area, leaving ample alternative targets. Even around Moscow, the efficiency of the defences is dubious and efforts to improve the penetration capability of the British A3 may well serve to keep the Russian capital vulnerable. The British authorities may believe that retaining a capacity to hit Moscow has special deterrent value. Certainly Soviet efforts to build a defence for Moscow suggest that the Russians take this view. In the longer term the emergence of effective BMD systems is obviously serious for a small and rather impoverished nuclear strike force. For the moment the agreement between the Superpowers to limit their deployment of BMD will considerably reduce the penetration problems of the smaller nuclear powers.

The weakness of the British force to ASW arises from its small number of boats. According to all Western declarations, the chance of ASW proving an effective or reliable counter to missile-firing submarines is small. On the other hand there is always the possibility of a breakthrough in ASW. American interest in developing ULMS suggests concern about the long term future. Even at the present state of the art a deployed force of only one or two boats obviously constitutes a more vulnerable target for such countermeasures as trailing from its base than a more numerous force. Much would depend on whether the Soviet Union felt able to give priority to dealing with the lesser submarine forces at the price of reducing its efforts against that of the United States.

Overall it seems reasonable to conclude that the British Polaris force will possess, at least for most of the seventies, a fairly high technical credibility as an instrument capable of doing substantial devastation to Russian cities should the occasion arise. It must also be remembered that for several years to come Britain intends to retain fifty-six medium-range Vulcan bombers which, though officially relegated to the tactical and interdiction roles, still possess a capability for low level penetration that might succeed in delivering some of their Blue Steel missiles on Russian targets. Finally, the substantial British tactical air force, including eighty Buccaneer aircraft and the planned multiple role combat aircraft (MRCA) would afford a last resort capability of sufficient magnitude to increase Russian uncertainties. In combination, all this adds up to the most powerful nuclear force yet existing in other than Russian or American hands.

The French Force

Many of the technical and political questions that are raised by the British force are also relevant to that of France. Some need pursuing further when we come to possibilities of Anglo–French co-operation, and to the conception of an integrated Western European force.

The most notable characteristic of the French force is that it has been created in an ostentatiously independent manner. So far as technical matters are concerned, this independence has not always been as total as French publicists would suggest. The United States provided France with twelve KC135F tankers to refuel its strategic bomber force in flight – a facility without which it cannot reach Russian targets on two-way missions – and rather more other technical information has been passed to the French than is commonly realized. But there has certainly been nothing to compare with the Nassau relationship between Britain and the United States. The French force, with all its deficiencies, is substantially home-grown and consequently rests on a more completely self-sufficient, if in many details inferior, technological infrastructure than the British. This independence has been purchased only at the price of numerous technological errors and at great financial cost.

The French force consists of thirty-six Mirage IVA supersonic aircraft (mach 2·2), with some two dozen others in reserve. These aircraft have a small payload; consequently their operational radius is little over 900 miles and their strategic employment depends on in-flight refuelling by the KC135s. For the same reason the Mirage carry only one 60-KT bomb. Despite dispersal over about ten airfields, the Mirage force must be regarded as vulnerable to counterforce action and of rather doubtful capability for penetrating Soviet defences.

A second component of the French force is composed of eighteen IRBMs with a range of 1900 miles and a single warhead of 150 KT. These solid-fuelled missiles, all of which are now said to be in service, are emplaced in hardened silos in Haut-Provence. This force, while far from negligible, is presumably open to the same doubts about survivability as now surround all the land-based missile forces of the Superpowers in a period of increasing missile accuracies.

For its third component and as a longer term investment, France, like Britain, has turned to the submarine-launched missile. The first of a projected force of five French-built nuclear-propelled submarines carrying sixteen missiles, also of French manufacture, is now in commission, although the full five boats are unlikely to be ready before 1978. The French SLBM has a range of only 1350 miles and a boosted fission warhead of 500 KT. As a result of severe developmental delays, true fusion warheads are not expected to be available before 1975.

France has set about providing its own command and control system for the submarines and has presumably achieved an adequate solution of the problem of accurate navigation involved in SSBN operation. It is possible, however, that in these respects French standards have yet to match those of the Anglo–American forces. Moreover, the restricted range of the French SLBM confines the submarines to smaller potential firing areas, with consequent reduction of time on firing station and increase in vulnerability to ASW.

The differences between the French and British forces and the respective infrastructures of nuclear and other military technology underlying them arise, of course, from divergent national approaches to the question of independence. Britain created an initial nuclear force long before France. Even in the early stages Britain used its nuclear force as part of an intimate relationship with the United States, sharing intelligence and engaging in joint targeting. In later years, as the pace of technological sophistication grew, Britain was able to maintain an advanced and effective – if small – strategic force by accepting American assistance within a continued framework of political and strategic co-operation. The possibility of using the British force independently has been maintained but is played down as an unlikely contingency.

France, on the other hand, has made a fetish of independence. Admittedly it is doubtful how much assistance she could have obtained if she had wanted it. At Nassau, President Kennedy held out the possibility of offering France Polaris on the same terms as Britain. But France at that time did not possess the nuclear capacity to accept the offer without asking for further assistance with the warheads. Even if this had been forthcoming, the price would undoubtedly have been a much tighter degree of integration than that demanded for the bare boosters. It is, in fact, unlikely that the United States would have helped France with warheads under any conditions, if only because of the deep suspicion of France traditionally entertained by the powerful Joint Congressional Committee on Atomic Energy.

Be that as it may, successive French Governments, including the pre-Gaullist régimes of 1954–6 which set France definitively on the road to nuclear weapons, have consistently preferred conspicuous political independence to technical efficiency in nuclear matters. This determination seems to derive partly from the fact that the French force owes much of its impetus to essentially political purposes of prestige and international status, and partly from a genuine belief that no nation can be relied upon to take nuclear action on behalf of another when the consequence may be devastating retaliation. In the words of M. Debré, French Minister of Defence, 'nuclear risk is not divisible . . . that risk is so enormous that a people would accept it only as a final defence of their supreme self-interest . . .' To this may be added the fear, frequently expressed by General de Gaulle, that the Superpowers might be tempted to wage a limited nuclear war confined to Europe, if no European nation had the power to extend the nuclear consequences to the homelands of the Superpowers. At the height of Gaullist independence of spirit these views were taken to the extreme of a strategy of *tous azimuts* enunciated by the then Chief of Staff, General Ailleret. This strategy of 'all directions' suggested the need to retaliate globally against any conceivable power, obviously including the United States. Even before the fall of de Gaulle, however, this doctrine, with its extreme political, strategic and technological implications, had been modified so that now, though the keynote of French nuclear strategy is still independence, the weapons are clearly pointed eastward.

A European Nuclear Force?

The British and French nuclear forces and the reasoning underlying their existence suggest both the opportunities and the obstacles confronting the project for an integrated European force. Several distinguishable arguments support this project. If the existing European nuclear powers are to perpetuate their forces into new generations of weapons they must, given the rising cost of sophisticated equipment, be interested in any possibility of economy by co-operation in development, procurement, or operation. Should the rise of Russian strategic forces to parity with the United States erode the credibility of American guarantees to Europe, it could be argued that Europeans need to increase rather than merely maintain their existing independent power. The case for economy of effort would thereby be reinforced and other Western European nations become more interested in association with Anglo–French efforts. Even without any dramatic sense of decline in reliability of the American guarantee, many argue that it is unreasonable to expect the United States to underpin the European balance of power for ever, and that the emergence of an integrated framework of Western European defence, including a nuclear component, is a natural corollary of the wider process of economic and political unification.

The Western Europeans undoubtedly enjoy the technological capacity to produce strategic nuclear forces of high quality; the obstacles are almost entirely political. From the technical point of view Britain and France possess ample facilities for producing plutonium, uranium 235 and the other materials required for fission and fusion weapons. Britain is ahead of France in warhead design, in miniaturization, multiplication of warheads and hardening them against radiation effects. France has a more substantial indigenous capability for design and development of long-range missiles and for manufacture of solid rocket fuels. Britain has more experience in construction of nuclear submarines and a closer acquaintance with the inertial guidance systems essential both for missiles and for submarines. A considerable degree of complementarity thus exists between the two nations, while several other European countries, particularly Germany, have much sophisticated technology that could be applied to strategic nuclear forces.

Thus it is chiefly for political reasons that a European nuclear force may be

The Russian-designed Tupolev TU16 medium bomber is the main delivery-vehicle for the Chinese nuclear bomb. It is subsonic and has a 4000-mile range which would theoretically allow it to reach Moscow.

difficult to construct. Several of these political obstacles are implicit in what has gone before. France, though anxious to preserve a nuclear force independent of the United States, would like to do so on a national basis and hence independent of other Europeans also. Britain, though also anxious to keep its nuclear force, puts a premium on doing nothing to weaken the American guarantee and values the assistance she has received and may continue to receive in return for a co-operative attitude to America's strategy.

Thus Britain has shown most receptiveness to operational co-ordination with France, with an implied co-ordination with the United States, and nervousness about technological co-operation which might breach undertakings to safe-

The deployment of the strategic weapon systems of the lesser nuclear powers, and the intermediate-range systems of Russia and America.

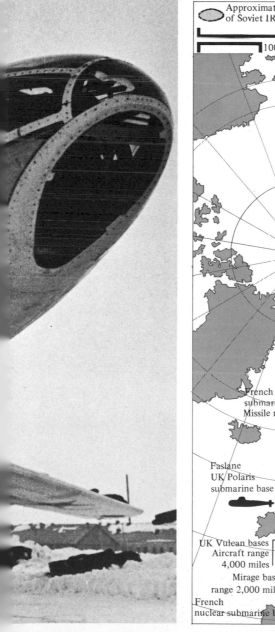

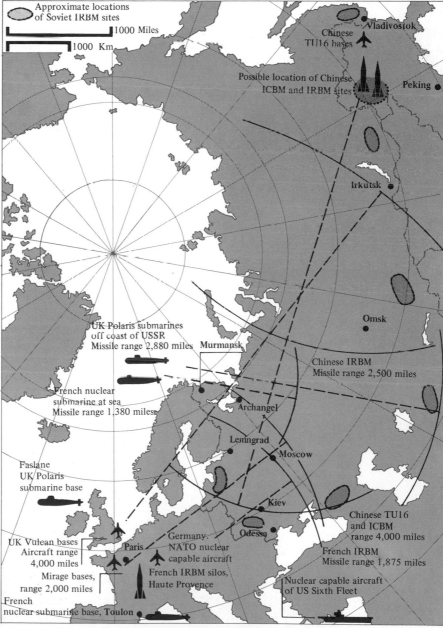

Approximate locations of Soviet IRBM sites

1000 Miles
1000 Km

Chinese TU16 bases

Vladivostok

Possible location of Chinese ICBM and IRBM sites

Peking

Irkutsk

Omsk

UK Polaris submarines off coast of USSR Missile range 2,880 miles

Murmansk

Chinese IRBM Missile range 2,500 miles

French nuclear submarine at sea Missile range 1,380 miles

Archangel

Faslane UK Polaris submarine base

Leningrad

Moscow

Kiev

Chinese TU16 and ICBM range 4,000 miles

UK Vulcan bases Aircraft range 4,000 miles

Germany NATO nuclear capable aircraft

Odessa

French IRBM Missile range 1,875 miles

Paris

Mirage bases, range 2,000 miles

French IRBM silos, Haute Provence

Nuclear capable aircraft of US Sixth Fleet

French nuclear submarine base, Toulon

The explosion of an atomic bomb at the Chinese test site at Sinkiang province.

guard secrets derived from America. France, by contrast, shows receptiveness to exchange of technical information but would wish to retain operational independence.

Many other problems are raised by the role of Germany, which has undertaken under the London and Paris Agreements of 1954 not to manufacture nuclear weapons on German soil, has signed the nuclear Non-Proliferation Treaty, and yet obviously constitutes the most powerful single industrial and economic component in emerging Europe. The German relationship, moreover, poses in very sharp form the possibility of adverse Superpower reactions as a price for developing a pan-European nuclear force.

Progress toward a European nuclear force may therefore be slow and much will depend upon whether the United States opposes it or comes to see it as a constructive devolution of responsibility for the balance of power in Europe. Nevertheless, certain nuclear measures of Anglo–French co-ordination are quite probable. Merely by agreed phasing of SSBN patrols, for instance, the two powers could go a considerable way to overcome the difficulty of maintaining several boats on constant patrol. This would complicate Soviet calculations even if the degree of Anglo–French agreement on how and when to fire their nuclear weapons remained obscure.

Agreement on this crucial question, whether between France and Britain or on a wider European scale, may very well have to await the emergence of a new European political authority. Some European equivalent of the co-ordinating machinery analogous to the Nuclear Planning Group within NATO might be possible in the interim. This might be all the more practicable if attention were concentrated upon such minimal purposes as threatening retaliation for nuclear attacks on European territory of the kind feared in General de Gaulle's conceptions.

The Chinese Force

Chinese nuclear forces are usually debated in a very different perspective from those of the Europeans because, impoverished though China may be today, no one seriously doubts her ultimate potential to become a major world power or her determination to maintain a nuclear force in the meantime. Since China has political unity, she tends to be taken more seriously as an ultimate disturbing factor for the bipolar, Superpower balance than the Europeans. Nevertheless, so far as the seventies are concerned, one should not fail to remember that Chinese short-term potential is limited. Virtually nothing about China is known with any precision, but few estimates put her Gross National Product (GNP) for 1970 over $100 billion or her defence expenditure over 10 per cent of that amount. This might be compared to French GNP for 1970 of $148 billion or British of $121 billion.

The obscurity surrounding the Chinese economy extends to her nuclear force. She detonated fission explosives in 1964 and her fusion test in 1967 pre-dated the French by over a year. Estimates of the total Chinese stockpile of nuclear weapons for early 1972 range from 120 to 280. Such estimates are based chiefly on assumptions about Chinese production of plutonium and U235.

For delivery of nuclear weapons, China could rely on her version of the Russian TU16 *Badger* medium-range subsonic bomber and on an MRBM modelled on the 1000-mile-range Soviet SS4. One Chinese nuclear test involved delivery of a 10–20 KT warhead by such a missile. The launching of a Chinese satellite in April 1970 and a second in March 1971 testified to Chinese missile capability. Development of a storable-liquid-fuelled IRBM of 2000–2500 mile range has been reported and the satellite launchings are believed by some to have involved components of a planned ICBM. Lower estimates of Chinese technical resources, however, now tend to suggest an operational Chinese ICBM force will not be deployed until after the middle of this decade. So far as submarines are concerned, the Chinese have long had a single version of the Soviet conventionally powered G class submarine designed to fire missiles from the surface, and are now said to be building their first nuclear-powered attack submarine. A nuclear-powered missile submarine is, however, thought to be at least 8–10 years away.

Thus, all imminent Chinese delivery systems are of medium or intermediate range. The significance of this depends very much on the supposed purposes of a Chinese force: whether to deter the United States and the Soviet Union, or to overawe Asian neighbours. For all but the first purpose intermediate range systems should have considerable potency, for even European Russia would be within range. At the same time, all the other major Asian powers must now take Chinese nuclear power into account.

Nuclear Proliferation

The problem faced by China's neighbours illustrates many of the questions raised by the prospect of nuclear weapons being acquired by more and more states. In the sixties, when France and China were becoming the fourth and fifth nuclear powers, there were alarmist predictions that there would be as many as twenty nuclear states by 1975. By now it has become clear that the process will be much slower and the Non-Proliferation Treaty (NPT) testifies to hopes that it may be arrested altogether. On the other hand several key states have either not signed or not ratified the NPT and it is in any case clear that the treaty is only a partial safeguard. With the technical capacity to acquire nuclear weapons rapidly spreading, the prospect of nuclear proliferation remains very real and overhangs many other strategic questions. (The term 'horizontal proliferation' is sometimes used to indicate the acquisition of nuclear weapons and 'vertical proliferation' to refer to the multiplication of nuclear weapons in the hands of states already possessing some. Others use the term 'nuclear dispersion' to refer to horizontal proliferation. Yet others use the term proliferation to denote the development of a new national capacity to make nuclear weapons and 'dissemination' to refer to the transfer of nuclear weapons from one state to another. But most commonly the term proliferation is used to identify the whole problem of new states acquiring independent control of nuclear weapons by any means.)

It is possible to analyse proliferation at two levels. One concerns the long-term

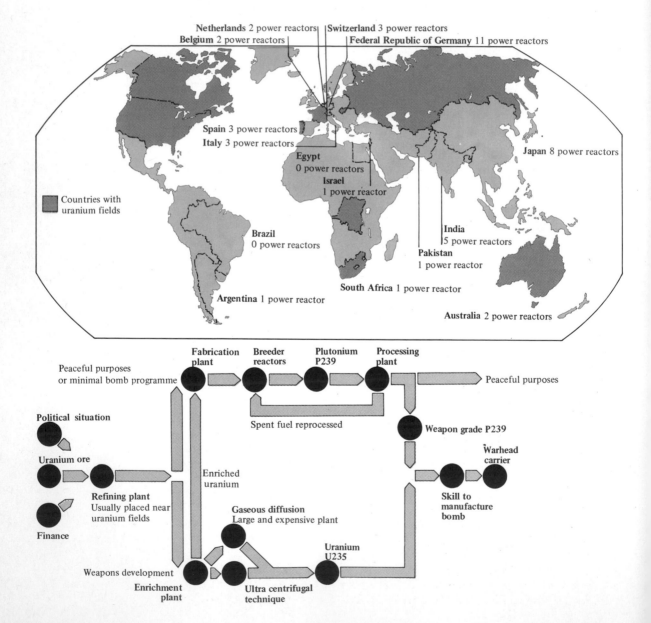

Status on NPT

	Signed	Not signed
Argentina		
Australia		
Belgium		
Brazil		
Egypt		
Federal Republic of Germany		
India		
Israel		
Italy		
Japan		
Netherlands		
Pakistan		
South Africa		
Spain		
Switzerland		

Signed
Not signed

Netherlands 2 power reactors
Belgium 2 power reactors
Switzerland 3 power reactors
Federal Republic of Germany 11 power reactors

Spain 3 power reactors
Italy 3 power reactors
Egypt 0 power reactors
Israel 1 power reactor

Japan 8 power reactors

Countries with uranium fields

Brazil 0 power reactors

India 5 power reactors

Pakistan 1 power reactor

South Africa 1 power reactor

Argentina 1 power reactor

Australia 2 power reactors

Fabrication plant
Breeder reactors
Plutonium P239
Processing plant

Peaceful purposes or minimal bomb programme

Peaceful purposes

Spent fuel reprocessed

Political situation

Weapon grade P239

Uranium ore

Warhead carrier

Refining plant
Usually placed near uranium fields

Enriched uranium

Finance

Gaseous diffusion
Large and expensive plant

Skill to manufacture bomb

Weapons development

Uranium U235

Enrichment plant

Ultra centrifugal technique

and largely unforeseeable problems implied by the need to manage nuclear power for the rest of history now that the genie is for ever out of the bottle. The other and more practical level concerns which nations might acquire nuclear weapons in the next few years, whether they will do so, and what the consequences would be.

These questions will be decided by the interaction of technical capabilities and political circumstances. In the short run, technical capability to produce nuclear weapons is sufficiently rare to provide some firm guidelines about immediate prospects. Such guidance is, however, chiefly negative; that is to say, while it tells us who could go nuclear, only political analysis can suggest who will. As the technical capabilities of nations rise, the dominating role of political considerations will become more and more apparent.

Technical Capability

While it is clear that nuclear weapons could spread by being distributed by the existing nuclear powers, at least to nations with sufficient military sophistication to use them, none of the present nuclear powers shows much current inclination to do so. This brief discussion therefore concentrates on the problems facing a nation trying to make weapons for itself. It must be realized, however, that even where no deliberate foreign assistance is given to make nuclear weapons, much equipment and knowledge of value for the purpose, such as computers, navigational equipment, precision engineering machinery and practice, is available through normal commercial channels.

So far as the strictly nuclear part of nuclear weapons is concerned, the prime requirement is a supply of the fissionable materials uranium 235 (U235), uranium 233 (U233) or plutonium 239 (P239). No significant use has yet been made of U233 which is obtainable by irradiating thorium in a reactor. Its chief interest lies in the fact that India has lots of thorium.

To manufacture U235 or P239 requires a supply of natural uranium. Deposits of uranium are plentiful and it can even be extracted from seawater; the latter process is, however, highly uneconomic unless combined with other purposes, such as fertilizer production. Largely due to the monopolistic efforts of the existing nuclear powers, no free and ready market exists in uranium. Outside the Communist world it has been obtainable virtually only under safeguards for peaceful use, once chiefly those overseen by the United States and now also those of the control accounting mechanisms of the International Atomic Energy Agency (IAEA) based in Vienna. This attempt to keep track of uranium and other fuels passing into nuclear reactors for ostensibly peaceful purposes (chiefly research and the generation of electricity) is now enshrined in the Non-Proliferation Treaty.

The readily fissile isotope U235 constitutes only 0·7 per cent of natural uranium, the rest being almost entirely U238. As the two materials are chemically indistinguishable, they can be separated only by methods exploiting their infinitesimally different weights. Of several theoretically possible processes the two found most practicable involve converting uranium into the gas uranium hexafluoride and then either spinning it at immense speeds in a centrifuge so that the heavier molecules containing U238 move to the periphery, or forcing it through successive thousands of filtering membranes so that the heavier molecules are slowly separated from the lighter. Both methods demand exacting engineering and large amounts of electrical energy.

Centrifuge technology is under development in the United States and jointly by Germany, Britain and the Netherlands. It is also said to have been used by

Opposite Some of the factors and stages involved in a nuclear weapons programme. At the top are the countries which could most easily initiate such a programme.

$ 5,000/lb

China. But overwhelmingly the bulk of U235 so far manufactured has been made by the filtering 'gaseous diffusion' process. All the existing nuclear powers possess gaseous diffusion plants, which are large, conspicuous and expensive. Weapon-grade U235 must be 90–5 per cent pure. The American plants are now thought to produce U235 at about $11,000 a kilogram. The required mass of U235 to sustain an explosion is about 12–14 kg; something over 20 kg is required to produce a fission yield of 20 KT.

Any really rich and technically sophisticated power opting for nuclear weapons will almost certainly seek to acquire U235 which, among other qualities, has generally been preferred in making triggers for thermonuclear weapons. The capital costs are, however, extremely high and it is both easier and cheaper to make plutonium. Cut-price nuclear weapons efforts may therefore be expected to begin with P239, which is also valuable for the manufacture of small weapons, the minimum explosive mass being only about 6 kg, with 8 kg yielding about 20 KT.

Plutonium, which does not exist in nature, is produced by bombarding U238 in a reactor. This produces both P239 and P240. P240 is of no use for weapons. The longer the uranium stays in the reactor, the more plutonium is produced, but its proportion of P239 declines in relation to P240. Similarly, if the reactor is fuelled with 'enriched uranium' – that is uranium in which the proportion of U235 has been increased – the lower quantity of U238 will entail less production of plutonium.

The importance of all this is, of course, that while the process of producing U235 would scarcely be worthwhile if it were not for nuclear weapons, plutonium is the inevitable by-product of reactors intended to produce electrical power. This is particularly true of the natural uranium reactors favoured by most nations other than the United States. Admittedly the need to remove the fuel rods before too much P240 is produced creates some conflict of interest between power production and weapons manufacture. To make weapon-grade P239 on a large scale it is economical to create special reactors for the purpose. But on a smaller scale the production of electricity can offset some of the costs of obtaining P239. While the price per kilogram will be very high (about $100,000) the total outlay will be far lower than that involved in going for U235. More important still, for the long run, is the fact that the spread of power reactors inevitably disseminates a capability to produce plutonium and, under present arrangements, creates plutonium under national ownership, even if at present under auditing safeguards and not usually in weapon grades. As we shall see, the step from plutonium to a weapon is not a small one. Nevertheless, a world full of plutonium, which is what we are achieving, is a world in which the time from the decision to make weapons to fulfilment is greatly abbreviated. Moreover, the peaceful nuclear programmes disseminate skills in nuclear engineering.

P239 is chemically distinguishable from uranium. Thus, although it is difficult stuff to handle, it can be processed in a 'chemical separation' plant at immensely less cost (and much less conspicuously) than gaseous diffusion. The costs of nuclear weapons programmes cannot be rigorously compared because of secrecy, disparate national systems of accounting, and the fact that costs for enterprises at very different times are expressed in current prices. But rough comparisons can be derived from the fact that the cost of a gaseous diffusion plant of 'economic size' is said to be between $750 million and $1000 million.

By contrast a minimal programme for producing 8 kg of P239 a year has been estimated at $22 million, with operating costs of $4·80 million a year. This includes reactor, fuel, and extraction of the P239. The capital cost of the extraction plant is estimated at only $1·25 million. At this rate the P239 would be costing $900,000 per kilogram. A larger programme based on a reactor designed to produce P239 could, however, cost $87 million, with yearly costs of $9·5 million, and provide 160 kg a year at $120,000 a kilogram.

These costs are, of course, only estimates based on prices in the late sixties. Cost overruns are notorious in the weapon business. The rough conclusion must be that producing fissile material is expensive, but that a modest plutonium-based programme could be vastly cheaper than the ambitious, across-the-board efforts of the existing nuclear powers. A very small production programme might be cheaper if combined with electrical power generation. Specialized reactors would be more economical for a larger programme (say 80 kg per year or more), though possibly there would be political advantages to integrating civil and military purposes. In any case civil nuclear programmes should afford valuable experience in the efficient operation of reactors and processing plants.

Certain additional special materials would be required for the manufacture of thermonuclear fusion weapons. It would be necessary to obtain deuterium, a heavy isotope of hydrogen, and preferably – though not, perhaps, essentially – another heavy isotope, tritium. Deuterium is expensive to produce but the materials and process are not hard to come by. It is also necessary to have lithium and to isolate its light isotope, Li6. Lithium is, however, very cheap and the isolation process is relatively simple.

Once the special materials are available, the steps toward nuclear weapons, particularly the fission variety, are widely understood if difficult to execute. The manufacture of nuclear weapons should no longer be regarded as a matter of secrets, so much as a matter of high standards of precision engineering. This engineering entails handling and shaping the nuclear materials, designing and shaping the high-explosive charges used to compress the material for detonation, and providing adequate means to ensure initiation of the explosion at the proper moment. All of this requires much narrower tolerances and higher reliability than most industry demands, if the weapons are to be both safe and usable. The secret experience of the advanced nuclear powers could obviously enable newcomers to achieve good weapons at less cost. But any advanced industrial nation, especially one with some conventional armaments industry, could be confident of ultimate success.

Manufacture of nuclear weapons is, of course, only part of the way to military nuclear capability, for the weapons have to be delivered. In some circumstances 'unconventional' methods of delivery might be considered – the use of merchant vessels, clandestine emplacement in embassy buildings etc. But these, as already remarked, would be of very doubtful reliability and would entail immensely high political and strategic risks. Thus delivery will probably require a force of bombers or missiles, though purely tactical purposes might be served by simply emplacing nuclear charges as land mines.

How difficult and expensive it is to provide an adequate aircraft or missile system will depend upon many variables. It will be closely related to how successful the nuclear engineers have been in achieving a good weight-to-yield ratio in the warheads. It will also depend upon the extent to which delivery systems are available by purchase. Above all, it will depend upon the range over which one wishes to operate and upon the sophistication of one's opponent and the nature of his target system. Thus, in relation to the Arab countries Israel possesses ideal delivery systems in the F4 Phantom and A4 Skyhawk aircraft obtained from America. Clearly the worst problem faces countries like France,

Britain and China, whose need is to deter distant Superpowers. These powers also face in extreme form the need to provide against counterforce pre-emption by a powerful nuclear opponent.

The five existing large nuclear powers have gone for a broad spectrum of capability, including thermonuclear weapons and advanced delivery systems. Their costs have consequently been high. One estimate of the cost of the French programme to the end of 1971 is nearly $13 billion. In Britain, during the period 1960–70, when much basic expenditure had already been made and substantial American assistance was being received, strategic nuclear forces are said to have cost nearly $5 billion.

But modest nuclear forces could be acquired much more cheaply. In 1968 the United Nations estimated that a 'modest but significant nuclear armament' of 30–50 jet bombers, 50 soft-based IRBMs and 100 plutonium warheads could be acquired and deployed for $1·7 billion spread over ten years. The same study suggested that a 'small, high-quality nuclear force' could produce 10–15 bombers and 15–20 warheads in five years and go on to create 20–30 thermo-nuclear weapons, 100 IRBMs and two SSBNs for a ten-year cost of $5·6 billion.

This is a much more optimistic estimate of costs than the actual experience of France in developing a not very dissimilar programme might suggest. But it must be borne in mind that France has been laying the foundations for a more substantial force. The future trend of nuclear weapon costs is unclear. Gradual leakage of information and spread of nuclear expertise may reduce costs of achieving basic explosive capability. On the other hand rising sophistication of offensive and defensive systems is likely to push up the price of serviceable and penetrating forces for the Superpower league. Quite different calculations may have to be made for nations with lesser local or regional ambitions.

Nuclear Candidates

On strictly technical grounds several countries must be regarded as capable of acquiring nuclear weapons quickly. Various lists of candidates are drawn up. Japan, India, Israel, Switzerland and Sweden figure high on all lists. Canada certainly has capability, but her disincentives are large. Similarly, West Germany has all the technical requisites but labours under many special inhibitions. For a somewhat longer future the list of technically competent can-didates includes Italy, the Netherlands, Australia, Argentina, Brazil, South Africa and several East European countries.

The extent to which advanced industrial countries have the technical capability to make nuclear weapons is very largely a matter of choice. Switzer-land, Sweden and India have all shown a tendency to direct their existing nuclear programmes so as to advance their 'option' on nuclear weapons. Thus it should be clear that, given a minimal technical competence, the decision to acquire nuclear weapons or to put oneself a very short lead time away from nuclear weapons depends on political circumstances.

The political determinants of decisions to acquire nuclear weapons raise complex questions that can only briefly be outlined here. In many respects the issue opens up the whole future of the international political system.

Arguments in favour of a national nuclear capability can be broken down into several categories. There are the primarily strategic considerations: the desire to have nuclear weapons to deter or overawe a foe who may or may not have nuclear weapons of his own. Nuclear weapons may also be desired for actual tactical use in military operations. Such uses have a more practical appeal to many military men than strategic deterrence, and Swiss, Swedish and Indian advocates have all foreseen special defensive tactical applications in their mountainous terrain. Strategic arguments may also include the utility of nuclear weapons in ensuring equal access to decisions within alliances.

The last argument blends with the second main category of incentives to obtain nuclear weapons: those concerned with political status and prestige. Such arguments have already been exemplified in the French and British cases. Prestige and status are very relative. Nuclear weapons might be thought useful by a nation seeking status as a world power – or, perhaps, anxious to arrest decline in such status – by one desiring regional primacy, or by one merely wishing to keep up with or outpace a local rival. It does not escape notice that permanent membership of the Security Council now coincides with possession of nuclear weapons. There are also domestic political influences on nuclear decisions. It seems clear that there were strong associations between the domestic prestige of French governments, their relations with the military establishment, and the decision to press forward with nuclear development. Nor must one neglect the interests and zeal of technologists, industrialists and military men associated with nuclear programmes. This element can be coupled with what some would regard as a distinct main category of nuclear incentives: the belief that a nuclear weapons programme can stimulate, help to justify, and advertise national competence in nuclear engineering and, indeed, in technological enterprises of all kinds. The restrictions imposed on non-nuclear-weapons states by the NPT have exacerbated anxieties that these states will be regarded as second rate and as less able to provide a complete and uninhibited service to importers of nuclear technology.

Arguments against acquiring nuclear weapons can also be broken down into categories. The most fundamental distinction is between the disadvantages for the candidate state and the alleged harm that proliferation may do to the international system as a whole. The latter dangers have been elaborately developed by advocates of nuclear disarmament and of non-proliferation agreements. In the first place it is argued that the multiplication of centres of independent nuclear decision increases the chances of nuclear war simply on a statistical basis. Each acquisition may serve to stimulate others; thus, it is argued, the immediate advantage foreseen by an acquiring state may soon be more than offset by the specific reactions of its opponents and the general deterioration of the world system.

A further source of concern is that nuclear proliferation may increase the danger of unstable behaviour. This danger may arise not merely from the possible acquisition of nuclear weapons by states with unsteady or irresponsible régimes, but also because small and crude nuclear forces may suffer technical accidents or be spurred into premature action by their lack of invulnerability to counterforce. An analogous fear concerns the pace and symmetry of proliferation: since there will typically be disparity in the rate at which rivals acquire weapons, the state which is ahead may be tempted to use its weapons before its rival catches up; alternatively, the power that sees its rival about to seize a nuclear lead might be impelled to a desperate conventional attack.

Obviously an assessment of such prospects ought to figure very largely in any national decision to go ahead with nuclear weapons. A major disincentive is the cost. This, as we have seen, may be large and the strain on the budget of any poorer country seeking nuclear power is seen by many students of economic development as an argument of general validity against proliferation. There are also strategic and political dangers. As we have already noted, the effort to acquire nuclear weapons may provoke enemies. It may also alienate allies who disapprove of proliferation or who fear being dragged into a nuclear war. This fear may be especially lively inasmuch as a common argument for the efficacy of quite small nuclear forces as deterrents suggests that they may serve as 'catalytic' agents to drag more powerful nuclear nations into war, thereby borrowing deterrent effect from the larger force. This argument is closely related to the prospect that calculations of nuclear balance will become increasingly difficult on a multilateral basis. Because the Superpowers see this and have so far tried to preserve their nuclear monopoly, a would-be nuclear nation has to reckon on their displeasure.

One quickly reaches the point at which such general analysis ceases to be helpful. There are clearly dangers as well as advantages in acquiring nuclear weapons. Equally there are dangers for the international system, though there is one school of thought, typified by the French General Gallois, which argues that a world of nuclear powers would be one of stability based on universal deterrence. Whether proliferation progresses and at what pace will clearly depend on each particular candidate nation's analysis of the balance of general and specific advantages and disadvantages for itself.

From this perspective it becomes apparent that several of the technically competent candidates are also delicately poised so far as political incentives are concerned. These frontrunners can be classified, with some falling into more than one class. There are the potential Superpowers, Japan and perhaps Europe. Failing Europe there is West Germany, which, like Japan, can also be classified as an 'exposed ally'. There are the contenders for regional primacy, like India and Brazil. There are the parties to bitter local quarrels, like Israel, and India *vis à vis* Pakistan and perhaps also *vis à vis* China. There are the traditional armed and independent neutrals, Sweden and Switzerland.

All these states must come fairly high on any list of early probabilities, and several of them have taken care to go part if not yet all the way to acquiring an 'option' on nuclear weapons. India, for example, is one of the few countries to provide herself with a chemical separation plant. To some degree it can be argued that a short-term option on nuclear weapons can bring many of the advantages of actual acquisition in terms of prestige, international leverage, technical learning and insurance against being taken unawares by a rival's nuclear programmes.

Control of Proliferation

It remains to say a word about efforts to control proliferation. Two major international efforts have been made by the Test Ban Treaty of 1963 and the Non-Proliferation Treaty of 1968. The Test Ban, which forbids nuclear testing in the atmosphere, underwater or in space, would obviously constitute a difficulty for any nuclear candidate which was unwilling to bear the stigma of breaching the treaty. It is unlikely that military authorities would be happy to acquire untested weapons from an untried national manufacturing process. Underground testing, however, though expensive if it seeks sophisticated data, would not be difficult to carry out, perhaps in an old mine, if mere proof of detonation and rough yield were desired. Tests would also advertise acquisition if that were thought desirable for deterrent or prestige purposes. Moreover, it can be argued that a nation really anxious to get nuclear weapons and to bear the reproaches of proponents of non-proliferation might very well regard the added stigma of even atmospheric tests as tolerable.

The NPT commits nuclear-weapon signatories not to transfer control of nuclear weapons to states that do not have them, or to help such states to acquire them. It commits non-nuclear states not to try to obtain nuclear weapons. The treaty serves to reinforce the stigma against acquisition, it endorses the view that proliferation is dangerous, it provides an excuse for nuclear-weapon states that might otherwise be embarrassed to refuse nuclear assistance to others, and it provides a lever for the domestic opposition to acquisition in candidate nations. But the treaty has built into it an escape clause permitting renunciation if changed circumstances seem to require it. More important still, several important candidates including India, Israel, South Africa, Australia, Brazil and West Germany have refused either to sign or to ratify.

It is clear that the Test Ban and the NPT are merely partial instruments within the overall network of considerations determining national decisions on acquisition. Each candidate faces an array of incentives and disincentives including inducements and threats from the major world powers. A most important ingredient in these factors is the extent to which the Superpowers offer functional substitutes for nuclear weapons by way of guarantees. Some states, such as the members of the large military blocs, already enjoy substantial guarantees. This is the basis of West German security and willingness to abstain from control of nuclear weapons. In the aftermath of the negotiation of the NPT, both the Soviet Union and the United States issued very general promises to consult and help any non-nuclear state threatened or attacked by nuclear weapons. But in times when even the guarantees within well-established alliances are queried, such promises do not go very far. Insofar as some of the motives to acquire nuclear weapons are concerned, such as prestige and status, guarantees may be not only inadequate but actually negative in effect.

The Future of Proliferation
The pace of proliferation will thus be decided by the general development of the international systems of power balances within which specific and deliberate non-proliferation policies, including international agreements, will play a part but by no means necessarily a decisive one. Should proliferation proceed, the major powers will have to decide upon a post-proliferation strategy, as they already have had to do in the case of each new nuclear power. There may well come a point, for example, when the interest of one of the Superpowers, and even international stability at large, may be better served by positive rather than negative responses to nuclear acquisition. Once a state is determined on nuclear weapons, for instance, it might be assisted to do so as economically as possible, in order not to retard economic development, or to do so with systems that offer minimum temptation to pre-emptive use. Moreover, if one party to a local balance is going nuclear, assistance to its rivals to do likewise might be a safer way to maintain stability than to permit asymmetry or intrude a Superpower guarantee.

The last consideration reminds us that the initial stages of proliferation will do much to set the course for later episodes. For if any of the candidates in one of the various categories suggested earlier acquires nuclear weapons, its example must be expected to have particular force on other members of the same category. In other words, it seems probable that if proliferation proceeds beyond the present nuclear powers, the next stopping point will be several, and not merely one, nuclear powers later.

PART II

The Technology of Limited War

CHAPTER THREE

The Land Battle

This chapter is chiefly devoted to hardware and the tactical considerations underlying its development. Some consideration of the strategic shape of a war in Europe is given in Part III, Chapter 8.

In some respects it is arbitrary and misleading to distinguish between warfare on land, at sea and in the air, for one of the most important effects of modern military technology has been to blur this traditional distinction between the armed services. Thanks in large part to the perfection of guided and ballistic missiles, weapons deployed in any one of the three environments, land, sea or air, can often be brought to bear on the others. One result of this development can be seen in competition among traditional branches of the armed services to perform similar tasks and a parallel tendency to merge or reorganize the services. But we must not allow these trends to obscure the fundamental differences that still make the mode of locomotion – by land, sea or air – the most convenient basis on which to organize a brief discussion of modern weapons and tactics.

Leadership in the design and manufacture of complex and sophisticated weapons is still confined to a relatively small number of nations. With the notable exception of Japan, which for political reasons has restrained its inherent capacity for a major arms industry, the leading weapon-manufacturing states are essentially the United States, the Soviet Union and their European allies. Quite naturally these nations design weapons chiefly with an eye to their most serious potential battlefield which is Europe. Consequently a survey of trends in modern weaponry is very largely a matter of observing preparations for war in Europe. The rest of the world tends to arm by acquiring and perhaps modifying either the latest or earlier generations of the weapons primarily designed for Europe.

Tanks

The centrepiece of modern land warfare is the tank. Certainly it is thought that the tank would dominate a future war in Europe if it occurred within the next decade or so. Superiority in tanks is usually cited as the chief index of Warsaw Pact superiority in the conventional European balance. Moreover, tanks have found themselves in other modern battlefields such as Korea, the Middle East, and on the border between India and Pakistan.

During the early stages of World War I, it became clear that improvements in the accuracy, rate of fire and killing power of small arms, particularly the machine gun, meant that infantry and cavalry could not dislodge well-entrenched defensive forces without prohibitive casualties. One solution was a much intensified use of artillery preparation to kill or stun the defenders and reduce their entrenchments and barbed wire. While these tactics often ensured short advances, they entailed loss of surprise and churned up the

Opposite The 39-ton Federal German battle tank, Leopard. Also used by the Belgians, Dutch and Norwegians this is the most widely deployed Western tank in the European theatre.

The simplified British inventory of tanks exemplifies the trend to standardization. The British reconnaissance tank Scorpion (**right**) and the 51·5-ton Chieftain main battle tank (**below**) whose 120-mm gun is the most powerful of any modern tank.

ground to create new obstacles. Moreover, the defenders could adopt new tactics of defence in depth, while the offensive artillery was not sufficiently mobile to follow up initial successes with further penetration.

The dominance of the defence and consequent strategic deadlock led to revival of an age-old military concept, that of providing an assault force with some mobile shield or protection. On this occasion the idea was combined with the internal combustion engine and the self-laying linked track to create the earliest tanks. Tanks could combine the virtues of cavalry, firing on the move, or of mounted infantry and horse artillery, moving forward to take up advantageous firing positions. The early tanks had armour no more than half an inch or so thick, giving protection only against small-arms fire. Committed at first in small packets, even when used later in mass, they were employed mainly to facilitate and reinforce infantry attacks to gain local successes.

Between the wars more thought was given, chiefly in Britain and in Germany, to the bolder, independent use of tanks to break through enemy lines and create havoc in the rear. It was still not fully realized, however, that the tank would become the chief enemy of the tank and that it would consequently need much heavier armour and an armour-piercing weapon. In 1939 more than 90 per cent of British tanks were armed only with machine guns and even the German proportion of heavier weapons was little higher. Nevertheless the Germans had seized on an important tactical innovation. For they had created a true armoured striking force in which tanks were combined with motorized infantry, many carried in half-tracks with cross-country capability, the whole under the close support of the Luftwaffe as mobile substitute for artillery. This was the conception that facilitated blitzkrieg and revolutionized armoured warfare into the form essentially still with us.

Thanks in large part to the new armoured tactics, World War II did not ossify into the static fronts of World War I. Even defence took on new mobile forms. The key role of the tank stimulated a race between armour and guns. Armour became many inches thick, guns grew to the 88 mm of the German Tiger, 76 mm of the British Centurion, 90 mm of the US Pershing and the 122 mm of the Josef Stalin. The prowess of Soviet tanks in Korea reactivated the armour–gun race, and confirmed the role of the tank. At the same time the advent of the tactical nuclear weapon provided a new argument for tanks. Only armoured forces, it was thought, could offer some protection against nuclear blast and radiation, and provide the speed to cross contaminated zones and close with the enemy so that his nuclear fire was inhibited. On the other hand the tank has acquired new and formidable foes in aircraft and, above all, the light missile. Indeed the whole future of the tank on the sophisticated battlefield is now in doubt. Given the central position of the tank in modern strategy, the outcome of this debate will decide the future shape of land warfare.

The tendency in all the leading nations has been to reduce the variety of tanks. Improvements in guns and the advent of missiles have made it possible to do away with the very heavy, cumbersome tank destroyers like the 65-ton British Conqueror and the 54-ton American M103. Instead there has been a move toward developing a single 'main battle tank' in the 40–50 ton range, supplemented by lighter reconnaissance tanks of about 10–20 tons.

Tanks combine three qualities which sum up the principles of successful military action: fire-power, mobility and self-protection. As the origins of the tank revealed, these three qualities are complementary; unfortunately for tank designers they are also competitive within any fixed weight and cost. There are pronounced differences between national solutions to this dilemma. The French view, shared in large part by the Germans, is that the power of modern offensive weapons has outrun the defensive properties of armour, and that safety must be sought above all in speed and manœuvrability. The British view is that, to prevail, a tank must be capable of standing up to and defeating other tanks. Consequently they favour fire-power and armour before speed. As a result the British 51·5-ton Chieftain is ten tons heavier than the German Leopard, and sixteen tons heavier than the French AMX 30. Moreover, the Chieftain mounts a 120 mm gun as compared to the 105 mm equivalent on the French and German tanks. American and Soviet practice falls somewhere between the two extremes.

In evaluating these philosophies it must be realized that mobility is of several kinds. In particular, speed on the battlefield must be distinguished from speed over the road for tactical deployment. The British view is that unknown and rough terrain limits the battlefield speed of any tank for reasons of caution and crew fatigue. But the Chieftain pays an undesirable penalty in road speed. Another factor, though not one of much present importance where main battle tanks are concerned, is that of air portability.

A further argument concerns the choice of offensive 'killing' systems. All nations have accepted the move toward equipping tanks with a single main weapon, supplemented by machine guns for defence against infantry and aircraft. Where provision is made for anti-aircraft defence it may increasingly be by light ground-to-air missiles. The choice of main armament has until recently lain only between various guns. Now, however, the missile provides an alternative and a sharp dispute exists as to their relative merits.

The majority of modern main battle tanks are armed with a gun of about 105 mm. This can fire two main types of anti-armour ammunition: Armour Piercing (AP) ammunition, which relies on the kinetic effect of firing a special hardened projectile at very high velocity – hence requiring a long-barrelled gun; and high explosive anti tank (HEAT) projectiles with 'shaped charges'. These rely not on the velocity of the projectile but on the concentrated force of explosive gases and metal particles focused on a small area when a charge with concave face is exploded from the rear at a precise distance from the defensive armour. Shaped charges are more effective if not rotated, so HEAT projectiles are commonly stabilized by aerodynamic fins or by allowing the inner charge to rotate in a ball-race within the shell casing. Another method of attack involves squashing plastic explosive against the armour to explode in a manner that 'spalls' deadly fragments of the tank's own inner lining.

Because a shaped charge is highly effective, increases in efficiency as the diameter increases, and is not dependent on high velocity, it can be very well delivered by a missile. It is, indeed, the shaped charge that has made anti-tank missiles practicable. The debate over the relative merits of gun and missile is a complex one, but the main points can be briefly summarized.

One advantage of the gun is that in addition to dealing with tanks it can fire a wide variety of general purpose high-explosive weapons against troops and fortifications; the ability to do this is one of the primary purposes of having tanks at all. Missiles are an unacceptably expensive way of doing this; indeed, one of the characteristics of the gun is that, while it is much more expensive than a missile launcher, the rounds of its ammunition are much cheaper than each missile. To solve this problem the Americans and the French have devised combined missile launchers and guns; the American system being named Shillelagh and the French ACRA (anti-char rapide autopropulsé). The resulting gun is, however, of relatively low velocity. This points in turn to another

The US Sheridan light tank firing a Shillelagh missile from its dual-purpose 152 mm low velocity gun.

advantage of the high-velocity gun: that it can fire both types of anti-armour munitions. The importance of this is that were shaped charges the only threat faced by tanks, they could be provided with 'spaced' armour, which causes the shaped charge to dissipate its energy on an outer skin, but is very vulnerable to high kinetic energy projectiles.

Another positive characteristic of guns is their capacity, because of rapid rate of fire and high-velocity projectile, to engage successive targets and, after being fired, to retreat to cover. These 'shoot and scoot' tactics are not possible with existing missiles which have to be tracked on to target. Moreover, some missiles leave a trail that betrays the source of attack. Another advantage of guns is that usually more rounds of ammunition can be carried, especially now that, as in Chieftain, the ammunition is in separable sections and the projectile casing is self-combustible, so that no spent cases have to be accommodated. A corresponding disadvantage of the gun, perhaps one of its greatest, is that the need to traverse, elevate and depress the gun, and to house its recoil, takes up space and requires a sizeable turret. An unusual solution to this problem is the Swedish 's' Tank, which has a fixed gun aimed by manœuvring the tank. This system sacrifices the ability to fire on the move, but gives a very low profile.

A major weakness of the gun has been ranging. World War II tanks usually ranged by trial and error. Most modern tanks use optical range-finders which are time-consuming and of far from perfect accuracy. The Chieftain uses a co-axial ranging machine gun, ballistically matched to the main gun. This has the great merit of automatically allowing for such variables as wind, atmospheric conditions and tilt of the gun mounting. The disadvantages are loss of time, betrayal of presence, and the fact that the machine gun cannot match the range of the main armament. However, the British argue that few good targets are seen under European conditions at more than the 2500 yards range of machine guns.

Completely new life may have been put into tank guns, however, by the advent of the laser range-finder now being fitted to tanks like Chieftain. The laser – which is a device for projecting an intense and very narrow beam of light (in the visual or infra-red wavelengths) – can be used like a radar to measure the time required for reflection of the beam back to the projector, thus calculating the range. Laser range-finders are quick and do not betray their presence. (Detectors may be devised but there would be little time to take advantage of warning.) As combined with other computational devices, such as the Belgian COBELDA, a laser range-finder and sight can, in no more space than an optical range-finder, provide the gunner not only with range, but with the proper compensation for wind, tilt, barrel wear, propellant temperature and, if the target is moving, the effects of turret traverse. The gun is thus given a new lease of life and it is noteworthy that the United States is said to be contemplating a gun,

NATO's potential opponent: Russian T55 battle tanks on manœuvres.

rather than Shillelagh, for the successor to its projected but abandoned MBT70.

Nevertheless, there is a case for the missile. Its greatest attraction is that it facilitates putting a heavy punch on to a light tank, both because of the inherent light weight of the system and the absence of recoil. Thus it has made practicable the air-portable reconnaissance tank, Sheridan. Such light tanks, with aluminium armour, as Sheridan and the British Scorpion (armed with a gun) are intended to scout for and to protect the flanks of the heavier tanks, substituting in many circumstances for armoured cars. When costs or the need for portability dictate they can, of course, be used as a second-best substitute for the battle tank. How they will perform in action remains to be seen.

A comparison of the main battle tanks in use today.

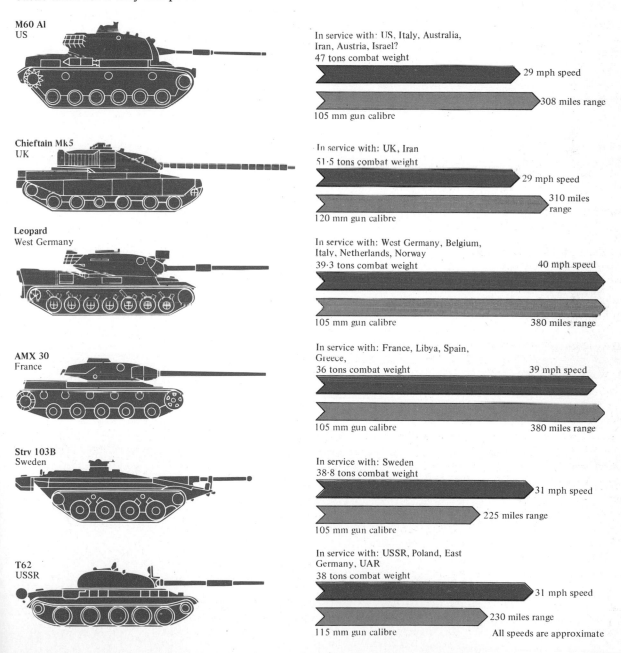

M60 AI
US

In service with: US, Italy, Australia, Iran, Austria, Israel?
47 tons combat weight
29 mph speed
308 miles range
105 mm gun calibre

Chieftain Mk5
UK

In service with: UK, Iran
51·5 tons combat weight
29 mph speed
310 miles range
120 mm gun calibre

Leopard
West Germany

In service with: West Germany, Belgium, Italy, Netherlands, Norway
39·3 tons combat weight
40 mph speed
380 miles range
105 mm gun calibre

AMX 30
France

In service with: France, Libya, Spain, Greece,
36 tons combat weight
39 mph speed
380 miles range
105 mm gun calibre

Strv 103B
Sweden

In service with: Sweden
38·8 tons combat weight
31 mph speed
225 miles range
105 mm gun calibre

T62
USSR

In service with: USSR, Poland, East Germany, UAR
38 tons combat weight
31 mph speed
230 miles range
115 mm gun calibre

All speeds are approximate

It remains to say a word about the armour of tanks with which the various guns and missiles have to deal. The armour of World War I was a few millimetres of hardened steel. The appearance of armour-piercing ammunition stimulated advances in the design of armour and a vast increase in the weight carried. Various alloys were adopted and riveted armour gave way to welded and cast armour. The thickest armour was – and still is – provided in front, to permit head-on engagements. By the end of World War II heavy tanks had up to six inches of frontal armour and two to three inches elsewhere. The consequent weight penalties are high: one-inch steel armour weighs about 50 lb a square foot. Advent of the shaped charge encouraged the development of spaced

The Russian BMP76 armoured personnel carrier. This carries eight infantrymen who can use their weapons from inside the vehicle and is armed with a 76 mm gun.

armour, mentioned above. Even tool boxes and other expendable equipment can afford some protection if arranged to predetonate projectiles. The latest development is aluminium armour.

Comparative performance of aluminium and steels depends on very complex considerations, but as a rough approximation aluminium gives about a third of the protection of steel, thickness for thickness. The direct savings in weight are thus not great, but the greater thickness of aluminium for a given weight permits many structural economies: the armour can itself form the structure and can contain many components. Thus aluminium is now widely used for light tanks and armoured cars. But the thickness required to afford the degree of protection sought in a battle tank would consume excessive space and in this category steels still predominate.

The effectiveness of armour depends very much on the angle at which projectiles strike. Tank designers therefore aim to give their vehicles a good 'ballistic shape', with a sloping front or 'glacis', and with an absence of overhangs or 'shot traps'. An extreme example of the latter consideration is to be seen in the inverted dish shape of Soviet turrets. Even the underside may be shaped so as to reduce the effect of mines. Some tanks still carry skirts to protect their tracks against small, infantry weapons; others have dispensed with them. Lower profiles can also be achieved by the design of suspension; a number of modern tanks have adjustable hydraulic suspensions to combine low profile with terrain-crossing capability. The importance of profile can be appreciated from the fact that tanks try to shoot 'hull down' and that the target they then offer may not be more than one metre high at a range of some 2000 metres.

One of the essences of a tank is the ability to move. We have already discussed the relative value of speed. All tanks move by linked tracks, the size being adjusted to the weight of tank and the type of terrain encountered. The ground pressure exerted will determine the capacity to cross soft ground. Most large tanks can scale a vertical obstacle three feet high. The tracks are pressed to the ground by a number of road wheels (sometimes rubber tyred to reduce track wear, a major limitation on tank endurance). Power is applied by a sprocket, usually at the rear, and the track suspended at the other end by an idler. There may or may not be return rollers at the top. Steering may be by clutch and brake applied to each track or by some form of automatic transmission. The power is supplied by engines typically of 1200–1500 h.p. in battle tanks. Some engines are 'multi-fuel', though mechanical adjustments are necessary to change fuels. The Swedish 's' tank combines a reciprocating engine with a gas turbine for peak power. Modern battle tanks tend to have an unrefuelled range of about 300 road miles, with an eye to a twenty-four-hour battle. Resupply of fuel and ammunition is a major constraint on tank tactics and experiments are made with auxiliary tanks or even separate fuel trailers. A further important aspect of mobility is amphibiousness. Most tanks can wade, some can cross on river bottoms (when reconnoitred) by means of air breathing tubes. Lighter vehicles can cross on the surface, sometimes after the erection of flotation screens. Propulsion may be by the tracks used as paddles, by propeller, or, in the case of many Russian vehicles, by water jets. Final mention should be made of ability to close down tanks and perhaps apply positive air pressure to permit traverse of areas polluted by nuclear or chemical weapons.

Other Armoured Vehicles

Mention of the lighter armoured vehicles that can be made amphibious points to the existence of many other members of the armoured category. In the heavier classes comes the variety of special purpose vehicles mounted on tank chassis. These include bridge-laying vehicles, tank-rescue vehicles, and the Soviet speciality of anti-aircraft tanks. Tank chassis can also be used to carry large surface-to-surface missiles. A major category which has become a ubiquitous feature of the modern battlefield is the self-propelled gun. This consists of a large gun capable of providing direct fire support for tanks and infantry, and mounted on a tracked carrier. In very large calibres the gun and parts of its auxiliary equipment, range-finder, and ammunition may occupy two or more vehicles. The truly self-contained, self-propelled gun differs from a tank chiefly in lacking a capability for all-round traverse or for firing on the move.

Typical modern anti-tank missiles.

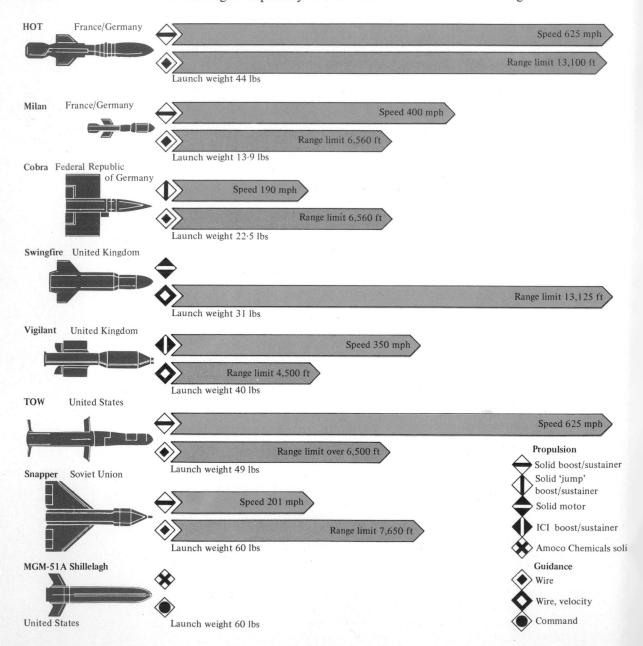

HOT France/Germany
Speed 625 mph
Range limit 13,100 ft
Launch weight 44 lbs

Milan France/Germany
Speed 400 mph
Range limit 6,560 ft
Launch weight 13·9 lbs

Cobra Federal Republic of Germany
Speed 190 mph
Range limit 6,560 ft
Launch weight 22·5 lbs

Swingfire United Kingdom
Range limit 13,125 ft
Launch weight 31 lbs

Vigilant United Kingdom
Speed 350 mph
Range limit 4,500 ft
Launch weight 40 lbs

TOW United States
Speed 625 mph
Range limit over 6,500 ft
Launch weight 49 lbs

Snapper Soviet Union
Speed 201 mph
Range limit 7,650 ft
Launch weight 60 lbs

MGM-51A Shillelagh
United States
Launch weight 60 lbs

Propulsion
Solid boost/sustainer
Solid 'jump' boost/sustainer
Solid motor
ICI boost/sustainer
Amoco Chemicals soli

Guidance
Wire
Wire, velocity
Command

Abandoning the need for traverse can permit abandonment of a turret and the consequent accommodation of a much larger breech and greater recoil than in a tank. Special hydraulic supports may be lowered into the ground to increase stability of the firing platform.

Perhaps the most important complement to the tank is the armoured personnel carrier (APC). The original purpose of the tank was to help the infantry advance. Even though the concept of deep mobile penetration by tank forces now prevails, experience shows that tanks cannot adequately protect themselves against enemy infantry, particularly at night, or exploit and hold their own gains without some infantry support of their own. Putting infantry into vehicles with cross-country capability to accompany the tanks was the basis of German successes in the early years of World War II. From this it is a natural step to provide the mechanized infantry with a degree of armoured protection. The modern possibility of nuclear or chemical warfare creates a further requirement for protecting infantry and giving them mobility to maintain the pace of battle.

As with the tank there are different philosophies for the use of APCs. British and American thought has centred around the 'battle taxi', using the APC to bring troops to the point of action but expecting them to dismount and fight on foot. This theory has rested partly on a firm faith in selective, aimed fire. The Russians and Germans have designed APCs from which the infantry can fire their personal weapons, assisted by a big machine gun or light cannon. APCs for this purpose need thicker armour, particularly in front, and provision for the troops to disembark, when essential, under cover of the APC itself. Rear unloading doors are therefore provided. Vehicles of this kind, which are expected to get into the line of fire as a matter of routine, need a lower silhouette than the box-like APCs of earlier vintages. Once dismounted the troops can still enjoy covering fire from the APC's gun. Experience in Viet Nam has now shifted American opinion towards the 'mounted fighting' vehicle and Britain is following suit. The appearance of a new American mechanized infantry combat vehicle prototype reflects this conversion, as does the design for a British aluminium APC70. Meanwhile the two most fully developed APCs are the German Marder and the Soviet BMP76. The latter has a crew of three, an infantry complement of eight, can swim, carries a 76 mm hollow-charge launcher, a machine gun, a guided-missile launcher, and has gas-tight firing ports for the infantry. In fully amphibious form such vehicles are closely related to modern landing craft; the US Marine's new LVTP7, carrying twenty-eight men and a machine gun, can traverse offshore waters and then proceed inland at a top speed of 40 mph.

Despite all this mobility we should note that some critics say it is insufficient for the modern battlefield and that only helicopters or hovercraft can fulfil the requirements. Thus the new American Tricap divisional organization (Tricapability) embraces air-mobile infantry in 100 mph helicopters and air cavalry in 150 mph helicopters. We will return to the virtues and vices of helicopters for the land battle later.

Anti-armour Systems

The toughest target of the anti-armour weapon is, of course, the battle tank. Any weapon that can kill tanks can deal with APCs, though it may well be wastefully overdesigned for the purpose. The modern tank faces a variety of threats several of which, as we have seen, are mounted on other tanks.

The capability of the shaped charge in a missile has already been described. The most important characteristic of the anti-tank missile is that it can be relatively light and much cheaper than the tank: a simple man-portable anti-tank missile can cost less than a thousandth of the price of a battle tank. This means that the exchange ratio is very unfavourable to the tank. It also means that, because small missiles are inconspicuous and can be provided in great numbers, the tank must now operate in a very nerve-racking environment where any bush may conceal a weapon capable of destroying tanks.

One method of firing shaped charges is by recoil-less rifle of the 'bazooka' type. These are cheap, but lack accuracy over all but short ranges and make a large backflash which betrays the operator's location. Guided missiles are generally regarded as much more effective and are coming to dominate the field of light anti-tank weapons.

Anti-tank guided missiles are of three main types. Simplest is the wire-guided missile with manual control. In this system the missile unreels one or more very fine wires. The operator watches the missile, aided perhaps by a flare on the tail, and steers it by means of a control lever, passing steering impulses along the wire. The missile may correct its course aerodynamically, by fins, or by directional jets. More complex are semi-automatic missiles. Once more these are wire guided but all the operator has to do is keep a sight trained on the target. A computer in the system calculates what corrections of course are necessary to bring the missile over the target. In the main, Western systems of this kind, the American tube-launched, optically tracked, wire-guided missile (TOW) and the French high-subsonic, optically guided, tube-launched (HOT), depend upon a sensor tracking an infra-red flare on the tail of the missile and calculating the divergence between this and the line of sight to the target. Fully automatic systems may dispense with the wires and transmit guidance information by modulations of the infra-red beams.

A number of considerations affect the performance of such missiles. They all require the operator to track on to the target. There can therefore be no quick engagement of successive targets and the operator cannot go for cover. In this respect the ultimate development would be a missile which, like the American TV-guided air-to-surface Walleye, could recognize a target when fired and home on it unattended. Such innovations would, however, be expensive, and increased expense negates the great cost-effectiveness of the simpler missiles mentioned earlier. From this point of view the ideal is a missile that can be regarded as a mere 'round of ammunition'. This ideal conflicts with the desire for greater sophistication. Similar considerations affect the expense of training. Some experts believe that simulators can train operators on the more complex missiles with few if any practice firings. Others believe that lack of live firing saps operator confidence and prefer a cheaper missile which can be expended in moderate numbers for training.

While several countries have moved toward the semi- or fully-automatic systems, the British have retained manual guidance in their new Swingfire. The main characteristic of this missile is that it can be fired by an operator as much as 50 metres away. The operator may have cover, so long as he can see the target; the launcher can be fully concealed if cover is available and can engage targets over a very wide arc of fire. This is because the missile is automatically 'gathered' into the vision of the operator. The problem of gathering the missile is a general one for these systems and accounts for a relative inability to deal with close targets. Tolerance is greater for the manually guided than for the infra-red guided missiles and one feature of Swingfire is its capability to deal with ranges from 300 to 4000 metres, whereas limits of 500–2000 are usually cited for the semi-automatics. Such highly sophisticated systems as Shillelagh and

The British Swingfire
missile just after firing.
The wire of its guidance
system can be seen
trailing behind it.

ACRA are said to be able to handle closer and more distant targets, and to do so at higher speeds than those achieved by missiles not gun-launched. Certainly manual guidance imposes certain limits on manageable speed. But the fully automatic systems still have to be watched on to target and their performance is only achieved at great cost. Part of this cost arises from the need to make the micro-wave or modulated infra-red guidance beams jam-proof.

A great variety of means of deploying anti-tank missiles is under development. The simplest are man-portable; the British Vigilant embodies a 12-lb 5-inch warhead in a system with total weight of 45 lb. Large weapons can be mounted on jeeps, APCs or tanks. Many projects exist for deploying anti-tank missiles on helicopters, which enthusiasts see as the best tank-killing system of the future.

The tank may acquire defences against some of these systems. It may acquire warning devices and perhaps a capability to shoot down the slower anti-tank missiles. But there can be no doubt that, for the present, tanks on a relatively sophisticated battlefield face a range of weapons that at least makes it possible to debate whether armoured forces will be able to dominate land warfare as they have for the last thirty years.

The problems of the tank cannot be left without a mention of new miniaturized anti-tank mines which can be pre-sown or distributed by missile or airdrop. A German innovation, Pandora, is a fist-sized mine which is difficult to find and capable of immobilizing if not destroying a tank. Another larger device, Medusa, is a magnetic hollow charge intended to penetrate the bottom plates of tanks. Combined with anti-personnel devices to hamper clearing operations, such devices may well interdict large areas to armoured fighting vehicles. The underlying principle of these weapons is that they are sufficiently cheap to be used in great quantity against expensive tanks. Thus, whereas the guided missile seeks efficiency by relatively expensive accuracy, the mine finds its effectiveness in quantity.

Artillery

Artillery remains an important instrument in the land battle but defining it becomes ever more difficult. At one time one might have secured fairly widespread agreement that weapons of 0·50 inch calibre and below were small arms while all large weapons were artillery. However, the man-portable recoil-less rifles and missiles would not now be normally considered artillery. To add to the confusion, tanks have taken over part of the role of artillery, while some of the functions of big guns can be performed by large missiles that merge almost imperceptibly into the long-range strategic categories. The United States has solved the latter problem by administrative fiat, confining the army to rockets of up to 400 mile range. Even within the category of 'tube artillery' there is room for confusion among the types. One classification would use the term 'gun' for long-barrelled weapons with a flat trajectory, 'howitzer' for shorter-barrelled weapons with a high curving trajectory, and 'mortar' for weapons with very short barrel and sharp up-and-down or hairpin trajectory.

As already mentioned, artillery, which had steadily increased in technical perfection and tactical importance during the nineteenth century, played a part of unprecedented intensity in World War I. Ammunition consumption soared far beyond estimates – not until 1917 did supply come close to demand – and both high explosive and shrapnel shells were in great use. A new departure was seen in gas shells. Ranges steadily increased, the ultimate exemplified in the German siege guns used against Paris with ranges of over seventy-five miles.

In World War II artillery retained its importance, although in more mobile warfare the methods of using it altered. Tanks and aircraft now afforded alternatives but artillery was found to be still superior for sustained accurate fire on precise targets. Guns became motorized, either by traction or by being self-propelled. An important step forward was taken by invention of the proximity fuse, a small radar set which could be used to detonate anti-aircraft shells close to aircraft or to achieve airbursts effective against troops in the field.

At present the classification of artillery continues to become more difficult. One end of the spectrum is affected by such innovations as the multi-barrelled 20 mm American Vulcan machine gun which achieves rates of fire of over 700 rounds a minute and even the 7·62 mm 'minigun' which can achieve 4000 rounds a minute at which rate its effect is said to be virtually explosive even against masonry. At the other end of the spectrum are the surface-to-surface tactical missiles for either conventional or nuclear warheads. Typical of these are the American Honest John, a free-flight solid-fuelled missile of over twenty-mile range; the Sergeant, also solid-fuelled with a range of over eighty miles, and the Pershing, solid-fuelled and carrying a nuclear warhead 400 miles. The Russian arsenal of FROG missiles (free rocket over ground) contains similar devices, many mounted on tracked carriers. Typical of large self-propelled weapons is the American tracked M107 175 mm gun which can fire its shell twenty miles and the M109 amphibious, aluminium armour, airportable 155 mm howitzer. Another variant is the multi-barrelled launcher for free rockets used to lay down a saturation bombardment. The Russian World War II Katyusha versions of this won wide fame and at present the West German army has a launcher for thirty-six 110 mm rockets mounted on a truck. The rockets can be fired singly or salvoed; an eight-vehicle battery can fire up to 300 rounds in half a minute.

The outstanding characteristic of most artillery is its capacity to deliver accurate indirect fire; that is, from behind some topographical cover. This requires accurate range-finding and gun-laying. Typically this is achieved by co-operation between a forward observer and a series of ranging shots to 'bracket' the range until fire for effect can begin. Modern technology has, of course, made for great advances in both fire and counter-battery fire. Observation from aircraft is long established and now helicopters afford an important variant. For counter fire, specialized radars can be used to observe the trajectory of hostile fire and deduce the position of the guns. These devices are particularly useful in locating otherwise elusive and deadly mortars.

Small Arms

Like most weapons, small arms have undergone considerable development in recent years, although not perhaps in ways that make for fundamental tactical changes. There has been a tendency to standardization of weapons. In the fifties the NATO countries agreed upon a common 7·62 mm calibre and, within the United States, the variety of small arms was reduced to three weapons in this calibre: the M60 machine gun, the M14 rifle, and the M15 heavy-barrelled version of the rifle as an infantry squad automatic weapon. Similarly the Warsaw Pact nations have standardized a 7·62 mm round which is in fact slightly wider and half an inch shorter than the NATO equivalent. The tendency to smaller calibres and to a smaller round, justified by higher propellant performance, has the double advantage of permitting a lighter weapon and reducing the logistic problem of ammunition supply. Pursuing this trend as a result of experience in Viet Nam, the United States has now broken the NATO standard by adopting the M16 rifle of 5·56 mm calibre for worldwide use and, as the AR18, some of these weapons have been adopted by the British Army.

The primary purpose of small arms is to kill or incapacitate the enemy soldier. Because no more than about 15 per cent of the area presented by a standing man represents zones where a hit will be immediately fatal it is desirable to fire a projectile that will deal an incapacitating blow wherever it hits, much as the ill-shooting cowboys of the West are supposed to have covered their deficiencies by using a 0·45 calibre bullet. If a small projectile is to deal a heavy blow it must yield up the bulk of its energy on initial impact; this suggests a bullet which, while stable and accurate in flight, becomes unstable on impact.

Another question concerns the range of engagement and manner of firing. The 7·62 mm NATO round can penetrate helmets and body armour with lethal effect at 1000 yards. But experience suggests that the soldier rarely sees his enemy or can hit him at much over 400 yards. Moreover, if the enemy is seen at a distance there are commonly other ways to deal with him than rifle fire. At the same time the average soldier is not a particularly good shot with even a good weapon. Thus some aids to ensuring a hit at shorter ranges may be more valuable than long-range accuracy. The United States has produced several devices to improve hitting power. One, the M198 dual or duplex bullet, houses a second projectile behind the first. The first flies on a normal trajectory; the second spirals around the first achieving about a foot of separation for every hundred yards flight. Another device is the flechette, a small dart about an inch long and one sixteenth in diameter. This is fixed within a sleeve that discards and could if necessary be arranged in multiples. So far, however, accuracy is very low and only close combat can be conducted.

The greatest practical aid to hitting is automatic fire. All modern rifles are self-loading from a magazine. Three types of fire are possible – single shot, automatic and short bursts – though not all rifles provide all three. A controversy exists between the advocates of fully automatic fire and selective single shots or bursts, typically of three rounds. Automatic fire is certainly the more expensive in ammunition and this compounds logistic problems. Nor, according to critics, is automatic fire necessarily more deadly, for vibration and rising of the barrel make for inaccuracy. British and American practice tends toward selectivity; the Soviet Union apparently gives more emphasis to automatic fire.

A great variety of new small arms is available and some concepts, like the flechette, are truly novel. But so far there is little to suggest improvement on the lightweight, post-war rifles that would justify the expense of re-equipment. In the NATO alliance the short-term future probably lies with the 5·56 mm rifle, perhaps with a higher-velocity round to afford a flatter trajectory and consequently simpler aiming at longer ranges. An important and increasingly common feature of rifles is provision for launching grenades beyond hand-throwing range at targets which cannot conveniently be brought under mortar fire.

Night Fighting

As the problem of effective ranges for rifle fire exemplifies, a weapon system is only effective if it can detect, identify and locate its target. Modern technology is producing a wide range of devices to perform this function. Radar for retracing trajectories has already been mentioned. In very recent years a considerable array of sensors have been introduced by the American forces in Viet Nam. Such sensors, operating by acoustic or seismic effects, can detect the passage of troops and vehicles. Sensors can be prelocated or dropped from the air and can be disguised as foliage. They are, however, useful chiefly for guerrilla environments or for the policing of perimeters, as their performance is severely degraded in a noisy area. Devices for jungle warfare include instruments for detecting humans by smell. Other devices can detect the electromagnetic effects of various forms of equipment.

Devices of this kind can be useful by night or day. Particularly energetic efforts are currently being made to improve capacity for night fighting so as to facilitate the 'twenty-four-hour battle'. Aids for night fighting may directly assist human vision or may actuate indicators. One such aid is doppler radar which can distinguish moving objects from their background. Modern equipment can readily pick out individual soldiers, rain, or the fall of shot. As yet, however, the equipment is relatively cumbersome, the smallest versions requiring two men to carry them.

Infra-red devices constitute perhaps the most important type of night vision aid. Infra-red can be used either actively or passively. In the active form an infra-red beam is projected and used to illuminate objects which are then observed through an infra-red sensitive viewer. This method is highly effective and is increasingly fitted to tanks and other weapons. The main drawback is that the infra-red emissions are readily detectable by a sophisticated enemy and may prematurely betray the men's presence and whereabouts. This difficulty is avoided by passive infra-red devices which depend upon sensing the differences in temperature between objects and their background. Passive detectors can be made sensitive to variations of 1°C, which makes it possible to detect men against vegetation. The engines of vehicles are readily detectable. Overall, however, the range and sensitivity of passive devices is somewhat limited, though they are, of course, particularly effective against camouflage.

A second major solution to the problem of night vision, which offers direct aid to the human eye, is image intensification. This entails a sensor, rather like a TV camera, which absorbs the available light and converts it into electronic

impulses which are then amplified, perhaps through three repeated processes or 'cascades', and ultimately re-converted into light. Image intensifications 200,000 fold are possible by such methods and devices are available commercially for around $5000. Image intensifiers can operate by available light, good results being achieved with moderate starlight, or by making use of a low level, artificial source of illumination. One British apparatus, the Pilkington Lolite, makes it possible to distinguish objects one yard square at ranges of over 2000 yards by starlight. This is available commercially for about $4000. Image intensifiers have already been made sufficiently small and rugged to be mounted as rifle sights. For this purpose they are, however, rather cumbersome and are better suited for the use of sentinels or in ambush than for mobile work in the field.

Night fighting aids are an area in which recent progress has been remarkable and in which future developments may well do more than in any other field of technology to revolutionize ground warfare. For the moment, however, there are several reasons for moderating expectations. The devices are still fairly, and in some cases extremely, expensive. They are also often heavy. As a result it is likely that for some time to come only a few, rather than all weapons in a category will enjoy sophisticated aids to night vision. The more expensive weapons, like tanks, will clearly merit universal application before the cheaper. Moreover, even the best night vision aids have ranges far below the effective range of the weapons with which they are associated. For some time to come, therefore, night will continue to make a considerable difference to tactics although the mere existence of night vision devices must inspire doubt in the mind of any force operating in the dark. To that extent the assurance of safety under cover of darkness is rapidly disappearing from the sophisticated battlefield.

Helicopters in Land Battle

In recent years the helicopter has become an increasingly pervasive participant in land warfare. Indeed, its role has become so closely entwined with that of specific 'land weapons' that it is in this connection that its potential for ground warfare can best be discussed.

The first war in which helicopters played an influential part was Korea. Here its functions were chiefly the evacuation of wounded, with consequent major reduction in combat deaths, the rescue of downed pilots, and the provision of reconnaissance and airborne command facilities. In the Suez crisis of 1956 Britain and France made the first substantial use of helicopters to effect a landing, thereby inaugurating the technique of 'vertical envelopment'. In Algeria the French made wide use of helicopters for the tactical movement of troops. They also used helicopters to salvage wrecked aircraft. But their most portentous innovation was to put 7·5 mm machine guns and 68 mm rockets on to helicopters, thus introducing the helicopter 'gunship'.

This photograph of Stonehenge was taken in starlight at 4 a.m. with the Pilkington Lolite, a typical image intensifier.

The Bell AH1G Cobra
gunship helicopter.

All of these beginnings have been followed up and extrapolated on a massive
scale in Viet Nam. Helicopters have been used to introduce troops and firepower quickly into areas where for topographical or tactical reasons it would
otherwise have been impossible to do so. They have made it possible to carry
out tactical movements with unprecedented speed. To do this in the face of
opposition has required the development of helicopters with high lifting capacity, good hover capability at high altitudes and temperatures, rapid acceleration, ability to land regardless of wind direction, substantial protection against
and capacity to survive damage, and a tolerable ease of maintenance.

As a result of this experience a wide range of military and combat helicopters is now available and many new versions are projected. One of the
most ubiquitous is the Bell UH1H Huey single-engined helicopter, of which
nearly 10,000 have been manufactured. This machine can carry a payload of
4500 lb, making possible the carriage of cargo, of fourteen troops in addition to
the pilot, or of six stretcher cases. Alternatively the pilot and ten troops can be
accompanied by two door-gunners. In this form the helicopter can fly missions
over a 100 nautical mile radius at 140 knots and hover at 4000 feet out of
ground effect. Experiments with loading this machine with external ordnance
for attack missions demonstrated the penalties paid because of drag and the
unsuitability of side-by-side seating if the pilot and gunmen were to have
adequate vision. The result has been one of the best known helicopters, the
AH1G Huey Cobra gunship which can, it is claimed, carry twice the payload
twice as far and twice as fast as the UH1. This machine can attain level speeds of
over 250 knots; with maximum payload it can fly level at 135 knots and dive at
190. The US Army version can include an XM28 turret with a 7·62 minigun
firing at 2000–4000 rounds a minute, grenade launchers, and 2·75 in rockets
mounted on the 'wings'. The maximum load of these rockets can be 86 and the
17 lb warhead is comparable to a 105 mm howitzer shell. An alternative is the
XM35 20 mm cannon firing at 750 rounds a minute. A limitation is that the
ammunition load for minigun or cannon is sufficient only for one minute's fire.

The logic of this system has been taken further in such projected attack
helicopters as the Sikorsky Blackhawk. This concept, now probably abandoned

was designed to have a low profile, automatic hovering controls, inertial naviga-tion equipment, and terrain-avoidance radar. The makers claim to have accepted the probability that military helicopters, and particularly attack helicopters which deliberately seek out combat, will receive hits and to have designed a great deal of survivability into the Blackhawk. Such measures can include light armour, particularly for the crew seats and fuel tanks, and the provision of redundant and robust controls. Twin engines offer additional survivability and in some models, although it is impracticable to armour the engines, an armoured partition can reduce the danger of losing both simultaneously.

The current Anglo–French series of helicopters, built collaboratively by Aérospatiale and Westland, comprises in British terminology the Gazelle, the Lynx and the Puma. Gazelle is a light helicopter for reconnaissance work, which can carry four men plus pilot at about 150 knots. Lynx is intended to be the standard utility helicopter with an all-up weight of 8000 lb. It has twin engines and an integrated navigational system to permit bad-weather flying. This system can provide the pilot with a digital reading of his position and also a map display. It can also give him instant range and bearing of up to ten destinations or targets fed into the computer before take-off. An automatic flight system can maintain speed, height, and heading. Automatic hover can also be added. The payload can be six troops at a radius of fifty nautical miles with thirty minutes in the target area.

Neither Britain nor France has ordered a specialized attack helicopter. There are, however, projects to add Swingfire to Lynx and it is claimed that with a load of twelve missiles (six for reload on the ground), Lynx could operate over a 100 nautical mile radius with ninety-five minutes on target.

Puma is intended to carry up to twenty troops or an all-up weight of 14,000 lb at 145 knots. This is still a relatively light helicopter by the modern standards of some nations. Thus the Sikorsky CH53, of which West Germany has ordered nearly 150, has an all-up weight of 42,000 lb, which makes possible carriage of up to sixty-four troops or the lift of heavy equipment. The Soviet Union has produced some very large helicopters, an important version being the Mi-6 with an all-up weight of 94,000 lb. A crane version with bare fuselage is designated Mi-10. A much larger Mi-12 is entering service.

Quite clearly helicopters of all types will play a major part in future land operations. Viet Nam has firmly established their role in guerrilla warfare. In different terrain, French campaigns in Algeria and British operations in the Middle East have conveyed the same lesson. The most important question is how far such experience can be extrapolated to the European battlefield where conditions would be very different. In Europe flying weather is frequently bad, the area is heavily urbanized, and overhead wires are ubiquitous. But most important of all, Europe would present an infinitely more intensive battle than Viet Nam. Ground-to-air fire would be heavy and sophisticated. Perhaps more important still, there would be no certainty of air superiority and the helicopter would have to compete with fixed-wing aircraft.

There can be no definite answers to these questions in advance. The debate is clearly bedevilled by enthusiasts on all sides. One can, however, venture some tentative observations on particular roles.

No one seriously questions the value of helicopters in the observation and reconnaissance role, especially as many of these missions can be conducted from the friendly side of the battle area. There may in practice be considerable doubt as to where that area is and it will be one invaluable task of the helicopter to find out.

Similarly, helicopters will certainly be useful for making tactical redeployments of troops. To move large units requires substantial inventories of helicopters and, if only for simplicity's sake, puts a premium on largish machines. Thus it has been estimated that to move an air-portable battalion group in one lift requires eighty helicopters like the Westland Wessex with a gross weight of 13,500 lb, fifty to sixty Pumas, or only twenty Boeing CH47 Chinooks. Less expensive uses for helicopters would be movement of smaller parties of troops into crucial positions, such as the insertion of anti-tank units to contain a break-through. In the same way essential supplies can be moved.

The most controversy centres around the attack helicopter, for this has to take its weapons to the enemy, thus entering his ground-to-air defences and coming within the area of his effort to maintain air superiority. Some British studies suggest that operations ten miles behind the enemy front would entail fifty per cent losses. This is a formidable figure when it is considered that rates of six or seven per cent were thought unacceptable for aircraft in World War II. Much of course depends on the expected duration of operations. American helicopter losses in Viet Nam have been over 16,000. Many of these have, however, been recovered for repair and it is said that the loss rate has been only one per 4000 sorties. However, many of these sorties have been unopposed and the attrition of helicopters coming under fire has been high.

As aircraft go, helicopters are vulnerable targets by reason of relatively low speed, a typical operational height accessible to light ground-to-air weapons and general fragility of construction. To offset these weaknesses it is suggested that helicopters can hug the ground, rising only to deliver their weapons. The attack helicopter may stay out of sight until its target has been located by smaller helicopters or by ground forces. Experience in the Six Day War suggests that helicopters (particularly the slower versions) are very vulnerable to fixed-wing aircraft if caught unawares, but can take very effective evasive action if warned in time. Efforts are now being made to improve the all-round, including upward, vision of helicopters. They can also be equipped to detect hostile radar transmissions.

Helicopters are expensive. The basic Cobra costs over $500,000 without weapons. Anti-tank missiles would increase the price some fifty per cent. The utility version of the Lynx is priced around $800,000. Maintenance can easily run at ten man-hours per hour of flight. It therefore seems likely that the lavish use of helicopters will remain a prerogative of the very rich. Whether use in the specialized attack role will continue to appear a lavish use depends very much on the outcome of future studies. But extensive use of helicopters in other roles will certainly be a feature of forces in the European theatre. Moreover, the use of helicopters, very often in small numbers, will continue to introduce new dimensions into conventional counter-insurgency operations everywhere.

Chemical Weapons

Even a brief survey of land warfare requires a mention of chemical weapons. Chemical weapons and the biological agents usually discussed with them can be used strategically as well as tactically. But there are good reasons for treating the tactical uses more seriously than the strategic. Chemical weapons, which will shortly be discussed in more detail, almost certainly cannot be effectively disseminated in sufficient quantities to do damage to civilian populations much more drastic than that obtainable by conventional explosions and certainly cannot compete with nuclear weapons. Biological weapons could do immense damage in much smaller quantities than chemical weapons. They are, however, relatively difficult to disseminate in a controlled manner and slow to act compared to other weapons. This slowness makes them useless for tactical purposes, except perhaps for such rather far-fetched notions as incapacitating a command headquarters. If used to substantial strategic effect against a nuclear power, the consequences would very probably be such as to remove any inhibition the victim felt about nuclear retaliation. For this reason a non-nuclear aggressor would probably be deterred from using biological weapons and a nuclear aggressor would probably use his own nuclear weapons from the start. Indeed the dubious utility and undoubted dangers of biological weapons has led to a general agreement on outlawing their use. Such prohibitions cannot be depended upon, of course, when self-interest dictates otherwise and it is impossible to rule out the possibility that biological weapons, which are easy and cheap to develop, if necessary in a clandestine manner, might one day become the strategic option of a less-developed country. Such a use, against another such country, might be facilitated by lower standards of public health and medical facilities.

We are left, then, with chemical weapons as a tactical instrument. This must certainly be taken seriously. Poisons have been used on a small scale in war for centuries. Modern technology makes possible the use of chemicals on a larger scale and they have already played a part in several twentieth-century wars. Poison gas was used extensively by both sides in World War I. It was used by the Italians in Abyssinia and the Japanese in China, and these wars involved the first uses against civilians. The UAR used several gases in its campaign in the Yemen and incapacitating gases and herbicides have been used extensively in Viet Nam. A special form of chemical weapon, napalm, was used in World War II. This jellified form of petroleum is highly effective against troops, particularly those in trenches or bunkers, and its use has been frequent and intensive in many modern wars. Indeed it has virtually come to be regarded as a perfectly normal element in the arsenal of conventional weapons.

The gas weapons have to be divided into the lethal and non-lethal categories. Some authorities define a non-lethal weapon as one producing less than 2 per cent fatalities among those affected; others maintain that certain agents can be used with no lethal effect at all. It is also possible to subdivide non-lethal agents into 'harassing' agents, which are intended to cause acute and disabling discomfort during the period of exposure but the effects of which quickly wear off, and 'incapacitating' agents, which disable victims for an appreciable period after exposure but which leave no permanent effects. This classification, like that between lethal and non-lethal, is only reliable as it applies to the intention of users. The actual effect of an agent on an individual will, of course, depend on many variables including the dose received and the individual's state of health.

The chief technical advantages of gases, in addition to their ability to kill or disable the enemy, is that they leave property and communications intact (though perhaps contaminated) and can compel hostile forces to don masks and protective clothing or to operate 'closed down', thereby reducing their efficiency. The legal aspects of using gas are discussed later under disarmament. In brief, the situation is that most nations have renounced the first use of lethal chemical weapons but preparations to use them are widespread. A great debate goes on as to whether harassing agents fall within existing bans or should be subsumed under them. Meanwhile the use of harassing agents continues in many instances.

Gas can be disseminated by simple release on to the wind, as it was at first in World War I, or can be dispersed by artillery shells, aircraft bombs or missiles.

It can also be sprayed from aircraft. Choice of gas will be dictated by whether or not it is intended to kill – a decision perhaps affected by whether friendly personnel will also be exposed – and by the state of preparation of the enemy. The 'tear gases', like chloracetophenone, the tear 'smoke', CS, and the vomiting gas, 'adamsite', are all thwarted by respirators and are thus ineffective against well-prepared troops, though the need to wear masks may be a handicap.

More potent, frequently lethal weapons, are the blister gases introduced during World War I. This group includes distilled mustard and lewisite. Also long established in military arsenals are the choking gases phosgene and diphosgene. Against all of these the wearing of a gasmask would provide effective protection, although in some cases deposit on the skin would cause local injury. For this reason the so-called 'nerve gases', developed before and during World War II, are more potent. There are three gases in this German family, tabun, sarin, and soman. The relevant characteristic of these gases is that they can penetrate not only through the respiratory tract, but also through the skin. They produce neither irritation nor blisters and may have no smell. Minute amounts absorbed in this way can kill in from two minutes to two hours by inhibiting the chemical processes necessary for control of muscles and nerves. The symptoms may proceed from difficulty in breathing, through sweating, vomiting, twitching, convulsions and coma to death. Less than one milligram is a fatal dose for an adult. Since World War II several new nerve gases have been developed. All of the nerve gases would necessitate protective clothing as well as respirators for survival. Effective protection is thus much less likely than with the older gases, and the inconvenience of taking protective measures correspondingly greater. Antidotes exist for nerve gases but they cannot be safely administered unless a dose of the nerve agent has been received. For this and other reasons early warning and detection devices are essential. They are, however, very difficult to introduce on a comprehensive basis.

Today there are also available psychic weapons, derived from drugs that act on the brain, such as LSD. These could be administered by inhalation or by contamination of food or water. In theory they could be used to incapacitate rather than kill, and might be regarded as an option where friendly and hostile forces are intermingled. In practice it would be next to impossible to ensure that measures intended to give all the target population a minimum dose did not result in an excessive, possibly fatal or permanently disabling dose for some. Moreover, the consequences of administering such drugs to men in control of weapons or in positions of command would be highly unpredictable.

Harassing agents of the lachrymatory type have acquired and seem likely to retain a widespread use in war. The main argument against their use is that they might encourage escalation to more harmful agents but it will continue to be difficult to prevent their use when they are widely used for police work and riot control. Harassing agents are likely to be most useful in counter-insurgency and other confused battlefields. In World War II, fear of retaliation and perhaps doubts about efficiency averted the use of lethal gases. It may well be that these inhibitions will persist. There are, however, several historical examples of the use of lethal gas, especially by combatants at a different level of military technology from their rivals. At the very least the potential of lethal gases will impose a need for at least defensive and perhaps retaliatory preparations on the major military powers.

The war in Viet Nam has demonstrated the military use of herbicides. These are commonly derivations of hormone weedkillers developed for agricultural use. In Viet Nam they have been used for two distinct purposes: the defoliation of areas of vegetation which might give cover to an enemy and the destruction of crops which the enemy might use. Because they are slow in operations, herbicides are unlikely to be used in other than guerrilla operations, except perhaps to clear fields of fire around prepared defensive positions. Another limitation on use is that to be effective herbicides must be rather carefully and evenly spread, which for large-scale use implies a high degree of air superiority to permit spraying. So far as guerrilla operations are concerned the chief disadvantages of herbicides would seem to be the stigma attached to use of chemical weapons which are suspected of having ill effects on humans also, and the likelihood of doing damage to the crops and environment of friendly populations, thereby alienating them. It is perhaps possible to imagine the use of herbicides as a strategic offensive weapon in conflict between less-developed and heavily agricultural countries. In this case the use of crop diseases as well as of plant poisons might be contemplated.

Command and Control

There are important developments afoot in the area of command and control which will affect operations at sea and in the air as well as on the ground. These developments arise chiefly from three related sources. First, the fact that military operations today take place within a context of nuclear deterrence gives governments an overriding interest in ensuring that military activity is strictly confined within the limits set by overall policy. Second, military forces are becoming so complex that the task of comprehending the situation and employing resources to the best effect within it is unprecedentedly complicated. Third, modern electronic communications and computers offer revolutionary new opportunities for commanders to enjoy comprehensive information and to exercise control in detail and from a distance. Indeed, it has been possible for remote higher commanders in Indo-China to activate weapon systems from afar on the basis of information received from distant sensors. At the more intense level of warfare, the possibilities of control are exemplified in aircraft interception systems, in which the pilot of an interceptor homing automatically on the enemy, and employing a missile fired automatically at the appropriate moment to home on the target, becomes little more than a machine minder.

Here the only point that can be made is that modern armies are installing elaborate communications and information systems to handle their operations as well as their planning and logistics. This raises many problems about the proper level of authority and delegation for decisions. In the Soviet states the development is adding new dimensions to the recurrent problem of relationships between party political control and military expertise; in less doctrinaire form the question is a universal one for advanced military nations. Perhaps the most difficult aspect of the problem is that, while armies dare not forego the opportunities offered by modern command technology, and indeed might not be able to use modern weapon systems without them, these systems are untested in intense war and they may well prove to be a source of weakness, giving unsuspected dimensions to battle. There exists a real possibility that weapons are outstripping the ability of men to use them to their full potential effect and that commanders may well have more information than they can digest. These problems are the more serious in so far as in intense war of the kind possible in Europe, the conflict may be decided before sufficient time has elapsed to sort out effective operating techniques by trial and error, as has been done in most previous wars.

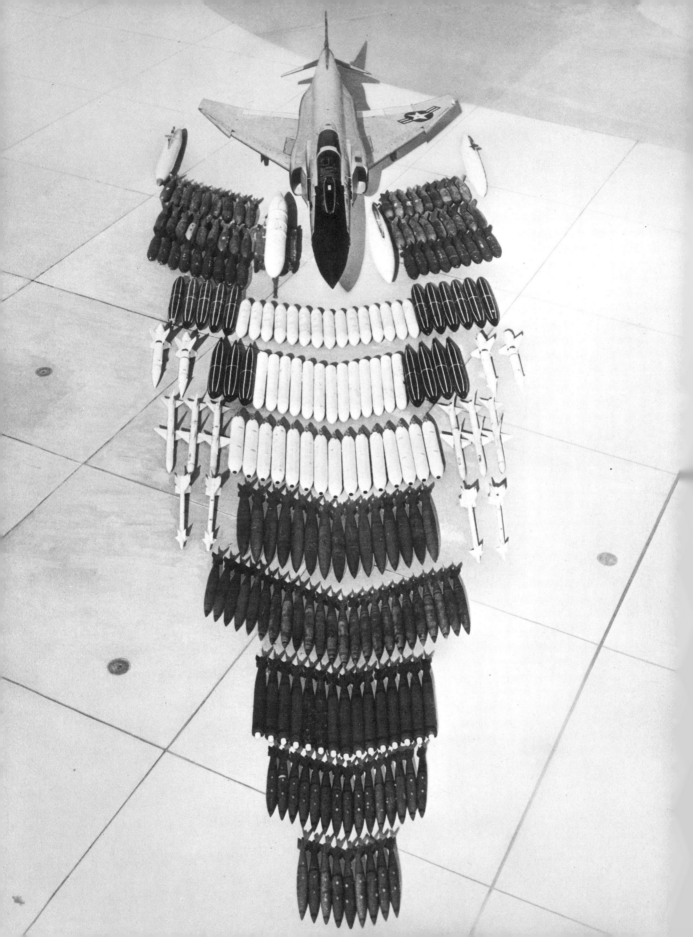

CHAPTER FOUR
The Air Battle

The military use of manned aircraft is greatly complicated today by the development of guided missiles. Both missile and combat aircraft are employed to carry and deliver weapons. For many purposes the manned aircraft can be regarded as a recoverable missile. On the same principle the missile can now compete in the efficient performance of many tasks which were possible hitherto only by the use of aircraft. This competition extends to the role of anti-aircraft interceptor. Thus missiles complicate analysis of the role of aircraft not merely as competitors but also as a new threat to the ability of the aircraft to perform its tasks at all.

A few years ago these developments seemed so revolutionary that many were prepared to predict the imminent obsolescence of military aircraft except for transport and, perhaps, reconnaissance. The process has gone furthest in the area of strategic strike, where targets are relatively few and well identified and where it is taken for granted that nuclear warheads would be employed. But even here it has become clear that prophecies of the demise of manned aircraft were premature. In the first place it has been recognized that the battle between the aircraft and anti-aircraft measures is not yet decided. Secondly, it is increasingly recognized that much warfare is likely to be limited and confined to conventional weapons. For many purposes of limited war the aircraft is still indispensable. Thus new generations of tactical aircraft continue to appear and both Russia and the United States seem to be developing new strategic bombers.

Trends in the development of modern military aircraft make classification difficult. In the thirties and forties one could draw a pretty clear distinction between bombers and fighters, based upon differences in size, weight, speed, payload and range. Towards the end of World War II the increasing use of lighter aircraft for the support of armies and interdiction of communications blurred the distinctions, as the term 'fighter-bomber' clearly indicated. Today the classification of aircraft has become very complex, because of the multiplicity of roles that a particular combination of airframe and engines can be made to serve. An aircraft like the well-known McDonnell Douglas F4 Phantom, originally conceived as a carrierborne strike aircraft and developed as a long-endurance naval interceptor, now serves as interceptor, as reconnaissance aircraft, as a close support weapon, and as a medium-range bomber. An interceptor in one role, it can also carry some 20,000 lb of bombs. Operating as a bomber, it can cover ranges comparable to those undertaken with difficulty by the four-engined Lancasters and B17s of World War II.

Another aspect of the same problem is illustrated by the British Hawker-Siddeley Vulcan, until recently the mainstay of the British strategic nuclear deterrent and now reallocated to tactical strike. The tendency is carried to its logical as well as verbal conclusion in the Anglo–German–Italian joint development of a multi-role combat aircraft (MRCA).

Opposite The American F4 Phantom fighter is the most widely used Western combat aircraft. It has now been developed for use in many roles from long-range interceptor to medium-range bomber. It is seen here with some of the typical loads of bombs or missiles which it can carry in its various roles.

Nonetheless, though classifications must be used with caution, it is still possible to distinguish tolerably well between some of the main functions of aircraft. Frequently the same nominal aircraft will be found performing several of these functions, but often this will be achieved only by giving the aircraft a radically different set of equipment or 'fit'. Thus the projected MRCA is intended for use as a close support aircraft by Germany, and therefore has a 'dry' wing, raising its weapon payload and decreasing vulnerability. The British version is intended for deep strike, and the wing will therefore be used for fuel. More common than such fundamental differences, are variations in the electronic equipment that is the determining characteristic of modern combat aircraft.

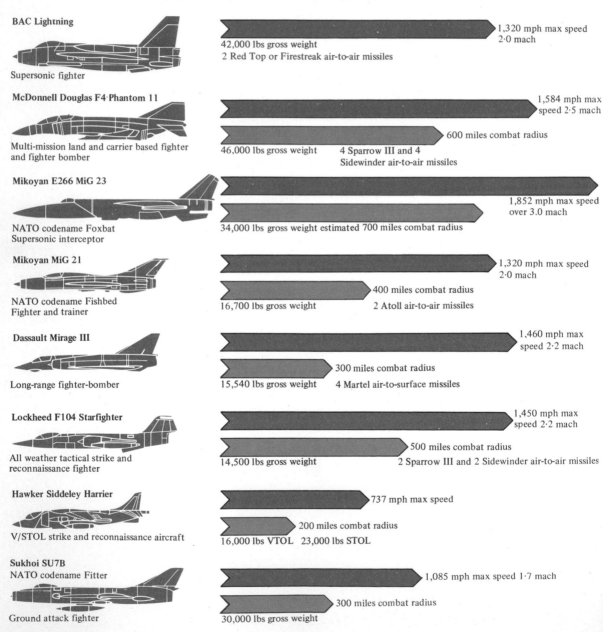

BAC Lightning

Supersonic fighter

1,320 mph max speed 2·0 mach
42,000 lbs gross weight
2 Red Top or Firestreak air-to-air missiles

McDonnell Douglas F4·Phantom 11

Multi-mission land and carrier based fighter and fighter bomber

1,584 mph max speed 2·5 mach
600 miles combat radius
46,000 lbs gross weight   4 Sparrow III and 4 Sidewinder air-to-air missiles

Mikoyan E266 MiG 23

NATO codename Foxbat Supersonic interceptor

1,852 mph max speed over 3.0 mach
34,000 lbs gross weight estimated 700 miles combat radius

Mikoyan MiG 21

NATO codename Fishbed Fighter and trainer

1,320 mph max speed 2·0 mach
400 miles combat radius
16,700 lbs gross weight   2 Atoll air-to-air missiles

Dassault Mirage III

Long-range fighter-bomber

1,460 mph max speed 2·2 mach
300 miles combat radius
15,540 lbs gross weight   4 Martel air-to-surface missiles

Lockheed F104 Starfighter

All weather tactical strike and reconnaissance fighter

1,450 mph max speed 2·2 mach
500 miles combat radius
14,500 lbs gross weight   2 Sparrow III and 2 Sidewinder air-to-air missiles

Hawker Siddeley Harrier

V/STOL strike and reconnaissance aircraft

737 mph max speed
200 miles combat radius
16,000 lbs VTOL   23,000 lbs STOL

Sukhoi SU7B
NATO codename Fitter

Ground attack fighter

1,085 mph max speed 1·7 mach
300 miles combat radius
30,000 lbs gross weight

A possible set of distinctive aircraft functions might be:

(1) Long-range weapon delivery
(2) Interception
(3) Medium-range strike and interdiction of the rear areas of fronts
(4) Close support over the battlefield, combining attack on ground targets and the contest for air superiority
(5) Reconnaissance, strategic and tactical
(6) Maritime reconnaissance and anti-submarine work
(7) Airlift or transport; (*a*) over strategic, intercontinental ranges, and (*b*) tactical, both within a military theatre and within the battlefield itself.

It is of interest to compare this classification with the actual structure of the Soviet air forces which are divided into: the Long-range Airforce, the Tactical Airforce, Fighter Aircraft/Air Defence Command, Air Transport and the Naval Airforce.

Before considering some current practices and problems within these classifications, some observations must be made about modern aircraft in general. In the first place we should recognize that it is the degree and subtlety of control provided by the human crew that accounts for the survival of the aircraft in the age of the usually much cheaper missile. The crew permit the recall of the mission without destruction of the vehicle should circumstances change. Moreover, the crew can search for targets and make late adjustments to tactical surprises, such as the disappearance of one target or appearance of another target of opportunity. All of this is particularly useful against targets on the ground where the complexity and clutter of the environment is intense and where automatic sensors are at a disadvantage.

Despite their residual limitations, the electronic aids that occupy so much of modern aircraft, the 'avionics', account for much of their capability and also for much of their expense. To a greater or lesser degree modern military aircraft contain a wide variety of equipment for communicating, both by speech and by transmission of data; radar for detecting, ranging, tracking and weapon firing both from aircraft to aircraft and from air to ground; infra-red devices to serve some of the same purposes; special facilities for identifying friend or foe (IFF); inertial navigation devices capable of errors of less than one mile for every hour of flight; digital computers to assess information from the sensors; and electronic equipment to confuse hostile radar. All of this makes aircraft capable of complex and precise missions, often in foul weather or darkness. It is achieved, however, at great cost not only in terms of initial investment but also in terms of maintenance and demands on skilled manpower both in the air and on the ground.

The increases in initial cost are well known. A World War II Spitfire cost about £10,000. At current prices the cost of a British Buccaneer low-level-attack aircraft is a little under £1,000,000; a so-called cheap and simplified interceptor/ attack aircraft, the F5, has been ordered by the United States for a unit cost of $1,600,000. Though all prices have risen, those of aircraft have done so with particular sharpness. The F4 is some 200 times the price of Spitfire, the modern tank is less than ten times the cost of its World War II predecessor. Much of the differential is to be found in the avionics, though modern aircraft engines are also peculiarly expensive to develop.

Complexity is accepted for the capacity it confers. But there is no doubt that numerous practical penalties are incurred. Crews are overburdened with tasks. Sophisticated though it is, a great deal of modern aircraft systems has been

Opposite Eight widely used modern combat aircraft, showing their maximum speed and radius. Precise comparisons are difficult because maximum speeds vary greatly according to the altitude the aircraft is flying, and to the external loads of the aircraft. Radius is governed by the payload to be carried. The diagram on page 92 shows how this can dramatically affect the performance of a Phantom.

The Anglo–French Jaguar which was designed as a relatively simple fighter and trainer aircraft.

developed *ad hoc* and there is a real need for more designing of aircraft systems *de novo*, within the concept of the total aircraft, to provide the crew only with the minimum information they need for the task in hand and to handle all other functions automatically. Another burden of complexity is unreliability. Unreliability can result either in aircraft unavailability or in the aborting of a mission and perhaps loss of an aircraft. Indeed, unavailability is itself a kind of lost mission. A frequently adopted cure is duplication or redundancy of systems. This, however, is further complexity and may purchase increased reliability in the air at the price of added difficulty on the ground.

Increasing complexity is thus one of the major problems of modern military aircraft. Some relief is afforded by major strides forward in inherent ruggedness of components. The problem is, however, also encouraging a movement back toward simplification of equipment for many tasks. This solution is forced on poorer countries, where it often takes the form of simply buying aircraft of an earlier generation. Even the richest countries have to grapple with the problem, however, particularly in the fields of close support and air superiority, where numbers are of special importance and are dictated by many external factors. Reluctance to make do with very small numbers of even superior aircraft is reinforced by the growing acceptance of limited conventional war as a likely contingency. As soon as conventional rather than nuclear weapons are envisaged, sheer numbers regain significance. The F5, already mentioned, and the new Anglo–French Jaguar represent responses to the need for relatively cheap aircraft. The cheapness of such machines is, however, very relative. A more striking example, perhaps, is the resuscitation of the World War II Mustang, with updated equipment, for counter-insurgency work.

The revived Mustang is not merely or even primarily a response to cost, however. It also responds to the need for low speed and high endurance for certain tasks. As such it represents, once more in extreme form, a general trend away from what a few years ago would have been regarded as the leading indices of aircraft performance, height and speed. A number of factors have served to demote these criteria. There are, to begin with, special engineering problems in going beyond the already commonly achieved speeds of mach 2·5–mach 3. (Mach 1 is the speed of sound at sea-level at normal temperatures. As an aircraft speed the mach number is the ratio of vehicle speed to the speed of sound in the same air. Up to about mach 0·80 is called subsonic, around mach 1 transonic, above mach 1·25 supersonic.) In particular, airframes can no longer be made of aluminium. A second consideration is that much modern airborne ordnance cannot be released at speeds much above 500 mph. Much more important is the fact that airborne missiles of supersonic speed relieve the aircraft of the necessity to maintain such speeds itself. Of the greatest importance is the fact that as aircraft have become vulnerable to guided surface-to-air missiles (SAMS), they have found their remaining best chance of survival at very low altitudes where high speeds cannot and perhaps need not be maintained. The rewards, in terms of survivability, of a capacity to fly lower are much greater than those of being able to fly faster.

Thus the search for speed and altitude has been largely replaced as the dominating concern of modern aircraft design. A current list of priorities would probably include: improved capacity for low flying, higher agility in air-to-air combat, greater payload and range (payload as fuel being the condition for range) at a given level of cost and other performance, greater capacity for all-weather operation, and added ability to operate from short, perhaps un-prepared landing strips. All-weather capability is, of course, chiefly a matter of electronics. Also chiefly electronic is the close struggle between aircraft and anti-aircraft systems. Success in this field depends not merely on electronic sophistication but also, as in the case of so many other problems, on payload to carry what technology provides. This makes heavy demands on power plants where, at the current plateau of speed demands, there probably lies more scope for development than in airframes, though the variable geometry (VG) wing affords one important exception. The development of advanced aircraft engines provides the clearest example of how the rise in sophistication and cost is confining the development of really advanced aircraft to only a few rich countries. It is striking that the whole Western alliance contains only three firms in the front rank of acro-engine design: Rolls-Royce, Pratt and Whitney, and General Electric. The recent trials of Rolls-Royce illustrate the strain of sustaining design leadership.

As this phenomenon also illustrates, it is the competition between the two great world alliances with particular reference to the European theatre that sets the standard for modern military aircraft. Yet aircraft are readily mobile and freely sold. Consequently the latest aircraft are quickly disseminated to other arenas of conflict. Indeed, given the armed stability that prevails in Europe, it is from such areas as South Asia and the Middle East that most combat experience with modern aircraft arises. Great caution must be observed, however, in extrapolating performance in those areas to the more intense military environment of Europe. Contrariwise, it may well be that simpler systems would prove more useful in other theatres than those developed for the hypothetical conditions of major war in Europe.

Strategic Strike

Aircraft entered military action to perform observation and reconnaissance. Efforts to interfere with them in this role gave birth to the concept of air superiority. Strafing the front lines initiated close fire support of ground forces. It was, however, the 'long-range' bombing of such targets as London and

Cologne by Zeppelins, Gothas and Handley Page bombers that caught the imagination of enthusiasts for 'airpower'. To this day the idea of an 'independent role' fascinates many airmen and influences, consciously or unconsciously, many decisions on procurement or operations. Extreme advocates of independent airpower, like the Italian Douhet, saw it as the decisive and sufficient instrument of victory, knocking out all resistance and terrorizing populations. Much more moderate analysts expected quick, catastrophic and decisive results in the early days of World War II.

Impressive though the damage was, the War revealed that the more extreme predictions had grossly exaggerated the capacity of the available bombers to penetrate defences or to find distant targets. Above all, they had overestimated the damage which conventional explosives could do and underestimated the resilience of societies under attack. Indeed, it was in the tactical support of ground forces that airpower did more to revolutionize war. Towards the end of the War, it is true, better equipment, and particularly better target selection, inflicted serious strategic damage on Germany and Japan. Even so, it is doubtful if the results would have been in any sense decisive except in association with the accompanying war on land and sea.

The key to strategic airpower's limitations lay in the low destructive power of conventional explosives, for it was this and the consequent need for multiple and repeated penetrations of the defence that gave such factors as the attrition rate its significance. Consequently the advent of the nuclear weapon transformed the situation. But as we have seen, putting immense destructive power into a small package, far from assuring the bomber a future, raised a new rival by making the long-range ballistic missile an economic proposition. During the fifties the bomber ceased to be the spearhead of strategic forces.

Nevertheless, the strategic bomber survives and is even showing signs of a resurgence. There are several reasons for this. First of all, the bomber shares with all manned aircraft the ability to be recalled or to be conspicuously alerted. The latter characteristic has practical advantages as a tool of crisis management and diplomacy. The former may be especially valuable in the strategic role where the consequences of irrevocable error are so grave. Moreover, the bomber's high payload still gives it advantages over the missile; the B52 with three or four 5-MT bombs, or a dozen or more short-range attack missiles, is a formidable multiple delivery vehicle. With its human crew it shares the aircraft's capability to retarget on the basis of late information according to changed circumstances. These circumstances may include the disappearance of the original target. Thus, in theory at least, the bomber is ideally suited to fly over the path beaten by an initial missile attack to clean up any targets left undamaged in a damage-limiting strategy.

Moreover, it is now thought that the bomber's chance of penetrating defences may be better than was commonly thought only three or four years ago. The foes of the bomber are the manned interceptor and the SAM. These two, and particularly the SAM, virtually rule out the fast, high-level attacks for which such aircraft as the B52 and the much faster but now discarded B58 Hustler were originally designed. According to current thinking, however, a low-level approach at subsonic or transonic speeds can still pose the defence with very difficult problems in detecting, tracking and intercepting the bomber. Experience shows that at least present-day SAMs find it very difficult to get on to course quickly enough against the fast, low aircraft, quite apart from the fact that the short radius of coverage of all ground-based systems against low targets, because of the closer horizon, demands multiplication of defences.

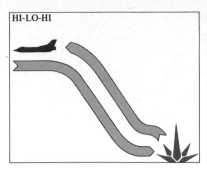
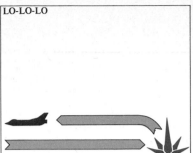
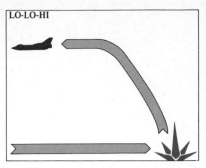

Achieving a low-level penetration puts very heavy demands on aircraft and crew. It requires a forward-looking terrain-avoidance radar to detect the contours of the land and automatically steer the aircraft safely above them at clearances perhaps as low as one or two hundred feet. Understandably, this system has to be reliable; for the confidence of the crew it also has to be conspicuously reliable. Because the low flight profile that restricts the detecting vision of the defences will also restrict the aircraft's field of view, special aids have to be provided for navigation and target location. Typically these would include a mapping radar, perhaps supplemented by infra-red detectors, to afford an illuminated display which the pilot can read 'head up' in front of him. Because the period in which objects ahead are in view is so brief, sideways-looking devices may also be desirable for navigational purposes. Inertial guidance will probably also be provided, the whole being assessed, of course, by computing devices.

High speeds at low altitudes produce 'buffeting' which is very hard on both airframe and crew. Swept wings do something to reduce this at transonic speeds but airframes must nevertheless be very strong and maintenance is heavy. The trouble this can cause becomes particularly plausible when it is realized that more than half of the faults grounding ordinary aircraft occur in the airframe. Obviously the effects of making long-range low-level flights are much graver than those over short ranges. The design of low-level strategic aircraft is therefore exacting. To cushion the shock to crew which, besides being unpleasant, will severely degrade their performance, special 'softride' systems have been developed. Nor should it be forgotten that at low levels jet engines are excessively heavy on fuel, thereby reducing either range or weapon load. Consequently, for both tactical and strategic strike, mixed mission 'profiles' may be adopted, flying high in zones of low risk and low where defences are thick. Thus, as the jargon goes, one may fly high to the target area, make the final run of some tens of miles low, and retreat high (hi-lo-hi), or, for maximum security may fly low all the way (lo-lo-lo). The latter is, of course, the most exacting of all the variety of profiles possible.

There are two other major approaches to the problem of penetrating heavy air defences. One is the adoption of 'stand off' bombs or missiles like the first generation British Blue Steel and American Hounddog, the Russian *Kangaroo*, and the newer American SRAM. In principle such missiles can be cruise missiles, usually with air-breathing engines and 'airborne', or rocket-propelled and ballistic. A second approach consists of electronic countermeasures (ECM) to degrade the defence. This stimulates electronic-counter-countermeasures (ECCM) and one is off on a chicken-and-egg spiral.

Electronic countermeasures can be active or passive. They can attempt to degrade the defence or they can attempt to deceive it. Passive measures can

Typical mission profiles of a modern strike aircraft.

involve such obvious – though not easy – measures as designing aircraft (or missiles) to reduce their radar cross-section and therefore detectability, or painting them with absorptive paint. To make such measures or, indeed, any ECM effective, it is highly desirable to know the nature of enemy radar so that ECM can be tuned to maximum effectiveness against the frequencies and other characteristics of enemy equipment. It is this consideration that explains the large investments made in electronic intelligence (ELINT). A defensive response to such ECM is to switch radar frequency. 'Agility' is thus a valuable quality in radars and some have the capacity to operate on several frequencies at once. Moreover, some frequencies of which equipment is capable may never be used in peacetime in the hope that enemies will not appreciate the full range.

Active confusion methods may include jamming by radiation of noise or deception by retransmitting received radar signals subtly altered to convey false information to the searching radar. Such noise will be made as similar as possible to noise arising from the nature of the detecting apparatus, and tampering with echoes will be done subtly, for any marked deviations from expected responses may be filtered out by discriminating equipment, leaving the true echoes for analysis. It is very relevant in this respect that the advantage of power will nearly always lie – at least in the case of relatively equally sophisticated combatants – with the ground equipment. Thus the detectors will try to transmit at high power and use relatively insensitive receivers so as to maximize the difficulty of any attempt to introduce false information into the system. One effort to redress the balance is the development of wholly specialized ECM aircraft to accompany missions. Attack aircraft can also be equipped with means to alert them when they are under surveillance. Developed forms of this equipment can tell the pilot what type of surveillance he is under, its range, and whether and what type of action he should take. One active countermeasure, available at least to large aircraft, is the launching of electronic decoys, cruise missiles shaped to simulate the radar signature of the real bomber. A now ageing device of this kind is the Quail carried by the B52, and the SCAD (subsonic cruise armed decoy), designed as its successor. An even more active countermeasure is the launching of missiles to home on and destroy the tracking radar. Examples of this are the American Shrike and the French Martel. Because a simple ECCM to this is to switch off the radar briefly, the missile needs a course memory. Dual sited radars, with transmitter and receiver at different locations, offer one partial response to such missiles.

How relevant and effective all this technology is depends very much on the environment. Between lesser military powers quite simple aircraft may still be effective strategic weapon carriers. Among the major powers, the challenge to a strategic bomber is very different from that to a tactical aircraft close to friendly ground forces. The evidence suggests that even the two Superpowers see a continued usefulness in manned strategic bombers, or at least that their air staffs are having success in arguing the point. In the United States, support for an advanced manned strategic aircraft, repeatedly suppressed by Secretary McNamara, has given rise to the development of the projected B1. The Soviet Union is introducing a new twin-engined, swing-wing bomber designated *Backfire* by NATO. It is estimated that this could reach the United States from Arctic bases or by aerial refuelling. We should also remember that of all the major powers, only the United States faces its more formidable opponents at solely intercontinental ranges. Russia, China and the Western Europeans have plenty of important strategic targets at medium range. One witness to this is the French force of Mirage IVA bombers, whose range is indeed so limited as to

CREW MORALE!!

cast doubt on their value. But in this respect one must recall that bomber ranges are normally cited on a two-way basis, a consideration that might not seem overriding in conditions of nuclear war.

Two other arguments for the bomber must be mentioned. The first is simply that maintenance of even a small nuclear bombing force imposes heavy costs of air defence on a potential enemy. The second is that when seeking a 'mix' of offensive nuclear forces to stabilize deterrence, bombers represent a greater variegation than land- and sea-based missiles do from each other. It can therefore be argued, though not necessarily decisively, that a bomber force is a stabilizing element because, if alert and embodying an airborne component in crisis, it greatly complicates the task of any power contemplating a first strike. For this reason we may yet see a return to the concept of the abandoned Skybolt, an airborne long-range ballistic missile.

As a result of such considerations, as well no doubt of some inertia, a large number of strategic bombers remain in service. To the American B52 and the small number of the bomber version of the F111 (the FB111), can be compared the oldish Russian TU20 *Bear*, and the TU22 *Blinder*. The medium TU16 *Badger* is obsolescent but a new version is now serially produced in China. The French Mirage IVA has already been mentioned. Britain's Vulcan II retains a strategic capability, being converted like the B52 to lower-level flight. The projected British version of the MRCA must also be regarded as a potential strategic weapon.

Interceptors

An interceptor is designed to locate, intercept, identify and, if necessary, destroy intruding aircraft. It is usually conceived as having a role against relatively sparse intruders over friendly terrain, where it can rely on a surface radar environment. It therefore needs rapid climb and high acceleration but can make do with relatively low payload, short range and a relatively narrow if sophisticated range of electronics. One exception in the matter of range and endurance is the naval interceptor, such as the F4 Phantom, that may face difficulties such as delay in returning to base or may have to fly a sustained air-cover.

In some respects the pure interceptor has been a vanishing breed because of the decline in manned bombers and the rival potential of the SAM. The great advantage of the manned interceptor is its capacity to operate at longer range than the SAM and its ability to identify and interrogate aircraft visually. The latter characteristic is particularly valuable in peacetime and in limited war. Speed and agility are less important to the interceptor than they once were, because the air-to-air missile (AAM) offers a method of shooting down aircraft without achieving the special relative positions imposed on a gun fighter.

There are at present two main types of AAM, those guided by radar homing and those guided by infra-red emissions. Infra-red has the advantage of not giving the enemy warning by radar emissions and of homing automatically once launched. Early versions like the American Sidewinder could only be used in pursuit from astern but new versions, including the British Red Top, permit a much wider spectrum of attack. Radar missiles like the American Sparrow permit wide-angle attack from collision courses, but require the aircraft to maintain constrained attitudes toward the target until the missile has closed with it. Disadvantages of this kind can be eliminated at a price of fully active homing, where all necessary equipment is in the missile itself. Even radar missiles continue to offer opportunities for ECM. One particular difficulty is that if visual

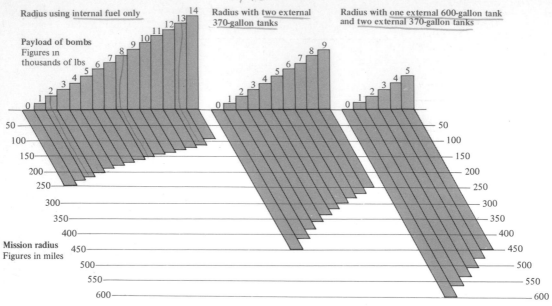

+740 GAL   + 1340 GAL

Radius using internal fuel only

Radius with two external 370-gallon tanks

Radius with one external 600-gallon tank and two external 370-gallon tanks

Payload of bombs
Figures in thousands of lbs

Mission radius
Figures in miles

The effect of increased load on the combat radius of a F4D Phantom.

Below A British Lightning interceptor with a Victor tanker in the background approaches a Russian *Bear*. The Lightning was designed as a short-range aircraft and needs in-flight refuelling to make long-range patrols.

identification is required, an interceptor may have to sacrifice much of the advantage of remote launching afforded by the missile. A tactic to deal with this can involve using aircraft in pairs, one to interrogate, one to shoot if necessary. But it is clearly an expensive method, which requires two aircraft and the possible loss of one. Partly for this reason guns are returning after a period of eclipse as interceptor armament; they give a close-range kill capability and confer a certain ground attack ability.

Ideally the interceptor should have an all-weather performance. This it achieves in collaboration with a friendly radar ground environment. The ground (or ship-borne) radars acquire and track the target, identify it so far as possible electronically, and guide the interceptor close enough for its own radars to take over. These will then fly the interceptor into an attack position and, unless overridden by the crew, may fire the weapons at the best time. Although the crew is there to deal with emergencies and to override the systems if desired, its role is otherwise subordinate to the electronics.

As we have seen, one tactic of an intruding aircraft is to fly low. This presents the surveillance radars and interceptor with the difficult task of detecting and tracking an aircraft which betrays itself late to ground radars and presents an image against confusing ground echoes or clutter to airborne radars. The emerging answer for sophisticated air defence is to exploit the so-called Doppler effect by which certain types of continuous-wave and pulse radars can discriminate moving targets from static objects. For use towards the ground, pulse radars are most effective and provision can be made to suppress the irrelevant static echoes. Thus interceptors can be equipped with 'snap down' systems to detect and to home missiles on to low-flying aircraft from above. These can operate in conjunction with long-endurance high-level surveillance aircraft. The United States has a project for such an airborne warning and command system (AWACS) in development, and the Soviet Union has flying a TU114 apparently adapted to this role. Aerial refuelling would permit sustained surveillance.

Close Air Support and Interdiction

Interdiction can be looked on as a venture midway between close air support and strategic strike. If anything, the problem is closer to the strategic end of the spectrum, for interdiction operations call for deep penetration of enemy defences. Thus the requirements for electronic counter measures and navigation are high. On the other hand, the target will probably be well identified and perhaps conspicuous. For many years it was assumed that any such operations in the European theatre would be nuclear. In that case they could also be performed by medium- or intermediate-range missiles. If, as current NATO strategy envisages, such operations were to be conducted conventionally, aircraft would be necessary and the task would be a demanding one.

It is possible, indeed, that political limitations would inhibit deep interdiction of any kind. Certainly such inhibitions have operated in Viet Nam and somewhat similar elements have entered calculations in the Middle East. All the more importance would then accrue to the tasks of close air support at the front.

The NATO concept of 'flexible response' has given renewed interest to the conduct of close air support with conventional weapons. Short-range tactical missiles cannot yet rival aircraft as a means of accurately delivering high explosive at tactical, frequently fleeting targets beyond artillery range. Nor, under many conditions, can sensors compete with men in the tasks of searching for targets and the general management of weapon delivery. The relative

Above One of the new generation of American fighter aircraft, the McDonnell-Douglas F15 air superiority fighter.

cheapness of short-range missiles, as compared to manned aircraft, provides a constant incentive to develop them as a substitute and one day, perhaps in conjunction with satellite observation, they may become a completely satisfactory alternative. That day, however, has not yet arrived.

Requirements for a good close-support aircraft are different from the specifications of an aircraft for deep strike. The support aircraft operates in an intense military environment where it encounters many dangers. Surface-to-air missiles force it to fly low. Once low it becomes a prey to heavy machine guns and cannon, perhaps radar assisted, and to new kinds of very light and portable anti-aircraft missiles. Electronic countermeasures will not help the aircraft against these missiles if they are guided by infra-red, although some evasive techniques are possible. Similarly it has no defence against the guns. Moreover, the investment that can be put into the equipment of the aircraft must be limited by the necessity to provide a sufficient number to deal with a wealth of targets and to react to them without undue delay.

The support aircraft needs an adequate payload to permit it to search for its targets and to carry the appropriate ordnance. How much is enough is a very hotly debated question. From one perspective it is hardly possible to have too much endurance, weapon load and avionics. On the other hand, such lavishness reduces numbers and may be superfluous if a lesser aircraft could nevertheless destroy the target, which, in tactical operations, may itself not be of overwhelming value. Thus we have seen the development of cheap aircraft such as the Jaguar and F5 mentioned earlier and the extension of the service of obsolescent types like the Hunter and the MiG 17 and MiG 19. For modest airforces a range of very cheap aircraft has appeared which can double as trainer and light attack aircraft. Examples are the British Aircraft Corporation Jet Provost in the guise of the 167 Strikemaster, the Cessna T37 as the A37, and the Canadian CT114 as the CL41.

The more advanced attack aircraft needs help in finding and hitting its target. At low level in a dangerous area – and by definition an attack plane seeks out dangerous areas – the aircraft cannot spare much time for search, both because of fuel consumption and because of the danger of prolonged exposure. It may therefore be provided with linescan radars and infra-red scanners, to help it find its way. It may also use low-light-level TV with image intensifiers, infra-red sensors and ignition sensors to help it locate its target. All are costly and many involve watching weapons all the way down to target. An alternative is to have a ground observer or a light aircraft or helicopter mark the target. A crude form of this is the smoke marker. A sophisticated variant is to have the observer 'illuminate' the target with a laser on the reflection of which a missile homes, allowing the carrying aircraft to break away once the weapon is launched.

Crew training is a vital component in the support operation. In this connection much depends on the duration of operations, for both crew and anti-aircraft defences are likely to improve in tactics and personal skill, other things equal, as the initial days of combat wear on. Most experts seem to believe that the passage of time will tell against the aircraft as the effect of initial surprise wears off and the ground forces learn. Proponents of this view compare the total success of the Israeli attacks on Egyptian airfields in 1967 with the rising attrition exacted against American aircraft in the drawn-out operations of Viet Nam. Clearly, however, such analogies must be drawn with great caution and due consideration of the variable factors in each situation.

A great many strike and support aircraft are in service. At the most powerful end of the scale is the F4 Phantom which can perform both close support and deep strike interdiction missions, having high speeds, a large payload and, hence, long range. No less than nine different versions of the Phantom have been put into operation and more than 4000 have been delivered. Very much in contrast to the heavy, twin-engined Phantom is the widely sold A4. This has a gross weight of only 24,500 lb, compared to the F4's 58,000 lb. Nevertheless the A4 can carry a 10,000 lb weapon load and has a range of over 2000 miles with external fuel. As with all aircraft, information about range and payload must be read cautiously, for commonly the maximum range is achieved only by accepting severely restricted payload and vice versa.

Below The French Dassault Mirage series of fighters have been widely sold. The F1 and F2 in the foreground of the picture are the latest variants of a line which began in 1960. The Mirage G in the background is an experimental swing-wing design.

An advanced low-level Soviet attack aircraft is the MiG 23, *Foxbat*, which has appeared in the UAR. Although capable of ground attack, this plane, which has flown·at over mach 3 and attained an altitude of over 98,000 feet, is probably more suited to be an 'air superiority' fighter. The requirements for an air superiority aircraft – that is to say, one capable of protecting friendly attack aircraft and opposing its hostile opposite number over the battlefield – are different from an ordinary interceptor. Ideally, such a plane needs considerable endurance either to facilitate escort missions or to permit sustained patrol. Such an aircraft is also much more likely than an interceptor to get into dogfight situations with aircraft of similar types. Consequently it needs agility and a weapon capable of kills at short range. Some missiles can fulfil this role and

The British Harrier close-support bomber. This is the first vertical take-off aircraft to go into regular military use. The outer pylons carry multiple rocket pods.

special new ones are under development, but many experts still favour the use of cannon, automatically fired at the best moment. These specifications for an air superiority aircraft are very demanding, especially on engines, for the combination of endurance with high performance in combat is difficult to achieve. It will usually dictate twin engines, a characteristic partly explaining why the ubiquitous F4 can add this role to its repertoire.

Two approaches are discernible to the challenge of designing close support and air superiority aircraft. One is to build all capability into one aircraft, or, more accurately, to make it possible to adapt one fundamental aircraft to the full range of strike, support and superiority tasks. The F4, the F111 and, very explicitly, the MRCA represent attempts to do this. A similar claim could be made for the Mirage series. An alternative is to build relatively simpler and slower aircraft for the support role and to create special aircraft for air superiority. The American A7 series of simplified light attack aircraft represents this trend and the projected A-X will continue it. At the same time the USAF has under development the F15, a specialized air superiority fighter. The difference in approach is illustrated by the contrast between A7's single 14,000 lb thrust engine, transonic speed and the F15's twin engines, each of 24,000 lb thrust and projected speed of over mach 2. The Mirage v, developed for (but not sold to) Israel is another example of simplified aircraft nevertheless capable of carrying 4000 lb of weapons to a radius of 275 miles flying lo-lo-lo.

An Achilles heel for most aircraft, particularly those required over the battlefield, is their dependence on conspicuous and vulnerable airfields. In tactical nuclear war there can be no realistic expectation that airfields would survive the very early phases of war. Israel's devastation of the Arab air forces in 1967 demonstrated what good tactics and surprise could achieve, even with conventional means. Aircraft needing long and specially prepared runways dictate conspicuous fields. Near the front, such fields are liable to bombing or to being overrun by ground forces. Removed from the fronts they impose long sorties on support aircraft. In all cases they restrict the flexible use of aircraft.

Several solutions can be tried. One is to disperse and shelter aircraft on airfields. The runways themselves, however, remain vulnerable, though special provision can be made for repair. Another possibility is to defend the airfields actively by anti-aircraft guns and missiles and by ground defence teams. A third approach and the one now being pursued with most originality, is to acquire support aircraft independent of conventional airfield. One method of doing this, already discussed, is to turn to the helicopter. Another is to create a fixed-wing aircraft capable of vertical or short take-off and landing (v/STOL). At the same time aircraft can be designed to make use of grass or only lightly prepared airstrips.

Only one true VTOL military aircraft is yet in service, the British Harrier used by the RAF and the US Marine Corps. The Soviet Union's prototype Yakovlev *Freehand* does not yet seem to be operational and the jointly developed German–Italian VAK 191B has been abandoned. Various approaches to vertical take-off are possible: pivotable wings and engines, separate propulsion and lift jets, and 'vectored thrust' using the same engine or engines for both purposes by deflecting the thrust. The latter principle, used by Harrier, is particularly flexible in permitting either vertical take-off or a short, adjustable run which greatly increases the possible payload. A run of some 300–400 feet is considered short (compared with up to 2500 for a high performance conventional aircraft) and the Harrier can take off some 6000 lb heavier with short roll than with truly vertical take-off.

This points to the short rather than vertical take-off for many purposes. Several military aircraft are now entering service which are capable of take-offs which are short in comparison with their airborne performance. Such results can be achieved by rocket-assisted take-off (which does not reduce landing distance and hence suggests special braking parachutes and other devices), special lift devices such as boundary-layer control, whereby the air near the wings is forced into favourable flows, and the thorough-going adoption of pivotable, swing wings as in the F111, the Russian MiG *Flogger* newly in service, and the projected Anglo–German–Italian MRCA. Swing wings permit minimal sweep for high lift at low speeds and swept positions for high speed at high altitude or for relatively smooth transonic performance near the ground. This effect is achieved, however, only at the price of considerable weight and loss of usable space within the wing or fuselage.

There is much controversy over the merits of VTOL and STOL aircraft. The performance is bought at some cost and the true VTOL performance is particularly prodigal with payload. On the other hand, it can be argued that release from large airfields may be the *sine qua non* of having any tactical air force survive at all, a point particularly convincing if nuclear operations are considered. Enthusiasts for VTOL maintain that it would permit wholly new tactics, with aircraft unprecedentedly close to the front and therefore capable of quick, short sorties. As a result the low payload may not be critical, for the VTOL 'loiters on the ground'. Close basing might also permit rapid turn-round to new missions. Quick turn-round is a vital factor in close support efficiency, as exemplified by the 1967 Israeli achievement of seven to eight sorties a day compared to the planned Egyptian three to four. Critics argue, however, that full dispersal is incompatible with supply and maintenance. To bring spares and munitions up to dispersed aircraft is not only troublesome but may betray positions. Helicopter supply may be the answer here, but one involving costs and vulnerabilities of its own.

The critics also argue that even from rearward bases the delay in reaction time of fast aircraft has little to do with flying time and most to do with deciding on targets and fitting the aircraft for each mission. Moreover, the danger of aircraft being overrun is compounded by forward dispersal. The U S Marine Corps solution is to envisage several categories of base, the main and rearward with full maintenance facilities, an intermediate forward base and, if appropriate, a very advanced and minimal pad for intimate integration with ground forces.

The Marines are doubtless encouraged to take this view by their long experience and great success in operating what is in effect a single-service air–ground team. For the question of operational control of support aircraft is a vexed one made particularly acute by the possibility for extreme dispersal

Russian and American swing-wing aircraft: the F111A multi-purpose fighter bomber (**below**) and the Russian MiG prototype which has the NATO code-name *Flogger* (**left and far left**).

The American Walleye
TV-guided bomb mounted
on a Phantom.

by VTOL. Air force commanders typically fear that devolution of control and intimate association with ground forces will lead to frittering away scarce aircraft on minor missions. Ground forces equally fear that centralized and air force control will result in slow reaction and reluctance to commit aircraft in time. This debate is endemic, though frequently suppressed, and affects the whole range of conventional, VTOL and rotary-wing support air power. The answer must be sought chiefly in tactical doctrine and military organization but there are also important technical aspects. In particular, truly effective use of flexible, quick reaction support requires easy, secure, voice communication between ground and air. Moreover, it will be essential to have good communications and control in the low air environment over the battlefield where, under present conceptions, conventional, VTOL and rotary-wing aircraft will all be mixed up together along with the enemy, the whole subject to help or attack by a proliferating variety of decentralized ground-to-air weapons.

What strike and support aircraft can achieve depends very much on the munitions available to them. The free-fall bomb is, of course, still very widely used. Dispersing clusters of small bomblets can be a much more effective method than larger bombs under many circumstances and new techniques are being developed to make this more practicable from low levels. Retarded bombs are also in use. This may be done simply to permit safe escape of the aircraft or as part of a technique to air burst the weapon or to 'lay it down' to explode on the surface, thereby maximizing blast and fragmentation effects. Alternatively it may be desirable to retard the bomb so as to make it penetrate deeply into the ground for maximum cratering effect.

Cannon are still in use for ground attack, some capable of very high rates of fire. Free-flight rockets are also used by fixed-wing aircraft as well as by helicopters. In Viet Nam the United States has employed quite large aircraft such as old DC3s and modern C130s as gunships to deliver heavy broadside barrages. For really accurate delivery, guided missiles are employed, accepting the inevitable weight penalty and high cost. The greater the sophistication, the less the weapon can be expended as casually as a mere 'round of ammunition'. To acquire targets, aircraft may have forward-looking radar or infra-red scanners, and new low-light-level TV is entering service. These systems can be automatically coupled to prepare and fire the weapon.

The actual guidance of the missile can be achieved in a variety of ways. Some weapons are guided by 'command' as in the case of the wire-guided anti-tank missiles already described in use by ground forces and helicopters. Other weapons may home on the target either actively or passively. Passive weapons home on a characteristic of the target, as infra-red missiles seek out sources of heat. Active weapons illuminate the target in some way and home on the reflected signals. A weapon may be fully active – emitting its own radiations and homing on them – or the target may be illuminated from somewhere else – the launching or other aircraft, or a ground observer. Command and many semi-active systems have the disadvantage that the launching aircraft must remain in position for observation during the flight time of the missile, thereby increasing vulnerability and reducing rate of fire. The ideal is a weapon one can 'launch and leave'. One such weapon is the American Walleye, a 'smart' bomb which has a TV head and homes automatically on a preselected optical image of the target. The Maverick is a follow-on adaptation of this principle being developed for the A-X and F4. Another approach is the TV-guided Martel, which has a TV head through which a command operator in a distant aircraft can see the target and steer the missile accordingly. The German Kormoran, on the other hand, depends on an inertial guidance system and terminal active radar homing. The technique of having an observer on the ground or in another aircraft to illuminate the target with a laser can be used to guide weapons as well as to identify targets.

Design of air-to-ground guidance is made difficult by the very heavy ground clutter. The guidance of ground-to-air weapons is correspondingly easier, and the aircraft now faces a great variety of new, light, anti-aircraft missiles. Again they may be steered by command or by passive, active and semi-active homing. An alternative method is the 'beamriding' missile, like the British naval Seaslug, which follows a radar beam which a surface-based system keeps locked on to the target. This system imposes a slow rate of fire but has an advantage of signal-power that makes jamming difficult. By contrast the famous Russian SAM2 system much employed in Viet Nam has proved very susceptible to ECM and also insufficiently agile to perform well against aircraft taking evasive action.

Even the larger surface-to-air missiles, like the American Hawk and British Bloodhound or Thunderbird, enjoy a cost advantage over aircraft. A Hawk battery of thirty-six missiles and six launchers is still substantially cheaper than a single F111. The real breakthrough has come in very light, portable systems. The new British Rapier is transported on a light vehicle and can be controlled by one man. The missile is steered by radio command slaved to binocular sights which can be replaced by radar. Accuracy is said to be sufficiently good to permit a small warhead to explode inside the target aircraft. This response to the threat of the low-flying aircraft is outstripped in cheapness and portability by the one-man systems now entering service. One of these, the British Blowpipe, weighs less than 40 lb in a canister ready for firing and with sights attached. Guided by radio link from visual tracking the range is said to be from 2000–7000 yards. The American Redeye is an infra-red weapon on a similar scale.

Such weapons have many faults but their cheapness permits wide dissemination. The resulting environment could be nerve-wracking for support aircraft. It will be an important consideration to ensure that friendly aircraft are not shot down by trigger-happy infantrymen. Later weapons such as Blowpipe have an integral IFF system. Many of the smaller surface-to-air missiles have only a fair-weather capability, but this defect is substantially offset by the difficulties which poor weather and darkness pose for aircraft.

Reconnaissance

Reconnaissance and observation are the oldest tasks of military aircraft. The famous U2 aircraft illustrate the potential of aircraft for strategic surveillance but as between the Superpowers this function has been increasingly replaced by the less politically sensitive use of space satellites. For both aircraft and satellites a great variety of sensors is now available, including optical photography, infra-red scanning, sideways-looking radar, and various kinds of television. A single RAF Victor can, in one seven-hour sortie, radar map the entire Mediterranean. All the information acquired can be processed and collated by computers. Equipment can be provided to record and compensate for the position and posture of the vehicle at the moment of acquiring any piece of data. Inertial navigation systems contribute to the accuracy of the work. Over distances of at least several hundred miles, drone aircraft can be used for reconnaissance and techniques exist to control formations of such aircraft precisely at considerable distances.

A special task is that of Airborne Early Warning (AEW), to extend the range

of surface-based systems. As already mentioned, such aircraft may be used to detect hostile aircraft and also to control intercepting planes and weapons. The concept of airborne control centre can be extended and the United States has several airborne National Military Command centres to take over complete control of American strategy if necessary. Current plans envisage putting more elaborate versions of this into an adaptation of the Boeing 747 Jumbo Jet.

Airlift

Air transport is a day-to-day feature of modern life and its military potential is obvious. It can be used strategically to move forces between theatres of

The British Rapier light-weight anti-aircraft missile system. This can be operated by three men and transported on a light vehicle.

(COMPANY PICTURE: NOTICE RIFLE)

combat or to secure supplies for the home or other base. It can be used tactically to secure flexibility within a theatre of operations, or close to the battlefield to ensure high mobility. The last role is very much the business of helicopters. The other two are the prime responsibility of fixed-wing aircraft, some now of tremendous size.

Typical of the tactical lift aircraft are the Franco–German Transall and the American C130 Hercules now in use by many nations. At the strategic level pride of place was briefly held by the Russian Antonov 22 with a range of over 6000 miles and payload of 176,000 lb over 2500 miles. Its status as largest military aircraft has now been usurped by the American C5 Galaxy. This monster, though a major financial disaster in development, has an impressive performance. It can carry a payload of 265,000 lb for 2950 miles, or 125,000 lb for 8000 miles. Its bulk enables it to airlift a main battle tank.

The subject of airborne logistics is a major study in its own right. Despite the performance of modern aircraft, many problems remain and airlift is not the answer to all problems. As the C5 illustrates, the cost of large transport aircraft is high. Many cargoes still cannot be airlifted satisfactorily either because of their absolute bulk or the sheer quantity required. Fuel is a main example of the latter problem and the transport aircraft is itself a major consumer of fuel. A brigade of some 5000 men on 'light scales' of equipment will still require some 1000 tons of freight. The payload of a C130 being about 20,000 lb over 4700 miles, some 200 sorties would be needed to move the unit. If the solution to some of these problems is dual provision of equipment – some where troops are based or train, some where they may be flown to fight – the costs in terms of capital outlay and maintenance are obvious. Particularly for strategic operations, another problem is the so-called air barriers; that is, the restrictions on flight over their airspace that countries very frequently apply to military aircraft. Such barriers can either make airlift impossible or impose penalties of range. Aerial refuelling is a partial solution, but one that again entails obvious costs. Moreover, much depends on military circumstances. Flights that are perfectly practicable in peacetime may become unacceptably hazardous once hostilities have broken out.

The conclusion must be that airlift has become an indispensable part of modern military capability but has not yet and probably never can supplant the use of ground and sea transport.

Maritime Aircraft

Aircraft from ships can operate over the land and land-based aircraft can operate over the sea. Purely for convenience the use of aircraft to attack or protect ships is discussed in the next chapter and the present discussion is confined to the large, shore-based aircraft which typically carry out long-range maritime reconnaissance and ASW operations.

This branch of aviation has long been important and as the likelihood of sustained battles between submarines and convoys has declined in the nuclear age, the advent of the missile-firing submarine has given ASW a new impetus. A great many large, fixed-wing shore-based reconnaissance aircraft are in service. The Russian TU95 turboprop *Bear*, TU16 twin-jet *Badger* and TU22 twin-jet *Blinder* have become familiar followers of Western naval forces. France operates forty Breguet Atlantic twin turboprops and Germany twenty of the same. The United States has some 400 Lockheed P2 Neptunes and the newer successor P3 Orion, the latter based on the four-turboprop Lockheed Electra. Britain operates the newest and most specialized maritime recon-

naissance aircraft, the Nimrod, a four-jet adaptation of the Comet airliner. This, the first pure jet built specifically for ASW work, is based on the theory of high-speed flight to patrol station followed by economical twin-engined patrol.

Modern ASW aircraft are equipped with a large variety of sensors and with elaborate computing equipment to collate and analyse the data acquired. Indeed, the need to carry all this equipment and a crew to handle it accounts for the existence of these large and powerful ASW aircraft. The crew of the Nimrod, for example, consists of three pilots, two navigators and no less than seven men to operate the detection equipment. This includes Jezebel sonobuoys, an Autolycus ionization detector to 'sniff' diesel fumes, magnetic-anomaly detectors (MAD) to detect metal objects below the surface, and, of course, various radars. The weapons of such aircraft usually comprise mines, depth charges, and homing torpedoes, some of which can be nuclear. It is also possible to use air-to-surface missiles which may be particularly valuable against surface craft.

Russia alone of the major powers still operates flying-boats for maritime operations. Her Beriev Be-10, a large twin-jet aircraft, holds the world speed record for water-based aircraft at over 565 mph. More numerous are the twin-turboprop Be-12 amphibians.

It must also be remembered that aerial reconnaissance against surface units is still valuable. A great deal of the Soviet naval air force's energy is devoted to this, and flights are carried out over great distances. Russian planes from Northern bases regularly fly missions over the Azores and Cuba.

The open nose of the American C5 Galaxy, the largest military aircraft in the world.

CHAPTER FIVE

The Maritime Battle

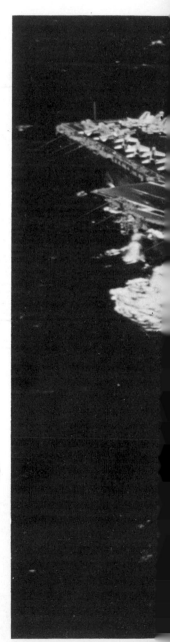

More than two thirds of the globe's surface is sea; more than half of the seas are deeper than 10,000 ft. The mean depth of the sea is about 12,500 ft, compared to a mean height of the land above sea-level of less than 3000 ft. It is consequently not surprising that the seas play an important part in man's military activities.

Seapower is largely a question of access; of using the seas to obtain supplies, to launch expeditions and to bombard the land. Although military forces constitute the means of assuring use of the seas for these purposes and of denying such use to others, it is important to recognize the importance of commercial uses of the sea. These are a source of politics and conflict, a target for military action, and an auxiliary to naval forces.

Three aspects of the commercial use of the sea deserve special mention. The oldest extractive activity at sea is fishing. Mundane though it may appear, fishing is of great political and strategic importance. It has given rise to most of the conflict that has had its origins at sea and efforts to protect fishing rights have done more than anything else to encourage nations to try to extend their territorial jurisdiction over the sea. In recent years fishing has caused serious international disputes involving the use of armed force, such as those between Britain and Iceland, France and Brazil, Peru and Ecuador. The growing possibility of over-fishing and the consequent need for conservation, together with wholly new concepts of fish farming (aquaculture), open up new political issues. Closely related is the problem of pollution, also raising questions of jurisdiction and hence of policing.

The second well-established use of the seas is shipping. It suffices to recall again that air transport, though taking over an increasing proportion of cargoes where value is high in relation to bulk, is no answer to the great mass of trans-oceanic freight. World shipping fleets totalled 61,000,000 tons in 1939, 95,000,000 in 1955, 154,000,000 in 1965 and 254,000,000 in 1972. One of the most noted aspects of this process has been the carefully nurtured and meteoric increase in Soviet merchant shipping, from 7,500,000 tons in 1965 to 12,000,000 in 1970, with a 1980 target of 24,000,000. Great developments in containerization, roll-on roll-off loading and the immense increase in ship size have accompanied this expansion of world shipping. The resulting fleets represent both great national assets and new sources of vulnerability. Destruction of shipping in war is a sufficiently recent experience to remain vivid, though the possibility of recurrence is debatable. By contrast the remarkably high level of order on the high seas in peacetime and absence of such phenomena as piracy is perhaps taken too much for granted. The recent spread of hijacking by air and of one or two examples at sea suggest the possibility of change.

The third and most striking aspect of exploitation of the seas is the newly created capacity to explore, and extract wealth from, the sea bottom. Until the middle of this century virtually the only commercial use made of the sea bottom

The 75,000-ton nuclear-powered attack aircraft carrier USS *Enterprise*, which can cruise more than four times round the globe before needing to refuel.

was for submarine cables and a little coalmining conducted from on-shore shafts. Now, as is well known, the extraction of oil and gas from the seabed is a major industry, while the offshore mining of solid minerals, though difficult, is slowly developing. The rewards to be won are rapidly accelerating the technology of working underwater from vehicles, fixed installations and, where necessary and within close limits, with men as free swimmers. The Polaris-type submarine can cruise at about 1000 ft and would collapse at 2000. But deep-search vehicles already approach 10,000 ft and bathyscaphes descend to 30,000. The bulk of future commercial use is, however, likely to be confined for a very long time to the Continental Shelf, a zone of varying width and shallow decline to 600 ft, beyond which a typically steep dive to the deep ocean begins.

Like all profitable activity, the exploitation gives rise to political issues. In particular it raises issues of ownership, for, beyond territorial waters of varying width, the high seas are common property. No international agreement has been reached on a uniform extent of territorial waters; most claims vary from three to twelve miles but some Latin American states claim up to 200 miles. The 1958 Geneva Convention on the Continental Shelf conferred exclusive rights on the littoral state to exploit the resources of the sea bottom out to a depth of 200 metres or such greater depth as proves practicable. Thus new frontiers are created beneath the seas. These may require policing and there may well be a tendency to assimilate the water over the shelf to territorial waters.

Such a tendency is reinforced by the development of new military uses for the seabed. While the emplacement of weapons of mass destruction on the seabed is now forbidden by the treaty of 1971, a wide variety of surveillance systems is already deployed or projected. As a result there have been suggestions for submarine identification zones analogous to the air defence identification zone (ADIZ) maintained around North America. There has also been a widespread tendency to extend national jurisdiction by such methods as simply claiming more generous territorial limits, redrawing the base lines from which limits are calculated, maintaining that archipelagos, like Indonesia, should enjoy a single, all-embracing territorial zone, and claiming to exercise jurisdiction over traditionally international straits. While there are generally recognized rights of innocent passage through territorial waters for merchant ships, these are customarily restricted where warships are concerned. Moreover, there is no right of passage by air over territorial waters, so that extended jurisdictions at sea have serious implications for the problem of air barriers. The possibilities for conflict are obvious and are compounded by the rapid post-war multiplication of sovereign states. There are now more than a hundred states with coastline. The phenomenon is particularly marked in the Indian Ocean and Gulf where, before 1945, Great Britain had jurisdiction over virtually the whole littoral and where tens of independent states now exist.

The nature of what may be called military seapower is complicated by several factors. Because the high seas are common property, naval power can be deployed at considerable distances. It was, indeed, the characteristic instrument of classic imperialism and of the extension of 'Western' power. In modern times the Western alliance has perhaps taken rather for granted the seapower which made possible creation of the Atlantic alliance and such overseas interventions as the Viet Nam war and British action in South-East Asia. As another result of the international nature of the high seas, seapower is a 'permeable' concept; there are no frontiers on the seas in peacetime and no clearcut battle area in war. Consequently, rival naval forces interpenetrate each other with many important implications for politics, strategy and tactics.

Maritime operations have also become exceedingly complex in terms of the instruments employed. For centuries the only instruments available were surface vessels, with the minor complication of shore batteries. The two World Wars introduced new dimensions with the aircraft and the submarine. Now space satellites for surveillance, navigation and communication take this diversification a stage further. All of these changes mean that, on the one hand, seapower which, short of amphibious invasions, could make only shallow penetrations beyond the shoreline, can now strike deep into the land with aircraft and missiles. At the same time, however, maritime forces are now open to attack from the land even when far out to sea. Thus war at sea is no longer a monopoly of naval forces.

One approach to classifying the complex array of maritime power would be to conceive it as having positive and negative aspects. Positive purposes might be those using the sea to seek results on land; negative purposes might be efforts to thwart the positive purposes. Thus one could regard the carriage of supplies, the mounting of invasions and the bombardment of the land as positive. Coastal defence, blockades, war on shipping could be regarded as negative. But, although such a classification seems to clarify some issues and to explain the characteristic make-up of superior and inferior navies, it breaks down in detail. Quite apart from the usual confusions that arise from the fact that defensive strategies can often serve offensive policies and vice versa, many of the specific instruments of seapower are adaptable to both negative and positive purposes. An anti-submarine capacity, for example, can be used to combat missile submarines, which are positive, or to thwart an attack on commerce, which is negative.

In an attempt to avoid some of these difficulties, the following discussion considers the wider issues concerning the use of maritime power and then concentrates in more detail on several of the more important tactical functions that are common features of a variety of strategies.

Seapower in General War

Seapower would obviously play a part if an all-out war arose between the major powers, but it is much more difficult than in former times to predict what that role would be.

Submarine-launched ballistic missiles are at the heart of strategic nuclear policy. They are likely to be retained, at least in part, as the residual bargaining retaliatory force, and ASW could clearly play an important part in damage limitation. As with BMD, a question arises as to the wisdom of attempting to undermine the forces on which mutual deterrence rests. The issue is complicated in the case of ASW, however, by the fact that ASW forces can serve many purposes other than countering the nuclear missile submarines (SSBN) and therefore cannot be simply abolished. Moreover, nations possessing SSBNs need to stay abreast of the art of ASW if only to preserve the invulnerability of their missile force. The prospects for ASW proving technically successful are considered later.

Attack aircraft carriers (CVA) can also launch strategic strikes. These were for several years the only naval contribution to strategic strike and much of the present Russian navy was constructed to neutralize the Western aircraft carriers. The increase in carrier aircraft performance, the miniaturization of nuclear weapons and the advent of the nuclear-power carrier (CVAN) have all increased the potency of carrier-borne strike. But in fact the aircraft carrier became a relatively unimportant and second-line part of the American striking force

because of the improvement in anti-aircraft defences, the increased vulnerability of the carrier in nuclear war and, above all, because of the better alternative offered by the SSBN. Nevertheless, the residual threat of the carrier imposes
a heavy precautionary defensive burden on the Soviet (and Chinese) navies and
air defence forces.

It is much more difficult to visualize other aspects of naval action in all-out
war. In the past there have been blockades and wars of attrition on shipping.
The modern submarine could do well in such a war. But an all-out land
campaign would probably be over before attrition could tell. Moreover, in
nuclear war the submarine bases, the commercial ports and perhaps most of

Assault practice by US
marines.

civil society might be annihilated. The campaign might begin but its purpose would be vitiated. Since the mid-fifties, when the implications of thermonuclear weapons were perceived, NATO has ceased to prepare for a sustained renewal of the Battle of the Atlantic.

There is also a place for naval operations in support of the land battle. NATO plans seaborne reinforcement and support for its Northern and Southern flanks. The Russian Navy has a role in coastal defence and, with its small amphibious force, an assignment to its traditional role of operations in support of the flanks of the Red Army. But the NATO flanks are very much subordinate to what happens on the Central Front, and there the effect of naval operations is likely to be minimal.

One is therefore driven to the conclusion that in all-out war between the Great Powers, conventional naval force may not be of major importance. Of course, between the lesser powers of the world, assuming no Great Power intervention, naval warfare could proceed much as in the past, complete with blockades and attrition. Naval forces have already played a modest but significant part in the Arab–Israeli conflict and the Indian navy was a vital factor in the victory over Pakistan in 1971.

Limited War at Sea

Should the Great Powers engage in a limited war with each other, refraining from use of nuclear weapons, traditional naval operations could play a part here also. The Western Powers have made great use of limited naval power in their peripheral wars against smaller powers or insurgent forces. Seapower has played an essential part in assuring supply, naval forces have been used for bombardment, amphibious landings have taken place, and new importance has been given to inshore and 'riverine' operations.

So far, however, the Great Powers have taken care not to get into naval combat with each other. A heated debate goes on in professional military circles as to whether limited wars at sea could in fact occur between the Great Powers and be successfully contained. Such collisions could occur when the Great Powers deploy their naval forces in support of policy in areas like the Middle East or Caribbean, or if their actual intervention on behalf of a client, as in Viet Nam, provoked a rival power to support the other side actively. With the growth of Russian naval power, the Soviet Union might emulate the Western disposition to intervene in local *coups* and crises, and a collision might again ensue. The growth and wider deployment of Russia's naval power certainly affords physical possibilities for a clash that have not existed hitherto and it is a question whether the obvious anxiety of the Great Powers to avoid direct confrontation will survive the new situation. This is a point on which the 'permeable' nature of seapower bears significantly.

A Russian Kynda class guided-missile cruiser passes through the Bosphorous on its way to join the Soviet fleet in the Mediterranean.

A special case of possible trouble concerns the harassment of merchant shipping. Some Western commentators look anxiously at the disproportionate dependence of the Western alliance and particularly its European members on shipping. Twenty-five per cent of the West European GNP arises from trade, and the seaborne portion of that trade, though declining relatively because of growing intra-European trade, is rising absolutely at 4 per cent a year. By comparison only 3 per cent of the Soviet GNP and 6 per cent of the American arises from trade. Europe is notoriously dependent on imports of oil and Japan derives no less than 90 per cent of its oil by sea from the Persian Gulf.

Modern submarines could wage a devastatingly effective war against this

Showing the flag: a Russian guided-missile destroyer during a visit to Lagos in Nigeria.

shipping, although, if the campaign were unlimited, it would presumably return us to the general war scenario discussed earlier, and if limited would, by definition, be more manageable. Even a limited war on shipping would, however, be exceedingly provocative and violate dramatically the principle of avoiding direct Great Power confrontation. To single out one nation for such attack, as sometimes suggested, would not be easy in practice in view of the great intermingling of ships, cargoes, crews and passengers under various national flags.

The reason why some commentators nevertheless believe there is a higher possibility of limited wars at sea is precisely because they believe war at sea would lend itself to limitation. Civilian casualties would be low and there need be no damage to homelands. Ships are well-disciplined, discrete units and therefore a high degree of command and control could be maintained. Indeed, some go so far as to say these characteristics would permit the use of nuclear weapons at sea with minimal risk of escalation.

Against this it can be argued that no war could really be so easily insulated. Most disputes likely to provoke such a war at sea would have their origins or some component on land where the normal processes of diplomacy and escalation might proceed. Undoubtedly war could begin at sea and a capacity to wage limited war at sea is a valuable insurance against being forced to a premature choice between defeat or escalation. But the Western powers clearly do not feel it necessary to prepare for a disproportionately long or extreme campaign at sea. As on the land, all that is provided for is a 'pause' for negotiation prior to escalation. Moreover, in the case of a Russian assault on Western sea communications, it must be recognized that, though by no means as dependent on shipping as the West, the Soviet Union now has in its merchant marine a growing hostage to Western naval power. Furthermore, such Russian clients as Cuba and the UAR are very vulnerable to naval action. A direct and open naval conflict between the two great blocs is therefore less likely than some suggest. The possibility of local interference with shipping of lesser powers, perhaps covertly encouraged or openly supported by greater powers, is perhaps more plausible. Interference of this kind might be covered by some legal pretexts concerning territorial jurisdiction and rights of passage.

Maritime Power and Peacetime Diplomacy

Any form of military power may be used not only in actual hostilities but also in indirect ways to advance policy. These ways may be simply a general reputation for military strength or may take more specific forms of demonstration and action short of war. Several features of seapower – its flexibility, mobility and permeability – suit it very well for this kind of modulated application. Indeed, some ways of using seapower short of war have become so typical as to acquire a well-defined character and generally-accepted name: showing the flag, gunboat diplomacy, pacific blockade. Whether such practices constitute acts of war in the narrowly legal sense is a complicated question depending on the circumstances attending each particular case. Whether they lead to a shooting war in practice depends on the reaction of the victim. For the risk of a violent response is inherent in any would-be limited application of maritime power.

At the lowest level, and furthest from the likelihood of violence, is mere showing of the flag – attempts to gain prestige and goodwill by visits, entertainment and perhaps rescue and relief operations. Higher on the scale come demonstrations of strength and minatory gestures to discourage foes and reassure friends. Such demonstrations may become continuous by the establishment of a permanent naval presence like that maintained by both the Soviet

Union and the United States in the Mediterranean or, on a much smaller scale, Britain in South-East Asia and the Caribbean. Occasionally, major deployments may be made to underline an interest, as when the American fleet entered the Bay of Bengal during the Indo–Pakistan war. Where more than one power maintains a presence, their forces may take advantage of the freedom of the seas to crowd and harass each other, such operations having already resulted in actual collisions between Russian ships and their British or American counterparts. Friction may also arise from the ubiquitous activities of electronic intelligence ships – the Russian ELINT trawlers and the ill-fated USS *Pueblo* affording examples.

The deployment of naval power in an attempt to mark out spheres of interest may extend to establishing special relations with lesser navies and affording them technical assistance. This activity is not confined to naval forces, of course, but perhaps because of the historic role of navies and naval bases in imperialist expansion, the penetration of Russian naval power in the Middle East and Indian Ocean, accompanied by dissemination of Russian naval vessels to local navies and the Soviet acquisition of port facilities, has attracted particular attention. In fact, the significance of naval bases has changed in an age of airpower, of potential nuclear war and of techniques for under-way replenishment. Given these techniques, any well-equipped navy can sustain forces at sea at almost any distance from home bases. But this is done at considerable expense. Thus, what is more valuable today is not a base that can support a fleet under siege, but facilities to shorten supply lines, permit some decentralization of maintenance, and offer some rest and recreation for crews.

A large navy could put some kind of peacetime force anywhere in the world without such local facilities. But having some friendly local ports very greatly increases the proportion of a force that can be kept on station to that which is engaged in rotation and support. Moreover, a standing naval presence constitutes a significantly different political instrument from a merely potential presence. There can be no doubt that the most important change in the global naval scene in recent years has been the extension of permanent deployment of Soviet naval forces. The Soviet Union now possesses options of quick intervention which it lacked previously. For this reason the United States and its allies must now reckon with new inhibitions arising from the potential for naval confrontation. Such actions as the landings in Lebanon in 1958 or the Cuban missile blockade, though perhaps still conceivable, would have to be approached in a radically different context.

Naval Support of Operations on Land

As we have already recognized, the most fundamental contribution of seapower to conventional military operations is the assurance of supply to the home base or to overseas expeditions. The lack of challenge to Western seapower since 1945 has partially obscured the fact that American operations in Viet Nam, and British operations elsewhere in South-East Asia have all depended on seapower. Despite the development of airlift, by far the greater proportion of military equipment goes by sea. Operations like those in Viet Nam consume vast quantities of such unglamorous and bulky commodities as structural steel, timber and petroleum products. As a consequence, no less than 98 per cent of the supplies for the Viet Nam war went by sea.

Many advances have been made in shipping techniques, some adaptable for either civilian or military use. Some of these innovations are roll-on roll-off loading, containerization, barge-carrying ships, ships to be unloaded by heli-

Russian marines going ashore in amphibious personnel carriers.

copter cranes, and ships to be unloaded across the beach. Nor should it be too easily assumed that the advantage of speed always lies with the air. For, disregarding the possibility of air barriers, the question of speed must be related to the scale and duration of the operation. For quick, almost instant delivery of small cargoes, the air is superior. But if the period under analysis is sufficiently long to permit the first ships to arrive – say ten days to two weeks at oceanic ranges – the cargo discharged by ships will rapidly outweigh that delivered by even a massive airlift over the same period. Schemes have been put forward for special ships to hover offshore from potential crisis zones to constitute floating stockpiles, capable of quick deployment to match up with airlifted troops.

Military expeditions can be regarded simply as a problem of supply if they can count on a friendly initial foothold, including port facilities. Where this is not available, we are brought into the area of amphibious landings. These may be what Americans call 'administrative' and the British 'red carpet' operations; that is to say, the amphibious force does not have to fight its way ashore but uses its specialized equipment to overcome the technical problems of disembarking without prepared ports. In extreme cases, however, the force may have to land under fire. Operations of this kind on the scale of D-Day are unlikely, if only because war on this scale would probably be nuclear and the massed

The strategic sea showing
the major shipping routes,
the straits and channels
of strategic importance.
Certain countries claim
wider jurisdiction
for specific purposes
than the limits shown –
such as most South
American countries,
Morocco and Iceland with
its fifty-mile claim
on fisheries.

forces necessary for such landings would form ideal nuclear targets. On a smaller scale, however, amphibious operations are still envisaged: NATO contemplates amphibious support for its flanks and the Soviet Union makes preparations for similar efforts. Amphibious forces have also played a part in limited wars, notably at Inchon in Korea, at Suez and during the Viet Nam war. There was also the famous peacetime landing in Lebanon in 1958, when troops waded ashore amongst holidaymakers.

Operations of this kind call for a variety of specialized ships and small craft. A new element has been added by the helicopter, which introduces the concept of 'vertical envelopment', first employed on a substantial scale at Suez. In the

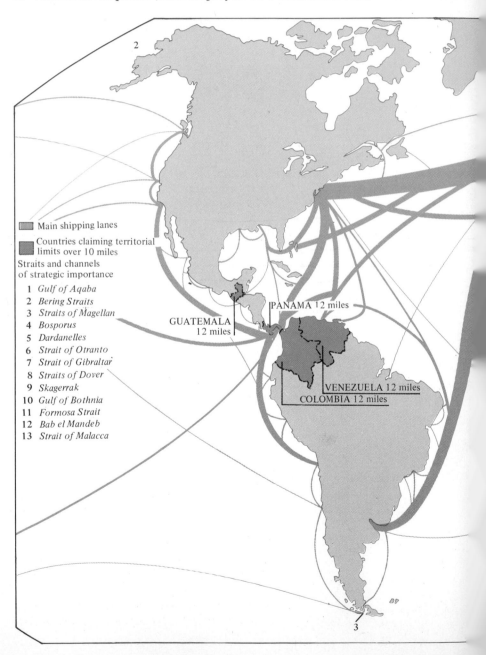

Main shipping lanes

Countries claiming territorial
limits over 10 miles

Straits and channels
of strategic importance

1   Gulf of Aqaba
2   Bering Straits
3   Straits of Magellan
4   Bosporus
5   Dardanelles
6   Strait of Otranto
7   Strait of Gibraltar
8   Straits of Dover
9   Skagerrak
10 Gulf of Bothnia
11 Formosa Strait
12 Bab el Mandeb
13 Strait of Malacca

GUATEMALA
12 miles

PANAMA 12 miles

VENEZUELA 12 miles
COLOMBIA 12 miles

future 'surface-effect vehicles' or hovercraft may also have a part to play. The larger navies dispose of helicopter carriers or commando ships (LPH), and of dock ships (LPD or LSD) which can disgorge fleets of smaller landing craft. There are also smaller landing ships capable of carrying tanks or other amphibious vehicles (LST or LSL). Many of the latter craft are designed to be beached. A modern British version of the LSL (landing ship logistic) is the Sir Lancelot class, of 5500 tons displacement, cruising at seventeen knots and capable of carrying 340 troops 'embarked' or 540 'hardlying', with an additional eighteen main battle tanks or thirteen Wessex helicopters, and a further nine helicopters or thirty-four 3-ton trucks.

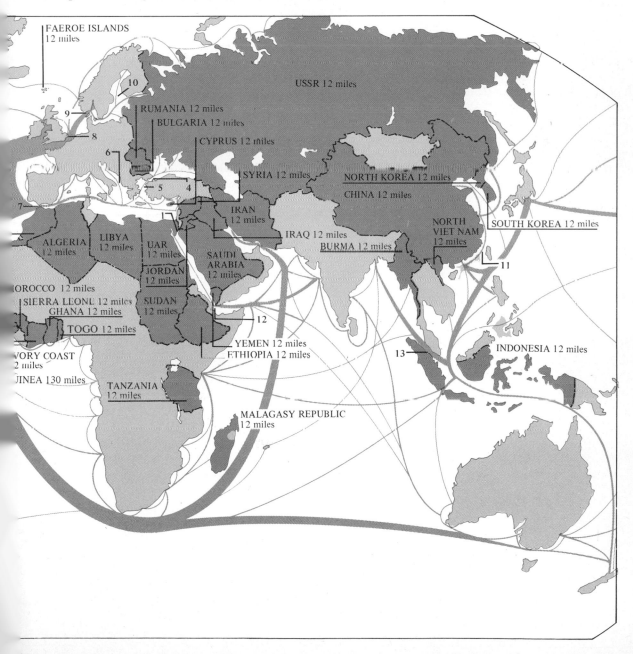

The Russian helicopter carrier *Moskva*.

The scale of amphibious forces varies a great deal between the major naval powers. Partly for historical reasons, the US Marine Corps is on a grand scale far beyond any other. The US Marines constitute a specialized, integrated armed force, embodying its own ground and air elements. Even after some reductions, the Marines maintain enough lift in both Atlantic and Pacific to move a Marine Force of reinforced brigade and associated air group at 20 knots. New helicopter ships are projected under the designation LHA, each of 40,000 tons, 820 feet long, 106 feet at the beam and capable of 22 knots cruising speed.

British forces are much more modest, comprising two LPH (converted from old CVAS), two new LSDs and a fleet of LSLs. France maintains a small Force Amphibie d'Intervention. The Russian force of naval infantry or marines, though expanded and rather energetically publicized in recent years, is still small, numbering about 12,000 men. As in other countries, however, elements of the Red Army are trained in amphibious action. Russia has a substantial fleet of smaller landing ships and her two helicopter carriers, though almost certainly given a primary role in ASW, could serve amphibious purposes. It is also possible that some of the Russian fleet of trawler depot ships could serve the function of LSDs.

The Russian helicopter carriers are a reminder that the Soviet Navy has no fixed-wing aircraft carriers. Opposed landings need air cover and beyond the range of aircraft based on friendly shores this can only be provided from aircraft carriers. The British Defence White Paper of 1966, which announced the winding-up of British CVA operations over the next few years, recognized this by acknowledging that henceforth British forces would be unable to undertake landings against 'sophisticated opposition' except with the help of allied carrierborne aircover.

As this testifies, an aircraft carrier is essential for certain types of operation. It also constitutes a possible alternative to airfields on land for the tactical air support of operations within convenient range of deep water. A fierce debate has raged between the rival advocates of land- or sea-based air power for such

THE MARITIME BATTLE 119

purposes; a debate inspired, of course, not merely by the technical merits of the alternatives but also by the fact that each is offered by a different armed service.

The carrier has many advantages. It is mobile and thus offers flexibility. Steaming at 500 miles a day a carrier on one side of the Indian Ocean can have its aircraft within range of the opposite shore in three days. A carrier has great endurance, especially with nuclear propulsion. The reactors of the CVAN *Enterprise* need refuelling only every four years and newer designs have a fuel life of over twenty years. This advantage is not quite so decisive as it may seem, however, for the carrier still needs frequent supplies of fuel for aircraft, munitions, food and other necessaries. These can be delivered by under-way replenishment from supply ships and, where smaller items are concerned, by carrier on-board delivery (COD) by special transport aircraft. The nuclear carrier does, however, enjoy the use of all the space that would be occupied by fuel for the ship's engines in a conventional carrier. Nuclear power also affords high acceleration and an absence of the smoke which sometimes impedes operations on oil-fired carriers.

As compared to land-bases carriers can put air power exactly where it is needed – assuming of course that the battle is relatively near the shore – and, by making short sorties possible, may increase the sortie rate, take immediate advantage of good weather in the battle area, and permit quick changes of aircraft 'fit' according to changing missions. The effectiveness of a carrier is very closely related to its size. A super-carrier of the recent American classes can accommodate over a hundred combat aircraft, with take-off weight up to 60,000 lb or more. With angled decks to permit overshooting without accident, multiple steam catapults, mirror landing systems and, increasingly, highly automated approach and landing control systems, the carrier can operate under most conditions. This effectiveness falls off rapidly if size is reduced. A 50,000-ton carrier can accommodate twice the aircraft possible on a 35,000-ton carrier at only 25 per cent more cost. Moreover, a small carrier will keep the sea less well than a large one in bad weather. This will result in more days when aircraft cannot fly and will increase the fatigue of crews, whose work is highly taxing under the best of conditions.

Efficient though the large carrier is, however, it is extremely expensive in absolute terms. A nuclear carrier like the CVAN *Dwight Eisenhower* can cost some $500,000,000 and the projected costs of future carriers are considerably higher. Moreover, a carrier needs a range of escorts and supply ships the capital cost of which can equal that of the carrier itself. Carriers are also very heavy consumers of manpower, itself an increasingly scarce and expensive resource. If this problem is solved, as the British Navy proposed to do, by having very few carriers, much of the vaunted flexibility of a carrier force is lost, especially when account is taken of the time needed for rest and refit. Thus a carrier force without a multiplicity of hulls may result in too many eggs in a few baskets: baskets which may frequently be in the wrong place. Moreover, Western carriers have operated in post-war years in virtually complete immunity from hostile action. In a more dangerous naval environment a carrier, though well protected, represents a tremendous potential loss. Even if the carrier itself were not lost, its effectiveness is very dependent on a vast array of electronic antennae which one lucky shot might disable. Such possibilities have to be set against the security problems of airfields ashore.

Perhaps the best conclusion to be drawn from all these considerations is that a carrier force is the only means of discharging some military tasks, above all the support of landing or other operations where air opposition can be expected and no land-bases are available near by. For other operations, land-based air power is an effective competitor, with the added advantage that land-based tactical air power is required on a large scale for operation in the main theatres of action. The consequence of such reasoning has been to bring about the prospective abolition of the British carrier force, to confine the remaining French carrier force to a very small scale, to leave one or two single-carrier forces scattered about Asia and Latin America and to make the United States the lone practitioner of carrier operation on a large scale. The decline of European carrier forces must be related to the reduced European enthusiasm for the kind of overseas military operation in which carriers have been most employed since 1945. One of the most interesting questions about naval affairs is whether the growth of the Soviet Navy and the extension of active Russian foreign policy will induce the Soviet Union to enter the field of fixed-wing carriers. Some kind of larger aircraft-carrying Russian vessels are now under construction.

Air War at Sea

The reciprocal aspect of naval forces' new capacity to strike inland by air is the ability of land-based air forces to attack ships far out to sea. This is one of the many reasons why modern navies need air cover and support if they are to enjoy really flexible operating. The commander of a fleet needs air support for many different purposes. Put briefly, he may want: reconnaissance, airborne early warning of air or surface attack, air defence against hostile aircraft, airborne strike against enemy ships, and help in conducting the anti-submarine battle.

For some, but not all, of these functions there are several options. Chief among these are: ship-based aircraft, fixed or rotary wing; shore-based aircraft, or seaborne surface-to-air and surface-to-surface missiles supplemented by guns. Aircraft occupy such a prominent part in this range of offensive and defensive operations that, except on the remotest oceans, the balance of land-based air power may well be more decisive in the naval balance than the relative strength in ships. This is especially obvious in such closed seas as the Mediterranean.

The advantages of carrier-based air power for operations at sea are closely related to the case for the carrier in support of land operations. The carrier can provide air support integrally combined with the fleet, operating within the same weather zone and under the close, direct control of the naval commander. This can ensure not only quick reaction and reliable support, but also a very desirable confidence on the part of the naval forces that their interests will prevail with the air commander. The disadvantages of carriers are again those already cited: high cost, consequent small numbers and possible vulnerability in combat. Because of this potential vulnerability – compounded, whenever aircraft are flying off or landing on the carrier, by the need to steer a steady upwind course – a great deal of the energy of the rest of the fleet is taken up in screening the carrier.

One alternative lies in the anti-aircraft fire power of the ships. A great deal of such fire power is provided whether the fleet possesses carriers or not. Most of the larger guns carried on modern ships are dual purpose, capable of engaging surface or aerial targets, and usually controlled by radar. A variety of smaller dual-purpose guns is also carried. Indeed, after a period of unfashionableness during early euphoria about guided missiles, guns are regaining a larger place in naval thought. It is now increasingly recognized that, heavy and space-consuming though guns are, without them ships may be incapable of bombarding the shore or of dealing with small hostile craft.

Nevertheless, the guided missile has come to occupy a dominant place in the anti-aircraft defence of ships. Naval SAMs fall into two broad categories: some, medium-range missiles like the British Seaslug, the American Tartar and Talos and the Russian *Goa*: others for close defence like the American Terrier and the very widely sold British Seacat. The former missiles are so large and their ancillary radar so complex that large ships are primarily devoted to deploying them (DLG). Where there are aircraft carriers, such missile ships provide a zone of defence; fleets without carriers may rely primarily on missiles for their air defence.

The chief deficiencies of the SAM solution to the air defence problem, as compared to air cover, are the relatively short range of the systems, their inability to contribute to many other tasks within the competence of aircraft, and the severe degradation of missile ships in intense action because of attrition of their stocks of the bulky missiles. Because of the beam-riding or semi-active homing

A French patrol boat fires the Exocet ship-to-ship missile. This has a range of about twenty miles and is typical of the new surface missiles being acquired by modern navies.

A model of the new British through-deck cruiser. These are designed to provide some measure of air support once the last British carriers are withdrawn.

usually employed, SAM ships are also unable to cope well with a number of simultaneous targets. This defect is modified, though not eliminated, by the development of automated and computerized tactical data systems (TDS) which help commanders assess the threat and assign weapons to targets in order of priority.

Missiles make no contribution to the problems of reconnaissance and airborne early warning. Helicopters, which most large naval ships now carry in one size or another, can do a good deal for reconnaissance but do not have range, payload or capacity to attain sufficient altitude to make good AEW platforms. The tendency in carrierless navies is to turn to large shore-based aircraft for AEW. Land-based aircraft have always, indeed, been the Russian way of providing air support for the fleet and the British intend to replace their carriers in this way to provide air defence and strike at sea, as well as AEW and reconnaissance.

This is certainly a cheaper recourse than carriers, but one viewed with misgivings in naval circles. Clearly land-based aircraft cannot substitute for carriers in mid-ocean in the strike and air defence roles, though inflight refuelling extends coverage. Nor will land-based aircraft be able to evade air barriers as carriers can. The greatest anxiety of naval commanders is that land-based air support might not be available when needed, either because of delayed reactions or because air commanders would set different priorities. It might be possible to fly permanent AEW over a fleet from the shore but it would certainly be prohibitively expensive to provide a permanent 'cap' of on-call strike and defensive aircraft.

Doubts about dependence solely on shore-based aircraft have led to speculation about the practicability of cheaper and simpler 'poor man's' carriers. There have been schemes to put flight decks on tanker hulls as was done in World War II. Others have looked approvingly on the two small French carriers *Foch* and *Clemenceau*. The British have taken up the idea of 'through-deck cruisers', small ships which could carry helicopters or offer a short-roll take-off for V/STOL aircraft. Faced with the two constraints of costs and numbers, even the United States has conceived of a moderate-sized sea-control ship (SCS) to serve in areas of 'low intensity threat'. An SCS would be of 15,000–20,000 tons and carry rather less than twenty helicopters or V/STOL aircraft.

The capacity to launch even a small number of fixed-wing, high-performance aircraft would be a very valuable asset. It would not permit air defence comparable to the capability of CVA, but it would provide a means of dealing with the shadowing reconnaissance aircraft and of striking at hostile surface craft before they were within range. It could also offer an answer to the enemy aircraft which might be providing guidance for a long-range surface-launched missile. But this capacity is not to be had easily. No V/STOL aircraft yet exists with a good maritime capability. The nearest thing, the Harrier, would need a search-radar and engine development to extend its range. One approach, again only to be had at a price, is to retain catapult launching, using vertical landing to dispense with a large, strong deck; one incidental advantage of VTOL capability being much wider tolerances in landing on a small, shifting deck under bad conditions. Another great problem is the provision of adequate maintenance for complex aircraft and avionics in a small ship. This is a problem of space for equipment and for spares. Maintenance also greatly extends the cost of an air-capable ship in both men and money. Similar problems are presented by the need for aircraft control and guidance radar and communication systems. These facilities will, however, have to be provided by some vessel in the fleet if the full value is to be extracted even from shore-based aircraft.

A small aircraft-carrying ship would be no replacement for a CVA but it would be a great deal better than nothing. It remains to be seen whether carrierless navies actually build such ships. The pressure to do so will almost certainly continue, for the loss of integral air support is a major handicap to any navy with pretensions to operate as more than a merely coastal force. Moreover, the inevitable development of V/STOL aircraft for other purposes is likely to sustain interest in that particular solution.

Ship-to-Ship Action

The submarine and air battles have come to overshadow combat between surface ships. Indeed, the design of ships to specialize in the ASW or anti-air roles has led to the eclipse of the gun, the virtual abandonment of armour and a generation of ships with remarkably little capability to fight other surface ships. This deficiency was acceptable to the larger Western navies because they or their allies regarded carrier aircraft as the decisive strike weapon, able to sink enemies far beyond gun range. Faced with this threat, and lacking carriers of its own, the Soviet Union has taken the lead in developing long-range surface-to-surface missiles for naval use.

This solution has been applied in two main forms. One consists of relatively short-range missiles mounted on small craft of the patrol boat type. The missile used is the *Styx*, a rocket-powered, aircraft-like missile launched from a ramp by a booster which is discarded. These missiles are mounted on two classes of boat, the Osa and the Komar, the former carrying four and the latter two missiles. The effectiveness of the system, at least under some conditions, was demonstrated by the sinking of the Israeli destroyer *Eilat* in October, 1967.

Some typical modern warships shown with the British 8000-ton World War II cruiser HMS *Belfast* as a size comparison. It should be noted that the greater part of the submarine hull is under water.

The *Styx* is thought to be radar-homing and to have a range of over twelve miles. Osa and Komar boats have been distributed to several other navies by the Soviet Union and constitute a cheap and apparently cost-effective inshore threat to even major naval units. Lack of endurance and seakeeping qualities would prevent their use far out to sea.

It is a testimony to the concept of a missile-firing patrol boat that several Western navies are hastening to develop similar systems. The most successful Western missile so far is the French Exocet which has a two-stage rocket motor and an active homing warhead. It is designed to fly, a few yards above the water, at transonic speed. Exocet is an all-weather system with ECCM capability

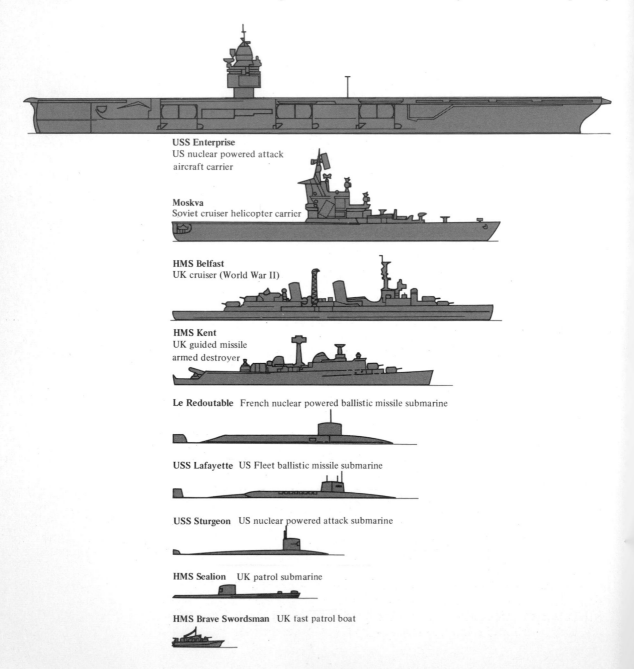

USS Enterprise
US nuclear powered attack aircraft carrier

Moskva
Soviet cruiser helicopter carrier

HMS Belfast
UK cruiser (World War II)

HMS Kent
UK guided missile armed destroyer

Le Redoutable French nuclear powered ballistic missile submarine

USS Lafayette US Fleet ballistic missile submarine

USS Sturgeon US nuclear powered attack submarine

HMS Sealion   UK patrol submarine

HMS Brave Swordsman UK fast patrol boat

and has a range of forty miles. The launching vessel must have a considerable amount of radar and other electronic equipment. France intends to mount Exocet on cruisers and on high-speed patrol boats. Germany has ordered twenty such boats for the Baltic and the British Navy is also adopting the missile on a large scale.

The second Soviet system consists of larger, long-range missiles, mounted on big surface ships, the Kynda, Kresta and Krivak classes, and on over sixty submarines. One such weapon in service in large numbers is the *Shaddock*, a cruise missile with a range of nearly 250 miles at transonic speeds. Presumably it carries a nuclear warhead and is intended primarily as an anti aircraft-carrier weapon. To operate at long range it needs the co-operation of an aircraft or another vessel able to supply line-of-sight guidance information. Several new self-contained horizon range missiles are now entering service.

Defence against missile-firing craft can be approached in two ways. Either an effort can be made to sink the parent craft before launch or the missile can be treated as an air defence problem. Where aircraft are available the first solution is the more satisfactory. Where they are not, the defending ship must either outrange the enemy missile or must adopt the second solution. This is not impossible where present generations of surface-to-surface missiles are concerned, but as their successors become faster, fly lower and obtain more-independent guidance systems, the task of defence will be formidable. The threat is the more serious inasmuch as even with conventional warheads such missiles have a very good chance of destroying a larger ship's electronic arrays. Moreover, the relative cheapness of the missile patrol boat permits its deployment in numbers that will greatly strengthen coastal defence forces *vis à vis* larger assailants from overseas.

Costs are as important in the naval balance as in any other aspect of modern military life, indeed perhaps more so, for the reduction of numbers poses special problems for forces that must frequently deploy across very extensive areas. Under such conditions requirements are set by considerations of space, time and distance as well as by the opposing order of battle. Consequently a constant discussion goes on as to whether it might not be better to forego a degree of sophistication in order to procure a greater number of simpler warships. This is, of course, a debate with parallels in the areas of land and air weapons, but is given particular point for naval systems by the demands of dispersed deployment already mentioned, and by the wide range of relatively simple tasks that warships are required to fulfil in time of peace and limited war.

The dominant tendency has been to build highly sophisticated ships, full of elaborate electronics and intended to fight all-out actions against similarly advanced opponents, if necessary, in simultaneous air, surface and submarine engagements. As a consequence the price of ships has soared. Typically the weapon systems within the ships are considerably more expensive than the ships themselves. A 1937 destroyer had about 60 electronic valves; by 1957 the advent of radar had raised the number to 4000; by 1961 the total had exceeded 30,000, since when the steady introduction of computers has accelerated electronic complexity. A modern nuclear-powered submarine costs something over $150,000,000. A British Leander class frigate costs about $40,000,000, a Type 42 frigate about $50,000,000. Yet it is possible to produce smaller and cheaper craft for much less. Thus the British firm, Vosper-Thorneycroft, has developed a cut-price frigate for export costing around $18,000,000. The Mark 5 version displaces 1200 tons and can carry one 4·5 inch gun and an Exocet missile, with a crew of 100; in addition it has sonar and anti-submarine mortars. The projected British Type 21 frigates, at 2500 tons and $21,000,000 to $26,000,000 represent another move in this direction.

Advocates of the cheaper ships emphasize the need for absolute numbers and the frequent incidence of simple peacetime and limited-war tasks. Opponents argue that an inferior ship is a sunken ship when serious action begins, and that priority must be given to preparation for the most taxing battles, accepting that the resulting ships will be over-equipped for day-to-day work. To this some critics reply that in fact some of the more sophisticated ships, such as the DLGs, are actually ill-equipped for the tasks most frequently encountered and offer little more than a high capacity to defend themselves. The debate will continue and is stimulated in some naval quarters by an uneasy suspicion that the Russians are more successful in cramming a wide range of capabilities into a hull of given size than Western designers. This is partly, but not wholly, the result of offering worse living conditions to crews.

The debate over ship design will also be much affected by the type of national strategy envisaged. Smaller ships, for instance, may be good at coastal work near to base but may be grossly inefficient if asked to undertake tasks at oceanic range, calling for long endurance and good seakeeping. Some reaction away from size and sophistication to economy will almost certainly be seen over the next few years for, under budgetary restraint, all navies are recognizing that if they do not accept something less than the best conceivable new equipment, the exhaustion of the money for new ships will simply necessitate extended reliance on old ships.

Anti-Submarine Warfare

The submarine and its enemies are at the centre of modern naval warfare. In both world wars the submarine proved itself a powerful and effective weapon, especially against commerce. The successful application of nuclear propulsion to the submarine has, however, made the submarine an infinitely more potent weapon. Nuclear propulsion, which provides steam-power without need for recourse to the atmosphere, coupled with modern life-support systems, gives a submarine long endurance while totally submerged. At the same time, the new propulsion method and the design of hydrodynamically effective hulls (facilitated by the reduced need to consider performance on the surface) have made high underwater speeds possible. A nuclear submarine is actually faster submerged than surfaced and, with a typical underwater speed of 35 knots, is as fast as most surface vessels and faster whenever surface conditions become turbulent. While submergence for twenty-four hours severely taxed a World War II submarine, a nuclear submarine can cruise for 100,000 miles and stay submerged for two months or more.

The breakthrough in ASW after 1942 was largely due to the ability of radar to locate submarines which had surfaced or were using schnorkel tubes. The ability to remain totally submerged is thus a fundamental improvement of submarine capability, valuable in any submarine and the very essence of the SSBN's invulnerability.

Some weaknesses remain. The submarine cannot communicate without risk of betraying itself, although it can receive special very low frequency (VLF) communications by coming close to the surface. The submarine is rather short of methods to sense what is going on around it, although modern developments giving it modest underwater perception represent a 100 per cent improvement on the recent past. The weapons available to submarines have not made such revolutionary progress as the submarine itself. The main anti-ship weapon is the

A British Nimrod
long-range maritime
patrol aircraft.

homing torpedo, and the speed and reliability of torpedoes is a notoriously backward area of military technology. There are, however, certain developments. The Russians have deployed cruise and short-range ballistic missiles on submarines, most of which, however, must be launched from the surface. The United States has the Subroc system which, fired like a torpedo, breaks surface and flies some tens of miles to re-enter the water as a depth charge with nuclear head. Future development is likely to stress submarine-launched missiles which will surface and become air flight-guided missiles.

The nuclear submarine is frequently described as the capital ship of today. This description needs some qualification. The capabilities of a submarine, though great, are limited in scope. Thus it is of little use for many peacetime and limited-war tasks. Although efforts are being made to equip some submarines with small missiles, like Blowpipe, to give it a limited surface offensive capability, the submarine remains vulnerable on the surface and no one would wish to risk an expensive nuclear submarine in such encounters. If, however, the phrase 'capital ship' is meant to imply that the nuclear submarine would come off best in a mortal combat with any other type of vessel, then the claim is probably well founded.

The task of anti-submarine warfare is thus both an important and a difficult one. For the NATO powers, the very large Russian submarine fleet, a natural acquisition for a once much inferior and still geographically disadvantaged power, offers an obvious challenge. Nor should we forget the ASW problem that the Western SSBNs present to the Soviet Union. Indeed, the primary stimulus to the forward deployment of the Soviet Fleet in the Northern Atlantic, Mediterranean and Indian Ocean is probably the Polaris threat.

Once a submarine is firmly located it is a relatively easy task to destroy it, especially with a nuclear weapon. Locating submarines is, however, perhaps the most intractable military problem today.

Water has very low resistance to electricity. As a result, electromagnetic radiation is quickly absorbed and no underwater version of radar is possible. It is the same phenomenon that prevents underwater reception of radio communication except near the surface and at very low frequencies. Similarly, visible light and infra-red radiation are quickly diminished. Because water is eight hundred times as dense as air it is, however, a very good conductor of sound. Indeed, sound travels four-and-a-half times as fast in sea water as in air. Sound has therefore become the main method of underwater detection, using systems known as 'sonar'.

Sonar can be used passively or actively. Passive sonar consists of devices for listening for the noise generated by targets, especially their engines and their hulls as they move through the water creating vapour bubbles that collapse (cavitation). Passive sonar can detect sound over long distances but is ill adapted

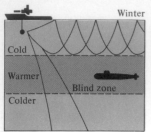
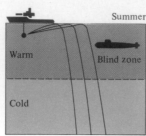
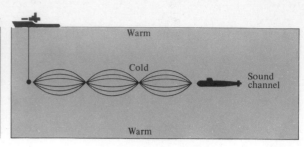

Sonar, showing how variations in temperature can affect its performance and create blind zones within which a submarine can escape detection.

to indicating the range of the target. Active sonar involves transmitting pulses of sound and calculating the range and direction of targets from the time elapsed before the return of echoes. It is thus analogous to radar and, like radar, can either be used in a beam or in an all-round radiation. High-frequency waves are rapidly attenuated; low-frequency waves give poor directional definition, so that in practice a compromise must be sought. A modification of the principle is sound ranging; the detonation of small charges in order to detect the echo from target objects.

There are very well known limitations to the effectiveness of sonar. The range of active sonar is limited under most circumstances to some thousands of yards; ten miles is still an extended range. Because a great deal of energy is needed to achieve even these ranges active sonar equipment is bulky and heavy, taking up a large part of a ship's payload. Active sonar also betrays its presence to passive detection devices over far greater distances than its own effective range. Moreover, sonar of all kinds is susceptible to interference from the noise of waves, marine life, and the sounds of its own vehicle. The last consideration means that surface vessels cannot operate sonar effectively at high speeds.

Above all, sonar is degraded by the fact that sound waves are refracted in water by changes in salinity, density and temperature. This means that sonar is not merely limited but erratic in performance. The refractions of sound create dead zones within which targets can lie undetected.

The temperature of the sea falls rapidly below 2000 ft depth (the thermocline) to about 38°F at 4000 ft and then falls very slowly to a constant temperature just below 30°F in the deep ocean. At the surface in summer, the water on top is warmest. In winter, however, the cooling of water at the surface leads to a cyclic mixing with warmer water below. Moreover, below 4000 ft the density of the water begins to rise more rapidly than the temperature is falling. Sound travels faster at higher densities and high temperatures. Where it encounters changes in velocity it is refracted toward the lower velocity. Thus, between 2000 and 4000 ft there is a zone of minimum velocity (the sound channel) in which sound is trapped and transmitted for long distances. Nearer the surface various patterns of temperature create shifting zones of refraction which may change rapidly during a single day. As modern submarines have hull-mounted sensors to detect water conditions, they can make skilful use of these blind areas. The submarine is also able to use sonar to detect its hunter; because the submarine is quiet, it can be made a rough rule of thumb that any sensor that can detect a submarine will do more to help the submarine detect a surface ship.

While sonar is the main recourse, there are other methods of hunting submarines. We have already mentioned magnetic-anomaly detectors (MAD) to discern the presence of large masses of metal underwater. These systems, deployed on aircraft, are of limited range (about half a mile) and of more use to confirm and pinpoint targets than to make initial contact. In shallow water magnetic sensors can be laid on the sea bottom. Devices also exist to detect temperature changes in the water around submarines and to 'sniff' diesel fumes where conventional submarines are concerned. Radar is, of course, still used so as to deny the surface to the submarine.

The various sensors can be deployed in several ways. Surface ships are the traditional vehicle and can use large variable-depth sonars (VDS) to penetrate below temperature layers. Helicopters use dipping sonars for the same purpose. Typically, several helicopters will work as a team to cross-fix the submarine, and another helicopter may be used to deliver the weapon. Fixed-wing aircraft use sonobuoys dropped in patterns as listening devices, frequently employing sound-ranging. Except in the latter case, aircraft have the advantage of being undetectable by the submarine. Submarines themselves constitute another way of getting below thermal layers, and share the target submarine's quietness and speed. As a result many believe the hunter–killer submarine to be the most potent if expensive ASW weapon.

A modern innovation in ASW is the use of fixed sonar devices on the sea bottom, linked to the shore by cable. The United States has for several years had a passive system of this kind (Caesar) off its Atlantic Coast and an active variant has been developed. For areas where the bottom is inconveniently deep, various kinds of moored buoy are being developed. Such systems can either be permanently linked to shore bases or intermittently interrogated by ships or aircraft. One great advantage of fixed installations is the ease with which their findings can be acquired and collated with other information. In the absence of any technical breakthrough in methods of detection it seems increasingly likely that progress in ASW must depend on numbers of hunting devices and of rapid collation of bits of information against a rising level of oceanographic knowledge. Various natural phenomena, types of vehicle and even individual vessels have characteristic sonar 'signatures' that can be built into computer-based recognition systems.

But if this approach is promising, it is also highly expensive. It will also have to be applied in an increasingly complex underwater environment. On the one hand, submarines are becoming more sophisticated and the development of longer-range missiles will make the ASW task increasingly difficult where SSBNs are concerned. For it has long been recognized that whereas the attack submarine must move (thereby creating noise) and come to its enemy, the SSBN need only get lost and lie low. And, on the other hand, the proliferation of submarines and of commercial underwater enterprises is making the subsurface waters an increasingly congested medium. Underwater sensors are ill-suited to provide positive identification of targets, yet this would be of great importance in limited war. When the rapidly increasing commercial activities under the sea are added to the many military considerations it becomes clear that underwater technology will inevitably be the subject of intense activity in the next few years.

CHAPTER SIX

Tactical Nuclear Weapons

Tactical nuclear weapons raise several issues of such importance that they deserve a separate discussion. The first difficulty is to decide what meaning to attribute to the term 'tactical'. As a rough guide we might agree to regard as 'strategic' any weapon used to do direct damage to the home base and war-making potential of an enemy state. We might regard as 'tactical' any weapon used to have relatively immediate effect on the course of military operations. Clearly the characteristics of a weapon will often indicate for which of these two purposes it is primarily intended: a field gun is indisputably tactical; a heavy, long-range bomber or an intercontinental missile may be considered strategic. Yet in many cases these distinctions break down. A heavy bomber can be used tactically, as the American B52s have been used in Viet Nam. Moreover, a weapon which may be chiefly intended for tactical use between the Superpowers, like a medium-range missile or an F4, might be used strategically in a Middle Eastern conflict. Thus while the characteristics of a weapon may classify it decisively as tactical in some cases, in others the distinction may have to be sought in the actual doctrine of use espoused by the owner.

This ambiguity is particularly important where nuclear weapons are concerned, because these weapons are so potent in their larger sizes. The use of nuclear weapons would bring into play a potentially decisive instrument and thus have profound effects on the prospect of escalation: the process whereby, intentionally or not, the level of violence rises to what, once nuclear weapons are employed, could be virtually total devastation. There is therefore a sharp debate as to whether a class of weapon so ominous and unmanageable at the higher end of its spectrum could be used safely and effectively at the lower.

At first nuclear weapons were thought of as exclusively strategic. The initial and only use of nuclear weapons, at Hiroshima and Nagasaki, was certainly strategic. Nuclear weapons were scarce and expensive; consequently they were reserved for the most important targets. The essential characteristic of a nuclear weapon is to extract a vast amount of energy from a small mass of material. It seems to follow from this that the appropriate and efficient use of nuclear weapons is destruction on a large scale.

In the early fifties, however, fissile material began to be available in more generous quantities. The United States, followed rather later by the Soviet Union, entered the age of 'nuclear plenty'. It thus became possible to think of sparing nuclear weapons from the strategic role to serve tactical tasks. This idea had arisen during the Korean War and scarcity had been one, though by no means the only, factor in inducing restraint. Also in the fifties, advances in weapon design made it possible to produce weapons that were much smaller and consequently much easier to deliver. For the most part these weapons were still of very high yield, but it also became possible to design weapons of smaller yield, chiefly by deliberately reducing the efficiency with which energy is extracted

Opposite A Russian Frog surface-to-surface tactical missile is raised to the firing position on its launcher.

A display of nuclear weapons showing how they have been miniaturized over the last twenty-eight years. **Right** The 20-KT bombs Fat Man and Little Boy of the type dropped on Japan in 1945. **Left** A tactical bomb (**top**) similar in yield to the previous weapons and (**bottom**) a bomb in the megaton range. Still smaller are the Davy Crockett mortar bomb (**front, left**) and the 8-inch howitzer shell (**front, right**) with a KT yield.

from the critical mass. Weapons of reduced yield could begin to be regarded, from the military perspective, as a better substitute for conventional explosives rather than as something on an utterly different scale. From that moment forward, the debate about the wisdom of using nuclear weapons tactically has continued unremittingly, bedevilled by the fact that the world has absolutely no practical experience as a basis for judgement. There are two main threads to this debate: one concerns the question of whether tactical nuclear weapons would be militarily useful; the other involves the question of whether such use would necessarily result in escalation toward strategic nuclear war.

Nuclear weapons could be used tactically in any of the three environments of land, sea or air. For aerial use several nuclear systems exist of both the surface-to-air and air-to-air variety. Examples in the American inventory are the Nike–Hercules anti-aircraft missile and the Genie air-to-air rocket. The purpose of using a nuclear warhead is, of course, to increase the kill-radius and thereby relax the requirement for accuracy. Used in one's own airspace defensively, such weapons might be regarded as relatively unprovocative. On the other hand, the need to avoid damage to the ground dictates limited warheads and such weapons would obviously be used only *in extremis* and probably only against aircraft thought to be carrying offensive nuclear weapons themselves. On this assumption the anti-aircraft category of missile is not of primary interest in considering the question of escalation.

There are also many maritime uses for nuclear weapons. Once again the primary motive is to compensate for inaccuracy by increased destructive potential. The Russians deploy nuclear cruise-missiles on aircraft, submarines and surface ships as part of their defensive effort against the American strike carriers. Once again one assumes that these weapons are unlikely to be used unless the Russians come to believe that the carriers are about to launch a nuclear strike.

The primary maritime use of nuclear weapons would be for anti-submarine work. Here the large kill-radius of nuclear weapons, compounded by the shock-transmitting properties of water, would be a valuable compensation for the difficulties of target-location discussed earlier. Nuclear warheads therefore figure largely in the arsenal of ASW weapons, as depth charges, torpedoes, and as the payload of such ASW missiles as the surface-launched ASROC and the submarine-launched SUBROC. Most underwater nuclear explosions would produce no fall-out. For this reason and because of the absence of any problem of 'collateral damage', many students of naval warfare believe nuclear weapons could be used with much less danger of escalation than in any other environment. Given the fact that naval vessels are relatively few in number and constitute discrete, highly integrated units, the problems of command and control might be handled more easily at sea than on land, though the deficiencies of submarine communication would present problems. As we shall see, however, the current climate of opinion about the danger of crossing the nuclear threshold makes it unlikely that permission to use nuclear weapons would be lightly given, even for maritime forces. Perhaps the most that can be said is that if the time comes when nations are ready to use nuclear weapons, tactical use at sea may recommend itself as one of the safer options.

It is the use of tactical nuclear weapons in the land battle that is most energetically recommended by enthusiasts and that arouses the sharpest controversy. The idea of using nuclear weapons in ground combat arose during the early fifties when it became clear that the NATO powers were unlikely to achieve the level of conventional rearmament thought necessary to deal with the Red Army

The American tactical missile Lance on its mobile launcher. This can deliver a kiloton-range warhead over seventy miles and is due into service shortly.

in Europe. At the same time the wars in Korea and in Indo-China suggested the need for some way to use advanced technology to offset disadvantages in sheer manpower. The Western powers were encouraged to think along these lines by the belief, not wholly unfounded, that the Soviet Union lagged behind the United States in both quantity and quality of nuclear weapons. In any case it was not thought that a war in Europe could be limited. Thus the tactical use of nuclear weapons would be accompanied by their strategic use. The problem of escalation would therefore not arise and hopes of decisive success for an American counterforce strategic strike held out some hope of quickly re-establishing a nuclear monopoly.

The major tactical nuclear rockets deployed today.

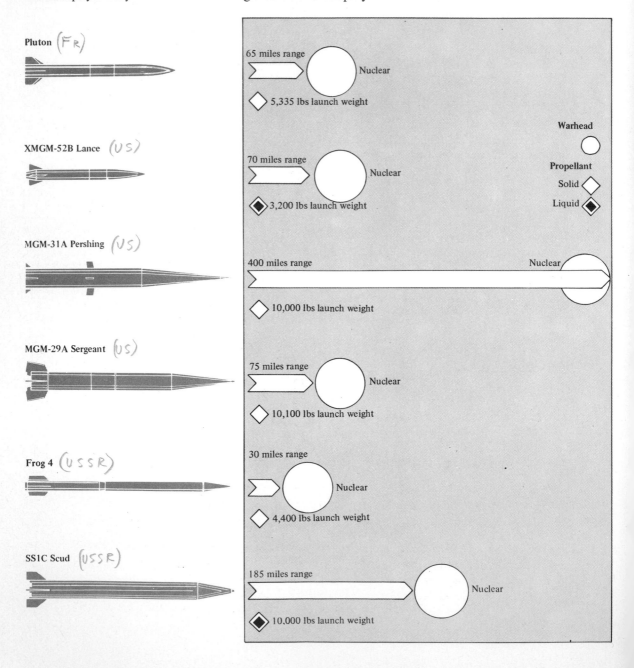

The French tactical missile Pluton.

Another factor encouraging the idea of using nuclear weapons tactically in the land battle was the desire of the US Army to acquire a share in nuclear weapons, which were seen as the most sophisticated and important form of modern military equipment. The army's enthusiasm was reinforced by the budgetary peculiarity, which still exists, whereby the cost of producing the actual warheads falls on the budget of the Atomic Energy Commission and not on that of the individual service. The miniaturization of nuclear warheads made specialized weapons for the army practicable and in 1953 a cumbersome 280 mm nuclear howitzer was introduced, firing a shell with a yield of 15 KT, not far short of the Hiroshima size.

In December 1954, NATO commanders were given permission to plan on the assumption that nuclear weapons would be used in a European war. In 1957 the United States offered to supply its European allies with IRBMs and with ground and air nuclear weapons which would be retained under American physical custody prior to release for use in war. The IRBMs were intended as a partial substitute for tactical airpower and when the missiles were withdrawn, in the early sixties, several Polaris submarines were assigned to SACEUR for application to high-priority targets relevant to the European battlefield. Also in 1957, the American Secretary of State, John Foster Dulles, suggested that tactical nuclear weapons might offer a limited alternative to 'massive retaliation' if war arose in Asia.

Since that time there has been a vast proliferation of nuclear weapons for tactical use. American statements suggest an American arsenal of not less than 10,000 tactical warheads and the Russian equivalent has been estimated at 3500–4500 with a higher average yield. Many specialized and multi-purpose delivery systems have been developed. The main classifications are the free-fall bombs and air-to-surface missiles of tactical aircraft, still one of the primary delivery systems; surface-to-surface missiles of ranges varying from some thirty to seventy miles in the case of the American guided missile Sergeant and the newer Lance, to 400 miles for the American Pershing; and the nuclear shells designed for the 8 inch and 155 mm howitzers. The Soviet Union has a similar arsenal, including the *Scud* and *Scaleboard* ballistic missiles, the latter of up to 500 miles range, the cruise missile *Shaddock* (also used at sea), the unguided *Frog* rockets and a 203 mm howitzer. France has developed and is about to deploy Pluton, a tactical missile of French design. As we have seen, IRBMs and MRBMs can also be used tactically and it is assumed that a portion of the large Soviet MRBM force in Western Russia would be so employed. At the other end of the scale the United States developed an infantry nuclear weapon, the Davy Crockett mortar, but this was withdrawn because of the great problems of command and control. *(No longer used – 1974)*

The proliferation of tactical nuclear weapons has not been accompanied by an equivalent refinement of satisfactory doctrine to justify and guide their employment. Initially the idea was to substitute for manpower, coupled with the belief that nuclear weapons would favour the defence. This assumption rested partly on the simple idea of putting more firepower into less hands and partly on the belief that, in order to attack, the aggressor would have to concentrate his forces and thereby offer worthwhile nuclear targets. Nuclear weapons were also thought useful for interdiction, to wipe out rail junctions, block passes and, in forested country, to clear large areas of cover.

These ideas presented several difficulties. The chief was the problem of collateral damage. Great destruction would be wrought on civilian populations and property, which the defensive side might expect to be friendly as the battle would be brought to them. For battlefield use there was also the difficulty of avoiding damage to one's own troops. These objections were rendered plausible by the very high yields of the so-called tactical weapons. All were in the kiloton range and some were many times the size of the Hiroshima bomb. This characteristic seems to have been perpetuated by a rather simple notion of efficiency, whereby it seemed uneconomic to design weapons to be less powerful than they might be.

Other difficulties concerned the question of control. Both because of the need to ensure that no needless damage was done to friendly troops or population and because of the danger that indiscriminate use would promote retaliation and escalation, control over the use of nuclear weapons must be close and precise. For this reason the traditional military control system of hierarchical administrative authority has been supplemented by the installation of physical controls on many nuclear weapons, which ensure that they cannot be activated except by someone in possession of an appropriate key or code. These expedients, however, must be weighed against the need for speed of response, especially desirable at the tactical level where targets may offer fleeting opportunities. Moreover, the effectiveness of a system of control might be expected to deteriorate rapidly under conditions of nuclear warfare.

Two exercises early in the period when tactical nuclear weapons were being introduced lent emphasis to these problems. One, *Sagebrush*, was held in the southern United States; the other, *Carte Blanche*, in West Germany. As the name of the latter exercise suggests, nuclear weapons were freely used, and the theoretical consequence was great collateral damage and a rapid breakdown of any semblance of order or control on the battlefield. *Carte Blanche* involved the use of 335 nuclear weapons with a consequent 1·7 million fatalities and a further 3·5 million casualties. The conclusion would seem to be that the use of nuclear weapons must be very selective if it is to remain orderly, yet the use of any nuclear weapons will itself do much to destroy the conditions for order. Closely related to this problem is the point that if the introduction of nuclear weapons is delayed much beyond the opening stages of war, the weaker side may find itself overrun in the conventional phase with a consequent loss both of good tactical opportunities to make use of nuclear weapons and of the degree of cohesion needed to maintain control. Indeed, supposing that the shorter-range nuclear weapons are deployed well forward, they themselves may be rapidly overrun. Some hope that this prospect might itself deter an aggressor, who would expect a violent response to the prospect of losing nuclear weapons by capture, and would thus be led to regard a nuclear response as credible.

The possibility that a nuclear battlefield might rapidly lose coherence is an important element in trying to assess the military utility of tactical nuclear weapons. It can be argued that the resulting stalemate would thwart the aggressor and thus serve the purposes of defence. This possibility must be weighed against the price to be paid in terms of collateral damage and in risk of escalation. Much would depend on how quickly and far forward the stalemate occurred. Nor is it certain that chaos would be symmetrical and produce stalemate. Instead, one side might prove the stronger.

The assumption that nuclear weapons would favour the defence was based partly on the belief that the aggressor would be the numerically superior Soviet Union and that nuclear weapons were a substitute for manpower. Critics, including such practical men as General Maxwell Taylor, have argued that this was wishful thinking. Nuclear weapons might dictate tactics of dispersal at the front, but would require even larger numbers of men in the rear areas and as reinforcements for units taking much higher casualties. It has been suggested, for instance, that casualty rates of some 6–10 per cent a month, typical on the Western Front after D-Day, would be replaced in nuclear war by rates of 20 per cent a day. Under such conditions advantage might still go to the more numerous forces. Even in peacetime, the custody of nuclear weapons – particularly in an alliance where one nation maintains control teams throughout the forces of 'non-nuclear' allies – consumes a great deal of manpower. Again, the idea that the attacker's need to concentrate makes him vulnerable must be partly offset by the need for the defence to disperse to avoid nuclear attack, and by the fact that the fixed installations of the defence will be much more readily located targets than the mobile forces of the attack and can be pinpointed by a prearranged and well-prepared nuclear offensive.

There is no escape from many of these problems by abandoning a tactical nuclear strategy so long as the enemy also has nuclear weapons. Forces must either be prepared to go at once to a nuclear strategy or they must be 'dual capable'. This is no easy task, for the pattern of deployment most suited to one type of operation may be very vulnerable in the other. Once again the advantage may lie with the more numerous force. The problem is partly mitigated by the fact that the qualities of modern conventional armament themselves dictate dispersed and mobile tactics. Soviet doctrine emphasizes that in a nuclear or potentially nuclear battle, the aim must be to maintain a fast offensive, closing as quickly as possible with enemy troops, including the use of airborne thrusts to the rear. This alone will inhibit nuclear fire. Moreover, the actual front-line troops will not often present very tempting nuclear targets because of their dispersed and relatively 'hard' nature. Because of the rapid attenuation of heat and blast over distance, the resistance of tanks and other protected vehicles to the immediate effects of nuclear explosions is relatively high. To put it another way, an immense explosion in one place is not the most effective way to dispense firepower on the battlefield.

Consequently, the most promising tactical use for nuclear weapons is for interdiction. This, however, presents problems of its own. Interdiction implies fairly deep penetration behind the front and thus blurs the distinction between tactical and strategic use, especially in an alliance where the rear area of the front may be the heart of a smaller ally's territory. Many interdiction targets, such as rail junctions, are situated in centres of population, with grave implications of collateral damage. In exercise *Sagebrush*, for example, interdiction strikes took place 1100 miles behind the front. Other important targets would be enemy airfields, in order to eliminate his tactical nuclear potential. This, however, indicates how tactical nuclear weapons may, if they are 'soft', generate temptations toward first and pre-emptive strikes, exactly similar to those feared at the strategic level. It is, however, probably harder to devise systems free of this characteristic at the tactical level. A further complication is introduced by such dual-capable weapons as tactical aircraft and missiles whose appearance may be misinterpreted as the onset of nuclear strikes.

The result of all these complexities has been to create a thoroughly confused situation where tactical nuclear weapons are concerned. Very roughly speaking, there seem to be three schools of thought.

One school, which numbers many senior military officers amongst it, maintains that the difficulties of using nuclear weapons, and above all, the inhibition against crossing the 'firebreak' between conventional and nuclear weapons, mean that tactical nuclear weapons are virtually unusable. In practice, this school suspects, political leaders will never give permission to cross this firebreak, for they regard it as the only clearcut distinction arresting a gradual escalation toward disaster. At least, the politicians are unlikely to give permission in time for good military use to be made of tactical nuclear weapons. Even if the political leaders wished to give permission, many regard the procedures for requesting use of nuclear weapons, consulting among allied governments as to the response, and passing the answers to commanders, as so cumbersome that the opportunity would be lost. These administrative difficulties at the highest level are duplicated by the complexity of identifying and approving targets at the operational level, where care will have to be

taken not to disrupt operations in one sector by nuclear action in another.

A war in Europe would presumably over-ride many other inhibitions that would deter the use of nuclear weapons elsewhere. Even in Europe, however, these inhibitions would not be negligible. There has grown up a great stigma around nuclear weapons; the side that first used them would suffer considerable political disapproval. This disapproval would arise in part from, and would be reinforced by, fear that one breach of the inhibition would greatly increase the likelihood of others. The danger inherent in making nuclear weapons appear 'usable' is closely related to fears of encouraging nuclear proliferation. While such inhibitions might appear secondary in a war in Europe, they have clearly had great and effective force whenever consideration has been given to the use of nuclear weapons in the peripheral wars in Asia.

The conclusion of this sceptical school of thought is therefore that nations had better create adequate conventional armed forces and not rely on tactical nuclear weapons as an economical substitute. There are, however, two great difficulties. One is that, as we have already recognized, a nation cannot safely prepare solely for conventional war if its enemies are prepared for nuclear war. At least it would be putting great reliance on the more general inhibitions just mentioned to do so. The second difficulty is that the Western alliance shows no signs of being prepared to match the Communist prowess in conventional armament.

Two Russian Frog missiles on manœuvres.

The official NATO solution to this dilemma has been to adopt, in 1967, the doctrine of 'flexible response', whereby an initial phase of conventional defence would be prolonged as long as possible. If and when this defence was overwhelmed, the alliance would resort to tactical nuclear weapons. Guidelines for the use of tactical nuclear weapons, officially adopted in 1969, are reported to direct that the initial application of nuclear weapons should be limited and designed to be militarily useful while minimizing collateral damage.

It is not at all clear that the alliance has made its mind up as to whether tactical nuclear weapons are to be introduced in the hope of successfully arresting the enemy offensive or to raise the spectre of escalation and thus bring about a negotiated settlement. There is a difference of perspective here between the United States, which would like to prolong the period before strategic weapons must be used, and the West Europeans who, though far from anxious to initiate strategic nuclear war, perceive that, for them, a prolonged tactical nuclear battle would not be so very different. The problem is compounded by the fact that a restrained nuclear war does not seem to be part of Soviet strategy. For although the Soviet Union has practised conventional manœuvres in recent years, particularly in the 1967 exercise *Dnepr*, and is grappling with the problem of dual-capable deployment, the basic Soviet assumption seems to be that war in Europe would be nuclear from the start. Moreover, her doctrine for tactical nuclear war calls for the use of large numbers of deep nuclear strikes with big weapons in the opening phase, probably coupled with chemical attacks. Indeed some Western critics of a limited initial use of nuclear weapons, particularly French commentators, argue that such a strategy gets the worst of both worlds, assuring a heavy Soviet strike and forfeiting the initiative. Both on tactical grounds and in order to act as a deterrent, these critics therefore urge that if nuclear weapons are to be used, they should be used to impose an immediate and decisive defeat on the enemy.

There is a third school of thought that believes most of the difficulties and inhibitions surrounding tactical nuclear weapons arise from the fact that the present arsenals of so-called tactical weapons actually consist of inappropriately high-yield weapons which would indeed cause unmanageable problems of collateral damage and disintegration of military control. Such high yields also justify fears that no distinction could be maintained between strategic and tactical weapons and that the only effective firebreak is indeed that between conventional and nuclear. This school therefore advocates the exploitation of modern techniques. Mini-weapons can be constructed with yields measured in tons rather than kilotons. Efforts should be pressed forward toward making 'cleaner' tactical weapons (the deliberate inefficiency of the reaction in many current tactical weapons results in large amounts of long-term radioactive debris). Collateral damage could also be reduced by using nuclear weapons only in airbursts or in underground explosions. With improved accuracy, it is argued, such weapons could bolster firepower with little or no collateral damage. One option, the atomic demolition mine or munition (ADM), combines underground emplacement with total accuracy.

From one perspective such a strategy would be expensive, for it would involve making large numbers of weapons that from the strictly engineering point of view would be very inefficient. Some compensation might be derived, however, from relaxing the requirements for safety and control of weapons which would be, by definition, far removed from the instruments of mass destruction that have dictated existing, accepted standards. More important, of course, would be the savings which might be derived from the increased effectiveness of the armed forces. It can also be argued that with such weapons one could threaten nuclear war from the start and that this would be an effective deterrent. If the hopes that the use of such small nuclear weapons would not be escalatory are justified, however, the deterrent effect would arise not, as in strategic deterrence, by the threat of annihilation but, as in the conventional deterrence of the past, by convincing the enemy that his attack could not succeed.

Such a strategy has by no means won acceptance. Two major doubts surround it. The first is whether such weapons really would permit a numerically inferior force to resist a superior one. Something could be done to resolve this dilemma by careful analysis. The second doubt is whether small nuclear weapons could be used without engendering escalation. This doubt is less amenable to analysis. It could be argued that small nuclear weapons would be a valuable way to initiate nuclear action, even if a purely conventional defence is tried first. But it might also be feared that, by making nuclear weapons seem less dreadful, the process of escalation would actually be accelerated. Moreover, it is only natural that Western analysts usually debate the potential of tactical nuclear weapons for defence. To round out the analysis one should perhaps consider how a would-be aggressor might seek to exploit the military and psychological potential of small tactical nuclear weapons. So far the Soviet Union, whether aggressive or not, has not shown much interest in weapons below the kiloton range.

It is a remarkable fact that relatively little attention has been paid by either analysts or the public to the implications of tactical nuclear weapons, despite the fact that, according to most current doctrine, it is the decision to use these that would have to be taken first. At present it seems unlikely that any doctrine calling for early Western recourse to nuclear weapons will overcome the inhibitions against their use. Equally it is unlikely that authority will be given to use a nuclear weapon merely because it seems the best solution to a particular tactical problem. Such is the awe surrounding nuclear weapons and so deeply rooted is the fear of escalation, that the decision to use even the smallest nuclear weapon would be weighed for its symbolic and deterrent effect rather than its direct utility. If the decision to use nuclear weapons were taken, however, the same inhibitions are likely to dictate an initially tactical use. The whole subject of tactical nuclear weapons is consequently one that seems to deserve much more interest than it has hitherto received.

The founding father of
modern guerrilla theory:
Mao Tse Tung during
The Long March in 1935 when
he led his forces more than
four thousand miles to find
a secure operational base.

CHAPTER SEVEN
Guerrilla Warfare

Strictly speaking, guerrilla warfare is simply a particular method of fighting that can be employed, under suitable circumstances, by any kind of belligerent. Militarily, guerrilla warfare is characterized by operations with lightly armed forces, of high mobility, making great use of concealment, covert manœuvres and depending on tenuous and frequently informal supply lines. Typically, guerrillas are irregular forces operating against conventional, regular troops. Guerrilla operations may be carried out as an auxiliary to conventional operations elsewhere, or may be the sole form of armed struggle. By their nature, guerrilla operations are the tactics of the weak against the strong. As such they may be employed by powerful combatants in places where they suffer local weakness – as in the case of operations behind enemy lines. Alternatively, guerrilla fighting may be the only military recourse of a belligerent who is inferior in all material respects.

Because guerrilla operations suit the weak and enable the inferior side to take the offensive, they are frequently the chosen instrument of revolutionaries. Guerrilla campaigns are most successful if conducted among a sympathetic population and over familiar terrain. Consequently, typical occasions for guerrilla operations are to mount resistance to foreign invaders or to advance a national or social revolution in situations where the government has lost or has never enjoyed the wholehearted allegiance of the people.

In recent years the conduct of guerrilla warfare by nationalist or social revolutionaries has been so endemic that the concept of guerrilla warfare has become almost synonymous with revolutionary warfare. As a result, military doctrines for guerrilla warfare have become closely entwined with prescriptions for social revolution. This tendency has been all the more natural in so far as guerrilla warfare in any case necessarily has a higher political content than conventional military operations. Nevertheless, insurgency is in fact only one of the possible purposes of guerrilla warfare. Equally, guerrilla warfare is only one of many strategies open to revolutionaries, who can also choose among such alternatives as political agitation, subversion, terrorism, *coups* and open civil war waged with regular forces.

An important characteristic of guerrilla warfare, as compared with some of these alternatives, is its protracted nature. If those who wage guerrilla war could win quickly, they would not need to resort to it. This distinguishes guerrilla warfare from the brief urban revolutions by street fighting characteristic of Europe in the nineteenth century and of the Russian revolutions of 1917. (The subsequent civil war *was* protracted.) The protracted character of guerrilla war dictates many of the principles for success in waging it or countering it. In his tactical advice to resistance fighters Mao Tse Tung laid special stress on the need for patience: 'however cruel the war may be, we must absolutely and firmly endure until the last five minutes of struggle'.

Police using tanks and tear gas to suppress a demonstration in Algiers. The struggle for independence from France which began in 1954 added a new dimension to guerrilla tactics for much of the fighting took place in the urban areas.

Guerrilla war, in the sense of irregular, harassing operations, has doubtless been a form of warfare throughout history. It is depicted in the Bible and was a feature of the American War of Independence as former Indian-fighters adapted the lessons they had learned to dealing with a sophisticated enemy. These American operations were precursors of nationalist movements which were to become a feature of the following century. The term guerrilla (little war) was coined to describe Spanish and Portuguese irregular operations against the French and in support of the British during the Peninsular War.

At Brussels in 1874, an international conference laid down conditions under which guerrillas could claim the legal rights of belligerents under the rules of civilized warfare. These conditions were taken over virtually unaltered by the Hague Conferences on the rules of land warfare in 1899 and 1907, and still embody the formal position today. To qualify, guerrillas must wear distinctive insignia visible from a distance and must carry their arms openly. They must be organized under an identifiable commander who can be held responsible for his troops. They must also themselves conform to the rules of war. More often than not these rules are ignored by the guerrillas, because observance would deprive them of many of the advantages inherent in guerrilla operations, and by the counter-guerrillas because of the guerrillas' own lack of observance and of the emotions which the practices of irregular warfare commonly arouse.

Despite the long history of guerrilla warfare, there is a widespread impression that it has become much more frequent and intensive since 1945. It is, of course, difficult to reach agreed definitions for operations that can range from isolated outrages to sustained and wide-ranging wars like that in Viet Nam. Several efforts have been made to keep score and the resulting statistics are formidable. Two of the more often quoted enumerations are an American count of 'internal wars' reported in the *New York Times* from 1946 to 1959, reaching a total of over 1200, and the famous assertion of Secretary of Defense McNamara, in 1966, that in the years 1956–66 there had been 164 'internationally significant outbreaks of violence', of which 150 had been civil conflicts. A more rigorous study, taking account only of conflicts in which states employed their armed forces rather than their police, suggests that there were thirty-one major insurgencies between 1948 and 1967, nine civil wars and nine *coups d'état* or violent mutinies.

Problems of commensurability and the inadequacy of earlier records make it impossible to decide with assurance whether the incidence of guerrilla warfare and insurgency is rising. Probably it is. There are certainly several special circumstances that have encouraged recent conflicts and raised the level of international attention paid to them. This account is primarily concerned only with the factors influencing the choice of guerrilla warfare as a military strategy, but it is important not to forget, at the outset, the underlying political and economic causes of unrest that provide the fertile soil and justification for worldwide revolutionary unrest. The most fundamental of these is the continued grinding poverty of many areas of the world which has been given new political force by the spread of the idea that it is no longer necessary or inevitable. The existence of pockets of extreme affluence in the poorest countries and the depiction of high standards of living elsewhere by the mass media have created optimistic expectations and exacerbated resentments.

The rapid process of decolonization since 1945 provided an initial focus for the social revolutionary forces. The great colonial empires offered a multiplicity of opportunities for national uprisings. After a while, the steady process of decolonization offered an encouraging precedent of success for those inclined to hurry the process and a correspondingly depressing set of expectations for the forces of resistance. Resistance was also sapped by a crisis of conscience in the democratic colonial powers which precluded a wholehearted effort to suppress revolt and indicated a readily available escape by the early conferral of independence.

The process of decolonization is now very nearly complete and not many further opportunities for guerrilla warfare will offer themselves in this guise. But dissatisfaction continues rife in the former colonial areas. Successful fights for political independence aroused expectations of economic benefits that have all too often failed to materialize. Economic conditions are bad and can be readily attributed to subservience of the new national régimes to alien economic influences. There is a plethora of overeducated and underemployed youth and the colonial frontiers have conferred a legacy of minority problems. The original decolonization struggles themselves have popularized the notions of revolt and secession. Thus the former colonial areas now display a variety of 'crises of succession' that afforded opportunities for guerrilla warfare. In many such areas the terrain is well suited to such wars.

Situations of this kind have provided the basic soil for revolutionary movements. The recourse to guerrilla warfare is doubtless due primarily to the existence of suitable terrain and to the particular local balance of forces. But there are several more general influences contributing to the popularity of guerrilla action as a strategy.

One such circumstance is the creation, in the works of Mao, General Vo Nguyen Giap and others, of a highly articulated theory of guerrilla and revolutionary warfare. Closely related to the influence of these writings has been the force of example of the immense success for the Communist forces in the Chinese Civil War and the establishment in China of a government prepared to encourage and, in a modest way, assist revolutionary forces. Elsewhere also, World War II gave rise to a large number of guerrilla resistance movements in the occupied territories, many of them under Communist leadership. These provided leaders, experience, prestige and, in several cases, the armaments for post-war movements. In Asia and in the Balkans, the establishment of new Communist governments provided some guerrilla forces with convenient sanctuaries.

A noticeable characteristic of recent guerrilla movements has been their close interconnection with the workings of the international system. One reason for this is that, by a coincidence, the great powers most intent on revising the international balance of power in their favour, China and the Soviet Union, are also the custodians of a universalist revolutionary ideology. They both also have experiences of successful guerrilla operations in the making or consolidation of their own revolutions. Another reason for the would-be revisionist powers to turn to the encouragement of insurgency and guerrilla operations as an instrument of foreign policy may be the increasing inhibitions on the use of open conventional military power in the nuclear age. This analysis was explicitly espoused by Khruschev when he modified his famous renunciation of war as a necessary instrument of Soviet foreign policy by making an exception for wars of 'national liberation'.

The interests of certain powers in the outcome of guerrilla contests elsewhere have led to the establishment of recognized international centres of encouragement for insurgency, notably the Soviet Union, China, Cuba, Algeria, North Viet Nam and Tanzania. In many respects the United States, Britain, France and Australia have served as equivalent sources of support for counter-revolutionary forces. One result of the existence of such centres is to encourage the spread of revolutionary attitudes and techniques. It would be quite wrong, however, to attribute the prevalence of revolutionary and guerrilla movements solely to the strategy of a few leading powers. Many movements are clearly the spontaneous result of local circumstance. Even these, however, are doubtless affected and perhaps occasionally inspired by the accounts of similar movements elsewhere which are quickly relayed by modern mass media. The media have, indeed, become a prime factor in revolutionary warfare and many operations are primarily intended to win effective publicity.

The Political Context of Guerrilla Warfare

The military strategy and tactics of guerrilla warfare are very similar whatever the occasion for fighting. Being weak and needing supplies and information, guerrillas always find local support desirable. For those who use guerrilla warfare in its chief modern application, as an instrument of revolution, popular attitudes become crucial. They are, indeed, the main concern of the operation. On the one hand, the government, whether colonial or indigenous, must be deprived of support and self-confidence so that it can be persuaded or compelled to abandon the struggle. On the other hand, a rising tide of popular sympathy will provide the guerrillas with information, shelter, supplies and recruits. The public are therefore a prime target of guerrilla strategy. In Mao's celebrated phrase, they are the sea in which the guerrilla swims.

An emphasis on the political context of guerrilla warfare accords fully with Marxist–Leninist theory. Marx and Engels had approved of guerrilla warfare as a possible instrument of nationalist revolution but, as in all their analyses, they stressed the need for a ripe, favourable political situation if the failures of the eighteen-forties were not to be repeated. Writing on guerrilla warfare in 1906, Lenin, while accepting guerrilla warfare as a tool useful for social as well as nationalist revolution, condemned as 'left adventurism' any attempt to resort to guerrilla action before favourable political conditions were fully developed. The same principle was the basic foundation of Mao's theory. Mao condemned mere 'guerrillaism' in the Red Army. Guerrilla warfare was only a part, and a subordinate part, of even the military component of revolutionary struggle, the ultimate military goal being to amass sufficient strength to defeat the enemy in 'mobile' or conventional operations. All military operations, however, could succeed only if primacy were given to political action. 'Modern warfare is not a matter in which armies alone can determine victory or defeat. Especially in guerrilla combat, we must rely on the force of the popular masses, for it is only thus that we can have a guarantee of success.' Similarly, General Vo Nguyen Giap notes, in his account of the Vietminh war against the French: 'the shifting from political struggle to armed struggle was a very great change that required a long period of preparation. If insurrection is said to be an art, the main content of this art is to know how to give to the struggle forms appropriate to the political situation at each stage, how to maintain the correct relation between the forms of political struggle and those of the armed struggle.'

The Russian revolution was made originally in the towns, and Lenin saw the urban proletariat as the key revolutionary force. Mao's contribution was to conclude that, because of the nature of Chinese terrain, the remoteness of some rural areas from the centres of governmental power and the dissatisfactions of the peasants, his revolution could be based in the countryside and on peasant support. This has become a dogma of Maoist thought and has, indeed, been translated to the world scene by depicting the underdeveloped world as the

Opposite Vo Nguyen Giap, one of the most successful guerrilla generals of modern times. He led the Communist Vietnamese forces in the defeat of the French and directed the subsequent war against South Viet Nam.

revolutionary area from which the advanced, urbanized countries will be surrounded and brought to submit. Vo Nguyen Giap, who, like Mao, initially enjoyed the benefit of nationalist sentiment against the invading Japanese, gave similar priority to the rural areas: 'in waging the resistance war we relied on the countryside to build our bases from which to launch guerrilla war in order to encircle the enemy in the towns and eventually arrive at liberating the towns'. To win over the peasants the guerrillas may put forward political programmes, such as the distribution of land, which may be far from their ultimate real intention.

When a colonial government is the foe, or where an indigenous government

Che Guevara: his experience of easy victory in Cuba led to over-ambitious extension of guerrilla activity in other parts of South America. He was killed by security forces in Bolivia in 1969.

depends very much on the support of a foreign power, the guerrillas acquire an additional political target in the public opinion and national will of the metropolitan or foreign nation. While an indigenous government may have no easy avenue of retreat – though wealthy leaders may well take to flight – a distant, alien régime can much more readily decide to cut its losses. Guerrilla operations may therefore be designed for the maximum impact on international opinion, aided and abetted by the modern mass media. Algeria and Cyprus both offer examples of revolutionary campaigns which broke the will of the colonial power long before the governmental forces faced anything close to military defeat. Viet Nam seems to have had a similar effect on American resolution.

Some of the leading Latin-American theorists of revolutionary war, such as Ernesto ('Che') Guevara and Régis Debray, have departed from the Leninist and Maoist insistence on the political prerequisites for successful guerrilla operations. The relatively easy success won in Cuba has encouraged this tendency. In Cuba circumstances were indeed very favourable: the Batista régime was unpopular, inefficient and perhaps no longer strongly motivated to resist. The Cuban population was highly politicized. These conditions allowed the guerrillas to win a quick victory with comparatively little sustained guerrilla warfare and a rapid collapse of government not dissimilar from the bourgeois revolutions of nineteenth-century Europe.

This quick and easy success seems to have convinced Guevara and others, not that the Cuban circumstances were peculiarly propitious, but that guerrilla activity itself may precipitate a revolutionary situation without waiting and working previously for the objective political preconditions to emerge. Guerrilla action achieves this result by creating a rallying point, by forcing the government into unwise repressive measures, and by polarizing society. Guevara did not go so far as to say that no preconditions at all were necessary. A certain degree of weakness in the government was essential. 'Naturally it is not to be thought that all conditions for revolution are going to be created through the impulse given them by guerrilla activity. It must always be kept in mind that there is a necessary minimum without which the establishment and consolidation of the first centre is not practicable. People must see clearly the futility of mounting the fight for social goals within the framework of civil debate.'

It is obvious, however, that Guevara believed that these necessary minimal conditions did exist throughout Latin America and, clearly, an eager would-be revolutionary would be greatly tempted to believe the time for action was ripe. He would thus fall into one of the errors regarded as most reprehensible in Leninist and Maoist theory, though it must be admitted that both Lenin and Mao were not always as patient in practice as their doctrine advocates. Régis Debray went even further than Guevara, and made a positive virtue of the guerrilla remaining aloof from the people and preserving his distinctive zeal undiluted. Guevara's own ill-fated guerrilla venture in Bolivia, which cost him his life, certainly seems to have been undertaken with a reckless misjudgement of the prevailing political climate. His largely alien force received scant support from the local peasants and its rapid defeat suggests the doubtful wisdom of departing too radically from the Maoist principle of giving priority to the political foundations of guerrilla activity.

Latin America has spawned another departure from Maoist principles in the recent upsurge of urban guerrilla movements. From one point of view urban guerrilla warfare is a contradiction in terms, for it will scarcely ever be possible to mount the large scale, almost conventional operations typical of advanced stages of traditional guerrilla campaigns. As a consequence the tactics as well

as the strategy are different. The so-called urban guerrilla specializes in terrorism, in kidnapping, in bank robberies, all to serve the purposes of 'armed propaganda'. In this way he hopes to raise funds, arouse support, unnerve the government, scare its adherents, win international publicity, discourage investment and generally create a revolutionary situation culminating not in mobile warfare but in the kind of governmental abdication characteristic of the nineteenth-century street revolutions. This approach runs counter not only to the prescriptions of Mao but also to those of Guevara, and of Castro, who has declared that 'the city is the graveyard of revolutionaries and resources'.

The reason for the move to the cities would appear to be twofold. Perhaps the more important is that a revolution must naturally be made where the people are, and in Latin America this increasingly means the cities. The Tupamaros, who derive their name from a sixteenth-century Inca hero, Tupac Amaru, have made Montevideo the most notorious centre of urban guerrilla activity in the world. This city contains more than half the population of Uruguay. Over two-thirds of the population of Argentina, Venezuela and Chile live in cities; the same is true of over half the population of Brazil and Colombia. There cities are growing at rates as high as 8 per cent a year.

Although the cities attract immigrants from the depressed countryside, they do not offer a satisfactory living. Rates of unemployment and underemployment run up to 40 per cent. Much so-called employment is in 'service industries', which is frequently a euphemism for thinly disguised begging. The cities are therefore concentrations of misery and their centres are surrounded by vast, almost impenetrable and therefore unpoliceable slums. Crime rates are high and organized criminals become a ready and frequently very troublesome source of recruits for revolutionary organizations. The second reason why Latin-American revolutionaries are turning to the cities is therefore that it is there that discontent is rife. While the peasants are declining in numbers, often apathetic and depoliticized, the cities are the home of dissatisfied intellectuals and students who provide a high proportion of the revolutionary leadership.

It is too early to speak with confidence of the future of urban guerrillas as a style of revolutionary. The phenomenon is chiefly Latin-American. So far it is rare in Asia, perhaps because, though Asia has large cities, they still constitute less than 15 per cent of the total population. Possibly the strong influence of Maoist doctrine with its rural emphasis has also discouraged a turn to the cities in Asia. As a rare exception, the Naxalites in North East India, though Maoists, have added urban violence to their repertoire, but this campaign has not yet reached impressive proportions.

It remains to be seen whether guerrilla tactics can really be developed in urban surroundings or whether such movements will remain essentially severe nuisances which may aggravate revolutionary situations but cannot win their own victory.

In recent years there have, of course, been outbreaks of politically motivated urban violence in the cities of advanced Western countries, and also in Eastern Europe. Only briefly, in Hungary, and, on a smaller but prolonged scale, in Northern Ireland, have the campaigns provided a real military challenge. The Irish situation is a quasi-colonial one, but it has demonstrated the capacity of a small force to be very effective against government troops who are compelled by principle and political expedience to use only a minimum level of force. It is, however, the colonial nature of the conflict that lends it prospects of success, for it is conceivable that the British government will decide to withdraw. Were it a revolutionary situation within an ethnically united country, the level of

Opposite British troops firing rubber bullets during a riot in Northern Ireland. The role of the army in trying to separate hostile communities and root out an urban terrorist organization has highlighted the problems of any military force trying to operate in a civilian environment.

disruption achieved by 1973 fell far short of what would bring down a government, even at the very moderate intensity of counter-insurgency effort yet being applied.

It is frequently observed that modern sophisticated cities are very vulnerable to disruption. But while this is true, they are also capable of remarkable feats of resilience and recovery. Advanced countries have very sophisticated and efficient police forces, powerful armies and a generally high degree of popular support where the fundamentals of economic and political life are concerned. Moreover, the type of alienated intellectual that seems to provide urban guerrilla leadership does not usually represent a very large, kindred proportion of the total population. The advance from serious nuisance to effective revolutionary force may therefore not be easy. As a British writer has observed, there were 4330 bomb explosions in the United States between June, 1970 and April, 1971, without producing any discernible effect on the American political fabric.

On balance, it seems likely that, where revolutionary situations exist, the progress of urbanization will ensure that armed insurrection embraces and sometimes begins in the cities. Mao's emphasis on rural operations and remote base areas can hardly be rigorously applied where the rural areas have ceased to be crucial to national life. But, under such circumstances, much of the rest of Mao's prescriptions may also cease to be relevant and we may come increasingly to recognize that we face a phenomenon falling more within the purview of police work than military strategy and to which the term guerrilla is scarcely appropriate.

The Military Strategy and Tactics of Guerrilla War

The strategy and tactics appropriate to the weaker side in a military conflict are very largely a simple matter of common sense. The key characteristic of guerrilla operations is that the weaker side has to find ways of taking the offensive. Because it is the weaker side, it has to do so selectively, choosing time and places of momentary superiority. In the words of Sun Tzu, endorsed by Mao, 'avoid strength, attack weakness'. The stages of Mao's classic guerrilla warfare are therefore strategic defence, equilibrium, strategic offensive, in the last of which the rebels move over to mobile warfare.

Much will depend on having some base or sanctuary. Mao, profiting from China's size, terrain and poor communications, established remote base areas and his doctrine makes this a fundamental principle. Many parts of the 'third world' offer opportunities to create such bases, but there are many prospective revolutionary areas that do not. Southern Africa offers an example where the landscape is fairly open. A substitute for base areas in the guerrillas' own country can be afforded by sanctuary in a neighbouring state. China served this purpose for the rebellion against the French in Indo-China, as North Viet Nam has done for the later insurgency in the South. Communist guerrillas prospered in Greece after World War II and declined when Tito closed the Yugoslavian frontier. If all else fails, the guerrilla must find his base by concealment among the people. This is the course forced upon the urban guerrillas but it is one that seriously constrains the type of operation possible.

Valuable though the base areas are, they are a means and not an end. The object of the guerrilla phase of operations is not to gain territory but to erode the war-potential and political stability of the enemy. According to Vo Nguyen Giap 'the main goal of the fighting must be the destruction of enemy manpower and ours should not be exhausted by trying to keep or occupy land'. This follows the precept of Mao: 'To gain territory is no cause for joy and to lose

Opposite Che Guevara broods over the heads of demonstrators in Venezuela. Despite his failure to lead widespread revolution his influence still inspires left-wing movements throughout the world.

Guerrilla troops move through the jungle of Angola. One of the longest lasting of modern guerrilla wars has been that of various nationalist movements against the Portuguese in Angola and Mozambique. More than 160,000 Portuguese troops have been fighting for more than twenty years and the war now takes about a quarter of the Portuguese national budget.

territory is no cause for sorrow. To lose territory or cities is of no importance. The important thing is to think up ways of destroying the enemy.' Similarly, though for reasons of morale and to conserve scarce resources, great care should be taken not to suffer defeats, particular defeats are no cause for despair if the general situation remains favourable and the campaign continues. For, unlike conventional operations where the side on the offensive is defeated if it does not win, in guerrilla operations it is the defensive side that loses if it does not secure a clear victory. This is because, so long as armed rebellion continues, the government is deprived of its most essential characteristic, that of possessing acknowledged authority and a monopoly of organized force.

With these basic distinctions between guerrilla and conventional operations in mind, the tactical principles involved are very much a matter of common sense. The emphasis is on alertness and intelligence, on mobility, concealment, offensive spirit and careful adjustment to the situation of the enemy. Large enemy forces are to be harassed and small ones annihilated. An idea of Mao's advice can be derived from some of the sub-headings in his brief book on Basic Tactics: 'We must not attack strong positions'; 'Do not fight hard battles'; 'Surprise attacks on isolated units'; 'Cause an uproar in the East, attack in the West'; 'Meeting a superior enemy. When the enemy advances we retreat. When the enemy retreats we pursue.'

There is patently no magic in such prescriptions, sound though they are. Success in guerrilla warfare is not something to be learned from a book. Probably the most important ingredients of success, given a reasonably suitable political context, are the elusive qualities of morale and, above all, leadership. A clear and ideologically compelling aim is a great asset against a frequently confused and demoralized government. Leadership is perhaps more important in guerrilla war than in any other kind because the weak must compensate for their material inferiority by skill. In T. E. Lawrence's phrase: 'guerrilla war is far more intellectual than a bayonet charge'. Successful guerrilla war through the ages seems to be closely related to the emergence of a series of strong personalities with compulsive zeal: Lenin, Trotsky, Lawrence, Mao, Tito, Ho Chi Minh and Castro offering fair examples.

Because most revolutionary guerrilla leaders would accept Mao's emphasis on the primacy of political action – even Lawrence, the agent of a great power, wrote that one 'had won a province when the civilians in it had been taught to die for the ideal of freedom; the presence or absence of the enemy was a secondary matter' – actual military operations must be geared to achieve political effects. Mere military success will itself win adherents. Many guerrilla leaders, however, stress the importance of treating the population well. Mao recommended paying for requisitioned supplies; Guevara suggested payment by IOU in bad times! Beyond mere compensation, guerrillas may work toward administrative and economic reform in the areas they occupy, actively beginning development programmes.

The other extreme is the use of terror. Terror is a long-acknowledged resort of the guerrilla. It may be exercised against the population to compel assistance and against supporters and agents of the government to demoralize them and paralyse administration. It is a delicate weapon that can misfire. Used injudiciously it can alienate popular support and stiffen the allegiance of government supporters by leaving them little hope of survival in the event of a guerrilla victory. Nevertheless, used judiciously, terror can do much to destroy the apparatus of government. Between 1966 and 1969 more than 18,000 South Vietnamese local officials are said to have been assassinated by the Viet Cong.

Under such conditions the government appears unable to offer the security that should be its prime service to the citizen. Allegiance may then shift to the guerrillas as the only remaining source of safety.

Counter-Insurgency Operations

The key to good counter-insurgency operations is obviously inherent in the principles of effective guerrilla warfare. At the military level the counter-insurgency forces must avoid the traps set by the guerrillas and must learn to exploit their material superiority in ways that are not counter-productive. But first the counter-insurgency effort must come to grips with the political dimensions of struggle that the revolutionaries themselves regard as all-important.

In itself the mere outbreak of guerrilla activity is a testimony to governmental failure. Very often, of course, the government's own legitimacy is questionable and its own origins may derive from force. If the insurrection is widely supported, the government has failed in its obligation to maintain at least a minimum level of satisfaction and consent among the people. In any case, its apparatus for the detection and suppression of subversion has proved defective. The best time to repress a guerrilla war is before it begins by removing the conditions that give rise to it. This calls for good police work and, perhaps, reform, concentrating on the most disaffected areas. In practice, however, the early stages of revolt often go unperceived or underestimated.

Once an open actual insurrection has challenged the government, the resulting blow to prestige makes the task of recovery all the more difficult. Restoring order is a complex and exacting process which must usually be executed by what is, by definition, an inefficient régime. In colonial situations, though the grievances of the rebels might be fundamental, the administration could frequently draw on a large metropolitan reservoir of administrative, political and military experience, and the apparatus of government itself was unlikely to be penetrated by subversives. A somewhat similar situation exists in Israel and South Africa, where the ruling group is clearly set off from the dissident forces and, moreover, has no line of retreat. Elsewhere, in social revolutionary situations, the loyalty of the government machine itself may be suspect.

Perhaps the critical factor is time. As we have seen, the guerrillas need time; equally the government must be prepared to endure a long campaign and not to lose the contest in patience. This has implications for the level of military effort, which must not impose strains on the society that cannot be sustained.

The insurgent campaign has two aspects: the actual guerrilla war and the underlying process of subversion and propaganda. For the modern revolutionary it is the political subversion that is primary. Consequently it should be the first concern of the counter-insurgents. The primary need for the government is to restore its claim to respect as a government by maintaining order, extending security to its law-abiding citizens and imposing retribution on the insurgents. This is not military but police work. The guerrillas, however, will use their large units of force to overwhelm the police and negate their efforts. Thus the prime task of the government's military forces is to protect the apparatus of civil government and police against *force majeure* while the police deal with subversion. Such police work calls for good intelligence and an intimate acquaintance with local conditions. Just as the work of the police will be negated if the guerrillas can over-run the areas policed, so the conquests of the military will be transient if their advance cannot be followed up by the establishment of effective police and administration. Only thus can the government prevent the frequent experience of villages ostensibly occupied by government troops being effectively under the covert control of the insurgents operating by subversion and terror. In such a campaign the order of priority recommended for earlier stages of insurgency must be reversed. Whereas, before insurgency is widespread, the police effort should concentrate on the most affected areas, once the rebellion is advanced the government must establish secure areas where this is most easily done, before moving out to reclaim the guerrillas' strongholds. In the meantime, the government may attempt, by military operations, to prevent the consolidation of rebel power in areas which it is not yet able to police.

A difficult problem is posed for the counter-insurgents by the question of whether or not to observe strict forms of legality. Most agree that, with regard to the general population, any resort to terror or extra-legal measures will almost always be counter-productive. Operating within a framework of law is indeed one of the hallmarks of a government and to depart from this principle is a confession of failure. French practice in Algeria and that of some government forces in Viet Nam have raised the special question of torture to extract the information that is so vital in counter-insurgency operations. Although torture has doubtless always been a common feature of guerrilla war, most Western analysts would recommend abstention, if only because of the debilitating effect of torture on the morale of government forces and its bad effect on public opinion. Similarly there is considerable scepticism about the value of collective punishments on communities that are suspected of collaboration with rebels. Such punishments arouse great resentment, yet offer a relatively weak counter-pressure to the terrorists' threat of assassination. Thus it may be better to preserve a framework of known and defensible law. This law may, however, be made very rigorous in periods of emergency. In Malaya the successful British operation against the Communists involved identity card systems, rights to search without warrant, death sentence for possession of illegal weapons, severe sentences for individuals convicted of helping the rebels, shooting on sight in prohibited areas and the resettlement of villages.

Despite the primary importance of police work and law enforcement, there will still be a military campaign if the guerrillas are strong enough to mount small-unit operations. The principles of military success for the counter-insurgents involve denying the guerrilla success in applying his own tactics. Government forces will naturally seek ways to exploit their material superiority but experience suggests the need for great caution. Large-scale sweeps by regular forces and the lavish use of bombing are generally ineffective against guerrillas who have not yet begun mobile warfare, while such operations usually do a great deal of incidental damage to the population and their property. The more heavy equipment is used, the more the government forces are tied to the roads. Many experts in counter-insurgency therefore stress the value of intensive patrolling by small units, spending long periods in the hills or jungle, getting to know and, indeed, living with the local communities. In recent years the helicopter has provided a new dimension to counter-insurgency operations. But, again, there is considerable evidence that the helicopter is best used to achieve mobility, putting units into place for sustained operations on the ground, rather than to permit troops to go home after brief forays, or as artillery to avoid going on to the ground at all.

The overriding principle would seem to be the correct orchestration of police and military efforts. Hard military action that would be counter-productive when the political climate is poor, may be well received when the government has re-established some credibility and the people are becoming weary of disruption. A classic example was provided in 1963 when President Betancourt of Venezuela, having bided his time while preparing free elections as a gesture of legitimacy, cracked down on the insurgents in large street battles. In the ensuing election the constitutional system was endorsed by a turn-out of 90 per cent of the voters.

The Prospects for Guerrilla Warfare

Guerrilla warfare is likely to remain a common feature of the world scene. Social unrest, weak administration, favourable terrain and the competitive meddling of the great powers offer favourable opportunities throughout the underdeveloped countries. The new urban variety will very probably continue to appear in the more urbanized poor countries. Partly in imitation, urban violence may extend to the cities of the richer nations, but in this case it is more likely to be a nuisance and a political catalyst than a self-sufficient revolutionary force.

The spate of guerrilla victories during the period of decolonization and the prolonged American agony in Viet Nam have created a widespread impression that guerrilla action is usually successful and resistance more or less hopeless. In fact the record is ambiguous. Indo-China, Cyprus, Algeria and Cuba were among the conspicuous successes. But in Kenya, Peru, Venezuela, Bolivia and Malaya there have been important if less-celebrated failures. Other defeats for guerrillas could be cited, as in the Philippines, Guatemala and Greece. In Israel and South Africa there are examples of the efficacy of tough and self-confident régimes. Moreover, we should not forget the highly successful record of control maintained by the Communist countries in the face of national and social unrest.

Another significant development that deserves attention is the wavering nature of international support for insurgent movements. For many years the Soviet Union and China have provided much encouragement and have been the chief ultimate suppliers of arms to insurgents. So long as the Soviet Union controlled the Communist bloc and the Western powers were the residual holders of colonial empires, the results of insurgency in the underdeveloped countries might be expected to further Russian interests. Since the Sino–Soviet split and the virtual completion of decolonization, the situation is not so simple. The Soviet Union shows many signs of preferring to extend its influence by improving relations with the governments of new states. Even China has demonstrated some similar tendencies. Chinese help to rebels has always been somewhat moderated by the Maoist insistence that revolutions must depend primarily on their own resources in keeping with the principle of waiting for ripe political conditions. In some areas the one-time sources of revolutionary inspiration have become props of the *status quo* and in 1971 one had the spectacle of Mrs Bandaranaike's government suppressing a leftist rebellion in Ceylon with the benevolent assistance of the United States, the Soviet Union, Britain, China and the UAR.

Thus, although guerrilla wars are almost certain to continue to occur, given the level of social dissatisfaction combined with political awareness that is typical of so many countries, it would be quite unwarranted to regard armed insurgency as an irresistible tide. As this brief survey illustrates, there are severe limitations on any attempt to conduct a general analysis of a phenomenon which displays rich variety in its manifestations. Any further attempt to predict the future would therefore require a careful analysis of the unique local circumstances that determine the outcome of each potentially revolutionary situation.

The main guerrilla move-
ments operating throughout
the modern world.

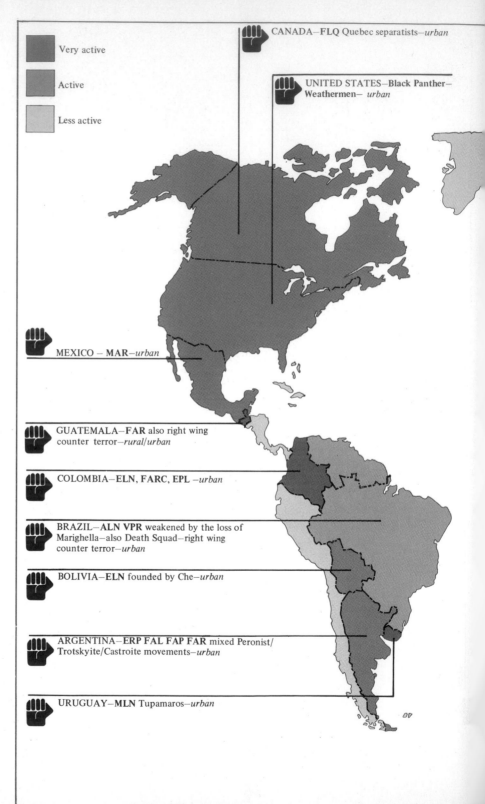

Very active

Active

Less active

CANADA—**FLQ** Quebec separatists—*urban*

UNITED STATES—Black Panther—
Weathermen— *urban*

MEXICO – **MAR**—*urban*

GUATEMALA—**FAR** also right wing
counter terror—*rural/urban*

COLOMBIA—**ELN, FARC, EPL** —*urban*

BRAZIL—**ALN VPR** weakened by the loss of
Marighella—also Death Squad—right wing
counter terror—*urban*

BOLIVIA—**ELN** founded by Che—*urban*

ARGENTINA—**ERP FAL FAP FAR** mixed Peronist/
Trotskyite/Castroite movements—*urban*

URUGUAY—**MLN** Tupamaros—*urban*

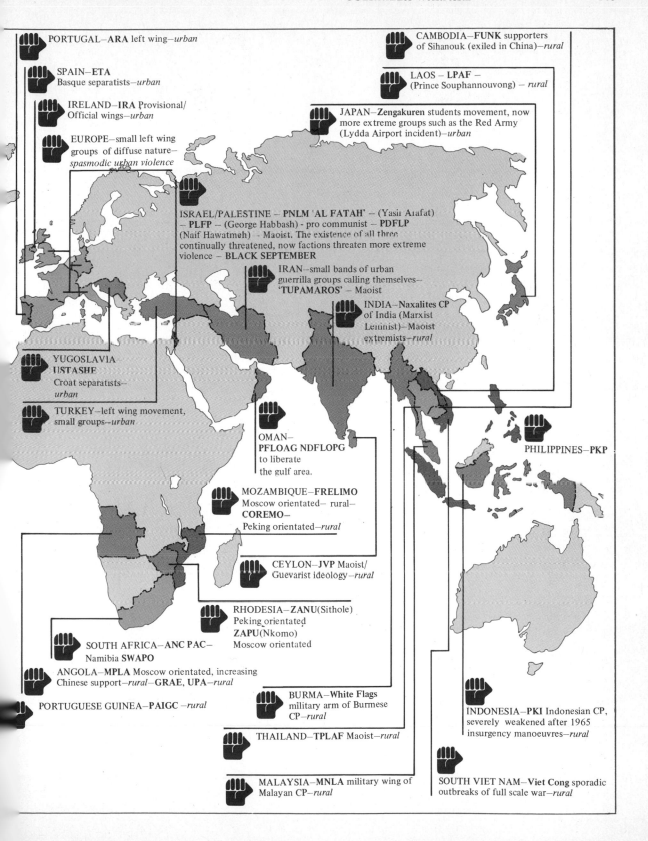

PORTUGAL—**ARA** left wing—*urban*

SPAIN—**ETA** Basque separatists—*urban*

IRELAND—**IRA** Provisional/ Official wings—*urban*

EUROPE—small left wing groups of diffuse nature— *spasmodic urban violence*

ISRAEL/PALESTINE – **PNLM 'AL FATAH'** – (Yasir Arafat) – **PLFP** – (George Habbash) - pro communist – **PDFLP** (Naif Hawatmeh) - Maoist. The existence of all three continually threatened, now factions threaten more extreme violence – **BLACK SEPTEMBER**

YUGOSLAVIA **USTASHE** Croat separatists— *urban*

TURKEY—left wing movement, small groups—*urban*

CAMBODIA—**FUNK** supporters of Sihanouk (exiled in China)—*rural*

LAOS – **LPAF** – (Prince Souphannouvong) – *rural*

JAPAN—**Zengakuren** students movement, now more extreme groups such as the Red Army (Lydda Airport incident)—*urban*

IRAN—small bands of urban guerrilla groups calling themselves— **'TUPAMAROS'** – Maoist

INDIA—Naxalites CP of India (Marxist Leninist)—Maoist extremists—*rural*

OMAN— **PFLOAG NDFLOPG** to liberate the gulf area.

MOZAMBIQUE—**FRELIMO** Moscow orientated— rural— **COREMO**— Peking orientated—*rural*

PHILIPPINES—**PKP**

CEYLON—**JVP** Maoist/ Guevarist ideology—*rural*

RHODESIA—**ZANU**(Sithole) Peking orientated **ZAPU**(Nkomo) Moscow orientated

SOUTH AFRICA—**ANC PAC**— Namibia **SWAPO**

ANGOLA—**MPLA** Moscow orientated, increasing Chinese support—*rural*—**GRAE, UPA**—*rural*

PORTUGUESE GUINEA—**PAIGC** –*rural*

BURMA—**White Flags** military arm of Burmese CP—*rural*

THAILAND—**TPLAF** Maoist—*rural*

MALAYSIA—**MNLA** military wing of Malayan CP—*rural*

INDONESIA—**PKI** Indonesian CP, severely weakened after 1965 insurgency manoeuvres—*rural*

SOUTH VIET NAM—**Viet Cong** sporadic outbreaks of full scale war—*rural*

PART III

Arenas of Conflict

CHAPTER EIGHT

Nato and the Warsaw Pact

Europe, where NATO and the Warsaw Pact confront each other, contains the most powerful concentration of military power that the world has ever witnessed. The demarcation lines between the blocs are sufficiently well drawn and the politico–military equilibrium so long established, that the situation appears relatively safe and stable. But it must always be remembered that the stakes in Europe are also the highest for which the Superpowers compete. Consequently, should a crisis arise in Europe, it might well have more potential for precipitating general war than any event elsewhere in the world.

The Second World War completed the collapse of the European balance of power begun in the First and the two Great Powers whose intervention had determined the outcome, Russia and the United States, remained in central Europe to establish the post-war equilibrium. Relations between the two rapidly deteriorated, multiplying the mutual suspicion that had been rife during the period of wartime co-operation. Preoccupied by the experience of invasion, Stalin was intent on retaining a strategic buffer in Eastern Europe and on preventing the resurgence of German power. Rightly or wrongly, these Soviet policies, when set against the ideological role of the Communist Party in Europe, revived pre-war Western fears of Bolshevik expansionism and led to the breakdown of any semblance of co-operation between Russia and the West. Soon two hostile military coalitions had emerged.

The North Atlantic Treaty was signed in the aftermath of the Czech *coup* of 1948 and the Berlin Blockade that followed. Both events made Russian military power seem more ominous and destroyed hopes of an early amicable relationship between East and West in Europe. The alliance was primarily an effort to reassure the West Europeans and give them confidence to pursue the work of economic reconstruction proceeding under the Marshall Plan. The core of the alliance was the guarantee that the United States would remain a factor in the European balance. This was the United States' first formal alliance since the War of Independence. The term of the treaty was twenty years, after which members could withdraw at one year's notice. Originally the members of the alliance were Belgium, Britain, Canada, Denmark, France, Iceland, Italy, Luxembourg, the Netherlands, Norway, Portugal and the United States. In 1952 Greece and Turkey acceded to the treaty. Under the treaty each signatory undertakes to regard an attack on any member of the alliance as an attack on itself and to give assistance by 'such action as it deems necessary, including the use of armed force'. To qualify, the attack must be on the territory of a signatory or on its forces, vessels or aircraft in the Mediterranean or Atlantic north of the Tropic of Cancer.

Russia's unexpectedly early detonation of an atomic device, late in 1949, gave warning that the alliance could not rest on a nuclear monopoly. The Korean War aroused a widespread belief, whether justified or not, that overt military

Opposite East German armoured forces during training. Like other armed forces of the Eastern bloc they are entirely equipped with Soviet weapons and fully integrated into a Russian-dominated defence system.

Left Paratroops landing during a Warsaw Pact exercise in Czechoslovakia. **Below** A signals unit of the East German army.

aggression was a more likely instrument of Russian policy than hitherto suspected. In this climate of opinion the allies undertook a major programme of rearmament. The United States reinforced its troops in Europe, which thus became part of a standing expeditionary force rather than residual occupation troops. Negotiations were begun to rearm West Germany and, after the failure of plans for a European Defence Community in 1954, West Germany became a member of the North Atlantic Alliance in 1955. Meanwhile, in 1950, the alliance had established a permanent headquarters, Supreme Headquarters Allied Powers Europe (SHAPE), and the United States had provided General Eisenhower as first Supreme Allied Commander, Europe (SACEUR).

The Soviet Union had tried very hard to discourage development of the alliance and above all the rearmament of Germany. Nine days after West Germany joined the alliance, the Soviet Union created the Warsaw Pact. An added incentive to do this stemmed from the signing of the Austrian peace treaty, which removed the existing legal basis for the presence of Soviet forces in Hungary and Rumania. The original members of the Pact, besides the Soviet Union, were Poland, East Germany, Czechoslovakia, Rumania, Hungary, Bulgaria and Albania. After a long period of non-participation, Albania denounced the treaty in 1968. Formally, however, the treaty was for twenty years, renewable in 1975 for a further decade.

The original Pact has been supplemented by a complex network of bilateral treaties of assistance and friendship both between Russia and the East Europeans and among the East Europeans themselves. These treaties bolstered East Germany and also ensure that, should the Warsaw Pact be abrogated as part of a deal to eliminate NATO, a legal basis would remain for the structure of Soviet defence in Eastern Europe.

Organization of the Alliances
The highest political body under the North Atlantic Treaty is the North Atlantic Council, which acts by unanimity. The chairman of the council is the

Secretary General, who controls an international staff at Brussels. A Committee of Political Advisers meets weekly. Since France left the military organization of NATO (but not the Alliance), in 1966, military affairs have been discussed in a Defence Policy Committee of thirteen (Iceland having no armed forces). Under the DPC is a Military Committee composed of national chiefs of staff. This committee issues instructions to the Supreme Commanders.

There are three such commanders: SACEUR (who has always been American), in Brussels; Supreme Allied Commander, Atlantic (SACLANT, also American), in Norfolk, Virginia; and Commander-in-Chief, Channel (CINCHAN), who is British and represents partly a belief that the problems of the 'Western

Approaches' need special treatment, and partly a concession to British naval prestige. Under SACEUR are four main area commands: Allied Forces, North (Oslo); Allied Forces, Centre (Brunsum, in Holland); Allied Forces, South (Naples); and Allied Forces, Mediterranean (Naples).

Because of the need for quick advice and constant surveillance, NATO air defences operate on an integrated basis even in peacetime. Otherwise, with few exceptions, the NATO command controls no forces in peacetime. Instead, forces are either 'assigned' to NATO – that is, they would definitely be placed under NATO command in war – or 'earmarked' for NATO – that is, they would probably be put under NATO command. Other national forces remain purely national. Because West Germany wanted to avoid the appearance of establishing a national military staff structure, all her forces are assigned.

Two other points are worth noting. In recent years with the exception of Iceland and Portugal, the European members of NATO have begun to operate together on certain issues. As such they are known as the 'Eurogroup'. Secondly, with the exception of the British (and French) nuclear forces, all the nuclear weapons in the alliance come under an American national chain of command.

The organization of the Warsaw Pact bears superficial similarities to that of NATO but the reality is far different, because the Soviet Union totally dominates the alliance and uses it as an adjunct to Russian national military institutions. For reasons of secrecy, even the formal structure of the Pact is obscure, not to speak of the actual day-to-day pattern of operations. Basically, the Warsaw Pact serves as a vehicle for Soviet diplomacy and as a framework and pretext for Soviet domination of Eastern European defence establishments. At times this dominance has been almost ostentatiously overt, such as the occasion when the Russian Marshal Rokossovsky was made Polish Chief of Staff.

The Pact has a Political Consultative Committee with a secretariat under a Russian Deputy Foreign Minister as Secretary General. There is also a Soviet High Command which, like the PCC, is in Moscow. This command is overwhelmingly Soviet and is run very much as a Soviet Military District. The

Soviet Units = 2/3 manpower of NATO units

In general the individual formations of the Warsaw Pact armies are smaller than those of NATO. Here the typical strengths of various West German formations are compared with those of the Soviet Union

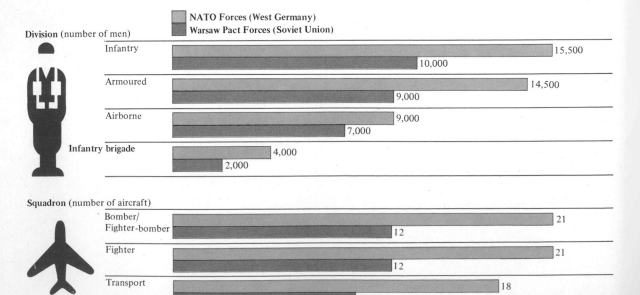

NATO Forces (West Germany)
Warsaw Pact Forces (Soviet Union)

Division (number of men)

Infantry   15,500 / 10,000

Armoured   14,500 / 9,000

Airborne   9,000 / 7,000

Infantry brigade   4,000 / 2,000

Squadron (number of aircraft)

Bomber/ Fighter-bomber   21 / 12

Fighter   21 / 12

Transport   18 / 10

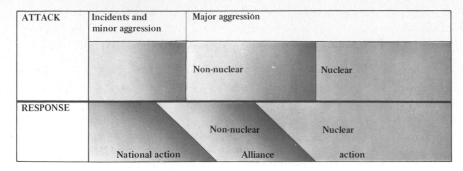

ATTACK	Incidents and minor aggression	Major aggression	
		Non-nuclear	Nuclear
RESPONSE		Non-nuclear	Nuclear
	National action	Alliance	action

This diagram illustrates the NATO strategic concept of flexible response. It shows the progression from national to Allied and finally nuclear response according to the scale and intensity of the attack and demonstrates NATO dependence on the first use of tactical nuclear weapons.

Commander-in-Chief is a Russian, as is the Chief of Staff. Since 1969, however, Eastern European officers have also been assigned to the command. The Russian Chief of Staff of the Pact is chairman of a Military Committee, founded in 1969, and controls a main staff. Soviet forces in Eastern Europe are divided into four groups: the Group of Soviet Forces in Germany, the Northern Group (Poland), the Central (Czechoslovakia) and the Southern (Hungary). The most important satellite armies, and those which get the best Russian equipment, are the Polish, the East German and the Czech. These forces are of debatable political reliability. Since 1969 the Soviet Union has made efforts to build East European forces into its order of battle. Thus, selected East European units are part of the Russian battle plan, but these units are those chosen by the Soviet Union, not a spontaneous national contribution to the alliance. Ever since Marshal Grechko became Commander-in-Chief in 1961, the Pact has put particular stress on elaborate joint exercises and manœuvres.

Aims and Strategies of the Blocs

NATO was founded to erect a deterrent against Soviet aggression. The very success of the alliance in erecting a framework of military strength in Western Europe has tempered the original fear, and the members of NATO now believe that open military aggression is very unlikely so long as a reasonable balance of power is maintained. The present purposes of NATO might therefore be described as: keeping up sufficient military strength, fundamentally supported by American nuclear power, to prevent military aggression from becoming an attractive option to the Soviet Union; avoiding a situation of weakness within which Soviet political pressures would become overwhelming; guarding against the possibility of limited acts of aggression; and providing for the containment and safe management of any crises that may erupt, perhaps unintentionally, on the East–West borderline. Since the so-called Harmel Report of 1967, it has been the official policy of the alliance to regard the maintenance of deterrence and the negotiation of *détente* as parallel and compatible policies.

The Warsaw Pact is allegedly intended to erect a defence against Western aggression, very probably incited by West German 'revanchism'. There is doubtless an element of genuine fear in this policy and it must be noted that one of the functions of NATO also is to contain German power safely. Whether Soviet purposes are aggressive or defensive, there can be no doubt that the Pact serves primarily to facilitate Soviet dominance over Eastern Europe. This dominance is necessary on political and ideological grounds but it is above all a military consideration, for Eastern Europe provides the Soviet Union with a defensive buffer against the West. Access to Eastern Europe during peacetime, through the Pact, enables the Soviet Union to deploy the Red Army for an offensive into the West. Thus the Red Army divisions in Eastern Europe serve a dual and closely interlocked purpose: they are deployed for war to the West and they guarantee the Russian hegemony over the Eastern European countries that makes that deployment possible. The Hungarian and Czechoslovakian invasions, together with several other smaller operations, testify to Soviet willingness to undertake limited wars to preserve this situation.

There are several conceivable ways in which war might occur in Europe. Since the fear of wilful, all-out Soviet aggression subsided, there have been fears of limited 'grabs', moves to seize such areas as Hamburg or Bornholm, creating a *fait accompli* which it would be difficult for NATO to handle and which would shatter the cohesion of the alliance. Such moves would, however, involve great risks of escalation and it is not easy to conceive of purposes that would seem worth the gamble. Thus, most analysts now believe that, if aggression took place on the central front, it would most likely take the form of pre-emptive action in some acute crisis. That action would probably constitute a full-scale attack. On the other hand, more limited actions are conceivable on the flanks of NATO, where the military situation is difficult for the West and where the stakes for the West might seem smaller. In the north, action against Norway is rendered less likely by the very stable political situation which offers few opportunities to create pretexts for action. In the south, the situation is very different, as there are acute political problems on both sides of the line and the area is closely entwined with the turbulent Middle East. The Rumanian–Russian tension, the unstable nationalities question in Yugoslavia, Albania, the Greek, Italian and Turkish political situations, the Greek–Turkish dispute over Cyprus, all offer possibilities for crises that might erupt quite unsought by either bloc. Finally we cannot altogether forget Berlin, despite the recent amelioration of day-to-day arrangements and the mutual understanding that any trouble over the city could quickly take on ominous proportions.

Soviet strategic intentions if war should come can only be surmised from Russian military writings. On the flanks, the Russians can envisage limited war confined to conventional weapons. On the central front they seem to believe war would probably be nuclear from the start. Where war 'in the main direction' is concerned, an official Soviet military writer suggests, 'one must regard the conduct of military operations with nuclear weapons as being the basic version'. It is consonant with this that, given their proclivity for artillery, the Red Army in Europe is relatively lightly provided with tube artillery and heavily endowed with missiles. The lavish provision of tanks and APCs fits this picture and indicates a mobile, offensive plan. If war occurred, the Russians would probably launch mass nuclear strikes up to 500 miles in depth, probably accompanied by chemical attacks where these offered surprise or served to protect their own forward elements. The Russians envisage battle by day and night, advancing seventy miles a day with mobile columns, open flanks and rapid river crossings. Airborne troops might be dropped 250 miles beyond the start line.

The NATO reply to this, as we have seen, would be the 'flexible response'. Under the strategy set in 1957 no conventional war with the Soviet Union was provided for, at least on the central front. In 1962 the so-called Athens Guidelines began the process of moderating the recourse to nuclear weapons and, in 1967, after the departure of France, new guidelines for the flexible response were adopted. Now the alliance will try to contain aggression conventionally (unless it is itself already nuclear). Should the initial resistance fail, tactical nuclear weapons would be used in defensive operations also intended to have a warning and deterrent effect. The sequence of response to acts of aggression

Opposite West German troops using a hand-flame cartridge in simulated attack on enemy armour.

therefore becomes: national action; direct defence by the alliance; deliberate escalation; general nuclear war. Some forms of escalation need not be nuclear; they might, for instance, involve war at sea or action on other fronts. Nuclear responses might be defensive use of demolition weapons, selective strikes on targets at the front or as interdiction, and other demonstrative uses. None of this doctrine for flexible response would be of much interest if, as seems likely, the Russian attack was nuclear from the start, although NATO would face a difficult situation if, by refraining from using strategic weapons, the Soviet Union exploited the divergence of interest between the United States and its European allies as to when to escalate beyond the battlefield. If the Russian attack were

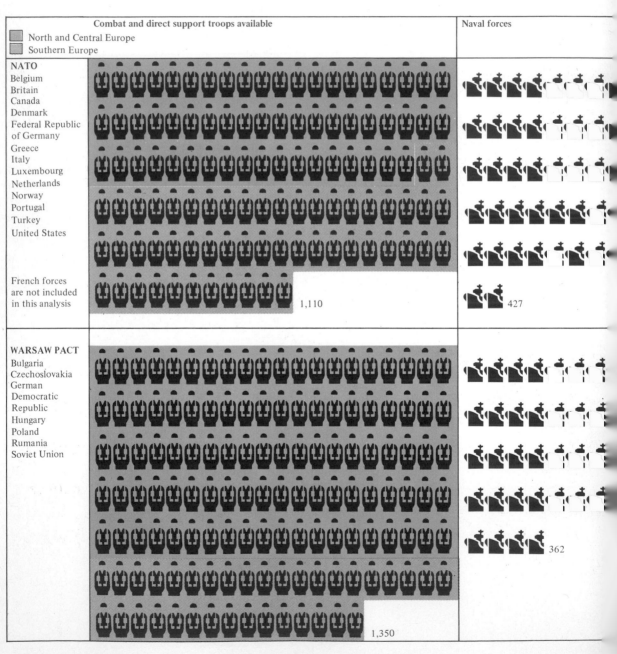

Combat and direct support troops available	Naval forces
☐ North and Central Europe	
☐ Southern Europe	

NATO
Belgium
Britain
Canada
Denmark
Federal Republic
of Germany
Greece
Italy
Luxembourg
Netherlands
Norway
Portugal
Turkey
United States

French forces
are not included
in this analysis   1,110   427

WARSAW PACT
Bulgaria
Czechoslovakia
German
Democratic
Republic
Hungary
Poland
Rumania
Soviet Union   362   1,350

conventional, the criterion for NATO escalation would be the progress of the battle and, in particular, whether the 'integrity' of a member of the alliance was threatened.

In 1969 NATO agreed rules for the use of ADMs and initial employment of tactical nuclear weapons. As we have seen earlier, there is little clarity as to precisely how to handle the next stage. This uncertainty reflects the divergence of interest between the European allies and the United States. The present ambiguity as to how much tactical nuclear action would be tolerable before escalation to strategic weapons, serves to assure the United States (which actually controls most of the weapons) that tactical use offers a real alternative

A comparison of the strength of NATO and the Warsaw Pact in the northern, central and southern theatres.

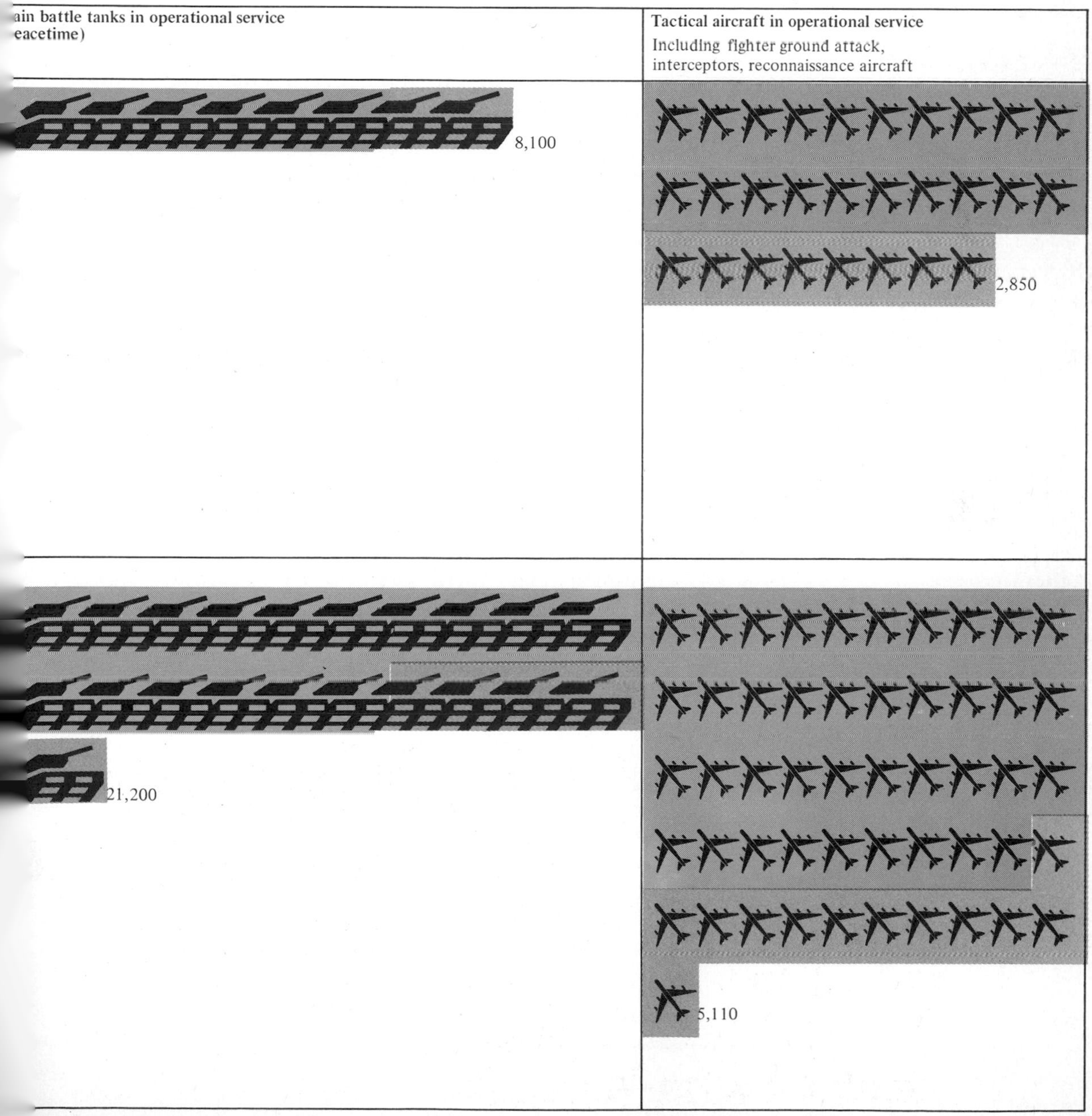

Main battle tanks in operational service (peacetime)

8,100

21,200

Tactical aircraft in operational service

Including fighter ground attack, interceptors, reconnaissance aircraft

2,850

5,110

to general war, and to persuade the Europeans that the situation is sufficiently dangerous and escalatory to deter the Soviet Union.

The Balance of Forces

The degree to which NATO would be forced to escalate depends on the balance of forces. This must be evaluated in the light of a new situation of rough strategic parity between the Superpowers. Estimating the balance of strength in the European theatre presents almost insurmountable problems of analysis. The task is much more difficult than at the strategic level because of the wide range of weapons involved, and the complicated effect of circumstances, terrain, weather and a myriad other variables.

If one considers the global strength of the two blocs, the balance appears not unfavourable to the West. The members of NATO (including France) have nearly $3\frac{1}{2}$ million men in their ground forces, while the Warsaw Pact have rather less than 3 million. The Soviet armed forces have remained fairly constant in size in recent years, with moderate improvement to land and air equipment and a much more marked naval development. There has been an eastward shift in the Soviet centre of gravity, with the number of Soviet divisions in the Far East rising from fifteen in 1968 to forty-four in 1972. This shift has taken place at the expense not of forces in the European theatre but of units and reserves in the Russian interior. There have been many indications that the Soviet Union feels the burden of military effort on its budget and its resources of skilled manpower, and this was underlined at the 24th Party Congress in 1971. It has not, however, led to any striking reallocations in the 1972–7 Plan and Russia will not suffer any severe general demographic pressures on manpower of military age during the seventies.

In the European theatre the overall picture is of superiority for the Warsaw Pact and Soviet Union, but this impression needs several qualifications. The northern and central fronts are best considered as a whole; the south can be treated separately. At present strengths, on the day when mobilization began (M-Day), NATO would have eight armoured and sixteen infantry divisions, as compared to twenty-eight armoured and thirty-seven infantry Warsaw Pact divisions. Nineteen of the armoured and twenty-two of the infantry divisions would be Soviet. These figures include the NATO divisions on the Continent and the Warsaw Pact divisions in Europe and those deployed and ready in the Western Soviet Union. To the NATO side one could probably add six French divisions (two armoured), but SACEUR cannot count on them in his plans.

The nominal balance of hardware also favours the Warsaw Pact. To NATO's 6000 main battle tanks, the Pact can muster 16,000 of which 10,000 are Russian. In tactical aircraft NATO has rather less than 2000 to the Pact's 3900. Of these 2400 are Russian.

In the south, counting forces committed to the Mediterranean area on both sides (with a low estimate of the forces in Southern Russia that would be so committed), the balance is thirty-seven NATO divisions to thirty Pact, of which six are Russian. The balance of tanks is 2100 NATO to 5000 Pact, and of aircraft 950 NATO to 1180 Pact. These figures exaggerate NATO effective strength however, as they include Italian forces, which are far removed from the likely battlefields in Southern Europe.

The relative strength in tactical nuclear weapons is over 7000 for NATO (not counting any British or French national capability), and 3500 for the Pact. These figures are believed to number warheads, not all of which will have a separate delivery system. The stockpiles are so large, however, that all that need be deduced is that neither side is likely to be constrained by a shortage of nuclear weapons, though it is possible that not all the types of weapon in the arsenals would prove convenient for particular tactical needs.

These crude figures of forces available on M-Day suggest a considerable advantage for the Warsaw Pact. There are two major qualifications to be entered: one concerning the quality of forces; the other the rate of mobilization and reinforcement.

In the early weeks of a crisis or war, mobilization and reinforcement would overwhelmingly favour the Warsaw Pact. This is the result of the much more favourable geographical position of the Pact's major ally, Russia, than of the

Czechoslovak and Russian troops fraternize during a joint exercise. Russia maintains more than 31 divisions in the territories of her Warsaw Pact partners.

United States. It is also the result of the Pact and particularly the Soviet Union maintaining larger forces in relatively ready reserve. Thus it is believed that within a month the Soviet Union could raise the thirty-one Russian divisions in Eastern Europe to seventy. In the same period the United States could bring across the Atlantic two brigades which are 'dual based'. It would also try to transfer two divisions for which equipment is stored in Europe, but it is not clear whether, even with improved air and sea lift, this operation could be completed in the time. In all cases the Soviet Union enjoys an advantage in the movement of heavy equipment, though the build-up envisaged would severely tax the road and rail facilities of Eastern Europe. Estimates for both East and West would, of course, have to be heavily revised if one assumes that hostilities have already begun. NATO would probably suffer the most, as airfields are very likely to be destroyed.

Estimates of reinforcement are very open to argument, but the inescapable conclusion is that for many weeks the NATO position would worsen. Over a period of months, NATO might regain lost ground from its large global potential. NATO relies upon a certain amount of 'political warning', but it is by no means certain that the coalition would make prompt use of this to begin mobilization, which might be regarded in some quarters as escalatory. While the long-term balance of strength is more encouraging, it seems likely that really serious crises would be decided in a few weeks. Certainly if war began, few NATO commanders believe the M-Day forces or those available in the next few weeks could resist long enough to make the more remote military resources relevant to the battle. NATO's disadvantage reaches a peak about five to six weeks after mobilization has begun. Efforts have been made, as in the following table, to establish the effect of mobilization on indices of relative strength.

	M-Day (without France)	M+30 (with France)
	NATO : WP	NATO : WP
Ground force men	1 : 1·6	1 : 2·1
Divisions	1 : 2·9	1 : 3·4
Tanks	1 : 2·5	1 : 2·9
Tac. Aircraft	1 : 1·8	1 : 2·0

Adjusting the figures to take account of quality is an even more difficult exercise. The chief talking point is the greater size of Western divisions. An American division has 16,000 men; a Soviet division has 10,500. Other NATO divisions are also several thousand men stronger than the Pact variety. The difference is accounted for in part by a different conception of a division. Soviet divisions are expected to fight in the line and be retired when exhausted. The Western division contains support forces that are intended to enable it to remain in the line for prolonged periods. Thus in one sense the reserve Pact divisions equate to the 'tail' of the Western divisions and to the high proportion of non-divisional formations in the total Western force. But one cannot simply deflate the crude number of Soviet divisions to arrive at a balance, because all the Soviet divisions have a high proportion of teeth. Thus the armoured Russian division has 330 tanks as compared to 364 in an American equivalent. In main battle tanks the proportion is an even closer 310:324. The majority of Western tanks are perhaps superior but the introduction of the Russian T62 is redressing the balance. There are other respects in which the Western divisions are more heavily equipped but it will be seen from the accompanying table that the Soviet division certainly cannot be written off as so markedly inferior as to compensate for the asymmetry in overall number of divisions on each side.

Similar calculations can be made about aircraft. In gross numbers, the balance of forces in the European area heavily favours the Pact. However, the Pact's apparent superiority is made up by a high proportion of interceptors. Optimists on the Western side point to the higher average performance of Western aircraft in range, payload, and loiter time, and to the supposedly higher standards of crew training. In his 1968 annual statement the American Secretary of Defense, Robert McNamara, set out these advantages in tabular form:

Characteristics of Air Forces – all regions

Primary Missions	NATO	WP
	%	%
Interceptors (high speed, low payload)	9	34
Multipurpose (high, high)	31	8
Attack (low, high)	24	20
Reconnaissance	7	2
Low Performance (low, low)	29	36
Payload index	100	35
Loiter time index	100	20–40
Crew training index	100	55

The significance of these figures, which change rapidly with re-equipment, depends on many external considerations. As we saw earlier, an inferior aircraft may be as useful as a superior if it is just good enough to perform its mission. The balance of interceptors to high-performance offensive aircraft must be related to the West's need to carry out interdiction to offset the Pact's advantage in reinforcement. It must also be related to the Pact's heavy inventory of anti-aircraft missiles and to its superiority in available airfields. On balance, NATO's air situation is probably better than that on the ground, but is still inferior. Moreover, many experts believe the air battle will be the decisive one.

Any evaluation of the balance should also take account of the advantage which the Pact's standardization on Russian equipment may give it in terms of logistics and operating flexibility over NATO with its variegated inventories. The Soviet Union itself also makes up a much higher proportion of Pact strength than does the United States within NATO. Moreover, as a result of national preferences and the historical legacy of the occupation period, the American troops may not be deployed to the best advantage in the relatively rugged terrain of Southern Germany. NATO supply lines are also defective in some respects and suffer a major handicap in the denial of French territory.

The military balance on the central front thus favours the Warsaw Pact. For the moment, however, NATO is sufficiently strong to deny the Pact a walkover and, under normal political circumstances, this is enough to make aggression unlikely. The questionable allegiance of the East Europeans offers the Soviet Union another inducement to caution, although, as we have seen, unrest in the satellites can also precipitate Soviet military action.

NATO faces special problems on its flanks. The central front makes up only some 600 miles of a total NATO land frontier of over 5000. In the north, NATO is very weak, partly as a result of Norwegian refusal to have foreign troops or nuclear weapons on its soil in peacetime. In Northern Norway about four Soviet

divisions face one Norwegian brigade. In Exercise *Sever*, in 1968, the Soviet Union practised moving forces right up to the frontier and associated amphibious operations. The military situation is therefore poor from NATO's point of view. On the other hand the political situation is very stable and is unlikely to offer any pretexts for limited aggression.

The situation is very different in the south where political affairs are very volatile. There are uneasy political situations in Greece, Turkey and Italy. The position of Yugoslavia and Albania is ambiguous and there are severe nationality problems within the former. Two members of NATO, Greece and Turkey, are at loggerheads over Cyprus and the whole region is close to the turbulent Middle East. The possibility of escalation from spontaneous local events is therefore higher than elsewhere on NATO's frontier.

With minor exceptions the southern frontiers of NATO are manned by national and not multi-national forces. In an effort to offset this weakness in its deterrent posture, which applies in the north also, NATO has set up a multilateral Allied Mobile Force (AMF) of eight battalions and five air squadrons which could be quickly moved into a threatened area. Its purpose is to act as a deterrent in crisis, emphasizing the involvement of all the allies in the problems of the flank nations, rather than to exert a great influence on the battle. In several areas, particularly in Thrace, the tactical situation is, indeed, fairly hopeless if the Soviet Union does decide to launch a serious attack. Some added deterrence is offered by the US Sixth Fleet, with its nuclear capability, and by the small British nuclear strike force based in Cyprus. The latter force is, however, chiefly designated for CENTO.

As the Sixth Fleet reminds us, the flanks are directly affected by the naval balance. This is even more difficult than the land balance to estimate because of the extreme mobility of naval forces. The growth, modernization and increasingly forward deployment of the Russian fleet has been much publicized. Though formidable, the actual increase in Soviet naval strength has been less than some of these accounts would suggest. Russian defensive requirements would be demanding in a full-scale war, leaving less for offensive operations. Russia still faces great difficulties, because geography divides her fleet areas. Strong emphasis has been placed on the northern area where deployment has been brought increasingly forward to cover the Iceland–Faeroes–Norway zone. This fleet is presumably intended to cover operations in northern Europe, to deal with the American carriers and any efforts to reinforce NATO's northern flank by sea, to deal so far as possible with NATO SSBNs, and to secure egress for the Soviet equivalents. In peacetime, the fleet serves to put political pressure on Scandinavia. The great weakness of the fleet is its dependence on a single main base at Murmansk and its relative lack of forward aircover. It is possible that these problems might recommend pre-emptive strategies should war seem near.

In the Mediterranean, the Soviet naval squadron serves a similar combination of defensive purposes in war and political influence in peace. The Soviet squadron is exceedingly inferior to Western forces and would certainly be easily defeated in a conventional war, the more so because of its difficult supply situation. In a nuclear war it might be able to inflict some substantial damage on Western forces before itself succumbing. The balance must be read in connection with the effect of land-based airpower. It must also be recognized that, whatever the course of the naval battle, Thrace and the Turkish Straits would probably quickly fall to Soviet land power in conventional war or if coherent military operations continued under nuclear conditions.

Opposite A Norwegian tank, part of the Allied Mobile Force on manoeuvres in the far north of the country.

In an effort to offset some of the effects of Soviet naval activity, NATO has taken several modest actions. In the Atlantic a Standing Naval Force, Atlantic (STANAVFORLANT) has been established. This force consists of some half-dozen destroyer-type vessels allocated by several nations to constitute a force under SACLANT's peacetime operational control. It is seen both as a symbol of solidarity and a test-bed for joint operations. Efforts to create an 'on call' force in the Mediterranean have proved much more difficult because of the political divisions among the allies. However, a special maritime reconnaissance command has been established in the Mediterranean (MARAIRMED) and this enjoys French co-operation.

Future Force Levels

Two factors suggest that the present balance will change and quite probably to NATO's disadvantage. One is the pressure within the members of NATO to reduce military demands on money and manpower. The other is the call to negotiate agreed reductions with the Warsaw Pact as part of the policy of *détente*. The notion of mutual balanced force reductions (MBFR) was introduced by NATO in 1968 in response to Warsaw Pact proposals for a European Security Conference. At first MBFR was ignored by the East, but in 1970 the Pact accepted the idea of discussing reductions in foreign ('stationed') troop levels and in 1971 the idea of reductions in general.

The pressure to reduce forces is general on the Western side but is rendered most serious by American desires to withdraw part of their expeditionary force. There has grown up in the United States a strong feeling that after over twenty years it is time a sub-continent as rich and populous as Western Europe did more for its own security. This feeling has been focused in the Mansfield Resolution in the Senate urging a drastic cut in American forces in Europe. There have already been considerable reductions over the years: from 430,000 in 1962 to 300,000 in 1972. Two quite distinct but frequently confused issues underlie American sentiment: one is the question of equitable 'burden

American and British
marines landing in Turkey
during an exercise designed
to test NATO's ability to
reinforce its southern flank.

sharing'; the other is the effect of overseas garrisons on the balance of payments.

It is very hard to ascertain what the budgetary cost of American contributions to NATO is. The forces in Europe themselves cost some $3 billion. But if one counts the proportion of total American forces chiefly intended for operations in Europe, the cost rises to at least $11 billion and in some estimates to over $23 billion. An official calculation in 1969 put the overall expenditure at $14 billion, this figure covering direct costs of troops in Europe, the cost of indirect support provided for those troops in the United States, the cost of other forces earmarked for Europe, and the cost of both the Sixth and Second (Western Atlantic) Fleets.

The higher estimates are almost certainly deceptive, for they imply that in the absence of the NATO commitment the United States would make much more drastic reductions in its military strength than is at all plausible. In other words, many of the forces in question are actually provided against a variety of contingencies of which NATO is only the most important.

American expenditure must be compared to that of the European allies if the question is one of equitable burden sharing. European members of NATO have military expenditures of about $26 billion which compares quite well with the American contribution. Calculated as a proportion of Gross National Product (GNP) the picture is less favourable to the Europeans: 1972 American military expenditure is about 7.8 per cent of GNP; European percentages range from just under 5 per cent to something under 3 per cent. On the other hand, American GNP is 50 per cent larger than that of the Europeans combined. Moreover, the figures are only a rough guide to actual economic sacrifice. A large proportion of expenditure is for manpower and here high American costs simply reflect high American wages. In estimating the effect of reductions on the American budget it must be realized that unless units brought home from Europe were disbanded the effective cost would rise rather than fall, as the provision of new accommodation would be expensive.

The balance of payments raises different issues. In gross terms the exchange

cost of American forces in Europe is about $1·9 billion a year, of which $1·7 billion is in the prosperous Western European countries. This expenditure is offset by European purchases of American military equipment, chiefly by Germany and to a lesser extent, Britain. The net American expenditure is thereby reduced to about $1·3 billion. West Germany also makes special purchases of US bonds which, while not constituting a real offset, postpone the impact on the US balance of payments. In the 1972–3 offset agreements Germany has broken new ground by making direct contributions to such American expenditures as provision and maintenance of barracks. Similar, smaller arrangements are made with Britain. The residual impact on the American balance of payments is not large when measured against the overall deficit, but the issue has strong political force, especially when some of the European countries oppose American policy with regard to international monetary affairs. As a result, several schemes have been put forward for a common fund that would handle exchange consequences of foreign stationing on a multilateral basis. Also, in an effort to defuse both the burden sharing and the exchange issues, the European members of NATO have been making conspicuous efforts to increase their military effort. In 1970 they announced a European Defence Improvement Programme involving added expenditure of $1 billion over five years, devoted chiefly to infrastructure works such as aircraft shelters. Similarly in 1971 the Eurogroup claimed to have added another $1 billion (at current prices) to their five-year costs.

MBFR is related to the pressures for unilateral reduction of Western forces in two ways. If unilateral cuts are politically unavoidable, it would obviously be wise to try to secure parallel reductions by the Pact. The possibility of a spontaneous erosion of Western strength may, however, undermine any Soviet incentive to offer any concessions on a mutual basis. Consequently the prospect of MBFR has been used within NATO as an argument against troop reductions, particularly American withdrawals, in order to preserve bargaining leverage with the Pact.

MBFR has distant antecedents in earlier proposals for 'disengagement' in Europe. It also constitutes a complement to SALT, as the forward-based nuclear systems that the Soviet Union would like to include in the strategic calculations (because they can hit the Soviet Union) are in Western eyes part of the European tactical balance. Working out a basis for 'parity' in MBFR is infinitely more complicated than striking a strategic balance because of the vast variety of weapons and the elusive relevance of such factors as terrain, morale, training and political circumstance. Western incentives to cut costs have already been

Ships of the United States, British, Italian, Portuguese, and West German navies lying in Phaleron Bay, Athens, during a joint exercise.

mentioned. Russia also faces economic pressures. However, she has a military tradition of seeking security in preponderance of numbers and her forces in Europe serve not only to balance NATO but also to discipline her satellites.

The Rome meeting of the North Atlantic Council in 1970 set out criteria for MBFR that are unobjectionable but also unrealistic. Amongst the principles was the prescription that reductions 'should be compatible with the vital security interests of the alliance and should not operate to the military disadvantage of either side having regard for the differences arising from geographical and other considerations'. Quite apart from the technical difficulties of deciding what constitutes a balance, the major obstacle is the existing inferiority of NATO and the inadequacy of its forces in many respects when measured against such rigid criteria as space and distance as well as against the level of Warsaw Pact forces. Moreover, whatever may be said, it will in practice be almost impossible to nullify the Soviet advantage of contiguity to central Europe if the reductions entail the withdrawal of American forces. A further difficulty is presented by the danger that any weakening of NATO's capacity for conventional resistance would, under present doctrine, accelerate the use of nuclear weapons; precisely what the flexible response tries to avert.

The only solution would be for the Soviet Union to make disproportionate cuts. At one time there was talk of equal cuts in absolute terms; clearly that would quickly render NATO's position untenable. Even equal percentages would have disproportionate effects on the weaker side. But the chances of securing unequal percentages across the board seem slim. An alternative is sometimes seen in asymmetric reductions in different armaments, each side cutting what it can most readily spare. The attraction for NATO here is to reduce the number of Soviet tanks. Unfortunately, there are few categories in which anyone believes NATO has a surplus, except perhaps the tricky case of tactical nuclear weapons.

Given all the difficulties it may be that, if there is to be progress in MBFR, it will come in rather crude agreements to make modest reductions in manpower, leaving it to each side to make what best it chooses of what is left. Many difficult problems would remain, not least of verification and, perhaps more important, what to do if violations of the understanding were detected.

Israeli troops during a
night action in the Six
Day War.

CHAPTER NINE

The Middle East

The military situation in the Middle East derives its explosive and dangerous character from the combination of acute local conflicts with a major confrontation of the Superpowers. There are several overlapping hostile relationships: the dispute between Israel and the Arab states, complicated by the separate identity of the Palestinians; the Superpower confrontation, which involves the southern flank of the European alliances, the support of local client states and an overall competition for prestige; a series of fluctuating disputes between the Arab states themselves, arising in part from the process of social revolution; a variety of insurgent movements with national or social revolutionary roots; and a related but distinguishable contest for superiority in the Persian Gulf. This last contest is merely the latest phase in the process of British withdrawal that has provided the occasion for all the Middle Eastern conflicts.

Strategically the Middle East is of great but changing significance. It lies on the southern flank of Europe, constitutes a possible base for attack on the Soviet Union and offers the Russians one of their few means of access to the outside world. Traditionally it has been the European and particularly British route to India and East Asia. This is of less importance today, given the British withdrawal from Asia and the increased use of the Cape Route for shipping, although the complete closing of the Middle Eastern air barriers would inconvenience British support for their remaining commitments in South-East Asia and Hong Kong. As the Middle East has declined in significance as a strategic route for the Western Powers, it has gained interest for the Soviet Union, for which it would offer easier access to its growing involvement in India, East Africa and the Indian Ocean. It is for this reason that the reopening of the Suez Canal may be a much more serious objective for the Soviet Union than for the NATO powers.

Although this discussion is solely concerned with military questions, a word should be said about the importance of Middle Eastern oil. Western Europe and Japan are heavily dependent on this oil and American dependence, now small, may rapidly increase. While Russian military interference with the oil trade is unlikely, it is possible that a great deal of military manœuvre and diplomacy in the area may involve efforts either to promote or undermine political conditions within which the oil continues to be available to the Western Powers at economic prices.

Approximately 80 per cent of the oil internationally transferred outside the western hemisphere comes from the Middle East and North Africa, three-quarters of this amount from the Asian Middle East. The Middle East and North Africa combined, supply over 80 per cent of Western Europe's oil needs, 72 per cent of Australia's and 90 per cent of Japan's. This situation is likely to continue in the eighties, with a slight shift in Western European reliance to North African sources. The most striking development, however, is likely to be increasing American importation of oil because of rising demand and falling domestic reserves. Thus it is estimated that the United States will import between a third and a half of its oil consumption as compared with a mere 3 per cent today. About half of this is likely to come from the Middle East and North Africa. It is possible that by the mid-eighties the Soviet Union and Eastern Europe will also become net importers of oil, but that is not likely to occur until after American dependence is well established.

The Military Balance

The complex military balance in the Middle East can best be approached historically. Israel established itself in 1948 by securing a decisive and unexpected military victory over the disunited efforts of its Arab neighbours to eliminate it. Since that time there have been two further Arab–Israeli wars, in 1956 and 1967, in both of which Israel easily defeated the Arabs. In 1956 American and Russian intervention saved the Arabs from the full consequences of defeat, but in 1967 Israel gained at least temporary possession of much territory.

During this period important alterations took place in the external context of the local conflict. By the mid-fifties the British and French military presences had both disappeared. The last British troops left Egypt in 1956. At the same time Soviet influence began to penetrate the area. The three main principles of Soviet security policy – assuring the safety of the Soviet Union, pursuing traditional Russian state interests, and extending the sphere of Soviet communist ideology – all have obvious applications in the Middle East. Stalin's efforts to penetrate the area immediately after World War II failed. The breakthrough came in 1955 when the Soviet Union arranged, partly through Czechoslovakia, for the delivery of large arms shipments in return for the Egyptian cotton crop. This began the pattern of competitive arms deliveries that still characterizes the Middle East.

The rising confidence of the Arabs coupled with attacks on Israel by Arab guerrillas or fedayeen from the Gaza Strip and west bank of the Jordan stimulated Israeli reprisals. Egyptian efforts to close the Straits of Eilat finally precipitated the war of 1956, in which Israel attacked Egypt in collusion with Britain and France. These events produced the UN force to police the Egyptian side of the truce line. They also brought about the more intensive involvement of the United States.

In 1957 the so-called Eisenhower Doctrine promised American support to Middle Eastern states resisting Soviet pressure. The Sixth Fleet was strengthened and in 1957 and 1958 British and American forces intervened in Jordan and Lebanon. Soviet naval presence also began in 1958 with the establishment of a short-lived submarine base at Valona in Albania. In another important change, the United States, which had hitherto influenced the local arms race by helping Israel, and such friendly Arab states as Jordan, to buy Anglo–French arms, now became a direct supplier. By 1956 the United States was transferring such advanced weapons as the A4 to Israel and the F104 to Jordan. Russian weapons were also flowing freely to Egypt, Syria and Iraq. The arms race was in full swing; indeed between 1945 and 1969 Middle Eastern countries received more than $10 billion worth of arms, 70 per cent going to Israel and Egypt. Typically these supplies are mutually exclusive; that is to say, a heavy recipient of Soviet arms receives no Western arms and vice versa, though a mixed inventory will persist for a time after a switch of allegiance. Indeed, it may well be that very heavy Soviet deliveries in the late fifties were

partly intended to purge Western weapons – and consequent dependence on spares and training – from Soviet client states.

Also during the late fifties and early sixties, the level of guerrilla activity reached new heights. The Palestine National Liberation Movement, known as al Fatah, was founded in 1956, though it remained little known. In 1964 a Palestine Liberation Organization was set up with the blessing of Arab states to create a Palestinian 'entity'. This Organization established a Palestine National Council and founded a Palestine Liberation Army.

This brings us to the origins of the 1967 war and thus to the present juncture. The precise origins remain partly obscure. Vigorous guerrilla incursions into Israel had provoked even more vigorous reprisals. In the spring of 1967 the Egyptian Government seems to have received reports that Israel was about to launch a major attack on Syria. President Nasser evicted the UN force and mobilized. Israel's strategy was that of a first strike, for she believed that with her small territory, difficult air defence problem, and limited population she could not await attack or accept a prolonged war of attrition. She therefore launched her famous low-level bombing strikes which eliminated the Arab air forces and paved the way for decisive victory on the ground.

While Soviet policy prior to the war had clearly tried to keep up tension, it seems unlikely that the Soviet Union desired the war. It seems possible that the Russians overestimated their control over Nasser and the military capacity of the Arabs, while underestimating the pre-emptive abilities of Israel. In the war Russia took a lead in agreement with the United States over the hot line to remain aloof. Both Russian and American fleets stood off 300 miles. The Arab defeat dealt a triple blow to Russian prestige, for it suggested the inferiority of Russian allies, equipment and training. On the other hand, the cautious American policy indicated that the United States was now rather more inhibited in the Middle East than in the late fifties when the Soviet presence had not materialized.

Two Egyptian aircraft destroyed on the ground during the Israeli raids which shattered the Egyptian air force at the beginning of the Six Day War.

The Post-war Rearmament

The present military situation in the Middle East must be seen against the background of these events. Russia's immediate response to the 1967 defeat of the Arabs was a massive and instant rearmament. Some $500 million worth of arms were shipped to Egypt by the end of 1968. Lesser amounts went to Algeria, Iraq, Syria and the Sudan. The Egyptian shipments included SA2 SAMS and MiG 21C and D interceptors, all intended to preclude a repetition of Egypt's disastrous aerial defeat.

A second consequence of the war was a rapid escalation in guerrilla activity, made possible in part by the fact that the territories now occupied by Israel

Israeli schoolboys inspect a SAM2 anti-aircraft missile captured by their forces.

Nasser looks across the Suez Canal at his lost territories.

offered an area of sympathetic population as a base. The guerrilla movements grew and multiplied confusingly. In 1969 a Palestine Armed Struggle Command was formed to unify commando enterprises but some groups still remained aloof, particularly the Popular Front for the Liberation of Palestine (PFLP). Guerrilla and terrorist activity in Israel reached substantial proportions. Over three hundred Israeli civilians and soldiers were killed in the four years following June 1967. Israel mounted a vigorous counter-campaign within Israel and the occupied territories and continued its policy of reprisals against the Arab countries, chiefly Syria and Jordan, from which the guerrillas operated.

Also during this period, sporadic fighting and artillery bombardments continued on the Canal line where Israel now occupied the east bank. The final ingredient in the present balance was created when, in 1969, the Israeli air force launched heavy attacks on Egyptian air defences west of the canal. This policy was intended to keep the area west of the canal open to Israeli air attack and thereby create a situation in which Israel could contain Egyptian forces along the canal without maintaining a high level of mobilization, which would be crippling to such a small state. Over 8000 tons of bombs were used in this campaign. The Russian SA2 missiles proved wholly ineffective against Israeli tactics and over 150 Egyptian pilots were shot down. The MiG 21C and D proved no match for the Israelis when in Egyptian hands.

Encouraged by this success the Israelis began deep penetration bombing near Cairo, using the F4 Phantoms they had now received from the United States. This posed a crucial challenge to Nasser who, in January 1970, demanded more Russian help. The strong Russian response transformed the strategic situation in the Middle East.

Soviet arms aid was again accelerated. Some $2500 million worth of military equipment was sent to Egypt in a year. This equipment included improved SA2s and a new SA3 missile specially designed to counter low-level attack. A four-barrelled 23-mm anti-aircraft gun was also sent. Much more important, however, was the Russian decision to send Russian troops to man the missiles and Russian pilots to fly the interceptors, which now included the superior MiG 21J. Up to 15,000 Russian military personnel were introduced. On 17 to 18 April 1970 Israeli pilots first encountered and discreetly withdrew from Russian air cover over Cairo.

At first the air defence missiles were set up to cover Cairo and Alexandria. There then began a creep of the missile sites toward the Canal. Israel tried to eliminate the sites by bombing and on occasion challenged Soviet pilots, near the Canal, shooting down several. However, Israel was also losing aircraft and had to reckon with the immense reserves of the Soviet Union should a war of attrition begin. Partly for this reason, a ceasefire was accepted on 1 August 1970, along with a so-called standstill in the area thirty-two miles on each side of the Canal. Despite this, the Russian missiles were pushed forward until some 40–50 sites comprising 500–600 missiles were close to the Canal. Half were SA3s and a third were within nineteen miles of the Canal. Roughly speaking, this system was effective for about ten miles on the Israeli side of the Canal. In response, the United States agreed to transfer another eighteen F4s to Israel and provided her with ECM equipment to neutralize the SAMs. Until this new balance of technology was tested it was impossible to determine exactly how the advantage had shifted. The short-term practical result, however, was certainly to increase Egyptian security.

The ceasefire presumably played a part in the domestic fate of the guerrillas. Israel had continued its actions against the guerrillas and their bases. The guerrillas had come into increasing conflict with the government of Jordan, one of their main hosts. After the sensational hijacking of four airliners by the PFLP in September 1970, war broke out between the guerrillas and the Jordanian army, with the former being heavily defeated after an incipient Syrian invasion of Jordan had been repelled. Renewed fighting and a further defeat for the guerrillas occurred in April 1971. The result was to greatly diminish the effectiveness of the guerrillas. There were signs that the Soviet Union and the Arab states were alarmed at the failure of the guerrillas to co-ordinate their activities with the policies of the states, and the sources of guerrilla funds became less generous. Within the Israeli-governed territories guerrilla activity fell sharply. Bombardments across the frontiers fell from a monthly average of 320 in early 1970 to less than forty in early 1971. Similarly, terrorist activity within Israeli-controlled territory fell in the same period from some fifty incidents a month to a sporadic few.

The Present Balance

The inventory of Israeli arms is formidable and it is coupled with a remarkable record of practical success. Unlike the other Middle Eastern countries Israel has a substantial indigenous capacity, carefully fostered, to manufacture its own weapons. Israel makes a light jet aircraft under licence and has comprehensive facilities for maintaining jet aircraft. Israeli designers are said to have contributed a great deal to the evolution of the Mirage V, a simplified version of the Mirage III, but this aircraft was never delivered as a result of French policy after the 1967 war.

Israel has shown great ingenuity in adapting imported equipment to Middle Eastern conditions and in standardizing for easy maintenance a heterogeneous collection of weapons. She is still dependent on imports for the more sophisticated weapons and this poses a problem inasmuch as she cannot lightly contemplate action that would entail substantial losses unless she has some assurance about resupply. The vigorous Israeli efforts to become more and more self-sufficient are a response to this weakness.

A much mooted question is whether Israel has or will acquire nuclear weapons. Her best known nuclear reactor at Dimona produces enough plutonium for about two bombs a year. As the reactor began production in 1964, Israel could have enough plutonium for about a dozen bombs. Whether she has been separating the weapon-grade material is unknown. So far as delivery is concerned, Israel's F4 and A4 aircraft are designed for carrying nuclear weapons. Moreover, Israel has been developing, at times in co-operation with France, a rocket with a range of 300 miles and a payload of 1000 lb. Thus Israel certainly has a fairly close option on a nuclear system. So far she has shown no signs of taking the politically dangerous step of announcing a nuclear programme. Instead she has been content to use her known potential in bargaining for supplies of such weapons as the F4. So long as her conventional superiority remains as convincing as it has been in recent years, it seems probable that this near option is best calculated to serve Israeli interests.

The most important recent change in Israel's defensive position is the much more favourable strategic frontiers which she attained in the 1967 war. The Suez Canal, the Jordan and the Golan Heights in Syria – where Israeli forces are only some fifty level miles from Damascus – constitute probably the best natural defensive position that Israel could hope to enjoy. Egyptian aircraft are now at least some 150 miles from Israeli cities. This may enable Israel to modify its

The Arab–Israel theatre of war.

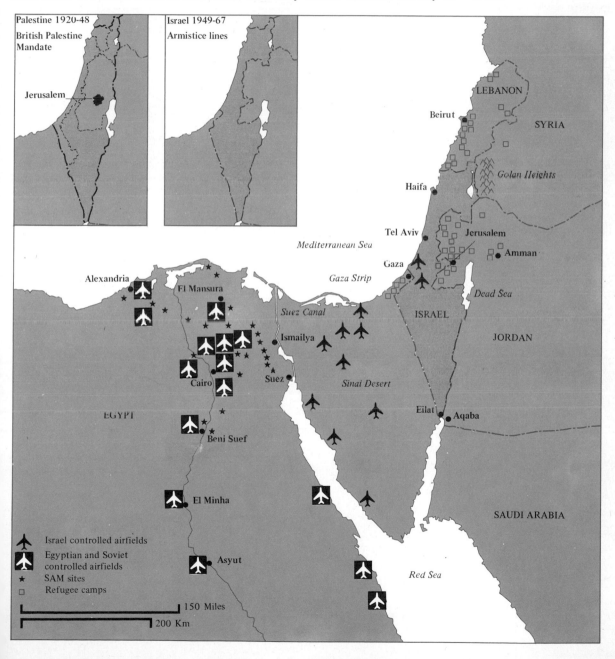

Palestine 1920-48
British Palestine Mandate
Jerusalem

Israel 1949-67
Armistice lines

LEBANON
Beirut
SYRIA
Golan Heights
Haifa
Mediterranean Sea
Tel Aviv
Jerusalem
Amman
Gaza
Gaza Strip
Dead Sea
ISRAEL
Alexandria
El Mansura
Suez Canal
JORDAN
Ismailya
Cairo
Suez
Sinai Desert
Eilat
Aqaba
EGYPT
Beni Suef
El Minha
SAUDI ARABIA
Asyut
Red Sea

Israel controlled airfields
Egyptian and Soviet controlled airfields
SAM sites
Refugee camps

150 Miles
200 Km

pre-emptive first-strike policy. The possibility of being a little less quick off the mark appears all the more valuable now that the Soviet presence in Egypt gives a new and dangerous dimension to an offensive strategy. Nevertheless the Israelis were careful to demonstrate that they were willing to bomb Soviet-manned sites and to engage Soviet aircraft at least near the Canal. Thus Israel preserves her chief military assets: tactical brilliance and a reputation for competent and ruthless execution.

On the Arab side the inventory of weapons is also impressive. Indeed, on paper it is if anything superior to Israel's. The chief Arab weaknesses are lower standards of training, leadership and morale. They also suffer from an appar-

Part of Israel's sophisticated modern armoury: an American-supplied CH53 helicopter and a M109 155-mm howitzer.

ently persistent lack of unity. Both Syria and Iraq are distracted by factional dissension, and Iraq contends with endemic Kurdish rebellion. Despite the commendable performance of the Jordanian army, Jordan's poverty, smallness and internal troubles ensure that she can never be more than an auxiliary factor. The main Arab element in the equation is therefore Egypt.

Unlike Israel, the UAR has no large pool of technical skills and no significant indigenous arms industry. She has not displayed any great ingenuity in adapting and modifying Russian arms to her own purposes. Nevertheless, her technical standards are said to be slowly improving at both the level of maintenance and operation. Her pilots fly the MiG 21 and some have even mastered the MiG 23. She has tried to preclude a repetition of 1967 by dispersing her aircraft and building shelters for them. The Egyptian air defence system, looked at from a purely material point of view, is probably the most sophisticated outside central Europe and, perhaps, North Viet Nam. Thus there have been improvements in the Egyptian situation and the long-term advantage of numbers is theirs. But in the perspective of the next few years the UAR will remain dependent on external sources of assistance if it wishes to sustain its side of the Arab–Israeli dispute and a claim to primacy among the Arabs. This is where the uneasy relationship with the Soviet Union is crucial. The Soviet–Egyptian Treaty of Friendship was a new departure in Soviet overseas commitments when signed in May, 1971. Subsequent Egyptian dissatisfaction with Soviet restrictiveness, however, suggests that the treaty was intended by the Russians as a substitute for rather than a promise of wholehearted support in achieving ultimate Egyptian purposes. Mutual irritation led to the expulsion of Soviet forces in mid-1972. By the end of the year, however, some of the forces had returned and Russians appeared to be manning some Egyptian defences again. It remained uncertain whether Egyptian and Soviet interests could be reconciled and whether this could be done without upsetting the wider balance in the Middle East.

The future of the guerrillas is obscure. They suffered a severe setback in their defeats at the hands of the Jordanian army. But this defeat may not be final. The Jordanian régime is isolated and can look only to Saudi Arabia and Kuwait for much sympathy. Should the regime fall, the situation would be transformed, perhaps by offering the guerrillas a secure base, perhaps by precipitating an Israeli occupation of Jordan. In 1970 the guerrillas set up a Unified Command, including the PFLP, but there is little sign that the divisions of the past have been healed. Nevertheless, if the existing stalemate continues between Israel and the Arab states, the occupied territories are likely to produce periodic revivals of insurgency. Meanwhile terrorist activities against Israel's interests around the world continue to present a global security problem.

The Superpowers

The two Superpowers are locked into the Middle East by their respective clients. So far as possible they have tried to avoid direct involvement and to contend by arming the local states. To some extent they have tried to exercise control by arming the locals along defensive lines, but this resolve has frequently broken down. There are important asymmetries in the Russian and American positions. The United States cannot afford to write off the goodwill of the Arabs as readily as the Soviet Union can align itself against Israel. Yet the United States is constrained to play a role in the Middle East by its political-ethnic ties with Israel, its concern for the Southern flank of NATO and for the Middle Eastern oil resources, and its general contention with the Soviet Union for primacy in the world. These American interests, however, especially in the present American national mood, do not inspire American Middle Eastern policy with a drive to match that of Russia. The Soviet Union has at last secured a fairly firm footing in an area of long traditional interest to her. From her present foothold in Egypt the Soviet Union could push influence westward along North Africa, outflanking NATO or southward toward the Persian Gulf, India and East Africa.

Already the Russians have secured what appear to be permanent and widely defined rights to naval and air bases in Egypt and perhaps Syria. This development represents a considerable departure for the Soviet Union and

Right Soviet involvement in the Middle East. Although their forces in Egypt were greatly reduced in 1972, the representation of Soviet air coverage from Egypt indicates the potential advantage to the Soviet Union of bases on the shore of the Mediterranean

Below The balance of power in the Middle East.

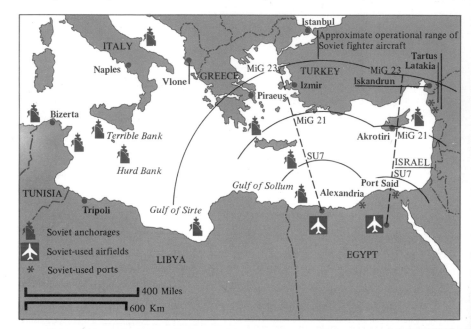

	Army			Combat aircraft		Ocean-going warships	Patrol boats carrying missiles	Submarines
	◉ = 10			◉ = 1		◉ = 1	◉ = 1	◉ = 1
Israel	●●●●●●○○○○○○○○○○○○ ○○○○○○○ 11,500 regular, 60,000 conscripts full mobilisation 275,000			●●●●●●●●●●●●● ●●●●●●●●●●●●● ●●●●●●●●●●●●● ●●●●●●●●●●●● 432		●1	●●●●●●●● ●●●● 12	●● 2
Egypt	●●●●●●●●●●●●●●●●●●●● ●●●●●●●● 285,000			●●●●●●●●●●●●●●●●●● ●●●●●●●●●●●●●●●●●● ●●●●●●●●●●●●●●●●●● ●●●●●●●●●●●●●●●●●● ● 568		●●●●●●●7	●●●●●●●●●●●●●●●● ●● 18	●●●●●●●●●● ●●●● 12
Jordan	●●●●●● 65,000			●●●●● 50				
Syria	●●●●●●●●●●●●●● 100,000			●●●●●●●●●●●●●● ●●●●●●●● 210		●● 2	●●●●●● 6	
Libya	●● 20,000			●● 22		●1	●●● 3	

would seem to mark a new stage in her techniques for extending military and political influence. Russian ships make constant use of port facilities in Alexandria and Port Said. Should the Canal open, it is possible that tentative arrangements in Hodeida (Yemen), Aden and Berbera (Somalia) would be consolidated. Russian naval reconnaissance aircraft operate from Cairo West airport and two new air bases have been located near Aswan and in the desert near the Libyan frontier. Two or three other Russian-controlled airfields are thought to exist. At the peak in 1972 there were thought to be about 120 Russian-manned MiG 21s, thirty Su 11s and a few MiG 23s in Egypt, as well as the longer-range maritime reconnaissance aircraft.

The Gulf

The situation in the Persian Gulf is dominated by the immediate after-effects of British withdrawal in December 1971. In anticipation of this event Iran prepared to become the dominating military power. Having negotiated an understanding with Saudi Arabia – whose defence capabilities face more to the north west – and having renounced its claims to Bahrein, Iran has established a military force that makes it plain she intends to be the arbiter of the Gulf. The Iranian defence budget for 1971–2 grew by 30 per cent to exceed $1 billion. With 30 F4s and 100 F5s the Iranian air force outclasses all others around the Gulf. Similarly the Iranian army, with 150,000 men, M60 tanks and an order for 800 Chieftains, will be a very powerful force if its competence can match its equipment. Iran has also developed its navy with an eye to the security of its oil and other traffic. For the same reason Iran demonstrated its new vigour by annexing the three small islands (the two Tumbs and Abu Musa) that dominate the entrance to the Gulf, in November 1971.

The most obvious rival to Iran is Iraq, but her forces are inferior and she is, as we have already noted, much distracted by internal problems. Iraqi–Iranian relations are bad and several frontier disputes exist, so that armed clashes are far from unlikely.

Great Britain has withdrawn its commitments to aid the Gulf states militarily, although Britain is still linked to Iran within the Central Treaty Organization (CENTO). British forces do intend to return to the Gulf on a visiting basis and for training. As a framework for local defence for the really tiny sheikdoms, whose main problems are thought to be internal subversion and some petty quarrels, Britain cajoled seven small states into the Union of Arab Emirates. The seven are Abu Dhabi, Dubai, Sharjah, Ajman, Umm-al-Qawain, Fujairah and Ras-al-Khaimah. Abu Dhabi and Dubai have retained small defence forces; the others share in the reconstituted Trucial Oman Scouts (now the Union Defence Force). All these forces retain British officers on loan.

Following the British withdrawal of a permanent naval presence, the United States has negotiated a special base agreement with Bahrein for its small Middle Eastern squadron of an unarmed flagship and two destroyers.

Farther round the south coast of Arabia an active war continues between the Government of Oman, whose forces have British officers and which are supported by units of the British Special Air Services Regiment, and rebels supported from the Peoples Democratic Republic of Yemen. This little war, in Dhofar, is extremely confused and it is uncertain whether the rebels are more supported by the Soviet Union or by China. Success for the rebels would indicate a pattern for action farther east among the Union of Arab Emirates.

CHAPTER TEN

Asia

The vast area of Asia contains an inexhaustible range of military activities and conflict. Much of the basic information is presented in the tables and appendices or is implicit in the general discussion of the various modes of warfare. There are, however, a number of particular issues that deserve a special mention.

India–Pakistan

The rivalry between India and Pakistan has provided a constant military competition ever since the two gained independence in 1947, several times punctuated by open warfare. Recent events have given this rivalry a decisive turn and have perhaps ended the contest in its established form.

From the very first India was much more powerful than Pakistan, having a population of over 500 million as compared to less than 150 million in Pakistan. Pakistan's strategic situation was also hopelessly impaired by the division of her territory between East and West. Upon partition the existing Indian armed forces were divided between India and Pakistan roughly in the proportion of two to one. Initially both obtained further arms from Britain. In the early fifties the American enrolment of Pakistan in the South-East Asian Treaty Organization (SEATO) initiated heavy American arms shipments to Pakistan. These were ostensibly intended to strengthen Pakistan against Communist threats from the north but Pakistan naturally valued them chiefly to improve the balance with India. American economic aid to India enabled the Indians to rearm also, chiefly with British and French weapons. Pakistan had perforce to accept an overall inferiority of over two to one. She partly compensated for this by maintaining an air strike capability against near-by Indian cities, including Delhi.

The small war between India and China in 1962, arising out of frontier disputes brought to life by the Chinese absorption of Tibet, stimulated a heavy flow of Anglo–American arms to India and also, in the deteriorating state of Soviet–Chinese relations, secured India Russian aid, including MiG 21 aircraft. These reinforcements and energetic Indian refurbishment of her armed forces, accompanied by accelerated establishment of an indigenous arms industry, left Pakistan relatively much weaker. Her inferiority now approached four to one. In particular, improved India air defences threatened to deprive Pakistan of her air strike capability.

In reaction to this process Pakistan moved closer to China. The general deterioration in Pakistan's position and fears that India was completing the absorption of the disputed territory of Kashmir precipitated the locally-confined but intense war between the two in 1965, fought chiefly in the Rann of Kutch. The result was something of a stalemate, with both sides running short of supplies. The war served to show Pakistan's vulnerability should India decide

Opposite A Phantom F4B of the US Navy launches its bombs against a Viet Cong strongpoint.

to attack in the East; this may have contributed a little to Eastern separatism. India moved even closer to the Soviet Union, as a result of a Western arms embargo. Over the next five or six years the United States transferred only about $70 million worth of military supplies to both countries combined, most of this being spares or transport items. By contrast China transferred $150 million worth to Pakistan and Russia no less than $700 million worth to India, including tanks, aircraft, submarines and missile boats.

This was the military background to the war of 1971. The political background was the victory in East Pakistan of the separatist Awami League in the elections of December 1970 and the severe repressive activity of the Pakistani

Recruits to the Pakistan Army during the 1971 war with India, training in Rawalpindi.

army. Prompted by the general tradition of hostility and by the immense refugee problem, India supported the guerrilla movement (Mukti Bahini) which began, rather ineffectively, in East Pakistan and then crossed the border with its own regular units on 27 November. An attack in strength began on 4 December after Pakistan had attempted a relatively unsuccessful Israeli-type pre-emptive strike on Indian airfields the day before. Meanwhile, India had been bolstered against the threat of Chinese intervention by the signing of a Treaty of Peace, Friendship and Co-operation with the Soviet Union in August. China made no significant military moves against India.

In the West, India stood chiefly on the defensive, successfully defeating Pakistani efforts to win territory for bargaining. Indeed India emerged holding the greater gains. In the East, Pakistan's forces were hopelessly inferior and were cut off by sea by the Indian fleet, which sank several Pakistani warships. They had only one squadron of old F86 Sabrejets and these, dependent on one airfield, were quickly eliminated. Their leadership was far from brilliant and their morale naturally deflated by their isolated position among hostile populations. By 17 December India had forced a ceasefire and the fall of the Pakistani government. A curious side issue had been the entry of an American fleet, headed by the CVAN *Enterprise*, into the Bay of Bengal, supposedly in an abortive effort to distract part of Indian air strength.

The result has been to overthrow the balance on the sub-continent. Pakistan has lost its Eastern territory. Nominally its armed forces, which have been partly re-equipped from China, remain not much diminished. They were always chiefly manned from the West. But it must remain doubtful whether the truncated state can maintain this level of effort. In any case India has proved its undoubted superiority. Ten years' work at raising the Indian armed forces from their unimpressive standards at the time of the Sino–Indian war had borne obvious fruit. The local balance between India and Pakistan, that had dominated military affairs on the sub-continent for decades, is now of much less interest. What now becomes more interesting is whether India will exploit her growing strength and new freedom from the balance with Pakistan to play a more active military and diplomatic role in her region. In particular the reduction in the power of Pakistan enables India to provide much more adequately for defence against any Chinese threat. The deterioration in Sino–Soviet relations and the new Soviet–Indian treaty will also increase Indian confidence in this respect. Looking in the other direction, the future of Indian naval development will attract close attention. Repeated rumours of the Soviet Union acquiring established naval facilities in India akin to those in Egypt may not be justified. Indeed in many respects India now has less need to pay a high and politically embarrassing price for Soviet help. But with the Soviet Union expanding its naval presence in the Indian Ocean and at the same time serving as India's chief source of modern weapons, a close working relationship between the two navies would be no surprise.

The Five Power Defence Pact
Until the present decade the area embracing Malaysia, Singapore and Indonesia was regulated chiefly by British power. The last major active British intervention was the so-called confrontation between Malaysia and Indonesia in which Britain fought a very successful campaign against insurgency and infiltration aimed at destroying the new Malaysian federation uniting Sarawak, North Borneo and Malaya. No less than 50,000 men were engaged on the British side and the campaign included intensive naval patrolling and the deterrent

deployment of bomber forces in addition to the infantry actions on the ground.

The situation was transformed by an anti-Communist change of régime in Indonesia in 1965 which unseated President Sukarno and led to the defeat and widespread massacre of Communist elements. The new government was much more amiable, concentrating attention on domestic issues, establishing very cordial relations with Malaysia, having a cool attitude toward the Soviet Union and an even more frigid one toward China. This change made much less painful the implementation of Britain's decision to run down its presence East of Suez.

Under the plans of the Labour Government the withdrawal of permanently based forces from the Malaysian area was to have been complete. Abandoning

The sailpast as the main British forces left Singapore.

any special provisions for action outside the NATO region, Britain was to have retained only a 'general capability' for intervention East of Suez. The Conservative Government which came to power in 1970 reversed this decision, albeit in a modest fashion. Instead it consented to the creation of a Five Power Defence Agreement under which a joint Australian, New Zealand and United Kingdom (ANZUK) defence force will be kept in the area to work in co-operation with the local forces. All the British bases and a good deal of the associated equipment were handed over to the two local powers, Malaysia and Singapore, including the jungle warfare school in Malaysia which Britain still intends to use under Malaysian management.

The Five Power Agreement is a rather qualified commitment. It is not embodied in a treaty but takes the form of a declaration of intent contained in a joint communiqué issued in April 1971. The scope of the commitment is expressed in the key affirmation of 'determination to work together for peace and stability . . . in the event of any form of armed attack externally organized or supported, or the threat of such attack, their governments would immediately consult together for the purpose of deciding what measures should be taken jointly or separately in relation to such attack or threat'. It is thus a conditional commitment and one clearly limited to external threats. Interpretation of the latter point is likely to be crucial, as by far the most likely form of external pressure would be through subversion, yet the guarantors are anxious not to get involved in the internal communal affairs that may well involve differences between Malaysia and Singapore themselves.

Almost certainly the British government regards the arrangement as transitional; a method of phasing withdrawal, not of perpetuating a presence or facilitating a re-entry. The intention is to create a framework of security and reassurance within which Malaysia and Singapore need not look too nervously at each other, and can deal more confidently with truly indigenous unrest. Equally, the guarantee prevents any would-be external troublemaker from regarding the two as an easy mark for aggression, subversion, or diplomatic pressure. But the Five Power Agreement clearly does not envisage large-scale military efforts by the ANZUK powers. Any decision to make such efforts might be influenced by the existence of the Five Power arrangement but is certainly not dictated by it.

Within the Five Power framework the three external powers contribute elements of a small but balanced force. The largest contribution is Australian, part of a 'forward defence' policy which is much debated in Australia. In recognition of this contribution the Commander of the ANZUK forces is an Australian officer, as is the Commander of the Integrated Air Defence system that has been established among the Five. This system is the most needed and welcome component in the external contribution.

Australia's contribution includes two squadrons of Mirage III-O based at Butterworth in Malaysia. A battalion group of infantry is stationed at Singapore, with a company detached to Butterworth. In addition there are a destroyer and a submarine. Altogether 3400 Australian personnel are involved. New Zealand contributes a battalion, a frigate and some transport aircraft, constituting a total of some 1200 men. The British contingent amounts to 2500 men comprising a battalion group, four Nimrod maritime reconnaissance aircraft, some Wessex helicopters and six ships of the destroyer–frigate type. These ships, however, also serve to maintain the Beira patrol against Rhodesia and to provide the 'guard ship' for Hong Kong. A British submarine alternates with the Australian boat. In addition the British plan frequent training visits of troops and combat aircraft, and occasional cruises by larger naval units. To complete the picture there is a Gurkha battalion in Brunei, where Britain's long-standing defence agreement has also been renegotiated to restrict it to external attack.

As we have seen, the Five Power Pact may prove to be an interim arrangement. Its future will doubtless be influenced by the course of American involvement in the more easterly parts of South-East Asia. It may also be affected by the proposal, made in November 1971, by the Association of South-East Asian Nations (ASEAN, a grouping of Indonesia, Malaysia, Thailand, Philippines and Singapore), for a neutralization of South-East Asia. Given the lively interest of several major external powers in the area the necessary degree of self-abnegation would obviously be hard to secure.

With Indonesia in its newly amiable mood the incidence of serious conflict in the area has temporarily abated. Guerrilla activity continues in several countries. This is true of the Philippines, where long-endemic insurgency is somewhat reinvigorated, of Indonesia where the huge territory spawns a variety of local restlessness, and of Malaysia where there are some 500–600 insurgents in Sarawak and where a residue of the Malayan Communist Party, perhaps 1200 strong, which gave the British so much trouble twenty years ago, still hold out on the Thai border.

Thailand faces several serious insurgent threats. It suffers its share of difficulty with the Malayan People's Liberation Army on its border with Malaysia. More serious are movements on the Burmese frontier, linked to Chinese-supported insurgency in Burma, and along the frontiers with Cambodia and Laos, where the activity is supported by the North Vietnamese in conjunction with their activities in the two neighbouring countries. The Thai People's Liberation Armed Forces are thought to have fielded about 5000 men in 1972. Thailand's problems are conditioned by the vigorous way in which the Thai government has assisted the United States effort in Viet Nam. At one time nearly 60,000 American military personnel were in Thailand supporting air operations from six airfields, one of which, a B52 base at U Tapao is the biggest airstrip in South-East Asia. Communist success in Viet Nam would create a dangerous situation for Thailand, making a neat test of the domino theory. Thailand shows some signs of attempting better relations with China as an insurance policy. There are also the beginnings of co-operative efforts by the local governments to deal with insurgency, such as the agreement between Malaysia and Thailand to concert action on their common frontier in 1970.

It should not be completely forgotten that the SEATO organization still exists on paper and as a skeleton administrative framework in Bangkok. Its nominal members are the United States, Britain, France, Australia, New Zealand, Thailand and the Philippines. A protocol extended protection to Laos, Cambodia and South Viet Nam. The United States, Australia and New Zealand have all used SEATO as part of a justification for their roles in Viet Nam. But the alliance is very much in decay. Pakistan has disengaged, France declares no forces to the alliance and since 1969 Britain has not declared any either. SEATO may still be used as a rationale for action members want to take anyway, but as a strategic conception it appears dead. The United States is more interested in keeping its relationship with Australia and New Zealand alive in the ANZUK agreement, and Americans co-operate very fully in Australian defence establishments. But with the arrival of the Nixon Doctrine there seems to be less American interest in exploiting the possibility of new American forward bases in Australia.

A new possibility of tension in South-East Asia has arisen since 1971 in the Strait of Malacca. Malaysia and Indonesia have united in demanding control over shipping in this strait, for the declared purpose of limiting the risk of accident and pollution by the greatly increased traffic including very large tankers. While some regulation is certainly desirable, other nations are exceedingly nervous about the principle involved which could obviously be extended for other purposes. The matter is of special interest to Japan, and the Soviet Union has also opposed the local claim to jurisdiction over what is commonly regarded as an international waterway. The potential for armed conflict involving the naval forces of the shipowning powers is obvious. The matter is the more important as there are many other narrow waters or 'choke points' where similar claims could seriously encroach on the freedom of navigation cherished by the larger maritime powers for both strategic and commercial purposes.

Viet Nam

It is clearly impossible to ignore the Vietnamese war. It is equally impossible to deal with it adequately in a brief survey. War in Viet Nam has dominated more than a decade of diplomacy and has provided the stimulus for many of the military innovations and practices described elsewhere in this book. It has also inspired a fundamental reorientation of American security policy. This account merely attempts a very simplified review of the military campaign.

Ho Chi Minh had led a nationalist resistance to the Japanese and in 1945–6 he formed a government in Viet Nam, supported by an army equipped with material provided by the Allies for use against Japan. Initially the American government was not ill-disposed to Ho and was markedly unenthusiastic about the reimposition of French rule in Indo-China. The French recognized Ho's government as a subordinate régime, but this did not satisfy Ho and he began a revolutionary war. Communist victory in China assured Ho a secure base and the French failed to establish a rival government with adequate popular appeal.

With the onset of the Cold War, American administrations came to regard the war in Indo-China as part of the general problem of containing Communism. Fear of Communist victory in Indo-China was the specific inspiration for the so-called 'domino theory', according to which, collapse of one portion of the Western defensive perimeter would lead to consequential further losses. By the early fifties the United States was providing some three-quarters of the equipment for the French campaign. Despite this aid, the French were forced to abandon their resistance, the siege and fall of Dienbienphu symbolizing their defeat. Plans for direct American intervention foundered on the opposition of some NATO allies, led by Britain, and on the reluctance of American army leaders to become entangled again in a war on the ground in Asia.

The Geneva Conference of 1954 gave independence to Cambodia and Laos and called for the withdrawal of foreign armed forces from those states. Viet Nam was also given independence and was divided at the seventeenth parallel, the north falling to Ho and the south to a régime headed by Ngo Dinh Diem. Presumably Ho accepted this as a price for getting the French out and on the assumption the arrangement was to be temporary. One of the complex and controversial agreements at Geneva called for all-Viet Nam elections in 1956, but the Southern régime refused to acknowledge or execute this understanding. The United States was not formally a party to the Geneva accords.

The South Vietnamese government was unexpectedly successful at first in establishing some order and stability. When the South did not collapse, the

North supported an insurgent movement in South Viet Nam, the armed wing of which, the Viet Cong, began a serious military campaign in rural areas in 1959, using arms stored from the previous war against the French. This campaign achieved widening control of the countryside.

South Viet Nam received heavy military assistance from the United States, including both arms and instructors. To the new régime of President Kennedy, wars of national liberation remained the one serious unclosed gap in the range of American defences against Soviet and Chinese military power. Counter-insurgency operations became a major preoccupation of American planners. Yet the Southern army was equipped by the United States in a fashion more suited to a Korean-type war. Over-supplied with equipment, the army tended to be tied to the roads and to launch heavy suppressive 'seize and hold' or 'search and destroy' operations that did a great deal of damage to the civilian population without establishing any substantial degree of security or control. Indigenous dissatisfaction with the course of events, coupled with American loss of faith in Diem, whose régime had become increasingly authoritarian and scandal-ridden, resulted in a *coup* in 1963 in which Diem was assassinated.

In the aftermath the guerrilla campaign made even more progress. Fighting had broken out again in Laos where the Communist Pathet Lao, aided by the North Vietnamese, gained control of large areas. The North Vietnamese used the famous Ho Chi Minh trail in Laos to infiltrate troops and supplies into South Viet Nam. They also established elaborate base areas in Cambodia and brought supplies in by sea through Sihanoukville (now Kompong Som). Continued Communist successes impelled President Johnson to begin the massive injection of American troops to take over the fighting, abandoning the previous posture of offering merely military 'advice'. At the same time he began bombing the North.

For a time the North Vietnamese shifted toward the use of major units in open battle. Though they had successes they suffered heavy losses in this kind of warfare which gave the Americans a chance to use their superior firepower. Perhaps out of anxiety about this course of events, the North launched an all-out co-ordinated offensive against several South Vietnamese cities in January 1968 (the Tet offensive). Their initial successes were shortlived and secured at the expense of crushing losses. As a military operation and indeed as a local political move the offensives were a serious failure, for the South Vietnamese were able to use the resulting period of Communist weakness to regain control over large areas of the country. But the offensive won a decisive political success in the United States where it was taken to belie the Administration's claims to have made military progress. President Johnson reduced and then halted bombing of the North to secure peace negotiations.

From that time until early 1972 the communists reverted to guerrilla operations. Under President Nixon the process of 'Vietnamization' began and American troop levels were rapidly reduced from their peak level of over half a million. This process was punctuated by a combined American and South Vietnamese incursion into Cambodia aimed at disrupting the heavy North Vietnamese build-up of forces. Just previously, in March 1970, a *coup* had overthrown Prince Sihanouk and established a more nationalist and anti-Communist régime.

While the offensive may have delayed Communist plans, the process of reinforcement continued along the trails in 1971. Russian arms supplies to the North also increased in quantity and quality. In the spring of 1972, when the withdrawal of American ground combat forces was virtually complete, the

North Vietnamese launched a major offensive on several fronts, reverting to the use of large units. Indeed this was the furthest the communists had gone in conventional warfare, involving the widespread use of armour. The American response was heavy renewed bombing of the North, making effective use of new 'smart' TV and laser-guided bombs. American ECM also proved very successful and B52s were able to operate with relative impunity.

The most dramatic American response, however, was the blockade of North Vietnamese ports by mining. This should perhaps be regarded as an early and specific test of American ability to exert a military influence on events on the Asian mainland when confined to an offshore air and naval strategy.

At the height of their involvement in the ground fighting in South Viet Nam, US troops build a fire-base.

It is hopeless to try to sum up the Vietnamese struggle, even now that a shaky peace has been concluded and American forces have been withdrawn. Whether the overall result of American policy is ultimately regarded as successful or not, there seems to be a general consensus that the politico-military handling of the war was misguided in several respects. Perhaps a fundamental failure was the inability to establish a good working relationship and mechanism for co-ordination between the South Vietnamese régime and a pre-eminent ally which was not formally at war and which, while not enjoying sovereign jurisdiction, did not greatly respect the susceptibilities of the local authority or seek to maintain a low political profile. Given the scale of American

The Viet Nam theatre of war.

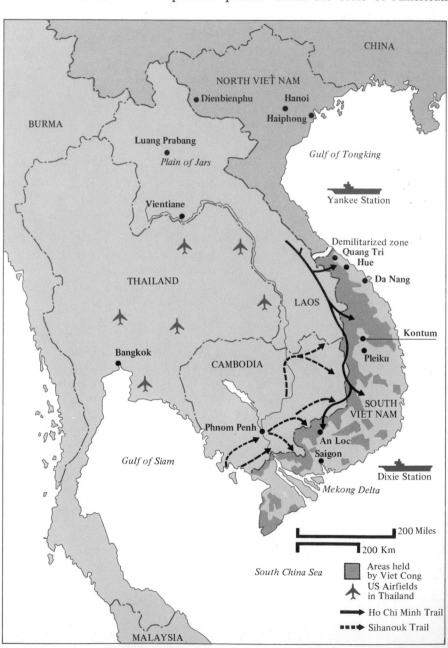

intervention, this failure was not surprising. But it may well be that that scale of intervention was itself an error on several counts.

In the first place it should have been clear that a presence of over half a million could not be long sustained. Thus the enemy were given notice that the Americans were not preparing to fight a long war. The scale of intervention also encouraged inappropriate tactics. Despite the fact that an alarming proportion of the half a million were support and not combat troops, the large forces lavishly equipped with helicopters encouraged search-and-destroy operations which did great collateral damage. The American forces used their mobility to avoid long periods living in the jungle. Yet many experts in counter-insurgency operations believe that only a policy of patrolling and ambushing can seize the real initiative and maintain that apparently vigorous search-and-destroy campaigns are actually merely reactive. If this was a failing, it was clearly related to intelligence services that were relatively poor. It is also related to the criticism that, while great energy was spent searching for the enemy, too little effort was directed to protecting and minimizing damage to the population. Police work was very neglected in favour of military operations. Yet it would be wrong to fall into the trap set for many British commentators who make unfavourable comparisons with British operations in Malaysia without recognizing that in Viet Nam the enemy himself had the capacity, which he often used, to mount large-scale attacks.

Finally, no comment would be complete that did not mention the bombing. This falls into two categories, that against the North intended to halt infiltration and damage the North's war potential, and that in the South. The military balance sheet remains obscure but clearly the effects of the bombing of the North were not sufficient to ensure success for the South. Nor did the bombing succeed in its other purpose of bargaining the North into halting its offensives. Whether a more sustained campaign would have done so is beyond knowing.

Equally it is impossible to say whether there is any merit in the view that the bombing would have been successful if it had begun in an allout rather than graduated fashion. Certainly the sharp and sudden bombing campaign begun in response to the Northern offensive of 1972 seemed to have a substantial effect, but this was in the face of much more orthodox military operations.

In the South bombing has doubtless served many military purposes well. It has also done a great deal of damage to civilians and their property. Whether it has done more to alienate civilian opinion or to boost the morale of Southern forces is debatable, but it seems improbable that the bombing need have been used so freely. What is clear, is that the bombing in general and particularly that in the North played a large part in alienating world opinion and in arousing resistance to the war in the United States. The impact of television reporting on this war has perhaps been the most revolutionary innovation of all. Henceforth, at least in limited wars, the management of the mass media will constitute a new and difficult aspect of military operations by the democracies.

China, Japan and the East-Asian Balance

After a long period of stability, not to say rigidity, the major power balance in Asia is changing rapidly. The four main actors are China, Japan, the Soviet Union and the United States. All of these powers have disputes with each other. China has a longstanding series of conflicts with the United States concerning South-East Asia, Taiwan – which the United States still guarantees – and Korea. China also looks with some misgiving on the rise of America's ally Japan. The Soviet Union has ideological and border disputes with China. Russia

An anti-aircraft gun crew of the North Vietnamese Army.

also must come to terms with the rise of Japan; relations between the two are affected by long memories of conflict and by Russian possession of several islands claimed by the Japanese. The United States has many troubled interests in Asia but, unlike the other three, she enjoys a certain degree of discretion as to how she pursues them. If she chose, the United States could abandon an active Asian policy. She is unlikely to do so given her extension through Hawaii into mid-Pacific and her pretensions to global power. But the possibility of a less active policy, embodied in the Nixon Doctrine, is one of the more important influences loosening the familiar pattern of Asian politics.

The possible permutations of alignment are many and commentators have a pleasant time hypothetically rearranging them. The most likely configuration consists of the United States, aligned with Japan but more loosely than hitherto, sometimes working tacitly with China to balance the Soviet Union. The Soviet Union may perhaps attempt to enlist the support of Japan in offsetting China, and that of the United States whenever a forward Chinese policy gives the two existing Superpowers cause for common alarm.

The military power of the United States and the Soviet Union is not in doubt; the only question concerns how it will be employed. From our narrow military perspective it is more interesting to look at the potential of China and Japan.

Left Soviet troops (in white) involved in a scuffle with Chinese guards.

Below A Russian patrol looks across the Ussuri river at the Chinese bank.

China

China assists North Viet Nam in a modest way with supplies of armament. She still maintains very considerable forces opposite Taiwan, despite the fact that an attack from that quarter seems unthinkable. As for a Chinese invasion of Taiwan, that seems almost equally unlikely, given the substantial military strength of the island's armed forces and the comparative weakness of Chinese maritime forces. It is much more likely that China expects to resolve her claims to Taiwan during the course of political evolution.

The Chinese have applied military pressure on India, but only moderately, and India's capacity to resist has become much greater. Undoubtedly, China's main military problem is the security of her long frontier with the Soviet Union, much of which is in dispute.

These disputes, which are set in the context of more general Sino–Soviet rivalry, have led to many border clashes. The series that occurred in 1969, particularly on the Ussuri river, were widely publicized. Negotiations have since taken place but with no apparent result. From the Russian point of view the clashes are probably only symptomatic of deeper concerns: one being the spectacle of increased Chinese settlement near the frontier as a warning of possible demographic pressure to come; another, a more generalized concern at the prospect of growing Chinese power, recently dramatized by China's acquisition of nuclear weapons. As a great power accustomed to overawe its neighbours by sheer size and numbers, the idea of being the smaller party to a relationship doubtless rests uneasily on Russian minds. Since 1969 Russian armed forces on the Chinese frontier have been strongly reinforced. By 1972 the

The Sino–Soviet border showing the disputed areas.

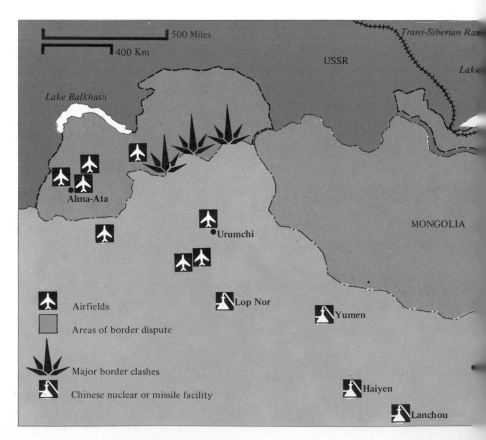

Soviet Union had forty-four divisions in the region as compared to fifteen four years earlier. Another two or three divisions are in the Mongolian People's Republic. Russian air forces in the area have grown to over 1000 aircraft. Tactical nuclear weapons have been deployed and medium and intermediate range missiles are also positioned for use against China.

Against all this might, China musters about forty divisions and a larger force of 'border troops'. The Chinese forces are much weaker in armour; in 1972 it was estimated there were only 2500 Chinese tanks to some 9000–10,000 Russian. Chinese armour is also inferior to Russian, being chiefly the T59 (a version of the Russian T54), and a light Chinese tank, the T62 (not the same as the Russian T62). The Chinese also lack logistic equipment. Soviet forces are thus superior in both mobility and firepower. Similarly the Chinese air forces are inferior. Out of some 1000 aircraft in the area many are early MiG types supplemented by a good many MiG 19s, a few MiG 21s (now being produced at about 100 a year in China), and a new twin jet, mach 2 aircraft of Chinese design, the F9. As we saw earlier, China is acquiring a small bomber force. By 1972 she also had deployed about twenty MRBMS of 1000-mile range and a few storable-liquid-fuelled IRBMS. China has a reasonable air defence system of improved SAM2s and a radar network partly of native design. It is probably inferior to the opposing Russian defence.

The Soviet Union obviously intends to maintain a decisive superiority in conventional forces. She would probably seek to avoid the use of nuclear weapons and her preparations in this field are presumably designed to deter any Chinese nuclear action. The resulting balance is something of a stalemate, in

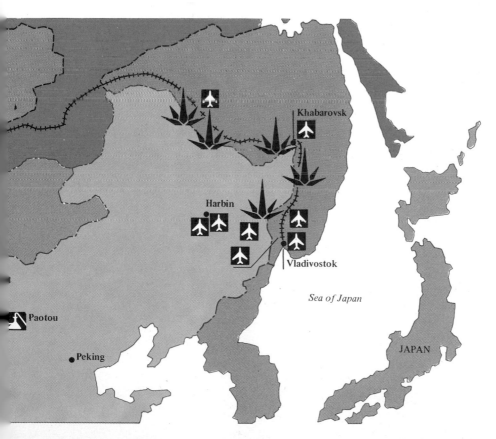

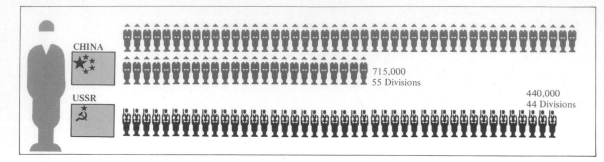

A comparison of the Soviet and Chinese forces available in the border areas.

CHINA

715,000
55 Divisions

USSR

440,000
44 Divisions

that China could not successfully invade Russia for lack of mobility and overall strength. For her part, Russia would not wish to penetrate China deeply, for Chinese strategy, as dictated by Mao and common sense, calls precisely for luring the enemy into a war of attrition on unfriendly soil. In such a war China's poor communications become a defensive asset. In localized border clashes, however, Soviet strength should prevail.

The situation on the border reflects the general condition of the People's Liberation Army. Although the PLA has an enviable fighting reputation, its present capabilities are strictly limited by lack of equipment. A moment's reflection will show that, rather surprisingly, it is a small army in relative terms. The total Chinese armed forces number less than three million, smaller than the recent size of either American or Russian forces, and a small proportion of a population of some 750 million. The airforce and navy are very small indeed. All the services are short of modern equipment except of the lightest kind. Only five of the 140 divisions are armoured. China's arms industry makes progress but it remains limited. It now makes MiG 21s, the Chinese F9, the TU16, tanks, an APC, missile patrol boats, and diesel submarines. China is also reputed to be building a nuclear submarine. This is supposed to be an attack boat and not an SSBN.

The PLA is heavily engaged in tasks of national administration and economic development. Its lack of mobility would severely limit the possibility of sustained offensive operations outside China. In any case, tough Chinese rhetoric should not obscure the fact that Chinese doctrine does not call for use of the PLA to promote the revolutionary situations Chinese diplomacy encourages. Modest help is given by supply of arms but the dominant message is self-help.

China's economy now shows signs of renewed growth and recent improvements in military equipment probably signify an increased rate of expenditure. One curb on military development may have been Mao's mistrust of military professionalism, coupled to the dogma of the superiority of the moral over the material elements in military success.

Another much more tangible factor has been the heavy investment in the nuclear programme. This has absorbed not just money but very scarce scientific manpower. The route China has taken, by way of gaseous diffusion and missiles, is initially very expensive, though it promises very substantial ultimate returns as thermonuclear weapons give a large yield for the price. Chinese space-satellite launchings confirm an energetic missile programme, though it remains uncertain how far China has progressed with guidance and re-entry systems. Most missile test firings have been from Manchuria to Sinkiang. Facilities for an ICBM range are said to be developing in Zanzibar and a missile-tracking ship has been prepared.

Chinese nuclear strategy appears to bear a resemblance to that of France in some respects. Since their disappointment with Russian support during the Quemoy crisis of 1958, the Chinese have emphasized the unreliability of guarantees from third parties. China has repeatedly renounced the first use of nuclear weapons. Her force is presumably intended to secure immunity from a first strike by establishing a second-strike retaliatory force. It remains to be seen whether, once such a deterrent is secured, China will use her conventional power more freely to coerce or overawe any of her neighbours.

Japan

For historical reasons Japan presents the unusual appearance of a state with immense technological capacity, the third highest GNP in the world, and a very small proportionate expenditure on armed forces. Even after some recent large increases, the Japanese defence budget absorbs less than 1 per cent of the GNP.

This phenomenon in a once highly militaristic nation is the result of defeat in World War II and the subsequent restriction on Japanese armed forces imposed by Japan's new constitution. Article 9 provides that 'the Japanese people forever renounce war as a sovereign right of the nation and the threat or use of force as a means of settling international disputes. In order to accomplish the aims of the preceding paragraph, land, sea and air forces, as well as other war potential, will never be maintained . . .' The Japanese Supreme Court has held that this does not eliminate an inherent right of self-defence and preparations for it. On the other hand, the prohibition is frequently interpreted as ruling out possession of such weapons as long-range bombers or missiles. At present it is also regarded as forbidding the overseas deployment of Japanese forces. Japan has been able to take a fairly restrictive view of these prohibitions, secure in the possession of the Japanese–American Mutual Security Treaty.

Japanese circumstances are, however, changing rapidly. The most important though imponderable factor is the reduced vigour of American overseas involvement and, in particular, the more relaxed tone of American policy toward the containment of China. China's rising power and her acquisition of nuclear weapons also arouse concern in Japan. The American military presence in Japan has been sharply reduced and Okinawa has been handed back to Japanese administration. Although this process has been partly in response to Japanese pressure, it nevertheless implies a greater Japanese responsibility for self-defence. Similar implications can be drawn simply from the meteoric rise in Japanese wealth and industrial capacity. A possible revision of Japanese attitudes toward overseas involvement may also be engendered by spreading Japanese trading interests and growing Japanese investment in South-East Asia.

The incentives for a normal country in Japan's position to arm would be strong. She is close to two large countries, China and the Soviet Union, each of which has big armed forces and an active foreign policy. She watches anxiously over the buffer state of South Korea and has also recently indicated a similar concern for Taiwan. She is entirely dependent for her immense prosperity on the security of the sea routes. In particular she depends on imported oil which gives her a vital interest in the sea lane to the Persian Gulf, in the stability of Indonesia and in the disposition of prospective oil resources on the continental shelf, much of which is linked to islands whose ownership is in dispute. Moreover, 12 per cent of her trade is now done with South-East Asia, an uncertain area over which Japan has, in discreetly shaded recent memory, exercised a dominant military influence.

Japanese inhibitions against following this logic are powerful. In addition to the constitution, the Japanese recognize that many other nations also remember

World War II and that vigorous rearmament would provoke hostile reactions. One of the few things on which China and the Soviet Union agree is denunciations of resurgent Japanese militarism. Nor are the Japanese unaware of the economic benefits they derive from an unusually low level of military expenditure.

Nevertheless, it would be a grave error to regard Japan as militarily negligible. Under the stimulus of recent events the Japanese five-year defence plan for 1972–6 envisages a sharp rise in expenditure of almost 150 per cent over the period. The present defence budget at just under $2 billion, though less than 1 per cent of the GNP, is large in absolute terms. If the five-year plan is fulfilled, the Japanese defence budget will be the seventh largest in the world.

The increased expenditure is to be devoted primarily to hardware. Service in the Japanese armed forces is voluntary, and the target for ground forces is only 180,000. The new programme calls for over 1000 tanks, including a new one of Japanese design, 158 F4 Phantoms, most built in Japan, and two large helicopter ASW ships. This programme is designed to enable Japan to take over more competently the tasks of island defence, replacing some of the American forces previously stationed in the North but leaving the tasks of regional stability and deterrence to the United States. However, as the ASW ships indicate, the repossession of Okinawa now gives an extended and maritime aspect even to the problem of home defence. It would presumably be a fairly easy task of reinterpretation to extend the notion of self-defence to cover the protection of Japanese ships on the high seas.

For the moment Japan still disclaims an overseas role. If such a role were to be assumed it might indeed be as a result of such problems as the challenge to shipping in the Strait of Malacca, though unless their overall mood changes, the Japanese would be cautious and reluctant in approaching such a venture. The possibility of the Japanese undertaking a military responsibility for shoring up stability in South-East Asia seems more remote. Hostile memories in South-East Asia have not yet subsided. The situation might change, however, if Chinese pressure on the area grew. Were Japan to take a hand, it might very well be by way of training and assistance initially, rather than by direct intervention. Such an approach would minimize the political and constitutional difficulties.

A very special interest attaches to the prospects for a Japanese nuclear force. The dominant popular mood is opposed to this idea, being very deeply coloured by memories of the war. But such moods can alter rapidly, especially after a change of generations. The abhorrence of nuclear weapons is, after all, founded on a fear of becoming their victim again. Under some circumstances possession of nuclear weapons rather than abstention might appear a better road to immunity.

Future Japanese thinking on this question will be largely dictated by the policies of the existing nuclear powers in the Far East. In particular it will depend on the credibility of the American guarantee. The presentation of the 1972–6 plan in 1970 contained a reaffirmation of abstention 'for the time being'. Nevertheless the subject is now debated on a more practical rather than moral or emotional level and already there have been declarations that small, defensive tactical nuclear weapons would be compatible with the principle of self-defence. The Japanese Atomic Energy Act clearly forbids the manufacture or possession of nuclear weapons. This could be amended but it would certainly constitute a practical obstacle to drifting imperceptibly into a nuclear posture.

About Japanese capability to produce nuclear weapons there can be no doubt. Japan's technical competence is in the first rank. Her existing atomic energy programme would provide her with enough fissionable material for about 100 weapons a year. As a civilian venture Japan has produced two large missiles, the Lambda and the Mu. The Lambda is comparable to the Minuteman and Japanese prowess was illustrated by the launching of a satellite in February 1970. Presumably Japan has not yet developed re-entry systems or the appropriate guidance systems for an ICBM. But should the political incentives to do so arise, there can be no doubt about the technical ability or material resources to make Japan into a formidable nuclear power.

An overall indication of Japanese military potential can be derived from the calculation that, assuming a reduced rate of economic growth, the Japanese GNP should reach $578 billion by 1985. Were she then to devote the roughly 5 per cent of GNP to defence that is typical of the Western European powers, her defence budget would be nearly $30 billion. Superpower rates of expenditure would result in a budget of $50 billion. The future application of this immense potential is probably the most important variable in the Asian military balance.

Southern Africa

Africa, like most other areas of the world, particularly the less economically developed parts, contains many minor conflicts, mostly domestic, that are too numerous and above all too changeable to characterize adequately in a brief survey. The problem of the Republic of South Africa's relations with neighbouring states is of a different order, not only because of its intrinsic importance, but also because it impinges on the relations of the great powers and on the changing military balance in the Indian Ocean.

The republic's foreign relations have undergone a cyclic change over the last twenty-five years. In the early days of the Cold War, South Africa expected to become linked with the Western security arrangements that were succeeding the

wartime alliance in which it had been an active member. If another war resembled the previous one, South Africa's position would again be vitally important to the Western side. For its part, South Africa saw the Middle East as its front line of defence. South Africans joined in Western strategic discussions and had expected to participate in the unrealized scheme for a Middle East Command. The South African air force played a part in the Berlin airlift and the Korean war. An agreement of 1950 made South African uranium available to Britain and the United States.

The other Western powers were, however, cautious about extending their commitments southward and about association with a state whose racial policies were already attracting adverse comment. As a result, the only formal defence arrangement that South Africa concluded was the much analysed Simonstown Agreement of 1955 with Great Britain. This exchange of letters was based on the explicit assumptions that the two countries had a common interest in the security of the sea routes round South Africa but that the internal affairs of the countries of Southern Africa were their own concern. The precise naval commitments are considered later.

From this modest watershed of co-operation South Africa sank into growing isolation as a result of her unique racial policy of apartheid. Antagonism in the United Nations grew and the Security Council imposed an embargo on sales of arms to South Africa. In 1961 South Africa left the Commonwealth and became

A Buccaneer bomber of the South Africa air force. Alone of the armed forces of Southern Africa the South Africans have the experience to operate very sophisticated modern weapon systems.

a republic. In 1963 the Organization of African Unity (OAU) was founded and set up a Liberation Committee to work toward the overthrow of the Republic. The advent of a Labour Government in Britain in 1964 led to the energetic implementation of the arms embargo. At the United Nations and elsewhere there was talk of wider economic sanctions and even of a blockade. South Africa seemed to be approaching a state of siege.

In the last decade, however, South African diplomacy has gone some way toward reversing this tide. The arms embargo proved to be very porous and the threat of sanctions never materialized. More important, a number of the black African states have begun to question the policy of ostracism. Led by Malawi, which is very dependent on South Africa economically, several states have begun more open relations with the republic. At the June 1971 meeting of the OAU, a bitter debate broke out over this policy and a split occurred over the idea of a 'dialogue' with South Africa, advocated by Ghana. A year later, at the 1972 meeting, support for dialogue seemed to have waned a little. The South African Government has responded eagerly to such overtures as it has received, for it sees better relations with the other African states as the key to resuming closer political *rapport* with the Western alliance. Perhaps paradoxically, the republic has also during these recent years undertaken a slightly more forward military role in suppressing unrest in bordering states.

This forward South African diplomacy rests on growing self-confidence. The South African GNP has been growing rapidly and some of this wealth has been directed toward establishing a strong military position. South African defence policy must provide against three dangers: internal subversion; attack by other African states; and the possibility of concerted international action enforcing sanctions or blockade. In addition there remains the possibility of South Africa becoming engaged on the Western side in a major war in which the Cape route might again appear vital.

To deal with these problems South Africa has built up its armed forces dramatically since the imposition of the arms embargo in 1961. The defence budget trebled between 1960 and 1963, and the growth has continued from a 1960 level of just over $62 million to a 1972 total of nearly $450 million. At the same time the republic set about diversifying its sources of arms and increasing its own capacity to manufacture weapons. Italy, and especially France, have been liberal suppliers. From the latter South Africa has secured Mirage aircraft, armoured cars, helicopters and three Daphne-class submarines. French sales are said to have totalled some $700 million over the last eight years. South Africa's own arms industry now manufactures a wide range of small arms and ordnance. A corporation, ARMSCOR, has been established to co-operate with foreign companies in setting up arms factories in South Africa. The Panhard armoured car is made in South Africa and the Italian Macchi MB326 is made under licence, the South African version going under the name of Impala. More recently an agreement has been made to manufacture Mirage aircraft under licence. South Africa also has a small guided-missile programme.

Development of an indigenous arms manufacturing capacity is, of course, intended to insulate South Africa against the effects of any more effective future embargo. South Africa's capacity to defy sanctions has also been increased, at least potentially, by the discovery of oil in neighbouring Angola. This would not, of course, enable South Africa to shrug off the economic effects of a general boycott but the chances of such a boycott being imposed would seem to have receded rather than advanced in recent years. South Africa's development of a capacity for maritime, air and naval operations may, however, be partly intended to suggest that an attempt to impose sanctions by blockade would not go unchallenged.

As a result of all these efforts and expenditures, South Africa has acquired a very respectable military force that far outmatches that of any near-by African state. The structure of the armed forces is designed to offset the racial composition of South Africa's population. In round figures there are four million whites to twenty million blacks. The armed forces are exclusively white. In the ground forces, therefore, there are only 10,000 professional soldiers, supplemented by about 22,000 conscripts serving for nine months. These conscripts later serve in a Citizen Force of about 45,000. In addition there are 75,000 Commandos, or militia, and a police force of 33,000, 3000 of which are organized in counter-insurgency formations with APCs.

The ground forces have 200 tanks, 100 of them Centurion V, and several hundred armoured cars. The air force has fifteen Buccaneers, sixteen Canberras, a variety of Mirages, a tactical airlift capacity with C130 and Transalls, the Impala armed trainer – well suited for counter-insurgency work – and a large force of helicopters to give counter-insurgency ground forces mobility. In this respect French deliveries of the new Puma will be a powerful reinforcement. France is also helping South Africa install the Cactus air defence system with the Crotale missile.

South Africa's navy has, in addition to its three Daphne submarines, two destroyers and six ASW frigates, though some of these ships are sometimes in reserve. There are also eleven minesweepers and five seaward defence boats. The navy's prime mission is the defence of the sea routes around South Africa but it also has a role in counter-insurgency. This role may grow. Arms for guerrillas have already been delivered by submarine and trawler to southern African coasts and guerrillas themselves might be infiltrated in this way. Heavy investments are being made in sonar and naval electronics. A very advanced naval communications centre is being established at Cape Town with a reported range extending from Australia to South America.

Given its supplies of uranium and its atomic energy programme, South Africa clearly has a nuclear potential. Nothing much is known about this, but South Africa, which has not signed the Non-Proliferation Treaty, could find an obvious rationale for nuclear weapons in its fear of having to face a hostile coalition without allies. It seems reasonable to assume that, in an economical way, South Africa will work systematically toward at least a short option on nuclear weapons.

For the present, South Africa faces only local threats which are scarcely of a kind to call for nuclear weapons. The immediate threat is of two kinds: one, the possibility of armed attack by the black African states; the other, guerrilla activity fostered by those states.

The first threat is negligible for the moment. On paper the armed forces of the OAU states are quite impressive, amounting to no less than 700,000 men; but a very high proportion of this total is made up by Egypt and Nigeria. The biggest black African forces other than the Nigerian are those of Zaire (Congo-Kinshasa) and Ethiopia, each of which has about 40,000 men under arms. Only Ethiopia, which is remote from South Africa, has much competently manned sophisticated equipment, and Ethiopia has severe internal conflicts of its own. Many of the African forces are receiving foreign training, and among South Africa's nearer neighbours Tanzania is said to be securing tanks and MiG 17s from China. But clearly it will be a long time before such armed forces become a technical match for those of South Africa. Moreover, the African forces suffer

Centurion tanks of the
South African army on
parade. South African
armed forces have a massive
conventional superiority
over any potential enemy.

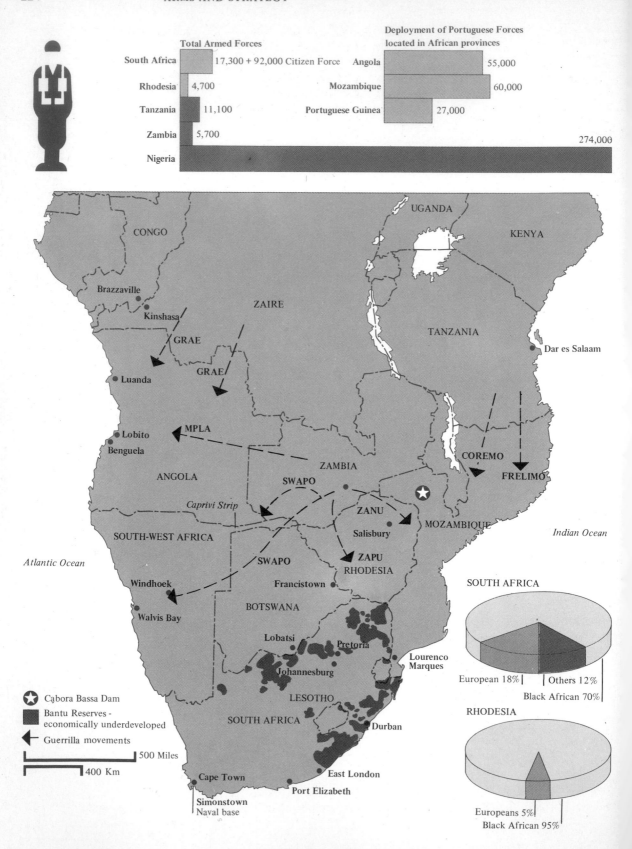

Total Armed Forces

Deployment of Portuguese Forces located in African provinces

South Africa — 17,300 + 92,000 Citizen Force

Angola — 55,000

Rhodesia — 4,700

Mozambique — 60,000

Tanzania — 11,100

Portuguese Guinea — 27,000

Zambia — 5,700

Nigeria — 274,000

CONGO

UGANDA

KENYA

Brazzaville

ZAIRE

Kinshasa

GRAE

TANZANIA

Dar es Salaam

Luanda

GRAE

Lobito

MPLA

ZAMBIA

Benguela

COREMO

ANGOLA

FRELIMO

SWAPO

Caprivi Strip

ZANU

Atlantic Ocean

SOUTH-WEST AFRICA

SWAPO

Salisbury

MOZAMBIQUE

Indian Ocean

ZAPU

RHODESIA

Windhoek

Francistown

Walvis Bay

BOTSWANA

Lobatsi

Pretoria

Lourenco Marques

Johannesburg

⭐ Cabora Bassa Dam

Bantu Reserves – economically underdeveloped

⬅ Guerrilla movements

LESOTHO

SOUTH AFRICA

Durban

500 Miles

400 Km

Cape Town

East London

Port Elizabeth

Simonstown Naval base

SOUTH AFRICA

European 18% | Others 12%

Black African 70%

RHODESIA

Europeans 5%

Black African 95%

A Mirage fighter-bomber of the South African air force.

Opposite The military situation in Southern Africa showing the armed strengths (**top**) and the major guerrilla movements (**bottom**).

from an almost complete lack of the logistical capability to launch an attack on the republic. Nor, despite repeated gestures, is there any semblance of an effective unified command. Some of the resistance to such a command arises from a fear among the African states that a unified force might become a powerful tool in the hands of an African leader with imperial ambitions. The response of several African states to the new dialogue with South Africa also suggests that many African leaders have no desire to seek a military solution to the South African problem.

A similar lack of will may contribute to the relative ineffectiveness of attempts to start a guerrilla movement in South Africa. The question of guerrillas has to be viewed in a wider perspective than the republic alone, for in this respect the situation in South Africa is closely bound up with that in Rhodesia and the neighbouring Portuguese possessions of Angola and Mozambique.

The OAU undertakes to give overall support to the guerrilla movements but, as we have said, it has not achieved a high degree of unity or efficiency in discharging this mission. Nor have the revolutionary groups within each white-ruled territory managed to put up a united front. Most of the effective support for the groups is channelled through individual African states, chiefly Zambia and Tanzania so far as Southern Africa is concerned. The movement in Portuguese Guinea, farther north, where some 10,000 rebels are contending with more than 25,000 Portuguese troops, is based in Guinea and Gabon. Ultimately, the main sources of arms for the guerrillas are the Soviet Union, China, East Germany, Cuba, Algeria and the UAR. There are training camps in Tanzania and Zambia and further training is given in Communist or Arab countries. As the list of patrons suggests, foreign support is by no means unified and these rivalries help to multiply the divisions among the Africans themselves. The African states have also developed a fairly shrewd appreciation of the dangers involved in permitting the Communists too much influence. The Summit Conference of East and Central African States on Southern Africa, held at Lusaka in 1969, provided a forum for private discussion of this danger.

Guerrilla and terrorist activity has not succeeded in achieving a foothold in the republic itself, although some small-scale sporadic incidents occur in South West Africa. The credit for this lack of success must go to the highly effective South African police and their network of intelligence. South Africa's elaborate systems of domestic controls, including the segregationist and pass systems, are of great assistance. The republic also resembles Israel inasmuch as the dominant race feels a sense of siege which intensifies solidarity. In 1972 some unrest appeared in the English-speaking universities but it remains impossible for the revolutionary elements to hope to infiltrate and subvert the machinery of government itself. In any case the would-be rebels are divided and weak. Precluded apparently from any significant organized existence within the republic, their substance consists chiefly of exiles trained in Tanzania and abroad. They are divided between the African National Congress (ANC) which receives Soviet support, the Pan-Africanist Congress (PAC) with Chinese support and the South-West Africa People's Organization (SWAPO). SWAPO is the only group maintaining a relatively active insurgency, chiefly in the Caprivi Strip. Its strength has been estimated at 1000.

There have been rather more guerrilla incursions into Rhodesia than into South Africa, and those on a larger scale. One intrusion was said to have mustered 225 men. The Rhodesian authorities claimed to have killed nearly 150 guerrillas between 1964 and 1968 and to have captured an equal number.

Guerrilla forces of ZAPU, one of the movements operating in Rhodesia.

Once again the resistance movements are divided, this time between the Zimbabwe African People's Union (ZAPU), based in Zambia, and the Zimbabwe African National Union (ZANU) also with Zambian links. ZAPU has been the more active of the two, but there are apparently factional differences even within this one organization. In 1971 an effort was made to merge the various Rhodesian groups into a Front for the Liberation of Zimbabwe (FROLIZI), and in 1972 it seemed that this organization, while not having absorbed the others, was taking a prominent position.

Although Rhodesia had succeeded in containing insurgency in the years following UDI, the months following the abortive Anglo–Rhodesian negotiations in 1972 saw a sharp rise in the level of guerrilla activity. The great weakness of the Rhodesian whites as compared to those in South Africa is their very small numbers. Out of a total population of over 5 million, 250,000 whites would obviously face severe problems if unrest grew to proportions which required a prolonged mobilization. South Africa has taken a very cautious attitude toward rendering assistance. The republic is caught in the dilemma that successful revolution in Rhodesia would set a disturbing precedent. Yet too deep an entanglement might draw a great deal of opprobium and entail an unnecessary involvement in a situation worse than that of South Africa itself. South African police have been committed to action in Rhodesia, but in a small-scale and inconspicuous fashion. In many ways South Africa might be better served by another compliant black state like Malawi than by the present white Rhodesia.

The really substantial guerrilla movements are to be found in the Portuguese territories of Angola and Mozambique. In Angola, activity was begun in the early sixties by the Angolan Revolutionary Government in Exile (GRAE), founded by Holden Roberto. More recently the lead has been taken by the Angolan People's Liberation Movement (MPLA) which operates from Zambia with Russian support. This group has won fairly extensive control over the eastern province of Moxico.

In Mozambique a very vigorous guerrilla war was carried on for several years by the Frente de Libertação de Mozambique (FRELIMO) under a charismatic leader Eduardo Mondlane. In 1969, however, Mondlane was assassinated and since that time the movement has suffered from factionalism. The main body is supported by the Soviet Union but a sub-group, the Comité Revolucionario de Mozambique (COREMO), espouses a Maoist line and has Chinese support. FRELIMO is thought to have between 6000 and 9000 active guerrillas and has established control over several areas of Mozambique. Its main base is, however, in Tanzania. Incursions are also made from Zambia into Têtê province where the Cabora Bassa dam is to be built. Rightly or wrongly this dam, which would supply power to the Rand in South Africa, has become a symbol of efforts to perpetuate white rule in Africa.

To combat these movements the Portuguese have mustered the largest armed force in Southern Africa. Unlike the South Africans, the Portuguese are willing to arm black soldiers. This policy is facilitated by the deep tribal divisions among the Africans concerned. The total Portuguese forces in Africa now number more than 230,000, of which 100,000 are Europeans. There are also 13,000 European police. The cost of the effort is some $130 million a year. By 1972 the Portuguese had confined the MPLA primarily to the province of Moxico in Angola and had won back a good deal of lost ground in Mozambique. Throughout Southern Africa the forces of counter-insurgency profit from the fact that, contrary to much foreign supposition, most of the terrain is open.

Women recruits of PAIGC, the guerrilla movement fighting the Portuguese in Guinea.

Nevertheless, the sparse population and vast areas make control by either side a rather ephemeral condition in rural districts. Thus claims of success and counter-success are subject to abrupt revision.

So far as the Republic of South Africa is concerned there seems little immediate possibility of serious guerrilla successes. Radical change in Rhodesia or the Portuguese territories might alter the climate and a determined campaign of urban violence might pose difficult problems. The repressive mechanisms are efficient and it may well be that no such determined campaign could get under way. If it did, the counter-insurgency forces are well prepared but a prolonged condition of unrest and repression might have very awkward repercussions on South Africa's external relations.

The rebellions in the Portuguese territories are well established if not yet tremendously successful. In purely military terms the Portuguese forces could probably maintain the present state of order indefinitely. The problem here is much more likely to be increasing exasperation with the wars in Portugal itself, where the constant drain on the budget, and small but steady casualties, are unpopular with all but the powerful groups with interests in Africa. Even these may one day come to prefer the option of a deal with the nationalist movements such as those that have been made in other ex-colonial territories.

There remains the question of South Africa's place in the wider world balance of power. The South Africans see themselves as a southern bastion of the Western alliance. As we have seen, Great Britain, South Africa's traditional link with the Western European powers, has regarded the political costs of a close association as outweighing the strategic advantages. Indeed, through the medium of the rather one-sided Simonstown Agreement, Britain has been able to enjoy the essential advantage of assured access to South African facilities without giving much in return. This attitude has been reinforced by the assumption that in any serious conflict with the Communist powers, South Africa would be compelled by sheer self-interest to throw its lot in with the West. In the late sixties, however, several factors enhanced the strategic attractions of South Africa and gave new arguments to the advocates of a closer military relationship between NATO and the republic. These factors included: the expansion of Russian naval power and its extension into the Indian Ocean; the closure of the Suez Canal and the diversion of shipping around the Cape; and the thaw in relations between South Africa and some of her African neighbours, which did something to reduce the stigma of associating with her.

The Cape Route is of undoubted importance. As South Africans were quick to point out, the closing of the Canal in 1967 represented the third occasion in just over twenty-five years when the Middle Eastern route had been severed. About fifty ships a day arrive at Western European ports having originated from, or having rounded, the Cape. Two thirds of these are diversions from Suez. About 12,000 ships a year call at the Cape and another 14,000 pass without calling. After a period in which very few British warships made use of the base facilities at Simonstown, forty-six warships and thirty-seven auxiliaries had visited within eight months of the closure of the Canal. In the event of a conventional war, the facilities of the Cape would be of irreplaceable value. Other minor anchorages exist up the East African coast and in Mauritius, but only South Africa offers an ideal position, elaborate dockyard facilities backed by an industrial hinterland, a small but efficient local navy, modern communication facilities and a fair degree of political reliability.

The new importance of the Cape Route is not a transient affair dependent solely on the closure of the Canal. In recent years the technology of ship

construction has made possible the building of very large tankers of 200,000 tons and even larger. These vessels make passage round the Cape economically competitive with use of the Canal even at pre-1967 tariffs. Most of the new supertankers could not pass through the Canal loaded and the very largest could not do so even in ballast. Europe's oil supplies from the Gulf are therefore increasingly tied to the Cape.

A mere shift in shipping habits will not create a strategic problem unless a plausible military threat appears. For many, the appearance of the Soviet Navy in the Indian Ocean has created just such a threat. Soviet naval deployment to the Indian Ocean began in 1968 with an extended series of courtesy visits. Since that time a more or less continuous presence has been maintained with a peak strength of about two dozen ships. Many of these ships have been non-combatant types associated with missile tests and satellite tracking. The Russians have laid mooring buoys off the Seychelles, Madagascar and Mauritius. They have secured port facilities in Aden, Hodeida, Mogadishu and Berbera. With Mauritius they have also concluded an agreement to facilitate the rotation of trawler crews; an arrangement that could be easily adapted to such naval uses as the servicing of submarines. Various ill-defined rumours have suggested the acquisition of base rights in India, at Vishakhapatnam and on South Yemen's island of Socotra.

There can be no doubt of Soviet determination to become a part of the naval scene in the Indian Ocean. What is debatable is the purpose the Russians have in mind. A naval presence accords well with Russian political penetration of the area. The wide range of port visits in India, East Africa, the Red Sea and the Gulf is a useful advertisement. With the Canal closed, the Indian Ocean is an immensely difficult area for the Russians from the logistic point of view and the reopening of the Canal would probably result in a more lavish deployment.

Strategic defence also offers a very good reason for the Russians to enter the Indian Ocean. The Bay of Bengal, Arabian Sea and Persian Gulf offer American Polaris submarines a field of fire over the Indian Ocean that is exceeded only

Left A Russian submarine rounding the Cape of Good Hope on its way to the Indian Ocean.

Below South African-built Macchi trainers. South Africa is developing its own arms industry in an attempt to ensure independence from Western pressure.

The naval base at
Simonstown.

from the Arctic Ocean. American construction of a VLF station on the North West Cape of Australia and interest in establishing a naval communication centre on the British island of Diego Garcia indicate that this possibility has not escaped American attention. A Russian naval presence can at least lay the groundwork for some countervailing capability. At the same time encouragement of local naval efforts will also help to crowd a hitherto rather uncongested sea.

There is no reason to believe, however, that the appropriate response to a Soviet damage-limiting naval deployment in the Indian Ocean – itself a rather forlorn task – would be an equivalent Western surface deployment. The case for an increased Western naval presence and, consequently, for placing a higher value on South African ports and the co-operation of the South African navy, must therefore rest either on a plan to offset the political effects of the Russian presence or on the belief that the Russians may launch an open attack on Western shipping.

The flurry of argument in favour of reviving the British naval relationship with South Africa that accompanied the return of a Conservative Government in Britain in 1970 laid heavy stress on the latter possibility. At that time the immediate question concerned the resumption of sales of maritime weapons to South Africa, following the precedent and, according to some, the actual or implied commitment, embodied in the Simonstown Agreement.

It seems clear that no such commitment can be found in the actual language of the agreement. South Africa undertook to buy six frigates and other ships from Britain. The Royal Naval Commander-in-Chief was to be responsible for the whole area but to have no authority over the South African navy unless the two countries became co-belligerents. In peacetime the South African navy was to have responsibility for a defined 'South African area'. Simonstown was to come under South African control in 1957 but Britain was to have the use of it in peace or war, whether South Africa was a belligerent or not.

Advocates of co-operation with South Africa maintain that the recognition of a common interest in defence of the area, in view of which South Africa gave Britain remarkably unfettered base-rights, entailed an obligation to help South Africa keep its maritime forces in good order. Without conceding a legal obligation, the new British Conservative Government of 1970 returned to the principle of standing ready to sell arms suited for the external defence of South Africa. The only early fruit of this policy, however, was the sale of seven Wasp helicopters. For South Africa the principle of acceptability and association was probably more important than any particular weapons. Certainly South Africa would be unlikely to return to dependence on any one supplier. Nor did the slight warming in British–South African military relations lead South Africa to cease efforts to diversify her security relationships. As the idea of extending the NATO commitment into the Southern Atlantic remained abortive, South Africa began to develop ties with Latin American nations. Some talk was heard of a South Atlantic Treaty Organization, but the project seemed to suggest a widening of outlook rather than a practical proposal for action.

Debate about the best response to Russian naval presence in the Indian Ocean continues. The reasons why an overt attack on shipping seems an unlikely occurrence were dealt with briefly in the discussion of maritime war. Such an attack would be very much out of keeping with the established ways in which the Soviet Union employs its armed force, though admittedly one cannot rule out completely the possibility that increased naval power might generate new behaviour. But the Soviet Navy is even yet ill-prepared to take on the Western powers in a long-range conventional war. So far as the special case of the Indian Ocean and the Cape route is concerned, these are areas which, if logistically difficult for NATO, are infinitely more so for Russia, especially if the Canal is closed or denied to the Russians, as it probably would be in a limited war. Even imagining a localized limited war, it is far from clear that the Cape would offer Russia its best point of interception for the crucial oil traffic. The bulge of West Africa or, if she had established a sizeable Indian Ocean fleet, the Gulf itself, might offer better pickings. Experience and theory both suggest, however, that political action at the source would offer a far more efficient and certainly less risky way of interrupting Western oil supplies, if that were the motive.

There remains the question of political influence. The Soviet fleet is only one of many instruments of growing Russian influence around the Indian Ocean. Indeed, it would be hard to say whether the fleet is more the agent or the beneficiary of this influence. This naval presence is not entirely welcome to the local states. Some view a prospective naval rivalry between East and West with apprehension and there have been proposals for neutralizing the Indian Ocean. So long as the Soviet presence continues, the Western powers will probably think it unwise to concede it an unchallenged predominance. Given the freedom of the seas and the hospitality of local states, there is no way to exclude the Russian fleet in peacetime but a symbolic countervailing presence can be sustained. It is, of course, possible that while avoiding any direct clash with the Western powers, the Russian fleet may begin to intervene in local disputes, shoring up friendly régimes and encouraging the enemies of others. A complete absence of Western naval power might be thought to give an unnecessarily free hand to such proclivities.

So long as Western powers, and Britain in particular, want to maintain a naval presence in the Indian Ocean, South African facilities will remain very useful. Their utility would rise if naval operations became active and intense. But, given modern methods of replenishment, the facilities are not essential. Any conspicuous *rapprochement* with South Africa to maintain or extend co-operation would have to reckon with unfavourable reactions in black Africa. If the danger were thought to be active combat with the Russians, these reactions would doubtless be discounted; if it were the political penetration of East Africa that was at stake, the price might well be thought excessive. Thus it seems likely that the present rather chilly marriage of convenience will continue.

PART IV

Current Problems

CHAPTER TWELVE

Disarmament and Arms Control

Some Problems of Disarmament and Arms Control

The terms 'disarmament' and 'arms control' are frequently used as if they were interchangeable. There is, however, a fundamental difference between the two conceptions. Disarmament describes the process of reducing or abolishing armaments. This may be done universally, by a small number of nations, or unilaterally. It may be done voluntarily, or it may be imposed, as in the case of Germany under the Treaty of Versailles. Arms control is a new phrase and a new conception which emerged during the nineteen-fifties. It entails efforts to regulate armaments in order to make war less likely and to mitigate its effects if it occurs. The effects of arms control can be attained by unilateral policies of restraint but the phrase is commonly used to refer to bilateral or multilateral understandings. An important feature of recent efforts to achieve arms control, however, has been the use of tacit rather than explicit agreement to abstain from dangerous or provocative military policies. Indeed, from the perspective of arms control, national military policy and international attempts to achieve restrictive agreements should both be regarded as part of an integrated effort to maintain national security.

Disarmament and arms control are thus closely related, and particular policies and agreements may contain elements of both. But, whereas all genuine disarmament agreements will be intended to contribute toward the purposes of arms control, not all arms control policies will necessarily involve disarmament. They may, like the Hot Line agreement, be concerned with ancillary matters, or, like a determination to maintain stable second-strike forces, may actually dictate a multiplication of particular weapons.

It is important not to allow the apparent purpose of a disarmament or arms control proposal to obscure its probable real consequences. Some well-intentioned agreements or policies, like the relative disarmament of the democracies in the thirties, may lead to serious instability and war. Other proposals may not even be well-intentioned, but designed either to make good propaganda or to secure a disproportionate military advantage. Moreover, just as some disarmament proposals may be made to secure military advantages, others may consciously accept military risks in order to promote a favourable political climate. Thus all disarmament proposals, like all military policies, need careful scrutiny to determine their likely practical effect. The mere aura of good intentions is no assurance of beneficial results.

Several different lines of argument can be used to support the general assumption in favour of disarmament and arms control. Disarmament, which, by definition, entails the reduction of armaments, offers appealing prospects of economy. Arms control is not necessarily so attractive in this respect, for it may actually require increased expenditure on more sophisticated weapons or on the mechanisms of command and control. Moreover, as in the case of underground

President Kennedy signs the
Test Ban treaty of 1963.
This was the first significant
move toward placing
limitations on
the nuclear race.

nuclear testing, arms control measures may stimulate more expensive methods of achieving results. Disarmament itself, so long as it is not complete, may also encourage the diversion rather than the cancellation of military expenditure, as military establishments seek substitutes for prohibited weapons or try to compensate by quality for restrictions on quantity. On the widest perspective, we must also remember that resources released from military enterprises will not be available for other purposes unless national economic management is skilful enough to manage the transition. Studies of proposals for complete disarmament have concluded that only careful and energetic policies could prevent a subsequent major economic recession. More modest military economies would not, of course, pose such severe problems. It is only necessary to realize that military economies are not automatically translated into increased national welfare.

The most earnestly argued case for disarmament and arms control is not that of economy but of peace. Although it is easy to assume otherwise, there is no axiomatic reason why disarmament should ensure peace. There are, however, several long-established theories as to how it might do so, and one or more of these is usually at least implicit in disarmament proposals.

One such theory argues that armaments are the tools of war which make it possible. Remove the instruments and the activity will be prevented. Another, rather more subtle, theory regards armaments as a cause, perhaps the main cause, of war. Armaments, it is argued, arouse anxiety and counter-arming. This results in an arms race and, at some point, the tension snaps, with one side launching war, perhaps in the belief that it has achieved superiority, perhaps out of the fear that it is about to be put in a position of hopeless inferiority. A variant of the argument that arms cause wars concentrates on the social consequences of armament and particularly on the influence acquired by the military and the arms industry within a heavily armed state. In the more sinister interpretations, the 'merchants of death' actually seek war; in other versions, the militarist groups simply promote the arms race that leads inadvertently to war. This argument about the undue influence of what, in recent times, President Eisenhower called the 'military-industrial complex', clearly has application also to the economic arguments for disarmament.

There is some truth in all these theories but study of particular cases reveals that they are not entirely valid and consequently do not point the way to a panacea for war. It is obvious, for instance, that wars can begin at any level of armament; removing weapons will not prevent war if nations want to pursue a conflict to the point of violence. Indeed, low levels of armament, especially if, as in the thirties, they are asymmetrical, may encourage war. A rearmament race may be faster and produce more tension than a steady high level of armaments. Without any rigorous proof being possible, it seems plausible to argue that political conflicts are primary and armaments only secondary in the causation of armed conflict. This observation, however, must be modified in two respects. First, although the belief that the existence of armaments is the main cause of war is certainly mistaken, there is no doubt that the military balance may be the catalytic element in particular conflicts. The state of the balance and the systems of mobilization in 1914 undoubtedly conditioned diplomacy in many important respects. Second, the advent of nuclear weapons has transformed the relationship between military means and political ends in one fundamental respect. There is now a form of war, that with strategic nuclear weapons, which is so destructive that the price outweighs any conceivable political purpose. In this respect, the regulation of military confrontations takes priority over other policies; at least, it does for rational men. It is this realization that explains the unprecedented seriousness with which governments now approach disarmament and arms control. It is, however, a narrow and negative basis for agreement. This, in turn, explains the strictly limited scope within which agreement has proved possible.

A major difficulty in arriving at agreement, even between states that desire disarmament, is that they naturally desire disarmament with security. In other words, they reject the simple notion that disarmament will guarantee security and demand, on the contrary, a framework of security as a precondition for disarmament. The task of affording security presents overwhelming problems. If disarmament is to be total, the problem is one of creating a system of world government, for there must be some kind of force to impose order, and control of that force would confer world domination. If disarmament is to be partial, the problem is one of creating an equitable balance.

This task is difficult for two distinguishable reasons. One is the sheer complexity of military affairs; as we have seen, the assessment of relative military strength is extremely difficult. In an unregulated military balance, nations do their best to acquire what security they can at a price they feel they can afford. In a negotiated disarmament agreement, they naturally demand a much higher degree of precision and perfection. The difficulty is compounded by the fact that, the lower the overall level of agreed armament, the more significant any absolute level of inequity or evasion will be. The extreme form of this problem is that of the decisive advantage a small residual stockpile of nuclear weapons would confer in an otherwise nuclearly disarmed world.

The second great difficulty in arriving at a world of equitable disarmament and security is that, at any particular time, the military balance already contains many inequities and much insecurity. Most schemes for disarmament specify that the result shall leave the balance unchanged, that no nation shall obtain an advantage, and that all nations shall be secure. These requirements are inevitably inconsistent. Any programme of disarmament which was applied in 1973 and left South Viet Nam militarily secure, would obviously have wrought a major alteration in the balance of power. Someone is always dissatisfied with the *status quo*. In every field of armament some nations are ahead and others are trying to catch up. This phenomenon is particularly well illustrated by the efforts of the existing nuclear powers to impose a non-proliferation policy on all others.

Problems of equity and balance affect not merely the ultimate level of armament envisaged in a scheme, but also the period of transition. One of the aims of schemes of 'general and complete disarmament' (GCD) is to resolve this problem by defining an equitable level of armaments as zero, and approaching it with considerable speed. The extreme example of this was the Soviet proposal, under Chairman Khruschev, for progress to GCD in four years. Political and propaganda motives impelled the United States to table a rival, though less precipitate, proposal, but the impracticability is obvious.

As we have already seen, a total abolition of armaments would imply a proposal for world government. Very low levels of armament would also exacerbate the problem of the covertly reserved force and hence set the requirements for verification very high. But in any case, the so-called GCD proposals do not really envisage complete disarmament. All schemes have to make some provision for internal security forces. In many countries the police forces already constitute quasi-armies. The internal security forces of a large state could serve as an army to overawe a small neighbour, and the difficulty is enhanced by the fact that subversion and insurgency are already a recognized instrument of international conflict. Thus GCD does not really evade the problems of equity, balance and security that beset more modest schemes. Indeed, by its patent impracticability, the notion of GCD brings more plausible ameliorative schemes into disrepute.

Many disarmament schemes would require some system of verification to be acceptable. The purpose of verification is to engender confidence by offering a good prospect of detecting evasions of the agreement. If evasions are detected, the problem of enforcement arises. Enforcement may be achieved by some process of compulsion applied by other parties to the agreement, or by a specially established force, or it may take the form simply of reprisal: the other parties may reckon themselves released from their engagement.

Verification may be secured by inspection. This may be performed by other parties to the treaty or by a special institution. The latter principle is embodied in the inspection arrangements among the members of the Western European Union and by the International Atomic Energy Agency. Verification may also be secured in other ways: by the supply of information and production of records, for example. The resistance of the Soviet Union in particular to 'on site' inspection has inspired several schemes to minimize the intrusiveness of inspection. One proposal is for verification by 'challenge': if a party to an agreement comes to suspect a violation, it may say so. It is then up to the alleged violator to produce proof that the allegation is false. One way of doing this would be to permit an *ad hoc* inspection.

There can be no doubt that the most decisive development in verification has been the immense increase in the capacity for unilateral inspection afforded by satellite reconnaissance. As a result, national military intelligence services have become capable of providing a vast amount of information that previously could have been secured only with the voluntary co-operation of other states. The precursor of these techniques, the high-flying U2 aircraft, led to serious international friction. This was partly because the aircraft violated accepted notions of sovereignty and partly because the idea of a mutual interest in disseminating certain kinds of reassuring military information had not become widely accepted. One of the major contributions of the concept of arms control has been to win precisely such acceptance. Thus satellites have not been inhibited by an analogous notion of sovereignty over areas of space and, after a period of uncertainty, the SALT agreement was concluded under a thoroughly well-understood assumption of effective unilateral verification.

In view of all the difficulties, it is not surprising that relatively few disarmament agreements have been concluded. The one substantial achievement between the wars was the Washington Naval Agreement limiting numbers of capital ships among the major powers. This was made possible by the fact that the other powers were willing to concede Japan superiority in the Western Pacific and that Japan was not yet ready to seek more. Several years of effort to follow up the hopes for general disarmament held out by the Versailles Treaty foundered on all the obstacles we have just surveyed.

Since 1960, however, there has been a considerable spate of arms control agreements. Not many of these can be regarded as disarmament in the strict sense; perhaps only the treaty on bacteriological weapons has entailed the destruction of weapons that existed. Rather, the recent agreements have taken the form of pledges not to do things that the signatories did not want to do anyway. This is not to imply that the agreements are valueless. Sometimes the will to abstain has been conditional on reciprocal restraint by others. This was probably the case with the treaties on demilitarization of the Antarctic, abstention from placing weapons of mass destruction in space and the similar self-denying ordinance applicable to the seabed. Moreover, while such agreements might not have been made even on a basis of reciprocity if one major power had had a strong inclination to pursue the military option in question, the treaties, once made, may well serve to inhibit a signatory from taking up an option under changed circumstances.

There are other cases in which arms control policies may be pursued even without reciprocity. The American decision to pledge itself not to use bacteriological weapons and to destroy its stocks seems to have been based on a conclusion that it would never be in the interests of the United States to use such weapons whatever others did. This assumption is shared by most nations and thus it has been possible to arrive at an unverified and unverifiable agreement. At a different level, the tendency of the nuclear powers to move toward secure second-strike systems that do not invite pre-emption does not depend on others doing likewise, though parallel developments are certainly welcome as a further contribution to stability. The same is true of unilateral efforts to improve command and control over nuclear weapons. Indeed, far more has been done to fulfil the purposes of arms control by unilateral policy than by explicit international agreement. One should not underestimate, however, the influence of mutual example and many ostensibly unilateral policies have in them an element of implicit understanding that may often be more politically acceptable than an overt bargain.

Existing Arms Control Agreements

The more important arms regulation and control agreements concluded since the Antarctic Treaty in 1959 are summarized briefly in Appendix ii. These are: the Antarctic Treaty of 1959, the Partial Test Ban Treaty of 1963, the Treaty on Activities in the Exploration of Outer Space of 1967, the Latin American Nuclear-Free Zone Treaty of 1967, the Non-Proliferation Treaty of 1968, the Seabed Arms Control Treaty of 1971, the Convention on Bacteriological Weapons of 1972, and the Strategic Arms Limitation Agreement of 1972. In addition there are the Hot Line Agreement of 1963, several-times amended for technical reasons, and some bilateral Soviet–American agreements arising out of the flurry of negotiations in 1971–2. These included agreements on procedures to limit the consequences of accidental nuclear attacks and a pact to avoid provocative harassment between naval units. Some of these call for brief discussion, especially where they have implications for further agreement. There are also one or two other areas in which agreement is being actively pursued.

The Test Ban Treaty prohibits nuclear weapons tests in the atmosphere, under water or in outer space. This treaty has been ratified by more nations than any other of the agreements, but the signatories do not include France or China. The purpose of the treaty was partly to end the gradual development of a serious menace to health from nuclear fallout. In this respect it has been extremely successful. Another purpose was to hinder the process of nuclear proliferation. In this respect its success is debatable: the ban might marginally add to the embarrassment of a would-be nuclear nation, but is unlikely to override the powerful motives that would inevitably underlie a decision to acquire nuclear weapons. A third purpose of the ban, in the eyes of at least some of its advocates, was to inhibit the development of weapons by the existing nuclear powers. In this respect it has been a complete failure; France and China have ignored the treaty. The other nuclear powers have resorted to underground testing. This has cost them more and may have prevented their acquiring some information on weapons effects in the atmosphere and in space. But, with few exceptions, weapon development has proceeded unhindered and some engineering techniques may actually have been stimulated.

Considerable efforts have been made to extend the ban to all testing. The obstacle, which partly explains the resort to a limited ban, has been the Russian refusal to accept on-site inspection (we cannot be sure that other objectors would not have appeared if the Soviet Union had not taken the onus of recalcitrance) and the inability of remote seismic techniques to distinguish smaller nuclear explosions (below 10 KT with the latest techniques) from earthquakes. Enthusiasts for a total ban now argue that improved seismic techniques could give adequate discrimination. As with some other disarmament problems, it is suggested that absolute certainty of detection is unnecessary. All that is needed is a high probability of detection; then no would-be violator would take the risk of discovery and consequent embarrassment.

Be that as it may, the pressure for a total ban is likely to continue. If it is achieved, several novel questions will arise. Very esoteric scientific definitions will have to be devised as to what constitutes a nuclear test. Nuclear research will not be forbidden, yet the point at which fission and fusion reactions could serve the purposes of weapon development is far from easy to define. A more general question also arises as to whether the elimination of all testing will gradually erode confidence in the stockpiles of existing weapons or in weapons that are designed and manufactured after the ban becomes total.

The non-proliferation purposes of the Test Ban have been somewhat superseded by the Non-Proliferation Treaty. This treaty declares – debatably – 'that the proliferation of nuclear weapons would seriously enhance the danger of nuclear war'. Non-nuclear signatories undertake not to receive the transfer of nuclear weapons or to manufacture or otherwise acquire them. Nuclear states agree not to transfer nuclear weapons or explosives or control over them and not to assist any non-nuclear state to acquire them. Non-nuclear states agree to accept safeguard controls over all raw or manufactured fissionable material. These safeguards are to be applied by the International Atomic Energy Agency under specially negotiated agreements. The IAEA approved the form of such agreements in April 1971.

Non-nuclear states had argued very strongly that the treaty was not merely discriminatory – which it is by nature – but excessively so. In particular they demanded assurances that their competitive access to peaceful nuclear energy would not be hindered and that the nuclear states should proceed rapidly toward real nuclear disarmament. To this end the treaty provides for an automatic conference of signatories to be held at Geneva five years after the treaty came into force in June 1970. Coupled with the clause permitting withdrawal at three months' notice if 'extraordinary events, related to the subject matter of this treaty, have jeopardized the supreme interests' of a party, the review procedure puts considerable pressure on the nuclear powers. This pressure has undoubtedly played a part in generating the Superpowers' enthusiasm for SALT.

A large number of non-nuclear states, whose capacity and incentive to acquire nuclear weapons is great, have either not signed or not ratified the treaty. In 1972 the non-signatories included Israel, South Africa, India and Pakistan; those who had not ratified included Australia, Italy, Switzerland, Japan and West Germany. These abstentions, together with the escape clause, make it clear that, while the treaty may reinforce the political inhibitions against acquiring nuclear weapons, it can only succeed as part of an overall strategic climate in which non-proliferation continues to serve the special interests of each non-nuclear state.

The history of the Convention on Bacteriological Weapons affords a good illustration of the principle that weapons of dubious utility are much more easily renounced than those that already have an established place in military practice. Interest in the problem of chemical and biological weapons was revived by the American use of herbicides and harassing gases in Viet Nam. In 1969 a committee of experts working for the UN General Assembly published a report emphasizing the dangers of such weapons and arguing that their abolition would not seriously impair any nation's security. The Secretary General of the UN thereupon recommended that all states adhere to the Geneva Protocol of 1925, which prohibits the use in war of asphyxiating and poisonous gases and of bacteriological weapons. He also urged agreement that the ban in the Protocol was comprehensive and proposed a new undertaking not to produce or possess the prohibited weapons, rather than merely not to use them.

As ratified by most of the important signatories, the Geneva Protocol entails renunciation of the first use of the specified weapons between parties to the treaty. The United States had never acceded to the Protocol, though it had long maintained that it would observe its principles. In November 1969, however, under pressure of opinion, President Nixon agreed to submit the Protocol to the Senate. This was done in August 1970, but by late 1972 the Protocol had still not been ratified.

In his 1969 and subsequent declarations, President Nixon made it clear that the United States would not only refrain from using bacteriological weapons and toxins but would also no longer manufacture or stockpile such weapons. As to gases, the United States would renounce the first use of lethal or incapacitating agents, but would not regard the prohibition as extending to harassing agents or herbicides. This went contrary to a 1969 resolution of the General Assembly interpreting the Protocol as embracing all chemical agents without exception. The United Kingdom took this opportunity to declare that it did not regard the use of CS 'tearsmoke' as coming within the prohibited category, despite the fact that British declarations in the interwar period were interpreted as explicitly comprehensive in their references to the illegality of lachrymatory agents.

It was obvious that none of the leading powers regarded bacteriological weapons as instruments of rational warfare. Gases, however, had many conceivable tactical uses, and harassing agents and herbicides were in regular use. As a consequence it has proved possible to agree upon a convention abolishing bacteriological weapons, but not as yet to extend the provisions of the Geneva Protocol with regard to chemical weapons. The reluctance of some powers to give up chemical weapons is compounded by the difficulty of establishing an adequate system to verify compliance. Unilateral methods of verification, which are adequate for relatively crude limitations on strategic missiles, would not be sufficient to deal with chemical weapons. Given the general consensus that bacteriological weapons would not be very useful, at least to the major military powers, governments are willing to dispense with any stringent system of verification. Consequently, the Convention on Bacteriological Weapons, which was submitted to the United Nations in September 1971, provides only for complaints of a suspected breach of obligation to be reported to the Security Council. Parties to the Convention are obliged to co-operate with any investigation the Council may launch. The Council operates, of course, under the principle of Great Power veto.

The differential treatment accorded chemical and biological weapons thus clearly reflects a disparate estimate of their potential military utility. Some who advocated treating the two types of weapon simultaneously and similarly were afraid that a ban on biological weapons alone might seem to legitimize chemical weapons. The Convention therefore contains a clause expressly declaring that the Geneva Protocol is in no way limited or weakened by the new Convention. A rather similar anxiety is widely felt about the trend toward distinguishing between the harassing and other chemical agents. The chief justifications for such a distinction are that harassing agents may be a humane instrument, when compared to lethal conventional weapons, and that it is illogical to ban in war

The current status of the Non-Proliferation Treaty.

Countries that have not signed

Algeria
Argentina
Brazil
Burma
Byelorussian Republic
Cambodia
Chile
Equatorial Guinea
France
Gabon
Guyana
India
Israel
Malawi
Mauritania
Niger
Pakistan
Portugal
Rwanda
Saudi Arabia
Sierra Leone
South Africa
Spain
Tanzania
Thailand
Uganda
Western Samoa
Zambia

Countries that have signed but not ratified

Australia
Barbados
Belgium
Ceylon
Colombia
Congo
Egypt
El Salvador
Gambia
Federal Republic of Germany
Honduras
Indonesia
Italy
Ivory Coast
Japan
Korea, South
Kuwait
Libya
Luxembourg
Netherlands
Nicaragua
Panama
Philippines
Sudan
Switzerland
Turkey
Venezuela
Yemen

agents that are commonly used by police forces in peacetime. The main source
of anxiety is that it is not easy to draw a clear line between harassing and more
potent agents and that permitting the former may lead to escalation, either from
one agent to a more deadly analogous substance, or simply as a result of a
belligerent regarding the use of any gas as opening up the whole category of
chemical weapons. In this respect it is interesting to note that several of the
recorded uses of gas in war began with lachrymatory agents and proceeded to
more deadly gases. This was the case in World War I, in the Italian war against
Ethiopia, the Japanese invasion of China and the recent war in the Yemen.

The Strategic Arms Limitation agreements signed in Moscow in May 1972

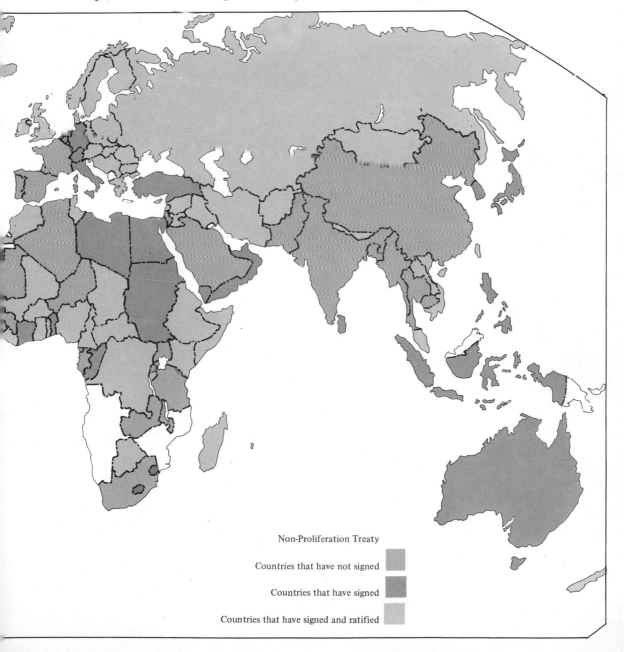

Non-Proliferation Treaty

Countries that have not signed

Countries that have signed

Countries that have signed and ratified

are undoubtedly among the most important of all arms control agreements yet concluded, for they directly restrict the most important weapons of the Super-powers. The agreements do not reduce the array of armaments that were in service at the time of signature; indeed, they permit certain substantial increases. Moreover, even these agreements fall into the category of agreement not to do things that neither really wants to do anyway. But, unlike the case of biological weapons, the willingness to abstain from certain lines of development in strategic weapons is very definitely dependent on a reciprocal restraint by the other Superpower. Thus the effect of the agreements is to register mutual restraint.

The origin of the SAL agreements can be traced back to proposals made by the American Administration under President Johnson between 1964 and 1967. In 1967 Mr Kosygin indicated Russian willingness, in principle, to pursue agreed limitations on strategic weapons, and actual negotiations began at Helsinki on 17 November 1969. During the years of negotiation, the positions of the two powers changed diametrically. Initially, the United States gave priority to restriction of ballistic missile defences as potentially destabilizing. The Soviet Union took the view that offensive as well as defensive weapons should be curbed. In the Russian view, defensive weapons should be regarded as benign elements in the strategic equation. After a time, however, the Soviet Union, having observed the pace of American ABM development, came to advocate curbs on defensive weapons and it was left to the United States, having seen the Russian build-up of offensive weapons, including the large SS9, to insist on an accompanying agreement on offensive systems. In May 1971 the two powers agreed to work primarily toward an ABM agreement with a parallel but subordinate understanding on offensive weapons.

Several factors have made the Superpowers receptive to a SAL agreement. As we saw earlier, the development of long-range nuclear missiles has brought about a situation in which either Superpower could devastate the other. This has engendered a sense of having attained a strategic plateau; no greater destructive power has any real value. Yet the development of ABM systems on the one hand and of MIRV on the other demonstrated that no technological plateau had been reached. Mutual vulnerability could be ensured but only at the expense of constant innovation and rising cost. The SAL agreements thus represent a pioneering attempt to avoid some of the expense by a pact to eschew certain lines of quantitative competition.

The agreement was made easier by the fact that the standstill of American procurement of missiles allowed the Soviet Union to catch up and, indeed, achieve some superiority. As a result, the Soviet Union could yield to its own need for economy and hope to avoid an expensive new cycle in the arms competition that the richer United States was better fitted to win. This was clearly expressed in *Pravda* on 7 July 1968, when it asserted that it was 'one of those rare moments in history . . . when both sides are ready to admit equality in the broadest sense and to view this as an initial position for reaching agreement concerning the freezing and subsequent reduction of arms'. For the first time, Russian writers depicted the arms race as a process of mutual interaction and not merely an evil necessity forced on the socialist camp by capitalist excesses. The recognition was, of course, all the easier because it represented an improve-ment on Russia's recent state of inferiority and a retreat from the previous American position of superiority.

The sense of futility about an expensive competition that resulted in no strategic advantage had, of course, developed before the agreements were reached. The agreements therefore registered a prior understanding. But this registration was by no means superfluous, as it serves not only as a basis for greater mutual confidence in the understanding, but also as a moderating influence on the internal debate over strategic policy that goes on within both Superpowers. A minor but palpable added incentive to achieve an explicit agreement was the obligation to make some gesture of arms limitation between the nuclear powers contained in the Non-Proliferation Treaty. The whole concept of strategic arms limitation between partners so mutually suspicious as the Soviet Union and the United States was made possible only by the development of satellite reconnaissance to a high state of perfection.

The agreements reached in May 1972 take two forms: one, a treaty limiting ABM deployment; the other an 'interim agreement' and a related protocol restricting offensive weapons. Adopting a less formal vehicle for the agreement on offensive weapons indicated an intention to go further in later negotiations and, perhaps, an American doubt as to the prospects for securing ratification of the latter arrangement by the Senate. Briefly, the treaty limits each side to one complex of up to a hundred ABMs around the national capital and another such complex around an ICBM site. Close restrictions are placed on the radar installations at such ABM sites to ensure that they are not capable of serving much more elaborate ABM systems, and other prohibitions preclude the building of similar radars elsewhere. This is important inasmuch as the radars are among the most easily detected elements in an ABM system and the component that takes the longest to deploy. The treaty provides for a bilateral commission to consider the working of the agreement and to form a channel for communication of reassuring information should doubts about compliance arise. Although the treaty is of unlimited duration, it can be denounced by a party at six months' notice if 'extraordinary events related to the subject matter of this treaty have jeopardized its supreme interests'.

Under the interim agreement the Superpowers agree not to start construction of ICBMs after 1 July 1972 and not to convert 'light' or old ICBMs into heavy ICBMs of types first deployed after 1964. This is aimed particularly at the SS9. The parties also agree to limit SLBMs and modern ballistic missile submarines to the numbers operational or under construction in May 1972, but reserve the right to construct new SLBMs and submarines to replace older types or to replace ICBMs. In the protocol the parties agree to interpret this confusing agreement on SLBMs to mean that the United States may have 710 SLBMs on 44 submarines and the Soviet Union may have 950 on not more than 62 submarines.

The full implication of these agreements will only emerge with time. Much depends on whether further agreements are made. As they stand, the 1972 agreements are important but strictly limited. They do nothing to limit qualitative development of weapons. The introduction and improvement of MIRVs can continue, though one indirect restriction arises from the limit on heavy missiles. Technical development of ABM may proceed; indeed, special provision is made for this in the treaty. It remains to be seen whether the spirit that gave rise to the agreements and the interchange of views on the bilateral commission and in continued SAL talks results in a general slowing down of the competition or whether, like the Partial Test Ban, the agreements merely divert energy into alternative strategic avenues, perhaps at increased rather than reduced expense. In the early days at least, both sides are likely to feel compelled to keep up a rapid pace of research and development as insurance against flaws in the arrangement. The agreements constitute an adjustment of the competitive strategic balance, not an alternative to it.

Minimum surviving force
to do unacceptable
damage to Soviet Union

Minimum surviving force
to do unacceptable
damage to US

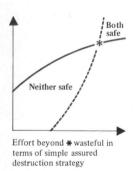

Effort beyond ✳ wasteful in
terms of simple assured
destruction strategy

An illustration of the
relationship between two
ICBM forces attempting to
maintain a secure assured
destruction capability
against each other's
counterforce potential.
At a certain point both
forces assure an adequate
retaliatory force and
further competition
becomes wasteful.

It is even more obvious that it will take a long time to show whether the agreements represent a triumph for peace and security. While it was undeniable that a race in strategic weapons was expensive, it was much more difficult to demonstrate that it increased the chances of war. Equally, it is hard to estimate the long-term effects of the Moscow agreements on the future political relations of the Superpowers and their allies. On the Western side, the mutual Soviet and American declarations of determination to avoid nuclear war are welcomed but only subject to certain interpretations. In particular, the allies of the United States must hope that the avoidance of war is achieved by Soviet forbearance from aggressive action and not by American acquiescence in it.

As soon as the Moscow agreements were made it was clear that the future course of arms control negotiations would provide an early test of alliance relationships. For the opening of talks on mutual balanced force reductions, perhaps within the framework of a European Security Conference, would inevitably link up with the SAL talks on the issue of forward-based nuclear delivery systems (FBS). This problem might present the United States with an explicit choice between the interests of its European allies and the pursuit of its bilateral relationship with the Soviet Union.

Some of the implications of MBFR for the relative strength of NATO and the Warsaw Pact were discussed earlier. As arms control proposals the notions of MBFR and an agreement on European Security have a long and devious history.

One line of ancestry can be traced from the various peace plans for Germany put forward in the early fifties. From the Soviet point of view these proposals were intended to keep West Germany demilitarized and out of NATO. A parallel campaign against 'foreign bases' suggested that a maximal Soviet objective was to secure American military withdrawal from Europe. After Germany entered NATO, Soviet attention turned to the Rapacki Plan of 1957 for denuclearization of central Europe. This was intended to ensure that West Germany did not acquire nuclear weapons, and to frustrate NATO efforts to adopt a nuclear strategy to offset Russian conventional strength. Also during the middle fifties, both East and West formulated a series of proposals for the reduction of forces in Central Europe, usually discussed under the rubric of 'disengagement'. These proposals all foundered, usually because of failure to resolve their implications for the future of Germany. The Russian suppression of Hungary in 1956 did not conduce to an atmosphere of mutual confidence.

By the mid-sixties Russian attention turned more towards the erosion of American military presence in Europe and to the undermining of the North Atlantic alliance, which was approaching the end of its initial twenty-year term in 1969 and was under attack from President de Gaulle. The chosen vehicle was a proposal for a European Security Conference (ESC). This idea was put forward in 1966 and with especial vigour by a conference of European Communist parties held at Karlovy Vary in 1967. The tone of the proposal was energetically ideological and it appeared that Canada and the United States would be excluded from the conference as non-Europeans. After the Czechoslovakian crisis of 1968 the Warsaw Pact reverted to the ESC but in a milder tone. A declaration issued at Budapest in 1969 emphasized that the negotiation should be between blocs – an idea that would have been anathema to de Gaulle – and appeared to admit Canadian and American participation. This concession was expressly confirmed in 1970. The suggested agenda concerned trade and a mutual renunciation of force; the chief purpose seemed to have shifted from expelling the United States to legitimizing Soviet hegemony in Eastern Europe. The preliminary stages of an ESC began at Helsinki in November, 1972.

Meanwhile the United States and NATO had introduced an emphasis on MBFR. The American National Citizens Commission, appointed by the President, had reported in favour of mutual force reductions in 1965 and the NATO Council formally proposed MBFR at its Reykjavik meeting in 1968. As we have seen, this proposal was repeated in elaborated form at the Rome meeting of 1970. After initial caution, partly related to unwillingness to seem to release American troops to fight in Viet Nam, the 1970 meeting of the Warsaw Pact Foreign Ministers at Budapest agreed that MBFR could be discussed at an ESC. The conclusion of an SAL agreement at Moscow in 1972 gave renewed impetus to the idea of ESC and the important bearing of the agreement on the FBS paved the way for MBFR negotiations that began in Vienna in 1973.

We have already noted that, starting from a position of weakness, NATO has little to hope for from MBFR in military terms unless the Soviet Union is unexpectedly generous. Looked at simply as a problem in designing an equitable measure of arms control, there are many technical difficulties to overcome. The area of reductions will need careful definition. Usually the so-called central region embraces Poland, Czechoslovakia, East and West Germany and Hungary. Possibly the Benelux countries might be included. There must also be a decision as to which nations make the cuts demanded of each alliance. These cuts must be made by 'indigenous' as well as 'foreign' forces if they are not to result in a very large reduction in the American presence. If indigenous forces are cut, they must presumably be demobilized, which raises a question of verification. Similar problems surround the question of replacement of equipment and 'roulement' of units into and out of the restricted area.

The question of verification could be made very difficult or relatively easy. If complete assurance of compliance were required, then a most elaborate and intrusive system of inspection would be necessary. The independent intelligence systems of each alliance – or, rather, of the member states of the alliances – are, however, fairly efficient. It could thus be argued that gross violations of an agreement would be readily detected and that small violations would be of little significance. But if this is true from the military point of view, an agreement on force levels might nevertheless become a source of political controversy. This might be particularly true during periods of crisis and high tension. Allegations and suspicion of violations might exacerbate relations between the alliances; differences as to how to interpret evidence and how to respond to violations might also prove a fruitful source of friction within the Western alliance. Indeed, the prospect of arms control in Europe will necessarily entail a reconsideration of the whole structure of Western defence and of the future relationship between Europe and the United States.

CHAPTER THIRTEEN

The Arms Trade with the Third World

The principle of comparative advantage, whereby it is most economically efficient for a country to export what it can produce most cheaply in exchange for imports of what it finds difficult and expensive to produce, applies to armaments as much as to any other commodity. As a consequence, there is a lively world trade in arms. The principle is, of course, never fully applied in any field of economic activity both because of inefficiencies in the market mechanism and because governments and individuals may have non-economic reasons to do differently and may be willing to pay an economic price to do so. The arms trade is especially subject to distortions of this kind. Those who might import weapons are usually very conscious of the loss of military self-sufficiency and independence this might involve. They may therefore accept a degree of economic inefficiency in order to maintain a domestic source of supply or at least to secure a variety of foreign sources. Sometimes the strictly strategic reasons for establishing or preserving an indigenous arms industry are believed to be reinforced by its indirect contributions to industrial development and sophistication. From the exporter's point of view, there are clearly important political and perhaps moral implications in providing other countries with the tools of war and coercion. Willingness to do so must obviously be much influenced by the supplier's attitude to the likely strategic behaviour of the recipient.

In many cases, trade in armaments consequently coincides with diplomatic alignments. Indeed, alignments and alliances are sometimes concluded and maintained precisely to secure supplies of arms. Most of the industrially advanced countries of the world are associated with one of the two great diplomatic blocs, centred upon the United States and the Soviet Union. These blocs are mutually exclusive so far as trade in armaments is concerned (with exceptions at the margins, such as computers and other electronics). Within the blocs, trade in weapons follows patterns chiefly determined by economic principles, modified by a degree of political deference to the leading ally.

The situation with regard to the so-called third world is more complicated. Most of the nations in this category have little or no capacity to produce modern arms at any level of economic sacrifice. They are therefore dependent on imports. Most of them are, however, far more politically indifferent than the industrialized nations as to where they secure their weapons. The third world's trade in armaments is thus a shifting and important element in world politics. It is also a subject of anxious debate for two particular reasons. One is that the vast majority of these nations are impoverished and their expenditures on arms are consequently a source of concern to those interested in their economic development. The other reason is that the incidence of actual armed conflict in the third world is high, and their trade in arms is therefore related with peculiar immediacy to questions of war and political change. This lends added gravity to the decisions of both supplier and recipient of armaments.

Opposite *Sovereignty*, a fast patrol boat built for the Singapore Navy by Vosper Thornycroft.

Right A comparison of sales of the four main modern arms suppliers.

Below Other producers and exporters of weapons.

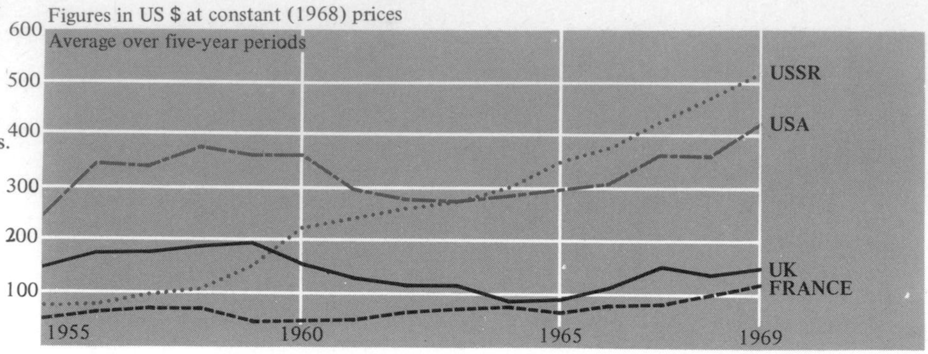
Figures in US $ at constant (1968) prices
Average over five-year periods
600
500
400
300
200
100
USSR
USA
UK
FRANCE
1955
1960
1965
1969

16 Categories (applicable)

★ Producer country's own design

☆ Produced or assembled not own design

	Aircraft					Missiles				Ships			Artillery		Tanks	
	SS Fighters	Subsonic	Trainers	Transports	Helicopters	SAM	SSM	ATGW	ASM/AAM	Submarines	Escorts	Patrol boats	Self-propelled	Towed	Medium	Light
Belgium 2/1	☆										★					★
Czechoslovakia 4/0 (13)			★										★	★		★
West Germany 10/5	☆	☆	☆	☆	★	★		★	★	★	★	★	★	☆	★	★
East Germany 2/0											★	★				
Italy 7/7	☆	☆	☆	☆	☆	★	★	★		★	★	★		★	☆	☆
Spain 5/5	☆	☆	☆	☆					★	★	★	★	★		☆	
Sweden 13/0	★	★	★				★	★	★	★	★	★	★	★	★	★
Switzerland 5/3 (13)	☆	☆		☆		★	★	★						★	★	
Yugoslavia 3/4		☆	☆		☆					★	☆	★		★		
Israel 3/3	☆		☆	☆			★					★		★		
United Arab Republic 1/1			☆				★									
South Africa 1/5	☆	☆	☆			☆								★		☆
Australia 2/4	☆	☆	☆				★				☆	★				
China 6/7	★	☆	☆	☆	☆	☆	★			★	☆	★		★	☆	★
India 1/9	☆	☆	☆	☆	☆			☆			☆	☆		★	☆	
Japan 9½/6½	☆	☆	★	☆	☆	☆		★	½★	★	★	★	★	★	★	★
Argentina 2/4		☆		☆						☆	★	★				☆
Brazil 4/4		☆	☆	☆			★	★	★		☆	★				
Canada 2/2	☆			☆							★	★				

In recent years concern about the implications of the arms trade has led several organizations to devote a great deal of energy to amassing information on the subject: notable among such organizations are the US Arms Control and Disarmament Agency, the Stockholm International Peace Research Institute, and the International Institute for Strategic Studies, based in London. Some of the relevant data are depicted in the accompanying tables and charts. What follows is a brief discussion of the more important trends and problems.

The Suppliers

In the interwar years there was much concern about the activities of private, capitalist armaments manufacturers, the 'merchants of death'. This is today a minor concern, for almost universally the arms industry is either nationalized or under very strict governmental control as to its activities. That is not to say that the profit motive has been eliminated but rather that, where it operates, it is within the limits of conscious official policy. The one remaining field for truly private enterprise is, perhaps, the supply of small quantities of arms, commonly second hand, to insurgents and revolutionaries. Here there still persists a certain amount of illegal traffic which is not without serious political consequences. Two recent examples are the supply of arms to the unofficial armies of Northern Ireland and a part, at least, of the provision of weapons to the Biafran rebellion. Even in such cases, however, it is never easy to be sure that ostensibly private activities are not connived at by governments as an instrument of covert policy.

Among the nations of the world, only four, the United States, the Soviet Union, France and Britain, manufacture a fairly full range of modern military equipment. During the post-war years these four nations have accounted for about 90 per cent of the world armaments production. Some weapons are made only by the two Superpowers, but most of these, such as ICBMs, are not those commonly required by other states. A more important consideration giving primacy to the Superpowers has been their willingness to supply weapons as gifts or on very favourable terms, whereas Britain, France and the other suppliers are constrained to primarily commercial dealings. For the more impoverished nations, therefore, the United States and the Soviet Union are virtually the only potential sources of expensive weapons. The picture is complicated, however, by the fact that the Superpowers have sometimes chosen to give military assistance through the medium of third parties. Nevertheless 65 per cent of all arms transfers to third-world countries over the last two decades have come from the United States and the Soviet Union.

After the big four, there comes a rather large group of states which can and do supply a varying range of equipment to the third world. These include: Italy, which has supplied aircraft, warships, tanks and small arms; West Germany and China, which have supplied aircraft, tanks and small arms; Czechoslovakia, aircraft and small arms; Sweden, aircraft, warships and small arms; Canada, chiefly aircraft, especially transports; the Netherlands, aircraft and small arms; Switzerland and Belgium, chiefly small arms; and Israel, small arms and a variety of captured equipment. Among other countries Spain, Yugoslavia, India, Argentina and Japan have either transferred arms to third world countries or show signs of doing so. None of these is as yet a supplier of major consequence.

The scale of the arms trade is considerable. It is estimated that the industrialized countries of the non-Communist world will trade some $35 billion worth of military equipment between each other in the decade 1965–74. This trade

Figures in US $ at constant (1968) prices

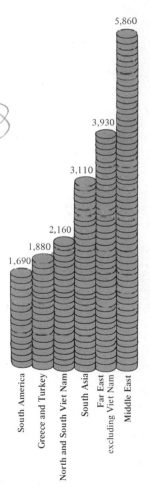

Arms imports by third-world countries divided by region.

An Israeli Phantom in action. Israel has relied heavily on the United States for its weapons.

bears upon that with the third world in that, like the developed countries' indigenous procurement, it releases large quantities of second-hand weapons for export and creates a financial incentive to do so. At 1970 prices the third-world countries themselves are thought to be spending about $6 billion a year on military hardware, of which a large proportion is imported. The pattern of these imports has shown significant fluctuations over the years. In the fifties and early sixties arms transfers ran at a high level as new sovereignties were created and the ex-colonial powers handed over defence responsibilities while at the same time the United States built up its network of alliances around the periphery of Russia and China. Since those years, there has been some tapering-off in exports, although special situations such as the Indo–Pakistan and Arab–Israeli wars have led to local increases. The Arab–Israeli war of 1967 led to particularly massive injections of Soviet arms to replace Arab losses, together with much smaller compensatory American supplies to Israel.

The major suppliers show certain individual characteristics. The United States is almost certainly the world's greatest arms manufacturer, but its own indigenous procurement is so massive that exports absorb only a tiny fraction of American output. This means that exports are not a major consideration for the American munitions industry as a whole, although foreign sales are naturally of importance to individual manufacturers. Although the proportion of exports to total production is small, the amount is very large in absolute terms and as a proportion of global trade. In recent years American export sales of arms to the third world have run at about $400 million a year, mostly to allies, with a roughly equal amount being given as grant aid. Over the whole period since 1945, the United States has probably supplied a little over half the world's arms exports. Moreover, these estimates do not include the heavy transfers of arms to South Viet Nam during American intervention in the Vietnamese war.

American policy has given priority to supply of arms to allied states in forward areas around Russia and China. Elsewhere the United States has supplied arms by sale or gift to countries displaying at least a moderate degree of benevolence toward American policy and co-operating with once strict, but now largely abandoned, embargoes on trade in strategic materials with the Communist nations. Hand in hand with the supply of arms has gone a large scale effort to provide military training to friendly countries, both in the United States and by means of military missions overseas.

At certain times and places the United States has tried to modulate its exports so as to establish a degree of local strategic stability. In these inter-mediate areas, however, American freedom of manœuvre was progressively confined by the appearance of the Soviet Union as a competitive supplier during the fifties. Previously the Soviet Union had tended to confine its supply of arms to confirmed opponents of the United States. Beginning in the mid-

fifties, however, the export of arms has become a more liberally used instrument of Soviet diplomatic influence. By thus providing an alternative source of supply, the Soviet Union both reduced the leverage that the United States had hitherto enjoyed from a monopolistic position and also increased American incentives to use arms supplies as a way to offset Russian influence.

American F5A fighters. These were designed as cheap and easy-to-run aircraft and have been widely supplied to more than fifteen air forces.

Up to the early sixties a very large proportion of American arms exports to the third world was by way of gift. In more recent years some relaxation in the American sense of urgency concerning the Cold War and increasing Congressional scepticism about military aid have engendered a shift towards sales. After 1970 and the American reduction of overseas military presence under the Nixon Doctrine, there were signs of a renewed impetus to grants of armaments as a means of devolving strategic responsibilities to local powers.

Something has already been said about the Soviet Union as a source of arms. Russian arms exports have run at an annual level of about $600 million, mostly in the form of sales at very favourable terms, often accepting in return the primary products of recipient nations. This figure does not take full account of the massive emergency supplies to the UAR after the war of 1967 and during the subsequent air battles along the Suez Canal. Nor does it give full weight to Soviet aid to North Viet Nam during the periods of intense war after 1968.

As with the United States, exports do not play a dominant part in the Russian arms industry, which is primarily geared to the Soviet Union's own lavish military procurement. There is no reason to believe that any Soviet arms exports are economically motivated and the entire business is therefore orchestrated to serve Russian diplomacy and military strategy. We have already remarked that the Soviet Union has progressively widened the range of countries to which it supplies arms, and the success attending this policy has resulted in an increasing number of Soviet customers and a somewhat reduced number of recipients for American arms. The initial breakthrough came with Czech and Russian replacement of Western nations as suppliers to Egypt in 1955. Another major step forward followed the Western embargo on sales to India and Pakistan during the war of 1965. In the five years that followed, the Soviet Union, which had only made its début as an Indian supplier three or four years previously, succeeded in providing more than 80 per cent of all Indian military imports. At the same time the Soviet Union kept a foot in the other camp by making limited shipments to Pakistan, particularly in the form of spare parts for Russian-made equipment that Pakistan had received from China. As this incident illustrated, the appearance of China as an arms supplier, however modest, creates competitive problems for the Soviet Union similar to those which the Russians themselves had posed earlier to the United States. After the war of 1967, for instance, Syria used approaches to China to overcome Russian temporizing about the supply of new aircraft.

Right A British-built Strikemaster aircraft in use with the Kuwait Air Force.

Below British SRN6 hovercraft of the Imperial Iranian navy.

British arms exports have averaged approximately $400 million a year, of which no less than half have gone to the Middle East. During the earlier post-war years, Britain exported a large quantity of arms to her former colonial possessions. Up to 1962 Britain was predominant as supplier to India. In the sixties general economic pressures and the special problem of trying to sustain a full range of arms industry with a contracting national military establishment became the chief incentives to export. The Labour Government explicitly recognized this in 1965 by the appointment of an overall co-ordinator of arms sales. Despite the traditional Labour Party suspicion of the arms industry, the Labour Defence Minister declared the next year that 'while the Government attaches the highest importance to making progress in the field of arms control and disarmament, we must also take what practical steps we can to ensure that this country does not fail to secure its rightful share of this valuable commercial market'.

These economic pressures ensure that most British military exports are on strictly commercial terms. As a result the British are frequently undercut by the two Superpowers which enjoy a larger industrial base and are ready to relax their terms for political reasons. British exports have also suffered in the past because the scale of British industry limits the range of products and these have frequently been designed to the highly sophisticated requirements of the British armed forces which, until recently, faced the dual demanding tasks of war in Europe and operations over long ranges East of Suez. The combination of simpler product and easier terms undoubtedly helped the Soviet Union oust Britain from the Indian market in the sixties.

On the other hand, Britain has done very well out of the sale of refurbished British aircraft – the Hunter and Canberra have been particularly ubiquitous. Much British army equipment, especially tanks, has also enjoyed a good reputation and, being rather less elaborate than aircraft, has been available at competitive prices. The performance of British armour in Israeli hands has been a good selling point and it must be recalled that almost continuous British counter-insurgency operations since 1945 have permitted the battle testing of many simpler weapons well suited to the third world. Meanwhile the rising sophistication of the military environment in the Middle East has facilitated the sale of British air defence systems. Another category in which Britain has done well is the sale of major naval vessels. This has been partly the result of British naval prestige and technological enterprise and partly due to the fact that shipbuilding is one area in which Britain is more than competitive with the United States so far as costs are concerned.

French arms sales have boomed in recent years, rising at 16 per cent a year in the sixties. This is largely the result of French freedom from the political inhibitions affecting the arms sales of other suppliers. French exports are chiefly impelled by the same economic considerations as dominate British policy. With these strong commercial incentives, France has moved decisively to take advantage of British and American political embarrassment in several lucrative markets. When South Africa accelerated its arms purchases after the declaration of the United Nations embargo in 1964, France became the main source of supply. Between 1961 and 1969 45 per cent of South African arms imports came from France. Similarly, France increased its exports to Pakistan after the Anglo–American embargo of 1965. In Latin America, France contributed to thwarting efforts by the United States to discourage the acquisition of supersonic aircraft by promoting sales of the Mirage. These French sales offer a particularly conspicuous instance of the way in which alternative

One of five gunboats built
by the French for the
Israeli navy.

suppliers undermine the political bargaining power of individual exporters.

In its efforts to use exports to sustain a French arms industry, France has met with remarkable success. No less than 30 per cent of French arms production is exported. Out of the first 700 Mirages produced, 400 were exported; similarly some 700 Alouette helicopters were sold abroad out of a production of 1300. On the other hand, it would be a mistake to overlook the political element in French export policy. There can be little doubt that French governments have welcomed the opportunity to undermine American preponderance in certain areas and similarly to challenge British influence. Diplomatic considerations overrode both economic advantage and domestic opinion in the French arms embargo against Israel imposed in 1967, which deprived the latter of a large consignment of Mirage v. The subsequent sale of these aircraft to the revolutionary government of Libya was also an obviously calculated political gambit. In French relations with South Africa, a special strategic consideration has been an arrangement for the supply of South African uranium to France.

With the exception of China, whose arms exports have been wholly in the service of foreign policy, the other substantial or potentially substantial exporters of arms have primarily economic motives, though these are frequently modified in detail by political inhibitions. Italy, which has become a major secondary source of arms supply, has done so on a fully commercial basis except for some small gifts to Somalia and the Congo. Much of what has been exported is American-designed equipment produced under licence. Italian naval vessels have sold well and Italy has developed a market for counter-insurgency weapons such as helicopters and light aircraft. The Macchi MB326 light jet armed trainer is now made under licence in Argentina as well as in South Africa.

West German foreign sales have been chiefly to the less-developed members of NATO, Greece, Portugal and Turkey. Like Japan, West Germany's defence industries have been kept small in proportion to overall industrial capacity as a result of political restrictions carrying over from defeat in World War II. Japanese exports so far have been chiefly small naval vessels, a few helicopters and training aircraft, and motor vehicles for military use. The resurgence of the Japanese armed forces and the corresponding increase in Japanese armaments production for indigenous use will, however, create a much larger potential for export and it remains to be seen whether Japan's role in the arms trade becomes more commensurate with her pre-eminent position in international trade.

The two European armed neutrals, Sweden and Switzerland, present interesting cases as exporters. Sweden is, for its size, unusually self-sufficient in arms production. This achievement is due partly to carefully phased and sustained production runs, which avoid over-capacity, and partly to the heavy use of foreign components which are built into native designs. In this respect Sweden's real self-sufficiency is less than might be incautiously deduced from the existence of a range of Swedish high-performance aircraft. Such independence as Sweden possesses has been achieved without heavy reliance on exports. Indeed, Sweden has probably been more inhibited by political considerations in its arms sales policies than any other major producer. At various times Sweden has applied arms embargoes against Portugal, South Africa, the Middle Eastern countries, India, Pakistan, and, because of Viet Nam, Australia and the United States. Nevertheless, some Swedish arms have found their way through devious channels to areas of combat, notably to Biafra during the Nigerian civil war.

Switzerland has presented a very different picture. Here the arms industry is chiefly in private hands and is engaged mainly in the production of light weapons. Over 70 per cent of Swiss military exports are of small arms and ammunition. These have flowed freely abroad and the system of governmental controls has been both permissive and, occasionally, ineffective. Switzerland is thus one of the relatively few places where there have been recent scandals concerning the exploitation of the arms trade for private profit.

The scale of arms sales to third-world countries, including licensed production, is very considerable. One estimate for the period 1955–68 suggests that during that time 7000 combat aircraft, nearly 2000 transport aircraft, 2500 training aircraft, 1500 helicopters, 12,000 tanks, 1600 APCs, over 100 large warships, and nearly 600 patrol boats were delivered. The type of weapon transferred depends chiefly, but not entirely, on the military problems of the recipient nations. These are typically counter-insurgency operations, although in some areas, notably the Middle East and India–Pakistan, the pattern is of highly sophisticated combat between states. In other areas also, however, considerations of prestige have created markets for advanced weapons. Some simplified versions of the most sophisticated weapons, such as the F5 and the Mirage V, have been developed as a compromise for export. Similar results have been achieved by refurbished second-hand weapons.

The motives of exports are, as we have seen, very mixed. For the Superpowers a prime motive is the extension of political influence and the winning of strategic advantages. Arms have been traded for bases and are supplied to friendly powers to retain their friendship, and to strengthen them to perform their role as allies and auxiliaries. For the United States, the chief purpose has been to shore up the countries bordering Russia and China. The problem for those trying to gain and preserve influence by the supply of arms is complicated by the appearance of alternative suppliers, particularly if they are hostile.

So long as one side enjoys a monopoly position it can use the control of arms supplies not only to obtain leverage over a recipient's foreign policy, but also to manipulate the local military balance. The United States has made several efforts to stabilize local balances. In the Middle East the United States, Britain and France made a tripartite agreement in 1950 to regulate arms supplies to the local powers. That policy foundered after Russian sales began in 1955 and the United States has since tried to measure its own supply unilaterally so as to offset Russian sales and thereby maintain an equilibrium. We have already referred to a similar American effort to regulate arms supply in Latin America. As elsewhere, the existence of alternative sources of supply has made the effort to use supplies as an instrument of control at best uncertain. That uncertainty is minimized, of course, where rigid confrontations narrow the field from which individual recipients can draw. The Middle East affords the most clearcut example of this. But as that example demonstrates, the recipients can frequently use a wide range of other political influences to negate efforts to withhold military supplies.

The Soviet record of using arms supplies to secure political influence is a mixed one, testifying to the volatility of political situations. In Indonesia and Ghana, Russia used substantial military supplies, particularly in the former case, to support pro-Soviet régimes. Political *coups* in both states overthrew the régimes and deprived the Soviet Union of its foothold. In Nigeria, however, well-timed assistance to the federal government during the civil war seems to have won the Russians considerable goodwill. In the Middle East, arms supplies patently play the central role in Russian ascendancy over several of the Arab states. The supplies have also become a dominant factor in the local strategic balance. Similarly, Russian supplies to India have been part of a steady growth

A Russian-built MiG 21 of the Indonesian air force.

in Russian influence and an important contribution to the rise of Indian regional predominance.

It is not easy to draw firm conclusions from this mixed record of efforts to use arms supplies to win influence and control events within the third world. Clearly arms supplies are a useful and probably inevitable part of the wider range of diplomatic instruments at the disposal of the Great Powers. Only the Superpowers have the resources to employ this instrument on a grand scale relatively indifferent to economic considerations. Where there are alternative suppliers, the influence of the Superpowers may be undermined. The lesser suppliers are chiefly motivated by economic considerations, and, where those considerations predominate, the political effects of sales are more likely to be discounted. Moreover, except in extreme cases, like the Middle East, the weapons most relevant to actual military situations are the simpler and cheaper kinds for which a multiplicity of suppliers exist. It is consequently far from easy for an arms-exporting nation to establish itself as a monopolistic supplier to any one recipient, and the possibilities for using arms supplies as an instrument of political control are correspondingly limited.

The Recipients

The pattern of behaviour among the third-world recipients of arms imports varies markedly between individual states, as we might expect, and also between the regions of the world. These patterns are determined by a variety of influences of which the three most important are probably the incidence of conflict in the area, the domestic system of the importer, and the intensity of Great-Power interest in the local situation. In the two decades since 1950 70 per cent of arms exports have gone to the Middle East and Asia. Of these 30 per cent have gone to the Far East, 25 per cent to the Middle East, and 15 per cent to India and Pakistan.

The Far East has been the scene of large indirect armed struggles between the United States and the Communist powers, chiefly in Korea and Viet Nam. More recently this conflict has been complicated by the split between Russia and China and the subsequent competition between them for influence over Asian revolutionary and nationalist movements. Under these stimuli the United States and Soviet Union have provided over 80 per cent of the arms supplied to the Far East, as compared with a 65 per cent contribution to exports to the world at large. North Viet Nam and North Korea have had some success in playing China and the Soviet Union off against each other; South Viet Nam, South Korea and Taiwan have been almost wholly dependent on the United States.

Competition between India and Pakistan has been primarily due to the territorial disputes between the two and to their more general political and ideological rivalry and antipathy. The fundamental asymmetry in the confrontation was partly offset by the disproportionate influence of the military within Pakistan, the weaker state. As we saw, the stimulus to Indian military efforts provided by the brief war with China in 1962 provoked India into realizing more of her superior military potential and culminated in the Indian victory over Pakistan in 1971. These experiences have also given a sharp impetus to India's arms industry and India could now play a significant part among the ranks of the suppliers.

The keen appetite for armaments in the Middle East is well known. In the twenty years after 1950 50 per cent of the arms supplied to this area came from the Soviet Union and 30 per cent from the United States, the balance coming chiefly from Britain and France. The Middle East vies with Viet Nam as the most intensive and sophisticated consumer of military exports. Israeli efforts to win a degree of independence from foreign supplies have, as in the similar case of India, accelerated development of an indigenous arms industry which has now become a modest exporter in its own right. Some of these exports have been aimed at winning friends, as in East Africa, but an arms industry with such a restricted basis as the Israeli economy will obviously have strong economic incentives to seek additional markets.

Black Africa provides a striking contrast to the military sophistication of the Middle East. Ethiopia alone has absorbed much advanced weaponry. The general propensity of Africa to import arms or maintain large armed forces is low. The civil war in Nigeria gave rise to a substantial military build-up and has left that country with by far the largest Black African armed forces. Nevertheless, the arms imports of the whole of Black or sub-Saharan Africa in the years 1966–71 were barely 70 per cent of those of the Republic of South Africa alone.

There are several reasons for this: a low incidence of interstate conflict and a preoccupation with internal security; a low level of disposable income; a shortage of technical skills; and relative insulation from the more intense areas of Superpower competition. Out of some thirty-five countries, less than a dozen possess any combat aircraft and several have no military aircraft at all. Only about half a dozen have tanks. As a result of the combination of recent colonial connections, the simple nature of the arms required, the relative indifference of the Superpowers and the African states' own desire to avoid involvement in the bi-polar alignment, arms suppliers other than Russia and the United States play a larger part in the pattern of arms supply in Africa than in any other region. Forty per cent of African arms come from Britain and France, 25 per cent from other suppliers and only 30 per cent from the Superpowers. The reported transfer of Chinese MiG 17s to Tanzania opens up the possibility of a more substantial role for China as a supplier. Though Chinese resources are limited, quite small injections of armament would be enough to have a significant impact on the sparse African military scene.

Latin America is also a region of only moderate importance to the world arms trade, though it is in all respects more active than Black Africa. Once again, the causes are to be sought in an extraordinarily low incidence of interstate conflict and a preoccupation with internal security operations requiring only simple arms. With occasional exceptions in the Caribbean and Central America, actual interstate warfare has been virtually unknown in Latin America for decades. On the other hand, the armed forces are an important and, in many cases, the dominant political force in all but two or three Latin American states. As a consequence, military budgets are higher than the apparent level of security problems might lead one to expect. Much of this expenditure is, however, devoted to personnel and the proportion allocated to hardware is unusually low: quite commonly no more than 10 per cent.

Some Latin American states have maintained this pattern of expenditure by being content with antiquated equipment. Latin America has been the last home of many venerable weapons of World War II vintage. In some cases, however, a desire for prestige, both on the domestic scene and vis-à-vis neighbouring states, has led to purchases of advanced equipment and this trend seems to be accelerating. Quite possibly the much publicized exploits of the Middle Eastern and Indian armed forces have inflated ideas of what is expected of a medium power's armed forces. American effort to curb this tendency has opened the way for European exports which now enjoy 60 per cent of the market. The breakthrough in supersonic aircraft has already been recorded and another noteworthy development has been the placing of sizeable orders for new naval vessels, several of them from Britain.

The Consequences of the Arms Trade

Those who are concerned with the economic development of the third world and those who subscribe to the view that supplies of armaments cause or exacerbate conflicts, fear that the nations of the third world pay a heavy economic and political price for their arms imports. In money terms these imports have been rising at 9 per cent a year, compared with a rise in overall military expenditure of 7 per cent and in GNP of 5 per cent. The question of the economic effects of this expenditure is a complex one. Given that the imports are frequently financed by generous credits that would probably not be available for other purposes, it is hard to determine how far the importer's real resources are being consumed. Another aspect of cost, the absorption of skilled manpower in the armed forces and for the maintenance of modern equipment, is also controversial. For there are those who argue that the armed forces constitute a constructive force by creating a centre of forced technical development and a nursery of administrative skills. Like arguments for the arms industry in advanced countries as a source of technological innovation, the concept of military expenditure as a positive ingredient in economic development is open to the objection that direct ways should be available to serve the purpose more efficiently. But whether such alternatives would actually be adopted remains speculative, and the speculation would have to take into account the fact that, for most countries, military necessities are not wholly imaginary and that consequently the clear-cut option of abolishing the armed forces is not a real one.

Whether the equipment of armed forces with modern weapons makes for conflict is a special case of the general argument, discussed earlier, as to whether disarmament would afford a panacea for war. Paradoxically it could be argued that, for many of the third-world nations, it is the simpler weapons that would be really useful in military terms and that, although sophisticated prestige weapons may consume resources, they do not pose much of a threat to others. This argument, however, needs to be modified by the consideration that advanced weapons might not prove useful in practice, but they may nevertheless alarm neighbouring states.

In some cases the state of the arms balance has certainly seemed to precipitate conflict. There was an element of pre-emptive alarm in Pakistan's reactions to Indian rearmament before the war of 1965 and the series of Middle Eastern wars and crises has clearly been related to assessments of shifting military advantage. In all cases, however, the perceived balance has been compounded of more than just the quantity and quality of hardware. The most one can say with assurance is that the acquisition of weapons has played a part in raising tension on occasion and in precipitating particular outbreaks of war. It is not possible to lay the underlying conflicts at the door of the arms trade or to be sure that the frequency or seriousness of actual outbreaks of violence would have been less if the arms had not been made available.

The Nigerian civil war offers an interesting example of a conflict that certainly began without any reference to the arms trade. It can be, and was at the time, argued that without the supply of foreign arms the conflict would have ended earlier. This is far from certain, as the belligerents' capacity for protracted low-level operations was great and the resulting casualties might have been high. Indeed, others argued that by supplying arms the conflict could be quickly terminated. As there was no consensus as to which side to supply, this policy also was less than decisive. Yet, as this difference of opinion illustrated, a decision to supply or not to supply arms in a situation of conflict amounts to intervention and implies a judgement as to the desirable political outcome. Thus a simple policy of never supplying arms to third-world countries would inevitably arouse difficult political questions in particular cases.

A similar ambiguity surrounds the argument that the arms trade entangles the suppliers in the conflicts of the recipients and may thereby lead to their extension. Quite apart from the fact that it is not easy to find cases where this has occurred, it can be argued that, to the contrary, the supply of arms is a substitute for intervention. It is a nice question as to whether American and Russian arms shipments to the Middle East should be regarded as entangling the Superpowers in the affairs of that turbulent region, or as a device whereby they manage to avoid the necessity for more direct involvement. Some arms supply is obviously intended as an instrument of disengagement: Vietnamization and Britain's provision of arms to the Persian Gulf states after withdrawal of the British military presence are recent illustrations. Whether such policies succeed in insulating the donors from local conflict depends in the first instance on how successfully the local balance is established and, in the second, on how rigorously the donors refrain from intervening if their protégés fail. The commitment of prestige entailed in the supply of arms may influence the decision to intervene, but there is no reason why it should dictate it.

The Control of the Arms Trade

Any proposal to restrict the transfer of arms to the nations of the third world must take account of the fact that this trade exists because the recipients want it. Although prestige plays a part, the bulk of the arms-transfers take place because armaments are the tools of conflict and the third world is full of conflict, both domestic and international. Suggestions that the supply of arms should be restricted have been almost universally resented and condemned by the third-world nations as an effort to undermine their independence and establish neo-colonialism. United Nations resolutions on the subject have been voted down. A General Assembly resolution of 1968, jointly sponsored by Denmark, Iceland, Malta and Norway, to set up a United Nations register of arms transactions met with strong opposition. Several Arab states and India pointed out that the sponsors either had no security problems or were members of powerful alliances. A Saudi Arabian delegate claimed that a register 'would place any small power or people, struggling for its independence, at a disadvantage'.

Given the facts that real conflicts and security problems exist among the third-world states; that they are prepared to resent as discriminatory any effort to apply restrictions on arms sales that are not universal to all states; that, because of their industrial backwardness, the third-world states are in fact disproportionately dependent on imports; and that there is a multiplicity of suppliers with diverse political purposes; the prospects for arriving at a comprehensive system of control for the arms trade are poor. Any comprehensive scheme would face all the difficulties of assessment and determination of balance that arise in schemes of disarmament; for, as the third world perceives, restriction of the arms trade is, in effect, an effort to impose a scheme of regional arms-limitation.

Such efforts as have already been made to regulate the export of arms to certain areas have, as we have seen, foundered on the rock of competition among potential suppliers. The most spectacular failure has been the UN embargo on South Africa, which has stimulated South African military preparations, encouraged South African arms manufacture, and resulted in a large increase in

South African arms imports. Western embargoes against India similarly led to diversification of sources of supply and stimulation of Indian arms manufacture to the point at which a new potential exporter has been created.

As an alternative to attempting a full embargo, exporters can try to regulate supplies so as to create a stable local balance. A variant of this policy is to encourage purchases of defensive arms and to discourage the acquisition of offensive weapons. Such a policy can only succeed if the suppliers of the local power likely to take offensive action want to curb it. The policy also raises all the difficulties of deciding what is an offensive weapon. An Egyptian air defence, for example, which relieved the UAR of anxiety about Israel's air power, might remove Egyptian inhibitions about the encouragement of guerrilla activity or about a renewed conventional offensive. Nevertheless, the United States has clearly tried to avoid delivery of too many offensive or provocative weapons to its clients in the Middle East and there are signs of a reciprocal caution in Soviet policy. Elsewhere similar examples can be cited. Taiwan has been denied amphibious equipment and South Korea has been kept short of attack aircraft and aircraft fuels. The Soviet Union has also conspicuously failed to supply Cuba with certain offensive weapons. In the extreme case one might cite the non-proliferation policies of the nuclear powers. Such policies are obviously more practical, the more the type of weapon in question is available only from a few sources or where the would-be recipient is restricted by ideological, political or economic circumstances to one potential supplier.

A military balance depends only partly on the relative inventories of weapons. Many other strategic factors come into play, such as terrain and the skill and standard of training of both leaders and led. While these factors will probably combine to decide the outcome of battle, many additional non-military considerations will play their part in determining whether or not there is to be war: the domestic and international political situations, the personal interests of leaders, reciprocal perceptions of intent and all the myriad determinants of diplomacy. With so many elements at work, any attempt to maintain stability by the regulation of arms supplies is unlikely to be successful except for a limited period and within a narrow range of favourable circumstances. Like other forms of arms control and disarmament, success depends on the effective manipulation of the whole arsenal of diplomatic means and not merely the isolation of one factor, the arms trade, which can, according to its context, be a force for good or bad.

CHAPTER FOURTEEN

Some Economic Aspects of Defence

Comparative National Defence Expenditures

In every country with a substantial defence establishment today there is great disquiet about the high and rapidly rising cost of modern military equipment, manpower and operations. Defence is, by any standards, a heavy consumer of resources and it becomes a major task of government to decide what proportion of national wealth the military should absorb and how that portion can be employed most efficiently.

For much of this century, from the moment, perhaps, when it became clear that World War I had become a battle of attrition, until some years after World War II terminated, the main problem in the economic management of defence was that of providing for the efficient mobilizing of national resources in time of war. This was a problem for solution during relatively short periods of high motivation and severe attrition. Very impressive rates of mobilization were achieved; at the peak of effort during World War II, Britain was devoting no less than 55 per cent and Germany 50 per cent of their GNP to military purposes. Under such conditions, much attention was devoted during the inter-war years and in the years immediately after 1945 to laying a framework for wartime mobilization. Offices of 'preparedness' and 'war mobilization' proliferated, 'shadow' munitions factories were established, 'strategic materials' were stockpiled and the armed forces set great store by their reserves.

The advent of nuclear weapons has done much to change this picture. With the prospect of decisive blows being delivered in the early days or even hours of a war, the Great Powers have moved from an age of wartime mobilization to an age of forces in being. This shift is reflected in high levels of peacetime military expenditure and readiness, and in correspondingly less interest in sustained wartime mobilization. The tendency is illustrated by such phenomena as the Soviet move away from the 'permanently operating factors' and new emphasis on the element of surprise, and in NATO's low level of stocks of war material and relative disinterest in the prospect of a renewed Battle of the Atlantic. The change is not, of course, complete. As we have seen, mobilization rates are still of great interest in the European theatre. But it is mobilization of forces for the supposedly decisive early stages of a campaign rather than the longer-term exploitation of 'war potential' that arouses concern.

A special problem apparently more reminiscent of sustained wartime mobilization has, however, continued to affect a few powers, chiefly the United States. This is the maintenance of high levels of military activity during prolonged periods of limited war, when national morale has not been galvanized as it usually is by an all-out war. The scale of the American economy and its rate of growth have, however, allowed the Viet Nam war to be handled with much less difficulty than the Korean, which came while real shortages of resources persisted from the preceding World War. Thus, although mobilization for

Opposite The Toulouse production line for the Jaguar fighter. This Anglo–French joint venture has been one of the most successful collaborative projects to date.

limited war has posed real problems of morale, it has not created problems, in strictly economic terms, which are very different from those of maintaining a high level of peacetime defence expenditure, coupled with a policy requiring a substantial amount of expenditure overseas.

Although commonly measured in terms of money, the resources that defence consumes are, of course, real. The chief ingredients, as of all economic activity, are labour of all kinds, real capital including industrial plant and materials, raw materials, inventories of manufactured goods, land, raw material reserves and 'overseas assets', which constitute claims on the resources of other states. Foreign resources may also be made available for political and strategic reasons arising from the policies of other states.

Money simply serves as a measure of these real resources. A reliable estimate or comparison of national military potential or of the true cost of defence would require a careful calculation of the real resources involved. On a small scale this can be done. A geopolitical analysis of a state's military potential can be conducted. Many practical difficulties will arise, however, in making an assessment of even the physical resources of a single country. Proper weighting will have to be applied to special critical factors, such as a dependence on imported oil, or to skill in areas of technology with military applications. The appropriate weighting will differ according to the contingencies envisaged. Moreover, the whole analysis will have to be complicated by building in various intangible factors like political will, administrative efficiency and technical skill.

In view of all this complexity, it is virtually impossible to make multilateral, across the board, comparisons in real terms and assessments commonly fall back on cruder indices of potential and effort. The most widely used indicator is the gross national product, sometimes coupled with demographic data, to yield, amongst other measures, an estimate of GNP *per capita*. The GNP expresses the aggregate at market prices – or, in administered economies, assigned prices – of all final goods and services. As a measure, the estimates of GNP commonly used suffer from many defects. In all countries the figure given for GNP can only be a questionable estimate, though some countries produce much more careful and plausible statistics than others. A particular defect when attempting to assess potential is that GNP accounts only for resources being actively employed. This is a proportion almost certain to change at different levels of military activity and likely to alter dramatically at times of extreme political stress or strategic danger. The exploitation of underemployed labour is, for example, a typical method of mobilization. A special difficulty also affects estimates of GNP in less sophisticated economies where many activities carried on commercially elsewhere are still conducted domestically.

The greatest single obstacle to using the GNP to make international comparisons, however, is that it is expressed in terms of national currencies which cannot be equated simply at official rates of exchange. This difficulty arises from the fact that each GNP is made up of different compositions of goods traded at different prices. Consequently the international exchange rates set by international agreement, or even by free trade in such goods as are internationally traded, do not accurately reflect relative purchasing power. Efforts are made to calculate 'purchasing power parity', by valuing the production of two or more countries at the prices of one, but the results vary very much according to which country's prices are chosen as a standard. Thus an EEC study some years ago calculated the British defence budget as $5·1 billion in British prices, but $7·1 billion in American. A common expedient is to take the mean of the two assessments, but this is a no more 'realistic' measure than either extreme.

Projections of GNP Figures in US $ at 1967 prices

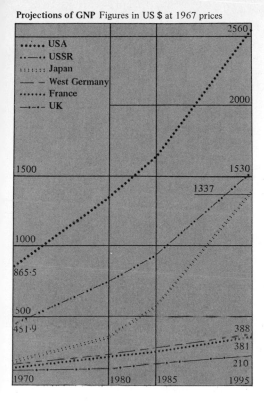

Defence expenditure as percentage of GNP

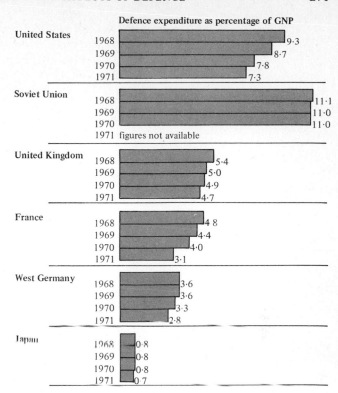

In comparisons of military power, it is common to relate the defence budget to GNP. Here there are special problems in trying to arrive at a purchasing power parity. First of all, much military expenditure is considered secret in many countries and comprehensive figures are not published. Even where secrecy is not consciously sought, countries have widely varying methods of accounting, so that military budgets do not cover the same range of expenditures. Moreover, the problem of assigning realistic comparable prices is especially acute in the military field, for no free market exists for much military equipment even within single countries. It is very rare for the land used by the armed forces to be assessed at a realistic price and, where there is conscription, an entirely arbitrary value is set upon the manpower consumed by the military, which is commonly the largest single item in the defence budget.

Nevertheless, with appropriate adjustments where possible, published military budgets and estimates of GNP offer the best basis of gross military comparisons that is available. It is some consolation that the results accord fairly well with common-sense impressions and that there are so many non-economic variables in determining military effectiveness that quite large errors in calculating material resources are unlikely to be decisive. The economic estimates are, however, likely to be much more critical if the purpose is to measure not military potential but the relative economic burden of defence efforts on national resources.

The accompanying table supports some rather obvious conclusions. There is a very close correlation between size of GNP and level of defence expenditure. Japan alone, for reasons we have discussed, is far out of her appropriate ranking. Countries with a high GNP are apparently countries with active foreign policies, lively concern with security, and are, even if members of

Comparisons of GNP and defence expenditure for the major powers. These figures provide a consistent standard of comparison with GNP at current prices. Other calculations, especially of GNP at factor cost, may afford higher figures for particular countries.

collective defence organizations, sufficiently rich to shoulder, willingly or not, a proportionate share of the military burden. Even so, the two Superpowers are quite clearly in a class of their own. Both in absolute terms and in the proportion of national resources employed, the United States and Soviet Union overshadow the other great powers. The United States, indeed, spends a good deal more than twice the combined defence budgets of the other members of the North Atlantic Alliance.

Comparisons with the Soviet Union raise all the problems of commensurability in a particularly acute form. Several factors combine to cast doubt on the accuracy of estimates concerning the Soviet defence effort. Soviet secrecy is pronounced and it is well known that large amounts of what most would regard as defence expenditure are not included in the published total of the official defence budget. Of course, nothing like the detailed breakdown provided by most Western governments is made public in the Soviet Union. A very large – but uncertain – proportion of the so-called 'science budget' is generally believed to be devoted to military development. According to Soviet figures, the science budget is equal to roughly a third of the ostensible defence budget. Some analysts assume that about half this science budget is devoted to military purposes; others put the proportion much higher.

There are other additional elements to be added to Soviet defence budgets to bring them into line with their Western equivalents. The largest of these remaining elements is probably the expenditure on frontier and security troops. Thus the International Institute for Strategic Studies, which allocates half the science budget to defences, grosses up the published Soviet defence budget by 30 per cent to account for all excluded items. By some standards this is a conservative estimate.

An even greater difficulty is presented by the task of estimating Soviet military prices; in other words, deciding what a defence rouble is worth and thus how much defence the Russians get for their expenditure. The answer is sought by trying to establish a purchasing power parity. This effort is bedevilled by the fact that the whole Russian price structure is artificial and that military prices are a very special case, both because the military sector of the Soviet economy is thought to be untypically efficient and because the price structure is probably deliberately managed to favour the military. Thus we must realize that estimates of the Soviet GNP are suspect and that calculations of the Soviet defence budget are particularly so.

The IISS estimates for 1971 suggest a Soviet defence expenditure of the equivalent of $55 billion, which amounts to 11 per cent of the Soviet GNP. There are, however, much higher estimates of both GNP and military spending. The IISS uses the mean of Soviet GNP expressed in dollars, using Soviet output weights, and in roubles, using American weights. As we have said, however, there is no conclusive reason for taking this figure. If, instead, one chose the 'dollar' figure, Soviet GNP would rise from about 50 per cent of the American GNP to nearly 70 per cent. Those who calculate on this basis maintain that Soviet defence expenditure is now roughly equal to that of the United States. Indeed, one noted study put Soviet defence expenditure at $84 billion in 1968 as compared to an American budget (including Viet Nam) of only $78 billion.

These high estimates are widely regarded as extravagant. On the other hand, the more modest figures of the IISS seem rather improbably low as a measure of Soviet outlays in real terms when one takes into account the impressionistic evidence of the rate and range of Soviet military procurement and the relatively lavish military use of manpower which, in most countries, is by far the heaviest

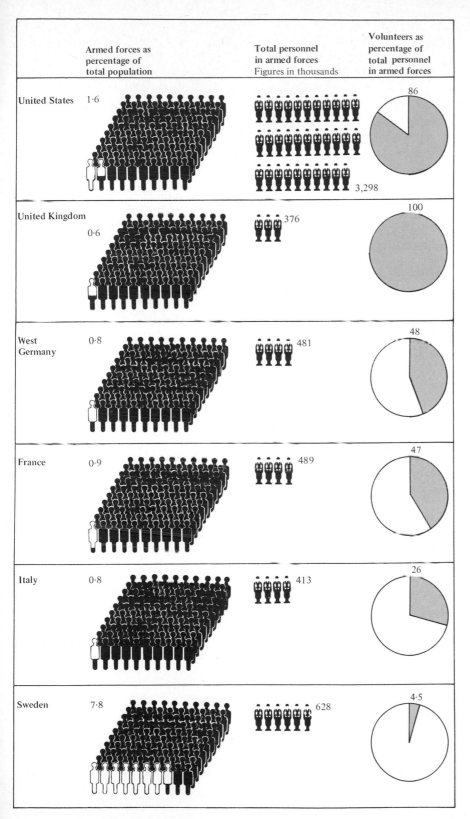

	Armed forces as percentage of total population	Total personnel in armed forces Figures in thousands	Volunteers as percentage of total personnel in armed forces
United States	1·6	3,298	86
United Kingdom	0·6	376	100
West Germany	0·8	481	48
France	0·9	489	47
Italy	0·8	413	26
Sweden	7·8	628	4·5

The armed forces of various countries in relation to their total populations and their methods of recruitment.

item of expenditure. Thus the figures given here for the Soviet Union, which follow the more moderate estimates widely accepted in the West, should be regarded as on the low side. By 1972 the IISS was ready to accept a figure of $91 billion to express the resources available to the Soviet military in US prices for equivalent research, development, equipment and operations.

As we noted, countries with high GNP tend to be among the most lavish spenders on defence, not merely in absolute terms, but also in terms of proportion of GNP allocated for military purposes. Six countries account for around 80 per cent of world military expenditure. Before we read too much into this, however, we must remember that, for various reasons, the higher GNPs tend to be disproportionately concentrated in North America and Europe and are therefore linked to the major East–West confrontation. Elsewhere in the world the proportion of GNP spent on defence tends to run between 2·5 per cent and 8 per cent, which is a far narrower range than one might expect from the vast differences between GNP *per capita*. Despite this tendency to set a norm for expenditure, there are, of course, marked divergences related to the level of local conflict. Thus Latin-American expenditures are low, being mostly under 3 per cent, with an exceptional and understandable 6 per cent for Cuba. In contrast, Middle Eastern outlays reach spectacular heights, rates of 6 per cent or 7 per cent being common, five countries reaching double figures and Israel an astronomic 25 per cent. Finally, we should notice that income *per capita* correlates very little with defence expenditure. The capacity to squeeze resources for defence out of impoverished populations is apparently high. Thus states with numerous, poor citizens, such as China and India, manage to support defence budgets that are proportionate to their GNP rather than to their *per capita* income. On the other hand, a low level of income *per capita* is an indication of the general level of economic development and technical sophistication, and therefore does provide some guide to the kind of defence establishment that can be maintained. Even this observation, however, must be interpreted with care and in the light of other variables. Thus China and Pakistan have roughly similar GNP *per capita*, but for reasons of scale and cultural history, China is far more able than Pakistan to nurse centres of high technological expertise within her overall industrial and military structure.

The task of deciding how much should be spent on defence is a complex and difficult one for governments. From the strategist's point of view one should decide what defences the country needs and then try to provide them as cheaply as possible. In practice, however, most countries most of the time do not find themselves beset by the sense of extreme danger that accounts for the degree of priority given to defence in such a beleaguered country as Israel. Thus, most countries set a figure for defence expenditure that modifies the preferences of defence advisers in the light of other national needs and priorities. The task is then to provide as much defence as possible with the resources made available. This entails both designing an optimal strategy and deciding how the resources devoted to it can best be extracted from the economy. Decisions have to be made, for example, as to whether to manufacture arms or import them, whether to raise forces by conscription or by voluntary recruitment in the labour market.

All countries have an existing level of expenditure on security and difficulties arise chiefly when some change is proposed. This may occur for many reasons: perhaps because the cost of the existing strategy is rising, perhaps because a new and expensive military policy seems necessary, perhaps because the country's economic situation deteriorates or new demands are made on it for national purposes other than defence. If there is to be an increase in real defence expenditure it must come either from an increase in national product or from a compression of civilian consumption, investment, other public expenditure and the running down of claims on foreigners. One possible solution is the mobilization of hitherto untapped resources, a consideration that complicates the problem by suggesting that increased defence expenditure could, in some circumstances, actually lead to a rise in general welfare by raising the level of economic activity. Obviously, accommodation to increased defence expenditure is easier within a growing economy, as no absolute reduction in other economic activities may be necessary. Thus, the vast American economy has been able to sustain the immense cost of the Vietnamese war while maintaining a high rate of growth in other expenditures also.

In theory, defence is like any other commodity and should be bought where it is cheapest. If a country is better at producing butter than guns it should export butter and buy its guns abroad. Similarly, if a nation wishes to station forces abroad it should regard the production of exports to raise the necessary foreign exchange as simply the appropriate mechanism for devoting a proportion of its resources to defence. In practice, things are not so simple. We have already referred briefly to the strategic reasons for not wishing to be dependent on imported arms. Looked at from the economic point of view, foreign expenditure on defence would only be a matter of indifference (within a given level of defence expenditure) if there were flexible exchange rates and if the resources necessary to pay for imports of weapons or overseas operations were readily transferable to the appropriate provision of exports. It is true that many crude calculations of the foreign exchange costs of defence need refinement. Troops stationed at home consume imports, for example, and even domestically produced weapons usually have an imported content. Overseas military commitments may stimulate export sales of arms. Thus, the important figure is the net effect on the balance of payments of particular military activities. But this being said, some military policies do constitute an effective rise in the propensity to import and this poses real problems of economic management. Thus, while it is true that the economic pressure to contract British overseas military commitments in the sixties resulted from a real scarcity of resources and the slow British economic growth rate, it is also true that, given the existing international monetary system and the rigidities of the British economy, it was not surprising that eliminating overseas military activity seemed an easier option than devaluation and a redeployment of industrial resources.

The International Procurement of Weapons

There are, as we have noted, several strategic considerations that may make governments reluctant to rely on foreign sources for the supply of weapons. The time-honoured reason, which has accounted in the past for policies of military self-sufficiency, stockpiling of strategic materials and subsidization of domestic food production, has been fear of being cut off from replenishment in time of war. This is clearly of more concern to some nations than to others, with the greatest anxiety arising in insular nations like Britain, or in countries, such as Germany, which were likely to get into conflict with nations astride their trade routes. So far as the Great Powers are concerned, the shift in emphasis to forces in being and the expectation of a war decisive in its early stages, has greatly modified this particular concern, but elsewhere, as in the recent cases of India, Pakistan, Nigeria and Israel, we see nations at least inconvenienced because of dependence on foreign supplies. As these cases and others also demonstrate, foreign suppliers can use their position to exert political leverage in time of peace as well as war. Even without any political intention, a foreign supplier may prove unreliable in the matter of delivery if, for instance, it decides to give priority to the needs of its own armed forces. Finally, foreign weapons are frequently less well suited to another nation's precise needs than a weapon tailored specifically to the latter's requirements.

Obviously, any or all of these considerations may make a government decide in favour of making its own weapons. If, as we assume, the foreign weapon would be cheaper in terms of the resources required to pay for it (otherwise the question of imports would not arise), then the added cost of domestic production must simply be regarded as a decision to devote rather more of the defence budget to avoiding one or all of the strategic objections to importation. The strictly strategic argument is often complicated, however, by the belief that other advantages may derive from domestic arms production. Manufacture at home may be justified on the grounds that it raises the national level of technical expertise, with a spill-over to other economic activity, that it increases the marketability of other products by enhancing the country's technological reputation, or that it is worth paying a price simply for the prestige attached to self-sufficiency and independence. It may also be argued that domestic manufacture will contribute to the full employment of national resources; that is, that the resources needed to make the weapon could not in practice be switched to earning the foreign exchange to pay for the apparently cheaper foreign weapon.

As was remarked in our discussion of the arms trade, most nations cannot manufacture a wide range of arms at anything like a competitive price. Indeed, very few of even the advanced industrial nations can compete with the Superpowers in this respect. The larger nations enjoy many advantages of which the chief is economy of scale. Domestic orders for large numbers of each weapon call for long production runs during which, thanks to a phenomenon known as the 'learning curve', the cost of production tends to fall; over several hundred aircraft the decrease in cost is typically around 20 per cent. At the same time, the heavy initial costs for research and development and for establishing production lines can be spread over a greater number of units produced.

From the wider perspective of the national arms industry as a whole, a large R and D establishment helps to maintain technical skills, increase industrial flexibility and encourage a high rate of innovation. The contrast between a few leading industrial nations and all the rest is most striking so far as R and D is concerned. In very rough terms the United States spent over $21 billion a year on all R and D in the mid-sixties. This was two or three times the total spent by all West European countries put together. Indeed, of all the non-Communist countries only Britain, France and West Germany spent over $1 billion on R and D. The imbalance was even more marked for military R and D, where the United States outspent the Western Europeans by seven to one at official rates of exchange and by five to one if a purchasing power parity is applied to compensate for lower research costs in Europe. Similar comparisons can be made among the Europeans: France and Britain accounted for over 80 per cent of the military R and D expenditure of Western Europe. To take a different standard, American aerospace industries employed over 1,400,000 people in the mid-sixties, while those of all Western Europe employed only 440,000. In industry at large the average expenditure on R and D of the twenty largest American firms was $1·4 billion, while that of the equivalent companies in Britain was $132 million, in France $65 million and in Italy $27 million.

In an effort to keep European defence industry alive by escaping from the disadvantages of small scale, there has been considerable enthusiasm in recent years for joint procurement and production on a multi-national basis. As an aggregate the arms producing capability of Western Europe is formidable. Between them the Western European countries make virtually every kind of modern armament, including nuclear weapons and long-range missiles. The Europe of the Nine, composed of the original EEC and the three newcomers, Britain, Denmark and Eire, have a combined population of about 260 million, which exceeds that of the Soviet Union or United States. Their combined GNP in 1970 was roughly $640 billion, which is 25 per cent more than that of the Soviet Union. The combined defence budgets of the nine are nearly $25 billion, which is a little less than half that of the Soviet Union. While this total reveals the lower inclination of the Europeans to undertake heavy defence expenditure, a budget of $25 billion would obviously permit military ventures on a grand scale, while the underlying GNP provides an even more substantial basis for military efforts should the political situation dictate an increase.

In the early seventies, however, the political problem for defence ministries in Western Europe was to sustain rather than increase defence expenditure and to try to reconcile the conflicting trends of rising military costs and a declining popular readiness to pay them. Joint procurement theoretically offers a contribution to solving this problem, not only by taking advantage of economies of scale but also by the increase in standardization of equipment that would automatically follow from purchases of identical equipment. This would bring about a direct improvement in military efficiency in addition to the hoped-for savings on procurement.

During the years when Britain was excluded from the EEC by the French veto, the British government's enthusiasm for joint procurement projects in Europe was reinforced by the belief that it might afford a backdoor to economic integration. Several very large joint-production projects were initiated in those years, notably the Anglo French strike-trainer aircraft, Jaguar (initiated 1965), the Anglo–German Italian multi-role combat aircraft, MRCA (1969) and an Anglo–French venture to produce a series of helicopters, the Gazelle, Puma and Lynx (1967). A great many other joint projects have been or are being carried out in Europe. Notable among these have been the multi-national production of the American F104 under licence, the Franco–German production of the Transall transport aircraft, and, at a somewhat different level, the effort involving many NATO countries to introduce the NATO Air Defence Ground Environment (NADGE) system.

The record of these ventures is mixed and it has become clear that joint procurement is no panacea. Perhaps the greatest difficulty is that participating nations usually demand a share in the economically and technologically rewarding tasks of design and production commensurate with their contribution to the purchase order. This principle of the *juste retour* runs counter to the fundamental purpose of increasing efficiencies of concentration and specialization. It is by no means necessary that the country wanting to buy the largest number of a weapon is best suited to produce it. One result tends to be continued duplication of effort. There are separate British and French production lines for Jaguar and no less than three national production lines for the RB199 power plant for the MRCA. Such practices prevent the full exploitation of the learning curve economies.

Among many other difficulties is the tendency for each nation to introduce somewhat different specifications into the weapon until it becomes considerably more expensive or even, by way of differing national models, almost ceases to be a common article. The British and French Jaguars have very different electronics and we have already noted the wide divergences between the British and German versions of the MRCA. Yet another disappointment for the advocates of international collaboration has been the fact that all such ventures have been *ad hoc*, combining different nations and different firms, and failing to create any lasting and coherent framework of collaboration. A particular difficulty in this connection is that of reconciling the various national systems of public accountability and budgetary control so as to provide the degree of financial stability desirable for a sustained programme. The difficulty of solving this problem, indeed we might think the unreasonableness of expecting to do so, can be appreciated by reflecting upon the frequency of false starts, cost overruns and cancellations in national procurement programmes.

These shortcomings in existing joint-procurement ventures have given rise to the belief in some quarters that real progress requires the establishment of a common budget into which a proportion of national procurement funds should be put for allocation to the development and production projects chosen purely on grounds of efficiency. It would obviously be difficult to eliminate hopes that over the long run each nation would receive a portion of the necessary work, but the main benefit to subscribers would be the procurement of weapons at economical prices. In this respect, however, a remaining difficulty would be the probability that nations which were chiefly consumers would frequently find a purchase from America even more economical. Moreover, any effort to discriminate against purchases from the United States in the cause of preserving a European arms industry and promoting European integration, while welcome to one strand in American policy, militates against the tendency to use the import of American weapons as an 'offset' to American foreign exchange outlays on a military presence in Europe. This consideration is complicated still further by the fact that many American firms can in fact participate in ostensibly European projects through the medium of their holdings in European companies.

Paradoxically the entry of new members to the EEC may slow down the progress of joint military procurement, at least temporarily. This is so because the incentive for Britain to use military procurement-projects as a backdoor to Europe is removed once the front door is open. At the same time it can be argued that the fundamental task is the integration of European industry as a whole, and that to single out the military sector for accelerated integration may lead to distortions and inefficiency. The fact remains, however, that private initiatives in co-operation, firm to firm, have been remarkably few so far within the EEC, and that the role of government as purchaser gives rise to special opportunities for action in the military area.

On balance, it seems clear that the logic of budgetary stringency and continued need for defence recommends inter-European collaboration at the level of both operations and procurement. The projected economic and ultimately political integration of Western Europe reinforces this logic. But it is too early to say whether military integration will be the bell-wether of a wider collaboration, or if any major step forward in this area will have to await some decisive progress in the more general process of political and economic unification.

Manpower

A large and, in many countries, rapidly increasing proportion of defence expenditure is devoted to manpower. Thus in fiscal 1973 $42·8 billion of a total defence outlay of $76·5 billion was devoted to 'personnel costs' in the United

States. In Britain 49·7 per cent of the defence budget was devoted to personnel as compared to 33·8 per cent on equipment. In principle there are two different ways of manning armed services: by compulsion or by the attraction of volunteers by financial and other inducements. Most countries employ a mixture of these two systems. Great Britain and Canada, however, with all-volunteer armed forces, occupy one end of the possible spectrum, while the Swedish and Swiss militia systems come close to the opposite pole of forces based entirely on compulsion. The latter are, however, dependent on a small core of voluntary professionals.

The mixed systems vary very much in the proportion of volunteers to conscripts. A similar variation can usually be discerned between services, with the armies being heavily dependent on conscripts in large, relatively unskilled numbers, and the air and naval forces on rather larger proportions of more highly skilled professionals. With their more heavily technical bias, air forces and navies both need and can recruit skilled manpower more intensively. As a consequence, the weight of the army within the national force structure tends to correlate positively, at least in democratic societies, with the proportion of conscripts in the nation's total military manpower. Thus Britain, with all-volunteer forces, has 47 per cent in the army, West Germany, with 52 per cent conscripts overall, has 70 per cent in the army, and Sweden, with 95 per cent compulsorily serving militia (when mobilized), has 95 per cent in the army. In normal times the Swedish proportions are less startling: 65 per cent conscript overall and 66 per cent of total active personnel in the army. The picture is further complicated by the fact that where there is compulsion, some shorter service volunteers are not truly voluntary members of the military, but have enlisted so as to secure an assignment of their choice or to avoid one particularly distasteful to them. Moreover, one must remember that, as in the Swiss and Swedish cases, even the most thoroughgoing system of universal compulsion needs a core of genuinely voluntarily motivated professionals to give continuity, experience and spirit. Also, some modern military tasks are increasingly too complicated to be mastered by any part-time militia man or by a conscript enlisted only for the relatively short period that is all most democratic societies will tolerate.

The debate as to which is the best system for manning the armed forces is not one that is decided solely on grounds of economy or of military efficiency, for it involves the liberty of the citizen and the nature of his relationship to society. Some societies may think compulsion to serve distasteful; others may put a positive value on a period of national service for youth. From the narrower economic and military point of view it seems clear that most states would find it hard to man sizeable armed forces without some element of compulsion. The two voluntary states, Britain and Canada, have the lowest proportion of population in the armed services of any of the NATO states. Conversely, the militia states, Switzerland and Sweden, have the highest proportion (when mobilized) and, indeed, have the largest armed forces in Europe outside Russia. Even the rich United States, which is attempting to attain 'zero draft', feels compelled to maintain residual powers of conscription and it seems quite probable that even high rates of pay will not save the American armed forces from very severe shortages of manpower.

Conscription gives the impression of offering a relatively cheap way to secure manpower. Conscripts are commonly paid not merely less than the rates needed to attract volunteers to military life but even far less than minimal civilian wages. Only the United States in the West pays its conscripts at the same rate for the job as volunteers. Yet although low military pay seems to reduce the burden of manpower in the military budget, and thereby to reduce the apparent burden of defence on the economy, the real costs of a conscript system are greater than they appear.

Conscription is like a tax in kind and, by diverting manpower from productive employment in the economy, imposes a burden which is understated by the soldier's nominal cost to the budget. Volunteer forces may also be more efficient, man for man, than conscript forces and therefore yield a greater military return for a given number of men. This greater efficiency may arise from the higher level of skill attained by longer service soldiers. Volunteer forces commonly enjoy higher morale than conscript forces, not merely because conscripts are frequently disaffected and lack professional pride in soldiering, but also because, in mixed forces, the disgruntlement of the conscript rubs off on to the professional. Volunteer forces, enlisted for longer periods, may also be more flexible than conscript forces both because individuals attain wider ranges of skill and because there may be less inhibition about assigning professionals to difficult or dangerous missions. A major source of inefficiency in conscript forces arises from rapid turnover of a high proportion of personnel and the consequent high burden of training that this entails. Not only do conscripts spend a very large fraction of their total service in training, but a correspondingly large number of the professionals must be devoted to conducting the training. This rapid turnover of personnel does, it is true, produce large reserves, but the quality of a reserve of ex-conscripts is not usually high unless special measures are taken to refresh their skills. Quite different standards apply, of course, to a militia system where the whole armed force is a kind of universal reserve in relatively frequent and consistent training.

A final defect of conscription that deserves attention is that if the system enrols all fit men of military age, the input is regulated not by military requirements but by the demographic characteristics of the nation. A shortage of men of military age will plague any manpower system, volunteer or conscript. A conscript system can, however, be equally embarrassed by an excess which can overburden the armed forces' capacity to train, equip, officer and employ troops. Expedients to regulate the flow by systematic exemptions or selection by lottery invariably engender inequities and social resentments. Meeting the problem by shortening the term of service exacerbates the problem of turnover mentioned earlier.

Despite all these shortcomings, conscription may well remain the normal way of providing the bulk of military and particularly army manpower. The system has much tradition behind it in many states and in some nations the pattern of conscription is historically and emotionally linked with the very essence of the state. The Swiss militia offers what is perhaps a supreme example of this. Nor should we underrate the positive advantage to governments and armed services of the illusory aspects of the economies afforded by conscription. Even if a voluntary system manned by high military wages could provide an efficient armed force at no greater or less cost than conscription, it might well be thought unwise to let the necessarily increased defence budget draw attention to the real cost of the security establishment. Moreover, in many countries it might in practice be necessary to pay quite astronomical rates of military pay to obtain large numbers of volunteers for the less attractive military tasks.

In many countries there is a tendency to alleviate the shortage of manpower in certain categories by turning many tasks over to civilians. This can be done with particular advantage in two contrasting cases: one, the discharge of relatively menial tasks such as clerical work, storekeeping or truck driving, which require no very high standards of physique or discipline and which may ill fit the martial image; the other, the performance of highly skilled technical maintenance or administration for which suitable recruits are scarce and expensive. Civilization of this kind can release military men for tasks where discipline, mobility and martial qualities are essential. Militia forces, with small professional cores and a necessarily low standard of technical training among the troops at large, could not operate modern electronic and aviation systems without delegating the work of maintenance to civilians.

Quite clearly the extent to which civilians can be substituted for military men is very much determined by national strategy. Civilianization can go far if home defence or deterrence by home based systems is what is required. If, on the other hand, distant operations by expeditionary force are intended, a much greater proportion of the work must be done by embodied troops. The recent trend to civilianization is therefore partly the result of the decline in overseas garrisons and operations. It may become important to remember that the opposite is also true; that is, that a force heavily dependent on civilians is severely restricted in the type of operation it can mount.

Obviously, all armed forces depend to some extent on recruiting volunteers, though the militia systems are less dependent than most. The most pressing need is to recruit and to retain officers and senior NCOS. In recent years socio-economic conditions have made recruiting difficult. Civilian life offers good rewards in affluent societies and some of the ways affluence is enjoyed are difficult to reconcile with the military life and ethic. A particular problem is presented by the military need for men in the prime of life, to whom it cannot offer a satisfying career in later years. To meet this problem armed forces are increasingly emphasizing preparation for post-military careers. In some cases this approach is combined with and related to efforts to make the armed forces directly useful to civil society by such services as bridge building and airfield construction. All of these activities, however, represent a distraction from the true military task of preserving a pugnacious spirit and preparing for combat. Moreover, it is far from proven, as yet, that the effort to make military life and service more similar to that of the civilian is the most effective way to bolster security and foster support for the armed forces in the long run. The problem is a serious and complex one and, if the affluent, democratic states continue to be spared large scale war, the sociological basis for the 'armed forces of deterrence' is likely to become the most important military question of all.

Defence Management

An important feature of recent years has been the intrusion of the techniques of economic analysis into the business of defence management. This has had a radical effect on the approach both to the management of resources and to the determination of strategy itself. Several incentives have contributed to this development. We live in an economizing age, in which decisions of all kinds are subjected as never before to explicit analysis to assure 'cost-effectiveness'. Military affairs have not merely shared in this evolution; in many respects they have taken a lead, spurred on by the heavy pressure of strategic demands on economic resources. We also live in an age of deterrence, as a result of which the most important strategies cannot be tested by the trial and error of actual wartime experience. It is only to be expected that policies which cannot be put to the test, yet are of such grave import, should be subjected to never-ending analysis and that no effort should be spared in trying to refine the machinery of judgement.

The cube illustrates how the resources available for defence can be divided from three different perspectives for the purposes of planning. The content and relative proportions of the 'slices' shown here are hypothetical.

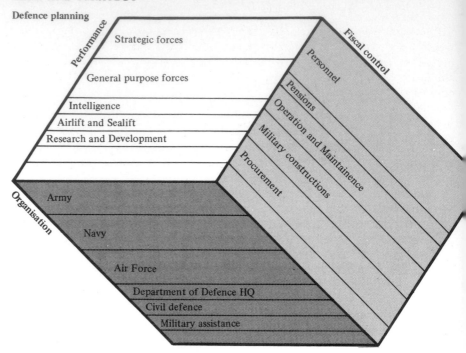

The introduction of new management techniques started first and went furthest in the United States. Early imitation, not unmixed with native modification, took place in Britain, Canada and West Germany. Now there are few Western defence establishments that have not been somewhat affected and it is clear, though the details are obscure, that the Soviet Union has also adapted the new techniques to its own elaborate structure of national planning.

The essence of the new approach is to identify the real costs and outputs of the defence establishment with greater clarity. In this way it is hoped to reveal what 'trade-offs' are entailed in the selection of strategic options. To a very large extent the pioneering of this approach is identified with the names of the American Secretary of Defense, Robert McNamara and his associates, though the pressures of American defence policy were already pushing the Pentagon in this direction before McNamara came to power.

Only a few aspects of this immense subject can be discussed even briefly here. The essential task is to identify very precisely the military functions to be performed and then to find ways of discharging them with a minimal consumption of resources. What constitutes an essential military task and what level of performance is adequate, are questions ultimately for decision on the basis of military and political judgement and experience. There is no simple, interchangeable measure of performance such as profit in money terms affords for private enterprise. Indeed, even large-scale modern businesses increasingly reckon with long-term considerations that rapidly escape simple financial analysis. Political and military judgement can be improved, however, if modern analytical techniques, applied where possible in quantitative terms, illuminate the options and costs. Even the richest nation with the most lavish military budget must face the essential economic fact of scarcity of resources, and the choices, which are the inevitable consequence of this fact, have to be made whatever strategic assumptions are accepted. More of something inevitably means less of something else. Even arbitrarily increasing the defence budget will not relieve the dilemma of those who allocate military funds. The admiral who refuses to choose between a nuclear carrier and a conventionally powered carrier with four escorts, and demands both the nuclear carrier and the escorts, still must decide whether the resulting larger sum would not be better spent on a conventional carrier and eight escorts.

One of the most important, if simplest, steps in establishing a new system of analysis and management has been the recasting of military budgets to express outputs rather than inputs. Instead of such elements as manpower and weapons, or air force and army, which are inputs, the categories for decision become military missions, such as 'strategic deterrence' and 'research and development'. In his original system, McNamara employed eight main 'performance' categories: strategic retaliatory forces, continental defence, general purpose forces, airlift and sealift, reserves, research and development, general support, and military assistance. These categories were then broken down into nearly a thousand 'programme elements', such as Minuteman and Polaris. For presentational purposes the budget also continues to be divided in more traditional ways: by 'component', that is to say, army, navy, air force, civil defence etc.; and by the 'functional' categories, such as 'procurement', 'operations', preferred by the Congress for much of its work of fiscal control. But it is in the performance or output categories that the planning is done and the government's decisions on allocation are taken.

Whether a certain level of forces will produce the right amount of international influence or the adequate degree of deterrence are ultimately matters for the highest politico–military judgement. No quantitative analysis can end the debate. But presenting the budget functionally at least reveals what deterrence is costing, and what else could be done if the effort were reduced. This form of presentation also helps to clarify the issues involved in functions to which more than one of the traditional armed services contribute. It also combats the tendency of the services to favour functions which appeal to them and to neglect those which do not. Air forces, for example, often prefer to spend their money on combat aircraft rather than transport aircraft to move the army, and on any kind of aircraft rather than on airfields. Functional or performance analysis can isolate the element of lift or assess precisely what contribution more aircraft or more airfields on which to disperse existing aircraft would make to survivability. A further refinement of this type of analysis is to project it over a longer period than the budgetary year – typically over five years – to illuminate the future impact of programmes on performance and costs and to undermine the technique of the 'foot in the door' – beginning a programme in the hope of securing extra funds for it in the future on the plea of not wasting the money already spent.

Good performance and cost analysis requires on the one hand skilful and imaginative conceptualization of options and, on the other, accurate attribution of costs. The main technique for doing this is known as systems analysis: rigorous and usually quantitative analysis to determine the characteristics of military tasks and systems and to ensure that each system has attached to it all the relevant costs and only the relevant costs. Typically, systems analysis takes a cost effectiveness approach which carefully compares options in terms of the input or resources required for each. In practice, the question is usually either how best to expend a given sum of money to achieve a performance objective, or how a prescribed performance can most cheaply be attained. To answer these questions calls for the close co-operation of system designers, cost analysts and military users. It also requires the collection and processing of vast amounts of information in a fashion that would not have been practicable before the advent of the computer.

There is little room to doubt that the introduction of such techniques and above all the adoption of cost effectiveness as an attitude of mind has had a very beneficial effect on defence management. Nevertheless, there are serious dangers and shortcomings which are increasingly widely recognized. One of the most obvious is the temptation to regard the most readily quantifiable factors as necessarily the most important, an error compounded when, as frequently happens, the quantification that exists is faulty. It is simply impossible to quantify many considerations, or to imagine all future military situations. Much depends on how wisely the boundaries of a system study are set: if they are too narrow, the full range of costs and benefits is not taken into account; if they are too wide, the field becomes almost synonymous with defence policy as a whole, and the study becomes unmanageable. This problem is particularly relevant to general purpose forces. The greatest apparent successes of systems analysis in giving new clarity and an explicit rationale to defence policy have been in the field of strategic deterrent systems. These systems have not, of course, been put to any practical test. The contribution of strategic forces to the deterrence of nuclear war can only be surmised and, so long as deterrence continues, the systems remain unproven even as forces of destruction. Thus an unkind critic might say that the success of systems analysis in this area is success confirmed only by further analysis.

Other critics have been concerned with the results of systems analysis when it enters the field of operations rather than procurement. The Viet Nam war has, according to some observers, provided practical examples of an undue fascination with the quantifiable as an index of success. If this has been so, it may be an illustration of a further danger of systems analysis: that, being only a partial and imperfect tool, it can become simply a more powerful weapon with which to enforce preconceived notions. Thus it has been suggested that, in the Mc-Namara Pentagon, it became widely appreciated that analyses concluding in favour of high cost or duplicatory solutions were unlikely to be welcome. In a wider perspective, it can be argued that cost effectiveness analysis, with its demand for quantitative justification at all stages, can stifle innovation and initiative. It is worth remembering that two of the most dramatically effective systems, the F4 Phantom and the Polaris submarine, were each at some stages in their evolution regarded as bad examples of parochialism and interservice rivalry on the part of the US Navy. Similarly, Mr McNamara of necessity set the main lines of his distinctive strategic policy before his managerial innovations had had time to bear fruit.

The conclusion must be that cost effectiveness is inherent in any rational approach to defence policy and that modern analytical techniques have made possible an unprecedented degree of precision in pursuing it. The precipitate multiplication of technological options and inflation of military costs makes efforts to achieve cost-effectiveness more necessary than ever before and the untestable nature of policies of strategic deterrence puts a new and novel premium on analysis. It will be constructive analysis, however, only if it is truly dispassionate and accords those with practical military and political experience a proper role in decision, along with those whose profession is quantitative analysis. The quality of results still depends on the quality of judgement that is brought to the business of analysis and management. If the higher direction is misguided, the new techniques may contribute only to more spectacular errors.

Glossary

AAM	air-to-air missile
ABM	anti-ballistic missile
ACRA	anti-char rapide autopropulsé
ADIZ	air defence identification zone
ADM	atomic demolition mine
AEW	airborne early warning
AMF	Allied Mobile Force
ANC	African National Congress
ANZUK	Australia, New Zealand, United Kingdom
AP	armour piercing
APC	armoured personnel carrier
ASEAN	Association of South-East Asia Nations
ASM	air-to-surface missiles
ASROC	anti-submarine rocket
ASW	anti-submarine warfare
AWACS	airborne warning and control system
BMD	ballistic missile defence
CENTO	Central Treaty Organization
CEP	circular error probable
CINCHAN	Commander-in-Chief, Channel
COREMO	Comité Revolucionario de Mozambique
CVA	attack aircraft carrier
CVAN	nuclear-power attack carrier
DLG	destroyer/leader, guided missile
DPC	Defence Policy Committee
ECCM	electronic counter-counter-measures
ECM	electronic counter-measures
EEC	European Economic Community
ELINT	electronic intelligence
ESC	European Security Conference
FBS	forward-based nuclear delivery systems
FDL	fast deployment logistic ship
FOBS	fractional orbital bomb system
FRELIMO	Frente de Libertação de Mozambique
FROG	free rocket over ground
FROLIZI	Front for the Liberation of Zimbabwe
GCD	general and complete disarmament
GNP	gross national product
GRAE	Angolan Revolutionary Government in Exile
HEAT	high explosive, anti-tank
HOT	high-subsonic, optically tracked, wire-guided missile
IAEA	International Atomic Energy Agency
ICBM	intercontinental ballistic missile
IRBM	intermediate-range ballistic missile
KT	kiloton
LHA	landing ship, helicopter, assault
LPH	landing platform, helicopter
LSD	landing ship, dock
LSL	landing ship, logistic
LST	landing ship, tank
MAD	magnetic-anomaly detector
MARAIRMED	Maritime Air Forces, Mediterranean
MBFR	mutual balanced force reductions
MIRV	multiple independently targetable re-entry vehicle
MPLA	Angolan People's Liberation Movement
MRBM	medium-range ballistic missile
MRCA	multiple role combat aircraft
MRV	multiple re-entry vehicle
MT	megaton
NATO	North Atlantic Treaty Organization
NPT	Non-Proliferation Treaty
OAU	Organization for African Unity
OTH	over-the-horizon-radar
PAC	Pan-African Congress
PENAIDS	penetration aids
PFLP	Popular Front for Liberation of Palestine
PLA	People's Liberation Army
RV	re-entry vehicle
SACEUR	Supreme Allied Commander, Europe
SACLANT	Supreme Allied Commander, Atlantic
SALT	Strategic Arms Limitation Talks
SCAD	subsonic cruise armed decoy
SCS	sea-control ship
SEATO	South-East Asian Treaty Organization
SLBM	submarine-launched ballistic missile
SRAM	short-range attack missile
SSBN	nuclear-powered, missile-firing submarine
STANAVFORLANT	Standing Naval Force, Atlantic
STOL	short take-off and landing
SUBROC	submarine-launched (ASW) rocket
SWAPO	South-West Africa People's Organization
TDS	tactical data systems
TOW	tube-launched, optically tracked, wire-guided missile
TNT	Tri-nitro-toluene
UAR	United Arab Republic
UDI	Unilateral Declaration of Independence
ULMS	undersea long-range missile system
VDS	variable-depth sonar
VLF	very low frequency
VTOL	vertical take-off and landing
ZANU	Zimbabwe African National Union
ZAPU	Zimbabwe African People's Union

Main Centres of Training and Assistance of Guerrilla and Revolutionary Movements

Main centres of training and assistance for guerrilla and revolutionary movements

Algeria: Arms aid for various revolutionary movements.

China: Training in China; instructors in Tanzania and Congo-Brazzaville. Arms aid.

Congo-
  Brazzaville: Training bases for Angola. Cuban instructors.

Congo-Kinshasa
  (now Zaire): Base for Angolan guerrillas.

Cuba: HQ of Tricontinental Solidarity Organization, concerned with Latin America, Asia and Africa.
Training for guerrillas for Latin America and Africa.

Guinea: Bases for guerrillas in Portuguese Guinea.

North Viet Nam: Assistance to guerrillas in Burma, Cambodia, Laos, Thailand.

Soviet Union: Training bases for Africans in Crimea. Arms and other aid for various movements.

Tanzania: Base for guerrillas in Mozambique and South Africa. Centre of Chinese activity.

UAR: Arms aid for various revolutionary movements.

Main centres of guerrilla and revolutionary activity

AFRICA

Angola: Movimento Popular de Libertação de Angola (MPLA)
Leader: Agostinho Neto.
Governo da Republica de Angola no exilio (GRAE), and
União das Populações de Angola (UPA)
Leader: Holden Roberto.

Mozambique: Frente de Libertação de Mozambique (FRELIMO)
Leader: Marcelino dos Santos.
Comité Revolucionario de Mozambique (COREMO)
Splinter with Chinese support.

Portuguese
  Guinea: Partido Africano de Independencia de Guiné e Cabo Verde (PAIGC)
Leader: Amilcar Cabral (assassinated in January, 1973).

Rhodesia: Zimbabwe African National Union (ZANU), Rev. Sithole, Peking-oriented; split from ZAPU 1963. Zimbabwe African Peoples Union (ZAPU), Nkomo.
Front for the Liberation of Zimbabwe (FROLIZI), Siwela, formed 1971 in an attempt to unite rival factions of ZANU and ZAPU.

South Africa: African National Congress (ANC), military wing 'Spear of the Nation' (SON), Winnie and Nelion Mandela.
Pan-Africanist Congress (PAC), splinter group from ANC, Peking-oriented. The activities of both organizations severely limited by the nature of the South African regime.

South-West
Africa
(Namibia): South West African Peoples Organisation (SWAPO); activities very limited.

ASIA

Burma: Kachin Independence Army (Nationalist).
White Flags (Burmese Communist Party, pro-Chinese).

Ceylon: Peoples Liberation Front (JVP), Maoist-Guevarist ideology.

India: Naga and Mizo tribes, ethnic movements in north-east Indian hills.
Naxalites, Maoist extremists, terrorist activities in West Bengal and Andra Pradesh.

Indonesia: Revived Communist activity, split between pro-Pekin and pro-Moscow wings. Main areas: South Sumatra, Central Java, Celebes.

Japan: All Japan Federation of Students Councils (Zengakuren), split into many factions some advocating the use of indiscriminate terror, such as the Red Army, Lydda Airport incident.

Laos, Cambodia: North Vietnamese-supported Communist rebels.

Malaysia: Malayan National Liberation Army (MNLA), military wing of the Communist Party of Malaya. MNLA also known as Counter Terror Organisation (CTO).

Philippines: Remnants of the Hukbong Mapgapalayang Bayan (Huks), army of Philippine Communist Party, now Peking oriented. Military arm now the New People's Army.

South Viet Nam: National Front for the Liberation of South Viet Nam (NFLSV); military wing Viet Cong; now assisted by regular troops from North Viet Nam.

Thailand: Thai People's Liberation Armed Forces. Communist–Chinese support.

LATIN AMERICA

Argentina: Fuerzos Argentinos de Liberación: Castroite urban terrorists
Montoneros Command: revolutionary Peronists; terrorists.

Bolivia: Ejercito de Liberación Nacional (ELN): Castroite; revival after defeat of Che Guevara.

Brazil: Ação Libertade Nacional (ALN): Castroite; organisation of the late Carlos Marighella (d. 1969) author of *Manual of the Urban Guerrilla*.
Vanguardia Popular Revolucionaria (VPR): Castroite.

Colombia: Ejercito de Liberación Nacional (ELN): Castroite.
Fuerzas Armadas Revolucionarias de Colombia (FARC): Soviet support.
Ejercito Popular de Liberación (EPL): Maoist.

Guatemala: Fuerzas Armadas Rebeldes (FAR): Castroite.

Mexico: Movimento de Accion Revolucionaria (MAR), sporadically active urban guerrilla group.

Uruguay: Movimiento de Liberación Nacional (MLN): Castroite (Tupamaros) Urban terrorism.

NORTH AMERICA

Canada: Front for the Liberation of Quebec (FLG); urban guerrilla group activities have diminished.

The United
States: Black Panther Party for Self Defence (BPP), programme of revolutionary black nationalism, very divided.
Weathermen, small urban guerrilla group, sporadic activities.

EUROPE

N. Ireland: Irish Republican Army (IRA): Marxist; 'The Officials'.
The Provisional Irish Republican Army (separated 1969).

Portugal:	Ação Revolucionara Armada (ARA), small left-wing urban guerrilla group.
Spain:	Freedom for the Basque Homeland (ETA), militant wing of the Basque Nationalist Party.
Yugoslavia:	USTASHE Croat separatists, mainly emigres.

MIDDLE EAST

Iran:	Small urban guerrilla groups calling themselves 'Tupamaros'.
Oman:	Popular Front for the Liberation of the Occupied Arab Gulf (PFLOAG) Operates in Dhofar – Chinese support. National Democratic Front for the Liberation of Oman and the Persian Gulf (NDFLOPG).
Palestine/Israel:	Palestine National Liberation Movement (Al Fatah) Leader: Yasir Arafat. Popular Front for the Liberation of Palestine (PFLP) Leader: George Habash. Popular (Democratic) Front for the Liberation of Palestine (PDFLP) Leader: Nail Howatauch. (These are the more active of a great variety of organizations.)
Turkey:	Turkish Peoples Liberation Army (TPLA), mixed ideological basis – sporadic urban activity.

Major Arms Control Agreements

Antarctic Treaty: signed 1959, in force 1961.
Signatories renounce military activity in Antarctic and consent to free movement to verify compliance. No derogation from territorial claims.

Treaty banning Nuclear Weapon Tests in the Atmosphere, in Outer Space and Under Water: signed 1963, in force 1963.
Signatories agree to 'prohibit, to prevent and not to carry out any nuclear weapon test explosion, or any other nuclear explosion, at any place under its jurisdiction or control:

(*a*) in the atmosphere; beyond its limits, including outer space; or underwater, including territorial waters or high seas, or

(*b*) in any other environment if such explosion causes radioactive debris to be present outside the territorial limits of the State under whose jurisdiction or control such explosion is conducted'.

A signatory has a right to withdraw at three months' notice 'if it decides that extraordinary events, related to the subject matter of this Treaty, have jeopardized the supreme interests of its country'.

Treaty on Principles Governing the Activities of States in the Exploration and Use of Outer Space, including the Moon and other Celestial Bodies: signed 1967, in force 1967.
Signatories are committed not to station nuclear weapons or other weapons of mass destruction in space or on celestial bodies, to use celestial bodies exclusively for peaceful purposes, not to create military bases or conduct military tests on celestial bodies, and to make all installations on celestial bodies 'open to representatives of other States Parties to the Treaty on a basis of reciprocity', subject to reasonable notice.

Treaty for the Prohibition of Nuclear Weapons in Latin America, with additional Protocols I and II: signed 1967.
The signatories agree to use nuclear material and facilities exclusively for peaceful purposes and to prevent in their territory 'the testing, use, manufacture, production or acquisition by any means whatsoever of any nuclear weapons' or 'the receipt, storage, installation, deployment and any form of possession of any nuclear weapons' by the parties or anyone else. They also engage not to help or encourage the manufacture or possession of nuclear weapons anywhere. The treaty establishes procedures for verification and control under an Agency for the Prohibition of Nuclear Weapons in Latin America. By Protocol I external states possessing territory in Latin America agree to accept the main prohibitions, though not all the controls. By Protocol II nuclear-weapon states agree to respect the provisions of the treaty and not to use nuclear weapons or threaten such use against the parties to the treaty. The treaty comes into force when all eligible parties to treaty and protocols have ratified and the IAEA safeguards are established. But signatories may agree to observe the treaty before these conditions are met.

Treaty on the Non-Proliferation of Nuclear Weapons: signed 1968, in force 1970.
The signatories affirm that benefits from peaceful applications of nuclear technology should be available to all parties to the treaty, and declare an intention to achieve an early cessation of the nuclear arms race. Each 'nuclear-weapon state' undertakes 'not to transfer

to any recipient whatsoever nuclear weapons or other nuclear explosive devices or control over such weapons or explosive devices directly or indirectly; and not in any way to assist, encourage, or induce any non-nuclear-weapon state to manufacture or otherwise acquire nuclear weapons or other nuclear explosive devices, or control over such weapons or explosive devices'.

'Each non-nuclear-weapon state ... undertakes not to receive the transfer from any transferer whatsoever of nuclear weapons or other nuclear explosive devices or of control over such weapons or explosive devices directly or indirectly; not to manufacture or otherwise acquire nuclear weapons or other nuclear explosive devices; and not to seek or receive any assistance in the manufacture of nuclear weapons or other nuclear explosive devices.'

The non-nuclear-weapon parties agree to accept safeguards to be negotiated with the International Atomic Energy Agency to prevent diversion of nuclear energy from peaceful purposes to nuclear weapons. (The IAEA approved the contents of agreements in April 1971.) These safeguards apply to 'source or special fissionable material in all peaceful nuclear activities'. All the parties agree not to provide nuclear material or equipment for processing it for peaceful purposes, unless under safeguards. The safeguards are not to hinder economic or technological development. Parties are to ensure that benefits from peaceful uses of nuclear energy, including nuclear explosions, are available to all non-nuclear-weapon states at low cost. The parties are to pursue total nuclear disarmament in good faith. A conference is to be held at Geneva five years after the treaty enters into force to review its operation.

A party to the treaty may withdraw at three months' notice 'if it decides that extraordinary events, related to the subject matter of this treaty, have jeopardized the supreme interests of its country'.

Treaty on the Prohibition of the Emplacement of Nuclear Weapons and other Weapons of Mass Destruction on the Seabed and the Ocean Floor and in the Subsoil thereof: signed 1971. The parties undertake not to emplant on the seabed, ocean floor or subsoil thereof 'any nuclear weapons or any other types of weapons of mass destruction as well as structures, launching installations or any other facilities specifically designed for storing, testing or using such weapons'. The prohibition does not apply to a coastal state in respect of its own coastal waters defined as coterminous with the twelve-mile outer zone referred to in the 1968 Geneva Convention on the Territorial Sea and Contiguous Zone.

The parties may verify compliance by observation of seabed activities beyond the zone provided observation does not interfere with the activities. If doubts persist, the party suspicious and the party suspected shall consult. If suspicion persists the suspicious party shall consult other parties who may carry out joint investigations. Ultimately complaints may be referred to the Security Council.

There is to be a review conference five years from the entry into force of the treaty. Similar withdrawal provisions exist as in the Non-Proliferation Treaty.

Convention on Bacteriological Weapons: signed 1972.
The parties agree 'never in any circumstances to develop, produce, stockpile or otherwise acquire or retain:
  (1) microbial or other biological agents, or toxins whatever their origin or method of production, of types and in quantities that have no justification for prophylactic, protective or other peaceful purposes;
  (2) weapons, equipment or means of delivery designed to use such agents or toxins for hostile purposes or in armed conflict.'

The parties agree to destroy or divert to peaceful use any excessive existing stocks. They agree not to assist other states to acquire the prohibited weapons. If a party discovers a breach of the treaty by another party it may complain to the Security Council. All parties undertake to co-operate if the Security Council initiates, 'in accordance with the provisions of the United Nations Charter', an inquiry into alleged breaches.

The parties affirm the 'recognized objective of effective prohibition of chemical weapons' and agree to negotiate to this effect. There shall be a conference at Geneva five years after the entry into force of the treaty, to review its operation and the progress of negotiations on chemical weapons. A similar withdrawal provision to the Non-Proliferation Treaty is included.

Agreement between the Soviet Union and the United States on Reducing the Risk of Nuclear War: signed 1971.

The parties agree to maintain arrangements to guard against accidental or unauthorized use of nuclear weapons. They undertake to notify each other immediately in the event of an accidental, unauthorized or any other unexplained incident involving a possible detonation of a nuclear weapon which could create a risk of outbreak of nuclear war. They will try to reduce the consequences of such incidents. They will notify each other of detection by missile warning systems of unidentified objects, or of signs of interference with these systems if the incidents create a risk of war. They will notify each other of planned missile launches beyond their territory toward the other party. The parties may request information from each other to avert misinterpretation. They agree to continue consultations concerning implementation of the agreement.

Treaty between the United States and the Soviet Union on the Limitation of Anti-Ballistic Missile Systems: signed 1972.

The parties undertake not to deploy ABM systems except within
(a) one system with a radius of 150 km centered around the national capital and having no more than 100 ABM missiles and no more than six ABM radar complexes, the complexes being circular and no more than 3 km in diameter, and
(b) one system with a radius of 150 km within an area containing ICBMs, including no more than 100 ABM missiles, two large phased-array radars, and eighteen ABM radars, each of the latter to have less potential than the smaller phased-array radar. There are no restrictions on the configuration of test ABM systems in established test ranges. For this purpose up to fifteen ABM launch-sites may be maintained.

The parties agree not to develop ABMs which are sea, air or space based or are mobile on land. They will not develop multiple interceptor missiles. They will not deploy early-warning radars except at the periphery of their territory and facing outwards.

For assurance of compliance each party 'shall use national technical means of verification at its disposal in a manner consistent with generally recognized principles of international law'. The parties shall establish a standing consultative commission to consider implementation of the treaty, provide on a voluntary basis information to assure confidence in compliance, and consider possible changes in the strategic situation affecting the treaty. The parties have a right to withdraw at six months' notice if extraordinary events related to the subject of the treaty jeopardize their interest.

Interim Agreement and Protocol between the United States and Soviet Union on the Limitation of Strategic Arms: signed 1972.

The parties agree not to start construction of additional fixed land-based ICBMs after 1 July 1972 or to convert land-based launchers for light ICBMs or for ICBMs of older types deployed prior to 1964 into land-based launchers for heavy ICBMs of types deployed after 1964. They agree to limit SLBMs and modern SSBNs to the number operational or under construction on 26 May 1972 and to SLBMs and SSBNs constructed by agreement as replacements for SLBMs on older submarines or for pre-1964 ICBMs. Otherwise modernization and replacement of offensive missiles may proceed.

The agreement shall be verified by national means. The parties agree not to use deliberate concealment to impede verification but need not abandon any current practices.

The agreement is to be overseen by the commission established by the ABM treaty and depends upon ratification of the ABM treaty. The same right of withdrawal exists.

The Protocol interprets the agreement to mean that the United States may have no more than 710 SLBMs on 44 submarines; the Soviet Union may have 950 SLBMs on 62 submarines. Any build-up to these ceilings over 656 SLBMs for the United States and 740 for the Soviet Union must be done as replacement of older, pre-1964 ballistic missiles of older types or of ballistic missiles on older submarines.

The Military Balance

THE UNITED STATES AND THE SOVIET UNION

The United States

Population: 210,000,000.
Military service: selective service for two years.
Total armed forces: 2,391,000.
Estimated GNP 1971: $1072·9 billion.
Defence budget 1972–3: $83·4 billion.

STRATEGIC FORCES

(a) Offensive
ICBM: 1054 (Strategic Air Command (SAC))
300 Minuteman 1. 500 Minuteman 2. 200 Minuteman 3.
54 Titan 2.
SLBM: 656 in 41 SSBN (US Navy)
10 SSBN each with 16 Poseidon. 23 SSBN each with 16
Polaris A3. 8 SSBN each with 16 Polaris A2.
AIRCRAFT (SAC)
Bombers: 522. 67 FB111A in 4 squadrons. 150 B52D/F
in 10 squadrons. 240 B52G/H in 16 squadrons.
Bombers in active storage or reserve include 9 FB111A,
22 B52D/F and 43 B52G/H.
Tankers: 390 KC135A in 38 squadrons, plus 130 in
reserve.
Strategic Reconnaissance: SR71A; 2 squadrons.

(b) Defensive
North American Air Defense Command (NORAD) is a
joint American–Canadian organization. 593 combat
aircraft (excluding Canadian): 9 squadrons F106.
National Guard with 5 sqns F101, 11 sqns F102, 2 sqns
F106. AEW: 3 sqns EC121. Missiles: 21 Nike Hercules
Batteries, 5 Bomarc B Batteries. National Guard with
27 Nike Hercules Batteries.

ARMY: 861,000.

3 armoured divisions. 1 cavalry division. 4 mechanized
infantry divisions. 3 infantry divisions. 1 airborne
division. 1 airportable division. 2 independent infantry
brigades. 1 independent airborne brigade. 5 armoured
cavalry regiments. 5 special forces groups. 30 SSM
batteries with Honest John, Pershing, Sergeant SSM;
(Lance is being introduced to replace Honest John and
Sergeant). M48, M60 and M60A1E2 med tks; M551
Sheridan lt tks with Shillelagh ATGW: M107 175 mm

SP guns; M109 155 mm and M110 203 mm SP hows;
TOW ATGW; Vulcan 20 mm AA arty system; Redeye.
Chaparral and HAWK SAM. Army Aviation:
about 200 units with 9000 hel and 2600 fixed-wing ac.

Deployment
CONTINENTAL UNITED STATES
(i) Strategic Reserve: 1 cav div; 1 armd div; 1 mech inf
div; 1 inf div; 1 AB div; 1 airportable div; 1 armed cav regt.
(ii) To reinforce 7th Army in Europe: 1 mech inf div
(less one bde); 1 armed cav regt; 1 special forces gp.
(iii) Other: 1 inf bde; 1 armed cav regt; 2 special forces
gps.
(iv) Hawaii: 1 inf div.
EUROPE
(i) Germany: 7th Army: 2 corps incl 2 armd divs, 2 mech
inf divs, 2 armd cav regts and 1 mech inf bde: 190,000.
(ii) West Berlin: 1 infantry brigade: 1700.
Italy: Task force: HQ elms and 1 SSM bn.
PACIFIC
(i) South Korea: 1 infantry division: 20,000.

Reserves
Authorized strength 660,000; actual strength 635,000.
(i) Army National Guard: 400,000, capable five weeks
after mobilization of manning 2 armd, 1 mech and 5 inf
divs and 19 indep bdes plus reinforcements and support
units to fill regular formations; 27 SAM btys.
(ii) Army Reserves: 235,000.

MARINE CORPS: 198,000.

3 divisions (each of 19,000 men), each supported by
1 tk bn and 1 HAWK SAM bn. M48 and M103A2 tks;
175 mm guns; 105 mm SP hows; 105 mm and 155 mm
hows. 3 Air Wings; 550 combat aircraft. 14 fighter sqns
with F4B and F4J (with Sparrow and Sidewinder AAM).
12 attack sqns with A4 and A6A. 1 close-support sqn
with 30 AV8A (Harrier). 3 recce sqns with RF4B/C, and
RF8A. 45 AH1 gunship hel. 6 heavy hel sqns with
CH53D, RH53D. 9 med assault hel sqns with CH46A.
3 assault tpt sqns with 46 KC130F.

Deployment
(i) *Continental United States*: 2 divisions, 1 brigade.
(ii) *Hawaii/Okinawa*: 1 division.

Reserves

Authorized strength 45,849; actual strength 42,000.

NAVY: 602,000

Submarines, attack

56 nuclear-powered, 35 diesel-powered.

Aircraft carriers

(i) Attack: 14:

1 nuclear-powered (USS *Enterprise* 76,000 tons).
8 Forrestal/Kitty Hawk-class (60,000 tons). 3 Midway-class (52,000 tons). 2 Hancock-class (33,000 tons). The larger carriers have a normal complement of 80–90 aircraft and the smaller ones between 70–80. These are organized as an air wing of 2 fighter sqns with F4 (F8 in the Hancock-class), 2 light attack sqns, all-weather attack sqn with A6; and AEW, tanker and reconnaissance aircraft. Light attack aircraft include A4 and A7 (the A7 due eventually to replace the A4). RA5C are used for reconnaissance (RF8G in the Hancock-class). E2A and E1B are used for AEW and a few KA3B as tankers.

(ii) Anti-Submarine (ASW): 2:

2 Essex-class (33,000 tons) each with 40–47 aircraft in two air groups with 3 sqns of 21 S2E, 2 sqns 16 SH3 hel, 4 E1B AEW and A4 or F8 light attack aircraft.

Other surface ships

1 SAM cruiser (nuclear). 3 SAM cruisers. 1 gun cruiser.
4 SAM light cruisers. 2 SAM frigates (nuclear). 28 SAM frigates. 29 SAM destroyers. 97 gun/ASW destroyers. 6 SAM destroyer escorts. 53 gun escorts (radar picket). 3 frigates (radar picket). 72 amphibious warfare ships. 100+ minor landing craft. 20 MCM ships (plus numerous small craft). 155 logistics and operations support ships. Missiles include Standard, Tartar, Talos, Terrier, Sea Sparrow SAM; ASROC and SUBROC ASW.

Shore-based aircraft

24 maritime patrol squadrons with 216 P3. Transports include C47, C54, C118, C119, C130 and C131.

Deployment

Fleets: First (Eastern Pacific), Second (Atlantic), Sixth (Mediterranean), Seventh (Western Pacific).

Reserves

Authorized strength 129,000; actual strength 120,000; 3500 a year undergo short active duty tours.

AIR FORCE: 730,000; 6000 combat aircraft.

General Purpose Forces include:

(i) *Tactical Air Command:* 110,000; 2200 combat aircraft, about 1000 normally based in the United States. 18 fighter squadrons with F4, F105 and F111E, 1 attack squadron with A7D. 9 tactical recce squadrons with RF4C. 16 assault air-lift sqns with C130E. 4 STOL air-lift sqns with C7 and C123B. 2 electronic warfare squadrons. 7 special operations sqns with A37, AC119, C123K and AC130

(ii) *US Air Force, Europe* (USAFE): 50,000.

21 fighter squadrons (and 4 in USA on call) with 475 F4C/D/E and 75 F111E. 5 tactical recce sqns with 85 RF4C. 2 transport sqns with C130.

(iii) *Pacific Air Forces* (PACAF): 120,000. 5th Air Force: bases in Japan, Korea and Okinawa with F4, RF4C, and C130. 13th Air Force: bases in the Philippines, Taiwan and Thailand, with F4, F105, RF4C and C130. 7th Air Force: 15,800 in South Viet Nam: (the air component of the Military Assistance Command Viet Nam, co-ordinating the operations of the Vietnamese Air Force) with F4C, A37, RF4, A1E, AC119, AC130, C123 and C7A aircraft plus large numbers of light aircraft and helicopters.

(iv) *Military Airlift Command* (MAC): 90,000; 18 heavy transport squadrons with 35 C133, 260 C141 and 60 C5A (planned strength 79 C5A by mid-1973). 24 medical tpt, weather recce and SAR sqns.

Reserves

(i) Air National Guard: Authorized strength 88,191; actual strength 87,000; 1500 aircraft in 18 fighter-interceptor, 28 tactical fighter and attack, 11 tactical reconnaissance, 5 tactical air support, 4 special operations, 7 tanker and 20 air transport squadrons.

(ii) Air Force Reserve: Authorized strength 49,634; actual strength 47,000; 400 aircraft in 52 squadrons incl 1 C123K, 6 C124, 18 C130 and 13 C141 tpt sqns (the others have tactical support, special operations and SAR roles).

The Soviet Union

Population: 246,800,000.
Military service: Army and Air Force, 2 years; Navy and Border Guards, 2–3 years.
Total armed forces: 3,375,000.
Estimated GNP 1971: $536 billion.
Defence budget 1972: $91 billion (approx).

STRATEGIC FORCES

(a) Offensive

(Strategic Rocket Forces (SRF)) 350,000.

ICBM: about 1618.

210 SS7 *Saddler* and SS8 *Sasin*. 290 SS9 *Scarp*. 970 SS11 (including about 100 with variable-range capability sited within IRBM/MRBM fields). 60 SS13 *Savage*. The SAL agreement of May 1972 implies that about 70 SS11 or 13 and 25 SS9 are being added to these strengths.

IRBM and MRBM: about 600.

100 SS5 *Skean* IRBM. 500 SS4 *Sandal* MRBM. (The majority are sited near the western border of the USSR and the remainder east of the Urals.)

SLBM: 560 in 61 submarines (Navy). According to the SAL agreement about 240 more SLBM will be carried by additional SSBN under construction.

29 SSBN (Y-class) each with 16 SSN6 missiles. 10 SSBN (HII-class) and 10 diesel (GII-class), each with 3 SSN5

Serb missiles. 12 diesel (GI-class) each with 3 SSN4 *Sark* missiles.

AIRCRAFT
(Long Range Air Force).
Long-range bombers: 140. 100 TU95 *Bear* and 40 Mya 4 *Bison*. Tankers: 50 Mya 4 *Bison*. Medium-range bombers: 700. 500 TU16 *Badger* and 200 TU22 *Blinder*.

(b) Defensive
Air Defence Command.
AIRCRAFT: about 3000.
Interceptors: include about 1060 MiG 17, 19 and Yak 25; 800 SU9; 1140 Yak 28P *Firebar*, TU28P *Fiddler*, SU11 *Flagon A* and MiG 23 *Foxbat*.
AEW aircraft: 10 modified TU114 *Moss*.

ANTI-BALLISTIC MISSILES (ABM)
64 *Galosh* long-range missile launchers are deployed in four sites around Moscow. Work has been resumed on previously uncompleted complexes in the same area.
SAM: 10,000 launchers at about 1600 sites
SA2: about 5000; track-while-scan *Fan Song* radar; high-explosive warhead; slant range (launcher to target) about 25 miles; effective between 1000 and 80,000 feet.
SA3: Two-stage, short-range, low-level missile; slant range about 15 miles.
SA4: Twin-mounted (on tracked carriers), air-transportable missile with solid fuel boosters and ram-jet sustainer.
SA5: Two-stage, boosted AA missile; slant range about 50 miles, with a capability against ASM.
SA6: Triple-mounted (on tracked carrier), low-level missile.

ARMY: 2,000,000.
106 motorized rifle divisions. 51 tank divisions. 7 airborne divisions. SSM about 900 (units are organic to formations).
(1) FROG, range 10–45 miles.
(2) *Scud A*, range 50 miles.
(3) *Scud B*, range 185 miles.
(4) *Scaleboard*, range 500 miles.
SAM: SA2, SA4 and SA6

TANKS
T10 hy; T62 and T54/55 med; PT76 amphibious recce lt. At full strength, tank divisions have 316 medium tanks and motorized rifle divisions 188.

ARTILLERY
ISU 122 and ISU 152 SP guns; 100 mm, 122 mm, 130 mm, 152 mm and 203 mm field guns; BM 21 122 mm and M1965 140 mm RL; ASU 57 and ASU 85 SP and 85 mm, 100 mm and 130 mm ATk guns; *Sagger*, *Snapper*, *Swatter* ATGW; AA guns.

Deployment
CENTRAL AND EASTERN EUROPE
31 divs: 20 divs (10 tank) in East Germany; 2 tank divs in Poland: 4 divs (2 tank) in Hungary; and 5 divs (2 tank) in Czechoslovakia.

EUROPEAN USSR
60 divs.
CENTRAL USSR (between the Volga River and Lake Baikal) 8 divs.
SOUTHERN USSR (Caucasus and West Turkestan) 21 divs.
SINO-SOVIET BORDER AREA
44 divs, incl 2 divs in Mongolia.
The 31 divisions in Eastern Europe are maintained at or near combat strength, as are about half of those in the Far East. The other divisions in the Far East are probably in the second category of readiness: below combat-strength, but not requiring major reinforcement in the event of war. Most of the remaining combat-ready divisions are in European USSR, while the divisions in central USSR would mostly require major reinforcement, as would about half of the divisions in southern USSR.

NAVY: 475,000 (incl Naval Air Force 75,000 and Naval Infantry 14,000).

SUBMARINES
Attack: 34 nuclear (C, V, N-classes) 210 diesel (B, F, R, Q, Z, W-classes).
Long-range cruise missile: 26 nuclear-powered (E-class) and 25 diesel (J, W-classes) with 4–8 450-mile range SSN3 missiles.

SURFACE SHIPS
2 ASW helicopter cruisers each with 2 twin SAM and about 20 Ka25 helicopters. 1 Kara-class cruiser with SSM and SAM. 2 Kresta II-class cruisers with SSM and SAM. 4 Kresta I-class cruisers with SSM and SAM. 4 Kynda-class cruisers with SSM and SAM. 11 Sverdlov-class (1 with SAM) and 4 older cruisers. 3 Krivak-class destroyers with SSM and SAM. 5 Kanin-class destroyers with SAM. 3 Krupny-class destroyers with SSM. 4 Kildin-class destroyers with SSM. 17 Kashin-class destroyers with SAM. 6 modified Kotlin-class destroyers with SAM. 17 Kotlin-class destroyers. 40 Skory- and modified Skory-class destroyers. 112 other ocean-going escorts. 250 coastal escorts and submarine chasers. 6 Nanuchka-class escorts with SSM and SAM. 117 Osa- and 30 Komar-class FPB with *Styx* SSM. 250 torpedo boats. 180 fleet minesweepers. 125 coastal minesweepers. 105 landing ships and numerous landing craft.
Some trawlers are used for electronic intelligence.
Coasts are covered by a coast watch radar and visual reporting system. Approaches to naval bases and major ports are protected by SSN3 *Shaddock* coast defence missiles and by guns.

SHORE-BASED AIRCRAFT
Bombers: 450, most based near the north-west and Black Sea coasts of the USSR. 300 TU16 with one *Kipper* or two *Kelt* ASM. 60 TU22 *Blinder* strike and reconnaissance 40 II28 *Beagle* torpedo-equipped light bombers. 50 TU95 *Bear* long-range naval reconnaissance. 150 TU16 *Badger* reconnaissance and tanker.
Other aircraft and helicopters: 560.

80 BE12 *Mail* ASW amphibians. 140 Il18 May ASW aircraft. 240 Mi4 and Ka25 ASW helicopters. 200 miscellaneous transports.

NAVAL INFANTRY

(marines): 14,000. Organized in brigades and assigned to fleets. Equipped with standard infantry weapons, T54/55 med tks, PT76 lt tks and APC.

Deployment

Arctic, Baltic, Black Sea and Far East Fleets.

AIR FORCE: 550,000; about 9000 combat aircraft.
(i) Long Range Air Force (*see* p. 293).
(ii) Tactical Air Force: about 4300 aircraft, incl medium, light bombers and fighter bombers, fighters, helicopters, transport and recce aircraft. Some obsolescent MiG 17, MiG 19 and Il28 are still in service. The most notable high performance aircraft are the MiG 21J *Fishbed J*

and Yak 28P *Firebar* fighters, the ground-attack SU7 *Fitter* and the light bomber Yak 28 *Brewer*. The variable-geometry *Flogger* is now entering service.
(iii) Air Defence Command (*see* p. 294).
(iv) Naval Air Force (*see* above).
(v) Air Transport Force: about 1700 aircraft. Il14, An24, some 8000 An12 and Il18 medium transports and 10 An22 heavy transports.
About 800 helicopters in use with the ground forces, including troop-carrying Mi6 and Mi8 and the heavy load-carrier Mi10. The Mi12, a very heavy load carrier, may now be in service. The total helicopter inventory is probably around 1750.
(vi) Training units: about 1800 aircraft.
PARA-MILITARY FORCES
300,000.
125,000 security troops; 175,000 border troops

WARSAW PACT

Bulgaria

Population: 8,610,000.
Total regular forces: 146,000.
Defence expenditure 1970: $279,000,000.

ARMY: 117,000.

8 motorized rifle divisions (3 cadre). 5 tank brigades. Some hy tks; about 1900 med tks mainly T54, with some T34, T55 and T62; PT76 lt tks; BRD scout cars; BTR50, BTR60 and BTR152 APC; 85 mm, 122 mm, 130 mm and 152 mm guns; SU100 SP guns; *Frog* and *Scud* SSM; 57 mm, 85 mm and 100 mm ATk guns; *Sagger* and *Snapper* ATGW; 37 mm and 57 mm AA guns.

NAVY: 7000

2 submarines. 2 escorts. 8 coastal escorts. 20 MCM ships. 3 Osa-class patrol boats with *Styx* SSM. 15 motor torpedo boats (8 less than 100 tons). 20 landing craft. A small Danube flotilla. 6 Mi4 helicopters.

AIR FORCE: 22,000; 252 combat aircraft.

6 fighter-bomber squadrons with MiG 17. 3 interceptor squadrons with MiG 21. 3 interceptor squadrons with MiG 19. 6 interceptor squadrons with MiG 17.
1 reconnaissance squadron with Il28. 2 recce squadrons with MiG 17 and MiG 21. (12 aircraft in a combat squadron.) 4 Li2, 6 An2 and 10 Il14 transports. About 40 Mi4 helicopters.

Czechoslovakia

Population: 14,800,000.
Total regular forces: 185,000.
Defence expenditure 1972: $1,875,000,000.

ARMY: 145,000.

5 tank divisions. 5 motorized rifle divisions. 1 airborne brigade. Some hy tanks; about 3400 med tks mostly T55 and T62 with some T54 and T34; OT65 scout cars; OT62 and OT64 APC; SU100, SU122 and ISU152 SP guns; 122 mm how; 82 mm and 120 mm mortars; *Frog* and *Scud* SSM; 57 mm, 85 mm and 100 mm ATk guns; *Sagger*, *Snapper* and *Swatter* ATGW; 23 mm and 57 mm AA guns. About 200 Mi1 and Mi4 hel.

AIR FORCE: 40,000; 504 combat aircraft.

12 ground-support squadrons with SU7, MiG 15 and MiG 17. 18 interceptor squadrons with MiG 19 and MiG 21. 6 reconnaissance squadrons with MiG 21, Il28 and L29. About 50 Li2, Il14 and Il18 transports. About 90 Mi1, Mi4 and Mi8 helicopters. SA2 SAM.

German Democratic Republic

Population: 17,285,000.
Total regular forces: 131,000.
Defence budget 1972: $2,240,000,000.

ARMY: 90,000.

2 tank divisions. 4 motorized rifle divisions. Some hy tks; about 2000 med tks, T54, T55, and T62; several hundred T34 (used for training); about 130 PT76 lt tks; BRDM scout cars; BTR50P, BTR60P and BTR152 APC; SU100 SP guns; 85 mm, 122 mm, 130 mm and 152 mm guns; *Frog* 7 and *Scud B* SSM; 57 mm and 100 mm ATk guns; *Sagger*, *Snapper* and *Swatter* ATGW; 23 mm and 57 mm SP AA guns; and 100 mm AA guns.

NAVY: 16,000.

2 destroyer escorts. 25 coastal escorts. 49 minesweepers. 12 Osa-class patrol boats with *Styx* SSM. 65 motor torpedo boats (45 less than 100 tons). 18 landing ships and craft. 16 Mi4 helicopters.

AIR FORCE: 25,000; 304 combat aircraft.

2 interceptor squadrons with MiG 17. 17 interceptor squadrons with MiG 21. (16 aircraft in a combat squadron.) 30 transports, including An2 and Il14. 30 Mi1, Mi4 and Mi8 helicopters.

Hungary

Population: 10,500,000.
Total regular forces: 103,000.
Defence budget 1972: $558,000,000.

ARMY: 90,000.

2 tank divisions (1 cadre). 4 motorized rifle divisions (1 cadre). Some hy tks; about 1500 med tks, mainly T55, T54 and T62; some T34 for training; 50 PT76 lt tks; FUG-M and OT65 scout cars; FUG-M1970, OT64 and BTR152 APC; 76 mm, 85 mm and 122 mm guns; 122 mm and 152 mm hows; *Frog* SSM; 57 mm ATk guns; *Sagger*, *Snapper* and *Swatter* ATGW; 57 mm twin SP AA guns.

NAVY: 500.

Danube River Guard of small patrol craft.

AIR FORCE: 12,500; 108 combat aircraft.

9 interceptor squadrons with MiG 19 and MiG 21. (12 aircraft in a combat squadron.) About 25 An2, Il14 and Li2 transport aircraft. About 15 Mi1, Mi4 and Mi8 helicopters.

Poland

Population: 33,600,000.
Total regular forces: 274,000.
Defence expenditure 1971: $2,350,000,000.

ARMY: 200,000.

5 tank divisions. 8 motorized rifle divisions. 1 airborne division. 1 amphibious assault division. (Divisions are at 70 per cent strength, except those in the Warsaw Military District, which are at 30–50 per cent strength.)

Some hy tks; 3400 med tks, T54, T55 and some T62; some T34 for training; about 250 PT76 lt tks; FUG-M

and BRDM scout cars; OT62, OT64 and BTR152 APC; ASU57 and ASU85 AB assault guns; 122 mm guns, 122 mm hows and 152 mm gun/hows; *Frog* and *Scud* SSM; 57 mm, 85 mm and 100 mm ATk guns; *Sagger*, *Snapper* and *Swatter* ATGW; 23 mm and 57 mm SP AA guns.

NAVY: 19,000 (including 1000 marines).

5 submarines. 4 destroyers. 30 coastal escorts/submarine chasers. 55 MGM ships. 15 Osa-class patrol boats with *Styx* SSM. 20 torpedo boats. 22 landing ships. 55 naval aircraft, mostly MiG 17, with a few Il28 lt bomber/recce and some helicopters.

AIR FORCE: 55,000; 696 combat aircraft.

4 light bomber squadrons with Il28. 12 fighter-bomber sqns with MiG 17 and Su7. 36 interceptor squadrons with MiG 17, MiG 19 and MiG 21. 6 recce sqns with MiG 21 and Il28. (12 aircraft in a combat squadron.) About 45 An2, An12, Il12, Il14, Il18 and Li2 transports. 40 helicopters, including Mi1, Mi4 and Mi8.

Rumania

Population: 20,600,000.
Total regular forces: 179,000.
Defence budget 1972: $725,000,000.

ARMY: 150,000.

2 tank divisions. 7 motorized rifle divisions. 1 mountain brigade. 1 airborne regiment. Some hy tks; 1700 T34, T54, T55 and T62 med tks; BTR40, BTR50P and BTR152 APC; SU100 SP guns; 76 mm, 122 mm and 152 mm guns; *Frog* SSM; 57 mm, 85 mm and 100 mm ATk guns; *Sagger*, *Snapper* and *Swatter* ATGW; 37 mm, 57 mm and 100 mm AA guns.

NAVY: 8000.

6 coastal escorts. 30 MCM ships. 5 Osa-class patrol boats with *Styx* SSM. 12 motor torpedo boats. 4 Mi4 helicopters.

AIR FORCE: 21,000; 252 combat aircraft.

20 interceptor squadrons with MiG 17, MiG 19 and MiG 21. 1 reconnaissance squadron with Il28. (12 aircraft in a combat squadron.) 1 transport squadron with Il14 and Li2. 10 Mi4 helicopters.

THE NORTH ATLANTIC TREATY ORGANIZATION

Belgium

Population: 9,800,000.
Total armed forces: 90,200.
Defence budget 1972: $723,744,292.

ARMY: 66,000.

1 armoured brigade. 3 motorized infantry brigades. 2 reconnaissance battalions. 1 para-commando regiment. 2 SSM battalions with Honest John. 2 SAM battalions with HAWK. 4 air sqns with 80 Alouette II hel and 12 Do27. 330 Leopard and 175 M47 med tks; 135 M41 lt tks;

M75 and AMX-VTT APC; M108 105 mm, M44 and
M109 155 mm and M55 203 mm SP hows; 203 mm hows.
Honest John SSM; HAWK SAM.

Reserves
1 mech inf bde and one inf bde.

NAVY: 4200.

7 ocean minesweepers/minehunters. 9 coastal
minesweepers/minehunters. 14 inshore minesweepers.
2 support ships. 2 S58 and 3 Alouette III helicopters.

AIR FORCE: 20,000; 144 combat aircraft.

2 fighter-bomber squadrons with F104G. 3 fighter-
bomber squadrons with Mirage-VBA. 2 AWX squadrons
with F104G. 1 reconnaissance squadron with Mirage-
VBR. (A combat squadron normally has 18 aircraft.)
2 tpt sqns with 24 C119, 5 C47, 12 Pembroke and 4 DC6
tpts (12 C130 Hercules are to replace C119 by end 1973).
11 HS3-1 helicopters. 8 SAM squadrons with Nike-
Hercules.

Britain

Population: 56,250,000.
Total armed forces: 372,331.
Defence budget 1972–3: $6,900,000,000.

STRATEGIC FORCES

SLBM: 4 SSBN each with 16 Polaris A3 missiles.

ARMY: 180,458 (incl 8200 enlisted outside Britain).

12 armoured regiments. 5 armoured car regiments. 47
infantry battalions. 3 parachute battalions. 6 Gurkha
battalions. 1 special air service (SAS) regiment. 3 regts
with Honest John SSM and 203 mm howitzers. 24 other
artillery regiments. 1 SAM regiment with Thunderbird.
14 engineer regiments. 59 of the above units are
organized in two armd, twelve inf, one para and one
Gurkha bdes. 900 Chieftain and Centurion med tks
(Scorpion lt tk being delivered); 105 mm Abbot and
M107 175 mm SP guns; M109 155 mm SP hows; M110
203 mm SP hows; Model 56 105 mm pack hows; Honest
John SSM; Vigilant and Swingfire ATGW; L40/70 AA
guns; Thunderbird SAM; lt aircraft; 132 Scout and 265
Sioux hels.

Deployment
The Strategic Reserve: includes one div of three
airportable bdes and two para bns of the United
Kingdom Mobile Force (UKMF), and the SAS regiment.
GERMANY
British Army of the Rhine (BAOR), of 54,900, includes
one corps HQ, three div HQ, five armd bdes, one mech
bde, two arty bdes, two armd car regts and the
Thunderbird SAM regt. In Berlin there is one 3000-strong
inf bde.
SINGAPORE
one inf bn gp (ANZUK force).

BRUNEI
one Gurkha bn.
HONG KONG
two British and three Gurkha inf bns; one arty regt.
CYPRUS
one inf bn and one airportable recce sqn with UN force
(UNFICYP); one inf bn and one armd car sqn in garrison
at Sovereign Base Areas.
GIBRALTAR
one inf bn and one coy.
BRITISH HONDURAS
one inf coy.

NAVY: 82,024.

SUBMARINES, ATTACK: 6 nuclear (SSN); 24 diesel.
SURFACE SHIPS
1 aircraft carrier. 3 commando carriers. 2 assault ships.
2 SAM cruisers with Seacat. 9 SAM destroyers with
Seaslug II and Seacat. 3 other destroyers. 33 general
purpose frigates. 24 ASW frigates. 4 AA and 4 aircraft
direction frigates. 38 coastal minesweepers/minehunters.
6 inshore minesweepers. 5 coastal patrol vessels.
5 patrol boats. (Ships in reserve or undergoing refit
or conversion are included in the above totals.)
THE FLEET AIR ARM
96 combat aircraft.
THE ROYAL MARINES
8000; including 3500 men in commandos.

AIR FORCE: 109,849; about 500 combat aircraft.

8 medium bomber squadrons with Vulcan. 3 strike
squadrons with Buccaneer. 7 strike/attack/recce
squadrons with F4M. 4 close support squadrons with
Harrier. 8 air defence squadrons with Lightning. 1 air
defence squadron with F4M. 1 recce squadron with
Victor SR2. 4 recce squadrons with Canberra. 1 AEW
squadron with Shackleton. 2 maritime patrol squadrons
with Nimrod. (Combat squadrons have 6–12 aircraft.)
3 tanker squadrons with Victor K1/K1A. 5 strategic tpt
sqns with VC10, Belfast, Britannia. 7 tactical tpt sqns
with C130 Hercules. 2 light communication squadrons
with HS125. 7 hel sqns with 60 Wessex, Whirlwind and
30 SA330 Puma.

Deployment
The Royal Air Force includes one operational home
command – Strike Command – and two smaller
overseas commands – RAF Germany (8600), and Near
East Air Force. Squadrons are deployed overseas as
follows:
GERMANY
4 F4; 2 Buccaneer; 2 Lightning; 3 Harrier; 1 Wessex.
NEAR EAST
(a) Cyprus: 2 Vulcan; 1 Lightning; 1 Hercules; 1
Whirlwind. (b) Malta: 1 Nimrod; 1 Canberra.
SINGAPORE
dets Nimrod and Wessex hel (ANZUK force).

Canada

Population: 21,800,000.
Total armed forces: 84,000.
Defence expenditure 1972–3: $US 1,936,634,000.

The Canadian Armed Forces have been unified since February 1968. The strengths shown here for Army, Navy and Air Force are only approximate.

ARMY (Land): 34,000.

In Canada: Mobile Command (about 20,000).
1 airborne regiment. 3 combat groups each comprising: 3 infantry battalions. 1 reconnaissance regiment. 1 reduced light artillery regiment (of 2 batteries). Support units.
M113 APC, Ferret armd cars; Model 56 105 mm pack hows.

In Europe
One mech battle group of 2800 men, with 32 Centurion med tks, 375 M113 APC and 18 M109 155 mm SP hows (Centurion tks are to be replaced by Scorpion in 1974).

NAVY (Maritime): 14,000.

4 submarines. 9 ASW hel destroyer escorts (4 hel destroyers under construction). 11 ASW destroyer escorts. 6 coastal minesweepers. 3 support ships. The Maritime Air Element consists of: 4 maritime patrol squadrons with Argus. 1 maritime patrol squadron with S2 Tracker. 1 ASW squadron with SH3 Sea King helicopters.

Reserves
about 2900.

AIR FORCE (Air): 36,000; 162 combat aircraft.

In Canada
Mobile Command: 2 CF5 tactical fighter sqns (for use with AMF). 6 helicopter squadrons.
Air Defence Command (Canadian component of NORAD). 3 interceptor squadrons with F101C. 28 surveillance and control radar squadrons. 1 SAGE control centre. 1 CF100 electronic warfare training squadron.
Air Transport Command: 1 sqn with 5 Boeing 707 320C transport/tankers. 2 sqns with C130E Hercules. 4 sqns with CC115 Buffalo, CC138 Twin Otter and CH113 Labrador SAR hel. 1 sqn with CC109 Cosmopolitan and Falcon.

In Europe
Germany: 2300; 3 strike/attack/recce sqns with CF104. (Squadrons have 6–18 aircraft.)

Denmark

Population: 5,000,000.
Total armed forces: 43,400.
Defence budget 1972–3: $438,300,000.

ARMY: 27,000.

4 armoured infantry brigades. 1 battalion group. 3 artillery battalions. Centurion med tks; M41 lt tks; M113 APC; M109 155 mm SP howitzers; 203 mm howitzers; Honest John SSM; 12 Hughes 500M helicopters.

Reserves
65,000, including 2 armd inf bdes and support units to be formed from reservists within 72 hours.

NAVY: 6600.

6 coastal submarines. 2 destroyers. 4 frigates. 4 coastal escorts. 9 seaward defence craft. 13 fast patrol boats. 7 coastal minelayers. 12 minesweepers (4 inshore). 8 Alouette III helicopters.

AIR FORCE: 9800; 112 combat aircraft.

1 fighter-bomber squadron with 16 F35XD Draken. 2 fighter-bomber squadrons with 32 F100D/F. 2 interceptor squadrons with 32 F104G. 1 interceptor squadron with 16 Hunter. 1 recce sqn with 16 RF35XD Draken. 1 transport squadron with 6 C47 and 8 C54. 1 SAR squadron with 12 S61 helicopters. 4 SAM squadrons with Nike-Hercules. 4 SAM squadrons with HAWK.

France

Population: 51,700,000.
Total armed forces: 500,600.
Defence budget 1972: $6,241,000,000.

STRATEGIC FORCES

IRBM: two squadrons, each with 9 SSBS S2 missiles.
SLBM: two SSBN with MSBS M1 missiles.

Aircraft
36 Mirage IVA bombers (9 squadrons). 12 KC135F tankers (3 squadrons). 22 Mirage IVA bombers are in reserve.

ARMY: 328,000.

5 mechanized divisions. 1 airborne division (2 brigades). 1 airportable motorized brigade. 2 alpine brigades. 4 armoured car regiments. 2 motorized infantry regiments. 1 parachute battalion. 25 infantry battalions. 5 SSM battalions with Honest John. 3 SAM regiments with HAWK. M47 and about 575 AMX30 med tks; AMX13 lt tks; Panhard EBR hy and AML lt armd cars; VTT-AMX APC; AMX SP 105 mm guns and 155 mm hows; Model 56 105 mm pack hows. 30 mm twin SP AA guns; SS11/ Harpon ATGW.

Army Aviation (Alat): 4500.
450 Bell, Alouette and SA330 Puma helicopters. 300 light fixed-wing aircraft.

NAVY: 67,000 (including Naval Air Force).

19 attack submarines (diesel). 2 aircraft carriers. 1 helicopter carrier. 1 helicopter cruiser. 2 cruisers (1 SAM, 1 command). 17 destroyers (4 SAM with Tartar, 6 ASW,

4 aircraft direction, 3 command). 29 frigates (2 SAM with Masurca, and Malafon ASW). 15 fleet minesweepers. 61 coastal minesweepers. 15 inshore minesweepers. 23 patrol vessels. 5 landing ships. 18 landing craft.

Naval Air Force

12,000; 150 combat aircraft.
2 fighter-bomber sqns with Etendard IVM. 2 interceptor sqns with F8F Crusaders. 1 reconnaissance sqn with Etendard IVP. 3 ASW sqns with Alizé. 1 ASW helicopter sqn with Super Frelon. 4 helicopter sqns, 1 with Alouette and 3 with HSS 1. 3 maritime recce sqns.

AIR FORCE: 105,000; 500 combat aircraft.

Air Defence Command: 3 interceptor sqns with Mirage IIIC. 2 AWX sqns with 30 Vautour IIN (Mirage F1 to be delivered early 1973). 3 interceptor sqns with Super Mystère B2.

Tactical Air Force

8 fighter-bomber squadrons with Mirage IIIE. 1 fighter-bomber squadron with Mirage IIIB. 2 fighter-bomber squadrons with F100D. 2 fighter-bomber squadrons with Mystère IVA. 2 light bomber sqns with 30 Vautour II IB. 3 recce sqns with Mirage IIIR/RD.

Air Transport Command

7 tactical transport sqns; 3 with Transall C160 and 4 with 173 Nord 2501 Noratlas. 1 heavy transport sqn. 2 mixed transport sqns. 4 helicopter transport sqns with H34, Alouette II.

Federal Republic of Germany

Population: 59,520,000.
Total armed forces: 467,000.
Defence budget 1972: $7568 million.

ARMY: 327,000.

13 armoured brigades. 12 armoured infantry brigades. 3 motorized rifle brigades. 2 mountain brigades. 3 airborne brigades. (The above are organized in 12 divisions.) 11 SSM battalions with Honest John. 4 SSM battalions with Sergeant. 1050 M48A2 Patton and 2200 Leopard med tks; 1800 HS30, 225 Marder, 2374 Hotchkiss and 3170 M113 APC; 1100 tank destroyers; 280 105-mm hows, 150 155-mm hows; 660 155-mm, 150 175-mm and 75 203-mm SP guns; 209 multiple RL: 500 40-mm SP AA guns; about 540 H34, UH1D Iroquois and Alouette II hels and 18 Do27 lt aircraft.

NAVY: 36,000 (including Naval Air Arm).

6 coastal submarines. 11 destroyers (3 with Tartar SAM). 6 fast frigates. 6 fleet utility vessels. 13 fast combat support ships. 58 minesweepers. 40 fast patrol boats. 2 landing ships. 10 landing craft.

Naval Air Arm: 6000; 75 combat aircraft.

4 fighter-bomber/recce squadrons with 60 F104G. 2 MR squadrons with 15 BR1150 Atlantic. 23 S58 SAR

helicopters (being replaced by 22 SH3D Sea King Mk 41). 20 Do28 and 9 miscellaneous liaison aircraft.

AIR FORCE: 104,000; 459 combat aircraft.

7 fighter-bomber squadrons with 126 F104G. 3 fighter-bomber/interceptor sqns with 45 F104G. 8 lt ground-attack/recce squadrons with 168 G91. 4 interceptor squadrons with 60 F104G. 4 heavy reconnaissance squadrons with 60 RF4E. 4 transport squadrons with C160 Transall. 4 helicopter squadrons with 134 UH1D, 55 Bell 47 and Alouette II. (Fighter, fighter-bomber, reconnaissance and light-attack squadrons have 15–21 aircraft and tpt squadrons up to 18.) 2 SSM wings with 72 Pershing.

PARA-MILITARY FORCES

18,500 Border Police with Saladin armoured cars and coastal patrol boats.

Greece

Population: 9,030,000.
Total armed forces: 157,000.
Estimated defence expenditure 1972: $495,134,000.

ARMY: 118,000.

1 armoured division. 11 infantry divisions (3 close to full strength). 1 commando brigade. 12 light infantry battalions. 2 SSM battalions with Honest John. 1 SAM battalion with HAWK. 200 M47, 220 M48 and 30 AMX30 med tks; M24, M26 and M41 lt tks; M8 and M20 armd cars; M2, M3, M59 and M113 APC; 105 mm, 155 mm and 175 mm SP guns; 105 mm, 155 mm and 203 mm hows; 40 mm, 75 mm and 90 mm AA guns.

NAVY: 18,000.

2 submarines (1 more to be delivered in 1973, 3 in 1974). 8 destroyers. 4 destroyer escorts. 3 coastal patrol vessels. 2 minelayers. 20 coastal minesweepers. 13 fast torpedo boats (less than 100 tons). 4 fast missile patrol boats with Exocet SSM. 8 tank landing ships. 6 medium landing ships. 1 dock landing ship. 8 landing craft. 12 HU16 maritime patrol aircraft.

AIR FORCE: 21,000; 190 combat aircraft.

3 fighter-bomber squadrons with F84F. 2 fighter-bomber squadrons with F104G. 1 fighter-bomber squadron with F5A. 2 interceptor squadrons with F5A. 1 interceptor squadron with F102A. 1 reconnaissance squadron with RF5. 1 reconnaissance squadron with RF84F. (A combat squadron has up to 18 aircraft.) 3 tpt sqns of 15 C47 and 45 Noratlas. 1 helicopter squadron with 12 H19 and 6 AB205. 1 helicopter squadron with 10 Bell 47G. 1 SAM battalion with Nike-Hercules.

Italy

Population: 54,490,000.
Total armed forces: 427,600.

Defence budget 1971: $3,244,000,000.

ARMY: 306,600.

2 armoured divisions. 5 infantry divisions. 1 independent cavalry brigade. 4 independent infantry brigades. 5 alpine brigades. 1 airborne brigade. 1 SSM brigade with Honest John. 4 SAM battalions with HAWK. 800 M47 and 200 M60 med tks (deliveries of 800 Leopard have started); 3300 M113 APC; 155 mm, 175 mm and 203 mm SP guns; Model 56 105-mm pack hows; M42 SP AA guns.

Army Aviation: Agusta Bell 205, 206A (26 CH47C Chinook on order) hels; lt fixed-wing aircraft.

NAVY: 44,500 (incl air arm and marines).

9 submarines. 3 SAM cruisers with Terrier SAM and ASW helicopters (one with ASROC ASW msls). 2 SAM destroyers with Tartar. 4 ASW destroyers. 10 destroyer escorts. 12 coastal escorts. 4 ocean minesweepers. 37 coastal minesweepers. 20 inshore minesweepers. 5 fast patrol boats (Otomat SSM to be operational in 1973).

Naval Air Arm:
3 maritime patrol squadrons with about 30 S2 Tracker. (Delivery of an order of 18 Atlantic started mid-1972), HU16A, 24 SH3D, 9 SH34, 30 AB204B and 12 Bell47 helicopters.

AIR FORCE: 76,500; 320 combat aircraft.

3 fighter-bomber squadrons with F104G. 1 fighter-bomber squadron with F104S. 1 fighter-bomber squadron with G91Y. 4 light attack squadrons with G91R. 1 AWX squadron with F104G. 4 AWX squadrons with F104S. 1 AWX squadron with F86K. 3 recce squadrons with 27 RF84F and 20 RF104G. 3 transport squadrons with C119 (14 C130E Hercules to be delivered by mid-1973). (A combat squadron has 12–18 aircraft and a transport squadron 16.) 12 SAM groups with Nike-Hercules.

Netherlands

Population: 13,325,000.
Total armed forces: 122,200.
Defence budget 1972: $1562 million.

ARMY: 80,000.

2 armoured brigades. 4 armoured infantry brigades. 2 SSM battalions with Honest John. 400 Centurion and 485 Leopard med tks; 120 AMX13 lt tks; M106, M113 and M577 (amphibious) APC; AMX-VTT and YP408 APC; AMX 105-mm, M109 155-mm, M107 175-mm and M110 203-mm SP hows.

NAVY: 20,000 (including 2800 marines and 2000 naval air force).

6 submarines. 2 cruisers (one SAM with Terrier). 6 SAM frigates with Seacat. 12 destroyers. 6 corvettes. 6 support escorts. 5 patrol vessels. 26 coastal minesweepers/minehunters. 16 inshore minesweepers. 1 fast combat support ship.

Naval Air Arm: 2000; 44 combat aircraft.
2 MR sqns with BR1150 Atlantic and P2 Neptune.

AIR FORCE: 22,200; 144 combat aircraft.

2 fighter-bomber squadrons with 36 F104G. 3 fighter-bomber squadrons with 54 NF5A. 2 interceptor squadrons with 36 F104G. 1 reconnaissance squadron with 18 RF104G. 1 transport squadron with 12 F27. 30 NF5B trainers.

Norway

Population: 3,935,000.
Total armed forces: 35,900.
Defence budget 1972: $490,780,000.

ARMY: 18,000.

The peacetime establishment includes 1 brigade group in North Norway, independent battalions and supporting elements and training units. Leopard and M48 med tks; M24 lt tks; M8 armd cars; M113 and BV202 APC; M109 155-mm SP hows; L18 and L19 lt aircraft. Mobilization would produce 11 Regimental Combat Teams (brigades) of 5000 men each, supporting units and territorial forces totalling 157,000.

NAVY: 8500 (incl 800 coastal artillery).

15 coastal submarines. 5 frigates. 2 coastal escorts. 10 coastal minesweepers. 5 minelayers. 20 fast patrol boats (refitting with Penguin SSM). 26 torpedo boats.

AIR FORCE: 9400; 117 combat aircraft.

5 light attack squadrons each with 16 F5A. 1 AWX fighter squadron with 16 F104G. 1 photo-reconnaissance squadron with 16 RF5A. 1 maritime patrol squadron with 5 P3B. 1 transport squadron with 6 C130 and 4 C47. 2 helicopter squadrons with UH1B. 4 SAM batteries with Nike-Hercules.

Portugal

Population: 9,780,000.
Total armed forces: 218,000.
Estimated defence expenditure 1972: $459,400,000.

ARMY: 179,000.

2 tank regiments. 8 cavalry regiments. 35 infantry regiments. 17 coastal artillery regiments. M47 and M4 med tks; M41 lt tks; Humber Mark IV and EBR75 armd cars; AML60 scout cars; FV1609 and M16 half-track APC; 105 mm and 140 mm howitzers.

About 25 infantry regiments and supporting units are located in the African provinces. (The numbers from all armed forces, in each province, including locally enlisted, are: Angola: 55,000; Mozambique: 60,000; Portuguese Guinea: 27,000.)

NAVY: 18,000 (including 3300 marines).

4 submarines. 11 frigates. 6 corvettes. 16 coastal patrol vessels. 4 ocean minesweepers. 12 coastal minesweepers.

AIR FORCE: 21,000; 150 combat aircraft.

2 light bomber sqns with B26 Invader and PV2. 1 fighter-bomber squadron with F84G. 2 light-strike squadrons with G91. 1 interceptor squadron with F86F. 6 COIN flights with armed T6. 1 maritime patrol squadron with P2V5. (A combat squadron has 10–25 aircraft.) 22 Noratlas, 16 C47, 11 DC6 and 15 C45 tpts. 13 T33, 25 T37 and 35 T6 recce trainers. Other aircraft include 11 Do27 and about 85 Alouette II/III and SA330 Puma helicopters. 1 parachute regiment of 4000.

Turkey

Population: 37,000,000.
Total armed forces: 449,000.
Defence budget 1972–3: $573,324,000.

ARMY: 360,000.

1 armoured division. 1 mechanized infantry division. 11 infantry divisions. 4 armoured brigades. 2 armoured cavalry brigades. 1 mechanized infantry brigade. 4 infantry brigades. 1 armoured cavalry regiment. 1 parachute battalion. M47 and M48 med tks; M24, M26 and M41 lt tks; M36 tank destroyers; M8 armd cars; M59 and M113 APC; 105 mm and 155 mm SP guns; 105 mm, 155 mm and 203 mm hows; SS11 and Cobra ATGW; 40 mm, 75 mm and 90 mm AA guns; Honest John SSM; about 20 AB204 helicopters.

NAVY: 39,000.

10 submarines. 10 destroyers. 6 coastal escorts. 11 motor torpedo boats (2 less than 100 tons). 14 fast patrol boats. 20 minesweepers. 6 minelayers.

AIR FORCE: 50,000; 288 combat aircraft.

2 fighter-bomber squadrons with F104G. 6 fighter-bomber squadrons with F100D. 1 fighter-bomber squadron with F5. 2 interceptor squadrons with F86 (in store). 2 AWX squadrons with F102A. 3 recce squadrons with RF84F and RF5A. (A combat squadron has an average of 18 aircraft.) 3 tpt sqns incl C47, 8 C130 and 16 Transall. 2 SAM battalions (8 batteries) with Nike-Hercules.

OTHER EUROPEAN COUNTRIES

Spain

Population: 34,500,000.
Total armed forces: 301,000.
Defence budget 1972: $879 million.

ARMY: 220,000.

1 armoured division. 1 mechanized infantry division. 1 motorized infantry division. 2 mountain divisions. 1 armoured cavalry brigade. 12 independent infantry brigades. (All above are about 70 per cent strength.) 1 mountain brigade. 1 airportable brigade. 1 parachute brigade. 2 artillery brigades (1 coast artillery). 1 SAM battalion with HAWK. M47 and M48 med tks; M24 and M41 lt tks; Greyhound armd cars; AML60/90 and M3 scout cars; M113 APC; 105 mm and 155 mm SP guns; 105 mm, 155 mm and 203 mm hows; 90 mm SP ATk guns.

NAVY: 47,500 (including 6000 marines).

4 submarines. 1 helicopter carrier. 1 cruiser. 13 destroyers/fast frigates. 8 frigates. 2 frigate-minelayers. 2 corvettes. 1 ASW patrol vessel. 3 torpedo boats. 17 minesweepers. 18 landing craft. 3 ASW hel and 1 light hel squadrons.

AIR FORCE: 33,500; 215 combat aircraft.

36 F4E fighter-bombers. 30 Mirage-IIIE fighter-bombers. 70 F5 fighter-bombers. 55 HA200 fighter-bombers. 13 F86F interceptors. 1 ASW squadron with 11 Hu16B. About 150 tpt aircraft and hel, including C47, C54, 12 Caribou and 21 Azor.

Sweden

Population: 8,200,000.
Defence budget 1972–3: $1510 million.

ARMY: 11,700 regulars, 13,700 reservists and 36,500 conscripts, plus 100,000 conscripts on 18–40 days annual refresher training.

6 armoured brigades. 20 infantry brigades. 4 Noorlands winter brigades. 50 independent battalions. 23 Local Defence Districts with 100 independent battalions and 4–500 independent companies. 30 non-operational armoured, infantry and artillery training units to provide basic arms training for conscripts. Centurion and STRV103 med tanks; STRV74 lt tanks; IKV91 armoured ATk guns; Pbv302 APC; 105 mm and 155 mm SP how; 75 mm, 105 mm and 155 mm how; 90 mm ATk guns; SS11, Bantam, Carl Gustav and Miniman ATGW; 57 mm SP, 20 mm, 40 mm and 57 mm AA guns; Redeye SAM; Iroquois and Jetranger hel.

NAVY: 4700 regulars, 2600 reservists and 7400 conscripts plus 14,000 conscripts on annual refresher training.

22 submarines. 2 missile destroyers with Rb08 SSM. 4 missile destroyers with Seacat SAM. 2 destroyers. 5 fast anti-submarine frigates. 17 heavy torpedo boats. 16 motor torpedo boats (less than 100 tons). 2 minelayer/submarine depot ships. 18 coastal minesweepers. 20 mobile and 45 static coastal artillery batteries. 10 Vertol and 10 AB206A helicopters.

AIR FORCE: 5800 regulars, 1900 reservists and 6400 conscripts, plus 7500 conscripts on refresher training; 400 combat aircraft.

10 attack squadrons with A32A Lansen (with Rb04E ASM) and AJ37 Viggen (replacement of the Lansen by the Viggen started in 1971). 13 AWX squadrons with J35 Draken F. 8 AWX squadrons with J35 Draken A/D. 2 recce/fighter squadrons with S32C. 3 recce/day fighter squadrons with S35E. (A combat squadron has up to 18 aircraft.) 5 tpt sqns. 5 comm sqns with Saab 91 and 130 Saab 105 (suitable for light ground attack duties); 5 Bulldog (98 on order). 10 helicopter groups (3–4 aircraft each) with 10 Vertol-107, 6 Alouette II/III and 16 AB 204/206. 6 SAM squadrons with Bloodhound 2.

Switzerland

Population: 6,400,000.
Military service: 4 months initial training, followed by reservist training of three weeks a year for 8 years, two weeks for 3 years and one week for 2 years.
(Total mobilizable strength 600,000; reservists can be fully mobilized within 48 hours.)
Defence budget 1972: $561 million.
Swiss Air Force and Air Defence Troops are an integral part of the army, but are listed here separately for purpose of comparison.

ARMY: 2500 regular cadre (including Air Defence troops): 17,000 conscripts; 530,500 reservists.

1 corps (Alpine defence) of 3 mountain divisions. 3 corps each of an armoured division and 2 infantry divisions. 17 frontier, fortress or 'redoubt' brigades. 300 Centurion and 150 Pz61 med tks; 200 AMX 13 lt tks; 1000 M113 APC; 155 mm SP how; 800 105-mm guns and hows.

AIR FORCE: 3000 regular; 7000 conscripts; 40,000 reservists (maintenance is by civilians); 315 combat aircraft.

13 ground support squadrons with Venom FB50. 2 interceptor squadrons with Mirage IIIS. 5 interceptor squadrons with Hunter F58 (with Sidewinder AAM). 1 reconnaissance squadron with Mirage IIIRS. (A combat squadron has 15 aircraft.) 20 transports including 3 Ju52/3 and 6 Do27. 80 helicopters including 60 Alouette II/III. 2 SAM battalions with Bloodhound 2.

Yugoslavia

Population: 21,000,000.
Total armed forces: 229,000.
Defence budget 1972: $485 million.

ARMY: 190,000.

9 infantry divisions. 1 tank division. 9 armoured brigades. 24 independent infantry brigades. 1 airborne brigade. Several hundred T54/55, T34 and M47 and about 650 M4 med tks; some PT76 lt tks; M3, BTR50P, BTR60P and BTR152 APC; SU100 SP guns; 105 mm and 155 mm hows; 50 mm, 57 mm, 75 mm and 76 mm ATk guns; ZSU572 SP AA guns; SA2 SAM.

NAVY: 19,000.

5 submarines. 1 destroyer. 19 coastal escorts. 30 MCM ships. 10 Osa-class patrol boats with *Styx* SSM. 65 motor torpedo boats (55 less than 100 tons).

AIR FORCE: 20,000; 342 combat aircraft.

12 GA sqns with F84, Kragu and Jastreb. 8 fighter/interceptor sqns with 50 F86D/E and 82 MiG 21. 2 reconnaissance sqns with RT33. (A combat squadron has 15 aircraft.) 60 Galeb trainers. 25 Li2, Beaver and C47 and 13 Il14 tpts. 50 Whirlwind, Mi4 and Mi8, and some Alouette III helicopters. 8 SAM batteries with SA2.
PARA-MILITARY FORCES
1,000,000 Territorial defence force (planned to increase to 3,000,000).

THE MIDDLE EAST AND MEDITERRANEAN

Algeria

Population: 15,200,000.
Total armed forces: 60,200.
Defence budget 1971: $99,200,000.

ARMY: 53,000.

4 motorized infantry brigades. 1 parachute brigade. 3 independent tank battalions. 50 independent infantry battalions. 12 companies of desert troops. 5 independent artillery battalions. 200 T34, 340 T54 and 50 T55 med tks; 50 AMX13 lt tks; 350 BTR152 APC; 25 SU100 and 6 JSU152 SP guns; 85 mm guns; 122 mm and 152 mm hows; 140 mm and 240 mm RL.

NAVY: 3200.

6 SO1 submarine chasers. 2 fleet minesweepers. 1 coastal minesweeper. 6 Komar- and 3 Osa-class patrol boats with *Styx* SSM. 12 P6 torpedo boats.

AIR FORCE: 4000; 181 combat aircraft.

30 Il28 light bombers. 25 MiG 15 and 70 MiG 17 FGA. 30 MiG 21 interceptors. 26 Magister armed trainers. 8 An12, 12 Il18 transports. 4 Mi1, 42 Mi4, 6 Hughes 269A and 2 SA330 helicopters. 1 SAM battalion with SA2.

Egypt

Population: 34,900,000.
Total armed forces: 325,000.
Defence budget 1972–3: $1510 million.

ARMY: 285,000.

3 armoured divisions. 3 mechanized infantry divisions.
5 infantry divisions. 2 parachute brigades. 16 artillery
brigades. 28 commando battalions. 50 JS3 hy tks; 1500
T54/55, 10 T62 and 400 T34 med tks; 100 PT76 lt tks;
2000 BTR40, BTR50P, BTR60P, OT64 and BTR152
APC; about 150 SU100 and ISU152 SP guns; about 1500
122-mm, 130-mm and 152-mm guns and hows; 40
203-mm hows; 57 mm, 85 mm and 100 mm ATk guns;
Snapper ATGW; 24 FROG-3, some FROG-7 and 25 *Samlet*
short-range SSM; ZSU23-4 and ZSU57-2 SP AA guns.

NAVY: 15,000 (including coastguard).

12 submarines (6 W- and 6 R-class – ex-Soviet). 5
destroyers (including 4 ex-Soviet Skory-class). 2
corvettes. 12 SO1 submarine chasers. 9 fleet minesweepers. 2 inshore minesweepers. 12 Osa- and 6 Komar-
class patrol boats with *Styx* SSM.

AIR FORCE: 25,000; 568 combat aircraft.

200 MiG 17 fighter-bombers, 18 TU16 *Badger* medium
bombers. 10 Il28 *Beagle* light bombers. 220 MiG 21
Fishbed interceptors. 120 SU7 *Fitter* fighter-bombers.
200 MiG, *Yak* and L29 trainers. About 40 Il14 lt
and 20 An12 med tpts. 180 Mi1, Mi4, Mi6 and Mi8
helicopters. Air defence is provided by 100 SAM sites,
each of 6 SA2 and SA3 launchers; 20 mm, 23 mm,
37 mm, 57 mm, 85 mm and 100 mm AA guns;
all integrated, through a warning and command
network, with 9 Air Force squadrons of MiG 21
interceptors. At peak involvement Soviet-manned
equipment co-ordinated with the air defence system
included some 65 SAM batteries with SA2, SA3, SA4 and
possibly SA6 missiles, 6 interceptor squadrons of MiG
21J and MiG 21D, some SU11 and a few MiG 23.

Iran

Population: 30,500,000.
Total armed forces: 191,000.
Defence budget 1972: $915 million.

ARMY: 160,000.

2 armoured divisions. 5 infantry divisions (some
mechanized). 1 independent armoured brigade. 1 SAM
battalion with HAWK. 400 M47 and 460 M60A1 med
tks; 100 M24 lt tks; 400 M113, 300 BTR50 and 400
BTR60 APC; 75 mm, 105 mm and 155 mm hows; 40 mm,
57 mm and 85 mm AA guns; SS11, SS12, TOW, ATGW.
(800 Chieftain tks on order; delivery started in 1972.)
8 Huskie, 52 AB205 and 24 AB206A helicopters. 8 C45,
20 Li8, 20 Cessna 185, 10 O2A lt ac.

NAVY: 9000.

1 destroyer. 2 SAM frigates (with Seacat). 4 corvettes. 24
patrol boats. 4 coastal minesweepers. 2 inshore
minesweepers. 4 landing craft. 8 SRN6 and 2 BH7

Wellington hovercraft (less than 100 tons).

AIR FORCE: 22,000; 160 combat aircraft.

2 fighter-bomber squadrons with F4D, with Sidewinder
and Sparrow AAM. 6 fighter-bomber squadrons with F5.
9 RT33 reconnaissance aircraft. Transports include 5
C47, 26 C130E and 6 Beaver. Helicopters include 4
Huskie, 10 AB206, 16 Super-Frelon, 2 CH47C Chinook.
Tigercat SAM (Rapier SAM are being delivered).

Iraq

Population: 9,750,000.
Total armed forces: 101,800.
Estimated defence expenditure 1970–1: $237,160,000

ARMY: 90,000.

1 tank division. 1 mechanized division. 2 inf divs (each
of four bdes, 3 arty and one para bn). 2 mountain divs.
800 T54/55 and 60 T34 med tks; 45 PT76, 20 M24 lt tks;
50 AML245 armd cars; 60 Ferret scout cars; 300
BTR152 and other APC; 300 120-mm and 130-mm guns.

NAVY: 2000.

3 SO1 submarine chasers. 12 P6 torpedo boats. 4 patrol
boats (less than 100 tons).

AIR FORCE: 9800; 189 combat aircraft.

9 TU16 medium bombers. 48 SU7 fighter-bombers. 32
Hunter FGA. 80 MiG 21 interceptors. 20 MiG 17 fighters.
4 Mi1, 30 Mi4, 12 Mi8 hel. 4 An2, 7 An12, 10 An24, 8
Il14, 2 TU124, 2 Heron tpt ac.

Israel

Population: 3,155,000.
Total armed forces: 25,000 regular, 52,000 conscripts;
(mobilization to 300,000 in 72 hours).
Defence budget 1972–3: $1247 million.

ARMY: 11,500 regular, 50,000 conscripts (including
12,000 women); 275,000 on mobilization.

4 armoured brigades. 5 mechanized brigades. 5 infantry
brigades. 1 parachute brigade. 3 artillery brigades. 450
M48 (with 105 mm guns), 250 Ben Gurion (Centurion
with French 105 mm gun), 700 Centurion, 200 Isherman
(with 105 mm gun) and Super Sherman, 100 TI67
(T54/55 with 105 mm gun) and some M60 med tks;
AML60, 15 AML90 and some Staghound armd cars;
about 1000 M2 and M3 half-tracks; M113 APCs; 352
105 mm and 155 mm, and some 175 mm SP how;
155 mm how on Sherman chassis; 900 120 mm and
160 mm mortars on AMX-chassis; 122 mm guns and
how; 130 mm guns; 240 mm RL (captured equipment);
90 mm SP ATk guns and 106 mm jeep-mounted
recoilless rifles; Cobra, and weapons carrier-mounted
SS10/11 ATGW; 20 mm, 30 mm and 40 mm AA guns.
(The 280-mile range Jericho SSM is believed to be in

production, but has not yet been reported deployed operationally.)

Reserves
Would increase above formations to 10 armoured, 9 mechanized infantry and 5 parachute brigades.

NAVY: 3500 regular, 1000 conscripts; 5000 on mobilization.

2 submarines. 1 destroyer (plus 1 awaiting disposal). 12 FPB (with Gabriel SSM). 4 motor torpedo boats.

AIR FORCE: 10,000 regular, 1000 conscripts; 20,000 on mobilization; 432 combat aircraft.

10 Vautour light bombers. 90 F4E fighter-bomber/interceptors. 50 Mirage IIIC fighter-bomber/interceptors (some with R530 AAM). 125 A4E/H Skyhawk fighter-bombers. 27 Mystère IV A fighter-bombers (in reserve). 30 Ouragan fighter-bombers (used mainly for training). 9 Super Mystère interceptors. 6 RF4E reconnaissance aircraft. 85 Magister trainers with limited ground attack capability. 10 Stratocruiser transports (incl 2 tankers). 20 Noratlas, 10 C47, 2 C130E transports. 12 Super Frelon, 10 CH53C, 30 AB205 and 20 Alouette helicopters. 8 SAM batteries with 48 HAWK.

Jordan

Population: 2,460,000.
Total armed forces: 69,250.
Defence budget 1971: $90,400,000.

ARMY: 65,000.

1 armoured division. 1 mechanized division. 1 infantry division. 1 independent infantry brigade. 1 Royal Guards battalion (armoured). 1 special forces battalion. 3 artillery regiments. 190 M47 and M48, 14 M60 and 140 Centurion med tks; 130 Saladin armd cars; 140 Ferret scout cars; 280 M113 and 120 Saracen APC; 130 25-pounder guns, 50 105-mm and 155-mm howitzers, 10 155-mm guns, 200 M42 SP AA guns.

NAVY: 250.

11 small patrol craft.

AIR FORCE: 4000; 50 combat aircraft.

2 ground-attack squadrons with 35 Hunter. 1 interceptor squadron with 15 F104A.

Lebanon

Population: 2,950,000.
Total armed forces: 14,250.
Defence budget 1972: $709,000,000.

ARMY: 13,000.

2 tank battalions. 2 reconnaissance battalions. 1 commando battalion. 9 infantry battalions. 3 artillery battalions. 40 Charioteer med tks; 40 AMX13 and 20

M41 lt tks; M706, M6 and AEC Mark-3 armd cars; M113 and M59 APC; 155 mm how; M42 SP AA guns.

NAVY: 250.

2 patrol vessels. 6 small inshore patrol craft. 1 landing craft.

AIR FORCE: 1000; 18 combat aircraft.

8 Hunter FGA. 1 interceptor squadron with 10 Mirage IIIC with R530 AAM. 5 transports. 1 helicopter sqn with 3 Alouette II and 5 Alouette III. Some French early warning/ground control radars.

Libya

Population: 2,100,000.
Total armed forces: 25,000.
Defence budget 1972: $120 million.

ARMY: 20,000.

1 armoured brigade. 2 mechanized infantry brigades. 1 National Guard brigade. 1 commando battalion. 3 artillery battalions. 2 anti-aircraft artillery battalions. 6 Centurion Mk 5, 200 T54/55 and 15 T34 med tks; 40 Saladin armd cars; Shorland and Ferret scout cars; Saracen and 70 M113A1 APC; 70 122-mm, 75 105-mm and 18 155-mm hows; L40/70 Bofors AA guns; 300 Vigilant ATGW. 5 AB206, 7 OH13 and 4 Alouette III helicopters.

NAVY: 2000.

1 frigate. 1 corvette. 3 FPB each with 8 SS12 (M) SSM. 2 inshore minesweepers.

AIR FORCE: 3000; 22 combat aircraft.

1 interceptor squadron with 10 F5A. 1 fighter squadron with 12 Mirage IIIB/E. 2 AB206, 3 OH13, 10 Alouette III and 6 Super Frelon helicopters. 3 T33 trainers. (45 of a total order of 110 Mirage III have been delivered.)

Morocco

Population: 16,500,000.
Total armed forces: 53,500.
Defence budget 1972: $124 million.

ARMY: 48,000.

1 armoured brigade. 3 motorized infantry brigades. 1 light security brigade. 1 parachute brigade. 9 independent infantry battalions. 1 Royal Guards battalion. 2 camel corps battalions. 3 desert cavalry battalions. 5 artillery groups. 2 engineer battalions. 120 T54 med tks; 120 AMX13 lt tks; 36 EBR75, 50 AML245 and M8 armd cars; 40 M3 half-track and 95 Czech APC; 25 SU100, AMX105 and 50 M56 90 mm SP guns; 75 mm and 105 mm hows; 6 Alouette II/III hels.

NAVY: 1500 (including 500 marines).

frigate. 2 coastal escorts. 1 patrol boat. 11 patrol boats less than 100 tons). 1 landing ship.

AIR FORCE: 4000; 48 combat aircraft.

20 F5A and 4 F5B interceptors. 24 Magister armed rainers. 35 T6 and 25 T28 trainers. 10 C47 and 11 C119 ransports. OH13, 12 AB205 and 6 HH43 hels. (12 MiG 17 fighter-bombers are in storage.)

Saudi Arabia

Population: 7,960,000.
Total armed forces: 40,500.
Defence budget 1970–1: $383,000,000.

ARMY: 36,000.

4 infantry brigades. 10 SAM battalions with HAWK. 25 M47 med tks; 60 M41 lt tks; 200 AML60 and AML90, some Staghound and Greyhound armd cars; Ferret scout cars. (AMX30 tks on order.)

NAVY: 1000.

2 torpedo boats. 12 FPB. 9 patrol boats. 8 SRN6 hovercraft.

AIR FORCE: 3500; 71 combat aircraft.

1 fighter-bomber sqn with 15 F86 (27 F5B and 30 F5E are on order). 2 ground-attack sqns with 21 BAC167. 2 interceptor sqns with 3 F52 and 32 F53 Lightning. 10 C130 and 2 C140B transports. 1 Alouette III, 1 AB204, 8 AB205 and 20 AB206 helicopters.

Sudan

Population: 16,450,000.
Total armed forces: 36,300.
Defence budget 1971–2: $143 million.

ARMY: 35,000.

1 armoured brigade. 6 infantry brigades. 1 parachute brigade. 3 artillery regiments. 3 air defence artillery regiments. 3 air defence regiments. 1 engineer regiment. 20 T34/85, 60 T54, 50 T55 and some T59 med tks; 50 Saladin and 45 Commando armd cars; 60 Ferret scout cars; 50 BTR50 and BTR152, 49 Saracen and 60 OT64 APC; 55 25-pounder, 40 105-mm and some 122-mm guns and hows; 20 120-mm mortars; 80 Bofors 40 mm and some Soviet 85 mm AA guns.

NAVY: 600.

6 coastal patrol boats. 2 landing craft.

AIR FORCE: 700; 40 combat aircraft.

16 MiG 21 interceptors. 8 MiG 17 fighter-bombers. 5 BAC145 Mk 5, 8 Jet Provost Mk 52 and 3 Provost Mk 51 light attack aircraft. 10 Mi8 helicopters.

Syria

Population: 6,450,000.
Total armed forces: 111,750.
Defence budget 1972: $206,452,000.

ARMY: 100,000.

2 armoured divisions. 1 mechanized division. 2 infantry divisions. 1 parachute battalion. 5 commando battalions. 7 artillery regiments. 8 SAM batteries with SA2 and SA3. About 30 JS3 hy tks; 240 T34 and 900 T54/55 med tks; some PT76 lt tks; 50 SU SP guns; 500 BTR50/60, BTR152 APC; 122 mm, 130 mm and 152 mm guns; SA2; ATGW; 37 mm, 57 mm, 85 mm and 100 mm AA guns.

NAVY: 1750.

2 minesweepers. 2 coastal patrol vessels. 6 Komar-class patrol boats with *Styx* SSM.

AIR FORCE: 10,000 men; 210 combat aircraft.

80 MiG 17 day fighter/ground attack aircraft. 30 SU7 fighter-bombers. 100 MiG 21 interceptors. 8 Il14 and 6 C47 transports. 4 Mi1, 10 Mi4 and some Mi8 helicopters.

Tunisia

Population: 5,360,000.
Total armed forces: 24,000.
Estimated defence expenditure 1972: $28,728,000.

ARMY: 20,000.

1 armoured battalion. 5 infantry battalions. 1 commando battalion. 1 artillery group. About 50 AMX13 and M41 lt tks; 20 Saladin and some M8 armd cars; 105 mm SP and 155 mm guns. 40 mm Bofors AA guns.

NAVY: 2000.

1 corvette. 2 coastal escorts. 2 patrol boats with SS12 (M) SSM. 4 patrol boats (less than 100 tons).

AIR FORCE: 2000; 12 combat aircraft.

12 F86 fighters. 8 MB326, 12 T6 and 12 Saab 91D trainers. 3 Flamant light transports. 8 Alouette II helicopters.

SUB-SAHARAN AFRICA

Ethiopia

Population: 26,000,000.
Total armed forces: 44,570.
Defence budget 1971–2: $US 40,500,000.

ARMY: 40,940.

4 infantry divisions of 8000 men each. 1 tank battalion. 1 airborne infantry battalion. 1 armoured car squadron. 4 artillery battalions. 5 air defence batteries. 2 engineer battalions. 30 M41 med tks; 20 M24 lt tks; about 40 APC; 6 AB204B helicopters.

NAVY: 1380.

1 coastal minesweeper. 1 training ship (ex-seaplane tender). 5 patrol boats.

AIR FORCE: 2250; 46 combat aircraft.

1 bomber squadron with 4 Canberra B2. 1 fighter-bomber squadron with 12 F86F. 1 ground-attack squadron with 6 T28A (COIN). 1 ground-attack squadron with 9 Saab17. 1 fighter squadron with 15 F5A. 1 tpt sqn with 6 C47, 2 C54, 4 C119G and 3 Dove. 3 trg sqns with 20 Safir, 15 T28A and 11 T33. 5 Alouette II, 2 Mi6, 2 Mi8 and 6 AB204B helicopters.

Nigeria

Population: 57,900,000.
Total armed forces: 274,000.
Defence budget 1971–2: $757,600,000.

ARMY: 262,000.

3 infantry divisions. 3 reconnaissance regiments. 3 artillery regiments. Saladin and 20 AML60/90 armd cars; Ferret scout cars; Saracen APC; 25-pounder, 76 mm, 105 mm and 122 mm guns.

NAVY: 5000.

1 ASW frigate. 2 corvettes. 3 P6 torpedo boats (ex-Soviet).

AIR FORCE: 7000; 38 combat aircraft.

6 Il28 medium bombers. 12 MiG 17 fighter-bombers. 10 L29 Delfin and 10 P149D armed trainers. 2 MiG 15 trainers. Other aircraft include 6 C47, 6 Fokker F27 Friendship tpts; 20 Do27/28 comms aircraft; 8 Whirlwind and Alouette II hel.

Rhodesia

Population: 5,600,000 (258,750 white population).
Total armed forces: 4700.
Estimated defence expenditure 1970–1: $US 25,000,000.

ARMY: 3500 Regular; 10,000 Territorial Force.

2 infantry battalions (one has Ferret scout cars). 2 Special Air Service squadrons. 1 artillery battery. 1 engineer squadron. 20 Ferret scout cars; Model 56 105 mm pack hows. There is an establishment for three brigades, two based on regular infantry battalions, which would be brought up to strength by mobilizing the Territorial Force

AIR FORCE: 1200; 45 combat aircraft.

1 light bomber sqn with 10 Canberra B2. 1 FGA sqn with 12 Hunter F5A9. 1 FGA sqn with 11 Vampire FB9. 1 recce sqn with 12 T52 Jet Provost. 1 transport sqn with 4 C47 and 1 Beech 55 Baron. 9 Aermacchi-Lockheed AL60F5 and 3 Canberra T4 trainers. 11 helicopter sqns with 12 Alouette III.

Reserves
10,000 Territorial Force.
The white population completing conscript service is assigned for three years' part-time training to territorial units.
The establishment of the Army Reserves is 8 infantry battalions, one field artillery battery and one engineer squadron.
Ground personnel servicing regular Air Force units are Air Force reservists or non-white civilian employees.
PARA-MILITARY FORCES
8000 active; 35,000 reservists.
The British South African Police (BSAP) have some military equipment such as small arms and would be responsible for much of the internal security in the event of civil unrest or military threat from outside. The white population forms only about a third of the active strength but nearly three-quarters of the Police Reserves.

South Africa

Population: 21,050,000 (4,000,000 white population).
Total armed forces: 17,300 regular; 92,000 Citizen Force.
Defence budget 1972–3: $448,300,000.

ARMY: 10,000 regular.

100 Centurion Mark 5. 20 Comet med tks; 800 AML60 and AML90, and 50 M3 armd cars; 50 Ferret scout cars; 250 Saracen APC.

Reserves
80,000 Citizen Force, in 11 territorial commands.

NAVY: 2300 regular.

3 submarines. 2 destroyers with Wasp ASW helicopters. 4 ASW frigates with Wasp ASW helicopters. 1 escort minesweeper. 3 coastal minesweepers. 5 seaward defence boats. 1 fleet replenishment tanker.

Reserves
9000 trained reserves in Citizen Force (with 5 frigates and 7 minesweepers).

AIR FORCE: 5000 regular; 166 combat aircraft.

1 bomber sqn with 9 Canberra B2. 1 light bomber sqn with 14 Buccaneer Mk50. 1 fighter-bomber sqn with 20 Mirage III EZ (AS20–30 ASM). 1 fighter squadron with 21 F86 Sabre. 1 interceptor sqn with 16 Mirage III CZ (R530 AAM). 75 MB326 Impala armed trainers. 1 reconnaissance sqn with 4 Mirage III RZ. 1 maritime recce sqn with 7 Shackleton. 2 transport sqns with 9 Transall, 20 C47, C54, and 7 C130B/E. 60 Alouette II/III, 8 Wasp, 16 Super Frelon and 16 SA330 Puma helicopters (of an order for 20). Other aircraft include 200 Harvard armed trainers.
The Cactus (Crotale) short-range SAM system is being introduced and some units may now be operational.

Reserves

3000 Citizen Air Force, operates eight Impala squadrons, 200 Harvard armed trainers, and some C47 transports and Cessna 185.
PARA-MILITARY FORCES
75,000 Kommandos organized and trained as a Home Guard.

Tanzania

Population: 13,900,000.
Total armed forces: 11,100.
Defence budget 1968–9: $26,640,000.

ARMY: 10,000.

4 infantry battalions. 20 Chinese T59 med tks; 14 Chinese T62 lt tks; some BTR40 and 152 APC; Soviet field artillery and Chinese mortars.

NAVY: 600.

6 patrol boats.

AIR FORCE: 500; no combat aircraft.

1 An2, 5 DHC3 Otter and 12 DHC4 Caribou transports. 7 Piaggio P149 trainers.

Uganda

Population: 10,450,000.
Total armed forces: 12,600.
Defence budget 1968–9: $16,875,000.

ARMY: 12,000.

2 brigades each of 2 infantry battalions. 2 border guard battalions. 1 mechanized battalion. 1 parachute/commando battalion. 1 artillery regiment. 12 M4 med tanks; 15 Ferret scout cars; 36 OT64B APC (perhaps half are operational); (36 Saladin on order).

AIR FORCE: 600; 21 combat aircraft.

1 fighter squadron with 7 MiG 15 and MiG 17. 14 Magister armed trainers. 2 AB206 and 2 Scout helicopters. 1 Caribou transport; P149 and 12 L29 Delfin trainers; 7 Piper light aircraft.

ASIA AND AUSTRALASIA
China

Population: 700–800,000,000.
Total regular forces: 2,880,000 (including construction engineer troops).
Defence budget: Estimated from $8 billion to $16 billion.

STRATEGIC FORCES

IRBM: 15–20.
MRBM: 20–30.
AIRCRAFT
up to 100 TU16.

ARMY: 2,500,000 (including construction engr tps).

5 armoured divisions. 120 infantry divisions. 3 cavalry divisions. 2 airborne divisions. About 20 artillery divisions. Heavy equipment consists of Soviet items supplied up to 1960 including IS2 tks and 152 mm and 203 mm artillery; Soviet T34 and T54, and Chinese T59 (version of T54) med tks; T60 (PT76 type) amphibious tks; T62 lt tks; and APC; SP arty incl SU76, SU100 and ISU122.
The geographical distribution of the divisions (excluding artillery) is believed to be:
NORTH AND NORTH-EAST CHINA (Shenyang and

Peking MR):
40 divisions.
EAST AND SOUTH-EAST CHINA (Tsinan, Nanking and Foochow MR):
25 divisions.
SOUTH-CENTRAL CHINA (Canton and Wuhan MR):
20 divisions.
MID-WEST CHINA (Lanchow MR):
15 divisions.
WEST AND SOUTH-WEST CHINA (Sinkiang, Chengtu and Kunming MR):
30 divisions.
LAOS AND NORTH VIET NAM
Some construction engineer troops and supporting elements, in all 15–20,000 men.

NAVY: 160,000 (including Naval Air Force and 28,000 Marines).

1 G-class submarine (with ballistic missile tube). 32 fleet submarines. 3 coastal submarines. 4 destroyers. 9 destroyer escorts. 14 patrol escorts. 24 submarine chasers. 15 missile patrol boats. 30 minesweepers. 40 landing ships. 45 auxiliary minesweepers. 220 MTB and hydrofoils.

Naval Air Force

20,000; over 500 shore-based combat aircraft, including about 100 Il28 torpedo-carrying and some TU2 light bombers.

AIR FORCE: 220,000 (including 85,000 air defence personnel); about 3600 combat aircraft.

About 100 TU16 and a few TU4 medium bombers. 200 Il28 and 100 TU2 light bombers. About 1700 MiG 15 and MiG 17; up to 1000 MiG 19, 75 MiG 21 and some 200 F9 fighters.

PARA-MILITARY FORCES

About 300,000 security and border troops, including 19 infantry-type divisions and 30 independent regiments stationed in the frontier areas; the public security force and a civilian militia with an effective element of probably not more than 5 million.

Australia

Population: 13,000,000.
Total armed forces: 88,110.
Defence budget 1971–2: $US 1500 million.

ARMY: 47,760 (Conscripts 18,960).

1 tank regiment. 3 cavalry regiments. 9 infantry battalions. 2 battalions of the Pacific Islands Regiment (PIR). 1 Special Air Service (SAS) regiment. 1 medium artillery regiment. 3 field artillery regiments. 1 light anti-aircraft regiment. 1 aviation regiment. 6 signals regiments. 3 field engineer regiments. 7 construction and survey squadrons. 1 Logistic Support Force. 143 Centurion med tks; 265 Ferret scout cars; 758 M113 APC; 260 105-mm how including M56 105-mm pack how; Sioux and Alouette III hels; 26 light aircraft.

Reserves

27,100.
The Citizen Military Force of 26,500 is intended to form 24 infantry battalions with supporting arms and services.

NAVY: 17,500.

4 Oberon-class submarines. 1 aircraft carrier. 3 ASW destroyers with Tartar SAM and Ikara ASW msls. 4 destroyers. 6 destroyer escorts with Ikara. 4 coastal minesweepers. 2 minehunters. 1 fast troop transport (ex-aircraft carrier).

Fleet Air Arm

2 fighter-bomber sqns with A4G Skynawk. 2 ASW sqns with S2E Tracker. 2 ASW helicopter sqns with Wessex 31B. 1 helicopter sqn with Iroquois and Scout.

Reserves

6350. Navy Citizen Military Force: 5400.

AIR FORCE: 22,850; 210 combat aircraft.

1 bomber squadron with Canberra B20. 2 fighter squadrons with F4E. 4 interceptor/strike squadrons with Mirage IIIO. 1 MR squadron with 10 P3B Orion and 1 MR

squadron with 12 P2H Neptune. 75 MB326 trainers. 2 tpt sqns with 24 C130, 1 tpt sqn with 2 BAC111, 10 HS748 and 3 Mystère 20 and 2 tpt sqns with 24 Caribou. 2 helicopter squadrons with Iroquois. (24 F111C are on order.)

Reserves

1520. Citizen Air Force 780.

Republic of China (Taiwan)

Population: 14,700,000.
Total armed forces: 500,000.
Estimated defence expenditure 1971: $601,250,000.

ARMY: 350,000.

12 heavy divisions. 6 light divisions. 2 armoured brigades. 1 armoured infantry regiment. 2 airborne brigades. 4 Special Forces Groups. 1 SAM battalion with HAWK. 1 SAM bn and 1 SAM bty with Nike-Hercules. M47 and M48 med tks; M24 and M41 lt tks; M18 tk destroyers; LVT4 and M113 APC; 105 mm and 155 mm guns; SAM.

NAVY: 35,000.

11 destroyers. 18 destroyer escorts. 6 escorts. 12 submarine chasers. 8 patrol vessels. 3 fleet minesweepers.

MARINE CORPS: 35,000.

2 divisions.

AIR FORCE: 80,000; 237 combat aircraft.

80 F100A/D fighter-bombers. 70 F5A tactical fighters. 55 F104A/G interceptors. 20 F86F interceptors. 8 RF104G and 4 RF101 recce aircraft. About 95 C46, C47 and C119 transports.

India

Population: 571,000,000.
Total armed forces: 960,000.
Defence budget 1972–3: $1817 million.

ARMY: 840,000.

2 armoured divisions. 3 independent armoured brigades. 13 infantry divisions. 10 mountain divisions. 6 independent infantry brigades. 2 parachute brigades. About 20 AA artillery units. 200 Centurion Mk 5/7, 250 Sherman, 450 T54 and T55 and 300 Vijayanta med tks; 150 PT76 and 140 AMX13 lt tks; OT62 and Mk 2/4A APC; about 3000 guns, mostly 25-pounders, but incl Model 56 105 mm pack how and about 350 100-mm and 140 130-mm guns; SS11 and Entac ATGW.

NAVY: 28,000.

1 16,000-ton aircraft carrier. 4 submarines (ex-Soviet F-class). 2 cruisers. 3 destroyers. 8 destroyer escorts (incl 5 ex-Soviet Petya-class). 8 frigates. 6 Osa-class patrol boats. 9 patrol boats (4 less than 100 tons). 8

minesweepers (4 inshore). 1 landing ship. 2 landing craft. The naval air forces include 33 Sea Hawk attack and 17 Alizé maritime patrol aircraft, and 2 Sea King and 10 Alouette III helicopters. 10 Sea Hawk, 5 Alizé and 2 Alouette can be carried in the aircraft carrier at one time.

AIR FORCE: 92,000; 650 combat aircraft.

4 light bomber squadrons with Canberra. 6 fighter-bomber squadrons with SU7. 2 fighter-bomber squadrons with HF24 Marut 1A. 7 fighter-bomber squadrons with Hunter F6. 2 fighter-bomber squadrons with Mystère IV. 8 Interceptor squadrons with MiG21. 8 interceptor squadrons with Gnat. 1 reconnaisance squadron with Canberra PR57, Mystère IV and Dakota. 1 maritime recce sqn of L1049 Super Constellation. (8 to 25 aircraft in a combat squadron.) 13 tpt sqns with C47, C119, Il14, An12, Otter, HS748 and Caribou. About 12 sqns of Mi4, Alouette III and Mi8 hels. About 20 SA2 SAM sites.

Indonesia

Population: 128,500,000.
Total armed forces: 317,000.
Estimated defence expenditure 1971: $286,700,000.

ARMY: 250,000.

15 inf bdes, formed from about 100 inf bns. 8 armoured battalions. 1 paracommando regiment (RPKAD). About one-third of the army is engaged in civil and administrative duties.
Stuart, AMX13 and PT76 lt tks; Saladin armd cars; Ferret scout cars; Saracen and BTR152 APC; artillery includes Soviet 57 mm AA guns and associated radar.

NAVY: 34,000 (incl 14,000 Marines).

Only a very small part of the navy is operational.
12 submarines (ex-Soviet W-class). 1 cruiser (ex-Soviet Sverdlov-class). 4 destroyers (ex-Soviet Skory-class). 11 frigates (including 7 ex-Soviet Riga-class). 18 coastal escorts (14 ex-Soviet, 4 ex-USA). 12 Komar-class patrol boats with *Styx* SSM. 8 patrol boats. 21 motor torpedo boats. 6 fleet minesweepers. 20 coastal minesweepers (6 ex-USA). 18 motor gunboats. 25 seaward defence boats (less than 100 tons). 6 landing ships. 7 landing craft. 2 Marine brigades.

Naval Air Arm
This has been reduced to a few helicopters and is virtually non-operational.

AIR FORCE: 33,000; about 120 combat aircraft.
Most of the Soviet-supplied combat aircraft, and the SA2 have not been used for some years. Few can be regarded as operational.
22 TU16 and 10 Il28. 5 B25 and 4 B26 light bombers. 13 F51D light-strike aircraft. About 4 MiG 15, 8 MiG 17 and 15 MiG 21 interceptors (mostly in storage).

Japan

Population: 105,800,000.
Total armed forces: 260,000.
Defence budget 1972–3: $2600 million.

ARMY: 180,000.

1 mechanized division. 12 infantry divisions (7000–9000 men each). 1 airborne brigade. 1 artillery brigade. 1 signal and 5 engineer brigades. 1 helicopter brigade. 3 SAM groups with HAWK (90 launchers). 380 Type 61 and 15 M4 med tks; 30 M24 and 140 M41 lt tks; Type 60 APC; 30 M52 105 mm and 10 M44 155 mm how; Type 60 twin 106 mm SP recoilless rifles; Type 64 ATGW; 125 aircraft and 220 helicopters.

NAVY: 39,000.

11 submarines. 1 SAM destroyer with Tartar. 27 destroyers. 12 destroyer escorts/frigates. 20 submarine chasers. 2 minelayers. 42 coastal minesweepers. 3 tank landing ships. 1 medium landing ship.
Naval air component: 200 combat aircraft. About 60 helicopters incl S61, S62, Vertol 107, CM34 and UH19.

AIR FORCE: 41,000; 406 combat aircraft.

7 fighter-bomber squadrons with 230 F86F. 7 interceptor squadrons with 160 F104J. 1 reconnaissance squadron with 16 RF86F (8 of 14 RF4EJ to be delivered in 1972–3). (18–25 aircraft in a combat squadron.) 3 transport squadrons with 30 C46, 13 YS11 and 12 MU2.

Korea: Democratic People's Republic (North)

Population: 14,300,000.
Total armed forces: 402,500.
Defence budget 1972: $443,100,000.

ARMY: 360,000.

2 armoured divisions. 20 infantry divisions. 4 independent infantry brigades. 750 T34 and T54 med tks; PT76 lt tks; 950 BA64, BTR40 and BTR152 APC; 200 SU76 and SU100 SP guns; 2000 AA guns incl ZSU57; 6000 other guns and mortars up to 152 mm calibre; FROG 5 SSM; SA2 SAM.

NAVY: 12,500.

3 submarines (ex-Soviet W-class). 6 Komar- and 4 Osa-class FPB with *Styx* SSM. 3 torpedo boats. 2 fleet minesweepers.

AIR FORCE: 30,000; 578 combat aircraft.

70 Il28 light bombers. 28 SU7. 380 MiG 15 and MiG 17 fighter-bombers. 100 MiG 21 and some MiG 19 interceptors. About 40 An2, Li2, Il12 and Il14 transports. 20 Mi4 helicopters.

Korea: Republic of Korea (South)

Population: 32,000,000.
Total armed forces: 634,750.
Estimated defence expenditure 1972: $427,500,000.

ARMY: 560,000.

29 infantry divisions (10 in cadre only). 2 armoured brigades. 80 artillery battalions. 1 SSM battalion with Honest John. 2 SAM bns with HAWK and 1 with Nike-Hercules. M4 and M48 med tks; Stuart and M24 lt tks; M10 and M36 tk destroyers; M8 armd cars and M113 APC; guns up to 175 mm; SSM; SAM.

NAVY: 16,750.
3 destroyers. 3 destroyer escorts. 4 frigates. 6 escort transports.

MARINE CORPS: 33,000.

1 division.

AIR FORCE: 25,000; 235 combat aircraft.

18 F4D fighter-bombers. 110 F86F fighter-bombers. 77 F5 tactical fighters. 20 F86D AWX (with Sidewinder AAM). 10 RF86F reconnaissance aircraft. 35 transports including C46, C47 and C54. Helicopters include 6 H19.

Malaysia

Population: 11,200,000.
Total armed forces: 50,500.
Defence budget 1972: $US 314,700,000.

ARMY: 43,000.

7 infantry brigades, consisting of: 27 infantry battalions. 3 reconnaissance regiments. 3 artillery regiments. 1 special service unit. 3 signal regiments. Engineer and administrative units. Ferret scout cars; 100 Commando APC; 105 mm how; 40 mm AA guns.

NAVY: 3500.

2 ASW frigates (1 with Seacat SAM). 6 coastal minesweepers. 4 fast patrol boats (less than 100 tons).

AIR FORCE: 4000; 30 combat aircraft.

16 CA27 Sabre fighter-bombers. 20 CL41G Tebuan light training and strike aircraft. 8 Herald and 12 Caribou transports.

New Zealand

Population: 2,910,000.
Total armed forces: 12,637.
Defence budget 1972–3: $US 152,600,000.

ARMY: 5449.

1 infantry battalion. 1 artillery battery. Regular troops also form the nucleus of a Combat Brigade Group, a Logistic Group and a Reserve Brigade Group. These units would be completed by the mobilization of Territorials. 10 M41 lt tks; 9 Ferret scout cars; 41 M113 APC; 10 5·5-inch med guns, 28 105-mm hows, 16 25-pdr guns.

NAVY: 2966.

4 frigates with Seacat SAM (2 with Wasp hels). 2 escort minesweepers.

AIR FORCE: 4222; 29 combat aircraft.

1 fighter-bomber squadron with 10 A4K and 4 TA4K Skyhawk. 1 fighter-bomber squadron with 10 BAC 167. 5 P3B Orion maritime reconnaissance aircraft.

Pakistan

This entry relates only to the former West Pakistan which, since it is for 1971, also covers the former East Pakistan, now Bangladesh. No entry is included for the armed forces of Bangladesh because of the difficulty in establishing firm figures for them.

Population: 51,300,000.
Total armed forces: 395,000.
Defence budget 1972–3: $405,500,000.

ARMY: 278,000.

2 armoured divisions. 10 infantry divisions. 1 independent armoured brigade. 1 air defence brigade. 135 M47, 65 M48, 50 T55 and 200 T59 med tks; 140 M24, 50 M41 and 20 PT76 lt tks; 250 M113 APC; about 900 guns incl 25 pounder, 105 mm and 155 mm hows and 130 mm guns; Cobra ATGW; H13 hels.

NAVY: 10,000.

3 submarines. 1 light cruiser/training ship. 4 destroyer escorts. 2 fast frigates.

AIR FORCE: 17,000; 200 combat aircraft.

2 light bomber squadrons with B57B. 2 fighter-bomber squadrons with Mirage IIIE. 6 fighter-bomber/interceptor squadrons with F86. 4 fighter/ground-attack squadrons with MiG 19. 1 interceptor squadron with F104A. 1 recce squadron with 4 RT33A, 2 RB57 and 4 F104B. 35 Sioux, Huskie, Alouette III and Mi8 helicopters.

Viet Nam: Democratic Republic (North)

Population: 23,300,000.
Total armed forces: 513,250.
Estimated defence expenditure 1970: $584 million.

ARMY: 500,000.

15 infantry divisions plus an additional 2 training divisions. 1 artillery division (of 10 regiments). 2 armoured regiments (a third may be forming). About 20

independent infantry regiments. 46 SAM battalions (each
with 6 SA2 launchers). 12 AA (artillery) regiments. 20
T34 and 75 T54 med tks; 100 PT76 Type 60 lt tks;
BTR40 APC; SU76 and ISU122 SP guns; 75 mm,
105 mm, 122 mm, 175 130-mm and 152 mm guns;
57 mm, 75 mm, 82 mm and 107 mm recoilless rifles;
82 mm, 100 mm, 107 mm, 120 mm and 160 mm
mortars; 107 mm, 122 mm and 140 mm RL; Sagger
ATGW; 12.7 mm, 37 mm, 14.5 mm, 57 mm, KS12
85 mm and KS19 100 mm AA guns and ZSU57-2 AA SP
guns; Strela SAM, Firecon AA radar.

NAVY: 3250 regular, 2000 reserves.

3 coastal escorts. 24 motor gunboats (less than 100 tons).

AIR FORCE: 10,000; 228 combat aircraft.

8 Il28 light bombers. 60 MiG 21F/PF interceptors with
Atoll AAM. 30 MiG 19 interceptors. 130 MiG 15/17
interceptors. 20 An2, 4 An24, 12 Il14 and 20 Li2
transports. 12 Mi4 and 5 Mi6 helicopters.

PARA-MILITARY FORCES
16,000 Frontier, Coast Security and People's Armed
Security Forces; about 1,500,000 Regional Armed
Militia.

Viet Nam: Republic of Viet Nam (South)

Population: 19,300,000.
Total armed forces: 503,000.
Defence budget 1972: $435,700,000

ARMY: 410,000.

11 infantry divisions. 1 airborne division (3 brigades).
6 independent armoured cavalry regiments. 3 independent
infantry regiments. 27 ranger battalions.
1 special forces group. 35 artillery battalions. M47 and
M48 med tks; M24, M41 and AMX13 lt tks;
Commando and Greyhound armd cars; M3 scout cars;
M59 and M113 APC; 105 mm and 155 mm guns;
155 mm SP guns; 175 mm how; AA guns; TOW ATGW.

NAVY: 39,000.

7 destroyer escorts. 70 fast patrol boats. 20 coastal
gunboats. 11 minesweeping craft. 20 landing ships. 160
minor landing craft. 500 river patrol boats. About 350
motorized junks.

MARINE CORPS: 13,000.
1 division.

AIR FORCE: 41,000; 275 combat aircraft.

1 tactical fighter squadron with F5. 5 fighter-bomber
squadrons with A37. 3 fighter-bomber squadrons with
Skyraider. Some RC47 reconnaissance aircraft. 80
armed light aircraft. 16 AC47 and 16 AC119 armed
transport aircraft. (Combat squadrons have from 15–20
aircraft.) 20 C47, 16 C119 and 465 C123 transports. 465
UH1 and 15 CH47 hels.
PARA-MILITARY FORCES
Regional Forces – 280,000, Popular Forces – 240,000, a
home guard. People's Self Defence Force – 1,400,000;
part-time village militia. Police Field Force – 35,000,
including special internal security units with armoured
vehicles and helicopters.

LATIN AMERICA

Argentina

Population: 24,166,000.
Total armed forces: 135,000.
Defence budget 1972: $694 million.

ARMY: 85,000.

1 armoured brigade. 1 horsed cavalry brigade. 5 infantry
brigades. 2 mountain brigades. 1 airborne brigade. 10
artillery regiments. M4 Sherman medium tks; 90
AMX13 lt tks; M113 APC; 105 mm and 155 mm guns;
105 mm pack how and 24 French Mk F3 and 155 mm
SP hows; recoilless rifles; Cobra ATGW; Tigercat SAM.

NAVY: 33,000 (including the Naval Air Force and
Marines).

1 aircraft carrier. 4 submarines (2 in reserve; 2 more are
under construction). 3 cruisers. 8 destroyers (2 more
under construction). 4 frigates. 2 corvettes. 6 coastal
minesweepers. 5 landing ships.

Naval Air Force
3000; 47 combat aircraft.
10 F9B Panther fighters. 16 A4B Skyhawk fighter-
bombers. 6 MB326GB armed trainers (6 more on order).
6 S2A Tracker, 6 P2V5 Neptune and 3 PBY5 Catalina
maritime patrol aircraft. 15 C47 and C54 transports.
About 60 trainers, including T28, TF95 Cougar and
Beech C45. 6 Bell 47D, 4 UH19, 6 Alouette III and 4
SH3 Sea King helicopters (2 Westland Lynx on order).
Seacat SAM.

Marines: 5000.

AIR FORCE: 17,000; 72 combat aircraft.

12 Canberra bombers. 47 A4B Skyhawk fighter-bombers.
20 F86F Sabrejet fighters.

Brazil

Population: 100,000,000.
Total armed forces: 198,000.

Defence budget 1971: $1 billion.

ARMY: 120,000.

1 armoured division. 4 mechanized divisions. 7 infantry divisions. 1 airborne division. 150 M4 Sherman and 40 M47 Patton med tks; M3 Stuart and 100 M41 Walker Bulldog lt tks; 120 Veteli A1 Cutia recce/APC/armd car; 40 M113 and M59 APC. 1 helicopter COIN squadron with 7 Bell 206A and 8 Bell UH1D.

NAVY: 43,000 (including 10,000 marines).

1 aircraft carrier. 3 submarines (3 more on order). 2 cruisers. 11 destroyers (1 with Seacat SAM). 6 coastal patrol vessels. 10 corvettes. 4 coastal minesweepers. 11 seaward and river patrol craft. 15 Whirlwind, 5 Wasp and Widgeon, 2 Bell 47, 13 Hughes 269A, 9 Hughes 200, 6 Hughes 500, and 3 SH3D helicopters.

AIR FORCE: 35,000; 231 combat aircraft.

15 B26K light bombers. 15 A4F Skyhawk fighter/ bombers (16 Mirage IIIEBR on order). 15 TF33, 60 AT37C, 60 AT6G and 18 AT28 armed trainers. 13 Tracker, 14 Neptune, 12 Albatross and 9 PBY5 Catalina maritime patrol aircraft. About 180 transports.

Chile

Population: 10,200,000.
Total armed forces: 47,500.
Defence budget 1972: $180 million.

ARMY: 24,000.

6 cavalry regiments (2 armoured, 4 horsed). 16 infantry regiments (incl 10 motorized). 5 artillery regiments. Some anti-aircraft and support detachments. 76 M4 Sherman med tks; M3 Stuart lt tks; some APC; Model 56 105-mm pack how.

NAVY: 15,000.

2 submarines. 3 cruisers. 4 destroyers. 4 destroyer escorts. 4 motor torpedo boats. 5 patrol vessels. (2 Oberon-class submarines and 2 Leander-class frigates with Seacat SAM are on order.)

AIR FORCE: 8500; 41 combat aircraft.

12 B26 light bombers. 18 Hunter F71 and 11 F80C fighters. 45 T34, 10 T37B, 8 T33A and 5 Vampire trainers. About 90 transports.

Cuba

Population: 8,650,000.
Total armed forces: 108,000.
Estimated defence expenditure 1971: $290,000,000.

ARMY: 90,000.

15 infantry 'divisions' (brigades). 2 armoured brigades. 8 independent 'brigades' (battalion groups). Over 600

tks including hy tks, T34 and T54/55 med tks, and PT76 lt tks; 200 BTR40, BTR60 and BTR152 APC; 100 SU100 assault guns; 122 mm and 152 mm guns; 30 FROG-4 and 20 Salish SSM; 57 mm, 76 mm and 85 mm ATk guns; *Snapper* ATGW.

NAVY: 6000.

4 frigates. 2 escort patrol vessels. 18 submarine chasers. 18 Komar-class patrol boats with SSM. 2 Osa-class patrol boats with SSM. 24 motor torpedo boats. 50 Samlet coastal defence SSM.

AIR FORCE: 12,000 (including the Air Defence Forces); 185 combat aircraft.

20 MiG 15 fighter-bombers. 50 MiG 21 interceptors. 40 MiG 19 interceptors. 75 MiG 17 interceptors. About 50 transport aircraft. About 25 Mi4 and 30 Mi1 helicopters. 24 sites with 144 SA2 SAM.

Mexico

Population: 52,200,000.
Total armed forces: 73,200 regulars; 250,000 part-time militia.
Estimated defence expenditure 1971: $216 million.

ARMY: 54,000, plus 250,000 part-time conscripts.

1 mechanized brigade group (Presidential Guard). 1 infantry brigade group. 1 parachute brigade. Zonal Garrisons including: 21 independent cavalry sqns. 50 independent infantry battalions. 3 artillery regiments. Anti-aircraft, engineer and support units. 50 med tks; M3 Stuart lt tks; 100 armd cars; 75 mm and 105 mm hows.

NAVY: 13,200 (including Naval Air Force and marines).

2 destroyers. 7 frigates. 2 gunboats. 16 escort and fleet minesweepers. 16 patrol boats. 2 troop transports.

MARINES: 1566 men; organized in 14 companies.

AIR FORCE: 6000; 27 combat aircraft.

12 Vampire fighter-bombers. 15 T33A fighter-bomber/ trainers. 130 trainers, including 45 T6 Texan, 13 AT11 Kansan, 32 T28 Trojan and 10 T34 Mentor. (The T6 T11 and T28 aircraft can be used for ground support.) About 40 transports.

Venezuela

Population: 11,150,000.
Total armed forces: 33,500.
Defence expenditure 1971: $267 million.

ARMY: 20,000.

2 armoured battalions. 1 cavalry regiment. 2 tank squadrons. 12 infantry battalions. 13 ranger battalions. 4 artillery battalions. Engineer and anti-aircraft

battalions. AMX13 lt tks; M18 tank destroyers and
ome armd cars.

NAVY: 7500 (including 4000 marines).

submarines. 3 destroyers. 6 destroyer escorts.
Otomat ssm are on order.)

AIR FORCE: 6000; 111 combat aircraft.

15 B2 Canberra bombers. 15 B25 Mitchell light bombers.
15 Venom FB4 and Vampire FB5 fighter-bombers. 16
CF5A fighters. 50 F86F/K fighters. (15 Mirage IIIE
fighters are on order.) 45 tpt ac incl C47; 18 C123B and
4C130.

Index